# SAP HR
## OM, PD and Training
## Technical Reference and Learning Guide

**P. K. AGRAWAL**
Program Manager
Tata Technologies Limited
Pune

**PHI Learning Private Limited**
Delhi-110092
2014

₹ 595.00

**SAP HR OM, PD AND TRAINING: Technical Reference and Learning Guide**
P.K. Agrawal



**Warning and Disclaimer**
While every precaution has been taken in the preparation of this book, the author and the publisher do not guarantee the accuracy, adequacy, or completeness of any information contained in this book. Neither is any liability assumed by the author and the publisher for any damages or loss to your data or your equipment resulting directly or indirectly from the use of the information or instructions contained herein.

**Trademark Acknowledgements**
SAP, SAPconnect, SAPNet, SAPoffice, SAPscript, ABAP, Basis, ECC are registered or unregistered trademark of SAP AG.

All product and service names mentioned in this book are registered or unregistered trademarks or service marks of their respective companies. Use of any product or service name in this book should not be regarded as affecting the validity of any trademark or service mark.

**ISBN-978-81-203-3984-2**

The export rights of this book are vested solely with the publisher.

**Third Printing** ... ... **September, 2014**

Published by Asoke K. Ghosh, PHI Learning Private Limited, Rimjhim House, 111, Patparganj Industrial Estate, Delhi-110092 and Printed by Rajkamal Electric Press, Plot No. 2, Phase IV, HSIDC, Kundli-131028, Sonepat, Haryana.

*This book is dedicated to*
*SAP consultants and users*
*who deserve to understand SAP much better*

# *Table of Contents*

Each chapter is rated for its importance and relevance for functional consultants (FC), users (US), business process owners (PO) and senior managers (SM). In MR you can keep your own rating and in UL, your understanding level. These ratings are repeated at the beginning of each chapter, so that at the beginning of each chapter you know whether to read it, or skip it, without having to go back to the Table of Contents.

# SAP Menu

| *Sequence number* | *SAP Menu (ECC 6.0)* | *Where covered* | *Why not covered* |
|---|---|---|---|
| | SAP menu | | |
| 1 | Office | | OoS |
| 2 | Cross-Application Components | | OoS |
| 3 | Collaboration Projects | | OoS |
| 4 | Logistics | | OoS |
| 5 | Accounting | | OoS |
| 6 | Human Resources | | |
| 6.1 | PPMDT - Manager's Desktop | | OoS |
| 6.2 | Personnel Management | | |
| 6.2.1 | Administration | | OoS |
| 6.2.2 | Recruitment | | OoS |
| 6.2.3 | Personnel Development | | |
| 6.2.3.1 | PPEM - Planning for Organizational Unit | 3.5 | |
| 6.2.3.2 | Profile | | |
| 6.2.3.2.1 | PPPD - Display | 24.1 | |
| 6.2.3.2.2 | PPPM - Change | 24.1 | |
| 6.2.3.3 | Planning | | |
| 6.2.3.3.1 | PPCP - Career | 25.1 | |
| 6.2.3.3.2 | PPSP - Succession | 25.5 | |
| 6.2.3.3.3 | PPDPIM - Individual Development | 26.1.2 | |
| 6.2.3.4 | Appraisal | | |
| 6.2.3.4.1 | APPCREATE - Create | 27.1 | |
| 6.2.3.4.2 | APPCHANGE - Edit | 27.1 | |
| 6.2.3.5 | Information System | | |
| 6.2.3.5.1 | Reports | | |
| 6.2.3.5.1.1 | PEPM - Profile Matchup | 24.4 | |
| 6.2.3.5.1.2 | PEPP - Profiles | 24.5 | |
| 6.2.3.5.1.3 | Search | | |
| 6.2.3.5.1.3.1 | PPPE_SEARCH_FOR_Q - Fo | 23.4 | |
| 6.2.3.5.1.3.2 | PPDPSPFP - For Developmen | 26.2.4 | |
| 6.2.3.5.1.3.3 | PPDPSPFS - For Developmen | 26.1.2 | |
| 6.2.3.5.1.4 | APPSEARCH - Appraisals | 27.1 | |
| 6.2.3.5.1.5 | Catalog | | |
| 6.2.3.5.1.5.1 | PPQD - Qualifications | 23.2 | |
| 6.2.3.5.1.5.2 | PPDPCS - Development Plan | 26.3 | |
| 6.2.3.5.1.5.3 | PPAD - Appraisals | 27.2 | |

| *Sequence number* | *SAP Menu (ECC 6.0)* | *Where covered* | *Why not covered* |
|---|---|---|---|
| 6.2.3.5.1.6 | S_AHR_61015524 - Careers | 25.2.5 | |
| 6.2.3.5.1.7 | Organizational Unit | | |
| 6.2.3.5.1.7.1 | S_AHR_61015532 - Profile Match | 24.5 | |
| 6.2.3.5.1.7.2 | S_AHR_61015533 - Profiles | 24.5 | |
| 6.2.3.5.1.7.3 | S_PH9_46000017 - Succession ( | 25.5.7 | |
| 6.2.3.5.1.7.4 | S_AHR_61015536 - Expired Quali | 23.5 | |
| 6.2.3.5.1.7.5 | S_PH9_46000016 - Qualifications | 23.5 | |
| 6.2.3.5.1.7.6 | HRPDV00REPORT0001 - Maintai | 23.5 | |
| 6.2.3.5.1.8 | Profile | | |
| 6.2.3.5.1.8.1 | S_PH9_46000019 - Objects Witho | 24.5 | |
| 6.2.3.5.1.8.2 | S_PH9_46000018 - Objects With | 24.5 | |
| 6.2.3.5.1.9 | Others | | |
| 6.2.3.5.1.9.1 | S_AHR_61016214 - Prebookings | 36.14 | |
| 6.2.3.5.1.9.2 | S_PH9_46000022 - List of Alterna | 23.5 | |
| 6.2.3.6 | Settings | | |
| 6.2.3.6.1 | PPUP - User-Specific | 25.4 | |
| 6.2.3.6.2 | Current Settings | | |
| 6.2.3.6.2.1 | S_AHR_61003929 - Edit Qualification | 23.2 | |
| 6.2.3.6.2.2 | S_AHR_61007208 - Edit Careers | 25.2 | |
| 6.2.3.6.2.3 | S_AHR_61003917 - Qualifications Pr | 24.2.1 | |
| 6.2.3.6.2.4 | S_AHR_61007168 - Edit Developmer | 26.3 | |
| 6.2.3.6.2.5 | S_AHR_61003969 - Edit Appraisals ( | 27.2 | |
| 6.2.3.6.2.6 | S_AHR_61007222 - Define Authorizat | 17.4, 17.5 | |
| 6.2.3.6.2.7 | S_AHR_61003942 - Assign Authoriza | 17.6 | |
| 6.2.4 | Benefits | | OoS |
| 6.2.5 | Compensation Management | | OoS |
| 6.2.6 | Personnel Cost Planning | | OoS |
| 6.2.7 | Management of Global Employees | | OoS |
| 6.2.8 | Administrative Services | | OoS |
| 6.2.9 | Pension Scheme | | OoS |
| 6.2.10 | Position Budgeting and Control | | OoS |
| 6.3 | Time Management | | OoS |
| 6.4 | Payroll | | OoS |
| 6.5 | SAP Learning Solution | | OoS |

| *Sequence number* | *SAP Menu (ECC 6.0)* | *Where covered* | *Why not covered* |
|---|---|---|---|
| 6.6 | Training and Event Management | | |
| 6.6.1 | Attendance | | |
| 6.6.1.1 | PSV1 - Attendance Menu | 36.3 | |
| 6.6.1.2 | PV00 - Book: Attendee for Business Event | 36.7 | |
| 6.6.1.3 | PV07 - Book: Attendee List for Business Ever | 36.8 | |
| 6.6.1.4 | PV08 - Book: Attendee for Business Event Lis | 36.9 | |
| 6.6.1.5 | PV02 - Prebook: Attendee for Business Event | 36.4.5 | |
| 6.6.1.6 | PV06 - Prebook: Attendee List for Business E | 36.5 | |
| 6.6.1.7 | PV16 - Prebook: Attendee for Business Event | 36.6 | |
| 6.6.1.8 | PV03 - Replace | 36.10 | |
| 6.6.1.9 | PV01 - Rebook Attendance | 36.11 | |
| 6.6.1.10 | PV04 - Cancel Attendance | 36.12 | |
| 6.6.1.11 | PV34 - Appraisals | 36.13.1 | |
| 6.6.1.12 | Correspondence | | |
| 6.6.1.12.1 | PVK0 - History | 37.3 | |
| 6.6.1.12.2 | PP40 - Manual Output | 37.2 | |
| 6.6.2 | Business Events | | |
| 6.6.2.1 | PSV2 - Business Event Menu | 34.2 | |
| 6.6.2.2 | Dates | | |
| 6.6.2.2.1 | PV10 - Create with Resources | 34.4 | |
| 6.6.2.2.2 | PV11 - Create Without Resources | 34.3 | |
| 6.6.2.2.3 | PV1A - Change | 34.6 | |
| 6.6.2.2.4 | PV1B - Display | 34.7 | |
| 6.6.2.2.5 | PSVP - Planning Menu | 34.5 | |
| 6.6.2.3 | PV12 - Firmly Book / Cancel | 34.8, 34.9 | |
| 6.6.2.4 | PV14 - Lock / Unlock | 34.10 | |
| 6.6.2.5 | PV15 - Follow Up | 34.13 | |
| 6.6.2.6 | PV33 - Appraisals | 34.12.1 | |
| 6.6.2.7 | PV1D - Price Proposal | 34.14 | |
| 6.6.2.8 | Billing and Activity Allocation | | |
| 6.6.2.8.1 | PV1C - Cost Transfer Posting | 38.6.2 | |
| 6.6.2.8.2 | PV17 - Billing | 38.7.1 | |
| 6.6.2.8.3 | PV18 - Activity Allocation: Attendance | 38.5.1 | |
| 6.6.2.8.4 | PV19 - Activity Allocation: Instructor Functi | 38.5.2 | |
| 6.6.2.9 | Budget | | |
| 6.6.2.9.1 | PVB0 - Budgeting | 38.11.1 | |
| 6.6.2.9.2 | PVBA - Comparison | 38.11.2 | |
| 6.6.2.10 | PV1M - Materials Procurement | 38.8.1 | |

| *Sequence number* | *SAP Menu (ECC 6.0)* | *Where covered* | *Why not covered* |
|---|---|---|---|
| 6.6.3 | Resources | | |
| 6.6.3.1 | PSVR - Resource Menu | 33.6 | |
| 6.6.3.2 | Create | | |
| 6.6.3.2.1 | OORA - Room | 33.2 | |
| 6.6.3.2.2 | OOER - External Instructor | 35.5 | |
| 6.6.3.2.3 | OORE - Other Resource | 33.3 | |
| 6.6.3.3 | Change/Display | | |
| 6.6.3.3.1 | PO18 - Room | 33.2 | |
| 6.6.3.3.2 | PO19 - External Instructor | 35.5 | |
| 6.6.3.3.3 | PO07 - Other Resource | 33.3 | |
| 6.6.3.4 | PVG2 - Lock/Unlock | 33.4.3 | |
| 6.6.4 | Information System | | |
| 6.6.4.1 | PSV3 - Information Menu | 32.2 | |
| 6.6.4.2 | Reports | | |
| 6.6.4.2.1 | Attendances | | |
| 6.6.4.2.1.1 | S_PH9_46000434 - Attendee List | 36.14 | |
| 6.6.4.2.1.2 | S_PH9_46000433 - Attendance List | 36.14 | |
| 6.6.4.2.1.3 | S_PH9_46000432 - Employee List | 36.14 | |
| 6.6.4.2.1.4 | S_AHR_61016215 - Bookings per Attend | 36.14 | |
| 6.6.4.2.1.5 | S_PH9_46000431 - Attendee's Training I | 36.14 | |
| 6.6.4.2.1.6 | S_PH9_46000430 - Attendance Prerequi | 36.14 | |
| 6.6.4.2.1.7 | S_PH9_46000429 - Attendee's Qualificat | 36.14 | |
| 6.6.4.2.1.8 | S_PH9_46000428 - Prerequisites Match | 36.14 | |
| 6.6.4.2.1.9 | S_PH9_46000452 - Attendee Appraisals | 36.13.2 | |
| 6.6.4.2.1.10 | S_PH9_46000427 - Prebookings per Bu | 36.14 | |
| 6.6.4.2.1.11 | S_AHR_61016214 - Prebookings per Att | 36.14 | |
| 6.6.4.2.1.12 | S_PH9_46000426 - Attendees for Reboo | 36.14 | |
| 6.6.4.2.1.13 | S_ALR_87014085 - Attendance Statistics | 36.14 | |
| 6.6.4.2.1.14 | S_PH9_46000425 - Attendance and Sale | 36.14 | |
| 6.6.4.2.1.15 | S_PH9_46000424 - Cancellations per Bu | 36.14 | |
| 6.6.4.2.1.16 | S_AHR_61016216 - Cancellations per At | 36.14 | |
| 6.6.4.2.1.17 | S_PH9_46000423 - Budget Comparison | 38.11.2 | |

| *Sequence number* | *SAP Menu (ECC 6.0)* | *Where covered* | *Why not covered* |
|---|---|---|---|
| 6.6.4.2.2 | Business Events | | |
| 6.6.4.2.2.1 | S_AHR_61016220 - Business Event Den | 34.14 | |
| 6.6.4.2.2.2 | S_PH9_46000438 - Business Event Sch | 34.14 | |
| 6.6.4.2.2.3 | S_PH9_46000451 - Business Event Appı | 34.12.2 | |
| 6.6.4.2.2.4 | S_AHR_61016217 - Business Event Hier | 34.14 | |
| 6.6.4.2.2.5 | S_ALR_87014085 - Attendance Statistics | 34.14 | |
| 6.6.4.2.2.6 | S_AHR_61016218 - Business Event Broc | 34.14 | |
| 6.6.4.2.2.7 | S_PH0_48000476 - Business Event Infor | 34.14 | |
| 6.6.4.2.2.8 | S_AHR_61016219 - Business Event Date | 34.14 | |
| 6.6.4.2.2.9 | S_PH9_46000437 - Resource List per Bu | 34.14 | |
| 6.6.4.2.2.10 | S_PH9_46000436 - Resources Not Yet A | 34.14 | |
| 6.6.4.2.2.11 | S_PH9_46000435 - Material Requiremer | 34.14 | |
| 6.6.4.2.2.12 | S_AHR_61016221 - Business Event Pric | 34.14 | |
| 6.6.4.2.3 | Resources | | |
| 6.6.4.2.3.1 | S_AHR_61016224 - Resource Equipmer | 33.7 | |
| 6.6.4.2.3.2 | S_ALR_87014087 - Resource Reservatic | 33.7 | |
| 6.6.4.2.3.3 | S_PH0_48000096 - Instructor Informatior | 33.7 | |
| 6.6.4.2.3.4 | S_PH9_46000441 - Graphical Resource | 33.7 | |
| 6.6.4.2.3.5 | S_AHR_61016225 - Available/Reserved I | 33.7 | |
| 6.6.4.2.3.6 | S_PH9_46000440 - Resource Reservatic | 33.7 | |
| 6.6.4.2.3.7 | S_PH9_46000439 - Resources Not Yet A | 33.7 | |
| 6.6.4.2.4 | S_PH0_48000535 - Ad Hoc Query | 32.2.9 | |
| 6.6.5 | Tools | | |
| 6.6.5.1 | PSVT - Tool Menu | 32.3 | |
| 6.6.5.2 | Database | | |
| 6.6.5.2.1 | RE_RHDBST00 - General Database Statistic | 19.1.1 | |
| 6.6.5.2.2 | RE_RHVSTA00 - Database Statistics - Numb | 19.1.2 | |
| 6.6.5.2.3 | RE_RHVSTA10 - Database Statistics - Numb | 19.1.3 | |
| 6.6.5.2.4 | RE_RHVSTA20 - Database Statistics - Numb | 19.1.4 | |
| 6.6.5.2.5 | RE_RHVSTA30 - Database Statistics - Numb | 19.1.5 | |
| 6.6.5.2.6 | RE_RHCHECK1 - Check Consistency | 19.1.6 | |
| 6.6.5.2.7 | RE_RHCHECKV - Check Relationships | 19.1.7 | |
| 6.6.5.2.8 | RE_RHRHAZ00 - Display DB Records | 19.1.8 | |
| 6.6.5.2.9 | RE_RHRHDL00 - Delete DB Records | 19.1.9 | |
| 6.6.5.2.10 | RE_RHRHDC00 - Delete with List | 19.1.10 | |
| 6.6.5.2.11 | RE_RHREFDOC0 - Reference Document Re | 38.5.1 | |

| *Sequence number* | *SAP Menu (ECC 6.0)* | *Where covered* | *Why not covered* |
|---|---|---|---|
| 6.6.5.3 | Structural Authorization | | |
| 6.6.5.3.1 | RE_RHAUTH00 - Per User/Profile | 17.9 | |
| 6.6.6 | Settings | | |
| 6.6.6.1 | Current Settings | | |
| 6.6.6.1.1 | S_AHR_61011845 - Cost Items | 31.14.1 | |
| 6.6.6.1.2 | S_AHR_61011844 - Time Schedule | 31.5.4–31.5.5 | |
| 6.6.6.1.3 | S_AHR_61011841 - Location | 33.8 | |
| 6.6.6.1.4 | S_AHR_61011843 - Building Address | 14.15.2 | |
| 6.6.6.1.5 | Organizer | | |
| 6.6.6.1.5.1 | PSVQ - Create... | 29.1 | |
| 6.6.6.1.5.2 | PSVO - Change/Display... | 29.1 | |
| 6.6.6.1.6 | Attendee | | |
| 6.6.6.1.6.1 | PSV8 - Create... | 35.1 | |
| 6.6.6.1.6.2 | PSV9 - Change/Display... | 35.1 | |
| 6.6.6.1.7 | S_AHR_61011889 - Business Event Group | 30 | |
| 6.6.6.1.8 | S_AHR_61011888 - Business Event Type | 31 | |
| 6.6.6.1.9 | Resource Management | | |
| 6.6.6.1.9.1 | S_AHR_61011886 - Resource Type | 33.1 | |
| 6.6.6.1.9.2 | S_AHR_61011885 - Room | 33.2 | |
| 6.6.6.1.9.3 | S_AHR_61011893 - External Instructor | 35.5 | |
| 6.6.6.1.9.4 | S_AHR_61011901 - Other Resource | 33.3 | |
| 6.6.6.1.10 | S_AHR_61011887 - Master Data Catalog | 29 | |
| 6.6.6.1.11 | S_AHR_61011912 - Maintain Authorization P | 17.4, 17.5 | |
| 6.6.6.1.12 | S_AHR_61011911 - Assign Authorization Prc | 17.6 | |
| 6.6.6.2 | PSV4 - Set Plan Version | 15.3 | |
| 6.6.6.3 | PSVI - User-Specific Settings | 32.4 | |

| *Sequence number* | *SAP Menu (ECC 6.0)* | *Where covered* | *Why not covered* |
|---|---|---|---|
| 6.7 | Organizational Management | | |
| 6.7.1 | Organizational Plan | | |
| 6.7.1.1 | Organization and Staffing | | |
| 6.7.1.1.1 | PPOCE - Create | 1.2, 2.1, 3.2 | |
| 6.7.1.1.2 | PPOME - Change | 1.3, 2.1, 3.2 | |
| 6.7.1.1.3 | PPOSE - Display | 2.1 | |
| 6.7.1.2 | General structures | | |
| 6.7.1.2.1 | PPSC - Create | 2.2 | |
| 6.7.1.2.2 | PPSM - Change | 2.2 | |
| 6.7.1.2.3 | PPSS - Display | 2.2 | |
| 6.7.1.3 | Matrix | | |
| 6.7.1.3.1 | PPME - Change | 12.6.3 | |
| 6.7.1.3.2 | PPMS - Display | 12.6.3 | |
| 6.7.2 | Expert Mode | | |
| 6.7.2.1 | PO10 - Organizational Unit | 2.4, 3.2 | |
| 6.7.2.2 | PO03 - Job | 2.4, 5.2 | |
| 6.7.2.3 | PO13 - Position | 2.4, 4.2 | |
| 6.7.2.4 | PO01 - Work center | 2.4, 9.2 | |
| 6.7.2.5 | PFCT - Task Catalog | 8.2 | |
| 6.7.2.6 | PP01 - General | 2.4 | |
| 6.7.2.7 | Simple Maintenance | | |
| 6.7.2.7.1 | PPOC_OLD - Create | 2.3 | |
| 6.7.2.7.2 | PPOM_OLD - Change | 2.3 | |
| 6.7.2.7.3 | PPOS_OLD - Display | 2.3 | |
| 6.7.3 | Info System | | |
| 6.7.3.1 | Organizational Unit | | |
| 6.7.3.1.1 | S_AHR_61016491 - Existing Organizatio | 3.5 | |
| 6.7.3.1.2 | S_AHR_61016492 - Staff Functions for O | 3.5 | |
| 6.7.3.1.3 | Organizational Structure | | |
| 6.7.3.1.3.1 | S_AHR_61016493 - Organizational St | 3.5 | |
| 6.7.3.1.3.2 | S_AHR_61016494 - Organizational St | 3.5 | |
| 6.7.3.1.3.3 | S_AHR_61016495 - Organizational St | 3.5 | |
| 6.7.3.1.3.4 | S_AHR_61016496 - Organizational St | 3.5 | |

| *Sequence number* | *SAP Menu (ECC 6.0)* | *Where covered* | *Why not covered* |
|---|---|---|---|
| 6.7.3.2 | Job | | |
| 6.7.3.2.1 | S_AHR_61016497 - Existing Jobs | 5.5 | |
| 6.7.3.2.2 | S_AHR_61016498 - Job Index | 5.5 | |
| 6.7.3.2.3 | S_AHR_61016499 - Job Description | 5.5 | |
| 6.7.3.2.4 | S_AHR_61016500 - Task Description for Jobs | 5.5 | |
| 6.7.3.2.5 | S_AHR_61016501 - Complete Job Description | 5.5 | |
| 6.7.3.3 | Position | | |
| 6.7.3.3.1 | S_AHR_61018869 - Periods When Positions Ar | 4.7 | |
| 6.7.3.3.2 | S_AHR_61016502 - Existing Positions | 4.7 | |
| 6.7.3.3.3 | S_AHR_61016503 - Staff Assignments | 4.7 | |
| 6.7.3.3.4 | S_AHR_61016504 - Position Description | 4.7 | |
| 6.7.3.3.5 | S_AHR_61016505 - Task Description for Positic | 4.7 | |
| 6.7.3.3.6 | S_AHR_61016506 - Staff Functions for Position: | 4.7 | |
| 6.7.3.3.7 | S_AHR_61016507 - Authorities and Resources | 4.7 | |
| 6.7.3.3.8 | S_AHR_61016508 - Planned Labor Costs | 4.7 | |
| 6.7.3.3.9 | S_AHR_61016509 - Vacant Positions | 4.7 | |
| 6.7.3.3.10 | S_AHR_61016510 - Correct Vacancies | 4.7 | |
| 6.7.3.3.11 | S_AHR_61018831 - Obsolete Positions | 4.7 | |
| 6.7.3.3.12 | S_AHR_61016511 - Complete Position Descrip | 4.7 | |
| 6.7.3.3.13 | Report Structure | | |
| 6.7.3.3.13.1 | S_AHR_61016512 - Report Structure Withou | 4.7 | |
| 6.7.3.3.13.2 | S_AHR_61016513 - Report Structure with Pe | 4.7 | |
| 6.7.3.4 | Work Center | | |
| 6.7.3.4.1 | S_AHR_61016514 - Existing Work Centers | 9.3 | |
| 6.7.3.4.2 | S_AHR_61016515 - Work Centers per Organiza | 9.3 | |
| 6.7.3.4.3 | S_AHR_61016516 - Authorities and Resources | 9.3 | |
| 6.7.3.4.4 | S_AHR_61016517 - Planned Labor Costs | 9.3 | |
| 6.7.3.4.5 | Restrictions | | |
| 6.7.3.4.5.1 | S_AHR_61016518 - Work Centers with Rest | 9.3 | |
| 6.7.3.4.5.2 | S_AHR_61016519 - Single Work Centers wi | 9.3 | |
| 6.7.3.4.6 | Health Examinations | | |
| 6.7.3.4.6.1 | S_AHR_61016520 - Work Centers Requiring | 9.3 | |
| 6.7.3.4.6.2 | S_AHR_61016521 - Single Work Centers Re | 9.3 | |

| *Sequence number* | *SAP Menu (ECC 6.0)* | *Where covered* | *Why not covered* |
|---|---|---|---|
| 6.7.3.5 | Tasks | | |
| 6.7.3.5.1 | S_AHR_61016522 - Existing Tasks | 8.6 | |
| 6.7.3.5.2 | Activity Profile | | |
| 6.7.3.5.2.1 | S_AHR_61016523 - Activity Profile for Po: | 8.6 | |
| 6.7.3.5.2.2 | S_AHR_61016524 - Activity Profile of Pos | 8.6 | |
| 6.7.3.5.3 | Characterization | | |
| 6.7.3.5.3.1 | S_AHR_61016525 - Character of Tasks i | 8.6 | |
| 6.7.3.5.3.2 | S_AHR_61016526 - Character of Individu | 8.6 | |
| 6.7.3.6 | General | | |
| 6.7.3.6.1 | S_AHR_61016527 - Existing Objects | 10.1.9 | |
| 6.7.3.6.2 | S_AHR_61016528 - Structure Display/Mainte | 12.5 | |
| 6.7.3.6.3 | S_AHR_61016529 - Structure Navigation Ins | 12.5 | |
| 6.7.3.6.4 | S_AHR_61016530 - PD Graphics Interface | 2.5 | |
| 6.7.3.6.5 | S_AHR_61016531 - Display and Maintain Inf | 13.5 | |
| 6.7.3.6.6 | S_AHR_61016532 - Infotype Reporting | 13.5 | |
| 6.7.3.6.7 | HR Master Data | | |
| 6.7.3.6.7.1 | S_AHR_61016533 - Start HR Reporting v | 12.5 | |
| 6.7.4 | Tools | | |
| 6.7.4.1 | Plan Version | | |
| 6.7.4.1.1 | RE_RHCOPLPT - Compare | 15.8 | |
| 6.7.4.1.2 | RE_RHCOPL00 - Copy | 15.6 | |
| 6.7.4.2 | Object | | |
| 6.7.4.2.1 | PP03 - Actions | 2.6.1 | |
| 6.7.4.2.2 | PSO3 - Object description | 13.5 | |
| 6.7.4.2.3 | RE_RHDESC10 - Display infotypes | 13.5 | |
| 6.7.4.2.4 | RE_RHCOPY00 - Copy | 10.1.8 | |
| 6.7.4.2.5 | RE_RHCOPY10 - Copy with list | 10.1.8 | |
| 6.7.4.2.6 | RE_RHCOPYSTRUCT - Copy structures | 15.7 | |
| 6.7.4.2.7 | RE_RHAKTI00 - Change status | 16.4 | |
| 6.7.4.3 | Infotype | | |
| 6.7.4.3.1 | PSO4 - Individual maintenance | 13.5 | |
| 6.7.4.3.2 | RE_RHGRENZ4 - New end date | 13.5 | |
| 6.7.4.3.3 | RE_RHBEGDA0 - New start date | 13.5 | |
| 6.7.4.3.4 | RE_RHTRANS0 - Translate | 13.5 | |
| 6.7.4.4 | Integration PA | | |
| 6.7.4.4.1 | OOHQ - Batch input sessions | 18.1.1 | |
| 6.7.4.4.2 | RE_RHREPL20 - Replace user | 18.1.4 | |

| *Sequence number* | *SAP Menu (ECC 6.0)* | *Where covered* | *Why not covered* |
|---|---|---|---|
| 6.7.4.5 | Struct.authorization | | |
| 6.7.4.5.1 | RE_RHAUTH00 - Per user/profile | 17.9 | |
| 6.7.4.6 | Database | | |
| 6.7.4.6.1 | RE_RHDBST00 - Database statistics | 19.1.1 | |
| 6.7.4.6.2 | RE_RHCHECK1 - Check consistency | 19.1.6 | |
| 6.7.4.6.3 | RE_RHCHECKV - Check relationships | 19.1.7 | |
| 6.7.4.6.4 | RE_RHRHAZ00 - Display DB records | 19.1.8 | |
| 6.7.4.6.5 | RE_RHRHDL00 - Delete DB records | 19.1.9 | |
| 6.7.4.6.6 | RE_RHRHDC00 - Delete with list | 19.1.10 | |
| 6.7.4.7 | Data transfer | | |
| 6.7.4.7.1 | RE_RHMOVE30 - Manual transport | 20.3 | |
| 6.7.4.7.2 | OOMV - Create sequential file | 20.4.1 | |
| 6.7.4.7.3 | OODT - Legacy Data Transfer | 20.4.3 | |
| 6.7.4.8 | Distribution/ALE | | |
| 6.7.4.8.1 | PFAL - Distribute master data | 20.5.1 | |
| 6.7.4.8.2 | RE_RHALECPS - Display change pointers | 20.5.2 | |
| 6.7.4.8.3 | RE_RHALESMD - Evaluate change pointers | 20.5.3 | |
| 6.7.4.9 | Quota Planning | | |
| 6.7.4.9.1 | S_PH0_48000088 - Delete Unoccupied Posi | 14.14.6 | |
| 6.7.4.9.2 | S_PH0_48000087 - Copying Quota Planning | 14.14.6 | |
| 6.7.4.9.3 | S_PH0_48000086 - Copying the Current Rec | 14.14.6 | |
| 6.7.4.9.4 | S_PH0_48000085 - Freeze Planned Quota | 14.14.6 | |
| 6.7.4.9.5 | S_PH0_48000084 - Generation of Positions | 14.14.2 | |
| 6.7.5 | Settings | | |
| 6.7.5.1 | PSO0 - Set Plan Version | 15.3 | |
| 6.7.5.2 | PPOM_MODE - Set Maintenance Interface | 2.7 | |
| 6.7.5.3 | Current Settings | | |
| 6.7.5.3.1 | S_AHR_61003187 - Create Working Time Gr | 14.10.2 | |
| 6.7.5.3.2 | S_AHR_61007150 - Create Authorities/ Resc | 14.9.3 | |
| 6.7.5.3.3 | S_AHR_61003603 - Create Health Promotioi | 14.8.3 | |
| 6.7.5.3.4 | S_AHR_61007156 - Create Restrictions | 14.5.3 | |
| 6.7.5.3.5 | S_AHR_61003170 - Create Justifications | 14.5.4 | |
| 6.7.5.3.6 | S_AHR_61003172 - Create Building Address | 14.15.2 | |
| 6.7.5.3.7 | S_AHR_61003129 - Check Integration Consi | 18.1.1 | |
| 6.7.5.3.8 | S_AHR_61003751 - Define Authorization Pro | 17.4, 17.5 | |
| 6.7.5.3.9 | S_AHR_61003750 - Assign Authorization Prc | 17.6 | |

# SAP Customizing Implementation Guide

| *Sequence number* | *SAP Customizing Implementation Guide (ECC 6.0)* | *Where covered* | *Why not covered* |
|---|---|---|---|
| | SAP Customizing Implementation Guide | | |
| 1 | Activate SAP ECC Extensions | | OoS |
| 2 | SAP NetWeaver | | OoS |
| 3 | Enterprise Structure | | OoS |
| 4 | Cross-Application Components | | OoS |
| 5 | Auto-ID Infrastructure | | OoS |
| 6 | SAP xApp Resource and Portfolio Management | | OoS |
| 7 | Financial Accounting | | OoS |
| 8 | Financial Accounting (New) | | OoS |
| 9 | Financial Supply Chain Management | | OoS |
| 10 | Strategic Enterprise Management/Business An | | OoS |
| 11 | Controlling | | OoS |
| 12 | Investment Management | | OoS |
| 13 | Enterprise Controlling | | OoS |
| 14 | Real Estate | | OoS |
| 15 | Flexible Real Estate Management (RE-FX) | | OoS |
| 16 | Logistics - General | | OoS |
| 17 | Environment, Health and Safety | | OoS |
| 18 | Sales and Distribution | | OoS |
| 19 | Materials Management | | OoS |
| 20 | Logistics Execution | | OoS |
| 21 | Quality Management | | OoS |
| 22 | Plant Maintenance and Customer Service | | OoS |
| 23 | Customer Service | | OoS |
| 24 | Production | | OoS |
| 25 | Production Planning for Process Industries | | OoS |
| 26 | Project System | | OoS |
| 27 | Collaboration Projects | | OoS |
| 28 | Collaboration Folders | | OoS |
| 29 | Personnel Management | | |
| 29.1 | Global Settings in Personnel Management | | OoS |

| *Sequence number* | *SAP Customizing Implementation Guide (ECC 6.0)* | *Where covered* | *Why not covered* |
|---|---|---|---|
| 29.2 | Organizational Management | | |
| 29.2.1 | Basic Settings | | |
| 29.2.1.1 | Maintain Number Ranges | | |
| 29.2.1.1.1 | Set Up Number Assignment for All P | 15.5 | |
| 29.2.1.1.2 | Maintain Number Ranges | 10.2.4 | |
| 29.2.1.1.3 | Customer Enhancement (User Exit): | 10.2.6 | |
| 29.2.1.2 | Data Model Enhancement | | |
| 29.2.1.2.1 | Maintain Object Types | 22.1–22.6 | |
| 29.2.1.2.2 | Infotype Maintenance | | |
| 29.2.1.2.2.1 | Maintain Infotypes | 22.7–22.9 | |
| 29.2.1.2.2.2 | Maintain Subtypes | 22.10, 22.8 | |
| 29.2.1.2.2.3 | Maintain User-Defined Settings f | 22.11 | |
| 29.2.1.2.2.4 | Maintain Country-Specific Infotyp | 22.12 | |
| 29.2.1.2.3 | Relationship Maintenance | | |
| 29.2.1.2.3.1 | Maintain Relationships | 22.13–22.19 | |
| 29.2.1.2.3.2 | Define Time Constraint Dependi | 22.20 | |
| 29.2.1.2.3.3 | Specify Start Date as Variable for | 22.21 | |
| 29.2.1.2.4 | Check Consistency of Installation | 19.1.11 | |
| 29.2.1.3 | Maintain Evaluation Paths | 12.2, 12.3 | |
| 29.2.1.4 | Maintain Personnel Actions | 2.6.2–2.6.4 | |
| 29.2.1.5 | Authorization Management | | |
| 29.2.1.5.1 | Maintain Authorizations | 17.1.4 | |
| 29.2.1.5.2 | Maintain Profiles | 17.1.4 | |
| 29.2.1.5.3 | Maintain User Master Record | 17.1.5 | |
| 29.2.1.5.4 | Structural Authorization | | |
| 29.2.1.5.4.1 | Maintain Structural Profiles | 17.4, 17.5 | |
| 29.2.1.5.4.2 | Assign Structural Authorization | 17.6 | |
| 29.2.1.5.4.3 | Save User Data in SAP Memory | 17.8 | |
| 29.2.1.5.4.4 | BAdI: Structural Authorization | 17.1.8 | |
| 29.2.1.5.4.5 | BAdI: Define Assigned Structural | 17.1.8 | |
| 29.2.1.6 | Dialog Control | | |
| 29.2.1.6.1 | Specify Sequence of Languages Ava | 19.2 | |
| 29.2.1.6.2 | Set Up SAPscript Connection for Sub | 14.1.3 | |
| 29.2.1.6.3 | Set Search Function | 19.3 | |
| 29.2.1.7 | Activate Inheritance of Account Assignm | 14.7.2 | |
| 29.2.1.8 | Activate Change Documents | 17.1.7 | |

| *Sequence number* | *SAP Customizing Implementation Guide (ECC 6.0)* | *Where covered* | *Why not covered* |
|---|---|---|---|
| 29.2.2 | Transport | | |
| 29.2.2.1 | Set Up Transport Connection | 20.1 | |
| 29.2.2.2 | Lock Infotypes for Import | 20.2 | |
| 29.2.2.3 | Manual Transport | 20.3 | |
| 29.2.3 | Workbench Data Transfer | | |
| 29.2.3.1 | Data Transfer Workbench: Personnel Plann | 20.4 | |
| 29.2.4 | Integration | | |
| 29.2.4.1 | Integration with Personnel Administration | | |
| 29.2.4.1.1 | Workflow for Organizational Change (WS | 18.3 | |
| 29.2.4.1.2 | Workflow Message About New Employe | 18.3 | |
| 29.2.4.1.3 | Set up Integration with Personnel Admin | 18.1.2, 18.1.3 | |
| 29.2.4.1.4 | Transfer Data from Personnel Administr | 18.1.1 | |
| 29.2.4.1.5 | Prepare Integration with Personnel Adm | 18.1.1 | |
| 29.2.4.1.6 | Transfer Data to Personnel Administrati | 18.1.1 | |
| 29.2.4.1.7 | Check Integration Consistency | 18.1.1 | |
| 29.2.4.1.8 | BAdI: Return Validity Period of Persons t | 18.1.5 | |
| 29.2.4.2 | Set Up Integration with Cost Accounting | 14.7.3 | |
| 29.2.4.3 | Set Up Integration for Cost Distribution | 14.13.2 | |
| 29.2.4.4 | Integration with SAP Business Partner | | |
| 29.2.4.4.1 | Activate Integration | 18.4.2–18.4.4 | |
| 29.2.4.4.2 | Data Synchronization: Organizational Un | 18.4.4 | |
| 29.2.4.4.3 | Data Sychronization: Persons - Activate I | 18.4.3 | |
| 29.2.4.4.4 | Activate Logging/Error Analysis for Data | 18.4.5 | |
| 29.2.4.4.5 | Assign HR Key for Marital Status to Busi | 18.4.7 | |
| 29.2.4.4.6 | Assign HR Form of Address Key to Form | 18.4.8 | |
| 29.2.5 | Infotype Settings | | |
| 29.2.5.1 | Activate/Deactivate "Vacancy" Infotype | 14.6.5 | |
| 29.2.5.2 | Working Time | | |
| 29.2.5.2.1 | Maintain Working Time Groups | 14.10.2 | |
| 29.2.5.2.2 | Maintain Rule Values | 14.10.3 | |
| 29.2.5.3 | Set up Check Values for Authorities/Resour | 14.9.3 | |
| 29.2.5.4 | Set Up Check Values for Health Examinatio | 14.8.3 | |
| 29.2.5.5 | Set up Check Values for Restrictions | 14.5.3 | |
| 29.2.5.6 | Set Up Check Values for Reasons | 14.5.4 | |
| 29.2.5.7 | Set Up Check Values for Buildings | 14.15.2 | |

| *Sequence number* | *SAP Customizing Implementation Guide (ECC 6.0)* | *Where covered* | *Why not covered* |
|---|---|---|---|
| 29.2.5.8 | Quota Planning | | |
| 29.2.5.8.1 | Set Subtypes for Quota Planning | | |
| 29.2.5.8.2 | Define Planning Type and Periods | 14.14.4 | |
| 29.2.5.8.3 | Define Calculation in Full-Time Equivale | 14.14.5 | |
| 29.2.6 | Edit Organizational Plan | 2.3 | |
| 29.2.7 | Matrix Organization | | |
| 29.2.7.1 | Define Matrix Types | 12.6.2 | |
| 29.2.8 | Dialog Control | | |
| 29.2.8.1 | Set Up Editing Parameters for Staffing Sche | 19.4 | |
| 29.2.8.2 | Customer Enhancements (User Exits) | 19.5 | |
| 29.2.8.3 | Settings for "Simple Maintenance" | 19.6 | |
| 29.2.9 | Data Extraction | | |
| 29.2.9.1 | Define Scenarios | 20.6.1 | |
| 29.2.9.2 | Assign Queries | 20.6.2 | |
| 29.2.10 | Hierarchy Framework | | |
| 29.2.10.1 | Adjust Tab Pages in Detail Area | | |
| 29.2.10.1.1 | Change Text and Icons on a Tab Page | 21.1.3, 21.1.5 | |
| 29.2.10.1.2 | Change the Tab Page Sequence | 21.1.5 | |
| 29.2.10.1.3 | Hide/Show Tab Page | 21.1.5 | |
| 29.2.10.2 | Integrate New Infotype | | |
| 29.2.10.2.1 | Add Infotype as Tab Page in Detail Area | 21.1.3, 21.1.5 | |
| 29.2.10.2.2 | Display Infotype as Column in Object Ma | 21.2.3, 21.2.4 | |
| 29.2.10.3 | Integrate New Object Type | | |
| 29.2.10.3.1 | Add Object Type to Object Manager | 21.3.3, 21.3.6 | |
| 29.2.10.3.2 | Display Object Type in Detail Area | 21.1.3, 21.1.5 | |
| 29.2.10.3.3 | Display Object Type in Structural Overvie | 21.1.6, 21.1.7 | |
| 29.2.10.4 | Exclude Infotypes when Copying Internal Ob | 21.4 | |
| 29.2.10.5 | Column Framework | | |
| 29.2.10.5.1 | Define Your Own Column Groups/Chan | 21.2.3, 21.2.4, 21.3.5 | |
| 29.2.10.5.2 | Define Hierarchical Column Group | 21.2.6 | |
| 29.2.10.5.3 | Define Your Own Column | 21.2.3 | |
| 29.2.10.5.4 | Adjust Existing Column Group | 21.2.4 | |
| 29.2.10.5.5 | Define Your Own Coherence Relationsh | 21.3.5 | |
| 29.2.10.5.6 | Define Your Own Header Type | 21.2.7 | |

| *Sequence number* | *SAP Customizing Implementation Guide (ECC 6.0)* | *Where covered* | *Why not covered* |
|---|---|---|---|
| 29.2.10.6 | Object Manager | | |
| 29.2.10.6.1 | Define Your Own Scenario | 21.3.6 | |
| 29.2.10.6.2 | Define Your Own Search Node | 21.3.3 | |
| 29.2.10.6.3 | Adjust Search Area | 21.3.6 | |
| 29.2.10.6.4 | Redefine Column Headers | 21.3.6 | |
| 29.2.10.6.5 | Display Your Own Column Group in | 21.3.6 | |
| 29.2.10.7 | Set Up Backup Prompt | 21.5 | |
| 29.2.10.8 | Assign InfoSets to Object Types | 21.6 | |
| 29.3 | Personnel Development | | |
| 29.3.1 | Basic Settings | | |
| 29.3.1.1 | Maintain Object Types | 22.1–22.6 | |
| 29.3.1.2 | Maintaining Number Ranges | | |
| 29.3.1.2.1 | Set Up Number Assignment for All P | 15.5 | |
| 29.3.1.2.2 | Maintain Number Ranges | 10.2.4 | |
| 29.3.1.2.3 | Customer Enhancements (User Exit | 10.2.6 | |
| 29.3.1.3 | Maintaining Infotypes | | |
| 29.3.1.3.1 | Maintain Infotypes | 22.7–22.9 | |
| 29.3.1.3.2 | Maintain User-Defined Settings for Ir | 22.11 | |
| 29.3.1.3.3 | Define Country-Specific Infotypes | 22.12 | |
| 29.3.1.4 | Maintain Subtypes | 22.10, 22.8 | |
| 29.3.1.5 | Maintain Relationships | 22.13–22.19 | |
| 29.3.1.5.1 | Define Time Constraint Depending c | 22.20 | |
| 29.3.1.6 | Maintain Evaluation Paths | 12.2, 12.3 | |
| 29.3.1.7 | Maintain Personnel Actions | 2.6.2–2.6.4 | |
| 29.3.1.8 | Specify Sequence of Languages Availab | 19.2 | |
| 29.3.1.9 | Authorization Management | | |
| 29.3.1.9.1 | Maintain Authorizations | 17.1.4 | |
| 29.3.1.9.2 | Structural Authorizations | | |
| 29.3.1.9.2.1 | Maintain Structural Authorization | 17.4, 17.5 | |
| 29.3.1.9.2.2 | Assign Structural Authorization | 17.6 | |
| 29.3.1.9.2.3 | Save User Data in SAP Memory | 17.8 | |
| 29.3.1.10 | Tools | | |
| 29.3.1.10.1 | Set Search Function | 19.3 | |
| 29.3.1.10.2 | Check Consistency of Installation | 19.1.11 | |
| 29.3.1.10.3 | Set Up SAPscript Connection for Sul | 14.1.3 | |
| 29.3.1.11 | Activate Change Documents | 17.1.7 | |

| Sequence number | SAP Customizing Implementation Guide (ECC 6.0) | Where covered | Why not covered |
|---|---|---|---|
| 29.3.2 | Integration | | |
| 29.3.2.1 | Set Up Integration with Personnel Admin. ar | 28.2.1, 28.2.3 | |
| 29.3.2.2 | Transfer Qualifications from Personnel Adm | 28.2.2 | |
| 29.3.2.3 | Transfer Qualifications from Recruitment | 28.3.2 | |
| 29.3.2.4 | Transfer Appraisals From Personnel Admin | 28.2.4 | |
| 29.3.3 | Master Data | | |
| 29.3.3.1 | Edit Organizational Plan | 2.3 | |
| 29.3.3.2 | Edit Scales | 23.6 | |
| 29.3.3.3 | Edit Qualifications Catalog | 23.2 | |
| 29.3.3.4 | Edit Careers | 25.2 | |
| 29.3.4 | Functions | | |
| 29.3.4.1 | Define Profile View | 24.6–24.10 | |
| 29.3.4.2 | Set Up Control Parameters | 23.7 | |
| 29.3.4.3 | Define Suitability Ranges | 25.3 | |
| 29.3.4.4 | Define Criteria for Detail Selection | 21.6 | |
| 29.3.4.5 | Activate/Deactivate "Vacancy" Infotype | 14.6.5 | |
| 29.3.4.6 | Enhancements | | |
| 29.3.4.6.1 | BAdI: Authorization Check for Accessing | 24.11 | |
| 29.3.4.6.2 | BAdI: Selection Options for "Find Objects | 23.4.1 | |
| 29.3.5 | Tools | | |
| 29.3.5.1 | Copy Requirements Profiles to Position Hol | 24.2.5 | |
| 29.3.5.2 | Qualifications Profile: Mass Data Maintenan | 24.2.1 | |
| 29.3.6 | Employee Self-Service (ESS) | | |
| 29.3.6.1 | Define Root Qualification Group | 23.7 | |
| 29.3.7 | Development Plans | | |
| 29.3.7.1 | Edit Development Plan Catalog | 26.3 | |
| 29.3.7.2 | Define Development Plan States | 26.4 | |
| 29.3.7.3 | Define Permissible Further Processing | 26.5 | |
| 29.3.7.4 | Further Processing of Plan States | 26.6 | |
| 29.3.7.5 | Automatic State Management | 26.7 | |
| 29.3.7.6 | Set Up Control Parameters | 26.6.5, 26.8 | |
| 29.3.8 | Objective Setting and Appraisals | | |
| 29.3.8.1 | Edit Basic Settings | 28.6.1 | |
| 29.3.8.2 | Edit Templates | 27.2–27.7 | |
| 29.3.8.3 | Set Up Integration Between HR and SEM Sy | | |
| 29.3.9 | Appraisal Systems | | Obsolete |

| *Sequence number* | *SAP Customizing Implementation Guide (ECC 6.0)* | *Where covered* | *Why not covered* |
|---|---|---|---|
| 29.4 | Personnel Administration | | OoS |
| 29.5 | HR Administrative Services | | OoS |
| 29.6 | Recruitment | | OoS |
| 29.7 | Benefits | | OoS |
| 29.8 | Compensation Management | | OoS |
| 29.9 | Personnel Cost Planning and Simulation | | OoS |
| 29.10 | Enterprise Compensation Management | | OoS |
| 29.11 | Management of Global Employees | | OoS |
| 29.12 | Company Pension Scheme | | OoS |
| 29.13 | Pension Fund | | OoS |
| 29.14 | Position Budgeting and Control | | OoS |
| 29.15 | Manager's Desktop | | OoS |
| 29.16 | Expert Finder | | OoS |
| 29.17 | Human Resources Information System | | OoS |
| 29.18 | Employee Self-Service | | OoS |
| 29.19 | Employee Interaction Center (EIC) | | OoS |
| 30 | SAP E-Recruiting | | OoS |
| 31 | Time Management | | OoS |
| 32 | Payroll | | OoS |
| 33 | Training and Event Management | | |
| 33.1 | SAP Learning Solution | | OoS |
| 33.2 | Difference: SAP Learning Solution - Training | | |
| 33.3 | Basic Settings | | |
| 33.3.1 | Plan Version Maintenance | | |
| 33.3.1.1 | Maintain Plan Versions | 15.2 | |
| 33.3.1.2 | Set Active Plan Version | 15.4 | |
| 33.3.2 | Number Range Maintenance | | |
| 33.3.2.1 | Set Up Plan Version-Independent Nu | 15.5 | |
| 33.3.2.2 | Define Number Ranges for Objects | 10.2.4 | |
| 33.3.2.3 | Define Number Ranges for External | 38.5.4 | |
| 33.3.3 | Object Type Modeling Enhancement | | |
| 33.3.3.1 | Object Type | | |
| 33.3.3.1.1 | Define Object Types | 22.1–22.6 | |

| *Sequence number* | *SAP Customizing Implementation Guide (ECC 6.0)* | *Where covered* | *Why not covered* |
|---|---|---|---|
| 33.3.3.2 | Infotype | | |
| 33.3.3.2.1 | Maintain Infotypes | 22.7–22.9 | |
| 33.3.3.2.2 | Maintain User-Defined Settings for Infoty | 22.11 | |
| 33.3.3.2.3 | Maintain Country-Specific Infotypes | 22.12 | |
| 33.3.3.2.4 | Subtype | | |
| 33.3.3.2.4.1 | Maintain Subtypes | 22.10, 22.8 | |
| 33.3.3.2.4.2 | Set Up SAPscript Connection for Sub | 14.1.3 | |
| 33.3.3.2.5 | Activate Change Documents | 17.1.7 | |
| 33.3.3.3 | Relationship | | |
| 33.3.3.3.1 | Maintain Relationships | 22.13–22.19 | |
| 33.3.3.3.2 | Define Time Constraint Depending on T | 22.20 | |
| 33.3.4 | Control Options for Days Off | | |
| 33.3.4.1 | Specify Factory Calendar | 33.8.5 | |
| 33.3.4.2 | Check Factory Calendar | 33.8.5 | |
| 33.3.5 | Dialog Control | | |
| 33.3.5.1 | Current Settings | | |
| 33.3.5.1.1 | Maintain Personnel Actions | 2.6.2–2.6.4 | |
| 33.3.5.1.2 | Specify Data Screen Display | 38.14.2 | |
| 33.3.5.1.3 | Customer Enhancement for Master Data | 38.14.3 | |
| 33.3.5.2 | Technical Settings | | |
| 33.3.5.2.1 | Specify Sequence of Languages Availab | 19.2 | |
| 33.3.5.2.2 | Set Up Search Function | 19.3 | |
| 33.3.5.2.3 | Note Function | | |
| 33.3.5.2.3.1 | Notes for Infotypes | 38.14.4 | |
| 33.3.5.2.3.2 | Procedure for Entering Notes | 38.14.5 | |
| 33.3.5.2.4 | List Entry for Attendee Activities | 38.14.6 | |
| 33.3.5.2.5 | Dynamic Menus | 32.1.6, 32.1.7 | |
| 33.3.5.2.6 | Set Up External Search Engine | 38.13.1 | |
| 33.3.6 | Authorization Management | | |
| 33.3.6.1 | Basic Authorization | | |
| 33.3.6.1.1 | Maintain Authorizations | 17.1.4 | |
| 33.3.6.2 | Structural Authorization | | |
| 33.3.6.2.1 | Maintain Structural Profiles | 17.4, 17.5 | |
| 33.3.6.2.2 | Assign Structural Authorization | 17.6 | |
| 33.3.6.2.3 | Save User Data in SAP Memory | 17.8 | |
| 33.3.7 | Structural Graphics | | OoS |

| *Sequence number* | *SAP Customizing Implementation Guide (ECC 6.0)* | *Where covered* | *Why not covered* |
|---|---|---|---|
| 33.3.8 | Human Resources Information System | | PA |
| 33.3.9 | Tools | | |
| 33.3.9.1 | Check Consistency of Installation | 19.1.11 | |
| 33.3.9.2 | Data Transfer Workbench | 20.4 | |
| 33.3.9.3 | Make Pushbutton Settings for Batch Inpu | 38.14.7 | |
| 33.3.9.4 | Transport | | |
| 33.3.9.4.1 | Set Up Transport Connection | 20.1 | |
| 33.3.9.4.2 | Lock Infotypes for Import | 20.2 | |
| 33.3.9.4.3 | Manual Transport | 20.3 | |
| 33.3.9.5 | Business Workflow | | |
| 33.3.9.5.1 | Activate Event Linkage | 38.12.1 | |
| 33.3.9.5.2 | Define Event Types for Customer-Sp | 38.12.2, 38.12.3 | |
| 33.3.9.5.3 | Redefine Event Types for SAP Busin | 38.12.3 | |
| 33.4 | Integration | | |
| 33.4.1 | Time Management | | |
| 33.4.1.1 | Integration Yes or No? | 38.3.1 | |
| 33.4.1.2 | Specify Attendance Types | 38.3.2–38.3.4 | |
| 33.4.1.3 | Define Incompatible Attendance and Abs | 36.2.6 | |
| 33.4.2 | Materials Management | | |
| 33.4.2.1 | Wizard | 38.8.8 | |
| 33.4.2.2 | Integration Yes or No? | 38.8.2 | |
| 33.4.2.3 | Specify Organizational Elements | 38.8.4, 38.8.5 | |
| 33.4.2.4 | Define Cost Center of Cost Object | 38.8.6 | |
| 33.4.2.5 | Specify Control Elements | 38.8.7 | |
| 33.4.3 | Budget Management | | |
| 33.4.3.1 | Specify Budget Currency | 38.11.3 | |
| 33.4.3.2 | Define Budget Type and Attributes | 38.11.4 | |
| 33.4.3.3 | Specify Budget Period | 38.11.5 | |
| 33.4.4 | Billing and Activity Allocation | | |
| 33.4.4.1 | Billing | | |
| 33.4.4.1.1 | Wizard | 38.7.7 | |
| 33.4.4.1.2 | Integration Yes or No? | 38.7.2 | |
| 33.4.4.1.3 | Specify Organizational Elements | 38.7.3 | |
| 33.4.4.1.4 | Invoice Creation Settings | 38.7.4 | |
| 33.4.4.1.5 | Credit Memo Creation Settings | 38.7.5 | |
| 33.4.4.1.6 | Prices, Taxes and Account Assignm | 38.7.6 | |

| *Sequence number* | *SAP Customizing Implementation Guide (ECC 6.0)* | *Where covered* | *Why not covered* |
|---|---|---|---|
| 33.4.4.2 | Activity Allocation | | |
| 33.4.4.2.1 | Wizard | 38.5.9 | |
| 33.4.4.2.2 | Integration Yes or No? | 38.5.3 | |
| 33.4.4.2.3 | Specify Organizational Elements | 38.5.5 | |
| 33.4.4.2.4 | Define Cost Center of Cost Object | 38.5.6 | |
| 33.4.4.2.5 | Specify Activity Types | 38.5.8 | |
| 33.4.4.3 | Cost Transfer Posting | | |
| 33.4.4.3.1 | Wizard | 38.6.8 | |
| 33.4.4.3.2 | Integration Yes or No? | 38.6.3 | |
| 33.4.4.3.3 | Specify Organizational Elements | 38.6.5 | |
| 33.4.4.3.4 | Define Cost Center of Cost Object | 38.6.6 | |
| 33.4.4.3.5 | Maintain Cost Items | 38.6.7 | |
| 33.4.5 | Appointment Calendar | | |
| 33.4.5.1 | Integration Yes or No? | 38.10.4 | |
| 33.4.5.2 | Specify Appointment Types | 38.10.3 | |
| 33.4.6 | Mail Connection | | |
| 33.4.6.1 | Set Up RFC Destination | 37.14.1 | |
| 33.4.6.2 | Set Up Mail Connection | 37.14.2, 37.14.3 | |
| 33.4.7 | SAP Knowledge Provider | 38.9 | |
| 33.5 | Business Event Preparation | | |
| 33.5.1 | Define Cost Items | 31.14.1 | |
| 33.5.2 | Define Time Schedule | 31.5.4–31.5.5 | |
| 33.5.3 | Create Building Address | 14.15.2 | |
| 33.5.4 | Location | | |
| 33.5.4.1 | Business Event Location Switch | 33.8.1 | |
| 33.5.4.2 | Create Location | 33.8 | |
| 33.5.5 | Organizers | | |
| 33.5.5.1 | Specify Organizer Types | 38.14.8 | |
| 33.5.5.2 | Create Company | 35.6 | |
| 33.5.5.3 | Create Organizational Unit | 3.2 | |
| 33.5.6 | Create Business Event Group | 30 | |
| 33.5.7 | Create Business Event Type | 31 | |
| 33.5.8 | Maintain Master Data via Catalog | 29.2 | |

| *Sequence number* | *SAP Customizing Implementation Guide (ECC 6.0)* | *Where covered* | *Why not covered* |
|---|---|---|---|
| 33.5.9 | Resource Management | | |
| 33.5.9.1 | Control Elements | 33.5 | |
| 33.5.9.2 | Create Resource Type | 33.1 | |
| 33.5.9.3 | Resources | | |
| 33.5.9.3.1 | Create Room | 33.2 | |
| 33.5.9.3.2 | Create External Instructor | 35.5 | |
| 33.5.9.3.3 | Create Other Resource | 33.3 | |
| 33.5.9.3.4 | Locking Resources | | |
| 33.5.9.3.4.1 | Create Service | 33.4.1 | |
| 33.5.9.3.4.2 | Specify Service for Lock Adminis | 33.4.2 | |
| 33.6 | Business Event Catalog | | |
| 33.6.1 | Control Elements | 31.6, 32.1.5, 36.7.2 | |
| 33.7 | Day-to-Day Activities | | |
| 33.7.1 | Control Elements | 31.6, 38.14.1 | |
| 33.7.2 | Prebooking | 36.4.2 | |
| 33.7.3 | Booking | | |
| 33.7.3.1 | Specify Attendee Type Control Options | 35.11 | |
| 33.7.3.2 | Attendee Checks | 36.2.5 | |
| 33.7.3.3 | Conflict Reaction | 36.2.3, 36.2.4 | |
| 33.7.3.4 | Fee Handling | 36.7.4 | |
| 33.7.3.5 | Booking Priorities | 36.1 | |
| 33.7.3.6 | BAdI: Additional Checks for Booking | 36.2.7 | |
| 33.7.4 | Canceling Attendance | | |
| 33.7.4.1 | Control Options | 36.12.6, 36.12.7 | |
| 33.7.4.2 | Reasons for Attendance Cancellation | 36.12.6 | |
| 33.7.5 | Correspondence | | |
| 33.7.5.1 | Wizards | | |
| 33.7.5.1.1 | Correspondence Setup | 37.13 | |
| 33.7.5.1.2 | Form | 37.13 | |
| 33.7.5.1.3 | Text Variable | 37.13 | |
| 33.7.5.1.4 | Notification Abbreviations | 37.13 | |
| 33.7.5.2 | Notification Abbreviations | | |
| 33.7.5.2.1 | Define Recipient Groups | 37.6 | |
| 33.7.5.2.2 | Assign Notification Abbreviations an | 37.5 | |
| 33.7.5.2.3 | Assign Notification Abbreviations an | 37.4 | |

| *Sequence number* | *SAP Customizing Implementation Guide (ECC 6.0)* | *Where covered* | *Why not covered* |
|---|---|---|---|
| 33.7.5.3 | Output Control | | |
| 33.7.5.3.1 | Specify User-Specific Output Cor | 37.7 | |
| 33.7.5.3.2 | Assign Users and User Groups | 37.8 | |
| 33.7.5.3.3 | Define Output Control Options Ba | 37.9 | |
| 33.7.5.3.4 | Specify Default Values for Form ( | 37.10, 37.11 | |
| 33.7.5.4 | Form Layout | | |
| 33.7.5.4.1 | Edit Forms | 37.12.1–37.12.4 | |
| 33.7.5.4.2 | Specify Output Sequence of Text | 37.12.5 | |
| 33.7.5.4.3 | Specify Format for Text Variables | 37.12.6 | |
| 33.7.5.4.4 | Specify Name Format for Recipie | 37.12.7 | |
| 33.8 | Recurring Activities | | |
| 33.8.1 | Firmly Booking/Canceling | | |
| 33.8.1.1 | Control Options | 34.8.9 | |
| 33.8.1.2 | Reasons for Event Cancellation | 34.9.8 | |
| 33.8.2 | Follow-Up Processing | 34.13.6 | |
| 33.8.3 | Appraisals | | |
| 33.8.3.1 | Appraisal Conversion Program | | Obsolete |
| 33.8.3.2 | Form of Appraisal | | Obsolete |
| 33.8.3.3 | Edit Scales | 23.6 | |
| 33.8.3.4 | Edit Appraisals Catalog | 27.2 | |
| 33.8.3.5 | Set Up Control Parameters | | Obsolete |
| 33.9 | Information System | | |
| 33.9.1 | Maintain Evaluation Paths | 12.2, 12.3 | |
| 33.9.2 | Integrate Customer-Specific Reports | 32.2.8 | |
| 33.10 | Employee Self-Service (ESS) | | |
| 33.10.1 | Set Up Control Elements for ESS | 38.13.2–38.13.4 | |
| 33.10.2 | Business Add-Ins (BADIs) for ESS | | |
| 33.10.2.1 | BAdI: Set Up Customer-Specific Atter | 38.13.5 | |
| 33.10.2.2 | BAdI: Customer-Specific Setup of 'My | 38.13.6 | |
| 33.11 | Room Reservation Management | | OoS |
| 34 | SAP Global Trade Services | | OoS |
| 35 | Management of Internal Controls | | OoS |
| 36 | Incentive and Commission Management | | OoS |
| 37 | Discrete Industries | | OoS |
| 38 | Public Sector Management | | OoS |
| 39 | Integration with Other mySAP.com Components | | OoS |
| 40 | SAP Banking | | OoS |

## Reasons for 'why not covered'

| *Code* | *Reason* |
|---|---|
| Obsolete | These functionalities are obsolete. They are replaced by other functionalities. |
| OoS | These nodes are out of scope of this book. |
| PA | This topic is covered in the Personnel Administration book. |

# Preface

If you are a consultant or user of Organizational Management, Personnel Development, or Training and Event Management, and at some point you did not know what the values in a particular field meant, or what would be the impact of selecting a particular value, this book is for you. If you did not know whether a certain functionality was supported by SAP, this book is for you. This book is also for you, if you did not know why your system was behaving in a certain way.

This book has evolved from the difficulty that each one of us experiences in 'Managing SAP'. As I constantly struggled, trying to understand the concepts of SAP and explore their linkages with other concepts, I found memory to be a major handicap. So I started taking notes. Before long, I could not find what I had written. Then I started reorganizing my notes. And finally I started feeling more comfortable. I knew where to write when I learnt something new, and I could find things I was looking for.

The notes improved continuously, and then came the desire to share them with others. Hence this book. While writing this book, I have tried to be clear, crisp and comprehensive as possible.

This book is also meant for users of SAP, business process owners and senior managers of companies, who have implemented, or are in the process of implementation, or are planning to implement, or are evaluating modules of SAP HR. Their need to understand the subject is not as comprehensive as that of functional consultants. How all these category of readers should use this book is described below.

**How to use this book**

There are two ways in which you can use this book. You can use it as a learning guide, and you can use it as a technical reference. When you use this book as a learning guide, you have to cover it in several iterations. Each iteration is designed to enhance your knowledge and prepare you for the next iteration.

In terms of job roles one can classify the readers as senior managers, business process owners, users, and functional consultants. Senior managers need to know only the important concepts, and what SAP can do for them. BPOs need to know more of SAP concepts and have a good idea of how to perform different tasks in SAP. Users need to have a thorough understanding of different tasks they have to perform in SAP and concepts underlying them. Functional consultants need to know everything, or at least everything important.

In the table of contents, each topic is classified in terms of relevance and importance for each category of user. Each topic is given A, B, C, or X rating for each category of user. During each iteration, you can decide the role and importance level you intend to cover. You can select the role you are going to refer to in an iteration, based on your job role, but that is not essential. For example, if you are going to be a user of SAP, but do not know anything about SAP, you may select senior manager role in your first iteration. Having learnt important concepts, you may select BPO role in the next iteration. Finally you may select user role. Also, once you become a proficient user, you may go through the book from the perspective of a functional consultant. These ratings are repeated at the beginning of each chapter so that at the beginning of each chapter itself you know whether to read it, or skip it, without having to go back to the Table of Contents.

In the table of contents, I have left two blank columns. Although I have given an importance rating to each topic, you can decide the importance based on your requirements. For example, if Activity Allocation is not applicable to you, you may mark it as not relevant for you. Similarly, you can decide the importance rating. There is nothing sacrosanct about the rating given by me. You may note this rating in the blank column 'MR', meaning my rating. As you read a topic, you will achieve a level of understanding. You can record it in the column 'UL', meaning understanding level. You may use A/B/C/X, or any other rating scale. After you complete an iteration, these columns will help you decide, which topics to revisit.

When you are reading this book, you will need to work on the system. When you are reading only the important concepts as senior manager, it may be possible to read the book without hands-on experience. However, as you go deeper and deeper, working on the system will become more and more necessary.

If you are using this book as a technical reference, apart from the table of contents and index, you can also locate the relevant material by using 'SAP Menu', and 'SAP Customizing Implementation Guide (IMG)'. Expanded tree of both the SAP menu and IMG (ECC 6.0) is given after the table of contents. Once you find the node in these structures, you will be guided to the relevant chapter. If that node is not covered in the book, that is also mentioned along with the reason for not covering it. In such cases you have to look for information elsewhere; this book will not help you.

You can also use the structure of this book to keep your discoveries in an organized way. You can maintain a Word or Excel document where you record your discoveries either against page numbers or chapter numbers. You can also share your discoveries with me (agrawal.prem@gmail.com) and help make this book even more useful in future editions.

You can also use the structure of this book for guiding your discussion with the users and recording their input. That document will finally become the configuration manual.

**Acknowledgements**

I am deeply indebted to my employer, my colleagues (particularly M/s Anamitra Basu, D.V. Prasad, Sanjay Lavlekar, Sandeep Dalvi and Joyeeta Dasgupta), and my family, who contributed in different ways to make this book possible. I express my sincere gratitude to my publisher, PHI Learning, for putting their trust in me and for improving the presentation of this book.

**Individual social responsibility**

There is no doubt that we must excel in our chosen profession. But our responsibility does not end there. Indeed, we have a greater responsibility of making the world a better place to live in—to address the challenges the world faces, to analyze, to find solutions, to share, to network, and to make a difference. You may have wondered about the diagram on the cover page; it is a plan for a city without traffic lights. There are four articles at the end of this book. You will perhaps find them interesting to read. In particular, think about Samay Daan. You are welcome to get in touch with me (agrawal.prem@gmail.com). Let us make a difference together. It is our Individual Social Responsibility.

P. K. AGRAWAL

# *Organizational Management*

# Chapter 1 Organizational Plan

## 1.1 CONCEPTS

| *Functional Consultant* | *User* | *Business Process Owner* | *Senior Management* | *My Rating* | *Understanding Level* |
|---|---|---|---|---|---|
| A | A | A | A | | |

Organizations are built for serving specific purposes. In order to do so, they perform several activities. To perform these activities, organizations structure themselves. An organization is divided into parts, each of which are assigned specific responsibilities. These parts may be further subdivided into smaller parts with more specific responsibilities. The organizational plan given below is a typical representation of an organization's structure.

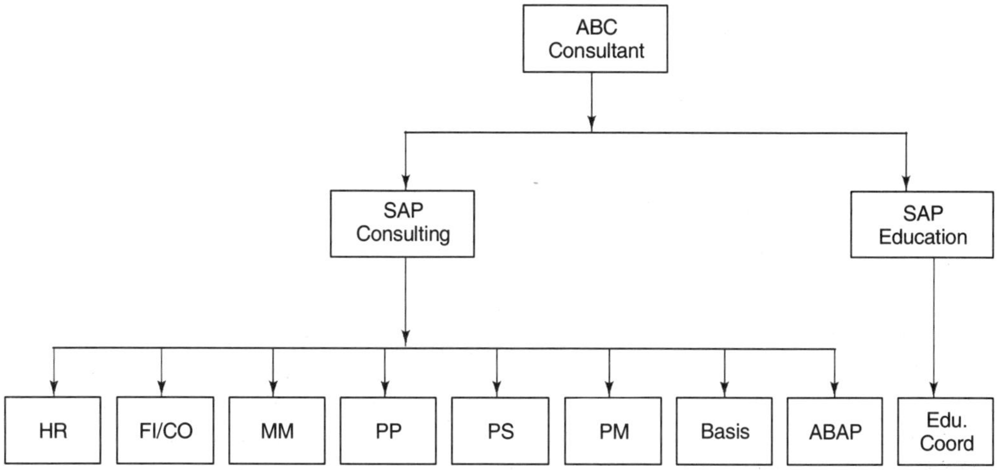

### Organizational unit

Organizational unit represents a functional unit in an enterprise. The entire organization is divided into organizational units. Organizational units form a hierarchy called organizational structure, where the lower level organizational units report to the higher level organizational units. An enterprise often has different names for organizational units at different levels, e.g. line of business (LOB), division, department, section, etc. In SAP, all these are called organizational units.

### Organizational structure

The organizational structure of an enterprise is a hierarchy of organizational units, where the lower level organizational units report to the higher level organizational units.

### Organizational plan

In SAP terminology, an organizational structure has only organizational units in it. Organizational plan is a broader structure which includes organizational structure, staffing of organizational units by positions and persons and assignment of jobs and tasks to organizational units, positions and persons. An organizational plan can include the following:

- An organizational structure
- Staff assignments
- A reporting structure
- A job index
- A work center plan
- A task catalog

### Position

In any organizational unit, the work is done by persons. But when you are planning an organization, you do not know who the persons would be. So you plan positions, which are later filled by employees. If an employee leaves, the position becomes vacant, and can be filled by another employee. Positions can also be filled by non-employees, e.g. contractors' employees.

### Person

SAP uses the term person for an employee. In an organization, persons occupy positions and perform the duties assigned to that position.

### Other holders of position

SAP recognizes that sometimes your positions may be occupied by people, who are not your employees. SAP therefore permits Business partners, External persons, Central persons and Users to occupy positions, and displays these position holders in the organizational plan in the same way as your employees.

## 1.2 CREATING THE ROOT ORGANIZATIONAL UNIT

| *Functional Consultant* | *User* | *Business Process Owner* | *Senior Management* | *My Rating* | *Understanding Level* |
|---|---|---|---|---|---|
| A | A | A | B | | |

You start creating an organizational structure in SAP by creating the root organizational unit. This is done using transaction PPOCE. When you run transaction PPOCE, the system will propose a validity period for the root organizational unit.

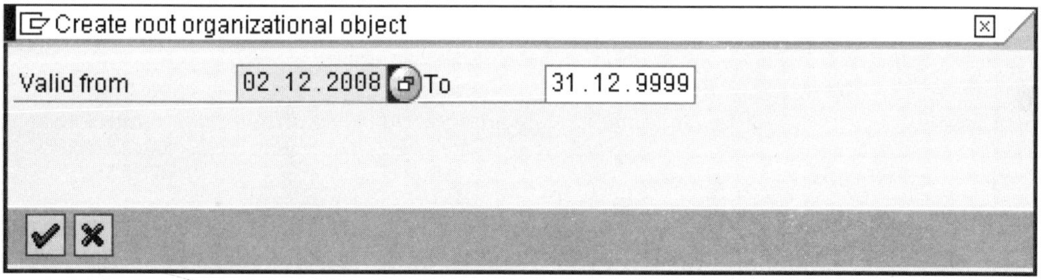


You can modify the validity period if you want. Once you accept it, the system shows the following screen.

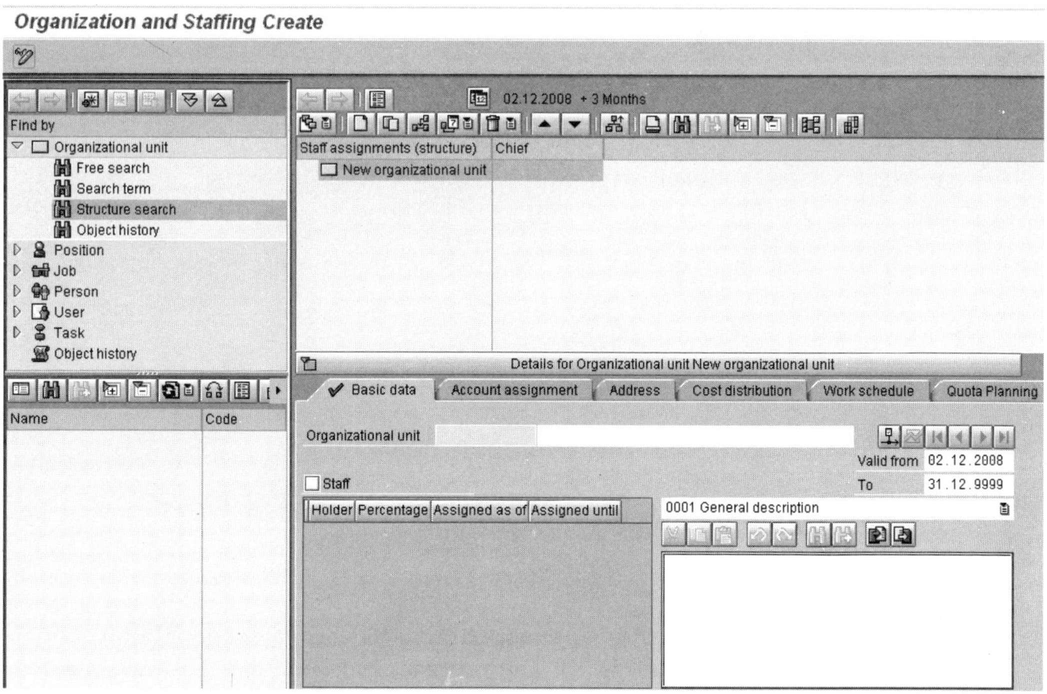

In the left part of this screen you can search and select an object, e.g. organizational unit, position, etc. and double-click it to transfer it to the right side to work on. At this point, you are creating a new organizational unit, so this functionality is not required. The system shows a 'New organizational unit'. You enter a short description (ABC Consult) and a long description (ABC Consulting) for the organizational unit. Validity dates that you entered in the initial screen are shown here. You can modify them if you want. You go to the tab, 'Account assignment' and enter cost center along with controlling area. In address tab you enter city and country. You then save. The root organizational unit is created. Note that the entry of cost center, controlling area, city and country is mandatory.

## 1.3 CREATING OTHER ORGANIZATIONAL UNITS

| *Functional Consultant* | *User* | *Business Process Owner* | *Senior Management* | *My Rating* | *Understanding Level* |
|---|---|---|---|---|---|
| A | A | A | B | | |

To create other organizational units, you run transaction PPOME and select the organizational unit you want to work on. To create an organizational unit under the selected organizational unit, you click [icon]. The system asks you whether you want to create an organizational unit, or a position.

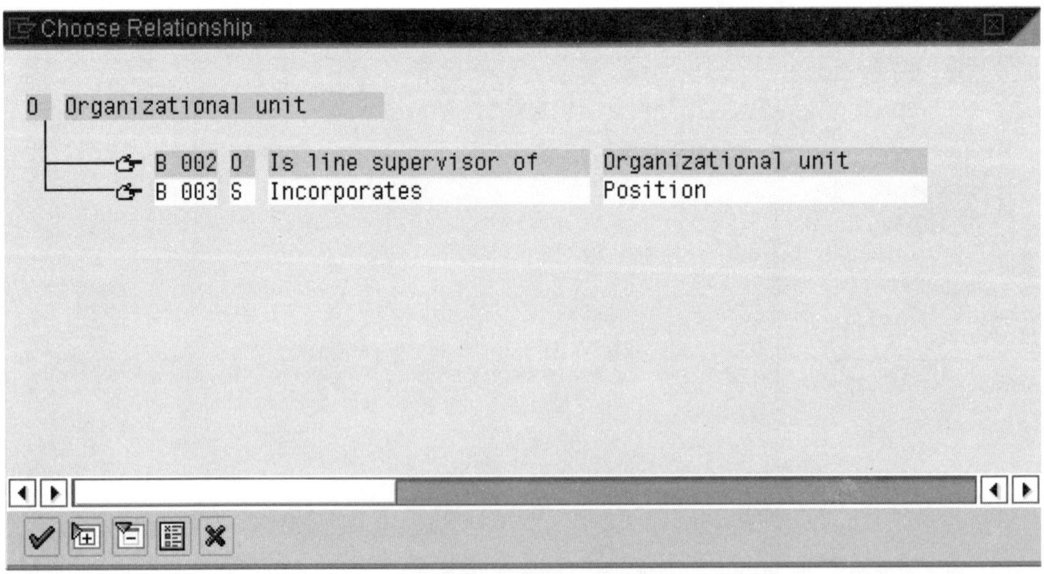


You select the organizational unit. The system creates a 'New organizational unit' under the root organizational unit. You select the 'New organizational unit' by double-clicking it, enter its short and long name, validity period, account assignment and save.

You can create other organizational units either by starting from a higher level organizational unit, and creating a lower level organizational unit by clicking , or by selecting the same level organizational unit and clicking .

## 1.4 CREATING POSITIONS

| *Functional Consultant* | *User* | *Business Process Owner* | *Senior Management* | *My Rating* | *Understanding Level* |
|---|---|---|---|---|---|
| A | A | A | B | | |

You create positions under organizational units. Select the organizational unit under which you want to create a position, click , and double-click the relationship 'Incorporates Position'. A 'New position' is created. You enter mandatory data, e.g. account assignment and address, and save. A position is created.

## 1.5 ASSIGNING PERSONS TO POSITIONS

| *Functional Consultant* | *User* | *Business Process Owner* | *Senior Management* | *My Rating* | *Understanding Level* |
|---|---|---|---|---|---|
| A | A | A | B | | |

Persons are hired in Personnel Administration using transaction PA40. They are also assigned positions there. This creates the link between positions and persons.

## 1.6 ASSIGNING OTHER HOLDERS TO POSITIONS

| *Functional Consultant* | *User* | *Business Process Owner* | *Senior Management* | *My Rating* | *Understanding Level* |
|---|---|---|---|---|---|
| A | A | A | B | | |

A position may be held by people other than persons (employees). To assign other holders to a position, you select the position and click 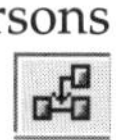.

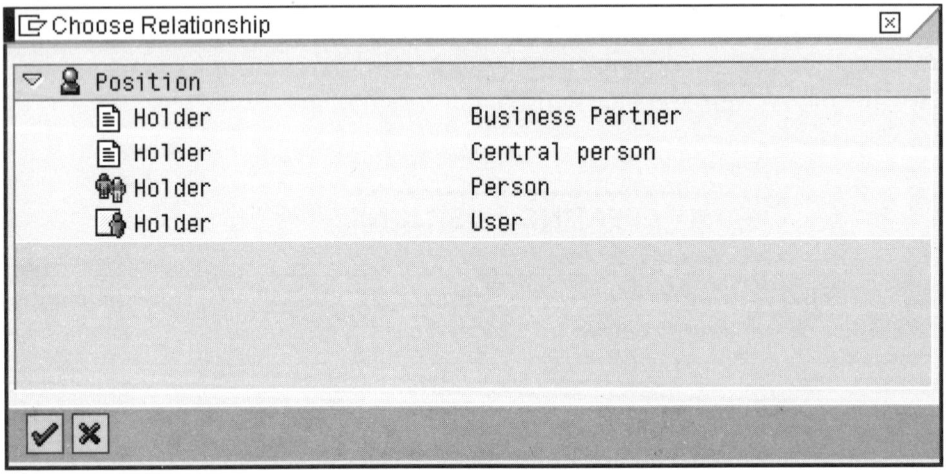


Select the type of the object and the object, who will hold the position. You need to create the object first, before assigning it.

## 1.7 ORGANIZATIONAL PLAN IN SAP

| *Functional Consultant* | *User* | *Business Process Owner* | *Senior Management* | *My Rating* | *Understanding Level* |
|---|---|---|---|---|---|
| A | A | A | B | | |

SAP provides standard reports to display organizational plan. If you want to see only the organizational units in the organization, you can use transaction S_AHR_61016493. If you also want to see positions along with organizational units, you can use transaction S_AHR_61016494.

| Object Name | Object abbr. | O.. | Extended ... | S | Start Date ... | End Date ... |
|---|---|---|---|---|---|---|
| ABC Consultants | ABC Consult | O | 50015902 | 1 | 02.12.2008 | 31.12.9999 |
| Chief Executive Officer | CEO | S | 50015968 | 1 | 02.12.2008 | 31.12.9999 |
| SAP Consulting | SAP Consult | O | 50015903 | 1 | 02.12.2008 | 31.12.9999 |
| SAP HR Consultant | SAP HR | S | 50016038 | 1 | 02.12.2008 | 31.12.9999 |
| SAP FI/CO Consultant | SAP FI/CO | S | 50016116 | 1 | 02.12.2008 | 31.12.9999 |
| SAP MM Consultant | SAP MM | S | 50016122 | 1 | 02.12.2008 | 31.12.9999 |
| SAP PP Consultant | SAP PP | S | 50016151 | 1 | 02.12.2008 | 31.12.9999 |
| SAP PS Consultant | SAP PS | S | 50016199 | 1 | 02.12.2008 | 31.12.9999 |
| SAP PM Consultant | SAP PM | S | 50016236 | 1 | 02.12.2008 | 31.12.9999 |
| SAP Basis Consultant | SAP Basis | S | 50016525 | 1 | 02.12.2008 | 31.12.9999 |
| SAP ABAP Consultant | SAP ABAP | S | 50016532 | 1 | 02.12.2008 | 31.12.9999 |
| SAP Education | SAP Educaton | O | 50015904 | 1 | 02.12.2008 | 31.12.9999 |
| SAP Education Coordinator | SAP Edu Coor | S | 50016540 | 1 | 02.12.2008 | 31.12.9999 |

***Key observations***

Business uses different terms for parts of organization, e.g. business unit, plant, division, department, section, etc. SAP uses a single term, 'organizational unit'. This is necessary because business does not use standard terminology, and SAP must use terminology which would make sense in diverse environments.

Different organizations have different number of levels in their organization. Some organizations are flat while some are deep. SAP lets you create your organizational structure as flat or as deep as you want. There is no limit on the number of levels in your organizational structure.

Usually business is accustomed to a top-down organizational plan as displayed in chapter 1.1 and the users generally demand that the same be provided from SAP. This can be done using structural graphics. However, you may note that the organizational plan display of SAP is much more compact than the traditional organizational plan display. It represents large structures which is not possible in the traditional top-down view. It is recommended that the users be made aware of the benefits of the left-to-right representation of the organizational plan.

## 1.8 OBJECTS, RELATIONSHIPS, AND INFOTYPES

| *Functional Consultant* | *User* | *Business Process Owner* | *Senior Management* | *My Rating* | *Understanding Level* |
|---|---|---|---|---|---|
| A | A | A | B | | |

Organizational Management is based on the concept of objects and relationships. Organizational unit, position, person, cost center are different types of objects. These objects are related to each other through relationships, thereby forming structures. SAP also lets you keep additional characteristics for objects in infotypes.

## 1.9 VALIDITY PERIOD

| *Functional Consultant* | *User* | *Business Process Owner* | *Senior Management* | *My Rating* | *Understanding Level* |
|---|---|---|---|---|---|
| A | A | A | B | | |

An enterprise's organizational plan is constantly undergoing change. For this reason, Organizational Management allows you to modify the organizational structure, staff assignments as well as other objects and structures from specified dates. You can see the modified organizational plan after the specified date, as well as the original organizational plan which existed before the specified date. The specified date may be in future, which means that you can also update changes which will take place in future.

## 1.10 PARTIAL ASSIGNMENT

| *Functional Consultant* | *User* | *Business Process Owner* | *Senior Management* | *My Rating* | *Understanding Level* |
|---|---|---|---|---|---|
| A | A | A | B | | |

If you have a productwise organization, but a sales manager in an area sales office looks after multiple products, how do you represent it? In SAP, you can assign a percentage to a relationship. Thus, a position may be assigned 60% to one organizational unit and 40% to the other. SAP lets you maintain a percentage for each relationship. By default this value is 100%, but it can be less than, or even greater than, 100%. You can see this field when you maintain infotype 1001 in expert mode. You can also see this field in some of the other interfaces.

## 1.11 PRIORITY

| *Functional Consultant* | *User* | *Business Process Owner* | *Senior Management* | *My Rating* | *Understanding Level* |
|---|---|---|---|---|---|
| A | A | A | B | | |

If an organizational unit has ten positions, you may want them listed in a certain sequence. The relationship infotype has a priority field, which is used for this purpose. The system automatically generates the priority number, but you can also maintain it manually for a relationship record. You may also change the sequence in structural display. The system will automatically make a change in the priority value so that next time they are displayed in the modified sequence.

CHAPTER 2

# Organizational Management Interfaces

SAP provides multiple interfaces for maintaining your organizational plan. You can use the interface you like most. No matter which interface you use, the data is updated in a common database, and is shown in all the interfaces.

## 2.1 ORGANIZATION AND STAFFING

| *Functional Consultant* | *User* | *Business Process Owner* | *Senior Management* | *My Rating* | *Understanding Level* |
|---|---|---|---|---|---|
| A | A | A | B | | |

SAP provides multiple methods of creating an organizational plan. You can create each object separately using 'Expert Mode' and create relationships between them. Alternatively, you can use the 'Organization and Staffing' interface where you create, change and display an organizational plan using transactions PPOCE, PPOME and PPOSE. The Organization and Staffing interface presents a more compact view of the organizational plan. In this interface you can search and select objects, display/modify structures and display/modify an object in the structure. This chapter explores various features of this interface. When you execute transaction PPOME, you would see the following screen which has five parts.

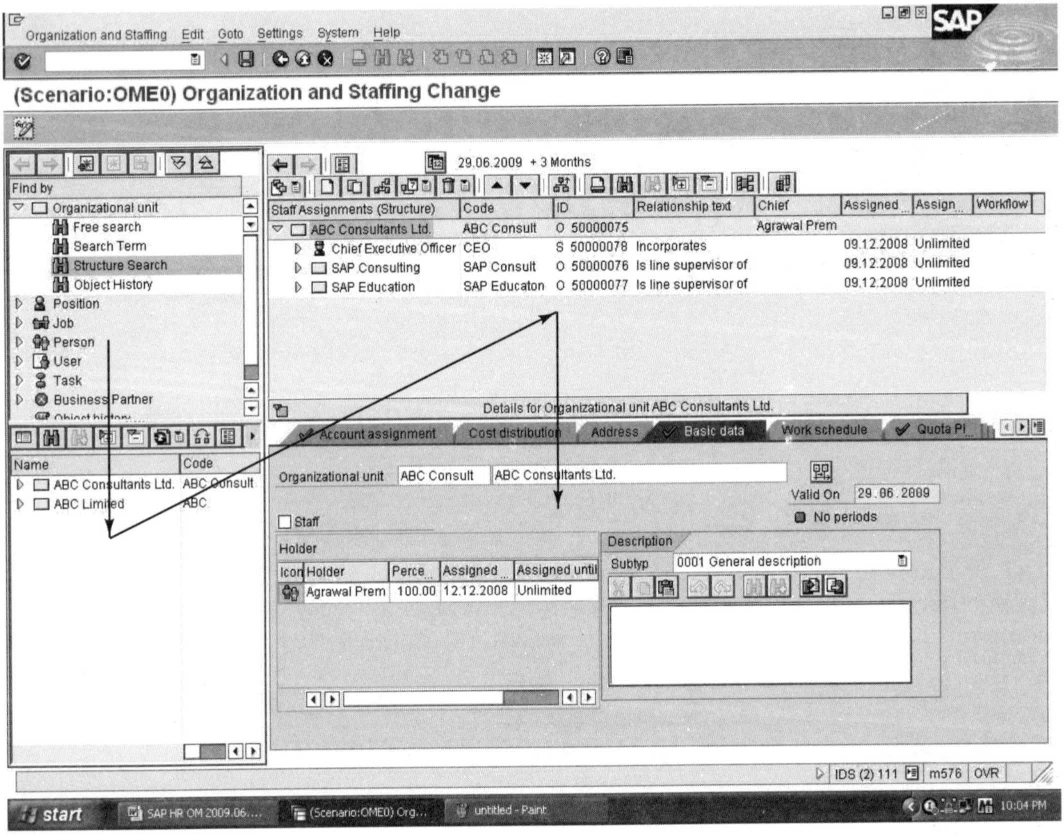

| *Area* | *Quadrant* | *Purpose* |
|---|---|---|
| Search area | Left-top | You can search for individual organizational objects such as organizational units, persons, jobs, positions, tasks and users according to search functions. The results of this search are displayed in the Selection area. |
| Selection area | Left-bottom | You can expand or contract structures and select an object in the Selection area, which can be transferred to the Overview area by double-clicking it. |
| Preview period area | Right-topmost | You can see and set the preview period here. |
| Overview area | Right-top | You can see different structures of the selected object in the Overview area, and select any displayed object to see its details in Detail area. |
| Detail area | Right-bottom | This area displays information on the object selected in the Overview area. This information can be edited and saved. |

### 2.1.1 Search Area

When you execute transaction PPOME, left-top part of the screen is the search area, where you decide the starting object type, e.g. organizational unit, position, etc. You then use one of the multiple search methods to select the objects, which are shown in the selection area.

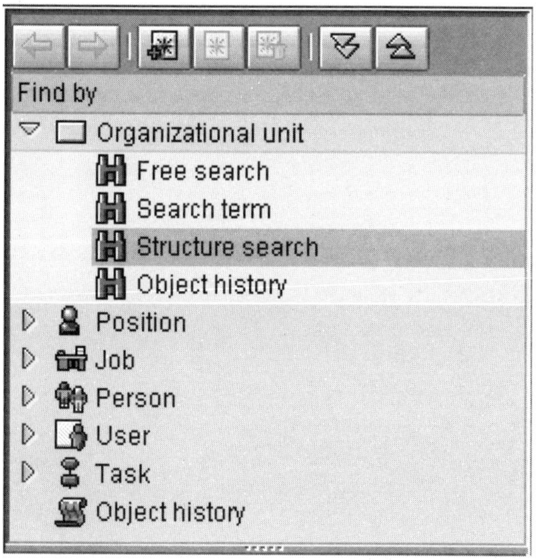


***Free search***

In free search the system gives you the infoset query screen, where you can specify different object characteristics, and the system finds objects matching your selection criteria.

***Search term***

You can search for an object by specifying either name or abbreviation. You can also search using the entry *. If necessary, you can start another search for the same object type and then choose Add to add the new hits to the earlier results in the selection area.

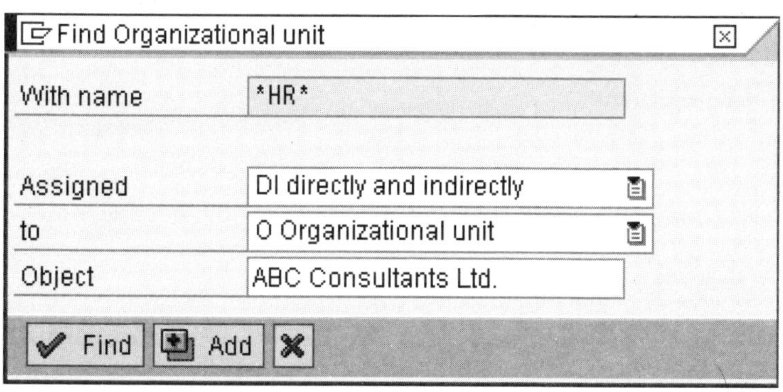

***Structure search***

If you choose structure search, the system gives you root organizational units in selection area which you can expand to reach the objects you desire.

***Object history***

***Search variant***

In the search area you can create search variants, so that you can reuse search criteria you have grouped together, or hits. You can add a search variant, select from search variants, and delete search variant using .

***Deleting all search variants***

You can use transaction DELETE_OM_SETTINGS to reset user-specific settings in the object manager.

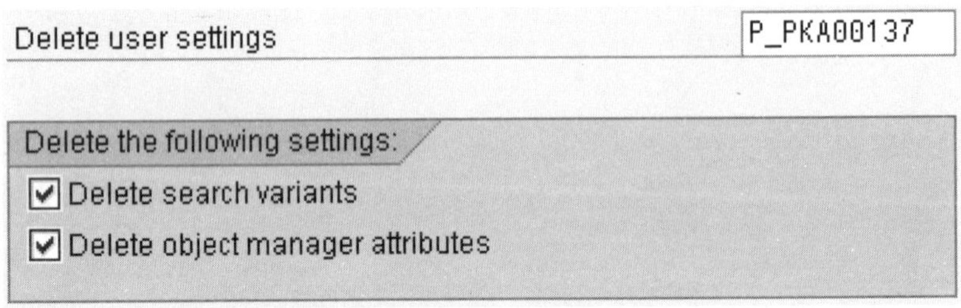


## 2.1.2 Selection Area

When you specify the criteria in the search area, the system selects all the objects that meet the selection criteria and exist on the key date and preview period you have set. These are displayed in the selection area. In the selection area you select the object. If the object is not visible, you can expand the organizational plan to reach it.

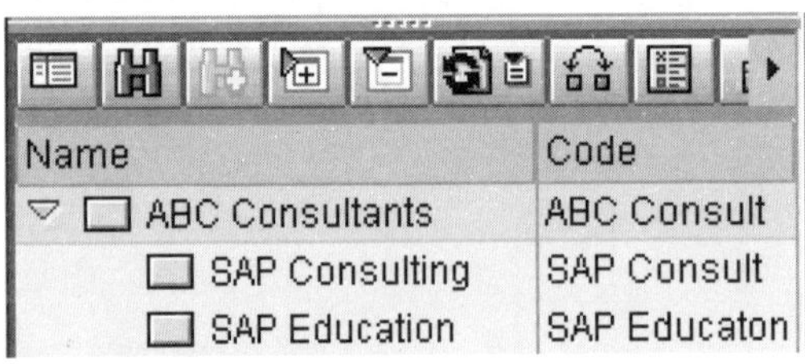


***Columns in selection area***

You can also decide which columns to display in the object list by clicking .

***Hiding the search area***

You can hide the search area and increase selection area by clicking . You click the same icon to display the search area again.

### *Transferring the object to overview area*

After selecting the object, you can select the view to be transferred to the overview area by doing a right click. The view shown in bold is the default view which can be transferred by double-clicking.

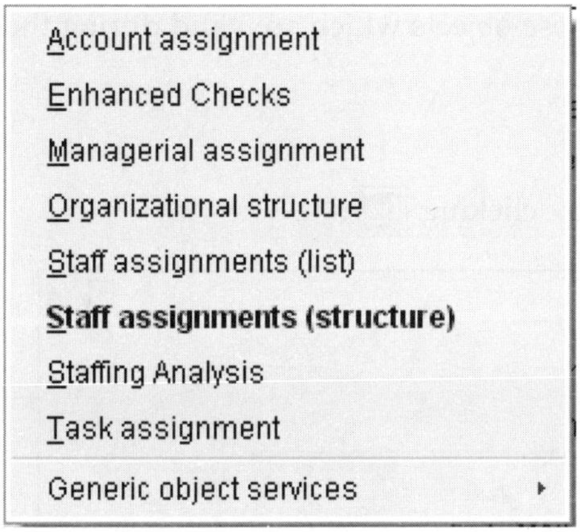


You can also drag an object (e.g. position) and drop it under the other object (e.g. organizational unit) to create a relationship.

### *Object manager*

Search area and selection area together is called object manager. You can either hide completely or display the object manager, so that the other screen areas get correspondingly bigger or smaller. To do that, choose Settings ➢ Show Object Manager/Hide Object Manager.

## 2.1.3 Preview Period Area

### *Key date*

Every time you logon, the current date is set as the key date. You can change the key date. Data valid on the date you have selected is displayed. If you create an organizational unit or position in the overview area, the validity of the object and the assignment begins with the key date set. Similarly, if you change any data in detail area, the change is effective from the key date. Before the key date, the data remains what it was before the change. If you have activated Query time period (Settings ➢ Query Time Period/Create Several Objects), the system asks you to specify the validity period of objects, relationships and infotypes instead of using key date as the start date.

### *Preview period*

You see the organizational plan on the key date. You may also want to see if any changes are going to occur in the near future. SAP lets you specify a preview period. When you logon initially, a preview period of three months is set and all changes to data that happen in this period are displayed. You can change this preview period. Next time you logon, the preview period which you selected is set. The organization and staffing interface displays data for the preview period. The key date and the preview period are displayed at the top-right quadrant of the screen 16.12.2008 + 3 Months . If the validity period of an object or relationship is entirely outside the preview period, that object or relationship is not shown. The search function also finds only those objects which are valid during the preview period.

### *Setting the key date and the preview period*

The key date and the preview period can be set by clicking .

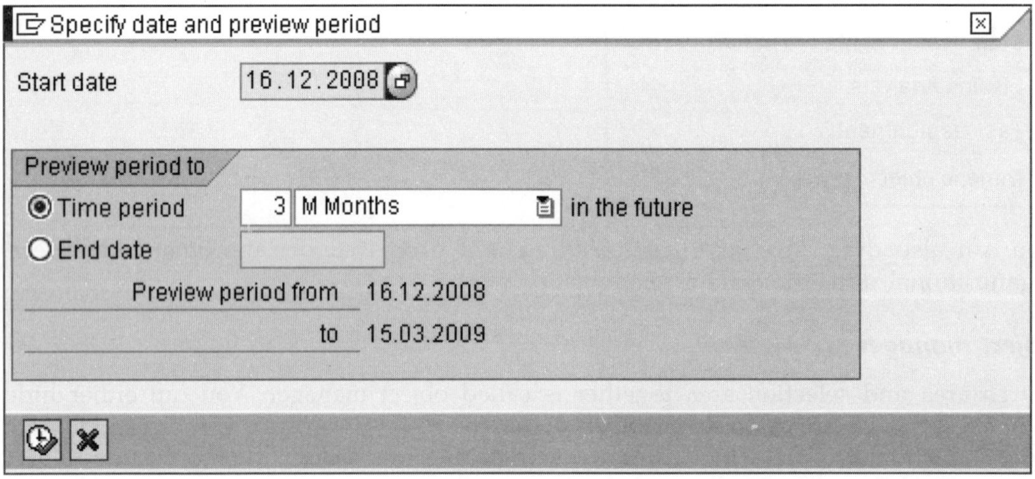


You can either specify a start date and a time period, or a start date and an end date. Start date is particularly important because all objects and relationships created using this interface are created from this start date. The period you set here is used in different areas of the interface.

### *Deleting the key date and the preview period*

You can use transaction DELETE_NF_SETTINGS to reset the last object selection and the preview period. The system then shows default preview period, current date + three months.

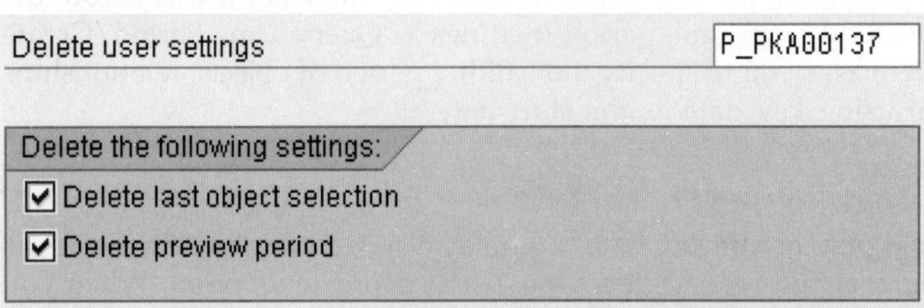

### *Use of preview period in search area*

The preview period is used to select the objects in the search area. If the validity period of an object is entirely outside the preview period, that object is not shown in the search area.

### *Use of preview period in selection area*

The objects, selected as per search criteria in the search area, are displayed in the selection area. The selected objects are also filtered for the preview period. If you are selecting the organizational units in your enterprise, and an organizational unit is not valid in the preview period, that organizational unit is not shown.

### *Use of preview period in overview area*

You see the structural view of an object in the overview area. This view shows only those objects and relationships which are either fully or partly valid during the preview period. Also, if you create an object or relationship in the overview area, the key date is the start date of the object or the relationship. The end date of the object is 31.12.9999 and the end date of the relationship is the lower of the end dates of the objects between which the relationship is being created.

### *Use of preview period in detail area*

The detail area shows the infotype data of the selected object. This data can change with time. Thus, there may be multiple records for the same infotype. By default, the detail area shows the data on the key date. You can, however, access data for other periods as well.

### *Query time period*

If you want the system to explicitly query the time period whenever you create an object or relationship, you can set it through Settings ➢ Query Time Period/Create Several Objects.

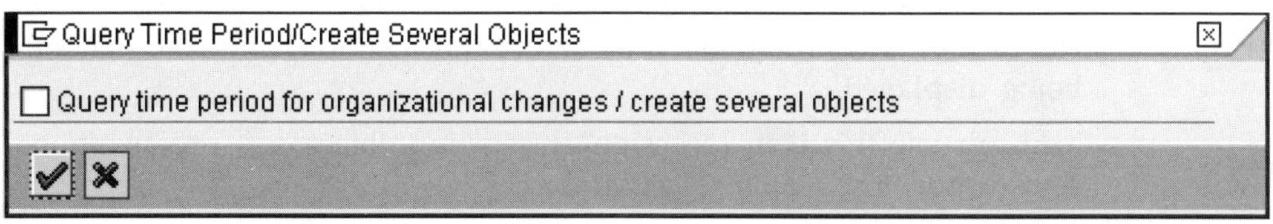


## 2.1.4 Overview Area

From the selection area, you transfer the selected organizational unit to the overview area. The overview area shows the structure of the selected object. There may be multiple structures, which display different information about the selected object. You can also modify the structures using the icons in the overview area. Some of the important icons are explained below:

---

You can use these arrows to move back and forth just like internet explorer.

You can click this icon to see the legend of icons.

| Icon | Description |
|---|---|
| | Business Partner |
| | Job |
| | Organizational unit |
| | Person |
| | Position |
| | Task |
| | User |
| | Chief |
| | Vacant position |
| | Unoccupied position |
| | Obselete Position |
| | Position with several holders |
| | Object to be added |
| | Object removed |

Objects whose validity, or assignment to other objects, begins only in the preview period set, are indicated by a [icon] in the selection area. Objects, whose validity ends in the preview period, are indicated by a [icon].

You can use this icon to set the period for which you are viewing the organizational plan.

Overview area displays the structure of an object. For an object, there can be multiple structures. You can use this icon to change the structure being displayed.

You can use this icon to assign an existing object, e.g. organizational unit or position, to the selected object.

You can use this icon to delimit the validity of an object, or its relationship with higher level object.

You can use these icons to change the order in which objects are displayed. If you want the change to be permanent, you should save the data after making changes.

If your current view shows only a part of the organizational plan, you can move up one level to show a larger part of the organizational plan.

SAP shows different views of the organizational plan by using different evaluation paths. You can see the evaluation path by clicking this icon. In the evaluation path window you can right-click to switch on, or switch off, the relationship key and text. You can also see the technical evaluation path by clicking .

If you want to see more data about the objects in the organizational plan, you can click this icon to add columns.

### Creating an object

You can create organizational objects (organizational units, positions, etc.) in the overview area and assign them to the objects that already exist.

### Copying an object

You can create a new object by copying an object which already exists.

### Assigning an object

To assign an existing object in the structure displayed in the overview area, search for the object in search area, select the object in selection area, drag the object to the overview area and drop in the structure at the object under which you want it to be. In case of list display, drop it in the field in which it should be.

### Moving an object

In the overview area, select the object that you want to move and drag it to the object to which you want to assign it. The old relationship is delimited and the new relationship is created.

### Repositioning an object

In the overview area, select the object that you want to reposition and move it up or down in the hierarchy using .

### Assigning/moving using a pushbutton

As an alternative to assigning or moving with drag and drop, you can also use the pushbutton. In the overview area, select the object that you want to assign to another object and choose . The Restrict allowed values dialog box appears. Search for the object that you want to assign, select it and then choose .

### Terminating/deleting objects or assignments

Select the object which you want to terminate/delete or whose assignment you wish to delete. Choose  if you want to terminate, or  if you want to delete. Choose whether you want to terminate/delete the object or the assignment.

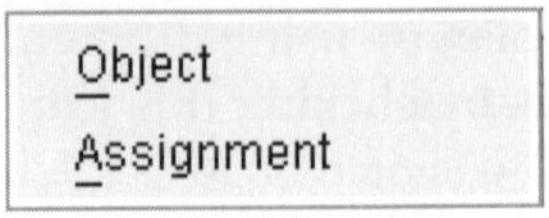


If you want to terminate, enter the date from which the object/assignment is to be terminated in the dialog box.

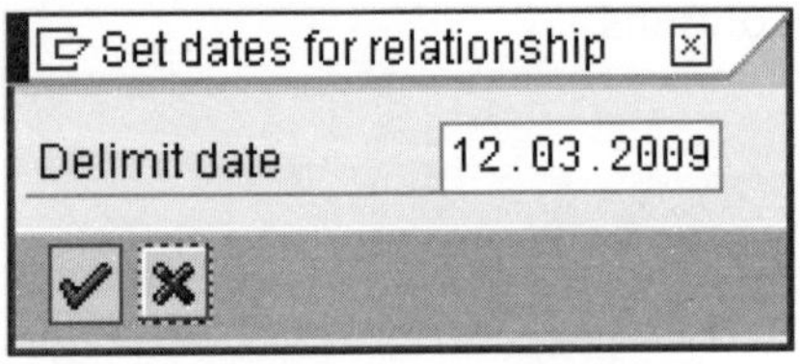


### *Undoing/recreating changes*

If you have already made changes to data in the overview area, but have not yet saved them, you can use [undo icon] to undo change and [redo icon] to recreate them. These icons appear if you make change or undo change.

### *Confirmation prompt*

Once you have carried out a specified number of changes to data (specified in view T77OMFRAMC), a dialog box appears asking whether you want to save these changes. This helps you avoid losing data.

### *Configuring columns*

You can decide which columns should be displayed in the overview area by clicking [icon].

### *Switching maintenance interfaces*

If you are in the Organization and Staffing interface and you choose Settings ➢ Maintenance Interface, the system takes you to the Simple Maintenance interface.

## 2.1.5 Detail Area

In the detail area, you see the details of the object selected in the overview area.

### *Hiding/displaying detail area*

You can click [icon] to hide the detail area, so that you can enlarge the overview area. You can display the detail area again by clicking [icon].

### *Detail area tabs*

The detail area has several tabs. These tabs and their contents depend on the type of object selected, whose details are being shown or edited. These are specified in view T77OMTABUS for each type of object.

### *Validity period*

The validity period concept is common to all types of objects. Detail area shows data about an object which is stored in infotypes. An object can have several records in an infotype, one for each period. The detail area shows the data on the key date, but you can access other records as well. In detail area there are two modes of displaying validity; key date mode and period mode.

### *Key date mode*

The key date mode shows the date for which data is being shown  Valid On 16.12.2008.

If there is a single record during the preview period, the system shows No periods. If there are multiple records during the preview period, the system shows Periods available. If you make any changes, they are made from the 'Valid On' date. The old record is delimited to one day before the new date. If you click , the system switches to period mode.

### *Period mode*

In the period mode, the system shows the validity period of the displayed record Valid from 12.12.2008 To 15.12.2008. You can click  to see all the periods, and select the validity period for which you want to see the record. You can also use  to navigate to first, previous, next or last record so as to see records of different periods. If you want to change data, you can specify the period and change the data. Validity of existing records is automatically adjusted. You can click 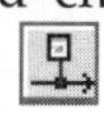 to switch to the key date mode.

## 2.2 GENERAL STRUCTURES

| *Functional Consultant* | *User* | *Business Process Owner* | *Senior Management* | *My Rating* | *Understanding Level* |
|---|---|---|---|---|---|
| A | C | X | X | | |

In Organization and Staffing, the system gives you predefined views which have predefined evaluation paths. You can use transaction PPSC to create general structures where you specify the evaluation path. Transaction PPSM can be used to change general structures and transaction PPSS to display them.

## 2.3 SIMPLE MAINTENANCE

| *Functional Consultant* | *User* | *Business Process Owner* | *Senior Management* | *My Rating* | *Understanding Level* |
|---|---|---|---|---|---|
| A | C | X | X | | |

### 2.3.1 Initial Screen

Simple maintenance is similar to Organization and Staffing. Organization and Staffing has richer features than simple maintenance, but some people prefer simple maintenance, and SAP continues to support it. You can create a new organizational structure using transaction PPOC_OLD, modify it using transaction PPOM_OLD and display it using transaction PPOS_OLD. All objects you create in Simple Maintenance automatically receive active status. When you run transaction PPOM_OLD, you see the following screen.

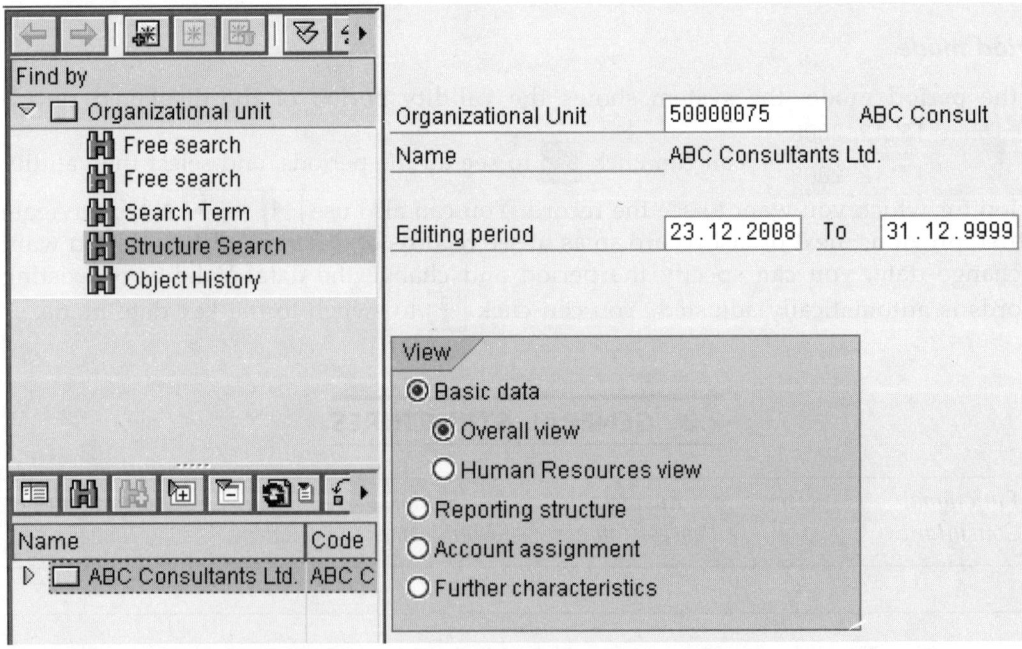


#### *Show/hide object manager*

The left-top and left-bottom quadrants are search area and selection area of object manager. Here you select the starting organizational unit, whose structure you want to see or maintain. You can hide or display the object manager, by choosing Settings ➢ Show Object Manager/Hide Object Manager.

### *Set plan version*

You can set the plan version by choosing Settings ➢ Plan version ..., or set active plan version by choosing Settings ➢ Active plan version.

### *Set editing period*

The editing period is equivalent to the preview period in Organization and Staffing. You can set the editing period either on the initial screen, or by choosing View ➢ Editing period.

### *View*

You select the view you want to display or maintain. Depending on the view chosen, you see different structures. These views are similar to the views in Organization and Staffing. In the overall view you can work with tasks, standard tasks, workflow tasks, workflow templates and rules, whereas in the human resources view you can work only with tasks and standard tasks.

### *Main screens*

In Simple Maintenance, you work with three main screens: Organizational Structure, Staff Assignments and Task Profile. You can change from one to the other using icons or menu item Goto. Each of these screens offers different editing functions.

| *Screen* | *Function* |
|---|---|
| Organizational Structure | Build up and maintain the organizational structure for your organizational plan. |
| Staff Assignments | Create staff assignments by creating jobs and positions, and by assigning holders to positions. |
| Task Profile | Create, maintain, and view task profiles for jobs, positions and organizational units. |

## 2.3.2 Maintaining Organizational Plan

You use Simple Maintenance to display or maintain organizational plan. In doing so, you create objects (organizational units, positions, jobs, tasks, etc.), create relationships, delete or delimit objects or relationships, etc. You change views to see staffing plan or task assignment. You also navigate to other screens, e.g. 'Maintain task catalog'. Some of the tasks you can perform are explained below.

### *Displaying tree structure*

When you click  or , you see the tree structure of the specified object in the specified view.

### *Switching between display and change modes*

You can switch between display and change modes by clicking .

### *Changing the selected item*

You can change the selected item by clicking .

### *Displaying the selected item*

You can display the selected item by clicking .

### *Setting editing period*

You can set editing period by clicking .

### *Creating an object*

You can create an object under the selected object by clicking . Both the object and its relationship with selected object are created. If multiple types of objects, or relationships, can be created, the system prompts you to choose from the possible options.

### *Reassigning an object*

If you want to reassign an object from one object to another, you click  or choose Edit ➢ Reassign. For example, you can move a position from one organizational unit to another.

### *Changing sequence of objects*

Objects in an organizational plan always appear in the same sequence. If you want to change this sequence, click .

### *Refreshing the screen*

You can click  to refresh the screen to show current status of data.

### *Expanding the tree structure*

You can click  to expand the tree structure below the selected object.

### *Collapsing the tree structure*

You can click  to collapse the tree structure below the selected object.

### *Displaying structural graphics view*

You can click  to see the selected object and the tree structure below it in the structural graphics view.

### *Deleting assignment*

You can delete assignment of the selected object with the higher level object by clicking .

### *Displaying organizational structure*

Organizational structure, Staff assignments and Task profile are sub-views of basic data view. You can switch from other views to the organizational structure view by choosing Goto ➢ Organizational structure.

### *Displaying staff assignments*

You can display the staff assignments view by clicking Staff assignments, or by choosing Goto ➢ Staff assignments.

### *Displaying task profile*

You can display the task profile view by clicking Task profile, or by choosing Goto ➢ Task profile.

### *Assigning an existing object*

You can assign an existing object to the selected object by choosing Edit ➢ Assign. You select the type of object, and in some cases, the relationship.

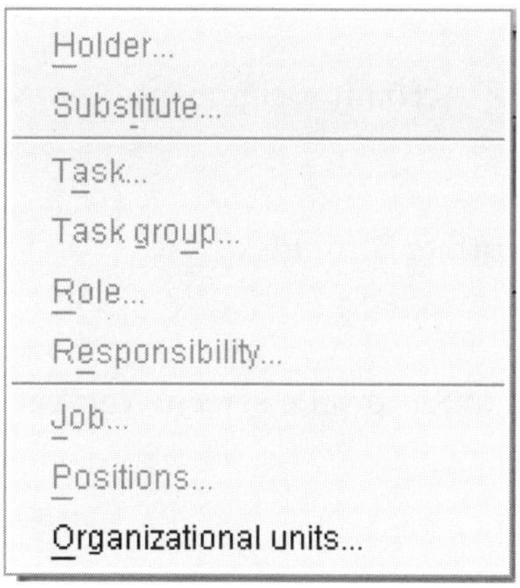


### *Maintaining chief position*

You can display, create, delimit or delete the chief position of an organizational unit by choosing Edit ➢ Chief position.

### *Delimiting object/relationship*

If you want to bring forward the end date of an object or relationship, you may do so by choosing Edit ➢ Delimit. If an object is delimited, its relationships are also delimited. You may also extend the end date.

### Deleting object/relationship

If you want to delete an object or relationship, you may do so by choosing Edit ➢ Delete. If an object is deleted, its relationships are also deleted.

### Renaming organizational units/positions

You can rename organizational units or positions by selecting the object to be renamed and choosing Edit ➢ Change ➢ Rename.

### Changing a position holder from user to person

If a position is held by a user and that user is an employee (user id of an employee is maintained in infotype 0105 subtype 0001), you can change the holder from user to person by selecting the user and choosing Edit ➢ Change ➢ Replace user.

### Changing staffing percentage of a holder

A holder (business partner, central person, person or user) can hold a position fully or partly. If you want to change the staffing percentage, select the holder and choose Edit ➢ Change ➢ Staffing percentage.

### Displaying reporting structure

You can display reporting structure by choosing Goto ➢ Reporting structure.

### Displaying account assignments

You can display account assignments by choosing Goto ➢ Account assignment.

### Displaying further attributes

You can display further attributes by choosing Goto ➢ Further attributes.

### Maintaining job profiles

If you choose Goto ➢ Job profiles, the system takes you to job profile screen. You can create or modify a job there.

### Maintaining tasks

If you choose Goto ➢ Task maintenance, the system takes you to task screen (transaction PFTC). You can create, modify or delete a task here. However, it is recommended that you maintain tasks in task catalog.

### Maintaining roles

If you choose Goto ➢ Role maintenance, the system takes you to role maintenance screen (transaction PFCG).

### *Displaying/hiding object data*

You can add or remove information columns for displayed objects through menu item View.

### *Viewing color legend*

SAP displays different objects in different colors. You can see the color legend by choosing View ➢ Color legend.

### *Showing/hiding object manager*

You can show/hide object manager (search and selection area) by choosing Settings ➢ Show Object Manager/Hide Object Manager.

## 2.3.3 Views

Like Organization and Staffing, Simple Maintenance can also be used to maintain multiple views of the organizational plan.

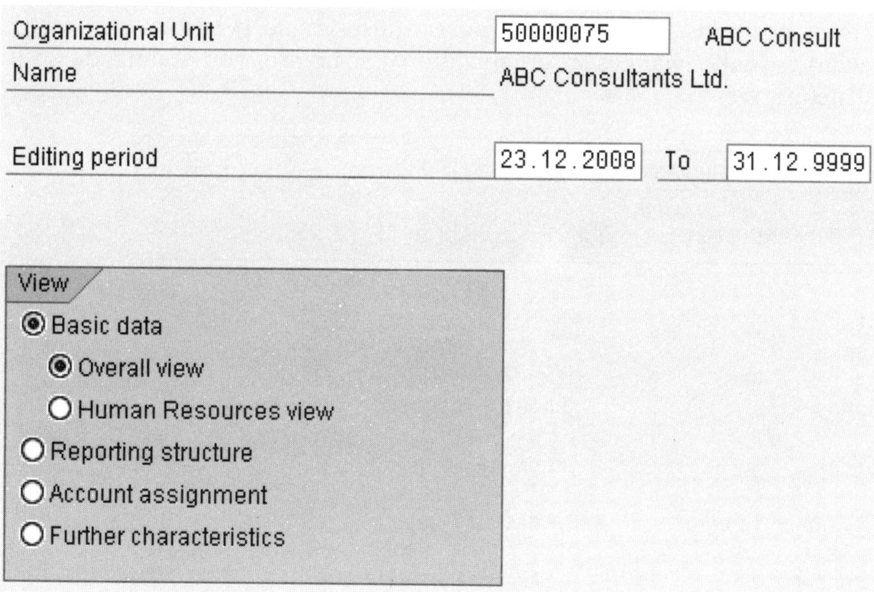


### *Basic data view*

In the basic data view you can maintain organizational structure, staff assignments and task profiles. In the overall view, you can work with tasks, standard tasks, workflow tasks, workflow templates and rules, whereas in the human resources view, you can work only with tasks and standard tasks.

***Organizational structure***

Organizational structure view shows relationships between organizational units. It also shows chief position of the organizational unit.

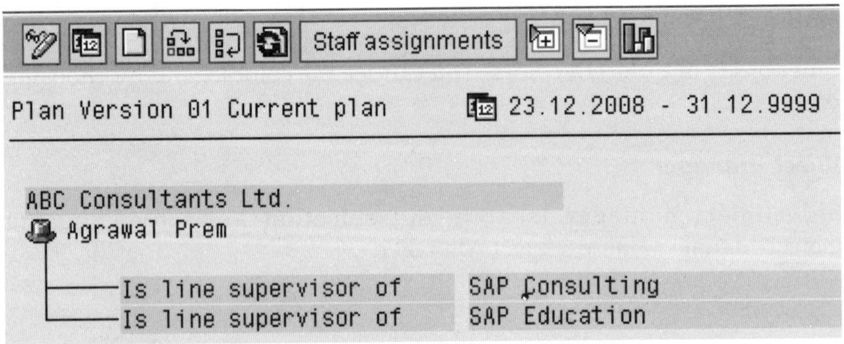


***Staff assignments***

Staff assignments view shows organizational structure, positions in the organizational units and holders of positions. In this view you can also create positions and assign holders. If you want to make changes in organizational structure, you should do so in organizational structure view.

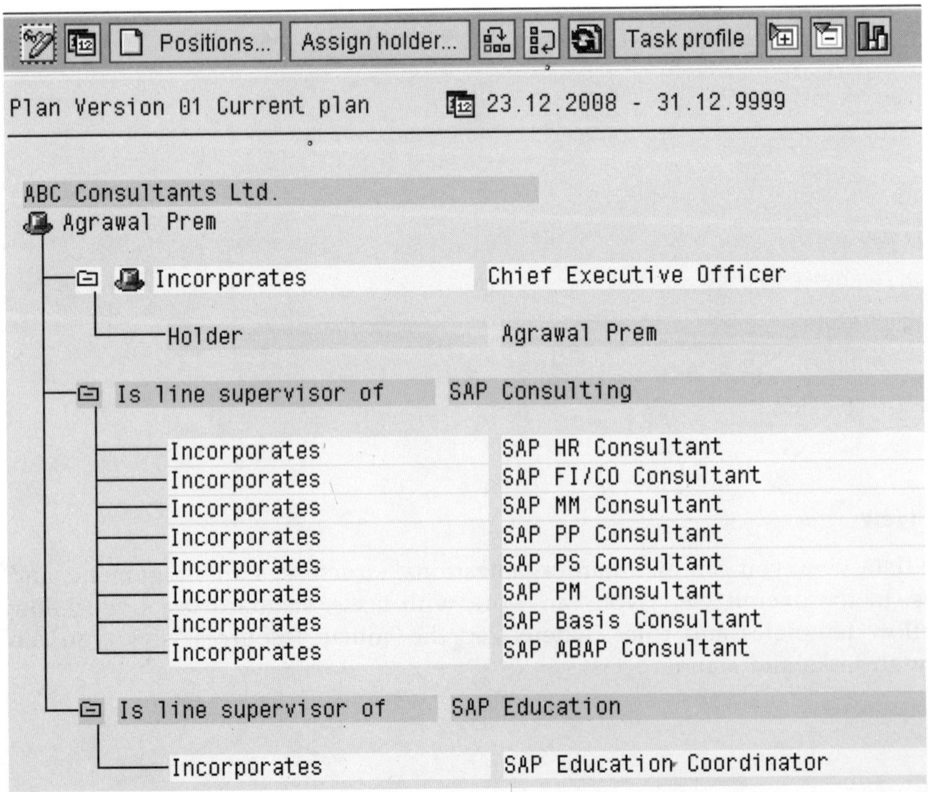

### *Task profile*

From the staff assignments view, you can select an object (usually position) and come to task profile. The system shows the tasks for the object, including those assigned through job. Here you can select the object and assign to it task, task group, role, responsibility or job. You can also delimit or delete an assignment.

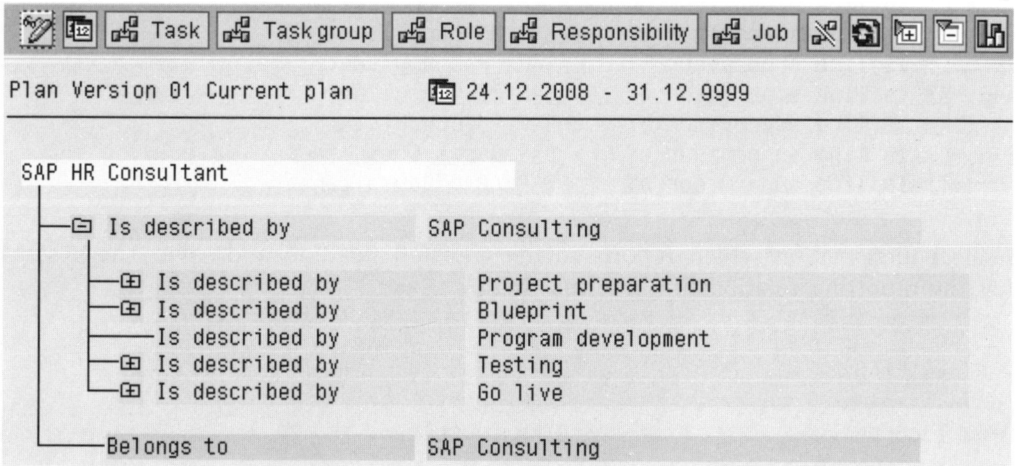


### *Reporting structure*

Usually an organizational unit has a chief position and all other positions in the organizational unit report to this chief position. However, some organizations have a more complex reporting structure and they directly define position to position reporting. This method gives more flexibility but the enterprise has to maintain both organizational structure and the reporting structure.

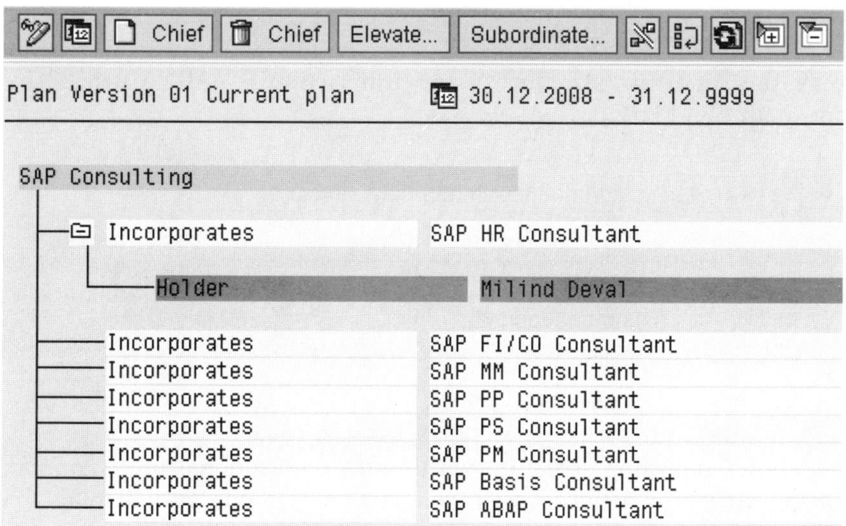

If you select a position and click [Elevate...], the system shows you the positions in that organizational unit which can report to the selected position.

SAP HR Consultant

| | |
|---|---|
| Holder | Milind Deval |
| ☐ Is line supervisor of | SAP FI/CO Consultant |
| ☐ Is line supervisor of | SAP MM Consultant |
| ☐ Is line supervisor of | SAP PP Consultant |
| ☐ Is line supervisor of | SAP PS Consultant |
| ☐ Is line supervisor of | SAP PM Consultant |
| ☐ Is line supervisor of | SAP Basis Consultant |
| ☐ Is line supervisor of | SAP ABAP Consultant |

You select the position which reports to the elevated position and save. The system creates the reporting relationship between them.

SAP Consulting

| | |
|---|---|
| Incorporates | SAP HR Consultant |
|     Holder | Milind Deval |
|     Is line supervisor of | SAP ABAP Consultant |
| Incorporates | SAP FI/CO Consultant |
| Incorporates | SAP MM Consultant |
| Incorporates | SAP PP Consultant |
| Incorporates | SAP PS Consultant |
| Incorporates | SAP PM Consultant |
| Incorporates | SAP Basis Consultant |

You can also display the reporting structure using transaction S_AHR_61016528 by specifying evaluation path O-S-PHIE.

Evaluation Path: O-S-PHIE Staff assignments with reporting structure

| No. | Obj.Type | A/B | Relat'ship | Relationship name | Priority | Rel.obj.type | Skip |
|---|---|---|---|---|---|---|---|
| 10 | O | B | 012 | Is managed by... | * | S | ☐ |
| 20 | S | A | 008 | Holder | * | * | ☐ |
| 30 | S | B | 002 | Is line supervisor of | * | S | ☐ |

This evaluation path shows reporting structure within an organizational unit. You can also maintain reporting structure between positions in Expert mode and display the complete reporting structure using transaction S_AHR_61016528 with evaluation path S-S. Evaluation path S-S shows reporting structure between positions without reference to organizational units.

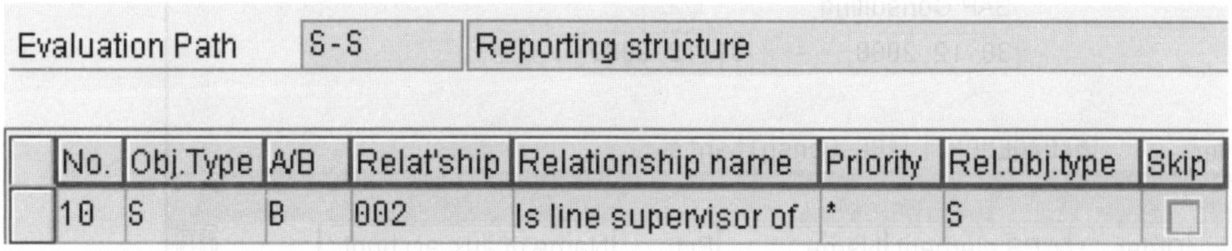


### *Account assignment*

You can use this view to create cost center assignment and cost distribution. You can also change account assignment features.

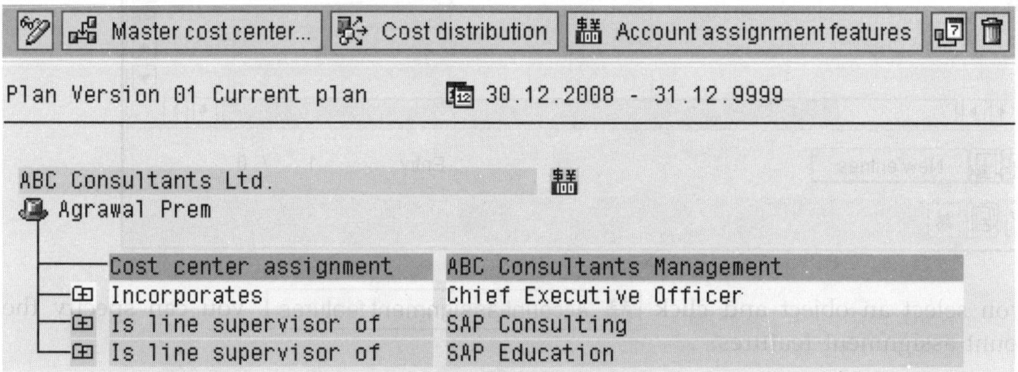


If you select an object and click Master cost center..., you can assign it a cost center.

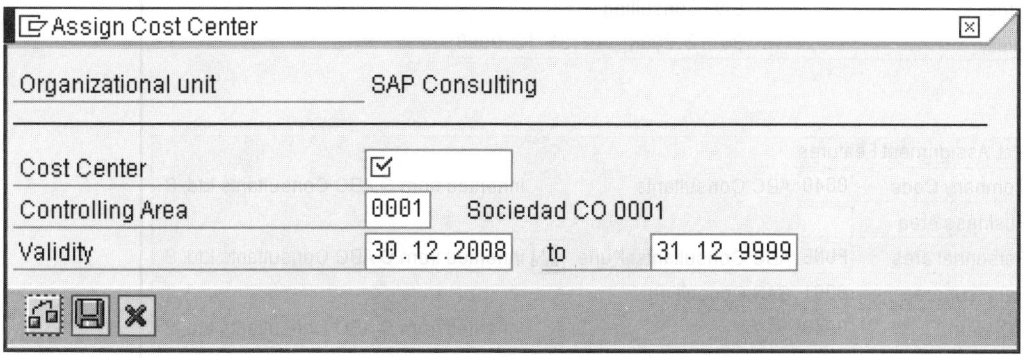


If you select an object and click Cost distribution, you can specify how the cost of the object should be distributed.

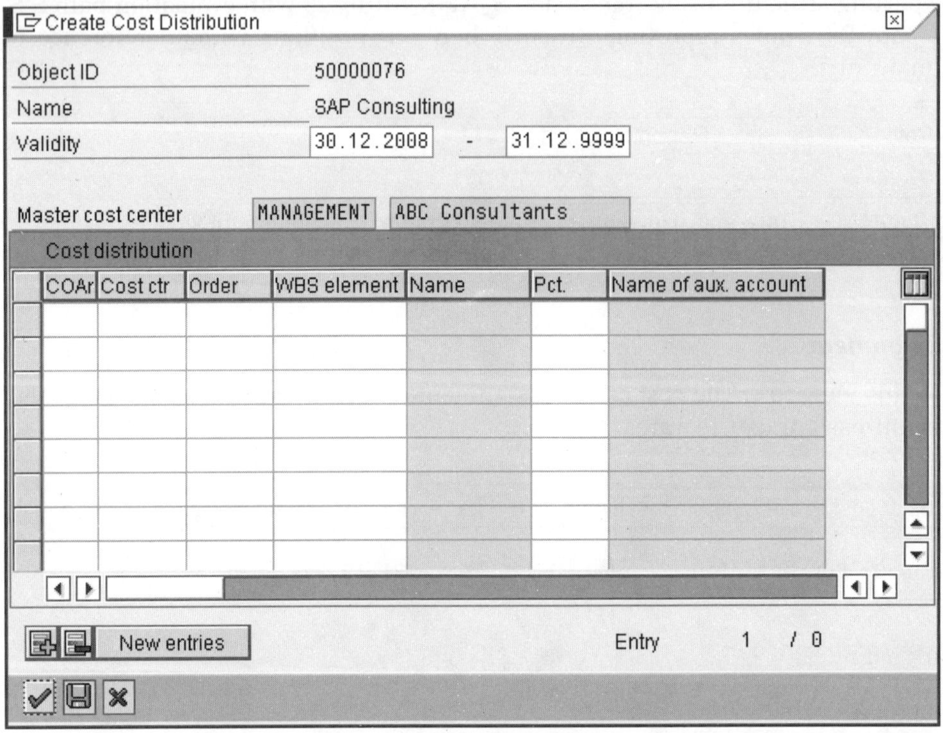


If you select an object and click Account assignment features, you can specify the account assignment features.

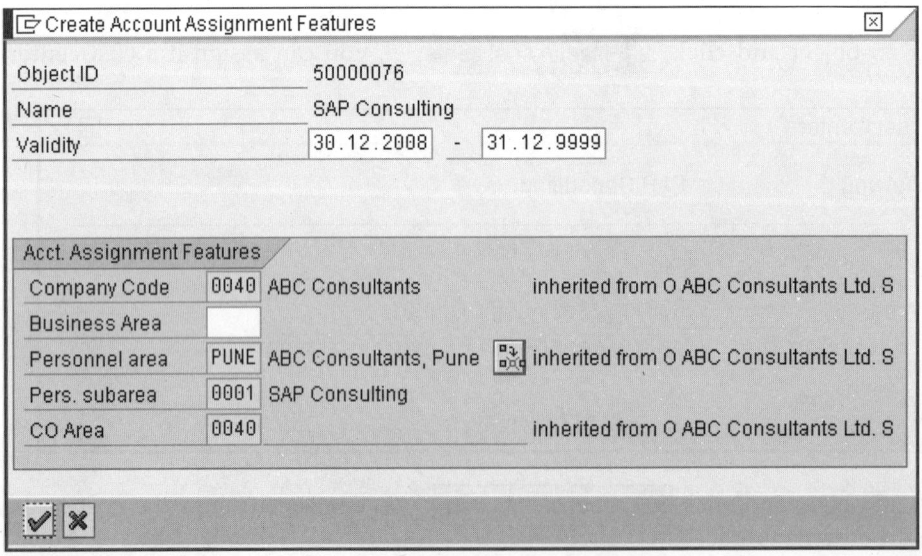


If you want to change the inherited values, click .

***Further characteristics***

You can use this view to edit further characteristics of organizational units and positions.

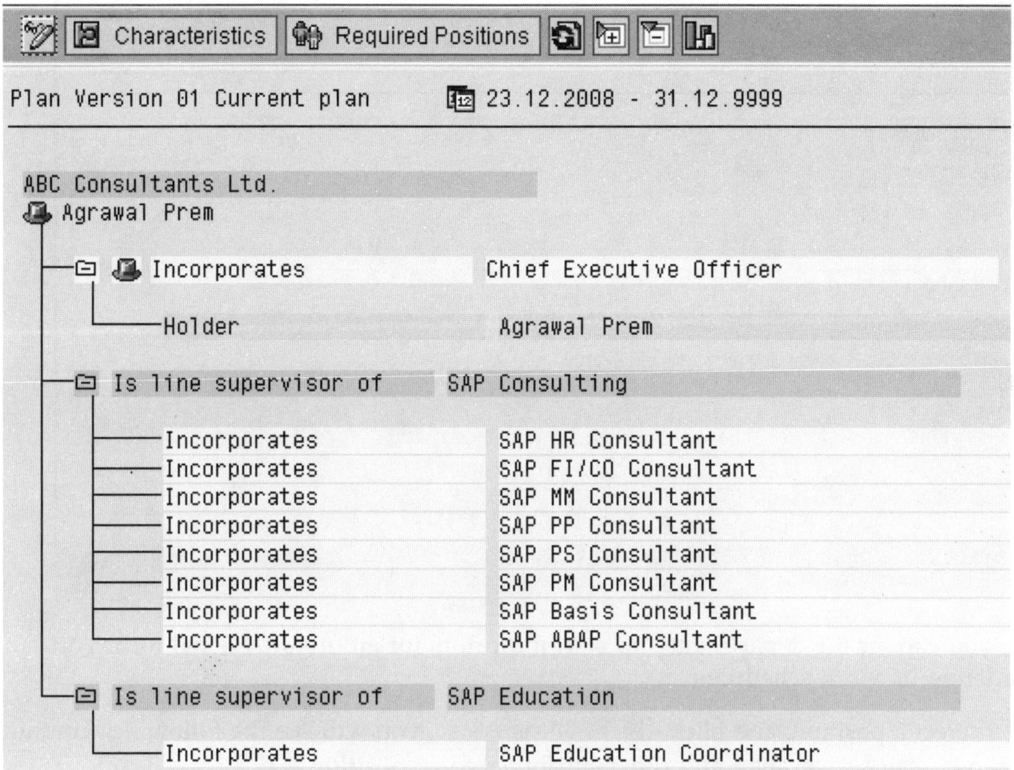


You can do quota planning here by clicking [Required Positions].

If you select an organizational unit, and click [Characteristics], you will see the following window.

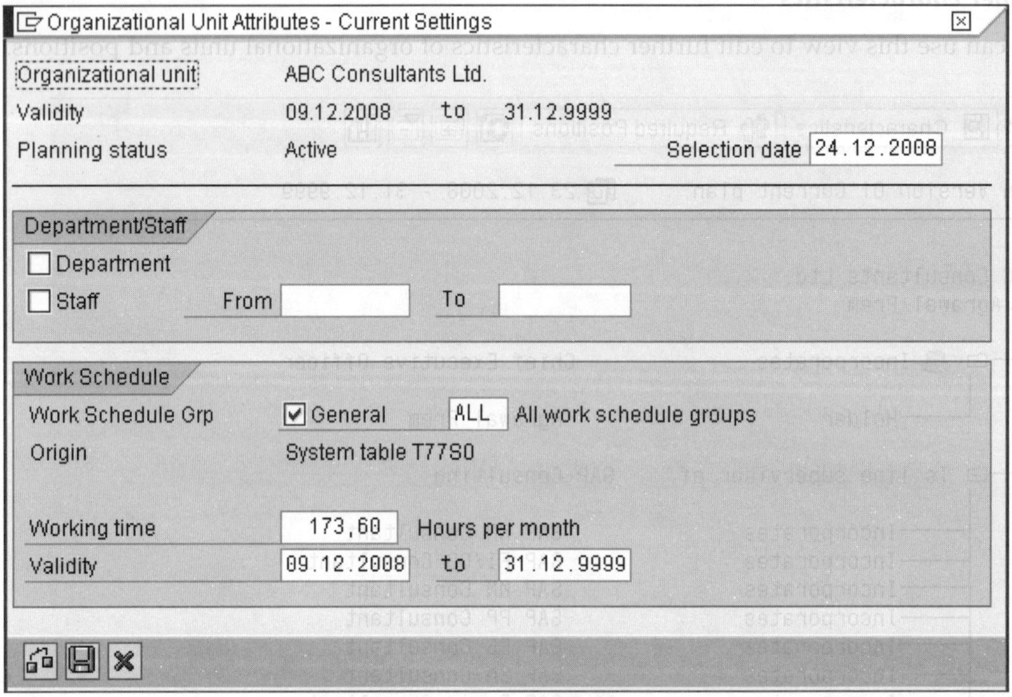


Here you can set the department and staff indicators for an organizational unit. You can also define its work schedule.

If you select a position, and click Characteristics, you will see the following window where you can set vacancy and other attributes for a position.

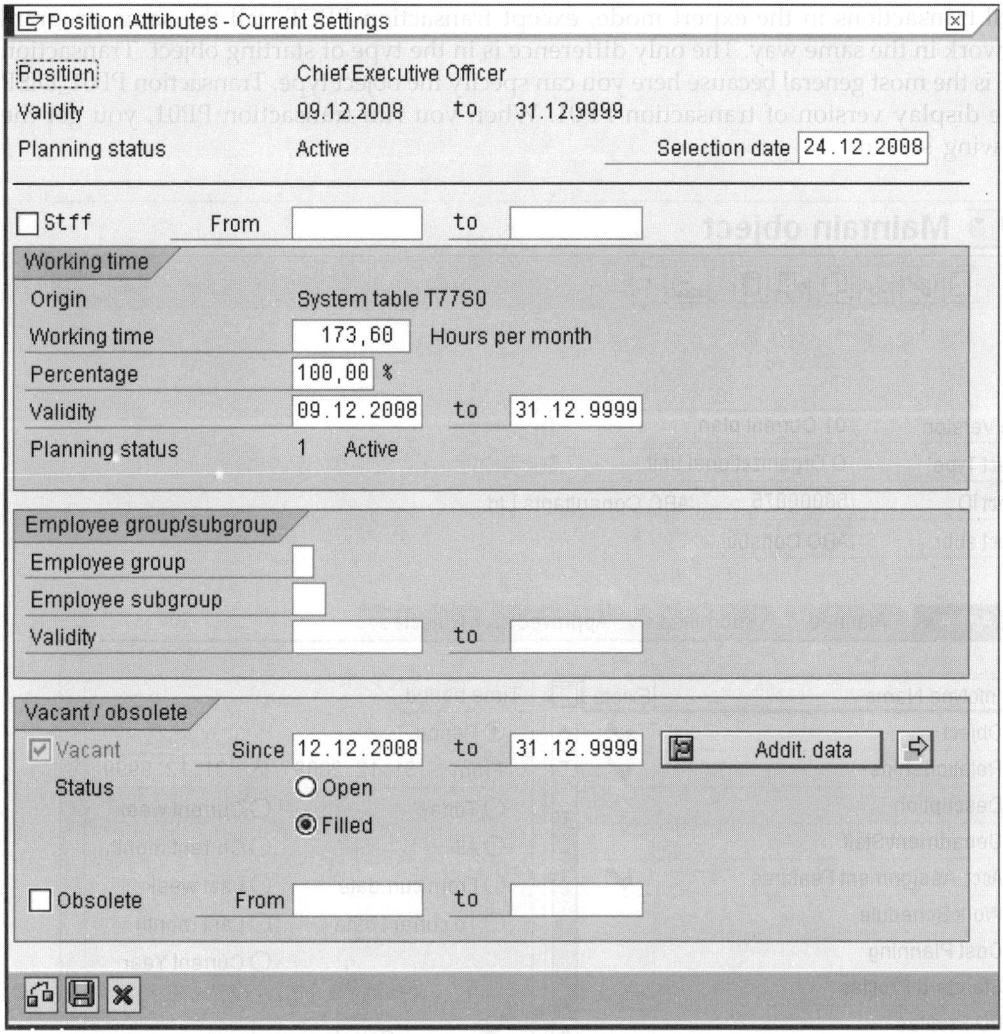


## 2.4 EXPERT MODE

| *Functional Consultant* | *User* | *Business Process Owner* | *Senior Management* | *My Rating* | *Understanding Level* |
|---|---|---|---|---|---|
| A | A | A | B | | |

Expert mode is ideal for users who clearly understand the concepts of objects, relationships and infotypes. The biggest advantage of the expert mode is that you explicitly specify the validity period of objects, relationships and infotypes. Another advantage is that you can build whichever relationship you want without looking for the view in which to create it. All transactions in the expert mode, except transaction PFCT, call the same program and work in the same way. The only difference is in the type of starting object. Transaction PP01 is the most general because here you can specify the object type. Transaction PP01_DISP is the display version of transaction PP01. When you run transaction PP01, you get the following screen.

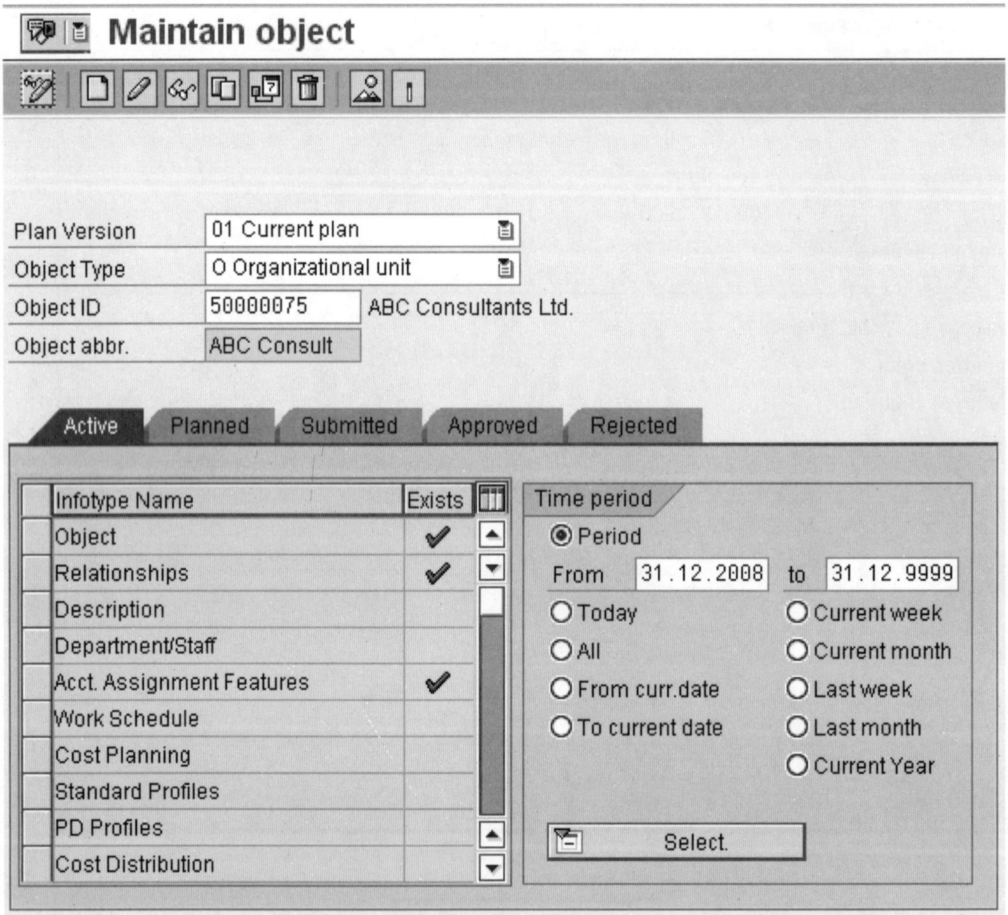


### *Using different plan versions*

Usually you work in current plan version 01. How to use other plan versions is discussed in chapter 15.

### *Maintaining different types of objects*

In transaction PP01, you can specify the object type on which you want to work. In contrast, transactions PO10, PO03, PO13 and PO01 have specified object types. This is the only difference between them and PP01. All these transactions have identical behavior and they call the same program.

### *Specifying object id*

If you are maintaining an existing object, you specify the object id. You are not expected to remember object ids, just select the object by clicking . If you are creating a new object, you leave the object id field blank. If you are using external number range, you specify the object id while creating the object as well.

### *Using possible infotypes*

When you specify an object type in transaction PP01, all the infotypes that can be maintained for that object type are shown. These include infotypes which are required for other applications, e.g. appraisal, shift planning, etc. Hence, you are not expected to maintain all of them. SAP stores objects in infotype 1000 and relationships in infotype 1001. That is why you see Object and Relationships in the list of infotypes.

### *Working with existing infotypes*

The infotypes that exist for an object are identified by a green tick in the Exists column. If an infotype exists, you may delimit, change or delete it. If you copy or create another infotype record, when an infotype record already exists, the previous infotype record will get delimited automatically (depending on the time constraint).

### *Selecting an infotype*

You select an infotype you want to maintain by clicking the button on the left side of the infotype name. The selected infotype is shown in a different color. Selecting another infotype automatically deselects the previously selected infotype.

### *Specifying validity period*

When you create an infotype, you need to specify its validity period. Even when you want to display an infotype, you can specify the period and the system will show you records which belong to that period. One of the key advantages of creating an infotype in expert mode is that you explicitly specify the validity period.

### *Switching between display and change modes*

You can switch from change mode to display mode, or vice versa, by clicking .

### *Creating an object*

To create an object, you leave the object id field blank, select infotype 'Object' and click . If you are using external number range, you specify the object id while creating the object as well.

### *Copying an object*

You can also create an object by copying an existing object. To do so, enter plan version, object type and object id of the object you want to copy from, and choose Object ➢ Copy. The system gives you the following dialog box.

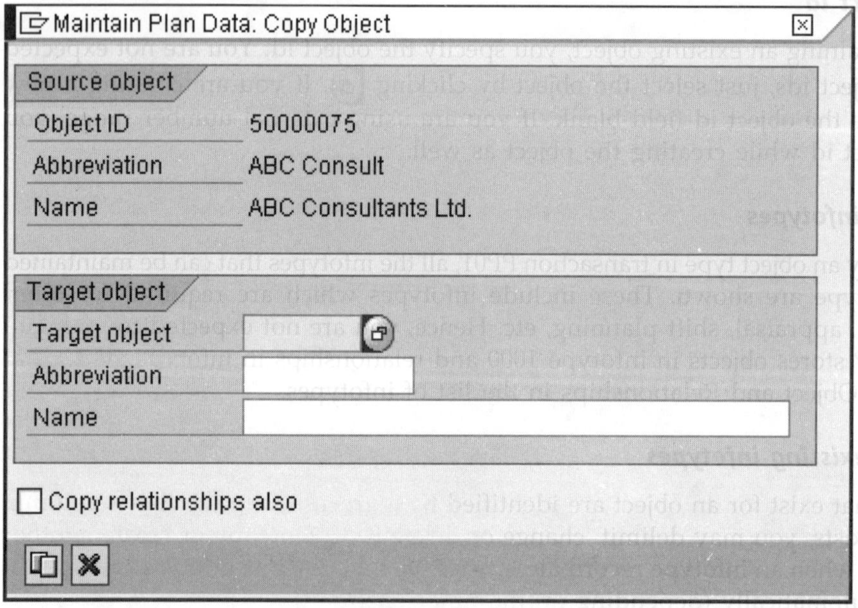


In this dialog box, you specify the name and abbreviation of the target object. If you are using external number range, you also specify the target object id. The system copies all infotypes except relationships. Relationships are copied, if you tick the 'Copy relationships also' checkbox. It shows you what it has copied.

| PV | OT | Object ID | Infotype | Subtyp | S | Start date | End Date | Var... | RNo | Data field | Comments |
|---|---|---|---|---|---|---|---|---|---|---|---|
| 01 | O | 50000243 | 1000 | | 1 | 09.12.2008 | 15.12.2008 | E | | test Te | |
| 01 | O | 50000243 | 1000 | | 1 | 16.12.2008 | 31.12.9999 | E | | test Te | |
| 01 | O | 50000243 | 1000 | | 3 | 31.12.2008 | 31.12.9999 | E | | test Te | |
| 01 | O | 50000243 | 1002 | 0120 | 1 | 06.02.2009 | 31.12.9999 | E | | IDS-----11 | |
| 01 | O | 50000243 | 1008 | | 1 | 09.12.2008 | 31.12.9999 | | | 0040 F | |
| 01 | O | 50000243 | 1019 | 0001 | 1 | 01.01.2009 | 31.12.2009 | | | 000000 | |

### *Delimiting an object*

You can delimit an object. To do so, enter plan version, object type and object id of the object you want to delimit. Select infotype Object and click . When you delimit an object, all its infotypes and relationships are also delimited.

### *Deleting an object*

To delete an object, enter plan version, object type and object id of the object you want to delete and choose Object ➢ Delete. When you delete an object, all its infotypes and relationships are also deleted.

### Creating an infotype

You specify the object id, select the infotype you want to create and click .

### Changing an infotype

You specify the object id, select the infotype you want to change and click . When you change an infotype, the data for the entire validity period changes. If you want to change data from a certain date, you should either create or copy infotype, specifying the start date.

### Displaying an infotype

You specify the object id, select the infotype you want to display and click .

### Copying an infotype

You specify the object id, select the infotype you want to copy and click . Copy facility is used to change an infotype from certain date. This can also be done by creating infotype, but copying lets you edit existing data thereby saving time and effort.

### Delimiting an infotype

When you create an infotype, you usually specify its end date as 31.12.9999, as you do not know the date till when it will remain valid. If it is subsequently determined when the validity of the information ends, you need to delimit that infotype by changing its end date. If the infotype remains valid with different data, you would create the infotype, which will automatically delimit the earlier infotype record. However, if the validity of information ends and no new values are available, then you delimit the infotype record. To do so, you specify the object id, select the infotype you want to delimit and click . If you delimit the object itself, all its relationships and infotypes are also delimited.

### Deleting an infotype

If you want to delete an infotype, you specify the object id, select the infotype you want to delete and click . If you delete the object itself, all its relationships and infotypes are also deleted.

### Displaying overview of an infotype

If there are multiple records of an infotype, you can see their important information in an overview mode by clicking . From the overview mode, you can select a record and display, change, copy, delimit or delete it.

Organizational unit: ABC Consult — ABC Consultants Ltd.

Planning Status: Active

Relationships

| Start | End | R | Rel... | Relat.text | R | Rel'd object ID | Abbr. | % Rate |
|---|---|---|---|---|---|---|---|---|
| 09.12.2008 | 31.12.9999 | A | 011 | Cost cente | K | MANAGEMENT | ABC Consulta | 0,00 |
| 09.12.2008 | 31.12.9999 | B | 002 | Is line su | O | 50000076 | SAP Consult | 0,00 |
| 09.12.2008 | 31.12.9999 | B | 002 | Is line su | O | 50000077 | SAP Educaton | 0,00 |
| 09.12.2008 | 31.12.9999 | B | 003 | Incorporat | S | 50000078 | CEO | 0,00 |
| 09.12.2008 | 31.12.9999 | B | 012 | Is managed | S | 50000078 | CEO | 0,00 |

### *Activating an infotype*

If you want to change the status of an infotype to Active, you may either choose Edit ➢ Status change ➢ Activate, or click .

### *Using planning status*

Most companies use only active planning status. However, SAP lets you create objects, relationships and infotypes in planned status, which may subsequently be accepted or rejected. You can change planning status of an infotype by selecting Edit ➢ Status change. Planning status is discussed in more detail in chapter 16.

### *Using object services*

If you click , the system shows you the object services tool bar.

Through this tool bar you can do the following.

- Enter personal or general notes for an object.
- Create attachments to an object.
- Create relationships between an object and documents that are in the optical archive or that are subsequently scanned in and stored.
- Start a workflow for an object.
- Display overview of all workflows, where an object is involved.

- Display overview of all business objects that are linked to an object. You can call the linked objects by double-clicking—independent of whether the objects are from the current system or another SAP System.
- Send an object as an attachment of a message.
- Subscribe to an object. The user is then notified of changes to the subscribed object.
- Add an object to the favorite list.

## 2.5 STRUCTURAL GRAPHICS

| *Functional Consultant* | *User* | *Business Process Owner* | *Senior Management* | *My Rating* | *Understanding Level* |
|---|---|---|---|---|---|
| A | B | C | X | | |

Structural Graphics lets you make structural changes to your organizational plan by simply moving objects around in the hierarchical structure. You can move single objects or substructures within your organizational plan. You can switch from many other interfaces to structural graphics interface by clicking . You can also start structural graphics by running transaction S_AHR_61016530. Depending on the structure you want to view or edit, you may specify the following evaluation paths.

| *Structure* | *Evaluation path* |
|---|---|
| Organizational structure | ORGEH |
| Organizational structure with positions | PLSTE |
| Organizational structure with persons | PERS-O |
| Staffing assignment (structure) | SBESX |
| Task assignments | WF_O_TTS |
| Account assignment | KOSTDIST |
| Staff assignments with reporting structure | O-S-PHIE |
| Reporting structure | S-S |

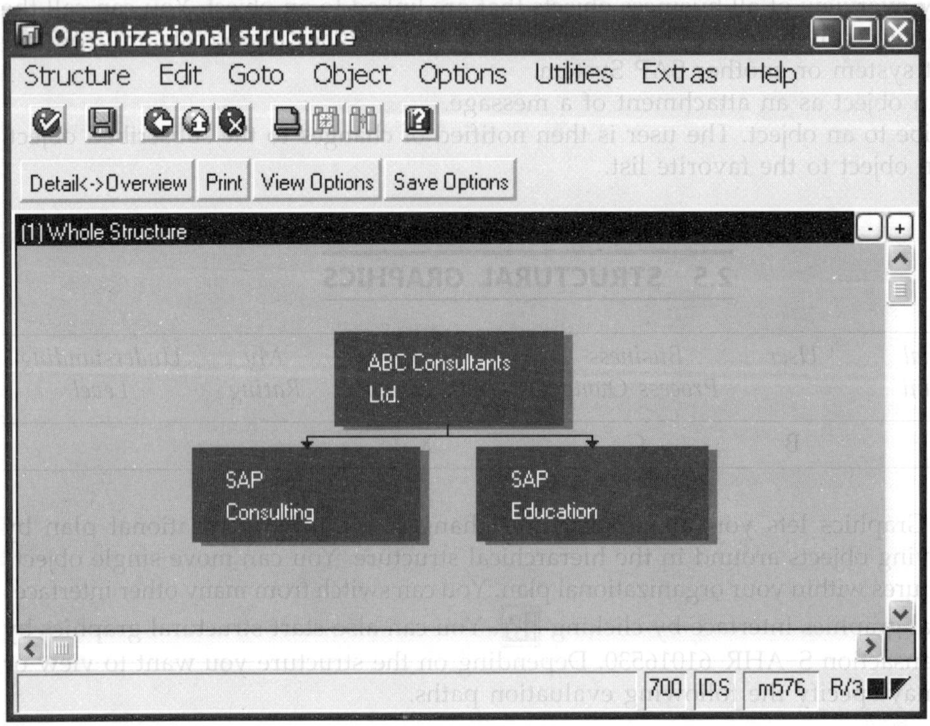


### *Displaying toolbox*

You can choose Edit ➢ Toolbox to show the toolbox in a separate window. The toolbox shows various actions you can perform on selected objects and is a substitute for menu.

### *Selecting objects*

You can select an object by clicking it. If you want to select multiple objects, press and hold the Shift key and click the objects. You can also select multiple objects by pressing the left mouse button, dragging the mouse to create a rectangle and leaving the left mouse button. All objects completely within the rectangle are selected. You can select a branch by pressing the Ctrl key and clicking an object. That object and all objects below it are selected. To select multiple branches, press and hold Shift and Ctrl keys and click the highest object of each branch.

### *Creating objects*

To create an object, select the parent object and choose Utilities ➢ Create objects. You can create up to five objects. You can also set the period and status. The system also creates relationship between the parent object and the created objects.

### Moving objects

To move an object, select the object and choose Utilities ➢ Move objects. The shape of the mouse pointer changes. Select the new parent object. The object moves below the new parent object.

### Inserting objects

To insert existing objects in the structure, select the parent object and choose Utilities ➢ Insert objects. The Relationship/Object type dialog box appears. Use the dialog box to select a relationship and click the green tick. The Possible Entries dialog box appears. Use the dialog box to select the object you want to insert and copy.

### Delimiting objects

To delimit an object, select the object and choose Utilities ➢ Delimit object. Click the green tick to delimit the object, its infotypes, as well as its relationship to the parent object. You can also change the default delimitation date and status of the object.

### Deleting objects

To delete an object, select the object and choose Utilities ➢ Delete object. Click the green tick to delete the object, its infotypes, as well as its relationship with all the objects.

### Displaying object description

To display the description of an object, select the object and choose Extras ➢ Object description.

### Displaying object data

To display the object data, select the object and choose Extras ➢ Object quick info. The system shows object details in a separate window.

### Maintaining infotypes

If you want to maintain infotypes of an object, select the object and choose Extras ➢ Maintain infotypes. The system takes you to Expert mode with the selected object. You can maintain the infotypes there.

### Changing staff mode

You can tick staff checkbox for an organizational unit or position in infotype 1003. To change the staff mode of a position or organizational unit, select the object and choose Utilities ➢ Change staff modes. If you choose Utilities ➢ Change staff modes when the staff checkbox is ticked, the tick is removed.

### Changing shapes, colors and line styles

You can change shapes, colors and line styles in structural graphics by selecting the appropriate option under Object in the menu.

### *Multiple views*

If you have difficulty in displaying the entire structure in the window, you can open multiple views by selecting Options ➢ Further view, or by clicking [+]. In each window, you can scroll independently or display different substructures. You can open up to four windows. You can close windows by clicking [-].

### *Overview and detail mode*

You can change from overview to detail mode and vice versa by clicking [Detail<->Overview]. In the Overview mode the system compresses the hierarchical structure so that you can see the entire structure in one view window. Because the objects are compressed, the complete object name may not be visible. In the Detail mode the system presents a hierarchical structure so that you can read the descriptions of the objects in the structure. However, you may not be able to see complete structure.

### *Displaying close-ups of a structure*

Choose Goto ➢ Choose Section. A rectangle appears in the window. Select the rectangle and hold down the left mouse button. Drag the rectangle over the section you want to view in close-up. Release the mouse button.

### *Displaying substructures*

Select the parent object in the substructure you want to view and choose Goto ➢ Display Substructure.

### *Displaying parent structure*

If you have displayed substructure in structural graphics, you can select Goto ➢ Parent Structure to display the structure of the parent of the highest object currently displayed.

### *Displaying whole structure*

If you have displayed substructure in structural graphics, you can select Goto ➢ Display Whole Structure to display the whole structure.

### *Selecting/deselecting all objects*

You can select all objects by choosing Edit ➢ Select All. You can deselect all objects by choosing Edit ➢ Deselect All.

### *Centering objects*

You can center the selected object by choosing Goto ➢ Center Selected Object. To center the root object, choose Goto ➢ Center Root Object.

### *Displaying paths*

You can display path of an object by selecting the object and choosing Object ➢ Display Path.

### *Searching for objects*

You can search for objects by selecting Object ➢ Search for Objects. You can specify whether the search should be case sensitive. The system highlights objects that match your entry. If you perform another search, the newly found objects are also highlighted. However, if you tick 'Remove Previous Selection' checkbox, only objects matching current search are highlighted. If you save options, this setting is also saved.

### *Sorting objects*

You can sort objects by priority, by key or by text in ascending or descending order by selecting Object ➢ Sort Objects. This only affects display. If you save options, this setting is also saved.

### *Suppressing subordinate objects*

You can hide substructure below an object by selecting the object and choosing Object ➢ Suppress Subordinate Objects.

### *Displaying subordinate objects*

You can display hidden substructure below an object by selecting the object and choosing Object ➢ Display Subordinate Objects.

### *Changing level of an object*

The system shows objects at different levels based on relationships.

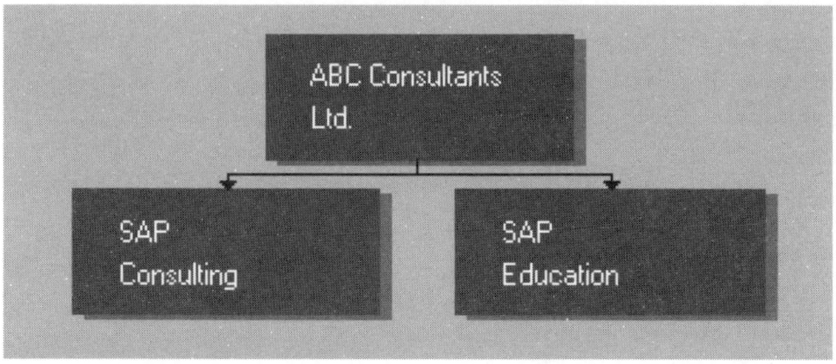


If you want to show an object at a lower level in structural graphics display, you can do so by choosing Object ➢ One Level Lower.

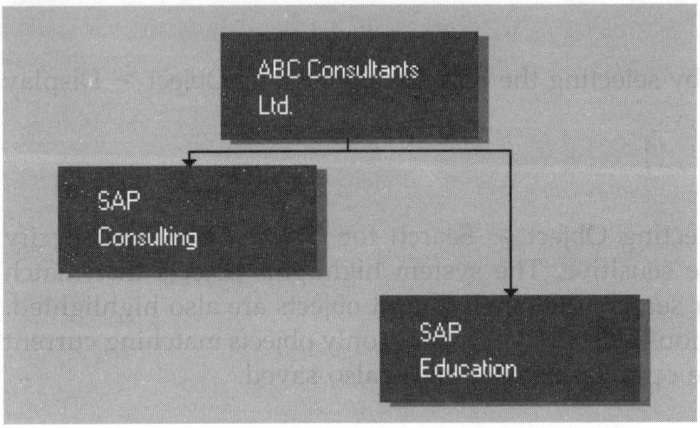


You can do it multiple times. If you have taken an object down more than required, you can move it up by choosing Object ➢ One Level Higher. These operations affect only display. The data does not change. If you exit the structural graphics and enter again, you will see the original structure.

### *View options*

You can change the structural graphics display by setting your view options (Options ➢ View options).

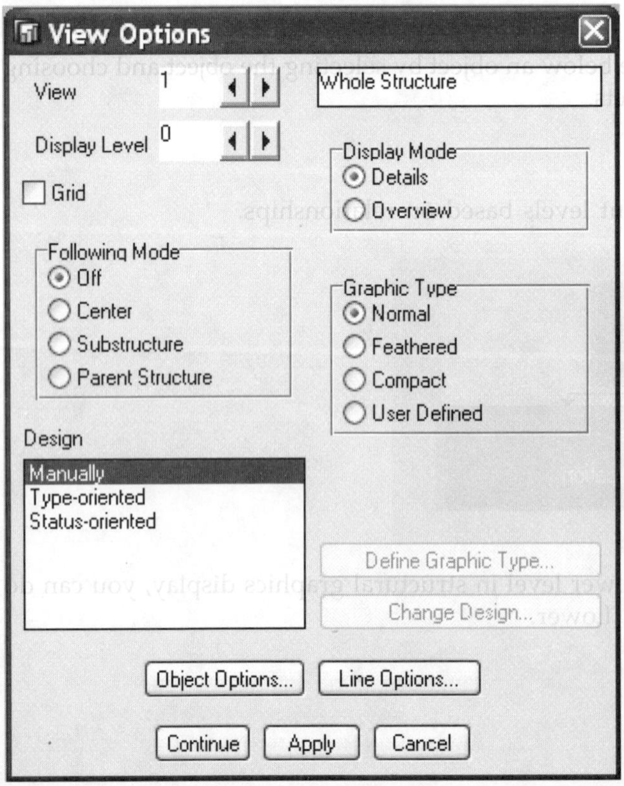

You can display up to four windows by changing the number in the View field. In each window you can scroll the structure independently. You can also set the mode independently. In the substructure mode, the substructure of the selected object is shown. In the parent structure mode, the parent structure of the object is shown. In the center mode, the selected object is positioned in the center of the window. In the off mode, the structure is shown in the normal way.

If you choose display level, only that many levels of the structure (starting from the top) are shown. If you choose 0, all the levels are shown. You can display hierarchical structures on a grid by ticking the Grid checkbox. You can choose between details and overview mode. These modes are explained earlier.

Feathered mode shows the graphics left-to-right, instead of top-down.

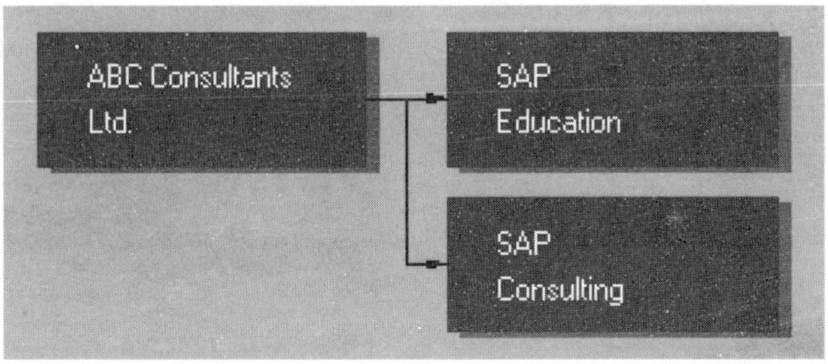


Compact mode is a combination of top-bottom and left-to-right modes.

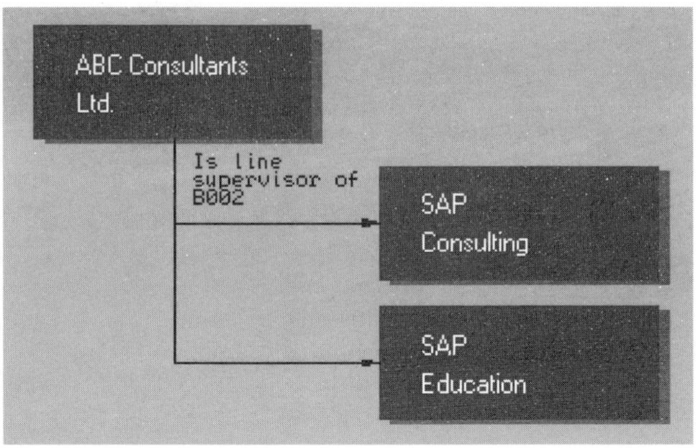


You can use different designs to display graphics. You may like to try them and select the one you like the best.

### *Object options*

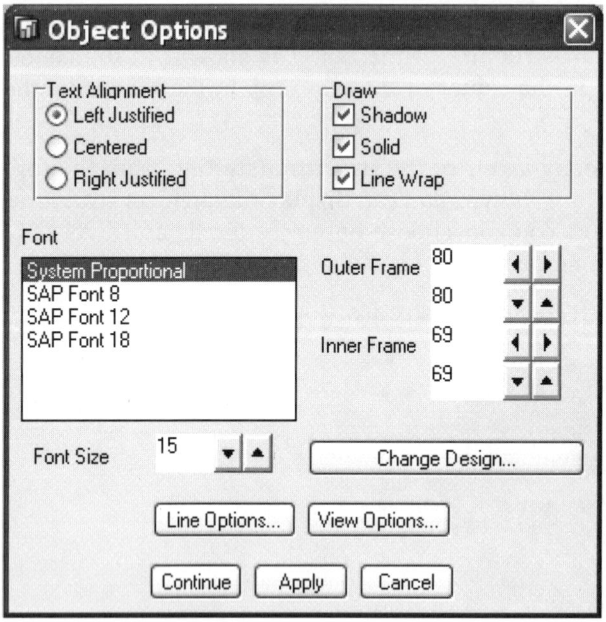


In the object options you can set the text alignment, font size and the object's look. You can increase or decrease the space between objects by changing the outer frame and the inner frame sizes.

### *Line options*

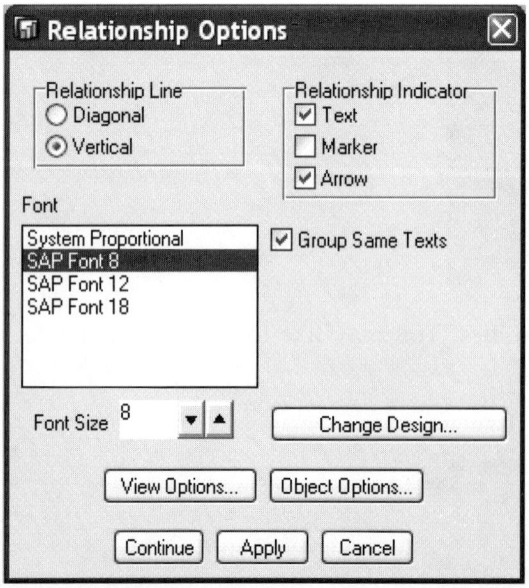


You can set the attributes of relationship lines here.

***Save options***

You can save the options by choosing Object ➢ Save Options.

***Delete options***

You can delete the saved options, and reactivate default options, by choosing Object ➢ Delete Options.

***Mailing structure***

You can mail the structure in the active window by selecting Structure ➢ Send.

## 2.6 ACTIONS

| *Functional Consultant* | *User* | *Business Process Owner* | *Senior Management* | *My Rating* | *Understanding Level* |
|---|---|---|---|---|---|
| A | B | C | X | | |

### 2.6.1 Running Actions

Actions provide another method of creating objects and updating information about them. When you run transaction PP03, you get the following selection screen.

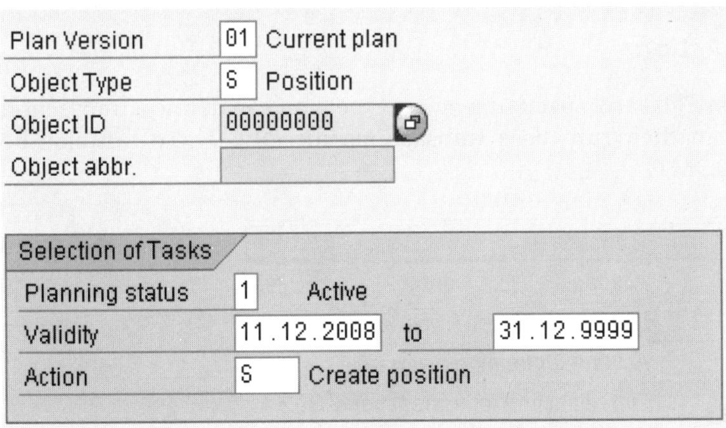


You enter the object type, select the action you want to perform, fill in the validity period, etc. and Execute. The system presents appropriate infotypes in the predefined sequence. The advantage of this method over the Expert mode is that you don't have to remember which infotypes have to be created.

### 2.6.2 Master List of Actions

Actions can be maintained using transaction OOMT. You may use the actions provided by SAP. If you create your own personnel actions, they should be between 001 and 999; you should not use alphabets. Each action can only be defined for one object type.

| Action | Info | Action text |
|---|---|---|
| A | i | Create work center |
| B | i | Create training program |
| C | i | Create job |
| D | i | Create Course Type Classroom Training |

### 2.6.3 Infotypes in Actions

When you define an action, you specify the infotypes which are to be presented when you run the action. This is also specified in transaction OOMT.

| Act. | Action text | SNo | Pla... | Obj... | Infoty. | Subtyp | Pla... | Varia... | Funct... | FCode... |
|---|---|---|---|---|---|---|---|---|---|---|
| 0 | Create organizational unit | 1 | ** | 0 | 1000 | | | | INSE | MASS |
| 0 | Create organizational unit | 20 | ** | 0 | 1002 | 0001 | | | INSE | MASS |
| 0 | Create organizational unit | 30 | ** | 0 | 1003 | | | | INSE | MASS |
| 0 | Create organizational unit | 40 | ** | 0 | 1001 | A011 | | K | INSE | |

### 2.6.4 Transactions for Actions

Instead of running transaction PP03 and specifying object type, you can define a transaction for each object type. You can then run these transactions directly. These can also be maintained in transaction OOMT.

| Group | Sem.abbr. | Value abbr | Description |
|---|---|---|---|
| TCODE | PQ01 | A | Actions for Work Center |
| TCODE | PQ01M | A | Default Action for Transaction PQ01 |
| TCODE | PQ02 | B | Actions for training program |
| TCODE | PQ02M | B | Default action for transaction PQ02 |
| TCODE | PQ03 | C | Actions for Job |
| TCODE | PQ03M | C | Default Action for Transaction PQ03 |

## 2.7 SETTING MAINTENANCE INTERFACE

| *Functional Consultant* | *User* | *Business Process Owner* | *Senior Management* | *My Rating* | *Understanding Level* |
|---|---|---|---|---|---|
| A | B | C | X | | |

You can set the maintenance interface by running transaction PPOM_MODE.

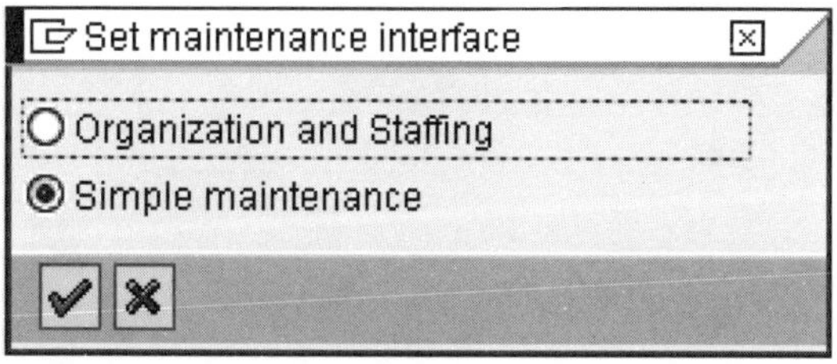


## 2.8 STANDARD SELECTION SCREEN FOR REPORTS

| *Functional Consultant* | *User* | *Business Process Owner* | *Senior Management* | *My Rating* | *Understanding Level* |
|---|---|---|---|---|---|
| A | A | B | C | | |

Reporting in organizational management uses the logical database PCH which contains a standard selection screen.

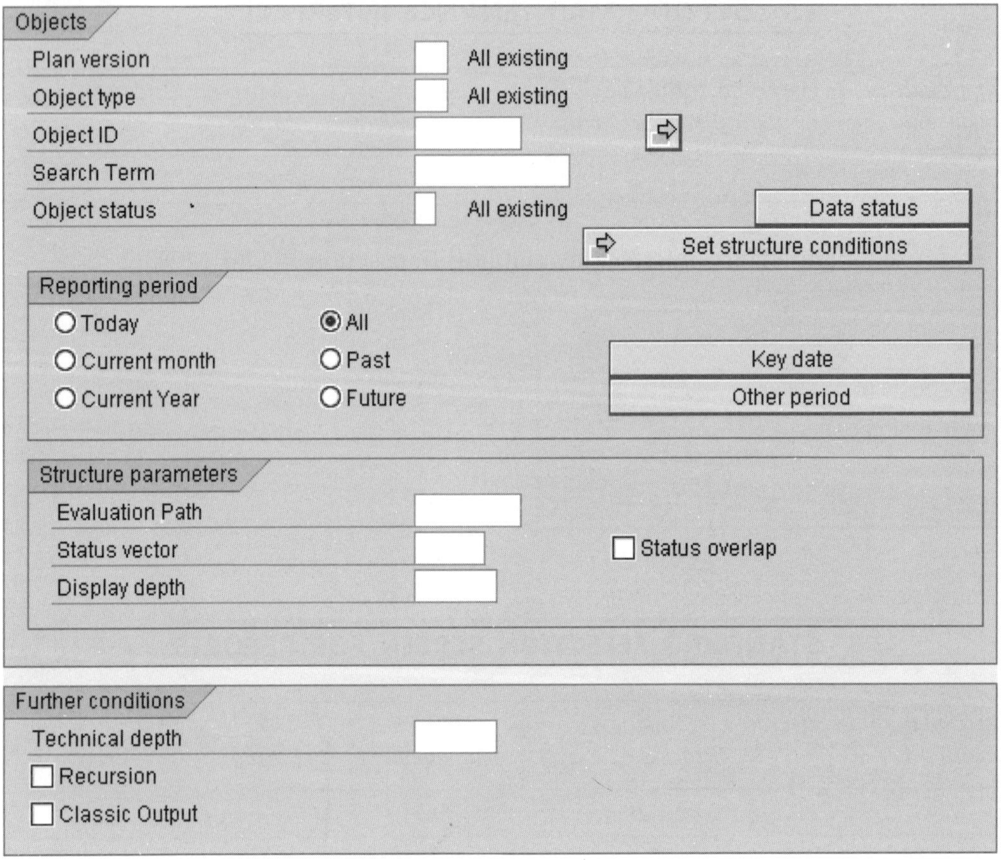


### *Plan version*

You can specify the plan version for which you want to start the report.

### *Object type*

You can specify the object type for which you want to start the report.

### *Object ID*

You can specify the object with which you want to start the report. If you don't know the object id, you can use the search term field to find the object.

### *Search term*

You can enter part of the description here to find objects. You may use * in the beginning, at the end, or in the middle of the search text for pattern matching. If a single object matches the search string, the id of that object is inserted in the object id field. If multiple objects match the search string, they are displayed and you select the one you want.

### *Object status*

You can specify that only objects with a certain status (usually Active) should be reported on.

### *Data status*

Even for active objects, there may be data in infotypes in planned status. Here you can specify that only data with certain status values should be reported on.

### *Set structure conditions*

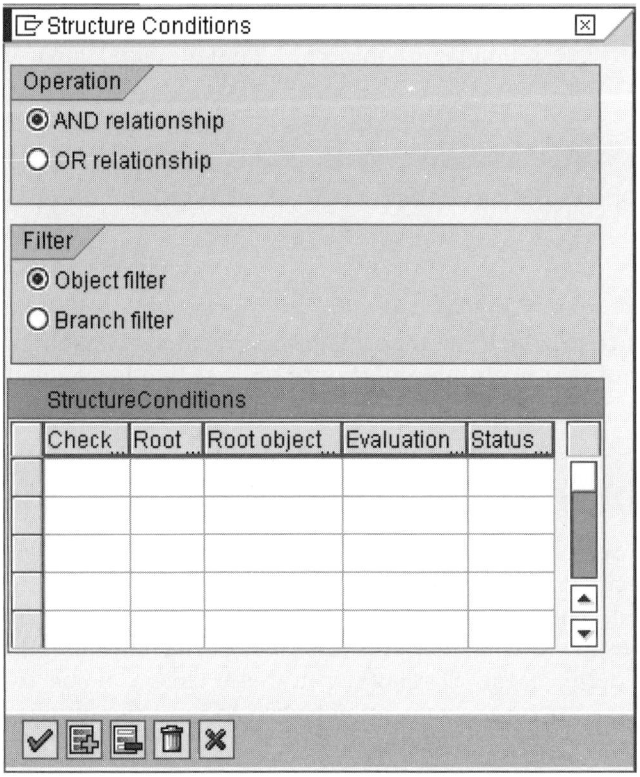


Here you enter the structure conditions for objects that should not appear in the displayed structure or list. You can identify a branch in the structure by Root object type, Root object ID, Evaluation Path and Status vector. You can specify that a certain object type (Check object type) in this branch should not be displayed.

If you specify multiple structure conditions, you need to specify whether they are to be combined using the AND operator or the OR operator.

When an object meeting the structure condition is found, you may decide not to display the entire branch under that object, or you may omit only that object, but show objects below that object, unless they are also filtered by the structure conditions.

### *Reporting period*

Here you specify whether you want the report on a given date, or for a period, specifying the date or the period.

### *Evaluation path*

Through evaluation path you specify which structure of the object is to be reported on. For standard SAP reports, the evaluation path is specified by SAP. If a report is not based on structure, this field is omitted from the selection screen.

### *Status vector*

You can specify that only objects whose relationship infotypes (assignments) have a certain status are to be reported on.

### *Status overlap*

You can execute a simulation that displays the results as though all relationship infotypes were active.

### *Display depth*

You can specify the level of a structure to which the report is to be executed. Thus, if an organizational plan has five levels, but you want the report only on first two levels, that can be done by specifying 2 in this field. If you do not wish to limit the number of levels, leave this field blank.

### *Technical depth*

You can write an evaluation path, in which you skip displaying intermediate objects. For example, you can display persons directly under the organizational units, without displaying positions to which they are attached. The actual structure has positions in it, but the display view skips them. In such cases, the display depth is less than the technical depth. You specify the limit on the display depth in the 'Display depth' field. Here you specify the limit on the technical depth of the structure. If you do not wish to limit the number of levels, leave this field blank.

### *Recursion*

This checkbox specifies whether the system should check the relationships among objects for recursions. A recursion occurs when the system traces the many relationships among objects in a structure, and finds no termination point.

### *Classic output*

If you tick this checkbox, the output is in classical report format. If you do not tick this checkbox, the output is more interactive. For example, you can adjust column widths and expand or collapse tree structures.

CHAPTER 3

# Organizational Unit

## 3.1 ORGANIZATIONAL UNIT DEFINITION

| *Functional Consultant* | *User* | *Business Process Owner* | *Senior Management* | *My Rating* | *Understanding Level* |
|---|---|---|---|---|---|
| A | A | A | A | | |

Organizational unit represents a functional unit in an enterprise. The entire organization is divided into organizational units. Organizational units form a hierarchy called organizational structure, where the lower level organizational units report to the higher level organizational units. An enterprise often has different names for organizational units at different levels, e.g. line of business (LOB), division, department, section, etc. In SAP, all these are called organizational units.

## 3.2 ORGANIZATIONAL UNIT CREATION

| *Functional Consultant* | *User* | *Business Process Owner* | *Senior Management* | *My Rating* | *Understanding Level* |
|---|---|---|---|---|---|
| A | A | B | X | | |

The highest organizational unit in an organizational structure is called the root organizational unit. You can create the root organizational unit using transaction PPOCE. All other organizational units can be created using transaction PPOME. You can also create organizational units using transaction PO10.

## 3.3 ORGANIZATIONAL UNIT STRUCTURES

| *Functional Consultant* | *User* | *Business Process Owner* | *Senior Management* | *My Rating* | *Understanding Level* |
|---|---|---|---|---|---|
| A | A | B | C | | |

When you select an organizational unit in Organization and Staffing (transaction PPOME), you can work on multiple views in the overview area. Each of these views is a structure starting from the selected organizational unit.

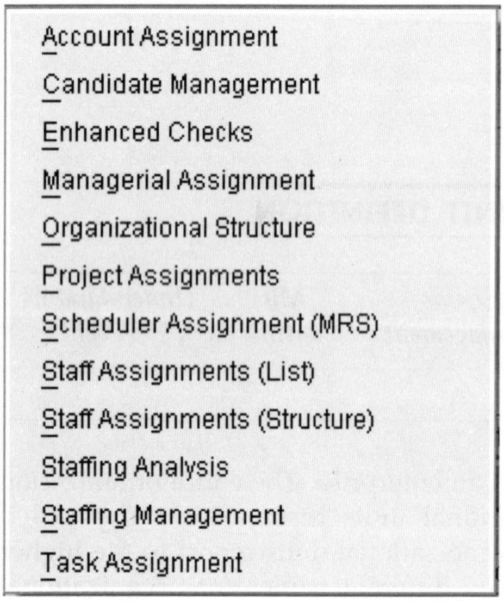

### 3.3.1 Staff Assignments (Structure)

***View***

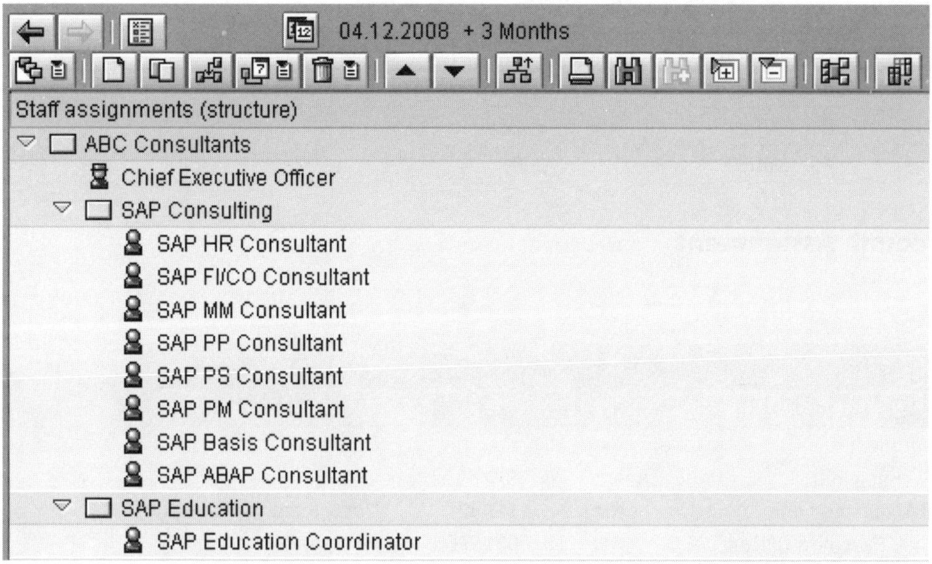


This is the most popular structure of an organizational unit. If you double-click an organizational unit in the selection area, the system shows this structure of the organizational unit in the overview area. In this structure, you see the organizational structure, positions in the organizational units and holders of positions.

***Evaluation path***

If you click , the system displays which structure it is showing.

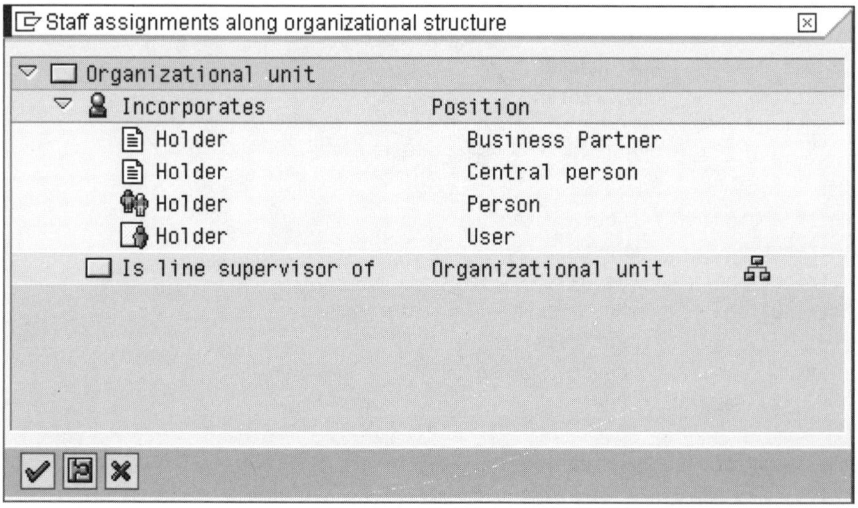

If you click , the system shows you the technical view of the evaluation path, SBESX in this case.

Staff assignments along organizational structure

| No. | Object Type | Rel... | Relat'ship | Priority | Rel.obj.type | Skip |
|---|---|---|---|---|---|---|
| 10 | O | B | 003 | * | S | |
| 20 | O | B | 002 | * | O | |
| 30 | S | A | 008 | * | * | |

### 3.3.2 Account Assignment

***View***

04.12.2008 + 3 Months

| Account assignment | Code | ID | Relationship text |
|---|---|---|---|
| ABC Consultants | ABC Consult | O 50015902 | |
| MUV - posting only | MUV - postin | K 1110001 | Cost center assignment |
| Chief Executive Officer | CEO | S 50015968 | Incorporates |
| SAP Consulting | SAP Consult | O 50015903 | Is line supervisor of |
| MUV - posting only | MUV - postin | K 1110001 | Cost center assignment |
| SAP HR Consultant | SAP HR | S 50016038 | Incorporates |

The above screenshot shows the account assignment view of an organizational unit. This view shows the cost center assignment and cost distribution of an organizational unit and positions under it. Holders of positions are also shown.

***Evaluation path***

| Organizational unit | |
|---|---|
| Cost center assignment | Cost center |
| Cost distribution | Cost center |
| Cost distribution | Request |
| Cost distribution | WBS element (project) |
| Incorporates | Position |
| Cost center assignment | Cost center |
| Cost distribution | Cost center |
| Cost distribution | Request |
| Cost distribution | WBS element (project) |
| Holder | Business Partner |
| Holder | Central person |
| Holder | Person |
| Holder | User |
| Is line supervisor of | Organizational unit |

The evaluation path is KOSTDIST.

### 3.3.3 Candidate Management

***View***

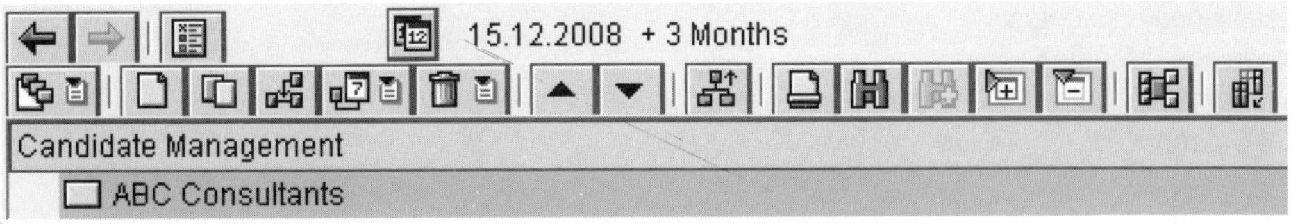


The above screenshot shows the candidate management view of an organizational unit. This view shows the candidate manager position of an organizational unit (relationship A440) and its holder. Candidate management is used in E-Recruitment.

***Evaluation path***

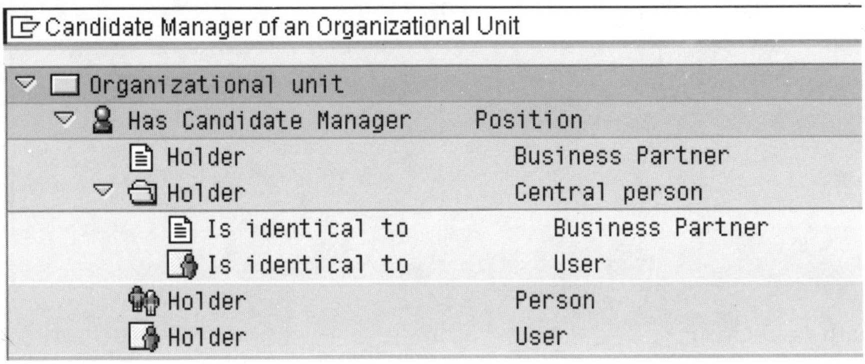


The evaluation path is WFM_CAND.

### 3.3.4 Enhanced Checks

***View***

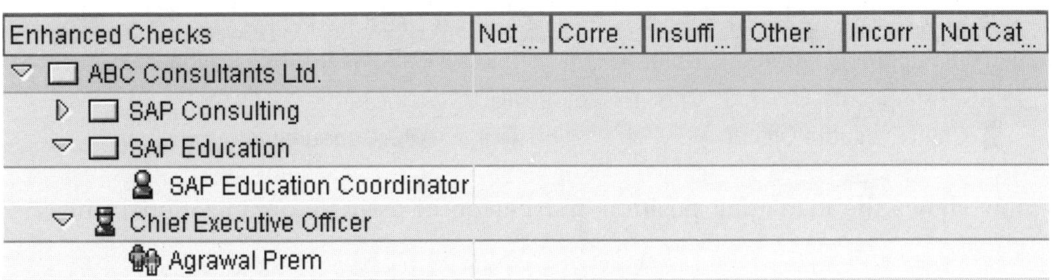

The important thing in this view is the columns.

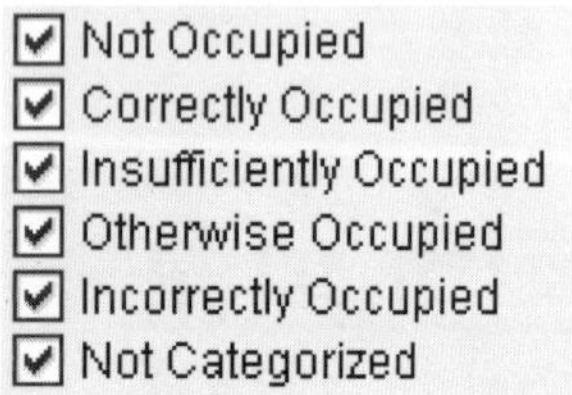


***Evaluation path***

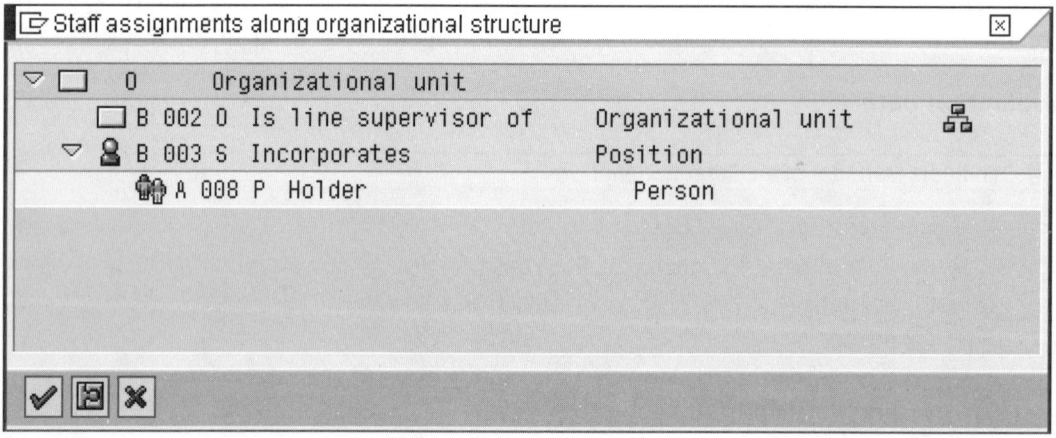


The evaluation path is O-O-S-P.

## 3.3.5 Managerial Assignment

***View***

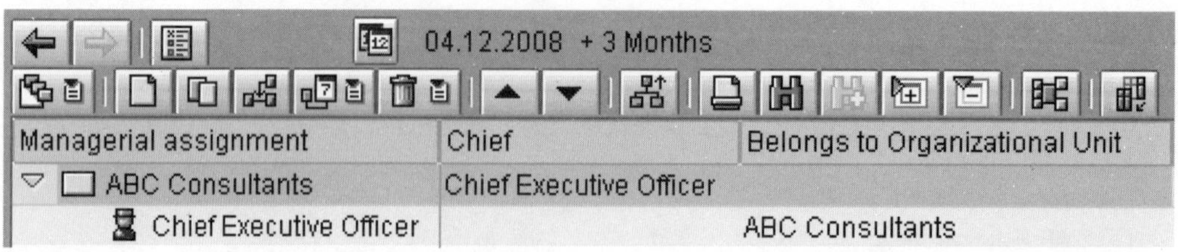


This view shows the managing position and person of a single organizational unit.

***Evaluation path***

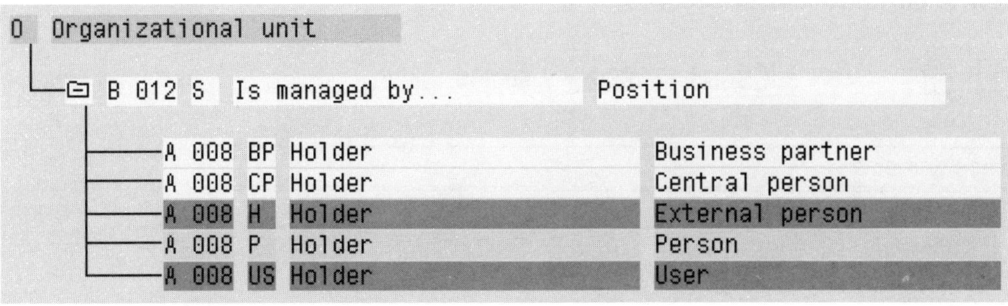


The evaluation path is BOSSONLY.

### 3.3.6 Organizational Structure

***View***

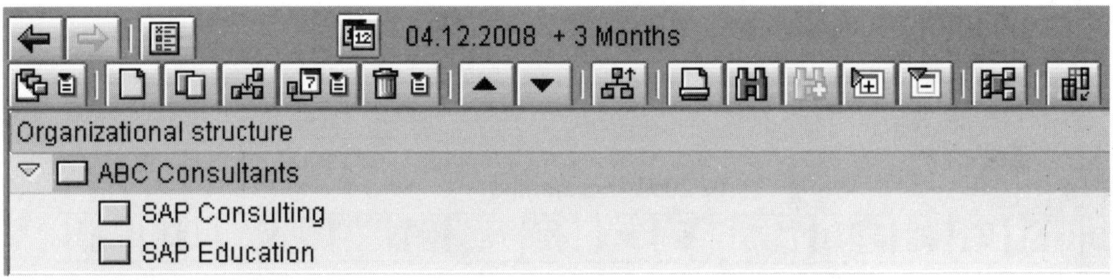


This view shows the organizational structure of an organizational unit.

***Evaluation path***

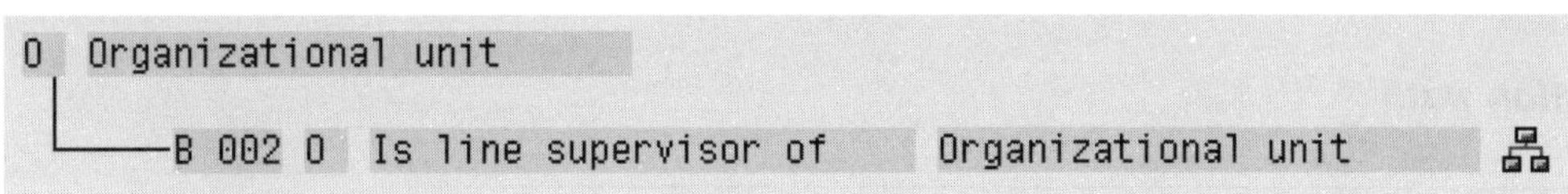


The evaluation path is ORGEH.

### 3.3.7 Project Assignments

This view is currently not in use.

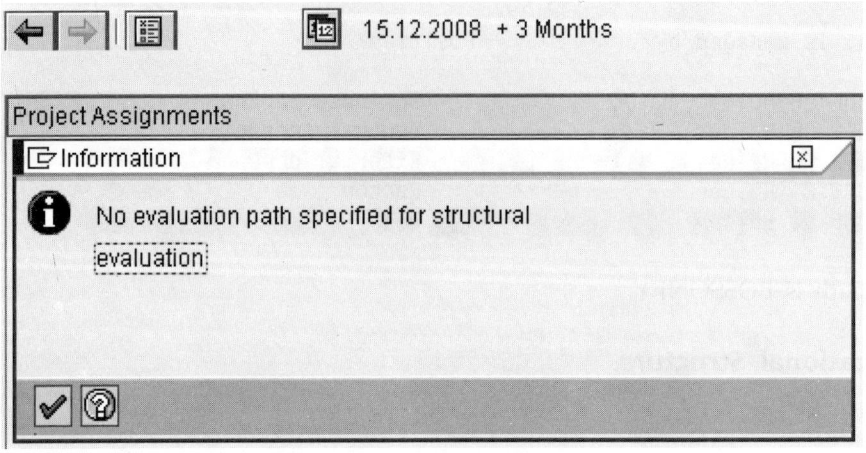


### 3.3.8 Scheduler Assignment (MRS)

***View***

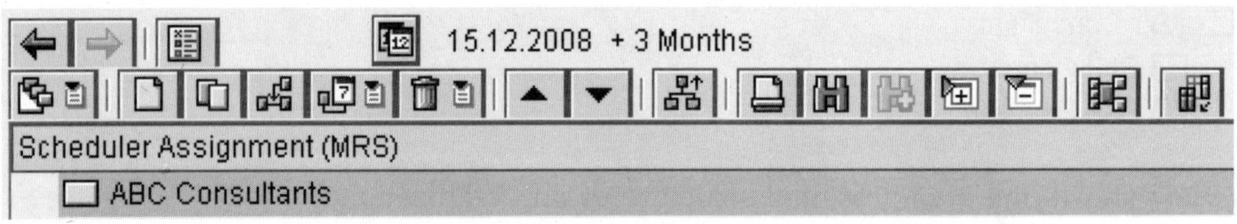


This view shows the shift planner position and its holders (only business partners and users, not employees) of a single organizational unit.

***Evaluation path***

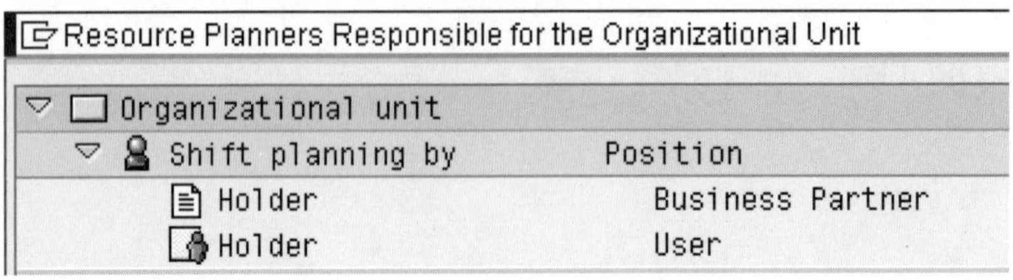


The evaluation path is OMDISPO.

## 3.3.9 Staff Assignments (List)

***View***

This view shows the list of positions in an organizational unit. It also shows detailed information about that position in various columns.

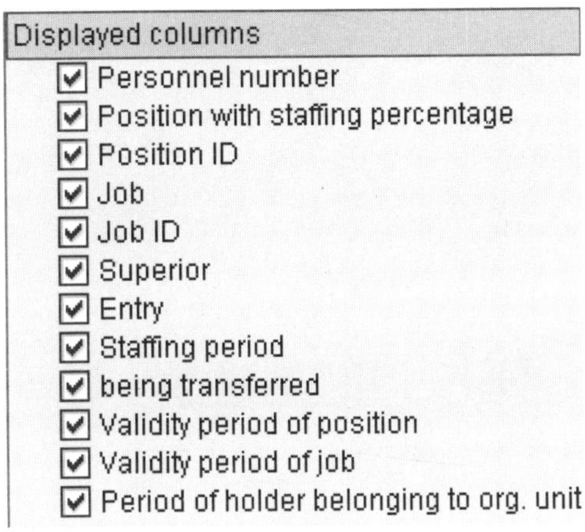


You can also create a position in this view by clicking .

## 3.3.10 Staffing Analysis

***View***

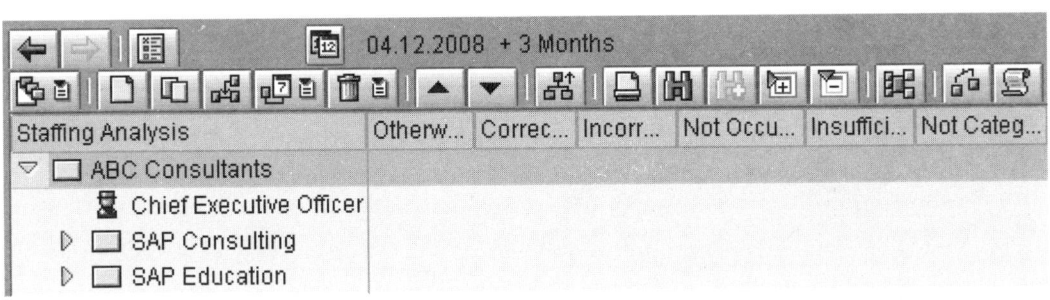

This view shows the staffing analysis of the entire organizational structure. This view is very similar to the Enhanced Checks view. It provides the same information in columns as the Enhanced Checks view.

***Evaluation path***

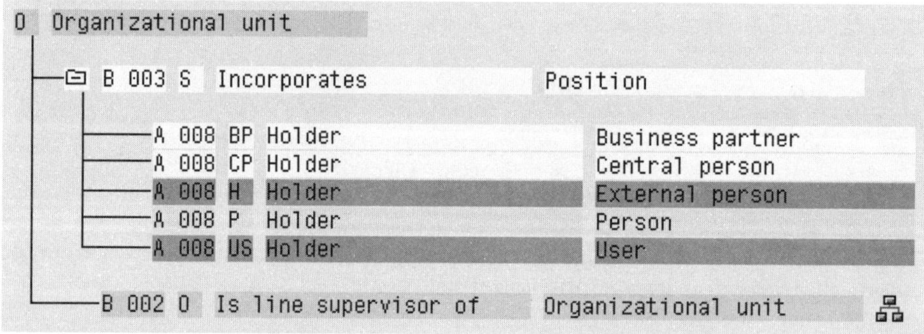


The evaluation path of this view is SBESX, which is very similar to the evaluation path O-O-S-P of the Enhanced Checks view.

### 3.3.11 Staffing Management

***View***

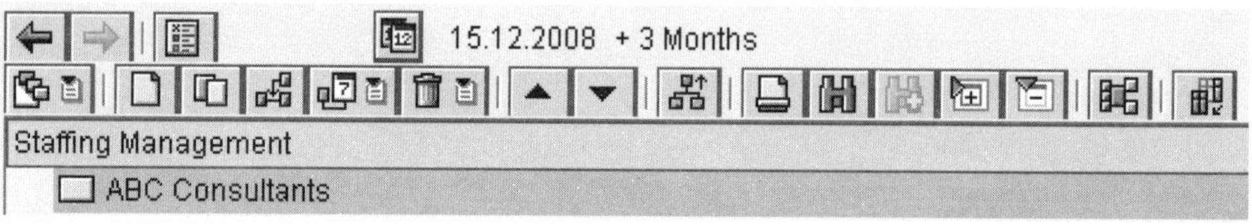


This view shows the staffing manager position and its holder of a single organizational unit.

***Evaluation path***

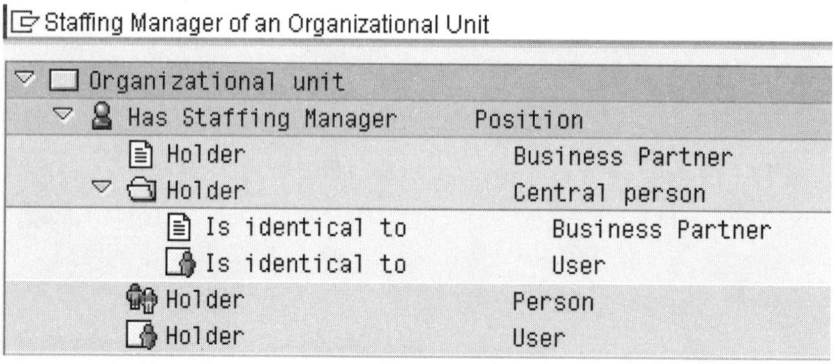


The evaluation path is WFMSTAFF.

### 3.3.12 Task Assignment

***View***

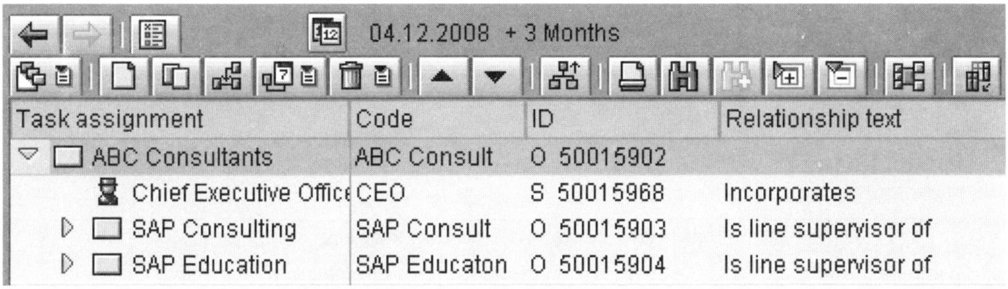


This view shows tasks associated with the entire organizational structure. Tasks may be associated directly or via job. Tasks may be associated with the organizational unit, position, holders of positions, or work center.

***Evaluation path***

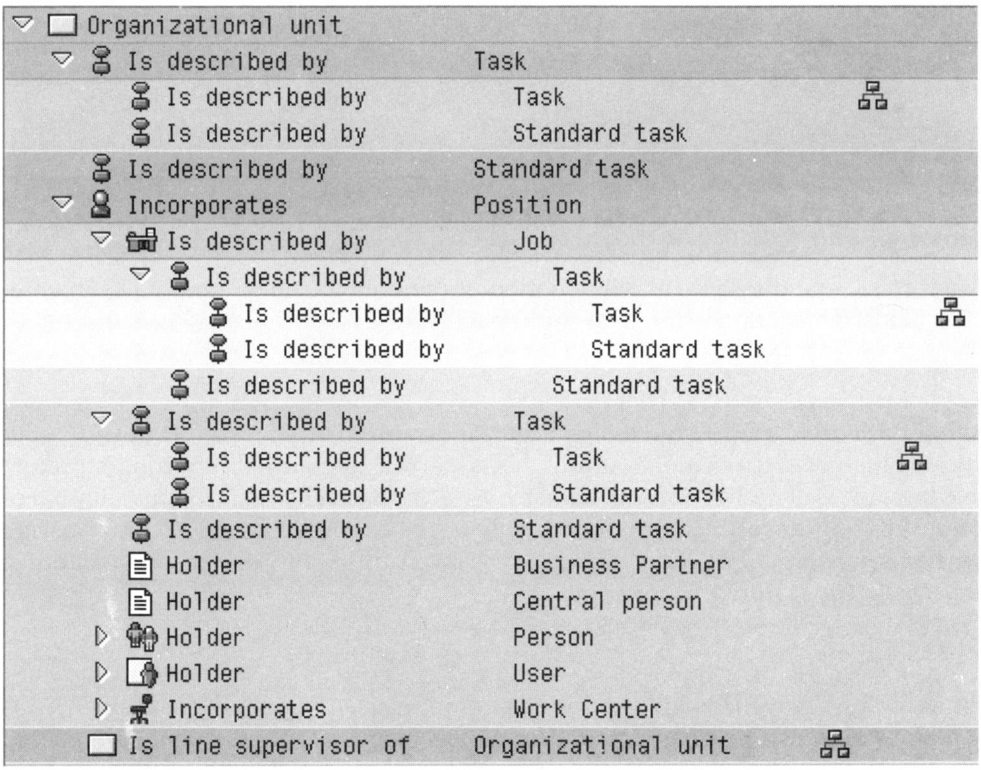


The evaluation path is WF_O_TTS.

## 3.4 ORGANIZATIONAL UNIT DETAILS

| *Functional Consultant* | *User* | *Business Process Owner* | *Senior Management* | *My Rating* | *Understanding Level* |
|---|---|---|---|---|---|
| A | A | B | C | | |

### 3.4.1 Basic Data

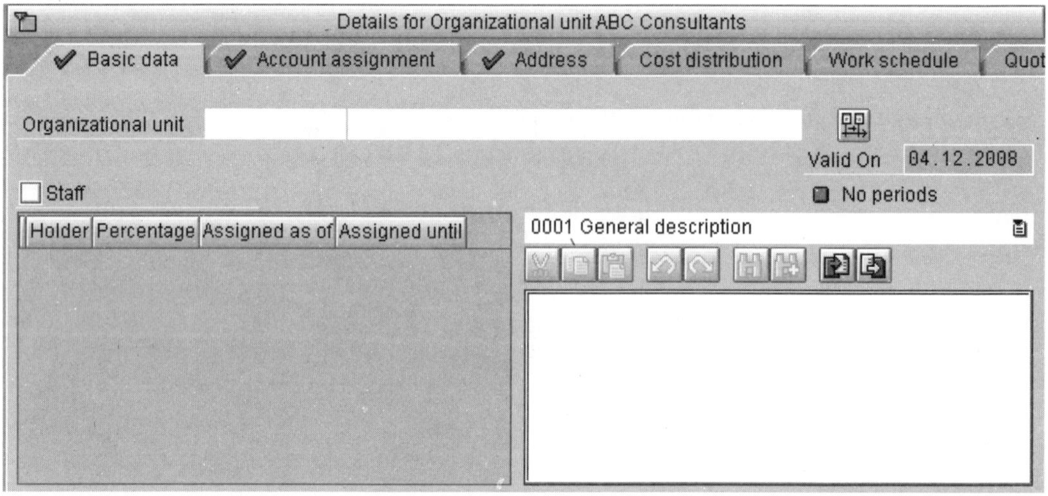


***Organizational unit***

If you want to change the name or abbreviation of the organizational unit, you can enter it in these fields. This data is stored in infotype 1000.

***Staff***

By selecting this checkbox, you can assign a staff indicator to organizational units. A staff flag indicates that an organizational unit is not a part of the normal reporting structure at your company, but rather reports directly to a high level organizational unit. For example, if the audit department reports directly to the executive board, you may assign it a staff flag. Staff organizational units are displayed differently in the organizational structure. This data is stored in infotype 1003.

***Holder***

This area shows the persons holding positions in the selected organizational unit. This is only display area, you can't change the information displayed here. This data is stored in infotype 1001 as relationships between organizational unit and position and between position and person.

***Description***

Here you can maintain the descriptions for an organizational unit which are stored in infotype 1002. You first select the type of description and then enter the description. You can import description from a file on the desktop. You can also export description to a file on the desktop.

***Validity***

The data displayed in Organization and Staffing is for a validity period. If the data for the entire period is the same, the system shows the date for which the data is shown Valid On 02.12.2008 and also indicates that there are no split periods No periods. If, however, the data is different for different periods, the system shows Periods available.

If you click, the system shows the validity period, instead of a single date. It also lets you move to different records or select a period by clicking.

If you change the data in this interface, it is changed from the date displayed, delimiting the existing record.

## 3.4.2 Account Assignment

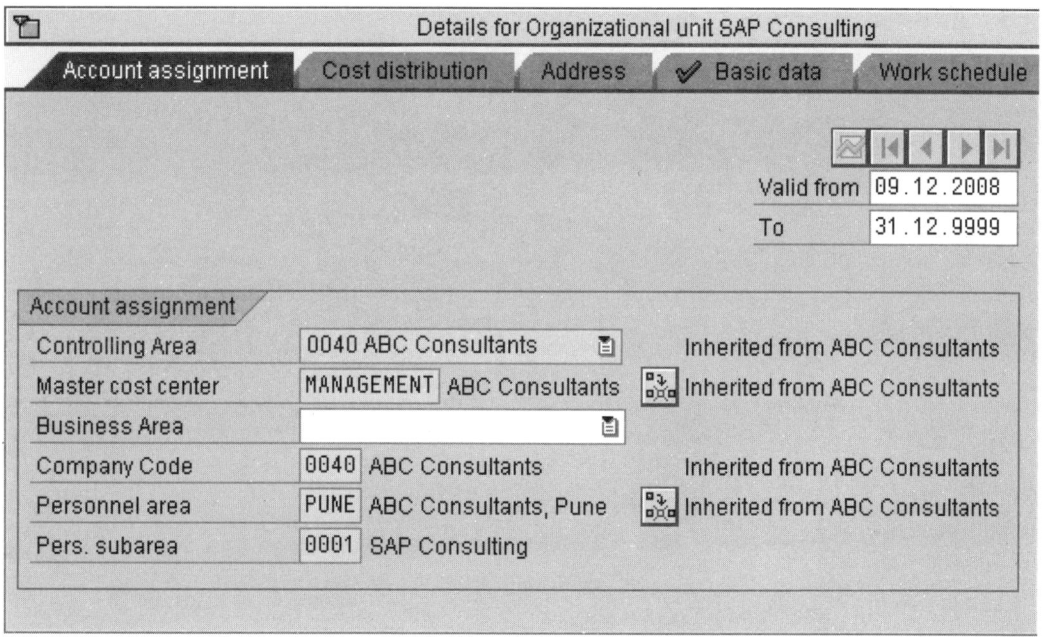


This tab shows data from infotype 1008 and cost center assignment which is stored as a relationship in infotype 1001. Account assignment of an organizational unit may be inherited from a superior organizational unit. If that is the case, the inheritance is shown by .

If the account assignment of the current organizational unit is different from that of the superior organizational unit, you can click and change the data. These fields are discussed in more detail in chapter 14.7.

***Enterprise organization***

In view V_TKA06_CC, you can specify the controlling areas for which enterprise organization is active (Controlling ➢ Cost Center Accounting ➢ Enterprise Organization ➢ Enter Settings for Enterprise Organization).

| CO area | Name | Ent. org. active |
|---|---|---|
| ZA01 | Kostenrechnungskreis ZA01 | ☑ |

Enterprise organization is based on the organizational plan in HR, and contains additional functions and organizational units specific to accounting. It integrates the HR organizational plan, the Cost center standard hierarchy and the Profit center standard hierarchy. If the enterprise organization is active for a controlling area, the HR organizational structure is maintained through transaction KEO1 (Controlling ➢ Cost Center Accounting ➢ Enterprise Organization ➢ Create Enterprise Organization). The account assignment of the organizational unit is specified here and not in the HR organizational structure.

## 3.4.3 Address

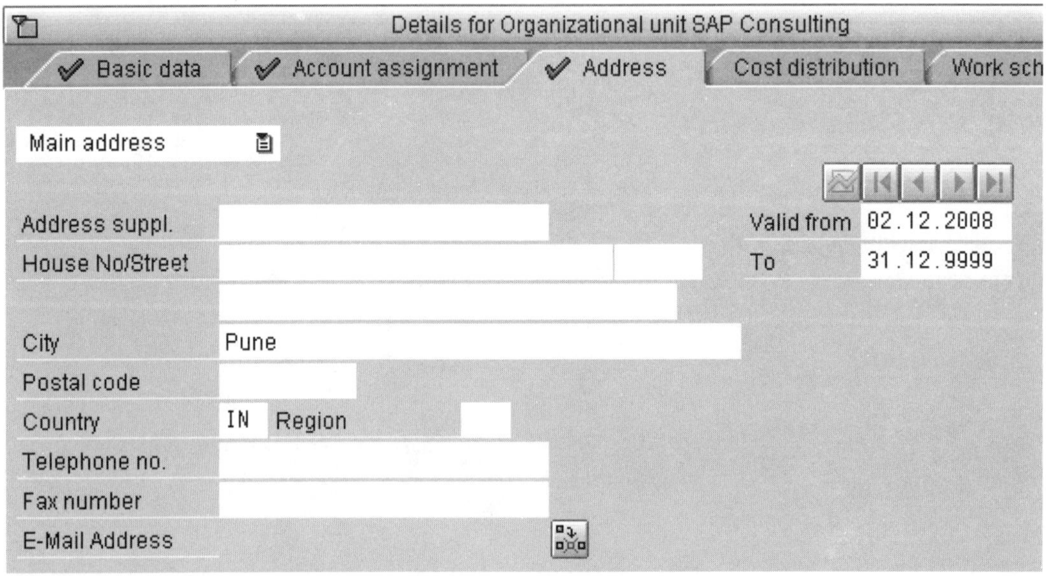


This tab shows data from infotype 1028 which is discussed in more detail in chapter 14.15. E-mail address is stored in infotype 1032. It is inherited from the superior organizational unit. You can change it by clicking . Infotype 1032 is discussed in more detail in chapter 14.16.

### 3.4.4 Cost Distribution

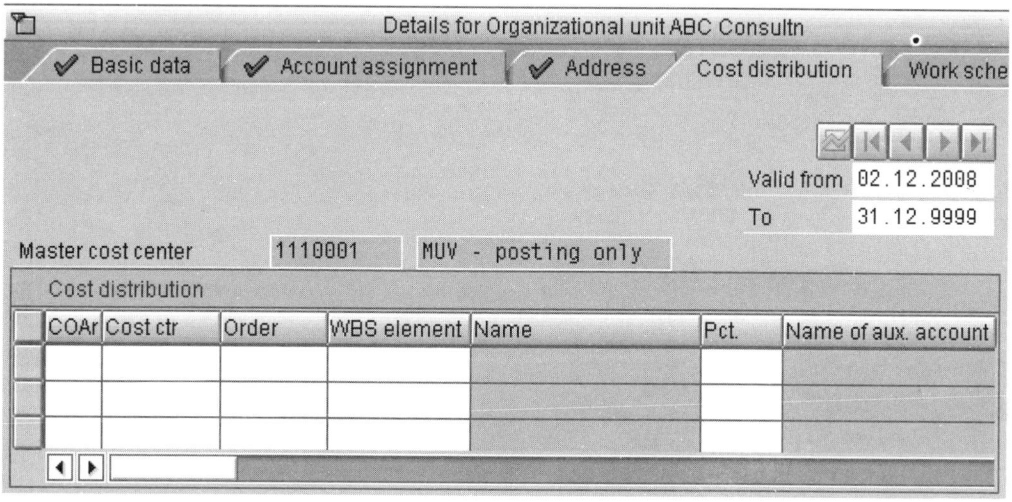


This tab shows you data from infotype 1018, which is discussed in more detail in chapter 14.13.

### 3.4.5 Work Schedule

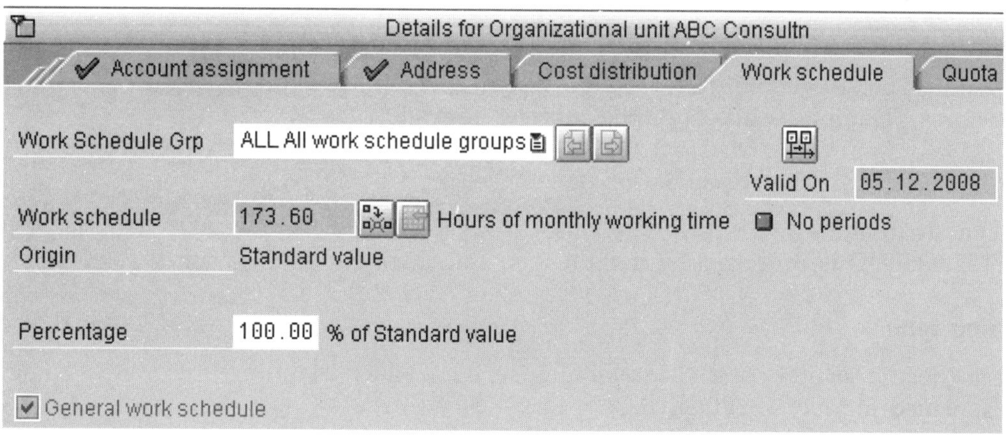


This tab shows you data from infotype 1011, which is discussed in more detail in chapter 14.10.

### 3.4.6 Quota Planning

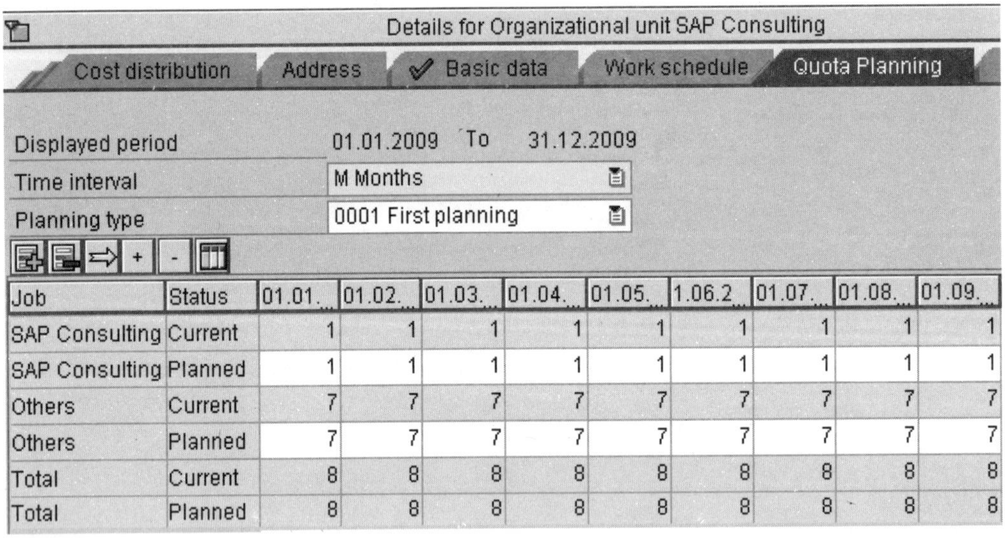


Quota planning is used to perform headcount planning for an organizational unit. You can plan how many and which positions are to be assigned in the staff assignments for an organizational unit in the future.

#### *Displayed periods*

The planning period is determined by the system based on planning type. The planning period for a planning type is specified in view T77POSBUD.

#### *Time interval*

You can do planning for different time intervals. The time interval specified in view T77POSBUD is proposed by default. You can change it if you want.

#### *Planning type*

You can execute several plans. The planning type for which planning is currently going on is specified in view T77POSBUD.

#### *Manpower plan*

Here you specify for each job, the number of positions required in each period. The screen also shows the actual manpower for the purpose of comparison. You can add a job by clicking and delete a job by selecting the job and clicking . You can enter the planned manpower directly in the cells, or increase or decrease it by clicking + - .

### 3.4.7 Tasks

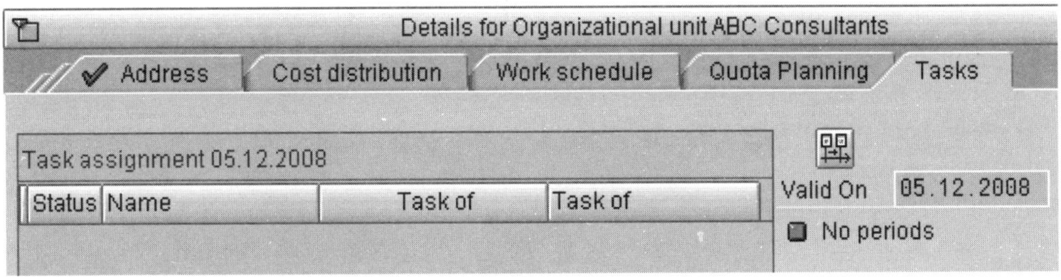


This tab shows tasks for an organizational unit. These are supposed to be performed by all position holders of the organizational unit.

## 3.5 ORGANIZATIONAL UNIT REPORTS

| *Functional Consultant* | *User* | *Business Process Owner* | *Senior Management* | *My Rating* | *Understanding Level* |
|---|---|---|---|---|---|
| A | A | A | B | | |

***Existing organizational units***

You can use transaction S_AHR_61016491 to list existing organizational units. You can also use this program to report all objects, or all objects of certain type. To do so, tick the checkbox 'Standard selection screen', Execute and then specify the object type.

| OT | Start date | End Date | S | Object name | Ext.obj ID |
|---|---|---|---|---|---|
| O | 16.06.1995 | 31.12.9999 | 1 | ALE department | 00000001 |
| O | 30.04.2003 | 31.12.9999 | 1 | FSCM Kreditorenbuchhaltung | 50000025 |
| O | 09.12.2008 | 31.12.9999 | 1 | ABC Consultants Ltd. | 50000075 |
| O | 09.12.2008 | 31.12.9999 | 1 | SAP Consulting | 50000076 |
| O | 09.12.2008 | 31.12.9999 | 1 | SAP Education | 50000077 |

***Staff functions for organizational units***

You can use transaction S_AHR_61016492 to list staff functions for organizational units. You can also use this program to report staff functions of all objects, or objects of certain type. To do so, tick the checkbox 'Standard selection screen', Execute and then specify the object type.

| Plan Version | Plan Version Text | Object Type | Object type text | No. of Staff Pos. |
|---|---|---|---|---|
| 01 | Current plan | O | Organizational unit | 1 |

### *Organizational structure*

You can use transaction S_AHR_61016493 to display the organizational structure. This transaction uses evaluation path ORGEH. You can change layout of the report by clicking . You can also see the output in structural graphics by clicking .

**Plan Version:** 01
**Evaluation Path:** ORGEH (Organizational structure)
**Depth:** 0
**Status Vector:** 1
**Evaluation Period:** 01.01.1900 - 31.12.9999

| Object Description | Object abbr. | Object Type | Extended object ID |
|---|---|---|---|
| ▽ ABC Consultants Ltd. | ABC Consult | O | 50000075 |
| SAP Consulting | SAP Consult | O | 50000076 |
| SAP Education | SAP Educaton | O | 50000077 |

### *Organizational structure with positions*

You can use transaction S_AHR_61016494 to display the organizational structure with positions. This transaction uses evaluation path PLSTE. You can change layout of the report by clicking . You can also see the output in structural graphics by clicking .

**Plan Version:** 01
**Evaluation Path:** PLSTE (Position overview along organizational structure)
**Depth:** 0
**Status Vector:** 1
**Evaluation Period:** 01.01.1900 - 31.12.9999

| Object Description | Object abbr. | O | Extended... | S | Start Date ... | End Date... |
|---|---|---|---|---|---|---|
| ▽ ABC Consultants Ltd. | ABC Consult | O | 50000075 | 1 | 09.12.2008 | 31.12.9999 |
| Chief Executive Officer | CEO | S | 50000078 | 1 | 09.12.2008 | 31.12.9999 |
| ▽ SAP Consulting | SAP Consult | O | 50000076 | 1 | 09.12.2008 | 31.12.9999 |
| SAP HR Consultant | SAP HR | S | 50000079 | 1 | 09.12.2008 | 31.12.9999 |
| SAP FI/CO Consultant | SAP FI/CO | S | 50000080 | 1 | 09.12.2008 | 31.12.9999 |
| SAP MM Consultant | SAP MM | S | 50000081 | 1 | 09.12.2008 | 31.12.9999 |
| SAP PP Consultant | SAP PP | S | 50000082 | 1 | 09.12.2008 | 31.12.9999 |
| SAP PS Consultant | SAP PS | S | 50000083 | 1 | 09.12.2008 | 31.12.9999 |
| SAP PM Consultant | SAP PM | S | 50000084 | 1 | 09.12.2008 | 31.12.9999 |
| SAP Basis Consultant | SAP Basis | S | 50000085 | 1 | 09.12.2008 | 31.12.9999 |
| SAP ABAP Consultant | SAP ABAP | S | 50000086 | 1 | 09.12.2008 | 31.12.9999 |
| ▽ SAP Education | SAP Educaton | O | 50000077 | 1 | 09.12.2008 | 31.12.9999 |
| SAP Education Coordinator | SAP Edu Coor | S | 50000087 | 1 | 09.12.2008 | 31.12.9999 |

### *Organizational structure with persons*

You can use transaction S_AHR_61016495 to display organizational structure with persons.

| Object Description | Object abbr. | O | Extende... | Start Date... | End Date (... | Percent... |
|---|---|---|---|---|---|---|
| ▽ ABC Consultants Ltd. | ABC Consult | O | 50000075 | | | |
| Agrawal Prem | Agrawal | P | 00121715 | 12.12.2008 | 31.12.9999 | 100,00 % |
| SAP Consulting | SAP Consult | O | 50000076 | 09.12.2008 | 31.12.9999 | |
| SAP Education | SAP Educaton | O | 50000077 | 09.12.2008 | 31.12.9999 | |

It uses evaluation path PERS-O. You can change layout of the report by clicking . You can also see the output in structural graphics by clicking .

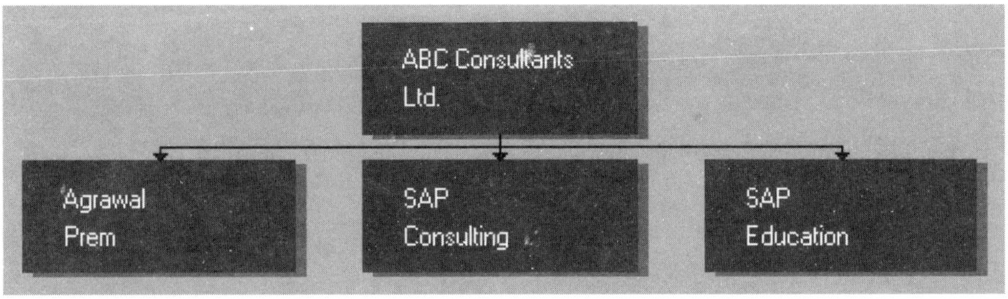


### *Organizational structure with work centers*

You can use transaction S_AHR_61016496 or S_AHR_61016515 to display organizational structure with work centers.

| Object Description | Object abbr. | O... | Extende... | Start Date... | End Date... |
|---|---|---|---|---|---|
| ▽ ABC Consultants Ltd. | ABC Consult | O | 50000075 | | |
| ▽ SAP Consulting | SAP Consult | O | 50000076 | 09.12.2008 | 31.12.9999 |
| SAP Consulting Work Center | SAP Cons Cen | A | 50000000 | 15.12.2008 | 31.12.9999 |
| SAP Education | SAP Educaton | O | 50000077 | 09.12.2008 | 31.12.9999 |

It uses evaluation path ARBP-O. You can change layout of the report by clicking . You can also see the output in structural graphics by clicking .

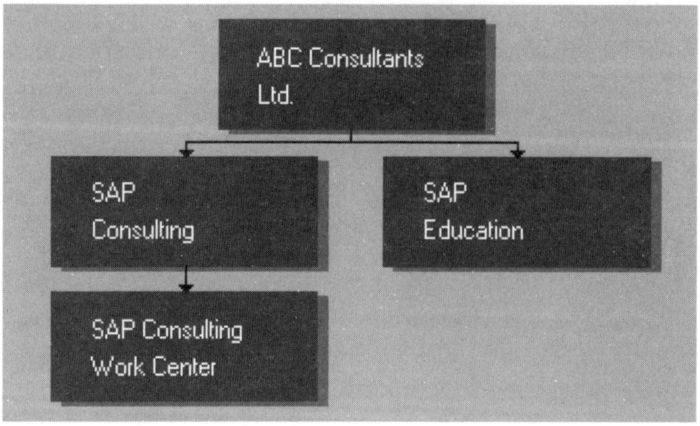


### *Staff assignments*

You can use the old staff assignments report (program RHSBES10) to see an overview of staffing of organizational units.

Overview of organizational units

Staff assignments 05.04.2009
Basic working hours Monthly

| Level | ID | Abbr. | Organizational unit | Planned hours | Actual hours | Deviation | Difference [%] |
|---|---|---|---|---|---|---|---|
| Name | Positions | | Employee | | | | |
| 1 | 50000075 | ABC Consult | ABC Consultants Ltd. | 173.60 | 0.00 | 173.60- | 100.00- |
| Direct | 1 | | 1 | | | | |
| Occupied | 1 | | | | | | |
| Obsolete | 0 | | 0 | | | | |
| Indirect | 9 | | 1 | | | | |
| Occupied | 1 | | | | | | |
| Obsolete | 0 | | 0 | | | | |
| 2 | 50000076 | SAP Consult | SAP Consulting | 1,388.80 | 173.60 | 1,215.20- | 87.50- |
| Direct | 8 | | 1 | | | | |
| Occupied | 1 | | | | | | |
| Obsolete | 0 | | 0 | | | | |
| Indirect | 0 | | 0 | | | | |
| Occupied | 0 | | | | | | |
| Obsolete | 0 | | 0 | | | | |
| 2 | 50000077 | SAP Educaton | SAP Education | 173.60 | 0.00 | 173.60- | 100.00- |
| Direct | 1 | | 0 | | | | |
| Occupied | 0 | | | | | | |
| Obsolete | 0 | | 0 | | | | |
| Indirect | 0 | | 0 | | | | |
| Occupied | 0 | | | | | | |
| Obsolete | 0 | | 0 | | | | |

By double-clicking an organizational unit, you access detailed information.

Key date 05.04.2009
Organizational unit 50000075 ABC Consultants Ltd.
Basic working hours Hours Monthly

| ID Abbr. Position | Target working hours | Chief | Obsolete | Vacant since | Unoccupied since |
|---|---|---|---|---|---|
| **ID Employee** | **Actual working hours** | **Staffing percentage** | **Employee group** | **Employee subgroup** | |
| 50000078 CEO Chief Executive Officer | 173.60 | 🎩 | | | |
| P 00121715 Agrawal Prem | 0.00 | 100.00 | Permanent | Executives | |

Staffing statistics

| | | | |
|---|---|---|---|
| Direct positions | 1 | Occupied | 1 |
| Obsolete | 0 | Occupied | 0 |
| Total | 1 | | |
| Direct employees | 1 | | |
| Obsolete | 0 | | |
| Total | 1 | | |
| Mean staffing percentage | 0.00 | Percent | |
| Target working hours | 173.60 | Hours | |
| Actual working hours | 0.00 | Hours | |
| Deficit | 173.60- | Hours | |

***Planning for organizational unit***

You can run transaction PPEM to do Personnel Development activities for objects in an organizational unit. When you run the transaction, the system shows you the organizational plan (Organizational unit, Job, Position, Person and User) of the default organizational unit specified in user settings. If the default organizational unit is not specified, the system lets you select an organizational unit. If you want to change the organizational unit, you may do so by choosing View ➢ Other Organizational Unit.

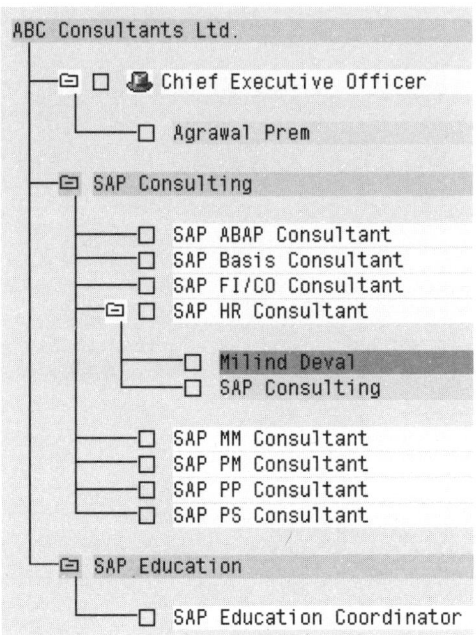

You can perform all the change, display and reporting functions of Personnel Development directly from the screen. You simply select the objects you require, and execute the function through menu or icon.

- Creating a Profile
- Displaying a Profile
- Evaluating a Profile
- Performing Profile Matchups
- Finding Objects for Qualifications
- Career Planning
- Succession Planning
- Evaluating Appraisals
- Calling Up an Individual Development Plan

# CHAPTER 4

# Position

## 4.1 POSITION DEFINITION

| *Functional Consultant* | *User* | *Business Process Owner* | *Senior Management* | *My Rating* | *Understanding Level* |
|---|---|---|---|---|---|
| A | A | A | A | | |

In any organizational unit, the work is done by persons. But when you are planning an organization, you do not know who the person would be. So you plan positions, which are later filled by employees. If an employee leaves, the position becomes vacant, and can be filled by another employee. Positions can also be filled by non-employees, e.g. contractors' employees. Positions can be 100% filled, partially filled or vacant. One position may also be shared by several employees, each working less than full-time. For example, two employees can hold 60% and 40% of one position. Positions differ from jobs. A job is not concrete but rather the basis for the creation of various positions with similar tasks and characteristics.

## 4.2 POSITION CREATION

| *Functional Consultant* | *User* | *Business Process Owner* | *Senior Management* | *My Rating* | *Understanding Level* |
|---|---|---|---|---|---|
| A | A | B | X | | |

You can create positions using transaction PPOME. You create positions under organizational units. Select the organizational unit under which you want to create a position, click 🗋, and double-click the relationship 'Incorporates Position'. A 'New position' is created. You enter mandatory data, e.g. account assignment and address, and save. A position is created. You can also create positions using transaction PO13.

## 4.3 STAFFING STATUS OF POSITIONS

| *Functional Consultant* | *User* | *Business Process Owner* | *Senior Management* | *My Rating* | *Understanding Level* |
|---|---|---|---|---|---|
| A | A | B | C | | |

| *Status of position* | *Icon in staff assignments* | *Text in person/ user column* | *Staffing status in detail area* |
|---|---|---|---|
| Occupied |  | Name | |
| Occupied by more than one person |  | Name | |
| Added during preview period |  | | |
| Removed during preview period |  | | |
| Newly hired person (employee) |  | | |
| Occupied, vacancy is filled |  | Name | Vacancy filled or withdrawn |
| Occupied and vacant |  | Name | Vacancy to be filled |
| Unoccupied and vacant |  | Vacant | Vacancy to be filled |
| Unoccupied and not vacant |  | Not vacant | |
| Unoccupied and not vacant, as vacancy has been withdrawn |  | Not vacant | Vacancy filled or withdrawn |
| Occupied and obsolete |  | Name | Obsolete |
| Occupied by more than one person and obsolete |  | Name | Obsolete |
| Unoccupied and obsolete |  | Not vacant | Obsolete |

## 4.4 CHIEF POSITION

| Functional Consultant | User | Business Process Owner | Senior Management | My Rating | Understanding Level |
|---|---|---|---|---|---|
| A | A | B | B | | |

You can define a chief position within an organizational unit, to which all other positions in the organizational unit report. Apart from displaying the information in the organizational plan, the chief position is also used by workflows to determine manager of a position. In many workflows the manager has to approve a request created by his subordinate. SAP determines the manager of an object in Organizational Management using the function module SWX_GET_MANAGER which uses the chief position to determine the manager.

## 4.5 POSITION STRUCTURES

| Functional Consultant | User | Business Process Owner | Senior Management | My Rating | Understanding Level |
|---|---|---|---|---|---|
| A | A | B | C | | |

If you select a position in transaction PPOME, you can view and maintain the following structures.

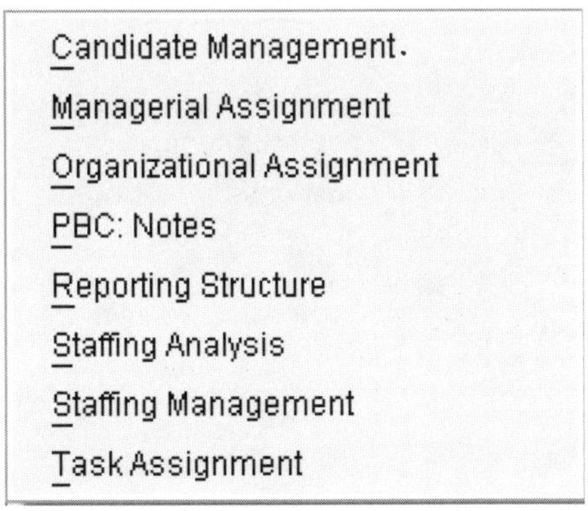

### 4.5.1 Task Assignment

***View***

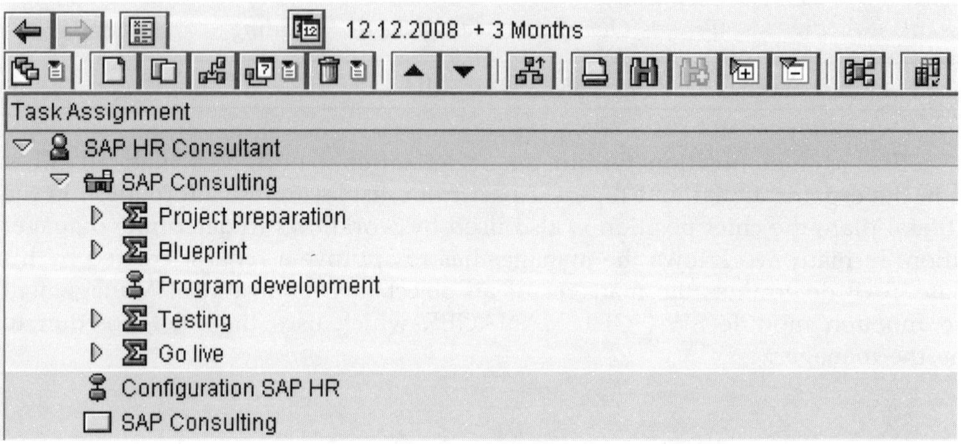


This view shows all the tasks for a position regardless of the route through which they are inherited.

***Evaluation path***

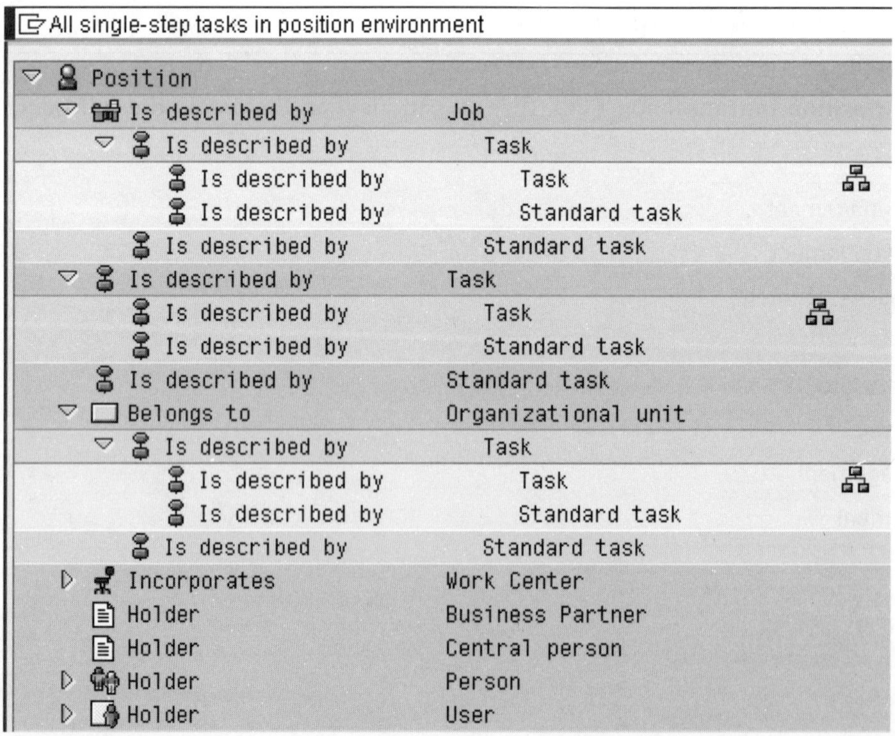


The evaluation path is WF_S_TTS.

### 4.5.2 Candidate Management

***View***

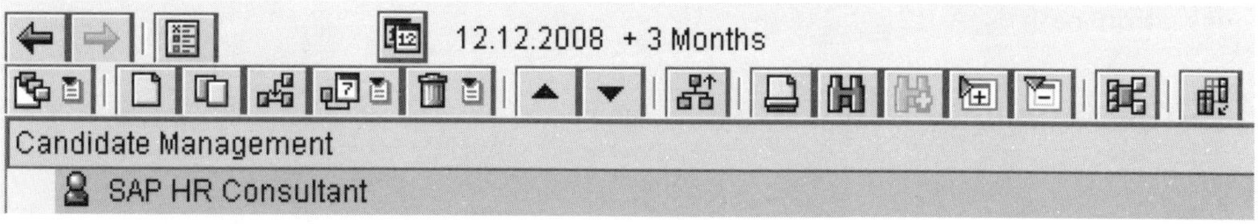


This view shows the candidate manager position of a single organizational unit, who could be an employee, user, central person or business partner. Candidate management is used in E-Recruitment.

***Evaluation path***

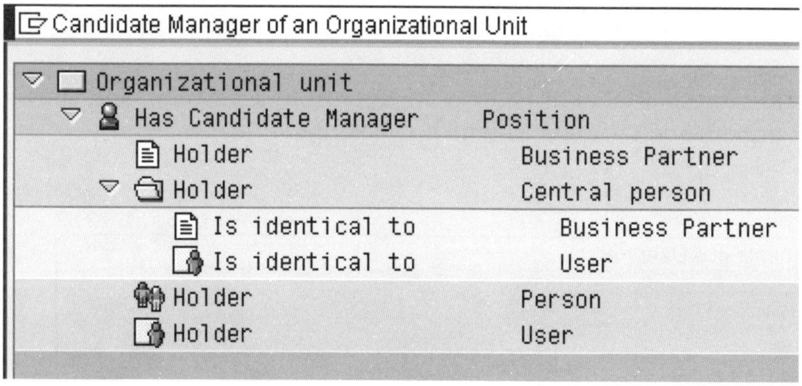


The evaluation path is WFM_CAND.

### 4.5.3 Managerial Assignment

***View***

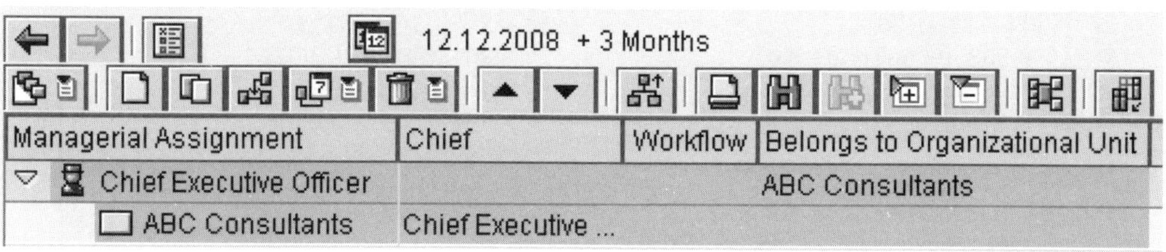


This view shows if a position is chief of the organizational unit to which it belongs.

***Evaluation path***

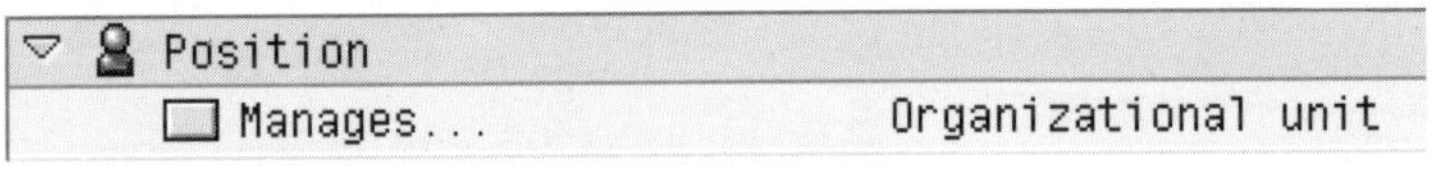


The evaluation path is A012.

### 4.5.4 Organizational Assignment

***View***

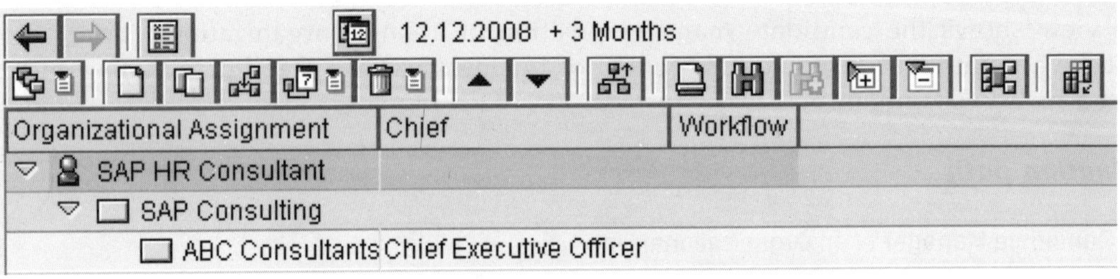


This view shows the organizational plan in reverse. It starts from a position, and shows the entire hierarchy of organizational units to which it belongs.

***Evaluation path***

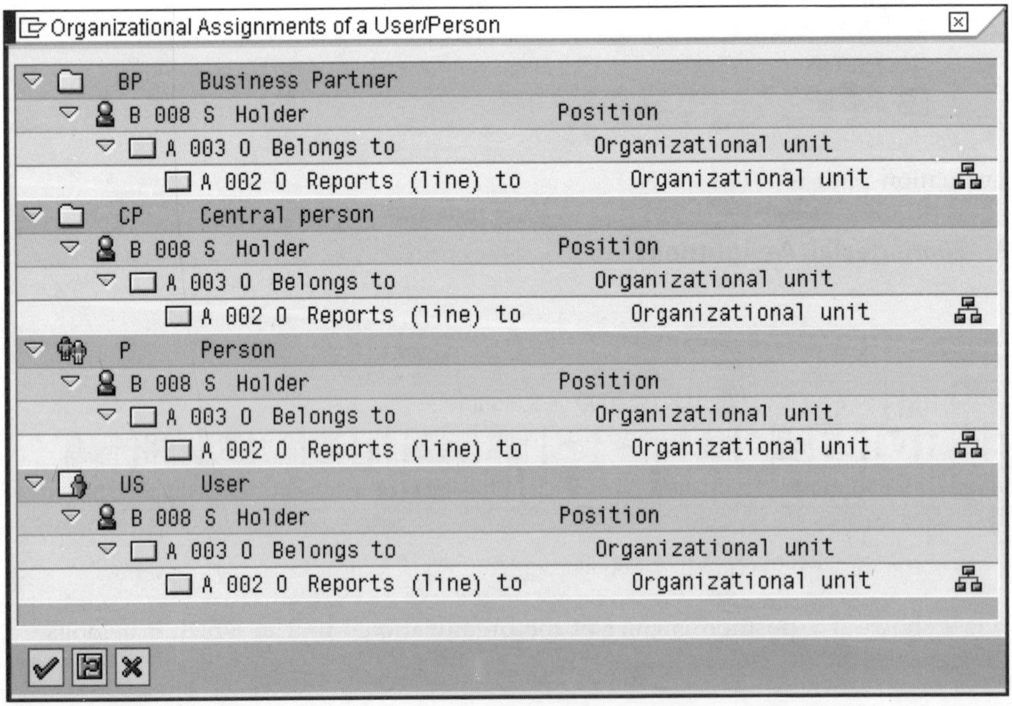


The evaluation path is SAP_PSOO.

### 4.5.5 PBC: Notes

***View***

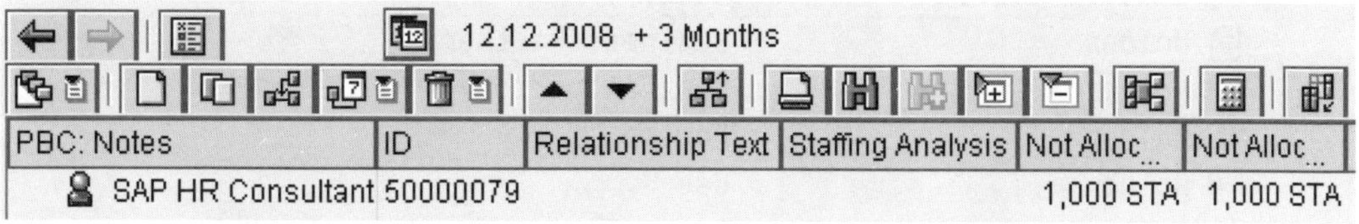


This view shows the following columns for the holders of position.

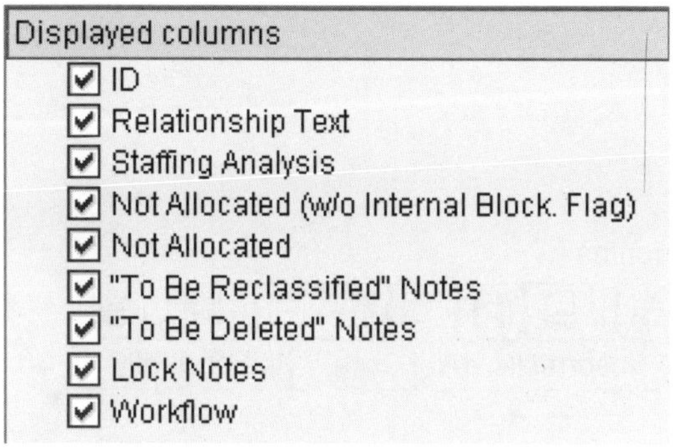


***Evaluation path***

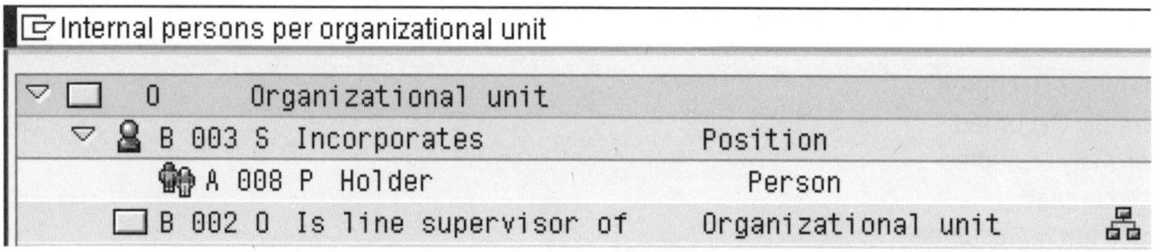


The evaluation path is O-S-P.

### 4.5.6 Reporting Structure

***View***

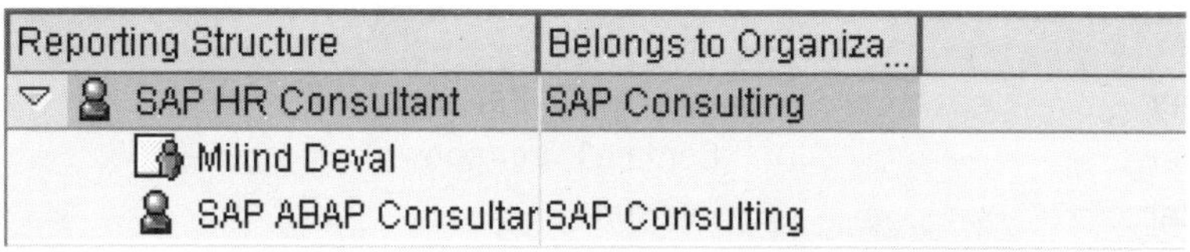


If you maintain a reporting structure between positions and positions, you can see that in this view. It also shows the holder of positions.

***Evaluation path***

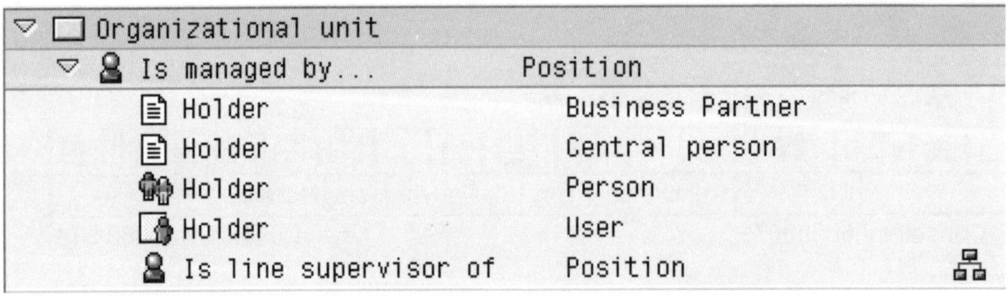


The evaluation path is O-S-PHIE.

### 4.5.7 Staffing Analysis

***View***

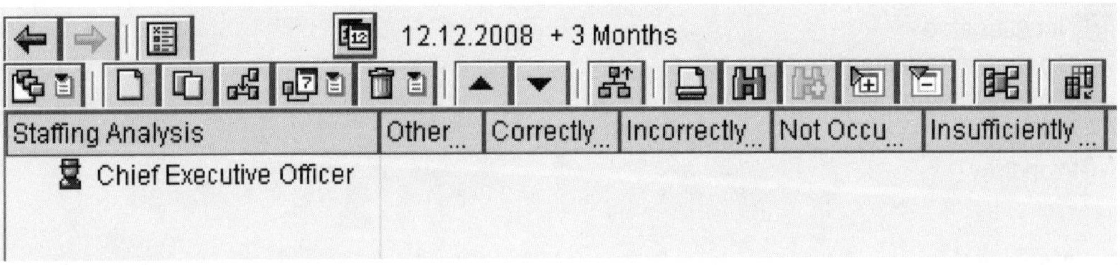


This view shows the holder of a position and information about the position. It displays important information about the position in the following columns.

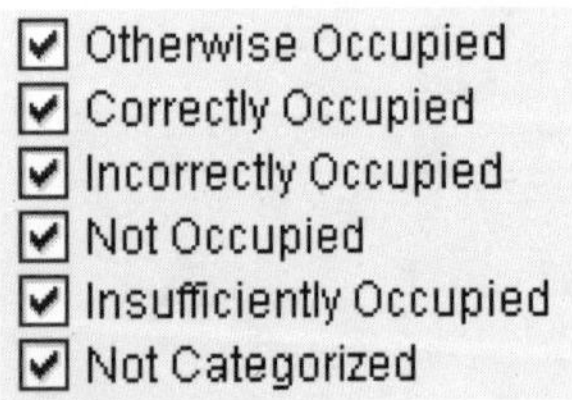


***Evaluation path***

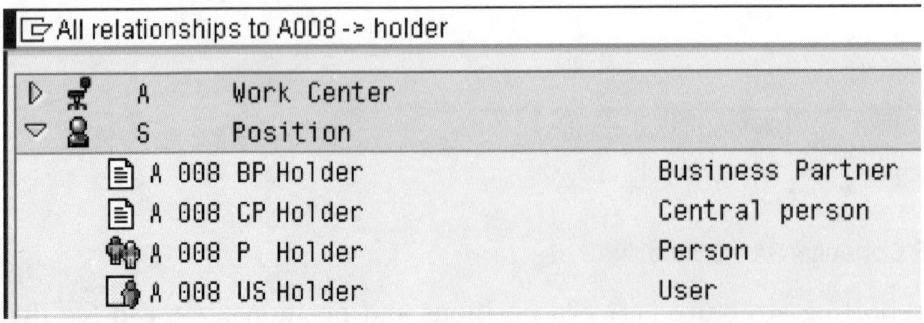


The evaluation path is A008.

### 4.5.8 Staffing Management

***View***

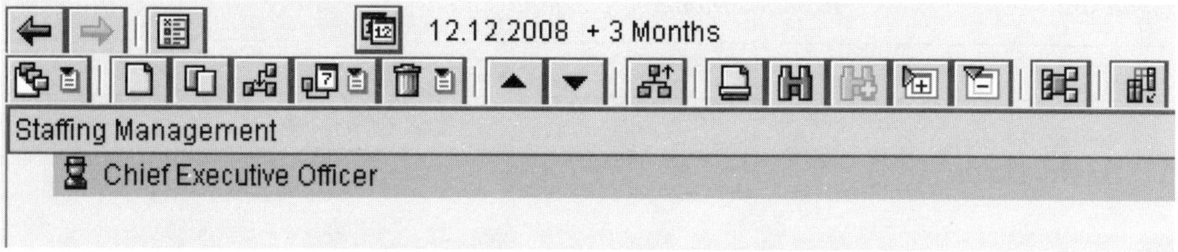


This view shows staffing manager of an organizational unit.

***Evaluation path***

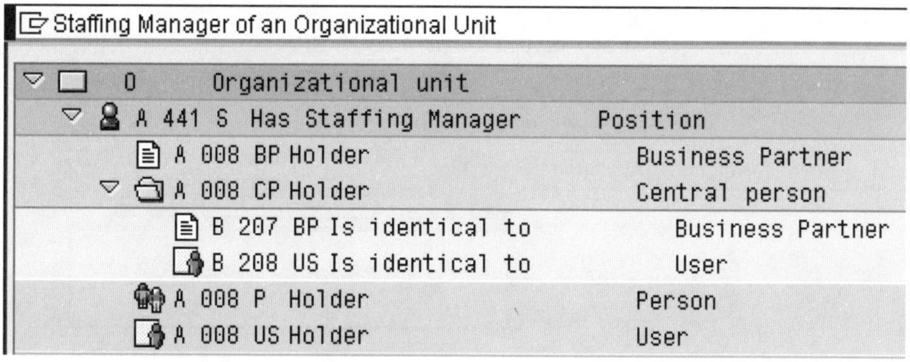


The evaluation path is WFMSTAFF.

## 4.6 POSITION DETAILS

| *Functional Consultant* | *User* | *Business Process Owner* | *Senior Management* | *My Rating* | *Understanding Level* |
|---|---|---|---|---|---|
| A | A | B | C | | |

### 4.6.1 Basic Data

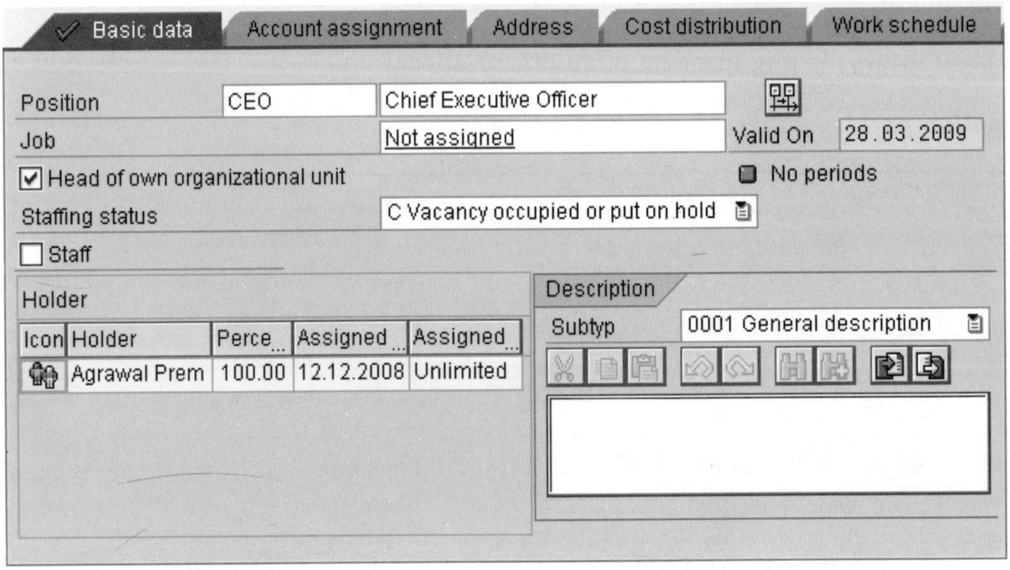


#### *Short and long names*

In the two Position fields, enter a short and long description for a position. These are stored in infotype 1000.

#### *Job*

The job assigned to the position is displayed in the Job field. You can assign a job directly by entering its name here. Otherwise, you assign a job to a position in the staff assignments. This data is stored as a relationship in infotype 1001.

#### *Head of own organizational unit*

By flagging this field, you mark a position as the chief position of the organizational unit to which it belongs. In many business processes you need to identify an employee's superior, e.g. for approving an employee's leave. This information is used for that. It is stored as a relationship between organizational unit and position in infotype 1001.

### *Staffing status*

You can enter the following statuses in this field. Vacancy is maintained in infotype 1007 and Obsolete status of position is maintained in infotype 1014.

| *Status* | *Description* |
|---|---|
| Vacancy open | The position is vacant, that is an employee is to be found for the position. The position is marked as vacant in Recruitment. |
| Vacancy occupied or put on hold | The position was vacant but the vacancy is put on hold and no person is to be found for the position at present. |
| Obsolete | The position will no longer be required in the future. |

### *Staff*

By choosing the Staff field, you can assign a staff indicator to positions. A staff flag indicates that a position is not part of the normal reporting structure at your company, but rather reports directly to a high level position, or organizational unit. In this way, a position can report directly to the chief executive officer. This information is maintained in infotype 1003.

### *Holder*

An employee or a user who occupies the position is displayed in the Holder table. There may be multiple holders of a position at the same time. Sometimes they may be part occupants of a position. Sometimes you may have a successor being groomed by the occupant of a position. This information is maintained as a relationship in infotype 1001.

### *Description*

You can maintain various types of descriptions for a position. These are stored in infotype 1002.

### 4.6.2 Account Assignment

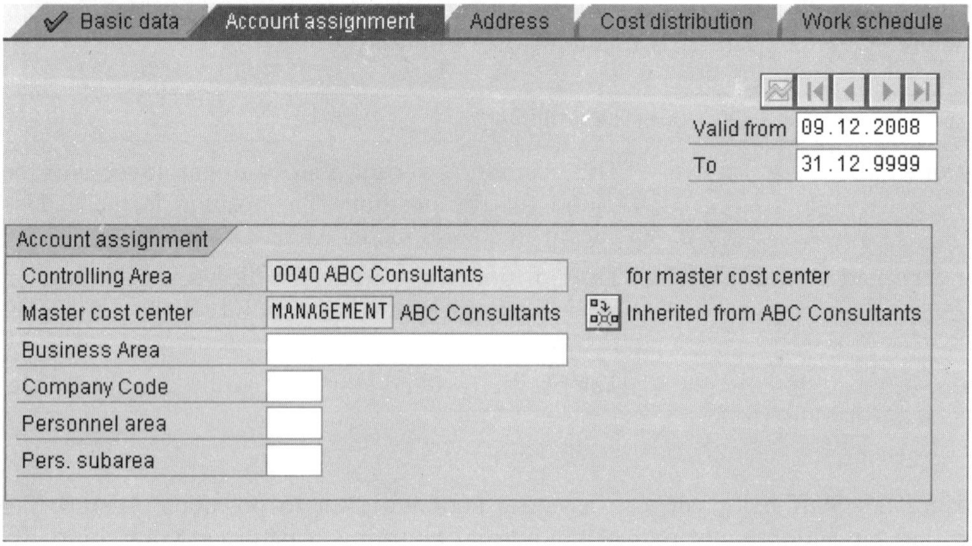


Data on the controlling area, company code, business area, personnel area and personnel subarea are used as default values in Personnel Administration. These values are inherited from the organizational unit to which the position belongs and can be changed. This data is stored in infotype 1008. Data on the cost center is stored in infotype 1001 and transferred to Personnel Administration in infotype 0001.

### 4.6.3 Address

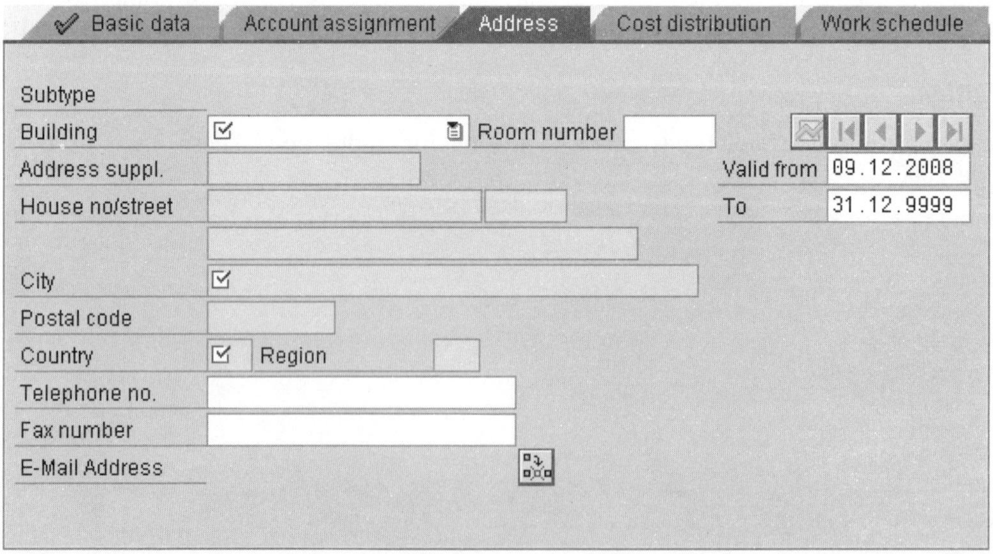


You can maintain the address details of a position in this tab which is stored in infotype 1028.

### 4.6.4 Cost Distribution

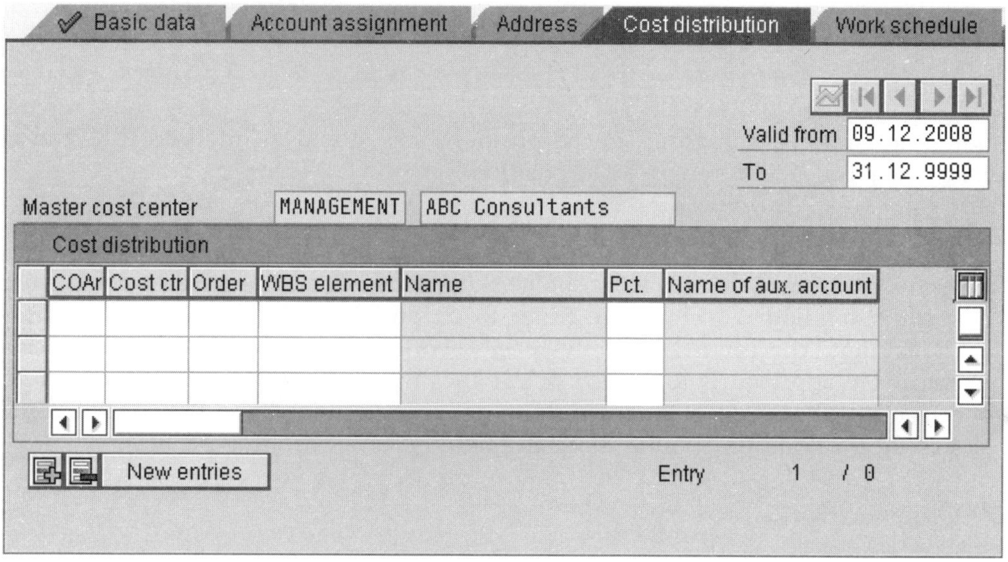


If you want to distribute the cost of a position between different cost centers orders or projects, you can maintain it in this tab which is stored in infotype 1018. The cost incurred by the person holding the position is distributed as specified here.

### 4.6.5 Work Schedule

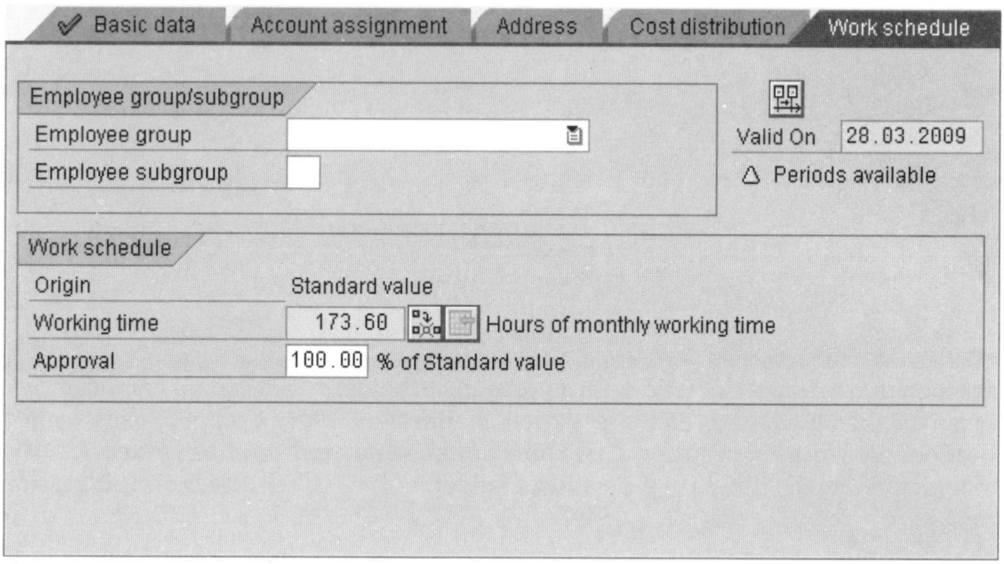

***Employee group***

You assign an employee group to the position. It is stored in infotype 1013 and is defaulted when you hire a person for a position.

***Employee subgroup***

You assign an employee subgroup to the position. It is stored in infotype 1013 and is defaulted when you hire a person for a position.

***Origin, working time, approval***

You may choose to have default value of working time, which may either come from enterprisewide standard working time (refer to chapter 14.10.3), or from the superior organizational unit. You can also directly specify working time for a position or enter a percentage in the approval field, which determines the working time. The origin field shows the method through which the working time is determined and the working time field shows the working time value. Working time is stored in infotype 1011.

## 4.6.6 Qualification

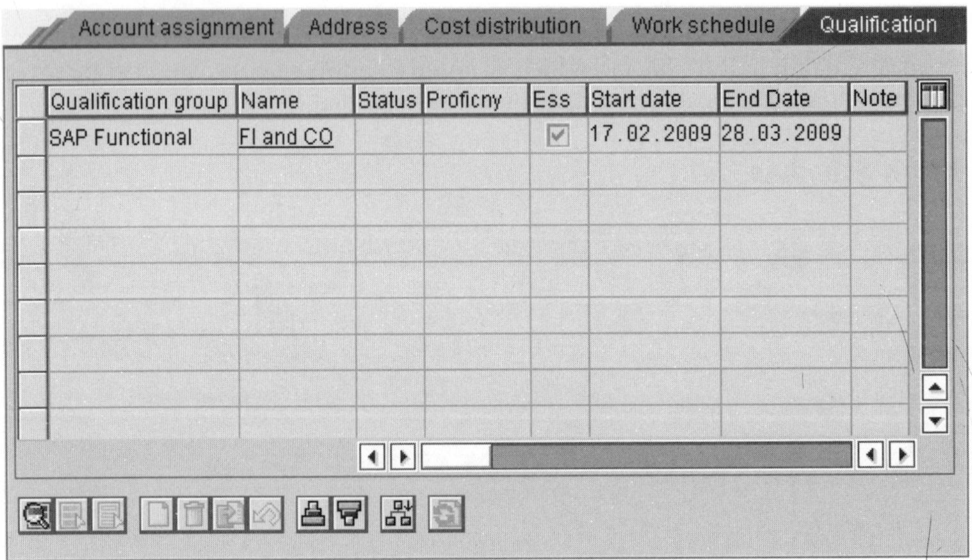


In order to perform tasks associated with a position, its holder needs certain competencies. These can be specified here and are stored in infotype 1001. Competencies (called qualifications in SAP) required for a position can be compared with competencies of a person to determine the fitness of a position's holder, as well as for career and succession planning.

### 4.6.7 Tasks

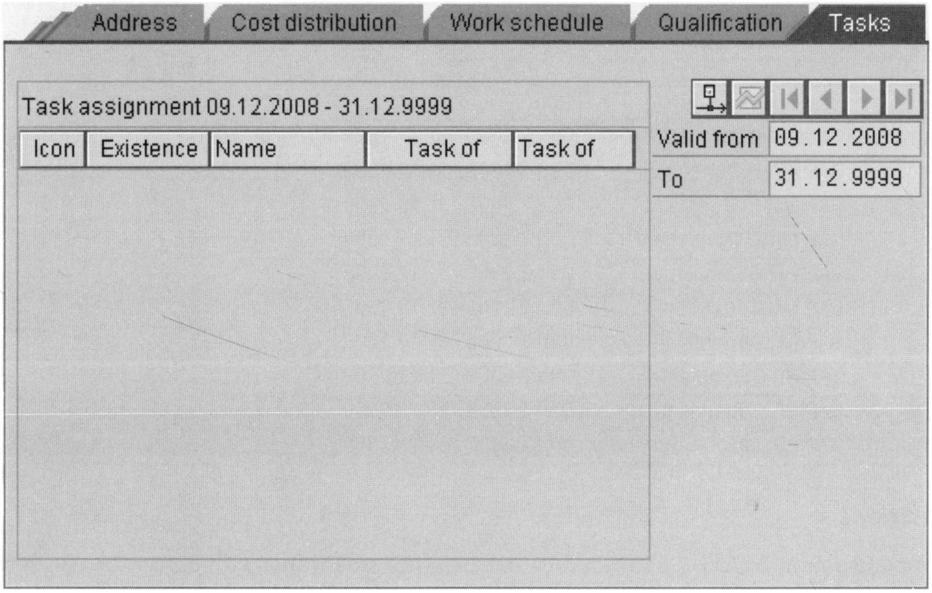


This tab shows the tasks that a position needs to perform. The tasks may be inherited by the position from the job which is assigned to it. Certain tasks may also be assigned to a position directly. This data is stored in infotype 1001.

## 4.7 POSITION REPORTS

| *Functional Consultant* | *User* | *Business Process Owner* | *Senior Management* | *My Rating* | *Understanding Level* |
|---|---|---|---|---|---|
| A | A | A | B | | |

***Periods when positions are unoccupied per organizational unit***

You can run transaction S_AHR_61018869 for information on unoccupied positions. It shows the number of days for which each position has remained unoccupied, and average number of unoccupied days for each organizational unit. This data is for the period you specify in the selection screen. You also have to specify the starting organizational unit. The system will show you positions in that organizational unit and all the organizational units below it. For this, it uses evaluation path SBESX. However, if you want to see positions only under the specified organizational unit, and not under the organizational units below the specified organizational unit, you can use evaluation path SBES. To change the evaluation path, you tick the checkbox 'Standard selection screen'.

## Periods when positions are unoccupied per org. unit

**Selection period:** 01.01.2008 - 31.12.2008

| Organizational unit | Position | Unocc. from | Unocc. to | New holder | Un... | Av... |
|---|---|---|---|---|---|---|
| ABC Consultants Ltd. | Chief Executive Officer | 09.12.2008 | 11.12.2008 | Agrawal Prem | 3 | 3 |
| SAP Consulting | SAP ABAP Consultant | 09.12.2008 | 31.12.2008 | | 23 | |
| | SAP Basis Consultant | 09.12.2008 | 31.12.2008 | | 23 | |
| | SAP FI/CO Consultant | 09.12.2008 | 31.12.2008 | | 23 | |
| | SAP HR Consultant | 09.12.2008 | 31.12.2008 | | 23 | |
| | SAP MM Consultant | 09.12.2008 | 31.12.2008 | | 23 | |
| | SAP PM Consultant | 09.12.2008 | 31.12.2008 | | 23 | |
| | SAP PP Consultant | 09.12.2008 | 31.12.2008 | | 23 | |
| | SAP PS Consultant | 09.12.2008 | 31.12.2008 | | 23 | 23 |
| SAP Education | SAP Education Coordinator | 09.12.2008 | 31.12.2008 | | 23 | 23 |

***Existing positions***

You can use transaction S_AHR_61016502 to list existing positions. You can also use this program to report all objects, or all objects of certain type. To do so, tick the checkbox 'Standard selection screen', Execute and then specify the object type.

| OT | Start date | End Date | S | Object name | Ext.obj ID |
|---|---|---|---|---|---|
| S | 16.06.1995 | 31.12.9999 | 1 | ALE administrator | 50000000 |
| S | 30.04.2003 | 31.12.9999 | 1 | Kreditorenbuchhalter | 50000028 |
| S | 30.04.2003 | 31.12.9999 | 1 | Kreditorenbuchhalter | 50000029 |
| S | 30.04.2003 | 31.12.9999 | 1 | Kreditorenbuchhalter | 50000050 |
| S | 09.12.2008 | 31.12.9999 | 1 | Chief Executive Officer | 50000078 |
| S | 09.12.2008 | 31.12.9999 | 1 | SAP HR Consultant | 50000079 |
| S | 09.12.2008 | 31.12.9999 | 1 | SAP FI/CO Consultant | 50000080 |
| S | 09.12.2008 | 31.12.9999 | 1 | SAP MM Consultant | 50000081 |
| S | 09.12.2008 | 31.12.9999 | 1 | SAP PP Consultant | 50000082 |
| S | 09.12.2008 | 31.12.9999 | 1 | SAP PS Consultant | 50000083 |
| S | 09.12.2008 | 31.12.9999 | 1 | SAP PM Consultant | 50000084 |
| S | 09.12.2008 | 31.12.9999 | 1 | SAP Basis Consultant | 50000085 |
| S | 09.12.2008 | 31.12.9999 | 1 | SAP ABAP Consultant | 50000086 |
| S | 09.12.2008 | 31.12.9999 | 1 | SAP Education Coordinator | 50000087 |

***Staff assignments***

You can run transaction S_AHR_61016503 to see positions and persons in an organizational plan or part of it. The report also shows other employee information, e.g. working time, staffing percentage, employee group and employee subgroup.

| Org. unit | Positions | Employee(s) | Chief | Staffing status |
|---|---|---|---|---|
| ABC Consult | Chief Executive Officer | Agrawal Prem | Chief | |
| SAP Consult | SAP HR Consultant | | | Vacant since 09.12.2008 |
| SAP Consult | SAP FI/CO Consultant | | | Vacant since 09.12.2008 |
| SAP Consult | SAP MM Consultant | | | Vacant since 09.12.2008 |
| SAP Consult | SAP PP Consultant | | | Vacant since 09.12.2008 |
| SAP Consult | SAP PS Consultant | | | Vacant since 09.12.2008 |
| SAP Consult | SAP PM Consultant | | | Vacant since 09.12.2008 |
| SAP Consult | SAP Basis Consultant | | | Vacant since 09.12.2008 |
| SAP Consult | SAP ABAP Consultant | | | Vacant since 09.12.2008 |
| SAP Educaton | SAP Education Coordinator | | | Vacant since 09.12.2008 |

You can refine this report by making the following selections in the selection screen.

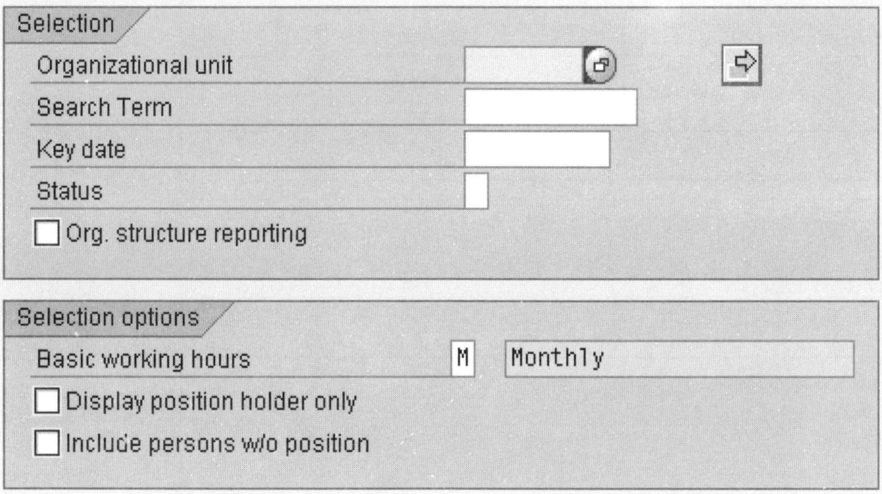


These are described below.

| *Selection parameter* | *Description* |
|---|---|
| Organizational structure reporting | If you tick this checkbox, all organizational units below the specified organizational unit are also taken. |
| Basic working hours | Here you specify the time period for which working hours are shown in the report. |
| Display position holder only | If you tick this checkbox, only position holders are included, substitutes are not shown. |
| Include persons w/o position | If you tick this checkbox, persons who do not have any position are also shown. |

### *Position description*

You can run transaction S_AHR_61016504 to see comprehensive description of a position. However, this report does not show information stored in description infotype 1002. If you want infotype 1002 to be included, use transaction S_AHR_61016511.

```
Plan version: Current plan                                   Page     1
Position Chief Executive Officer                  Key date: 07.01.2009

Basic data

   Name

 Name:                         Chief Executive Officer
 Valid                         From 09.12.2008

Integration in organizational structure

    Integration in organizational structure

  Organizational Structure    Text
  Position                    Chief Executive Officer
  Organizational Unit         ABC Consultants Ltd.

    Is head of organizational unit

 ABC Consultants Ltd.

Staffing

   Holder with Work Schedule

                                              Working hours per Month
                                              Total   Percent   Share
 Person Agrawal Prem

 Approved working hours        Organizational unit               173,60

 Difference                                                      173,60-

Requirements

   Required qualifications

                                  does not exist

Succession planning
 Staffing

    Holder

 Agrawal Prem                                     100,00 %
```

### *Task description for positions*

You can run transaction S_AHR_61016505 to see tasks for a position.

| Object Name | Object... | Abso... | Actual | (Total) |
|---|---|---|---|---|
| SAP HR Consultant | Position | 100.00 | | |
| SAP Consulting | Job | 100.00 | | |
| Project preparation | Task | 100.00 | 100.00 | |
| Hardware and software | Task | 100.00 | 100.00 | |
| Networking | Task | 100.00 | 100.00 | |
| Office space and facilities | Task | 100.00 | 100.00 | |
| Team building | Task | 100.00 | 100.00 | |
| Blueprint | Task | 100.00 | 100.00 | |
| Study and document old business process | Task | 100.00 | 100.00 | |
| Propose new business processes | Task | 100.00 | 100.00 | |
| Program development | Task | 100.00 | 100.00 | |
| Testing | Task | 100.00 | 100.00 | |
| Unit testing | Task | 100.00 | 100.00 | |
| Integration testing | Task | 100.00 | 100.00 | |
| Go live | Task | 100.00 | 100.00 | |
| Data Preparation | Task | 100.00 | 100.00 | |
| Data Upload | Task | 100.00 | 100.00 | |

### *Staff functions for positions*

You can run transaction S_AHR_61016506 to see all the positions which are staff functions.

| Plan Version | Plan Version Text | Object Type | Object type text | Number of Staff Positions |
|---|---|---|---|---|
| 01 | Current plan | S | Position | 1 |

### *Authorities and resources*

You can run transaction S_AHR_61016507 or S_AHR_61016516 to see authorities and resources for a position or for all positions directly belonging to an organizational unit. Authorities and resources may be maintained directly for positions. Alternatively, authorities and resources may be maintained for work centers which are linked to positions. The evaluation path used in the report is ARBPL. This evaluation path does not take you down the organizational structure.

```
Authorities and Resources
--------------------------------------------------------------------------
Plan version: 01     Status: 1       Selection period: 01.01.1900 -31.12.9999
--------------------------------------------------------------------------
O 50000075 ABC Consultants Ltd.
  S 50000078 Chief Executive Officer
      Authority/pwr of attorney
         Full commercial power
```

If you want to see authorities and resources along organizational structure, you should use evaluation path ARBPLX.

```
Authorities and Resources
--------------------------------------------------------------------------
Plan version: 01     Status: 1       Selection period: 01.01.1900 -31.12.9999
--------------------------------------------------------------------------
O 50000075 ABC Consultants Ltd.
  S 50000078 Chief Executive Officer
      Authority/pwr of attorney
         Full commercial power
. O 50000076 SAP Consulting
    S 50000079 SAP HR Consultant

      A 50000000 SAP Consulting Work Center
        Authority/pwr of attorney
           Limited commercial power
```

### *Planned labor costs*

You can run transaction S_AHR_61016517 or S_AHR_61016508 to see planned labor costs of an organizational unit in structural form.

| Organizational unit | Position | Σ Amount | Curre... |
|---|---|---|---|
| ABC Consultants Ltd. | Chief Executive Officer | 50.000,00 | USD |
| ABC Consultants Ltd. | | ▪ **50.000,00** | **USD** |
| SAP Consulting | SAP HR Consultant | | |
| | SAP Consulting Work Center | | |
| | SAP FI/CO Consultant | | |
| | SAP MM Consultant | | |
| | SAP PP Consultant | | |
| | SAP PS Consultant | | |
| | SAP PM Consultant | | |
| | SAP Basis Consultant | | |
| | SAP ABAP Consultant | | |
| SAP Consulting | | | |
| SAP Education | SAP Education Coordinator | | |
| SAP Education | | | |
| | | ▪▪ **50.000,00** | **USD** |

The selection screen has the following important fields.

| Controls | |
|---|---|
| Reporting along a structure | X |
| Values (1=mid,2=min,3=max) | 1 |
| Period | 1 |
| Conversion type as in TCURR | M |
| Currency | USD |

| *Selection parameter* | *Description* |
|---|---|
| Reporting along a structure | If you select this, the cost is reported for the entire organizational structure starting from the specified organizational unit, otherwise only for the specified organizational unit. |
| Values | Here you specify whether minimum maximum or midpoint costs are to be reported. |
| Period | Here you specify whether planned costs are for a month, week, etc. |
| Conversion type | In case the reporting currency is different from planned currency, the method of conversion to be used is specified here. |
| Currency | Here you specify the currency for reporting planned costs. |

### *Vacant positions*

You can run transaction S_AHR_61016509 to report vacant positions in the organizational structure under an organizational unit.

**Vacant positions**

**Key date** 07.01.2009

| Organizational unit | Position | vacant from/to | Staffing status |
|---|---|---|---|
| SAP Consulting | SAP FI/CO Consultant | 09.12.2008-31.12.9999 | Unoccupied since 09.12.2008 |
| | SAP MM Consultant | 09.12.2008-31.12.9999 | Unoccupied since 09.12.2008 |
| | SAP PP Consultant | 09.12.2008-31.12.9999 | Unoccupied since 09.12.2008 |
| | SAP PS Consultant | 09.12.2008-31.12.9999 | Unoccupied since 09.12.2008 |
| | SAP PM Consultant | 09.12.2008-31.12.9999 | Unoccupied since 09.12.2008 |
| | SAP Basis Consultant | 09.12.2008-31.12.9999 | Unoccupied since 09.12.2008 |
| | SAP ABAP Consultant | 09.12.2008-31.12.9999 | Unoccupied since 09.12.2008 |
| SAP Education | SAP Education Coordinator | 09.12.2008-31.12.9999 | Unoccupied since 09.12.2008 |

### *Correct vacancies*

One might consider every unoccupied position as vacant. In that case, whenever a position becomes unoccupied, it will be declared vacant and recruitment action will get triggered. Many companies don't want this to happen. They would like to review unoccupied positions, and declare them vacant selectively. Therefore, SAP provides a separate vacancy flag for positions. Thus, a position may be unoccupied, but not vacant. In a reverse scenario, you may declare an occupied position vacant so as to trigger recruitment action, because you are looking for a successor. Therefore, SAP allows vacancy flag for an occupied position. But it is possible that some occupied positions are erroneously declared vacant. Transaction S_AHR_61016510 lets you review occupied positions which have vacancy flag. If you find that some positions are erroneously declared vacant, you can correct it in the same report.

Vacancies to be corrected:

| OT | ObjectID | Start date | End Date | H | V | Object name |
|---|---|---|---|---|---|---|
| List contains no data | | | | | | |

### *Obsolete positions*

When a position is no longer required, you can delimit it. But, if the position is occupied, before delimiting it, you have to wait till it becomes unoccupied. You can declare such positions obsolete so as to avoid the risk of accidental vacancy creation. Once a position is declared obsolete, vacancy cannot be created for it. You can run transaction S_AHR_61018831 to view obsolete positions. If they are unoccupied, you may like to delimit them.

| Organizational unit | Position | Obs. from |
|---|---|---|
| Human Resource | Manager Resource | 19.06.2009 |

### *Complete position description*

You can run transaction S_AHR_61016511 to see complete description of one or more positions. The report contains the following information.

- Description
- Holder of a position
- Superior and subordinate positions
- Activity profile of the position
- Requirements profile if available
- Describing job
- Activity profile of the job
- Requirements profile of the job if available
- Work center assigned to the position
- Integration of the position in the organization

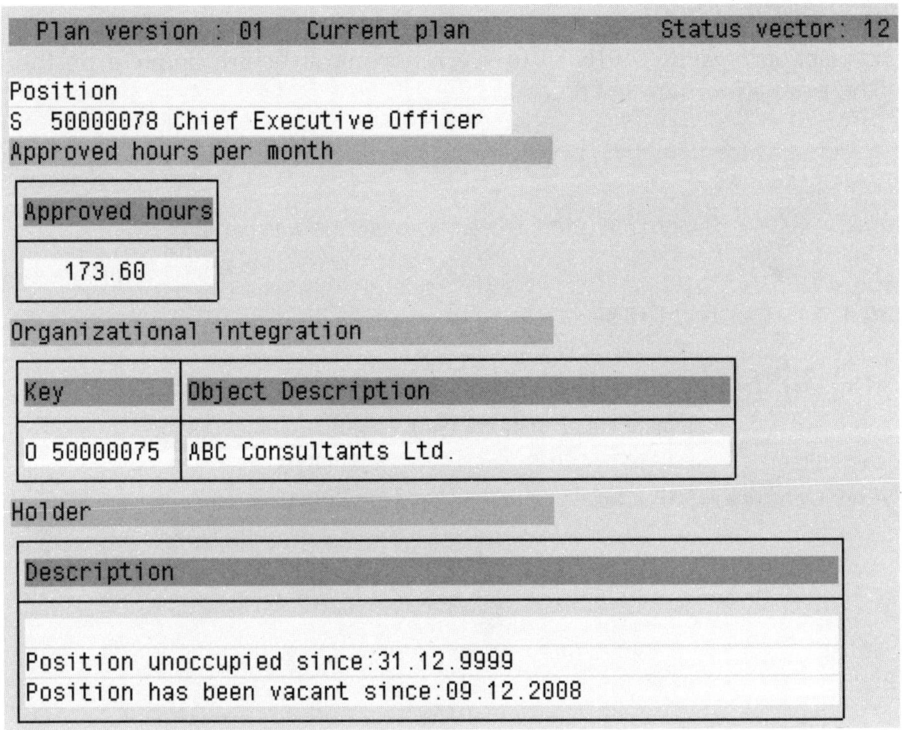


***Reporting structure without persons***

You can run transaction S_AHR_61016512 to see reporting structure under a position without persons. The evaluation path is ORGA.

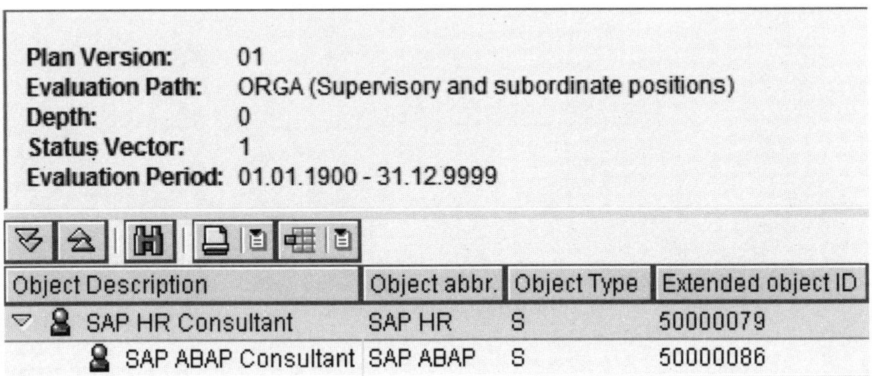

### *Reporting structure with persons*

You can run transaction S_AHR_61016513 to see reporting structure under a position with persons. The evaluation path is ORGA-P.

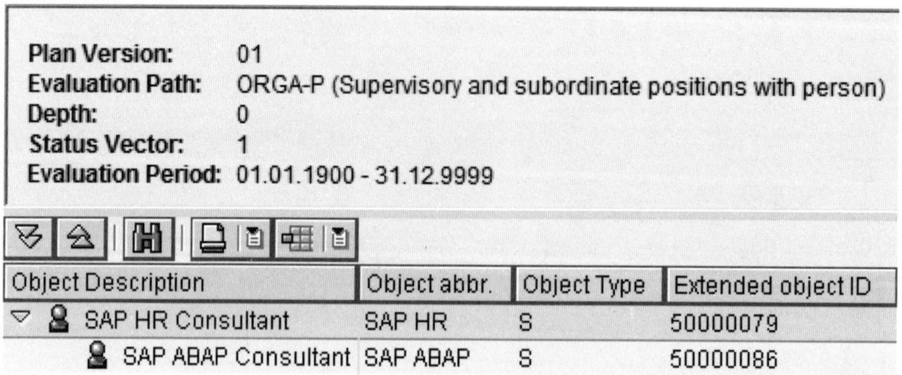

**Plan Version:** 01
**Evaluation Path:** ORGA-P (Supervisory and subordinate positions with person)
**Depth:** 0
**Status Vector:** 1
**Evaluation Period:** 01.01.1900 - 31.12.9999

| Object Description | Object abbr. | Object Type | Extended object ID |
|---|---|---|---|
| SAP HR Consultant | SAP HR | S | 50000079 |
| SAP ABAP Consultant | SAP ABAP | S | 50000086 |

CHAPTER 5

# Job

## 5.1 JOB DEFINITION

| *Functional Consultant* | *User* | *Business Process Owner* | *Senior Management* | *My Rating* | *Understanding Level* |
|---|---|---|---|---|---|
| A | A | A | A | | |

In an organization, work is done by persons, who hold positions. For each position, you need to define the tasks performed by that position. In a large organization, many positions perform similar tasks. For example, many managers in your organization may perform tasks which are very similar. Supervisors, on the other hand, would perform tasks which are different from those of managers. You can create different jobs, e.g. manager, supervisor, worker, etc. Each job is a set of tasks. A job can be used to create many positions which are similar in certain ways, but also have their individual characteristics. For example, Manager—Purchasing, Manager—Sales and Manager—HR all may perform the tasks of the job Manager, but each one has different responsibility. Positions are concrete and can be held by persons in an enterprise. Jobs, in contrast, are classifications of functions in an enterprise. A job describes a position. Through this relationship, the position automatically inherits the tasks and characteristics assigned to the job. This significantly reduces data entry time, as tasks and characteristics do not have to be assigned to each position separately. Specific tasks and characteristics can also be assigned directly to positions. When you create jobs, they are listed in a job index. A job index is a list of jobs maintained for an enterprise.

## 5.2 JOB CREATION

| *Functional Consultant* | *User* | *Business Process Owner* | *Senior Management* | *My Rating* | *Understanding Level* |
|---|---|---|---|---|---|
| A | A | B | X | | |

You can create a job using transaction PO03. When you run transaction PO03, you get the following screen.

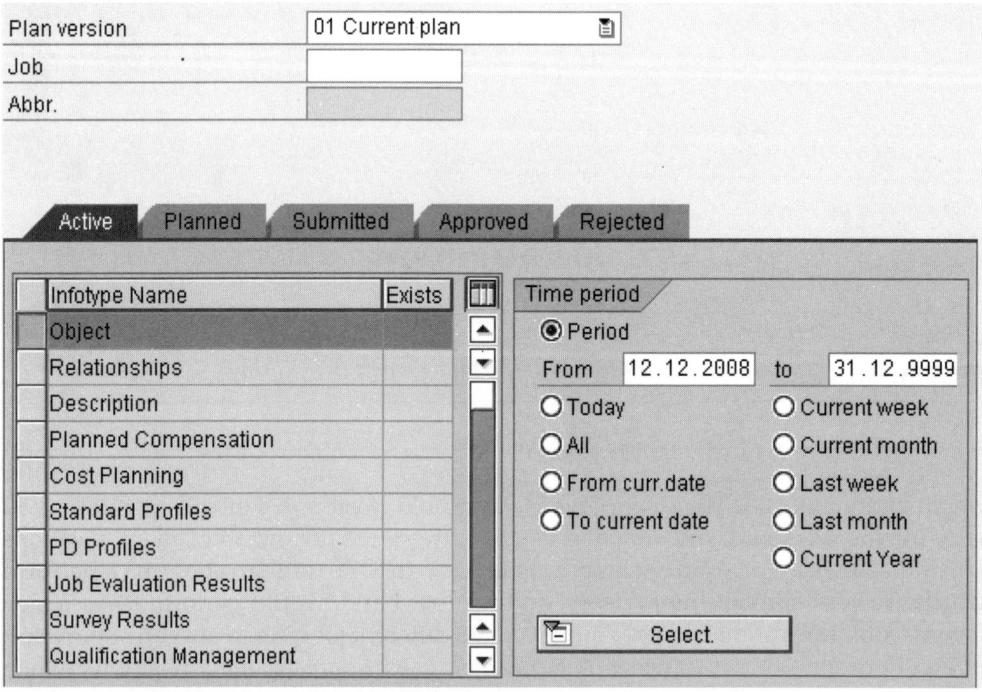


You select Object and click the create icon.

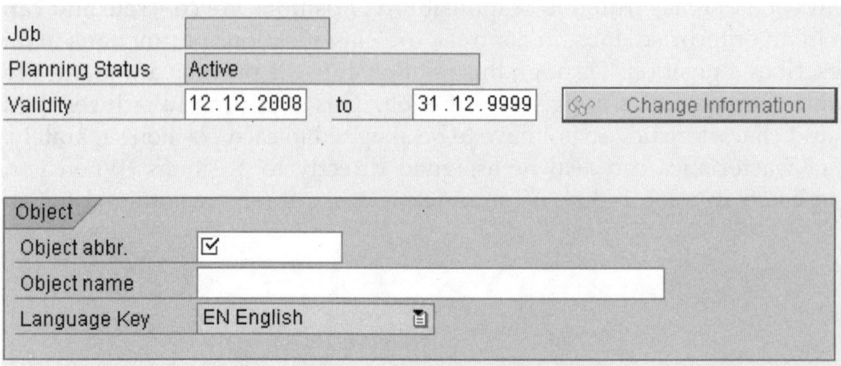


You specify the object abbreviation and name, and save. The job is created.

## 5.3 JOB STRUCTURES

| *Functional Consultant* | *User* | *Business Process Owner* | *Senior Management* | *My Rating* | *Understanding Level* |
|---|---|---|---|---|---|
| A | A | B | C | | |

Further activities on job, e.g. assigning tasks and assigning holders, can be done in transaction PPOME. You select a job in the Selection area and double-click it to transfer it to the Overview area. In the Overview area you see the task assignment view which shows tasks that constitute a job.

### 5.3.1 Task Assignment

***View***

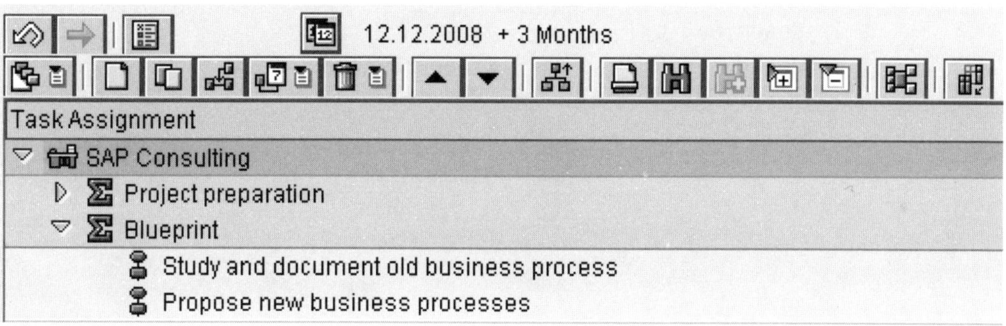


The task assignment view shows tasks for a job. You can create a new task here, but then it will not appear in the task catalog unless you specifically create that relationship. You can assign an existing task to a job. If you assign a higher level task, its lower level tasks are automatically included.

***Evaluation path***

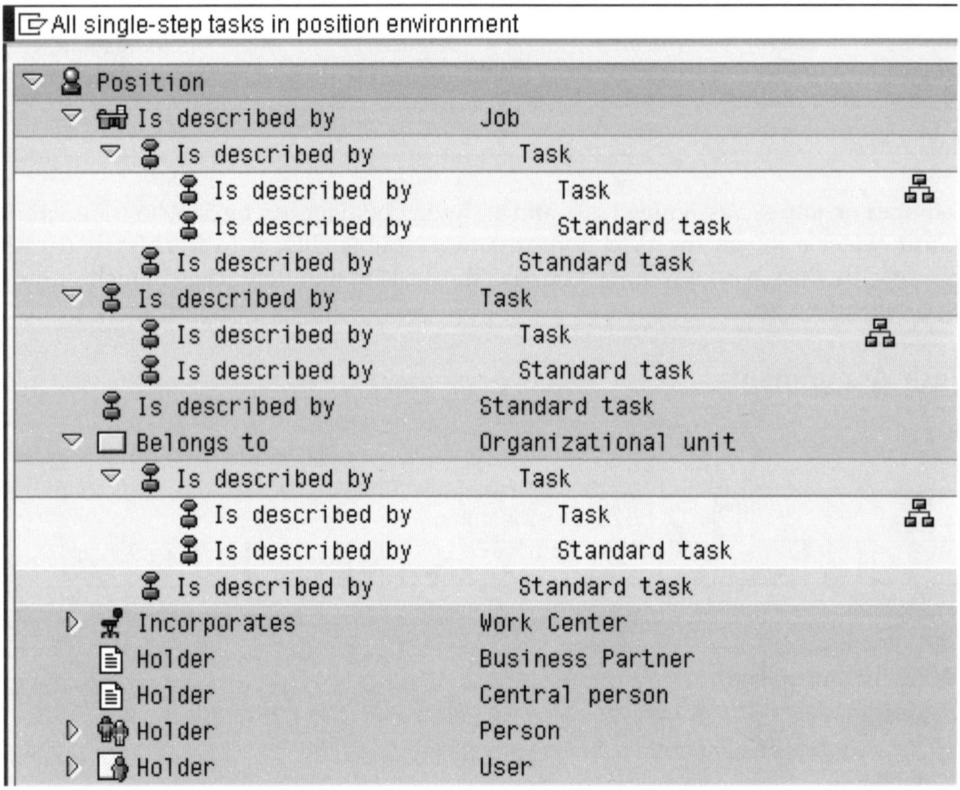


The evaluation path is WF_S_TTS.

## 5.3.2 Job Usage

***View***

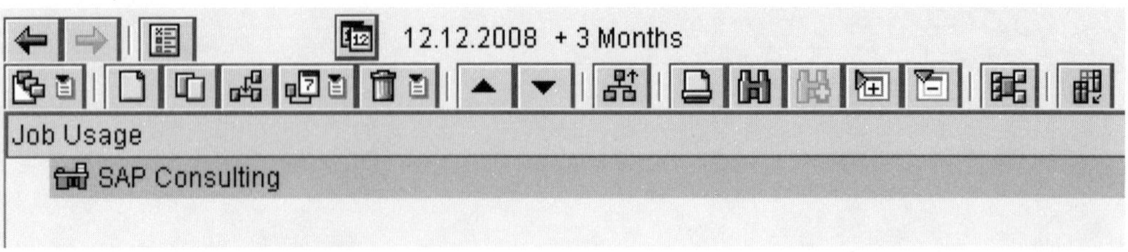


If you select the 'Job Usage' view, the system shows all the positions which are associated with the job, the organizational units of those positions, and the holders of those positions.

***Evaluation path***

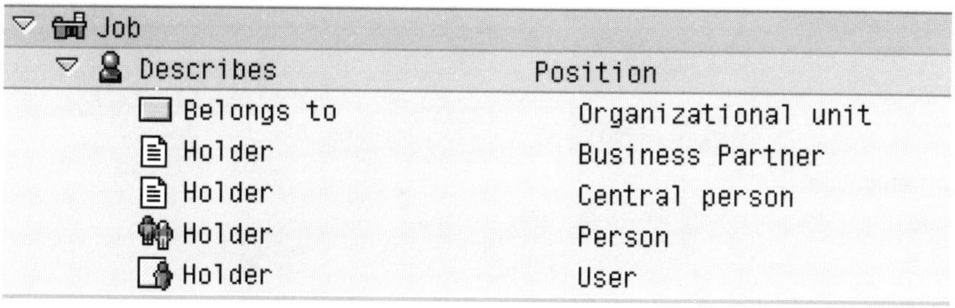


The evaluation path is WF_S_TTS.

## 5.4 JOB DETAILS

| *Functional Consultant* | *User* | *Business Process Owner* | *Senior Management* | *My Rating* | *Understanding Level* |
|---|---|---|---|---|---|
| A | A | B | C | | |

### 5.4.1 Basic Data

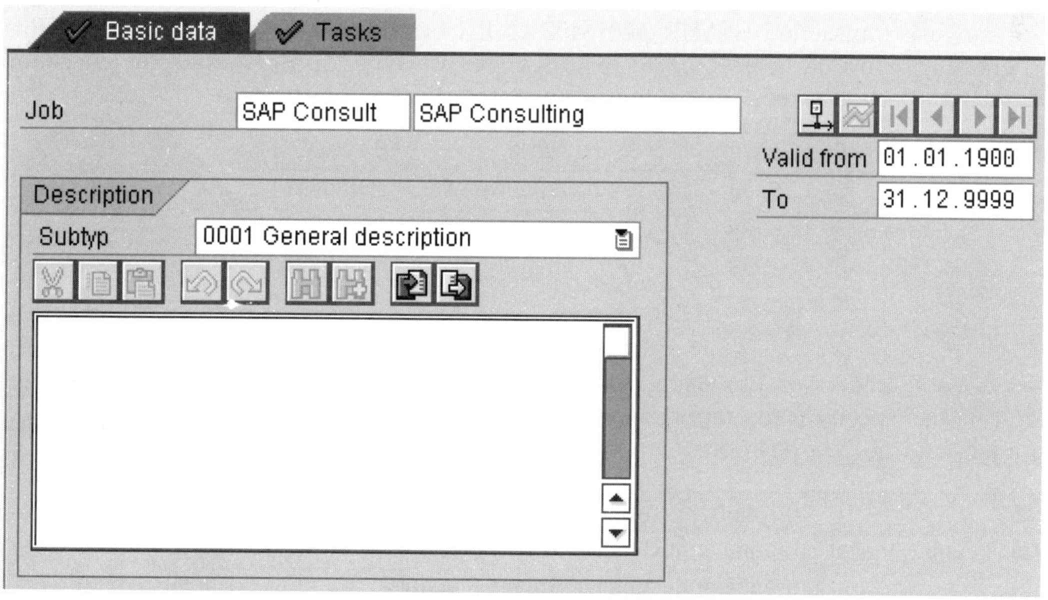


This tab has job abbreviation and job name which are stored in infotype 1000. It also has job description which is stored in infotype 1002.

### 5.4.2 Tasks

Basic data | Tasks

Task assignment 12.12.2008 - 31.12.9999

| Icon | Existence | Name | Task of | Task of |
|---|---|---|---|---|
| | | Project preparation | | |
| | | Hardware and software | | Project preparation |
| | | Networking | | Project preparation |
| | | Office space and facilities | | Project preparation |
| | | Team building | | Project preparation |

Valid from 12.12.2008
To 31.12.9999

This tab shows the tasks that constitute the job. These are stored in infotype 1001.

## 5.5 JOB REPORTS

| *Functional Consultant* | *User* | *Business Process Owner* | *Senior Management* | *My Rating* | *Understanding Level* |
|---|---|---|---|---|---|
| A | A | A | C | | |

***Existing jobs***

You can use transaction S_AHR_61016497 to list existing jobs. You can also use this program to report all objects, or all objects of certain type. To do so, tick the checkbox 'Standard selection screen', Execute and then specify the object type.

| OT | Start date | End Date | S | Object name | Ext.obj ID |
|---|---|---|---|---|---|
| C | 30.04.2003 | 31.12.9999 | 1 | Kreditorenbuchhalter 1 | 50000026 |
| C | 30.04.2003 | 31.12.9999 | 1 | Kreditorenbuchhalter 2 | 50000027 |
| C | 01.01.1900 | 31.12.9999 | 1 | SAP Consulting | 50000122 |

***Job index***

You can see holders of jobs using transaction S_AHR_61016498. In the selection screen you can also specify if the report should also display persons who are directly assigned to a job, and not via position.

| Job | Position | Holder | Staffing percentage |
|---|---|---|---|
| Kreditorenbuchhalter 2 | Kreditorenbuchhalter | Jürgen WEISS | 100,00 |
| | Kreditorenbuchhalter | Roland Stauder | 100,00 |
| | Kreditorenbuchhalter | CAROLINEKING | 100,00 |
| SAP Consulting | SAP HR Consultant | Position is vacant | 0,00 |

### *Job description*

You can run transaction S_AHR_61016499 to see all jobs and their job descriptions. The system first shows all the jobs.

| Object Name |
|---|
| ▽ ☑ Kreditorenbuchhalter 1 |
| ☑ Kreditorenbuchhalter 2 |
| ☑ SAP Consulting |

You select the jobs whose description you want to see and click Selected objects. You navigate from one job to another using arrow icons.

**Basic Data**

**Name**

| | |
|---|---|
| Name: | SAP Consulting |
| Valid | static |

**SAP Consulting**

| Tasks/Activities | | Percentages | | |
|---|---|---|---|---|
| Superior Task | Task | Absolute | Actual | (Total) |
| SAP Consulting | Project preparation | 100.00 | 100.00 | |
| | Hardware and software | | | |
| | Networking | | | |
| | Office space and facilitie | | | |
| | Team building | | | |
| | Blueprint | 100.00 | 100.00 | |
| | Study and document old bus | | | |
| | Propose new business proce | | | |
| | Program development | 100.00 | 100.00 | |
| | Testing | 100.00 | 100.00 | |
| | Unit testing | | | |
| | Integration testing | | | |
| | Go live | 100.00 | 100.00 | |
| | Data Preparation | | | |
| | Data Upload | | | |

### *Task description for jobs*

You can run transaction S_AHR_61016500 to see the tasks in a job.

| Object Name | Objec... | Absolute | Actual |
|---|---|---|---|
| SAP Consulting | Job | 100.00 | |
| Project preparation | Task | 100.00 | 100.00 |
| Hardware and software | Task | 100.00 | 100.00 |
| Networking | Task | 100.00 | 100.00 |
| Office space and facilities | Task | 100.00 | 100.00 |
| Team building | Task | 100.00 | 100.00 |
| Blueprint | Task | 100.00 | 100.00 |
| Study and document old business process | Task | 100.00 | 100.00 |
| Propose new business processes | Task | 100.00 | 100.00 |
| Program development | Task | 100.00 | 100.00 |
| Testing | Task | 100.00 | 100.00 |
| Unit testing | Task | 100.00 | 100.00 |
| Integration testing | Task | 100.00 | 100.00 |
| Go live | Task | 100.00 | 100.00 |
| Data Preparation | Task | 100.00 | 100.00 |
| Data Upload | Task | 100.00 | 100.00 |

### *Complete job description*

You can run transaction S_AHR_61016501 to list all jobs along with their description, requirements profile, task profile and authorities/resources.

Job
C 50000122 SAP Consulting
Task profile of job

| Key | Object Description | Percentage Assignment | Proficiency |
|---|---|---|---|
| T50000104 | Data Upload | 0.00 | Task |
| T50000103 | Data Prepare | 0.00 | Task |
| T50000101 | Go Live | 100.00 | Task |
| T50000106 | Integ. test | 0.00 | Task |
| T50000105 | Unit Test | 0.00 | Task |
| T50000100 | Testing | 100.00 | Task |
| T50000108 | Develop | 100.00 | Task |
| T50000110 | New BP | 0.00 | Task |
| T50000109 | Old BP | 0.00 | Task |
| T50000098 | Blueprint | 100.00 | Task |
| T50000114 | Team | 0.00 | Task |
| T50000113 | Office | 0.00 | Task |
| T50000112 | Networking | 0.00 | Task |
| T50000111 | Hard & Soft | 0.00 | Task |
| T50000097 | Preparation | 100.00 | Task |

# CHAPTER 6

# Person

## 6.1 PERSON DEFINITION

| *Functional Consultant* | *User* | *Business Process Owner* | *Senior Management* | *My Rating* | *Understanding Level* |
|---|---|---|---|---|---|
| A | A | A | A | | |

A person is an employee, who holds a position and carries out the tasks assigned to that position. Unlike other objects, persons are not created in Organizational Management. They are created in Personnel Administration and are linked to the organizational plan through their position assignment. They are external objects for Organizational Management. You will not find a record in infotype 1000 for them. Also, in infotype 1001, you will only find a single relationship pointing to a person and not the reverse relationship from person to another object. In an organization, there may be other holders of position, e.g. users, central persons, etc. They are not employees and are not called persons in SAP. Object person in SAP refers only to employees.

## 6.2 PERSON CREATION

| *Functional Consultant* | *User* | *Business Process Owner* | *Senior Management* | *My Rating* | *Understanding Level* |
|---|---|---|---|---|---|
| A | A | B | X | | |

Persons are created in Personnel Administration. You run the hiring action using transaction PA40. You also assign him a position in infotype 0001. Person is an external object in the Organizational Management. Once the person is created in Personnel Administration, you can see him in Organizational Management as well.

## 6.3 PERSON STRUCTURES

| *Functional Consultant* | *User* | *Business Process Owner* | *Senior Management* | *My Rating* | *Understanding Level* |
|---|---|---|---|---|---|
| A | A | B | C | | |

### 6.3.1 Organizational Assignment

***View***

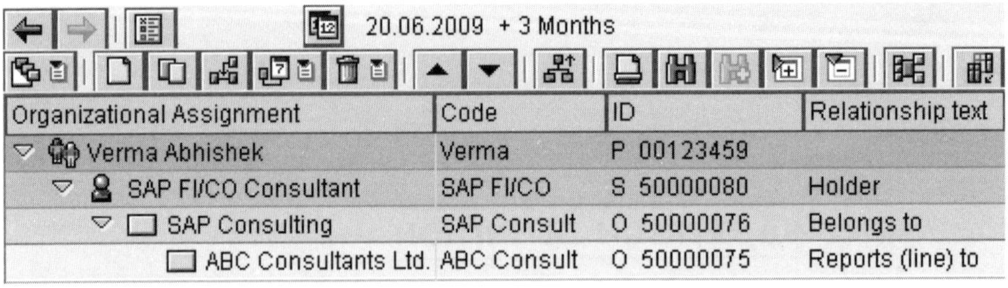


The organizational assignment of a person shows the person's position and the position's organizational structure as a reverse tree.

***Evaluation path***

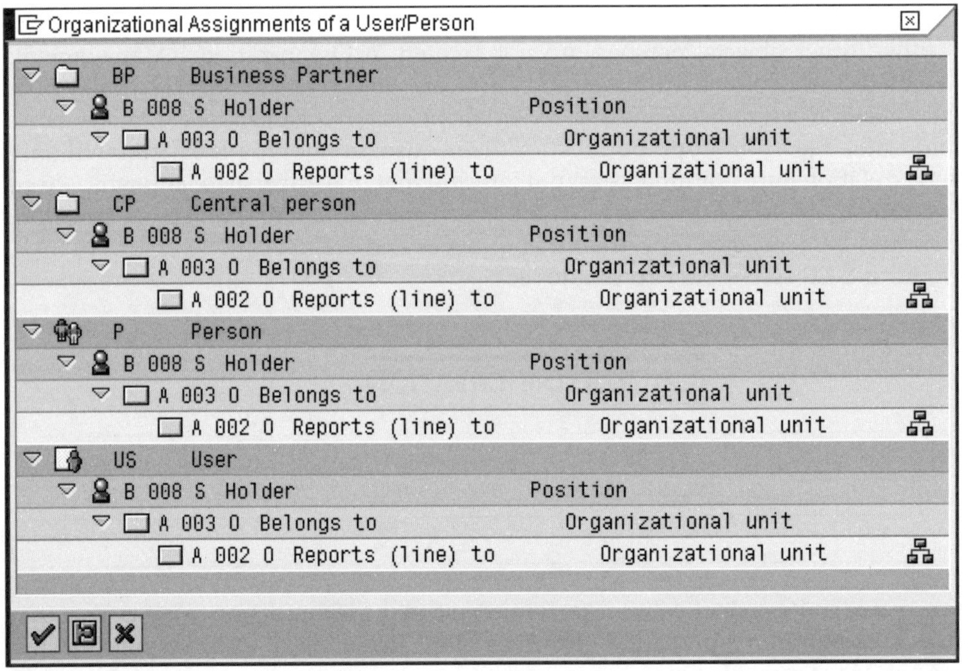


The evaluation path is SAP_PSOO.

### 6.3.2 Task Assignment

***View***

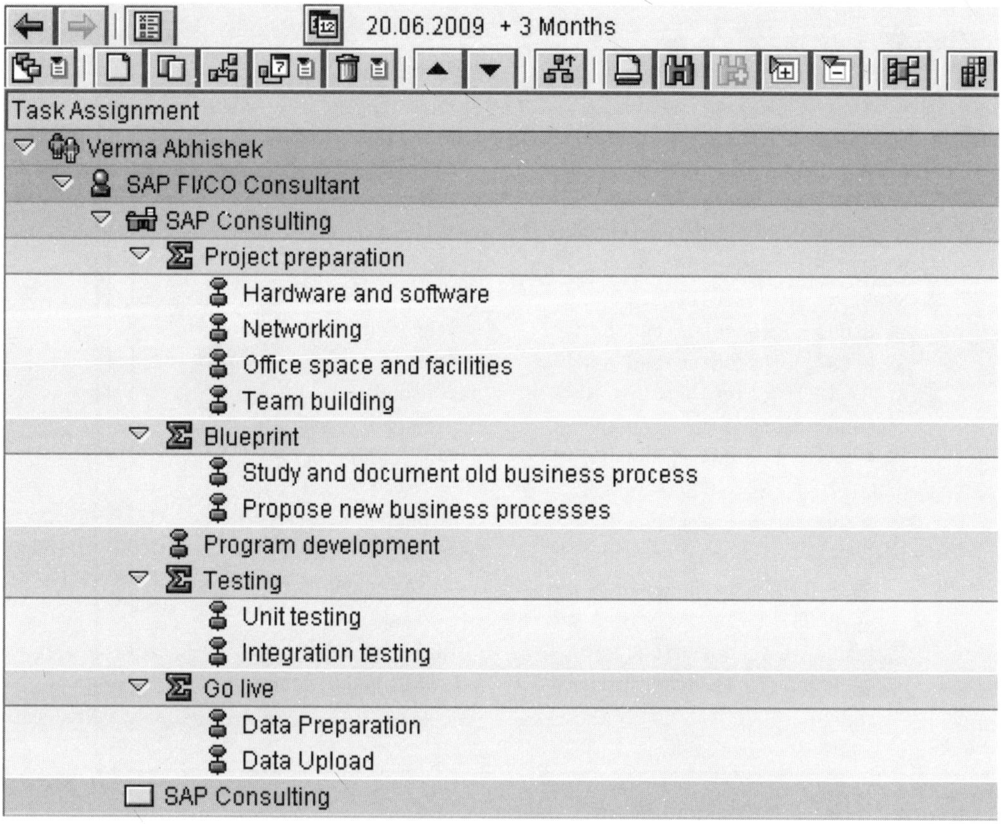


A person needs to know all the tasks he has to perform regardless of the route, e.g. position, organizational unit, etc. through which they are assigned to him. This view fulfils that need.

***Evaluation path***

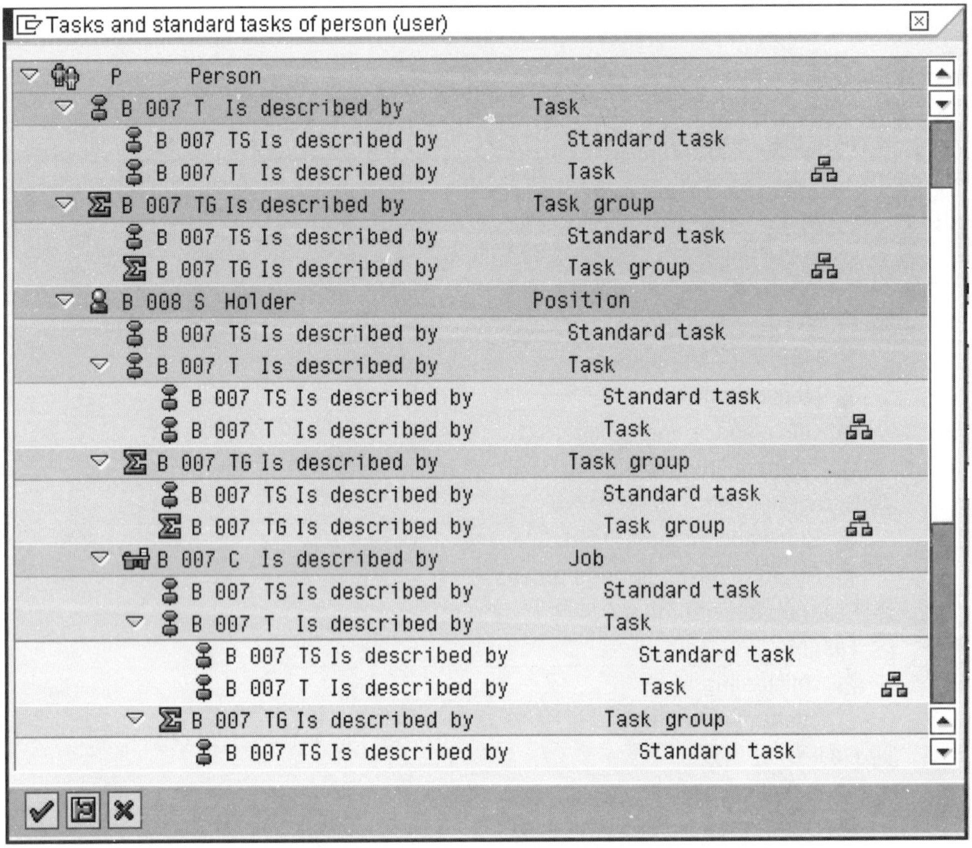


The evaluation path is TASKSOFP.

## 6.4 PERSON DETAILS

| *Functional Consultant* | *User* | *Business Process Owner* | *Senior Management* | *My Rating* | *Understanding Level* |
|---|---|---|---|---|---|
| A | A | B | C | | |

### 6.4.1 Basic Data

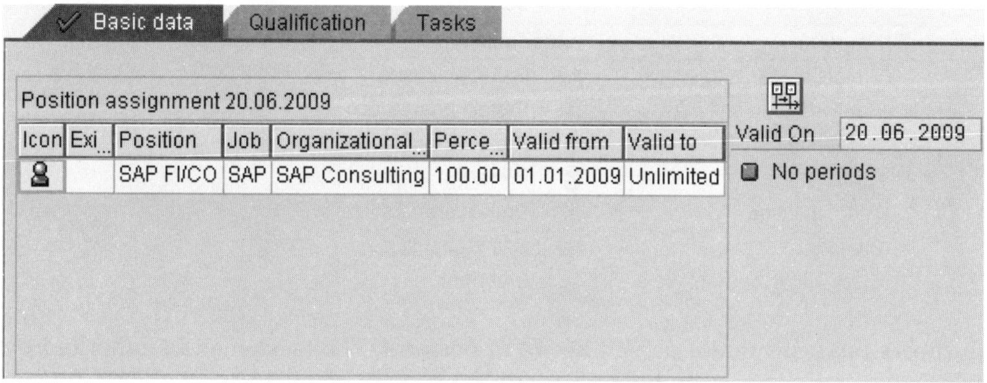


The basic data tab shows a person's position and the organizational unit of that position. If a person holds more than one position all the positions are shown.

### 6.4.2 Qualification

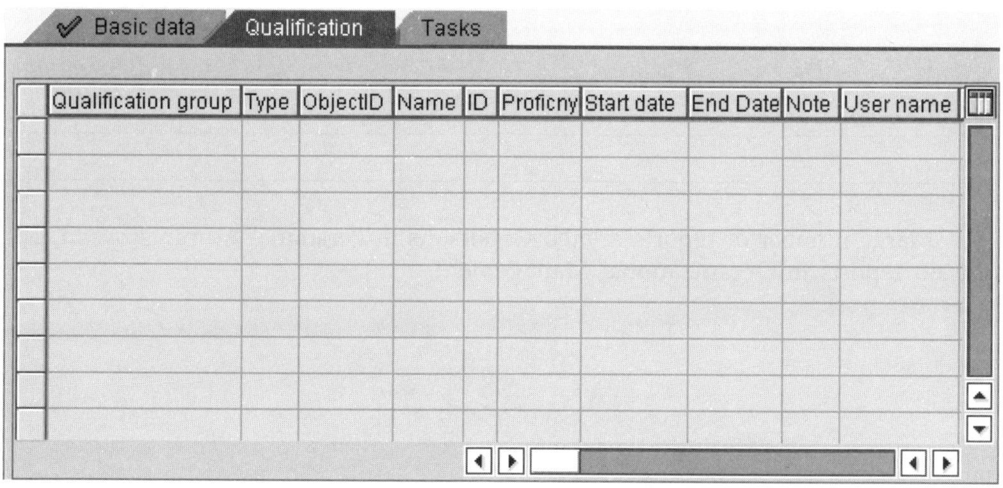


Just as a position has required competencies, a person has available competencies. The competencies of a person are usually maintained through infotype 0021 in Personnel

Administration, but they are actually stored in infotype 1001. Competencies (called qualifications in SAP) required for a position can be compared with competencies of a person to determine the fitness of a person for the position he holds. They are also used in career and succession planning.

### 6.4.3 Tasks

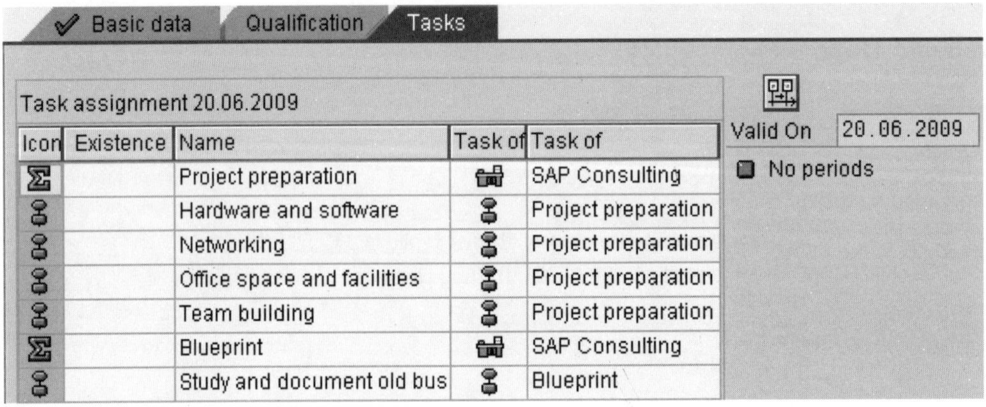
Basic data | Qualification | Tasks

Task assignment 20.06.2009

| Icon | Existence | Name | Task of | Task of |
|---|---|---|---|---|
| | | Project preparation | | SAP Consulting |
| | | Hardware and software | | Project preparation |
| | | Networking | | Project preparation |
| | | Office space and facilities | | Project preparation |
| | | Team building | | Project preparation |
| | | Blueprint | | SAP Consulting |
| | | Study and document old bus | | Blueprint |

Valid On 20.06.2009

No periods

This tab shows the tasks that a person needs to perform. The tasks may be inherited by the person from the position he holds. Certain tasks may also be assigned to a person directly. This data is stored in infotype 1001.

## 6.5 PERSON REPORTS

| *Functional Consultant* | *User* | *Business Process Owner* | *Senior Management* | *My Rating* | *Understanding Level* |
|---|---|---|---|---|---|
| A | A | A | C | | |

There are a large number of reports related to persons in Personnel Administration, but there are no reports in Organizational Management.

# Chapter 7

# User

## 7.1 USER DEFINITION

| *Functional Consultant* | *User* | *Business Process Owner* | *Senior Management* | *My Rating* | *Understanding Level* |
|---|---|---|---|---|---|
| A | A | A | A | | |

Users are objects that can hold positions within the organizational structure just like employees. Users are created to access the SAP system. Users may be employees or non-employees. If users are employees, the relationship between their personnel number and user id is maintained in infotype 0105, subtype 0001. Users can participate in workflows.

## 7.2 USER CREATION

| *Functional Consultant* | *User* | *Business Process Owner* | *Senior Management* | *My Rating* | *Understanding Level* |
|---|---|---|---|---|---|
| A | A | B | X | | |

Users can be created using transaction SU01.

## 7.3 USER STRUCTURES

| *Functional Consultant* | *User* | *Business Process Owner* | *Senior Management* | *My Rating* | *Understanding Level* |
|---|---|---|---|---|---|
| A | A | B | C | | |

### 7.3.1 Organizational Assignment

***View***

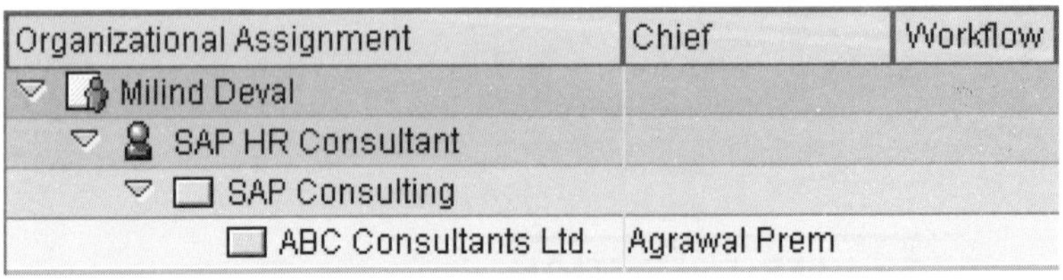


The organizational assignment of a user shows the user's position and the position's organizational structure as a reverse tree.

***Evaluation path***

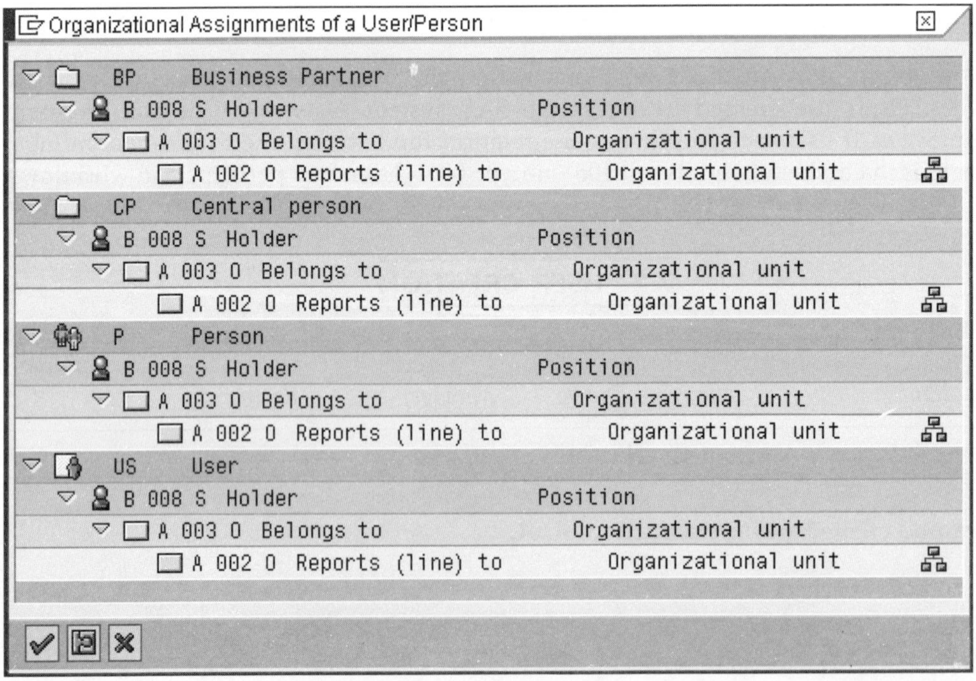


The evaluation path is SAP_PSOO.

### 7.3.2 Task Assignment

#### *View*

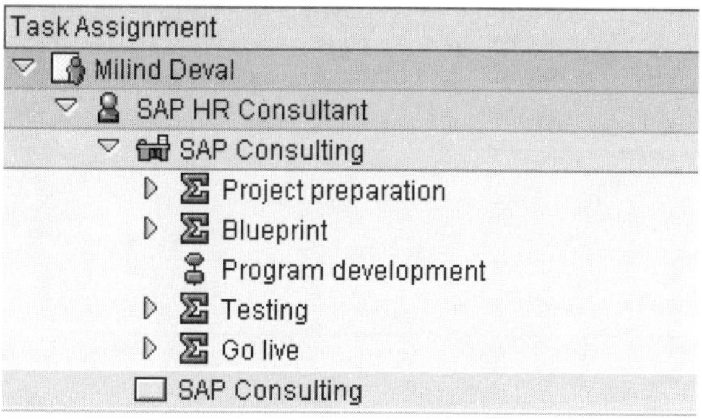


A user needs to know all the tasks he has to perform regardless of the route, e.g. position, organizational unit, etc. through which they are assigned to him. This view fulfils that need.

#### *Evaluation path*

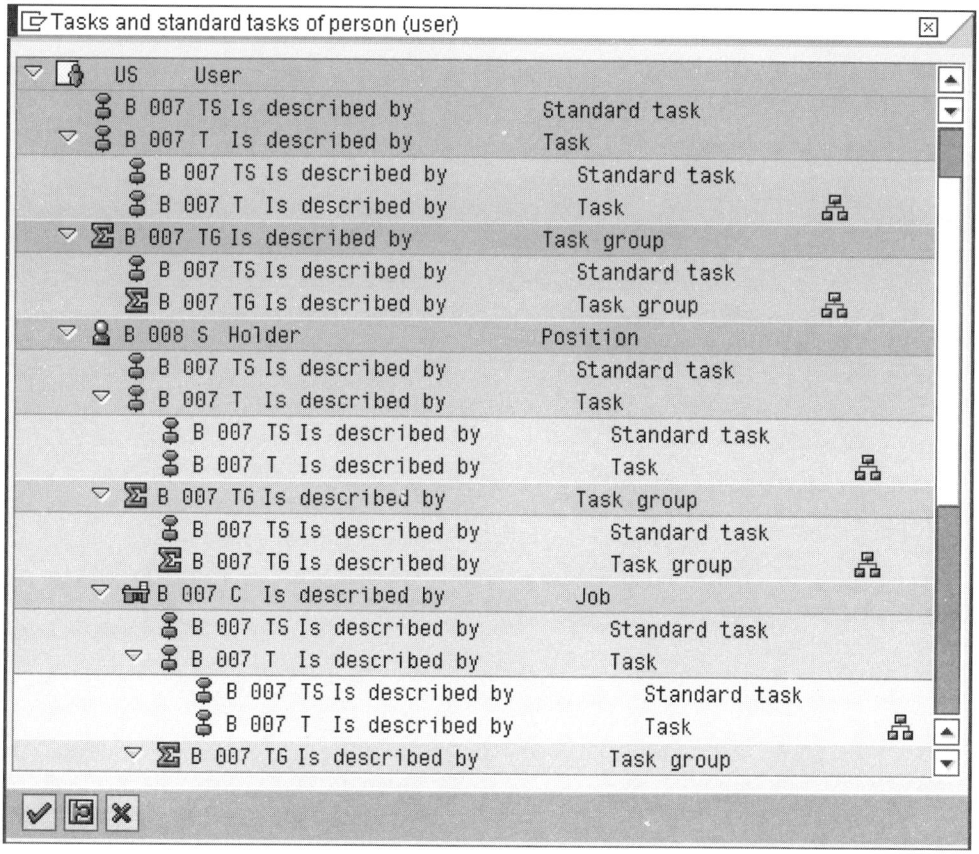


The evaluation path is TASKSOFP.

## 7.4 USER DETAILS

| *Functional Consultant* | *User* | *Business Process Owner* | *Senior Management* | *My Rating* | *Understanding Level* |
|---|---|---|---|---|---|
| A | A | B | C | | |

### 7.4.1 Basic Data

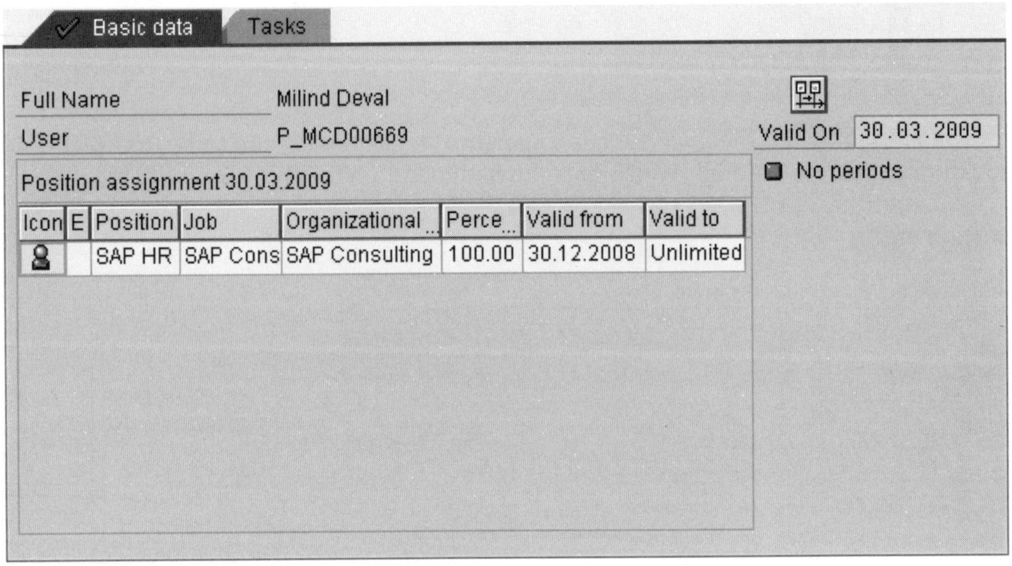


This tab shows the position assigned to a user.

### 7.4.2 Tasks

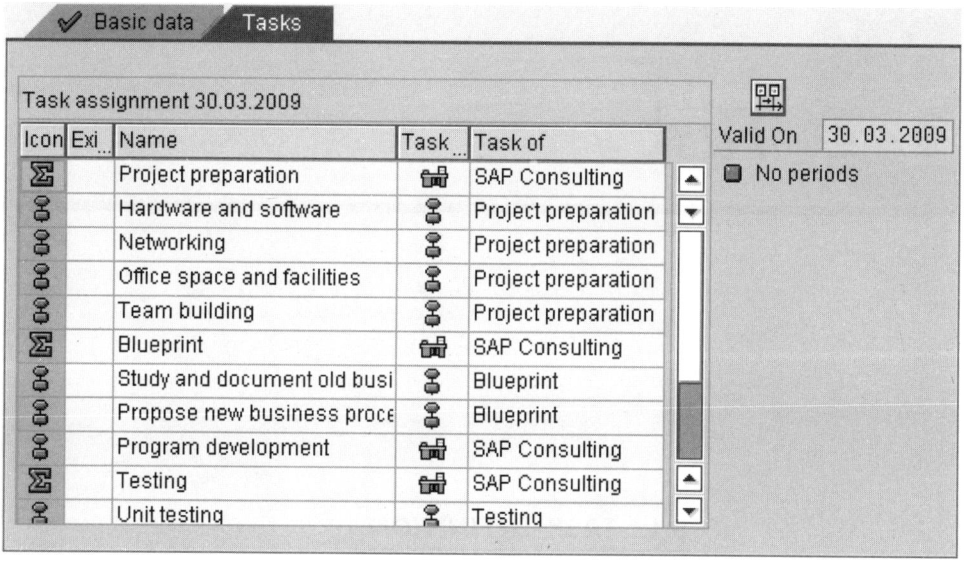


This tab shows the tasks that a user needs to perform. The tasks may be inherited by the user from the position he holds. Certain tasks may also be assigned to a user directly. This data is stored in infotype 1001.

## 7.5 USER REPORTS

| *Functional Consultant* | *User* | *Business Process Owner* | *Senior Management* | *My Rating* | *Understanding Level* |
|---|---|---|---|---|---|
| A | A | B | C | | |

You can get a lot of information about users in transaction SUIM.

CHAPTER 8

# Task

## 8.1 TASK DEFINITION

| Functional Consultant | User | Business Process Owner | Senior Management | My Rating | Understanding Level |
|---|---|---|---|---|---|
| A | A | A | A | | |

Tasks are micro level activities which are performed in your organization. You can create a tree structure of tasks called task catalog. Tasks are grouped into jobs, which are assigned to positions. Tasks of the job assigned to a position are automatically inherited by the position. Apart from tasks inherited from the job, individual tasks can also be assigned to positions.

## 8.2 TASK CATALOG

| Functional Consultant | User | Business Process Owner | Senior Management | My Rating | Understanding Level |
|---|---|---|---|---|---|
| A | A | A | A | | |

Tasks are maintained in task catalog for ease of search. You can maintain task catalog using transaction PFCT. When you run transaction PFCT, you get the following screen.

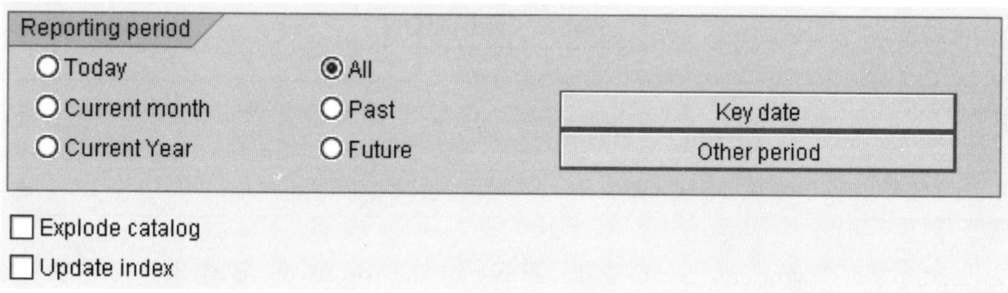


You fill the necessary information and Execute. You get the following screen.

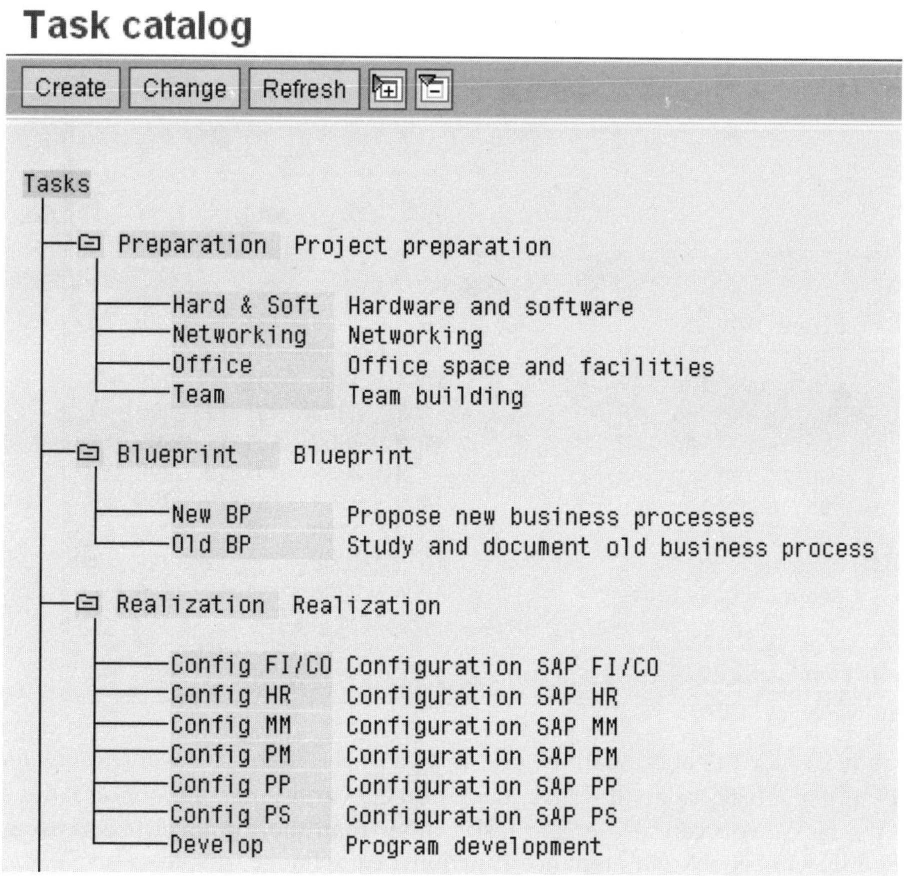

## 8.3 TASK CREATION

| *Functional Consultant* | *User* | *Business Process Owner* | *Senior Management* | *My Rating* | *Understanding Level* |
|---|---|---|---|---|---|
| A | A | B | X | | |

In transaction PFCT you can create tasks, either at the top level, or at the subordinate levels. To create a top level task, select Tasks and click Create.

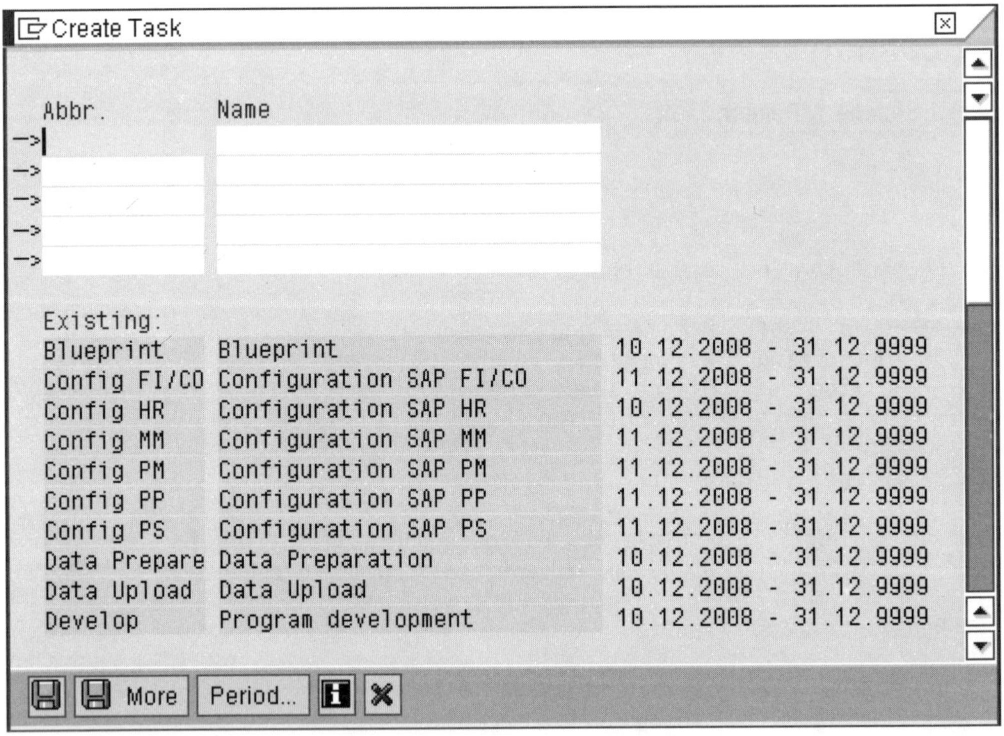


In the screen above, enter the abbreviations and names of the tasks you want to create. To create tasks under a task, select the task, click Create and enter the abbreviations and names of the tasks. You can also create tasks, other than the top level tasks, using transaction PPOME. Other task maintenance functions, e.g. change, display and delete, take you to the screen of transaction PP01, where you can maintain all the infotypes of the task. It is recommended that you create tasks using transaction PFCT and maintain tasks using transaction PP01 or PPOME.

## 8.4 TASK STRUCTURES

| *Functional Consultant* | *User* | *Business Process Owner* | *Senior Management* | *My Rating* | *Understanding Level* |
|---|---|---|---|---|---|
| A | A | B | C | | |

### 8.4.1 Task Hierarchy

***View***

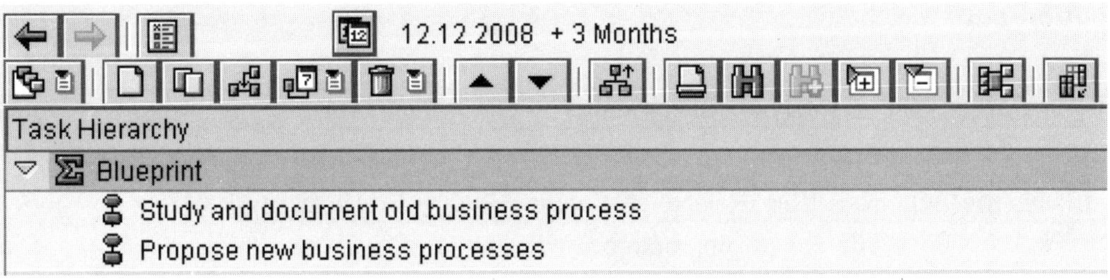


The task hierarchy shows the tasks under the selected task. Task hierarchy consists of task groups and tasks. Task groups are activities that are routinely performed together. If a task group is assigned to a job or position, all the tasks in the task group are assigned to that job or position.

***Evaluation path***

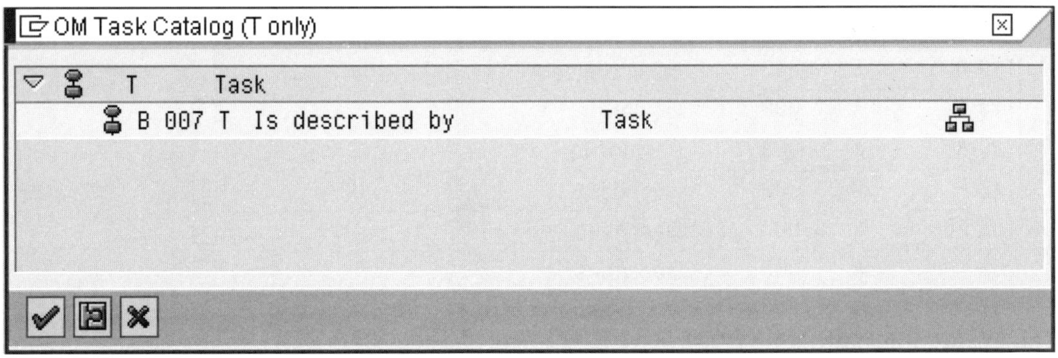


The evaluation path is TASKONLY.

### 8.4.2 Agents

***View***

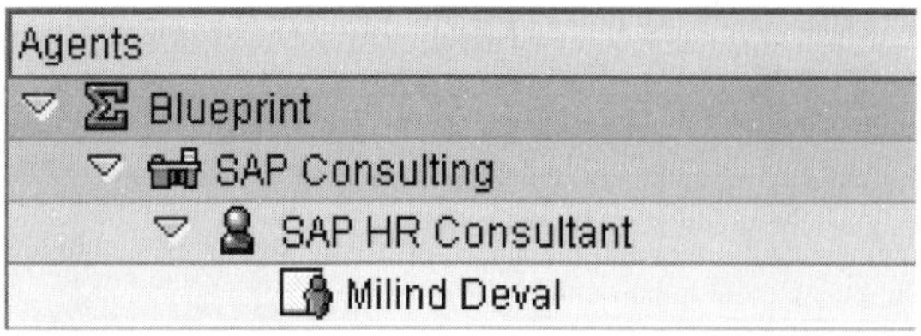


If you want to see who all will perform certain task, you can see it in the agents view.

***Evaluation path***

Evaluation Path SAP_CTSK Task customizing -> agent assignment

| No. | Obj.Type | A/B | Relat'ship | Relationship name | Priority | Rel.obj.type | Skip |
|---|---|---|---|---|---|---|---|
| 10 | FA | B | 003 | Incorporates | * | TS | ☐ |
| 11 | FA | B | 003 | Incorporates | * | T | ☐ |
| 20 | FA | B | 003 | Incorporates | * | WS | ☐ |
| 21 | FA | B | 003 | Incorporates | * | WF | ☐ |
| 30 | TS | A | 007 | Describes | * | * | ☐ |
| 31 | WS | A | 007 | Describes | * | * | ☐ |
| 40 | T | A | 007 | Describes | * | * | ☐ |
| 41 | WF | A | 007 | Describes | * | * | ☐ |
| 100 | C | A | 007 | Describes | * | S | ☐ |
| 110 | O | B | 003 | Incorporates | * | S | ☐ |
| 120 | * | A | 008 | Holder | * | * | ☐ |
| 130 | A | A | 003 | Belongs to | * | S | ☐ |
| 140 | P | B | 208 | Is identical to | * | US | ☐ |
| 150 | AG | A | 007 | Describes | * | * | ☐ |
| 200 | TG | A | 007 | Describes | * | * | ☐ |

The evaluation path is SAP_CTSK.

## 8.5 TASK DETAILS

| Functional Consultant | User | Business Process Owner | Senior Management | My Rating | Understanding Level |
|---|---|---|---|---|---|
| A | A | B | C | | |

### 8.5.1 Name

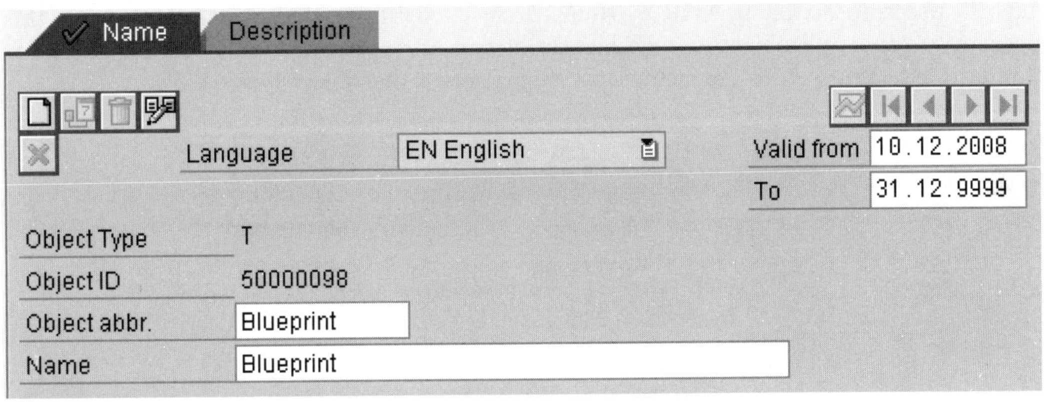


This tab contains the name and abbreviation of the task.

### 8.5.2 Description

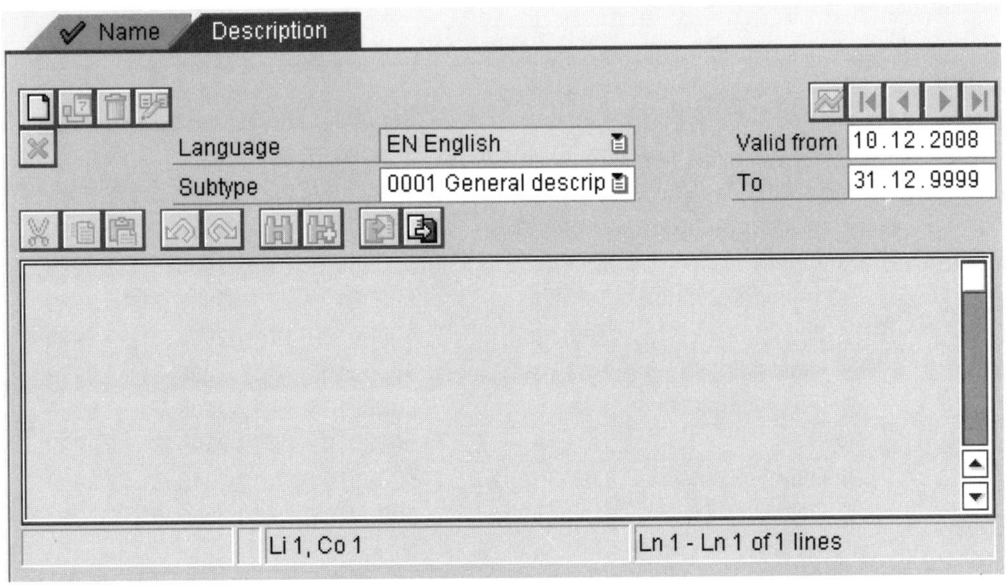


In this tab you can maintain various types of descriptions of the task.

## 8.6 TASK REPORTS

| *Functional Consultant* | *User* | *Business Process Owner* | *Senior Management* | *My Rating* | *Understanding Level* |
|---|---|---|---|---|---|
| A | A | B | C | | |

### *Existing tasks*

You can use transaction S_AHR_61016522 to list existing tasks. You can also use this program to report all objects, or all objects of certain type. To do so, tick the checkbox 'Standard selection screen', Execute and then specify the object type.

| OT | Start date | End Date | S | Object name | Ext.obj ID |
|---|---|---|---|---|---|
| T | 10.12.2008 | 31.12.9999 | 1 | Project preparation | 50000097 |
| T | 10.12.2008 | 31.12.9999 | 1 | Blueprint | 50000098 |
| T | 10.12.2008 | 31.12.9999 | 1 | Realization | 50000099 |
| T | 10.12.2008 | 31.12.9999 | 1 | Testing | 50000100 |
| T | 10.12.2008 | 31.12.9999 | 1 | Go live | 50000101 |

### *Activity profile for positions along organizational structure*

You can run transaction S_AHR_61016523 to show the tasks for positions along the organizational structure.

| Object Description | Object abbr. | C | Extende... | Start Dat... | End Date... |
|---|---|---|---|---|---|
| ABC Consultants Ltd. | ABC Consult | O | 50000075 | | |
| Chief Executive Officer | CEO | S | 50000078 | 09.12.2008 | 31.12.9999 |
| SAP Consulting | SAP Consult | O | 50000076 | 09.12.2008 | 31.12.9999 |
| SAP HR Consultant | SAP HR | S | 50000079 | 09.12.2008 | 31.12.9999 |
| Project preparation | Preparation | T | 50000097 | 12.12.2008 | 31.12.9999 |
| Blueprint | Blueprint | T | 50000098 | 12.12.2008 | 31.12.9999 |
| Program development | Develop | T | 50000108 | 12.12.2008 | 31.12.9999 |
| Testing | Testing | T | 50000100 | 12.12.2008 | 31.12.9999 |
| Unit testing | Unit Test | T | 50000105 | 10.12.2008 | 31.12.9999 |
| Integration testing | Integ. test | T | 50000106 | 10.12.2008 | 31.12.9999 |
| Go live | Go Live | T | 50000101 | 12.12.2008 | 31.12.9999 |
| Data Preparation | Data Prepare | T | 50000103 | 10.12.2008 | 31.12.9999 |
| Data Upload | Data Upload | T | 50000104 | 10.12.2008 | 31.12.9999 |

It uses evaluation path AUFGABEX which shows tasks and tasks in jobs for positions which are displayed in the organizational structure.

Evaluation Path AUFGABEX Activity profile of positions along organizational structure

| No. | Obj.Type | A/B | Relat'ship | Relationship name | Priority | Rel.obj.type | Skip |
|---|---|---|---|---|---|---|---|
| 10 | O | B | 003 | Incorporates | * | S | ☐ |
| 20 | O | B | 002 | Is line supervisor of | * | O | ☐ |
| 30 | S | B | 007 | Is described by | * | T | ☐ |
| 40 | S | B | 007 | Is described by | * | C | ☑ |
| 50 | S | B | 002 | Is line supervisor of | * | S | ☐ |
| 60 | C | B | 007 | Is described by | * | T | ☐ |
| 70 | T | B | 007 | Is described by | * | T | ☐ |

***Activity profile of positions with persons along organizational structure***

You can run transaction S_AHR_61016524 to show the tasks for positions along the organizational structure. Persons holding these positions are also shown.

| Object Description | Object abbr. | C | Extende... | Start Dat... | End Date... |
|---|---|---|---|---|---|
| ▽ ABC Consultants Ltd. | ABC Consult | O | 50000075 | | |
| ▽ Chief Executive Officer | CEO | S | 50000078 | 09.12.2008 | 31.12.9999 |
| Agrawal Prem | Agrawal | P | 00121715 | 12.12.2008 | 31.12.9999 |
| ▽ SAP Consulting | SAP Consult | O | 50000076 | 09.12.2008 | 31.12.9999 |
| ▽ SAP HR Consultant | SAP HR | S | 50000079 | 09.12.2008 | 31.12.9999 |
| ▷ Project preparation | Preparation | T | 50000097 | 12.12.2008 | 31.12.9999 |
| ▷ Blueprint | Blueprint | T | 50000098 | 12.12.2008 | 31.12.9999 |
| Program development | Develop | T | 50000108 | 12.12.2008 | 31.12.9999 |
| ▽ Testing | Testing | T | 50000100 | 12.12.2008 | 31.12.9999 |
| Unit testing | Unit Test | T | 50000105 | 10.12.2008 | 31.12.9999 |
| Integration testing | Integ. test | T | 50000106 | 10.12.2008 | 31.12.9999 |
| ▽ Go live | Go Live | T | 50000101 | 12.12.2008 | 31.12.9999 |
| Data Preparation | Data Prepare | T | 50000103 | 10.12.2008 | 31.12.9999 |
| Data Upload | Data Upload | T | 50000104 | 10.12.2008 | 31.12.9999 |

It uses evaluation path AUFGABEP which shows tasks and tasks in jobs for positions which are displayed in the organizational structure. Persons holding these positions are also shown.

| Evaluation Path | AUFGABEP | Activity Profile of Positions with Persons Along Org. Structure |
|---|---|---|

| No. | Obj.Type | A/B | Relat'ship | Relationship name | Priority | Rel.obj.type | Skip |
|---|---|---|---|---|---|---|---|
| 10 | O | B | 003 | Incorporates | * | S | ☐ |
| 20 | O | B | 002 | Is line supervisor of | * | O | ☐ |
| 30 | S | B | 007 | Is described by | * | T | ☐ |
| 40 | S | B | 007 | Is described by | * | C | ☑ |
| 50 | S | B | 002 | Is line supervisor of | * | S | ☐ |
| 60 | C | B | 007 | Is described by | * | T | ☐ |
| 70 | T | B | 007 | Is described by | * | T | ☐ |
| 80 | S | A | 008 | Holder | * | P | ☐ |

### *Character of tasks in organizational structure*

You can run transaction S_AHR_61016525 to display tasks having character definition in infotype 1004. It uses evaluation path AUFGABEX to show the tasks in the organizational structure.

| Object Name | O | Extended... | Description |
|---|---|---|---|
| ABC Consultants Ltd. | O | 50000075 | |
| SAP Consulting | O | 50000076 | |
| SAP HR Consultant | S | 50000079 | |
| Project preparation | T | 50000097 | Task With 1 Character |
| Character | T | 50000097 | Completion X |
| Character | T | 50000097 | Indicator: Execute X |
| Character | T | 50000097 | Indicator: Purpose Task X |

### *Character of individual tasks*

You can run transaction S_AHR_61016526 to see the tasks for which infotype 1004 (Character) is maintained and its character attributes

| Obj... | Object Name | Object ID | Description |
|---|---|---|---|
| | Project preparation | T 50000097 | With 1 Character |
| | Character | T 50000097 | Completion X |
| | Character | T 50000097 | Indicator: Execute X |
| | Character | T 50000097 | Indicator: Purpose Task X |

# CHAPTER 9

# Work Center

## 9.1 WORK CENTER DEFINITION

| *Functional Consultant* | *User* | *Business Process Owner* | *Senior Management* | *My Rating* | *Understanding Level* |
|---|---|---|---|---|---|
| A | A | A | A | | |

A work center identifies the physical location where tasks are performed. A work center can represent something as general as a geographical location, such as the Mumbai office, or it can be very precisely defined, such as a particular workstation with specific equipment in a specific building (Mumbai office, Room 105, Desk III, for example). Several positions may share one work center. For example, the reception desk may be shared by a number of different employees working in different shifts during the day.

## 9.2 WORK CENTER CREATION

| *Functional Consultant* | *User* | *Business Process Owner* | *Senior Management* | *My Rating* | *Understanding Level* |
|---|---|---|---|---|---|
| A | A | B | X | | |

Work centers can be created using transaction PO01 or PP01. When you run transaction PO01, you see the following screen where you can create the work center and maintain various infotypes for it.

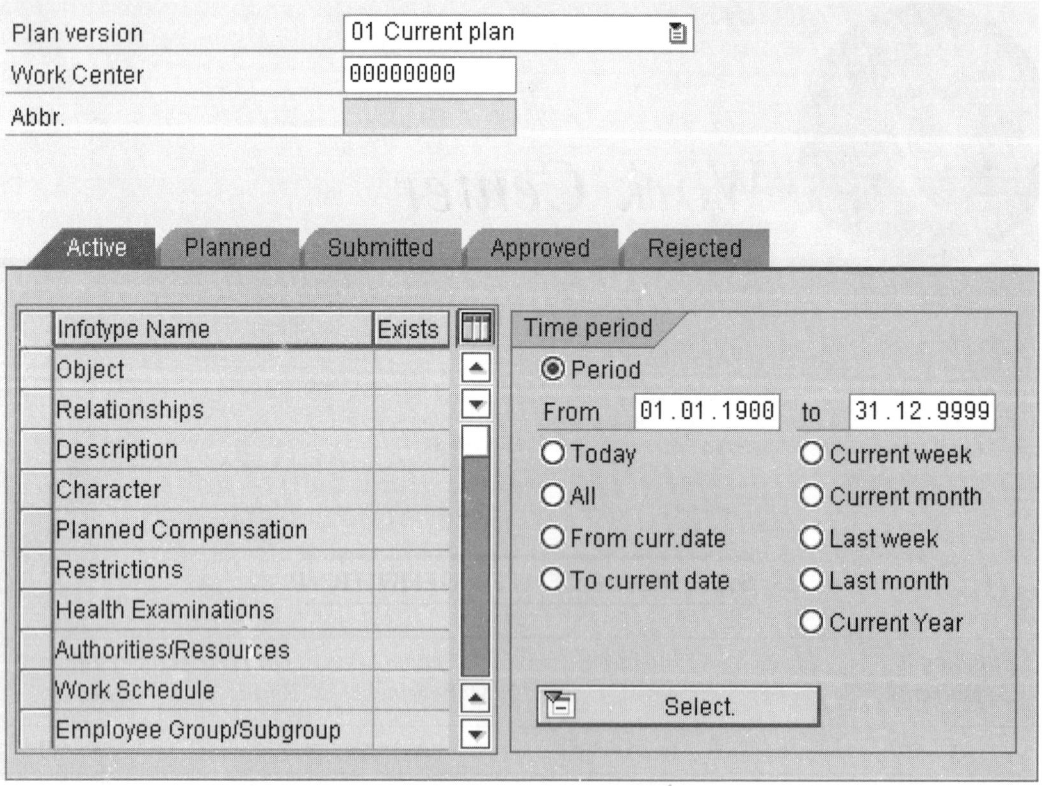


## 9.3 WORK CENTER REPORTS

| *Functional Consultant* | *User* | *Business Process Owner* | *Senior Management* | *My Rating* | *Understanding Level* |
|---|---|---|---|---|---|
| A | A | B | C | | |

***Existing work centers***

You can use transaction S_AHR_61016514 to list existing work centers. You can also use this program to report all objects, or all objects of certain type. To do so, tick the checkbox 'Standard selection screen', Execute and then specify the object type.

| OT | Start date | End Date | S | Object name | Ext.obj ID |
|---|---|---|---|---|---|
| A | 08.09.1995 | 31.12.9999 | 1 | SAP Consulting Work Center | 50000000 |

### *Work centers per organizational unit*

You can use transaction S_AHR_61016496 or S_AHR_61016515 to display organizational structure with work centers.

| Object Description | Object abbr. | O... | Extende... | Start Date ... | End Date ... |
|---|---|---|---|---|---|
| ▽ ☐ ABC Consultants Ltd. | ABC Consult | O | 50000075 | | |
| ▽ ☐ SAP Consulting | SAP Consult | O | 50000076 | 09.12.2008 | 31.12.9999 |
| SAP Consulting Work Center | SAP Cons Cen | A | 50000000 | 15.12.2008 | 31.12.9999 |
| ☐ SAP Education | SAP Educaton | O | 50000077 | 09.12.2008 | 31.12.9999 |

It uses evaluation path ARBP-O. You can change layout of the report by clicking . You can also see structural graphics by clicking .

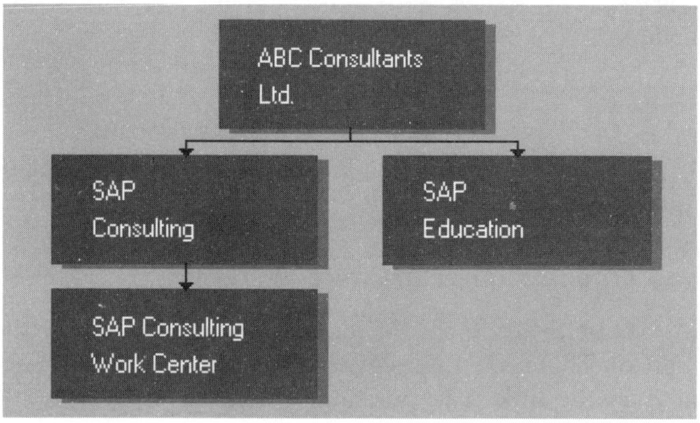


### *Authorities and resources*

You can run transaction RE_RHXHFMT0, S_AHR_61016507 or S_AHR_61016516 to see authorities and resources for a position or for all positions directly belonging to an organizational unit. Authorities and resources may be maintained directly for positions. Alternatively, authorities and resources may be maintained for work centers which are linked to positions. The evaluation path used in this report is ARBPL. This evaluation path does not take you down the organizational structure.

```
Authorities and Resources

Plan version: 01    Status: 1       Selection period: 01.01.1900 -31.12.9999

O 50000075 ABC Consultants Ltd.
  S 50000078 Chief Executive Officer
      Authority/pwr of attorney
         Full commercial power
```

If you want to see authorities and resources along organizational structure, you should use evaluation path ARBPLX.

```
Authorities and Resources

Plan version: 01     Status: 1      Selection period: 01.01.1900 -31.12.9999

O 50000075 ABC Consultants Ltd.
  S 50000078 Chief Executive Officer
      Authority/pwr of attorney
         Full commercial power
. O 50000076 SAP Consulting
    S 50000079 SAP HR Consultant

      A 50000000 SAP Consulting Work Center
        Authority/pwr of attorney
           Limited commercial power
```

***Planned labor costs***

You can run transaction S_AHR_61016517 or S_AHR_61016508 to see planned labor costs of an organizational unit in structural form.

***Work centers with restrictions along organizational structure***

You can run transaction RE_RHXIAW00 or S_AHR_61016518 to see work centers with restrictions along organizational structure. This report uses evaluation path ARBPLX. For this report to work, the work center must be linked to position.

**Plan version:** 01
**Infotype:** 1006 Restrictions
**Evaluation path:** Work center assignment along organizational structure
**Display:** With infotype only

| Object Name | C | Extende... | Description |
|---|---|---|---|
| ABC Consultants Ltd. | O | 50000075 | |
| SAP Consulting | O | 50000076 | |
| SAP HR Consultant | S | 50000079 | |
| SAP Consulting Work Center | A | 50000000 | Work Center With 1 Restrictions |
| Restrictions | A | 50000000 | Restrictions Not suitable for severely |
| Restrictions | A | 50000000 | Reason Constant night work |

### *Single work centers with restrictions*

You can run transaction RE_RHXIAW01 or S_AHR_61016519 to see restrictions on work centers.

**Plan version:** 01
**Selection period:** 01.01.1900-31.12.9999
**Infotype:** 1006
**Display:** With infotype only

| Obj... | Object Name | Object ID | Description |
|---|---|---|---|
| | SAP Consulting Work Cente | A 50000000 | With 1 Restrictions |
| | Restrictions | A 50000000 | Restrictions Not suitable for severely disabled cl. |
| | Restrictions | A 50000000 | Reason Constant night work |

### *Work centers requiring health examinations along organizational structure*

You can run transaction RE_RHXIAW02 or S_AHR_61016520 to see work centers with health examinations and exclusions along organizational structure. This report uses evaluation path ARBPLX. For this report to work, the work center must be linked to position.

**Plan version:** 01
**Infotype:** 1009 Health Examinations
**Evaluation path:** Work center assignment along organizational structure
**Display:** With infotype only

| Object Name | C | Extende... | Description |
|---|---|---|---|
| ABC Consultants Ltd. | O | 50000075 | |
| SAP Consulting | O | 50000076 | |
| SAP HR Consultant | S | 50000079 | |
| SAP Consulting Work Center | A | 50000000 | Work Center With 1 Health Examinations |
| Health examinations | A | 50000000 | Examination Type Eye test |

### *Single work centers requiring health examinations*

You can run transaction RE_RHXIAW03 or S_AHR_61016521 to see health examinations and exclusions for work centers.

**Plan version:** 01
**Selection period:** 01.01.1900-31.12.9999
**Infotype:** 1009
**Display:** With infotype only

| Obj... | Object Name | Object ID | Description |
|---|---|---|---|
| | SAP Consulting Work Cente | A 50000000 | With 1 Health Examination |
| | Health examinations | A 50000000 | Examination Type Eye test |

# CHAPTER 10 Objects

## 10.1 OBJECTS

| *Functional Consultant* | *User* | *Business Process Owner* | *Senior Management* | *My Rating* | *Understanding Level* |
|---|---|---|---|---|---|
| A | A | A | A | | |

### 10.1.1 Object Definition

An organization has a number of objects of different types, e.g. organizational units, positions, persons, cost centers, jobs, tasks, etc. Each object has a unique id. It also has a name and abbreviation which can change with time. Objects are stored in infotype 1000.

### 10.1.2 Creating an Object

Organizational Management of SAP is based on the concept of objects and relationships. You have already seen many important types of objects and relationships between them. You can create any type of object using transaction PP01. There are also other transactions which are used for creating specific type of objects. When you run transaction PP01, you get the following screen.

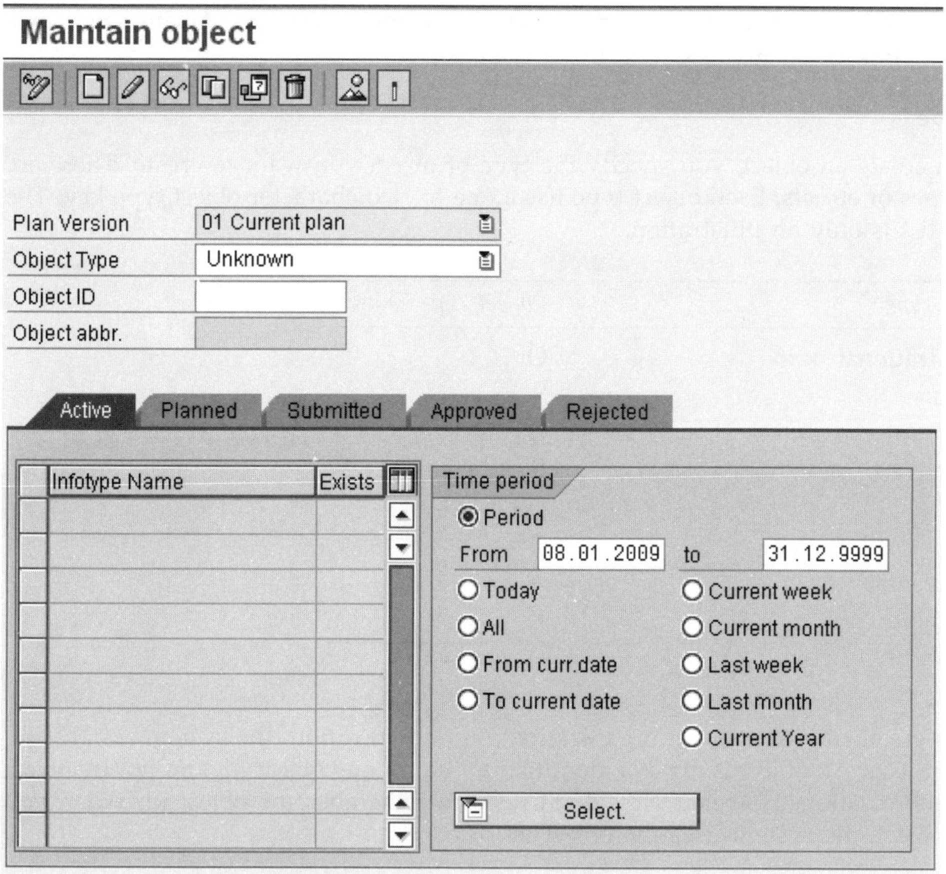


When you select the object type, the system shows all the infotypes which can be maintained for that object type. No matter which object type you select, the first infotype is 'Object'. Select that infotype, enter validity period and click the create icon.

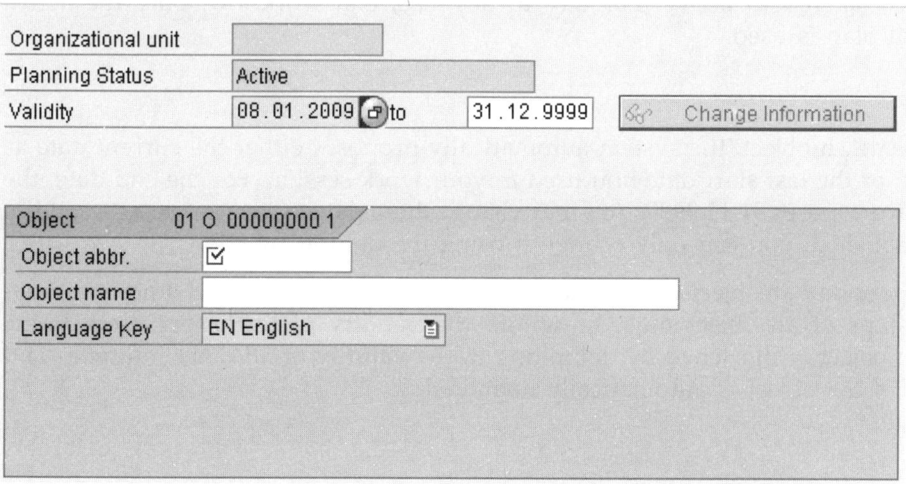

In the screen that follows, you enter the object abbreviation and object name and save. The system creates a new object and gives it an object id.

### Object type

When you create an object, you specify the type of object you want to create. There are various types of objects. Each object type has a one or two character object type key. The following list is only an illustration.

| *Object type* | *Object type key* |
|---|---|
| Organizational unit | O |
| Position | S |
| Job | C |
| Person | P |
| User | US |
| Task | T |
| Work center | A |
| Cost center | K |

### Object id

When you create any object, e.g. organizational unit or position, the system assigns it a unique object id. An object is always identified by its unique object id, and not by object name or abbreviation. However, you don't need to remember the object id. When you select an object, the system uses the object id.

### Planning status

SAP provides you facility for creating an object or infotype in planned status, which could be submitted for approval. It may then get accepted or rejected. If accepted, the status can be changed to active. For day to day use, e.g. workflow, only the active organizational plan is used.

### Validity

When you create an object, the system automatically proposes either the current date as the start date, or the last start date you used in your work session. For the end date, the system usually proposes 31.12.9999. You may change these dates. Once an object's validity period is established, you can only change it using the delimit function.

The validity period of an object has special significance. The validity of all other infotypes and relationships of an object must be within the validity of the object itself. If the validity of an object is shortened by delimiting it, the validity of all other infotypes and relationships of the object is automatically delimited.

***Object abbreviation and name***

When you create an object, you specify its name and abbreviation. You access the object using object name or abbreviation. Since the object is identified primarily by the object id, you can change the object name or object abbreviation. It is also possible to have different names of an object during different periods. Thus, if your company decided to change the name of an organizational unit from a certain date, you can do so in SAP. Depending on the date specified, the system will show either the old or the new organizational unit name.

***Language key***

You can maintain object name and abbreviation in different languages.

### 10.1.3 Creating Multiple Object Copies

If you want to create multiple positions from a job, you can use program RHMULT00. You specify the source object, target object type, number of target objects and relationship between the source and target objects. You should run the program in test mode first.

### 10.1.4 Changing an Object

If you wish to change the abbreviation or name of an object, you may do so by clicking the change icon. If you want to change the abbreviation or name of the object from a certain date, you create a new record for the object by clicking either create or the copy icon. You specify the abbreviation, name and validity period and save. The system automatically delimits the old record.

### 10.1.5 Delimiting an Object

You can change abbreviations and descriptions at a later time by editing object infotype records. However, you cannot change an object's validity period in this manner. This must be done using the delimit function.

### 10.1.6 Delimiting Multiple Objects

If you want to delimit multiple objects, you can do so using transaction RE_RHGRENZ0. The objects can be selected using evaluation path.

### 10.1.7 Deleting an Object

You can also delete the objects you create. However, if you delete an object, the system erases all records of the object from the database. You should only delete objects if they are not valid during any period. If an object was valid in the past, you should delimit it.

### 10.1.8 Copying an Object

SAP provides transaction RE_RHCOPY00 to copy an object. When you copy an object, all its infotypes are copied. You can specify whether relationships are also to be copied. You can specify new name and abbreviation for the created object; otherwise the name and abbreviation are also copied. You can display the copied records and do the copy in test mode. If you do not know which object to copy from, you can use transaction RE_RHCOPY10. You can first see the list of objects, and then choose the object to copy from.

### 10.1.9 Displaying Existing Objects

You can use transaction S_AHR_61016527 to list the existing objects.

| OT | Start date | End Date | S | Object name | Ext.obj ID |
|---|---|---|---|---|---|
| O | 16.06.1995 | 31.12.9999 | 1 | ALE department | 00000001 |
| O | 30.04.2003 | 31.12.9999 | 1 | FSCM Kreditorenbuchhaltung | 50000025 |
| O | 09.12.2008 | 31.12.9999 | 1 | ABC Consultants Ltd. | 50000075 |
| O | 09.12.2008 | 31.12.9999 | 1 | SAP Consulting | 50000076 |
| O | 09.12.2008 | 31.12.9999 | 1 | SAP Education | 50000077 |

## 10.2 NUMBER RANGES

| *Functional Consultant* | *User* | *Business Process Owner* | *Senior Management* | *My Rating* | *Understanding Level* |
|---|---|---|---|---|---|
| A | A | B | C | | |

### 10.2.1 Object Identification

Every object you create has a unique object ID. The object is identified by a combination of plan version, object type and object ID. Object IDs are numeric. They cannot be alphanumeric.

### 10.2.2 Internal and External Number Assignment

There are two types of number assignment.

| *Type of number assignment* | *Object ID allocation* |
|---|---|
| Internal assignment | The system automatically allocates an object ID from the corresponding number range. |
| External assignment | The user enters the object ID. |

As the search function is available, it is not generally necessary to enter meaningful numbers using external number assignment. It is recommended that you use the internal number assignment.

### 10.2.3 Number Assignment for All Plan Versions

If you are using multiple plan versions, you can decide whether objects of all plan versions will get their numbers from the same range, or whether there will be specific number ranges for specific plan versions. Whether your number assignment is for all plan versions, or it is plan version specific is specified in table T77S0 (discussed in more detail in chapter 15.5). Number assignment for all plan versions has the advantage that objects will not be overwritten when objects are copied from one plan version to another.

| Group | Sem. abbr. | Value abbr. | Description |
|---|---|---|---|
| NUMRG | COMP | | Number assignment for all plan versions |

### 10.2.4 Number Ranges

You can decide whether objects of all types will be given number from the same range, or different object types will get their numbers from different ranges. Number ranges can be maintained using transaction OONR.

| Subgroup | NR int.assgnmt | NR ext.assgnmt |
|---|---|---|
| $$$$ | IN | EX |
| | | |

The first two characters of the subgroup specify the plan version and the last two specify the object type. $$ in the first two characters indicates all plan versions and $$ in the last two characters indicates all object types. The standard entry $$$$ in the field subgroup stands for all number ranges not listed explicitly. This entry should not be deleted.

### 10.2.5 Creating a New Subgroup

If you want to assign a separate internal number range for organizational units in plan version 01, you would click [New entries], enter 01O in the subgroup and save. You would then create the number range by clicking [Number range maintenance]. The system will take you to the next screen.

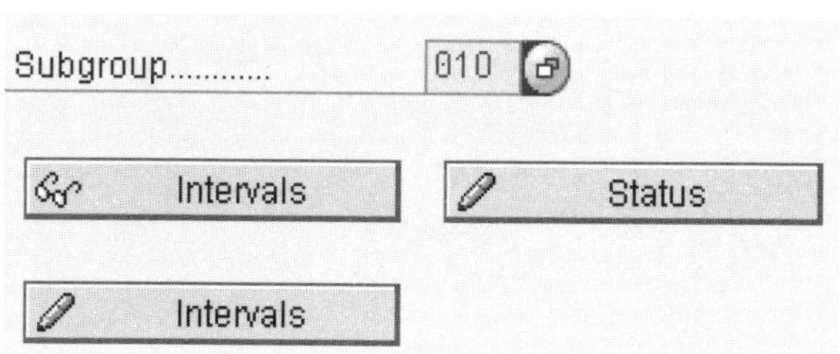

Click [Intervals], to create the number range for the subgroup. Add an interval by clicking [Interval].

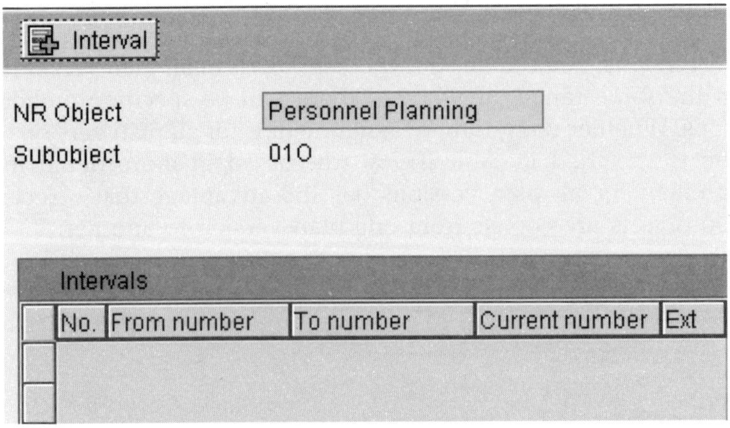


### 10.2.6 Customer Logic for Number Assignment

If you want to use your own logic for number assignment, you can implement the following User Exits of the enhancement RHIV001.

| *User exit* | *Description* |
|---|---|
| EXIT_SAPLRHIN_001 | Check number ranges for integration |
| EXIT_SAPLRHIV_001 | Internal number assignment |
| EXIT_SAPLRHIV_002 | Check external number assignment |
| EXIT_SAPLRHIV_003 | Check whether internal number assignment is available |

# CHAPTER 11

# Relationships

## 11.1 RELATIONSHIP DEFINITION

| *Functional Consultant* | *User* | *Business Process Owner* | *Senior Management* | *My Rating* | *Understanding Level* |
|---|---|---|---|---|---|
| A | A | A | A | | |

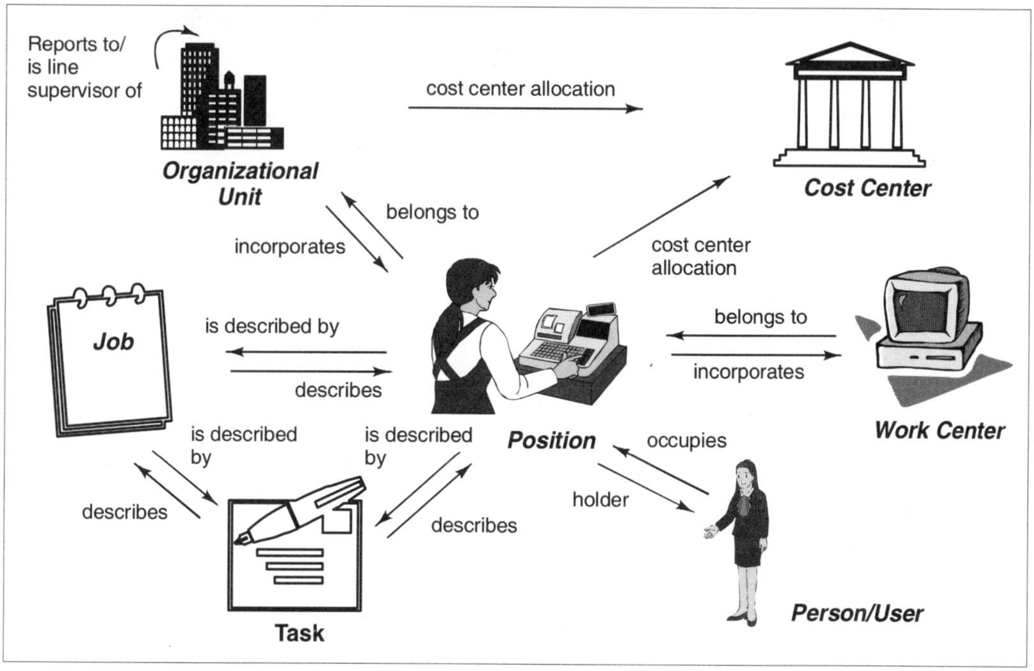

Objects are related to each other through relationships. For example, a position belongs to an organizational unit. Objects which are related to each other form structures. For example, organizational structure is a structure of organizational units which form a hierarchy. Most relationships are bidirectional. If a position belongs to an organizational unit, the organizational unit incorporates the position. Each relationship has a name in either direction.

## 11.2 RELATIONSHIP TYPES

| *Functional Consultant* | *User* | *Business Process Owner* | *Senior Management* | *My Rating* | *Understanding Level* |
|---|---|---|---|---|---|
| A | A | A | A | | |

Objects are related to each other in different ways, i.e. they have different types of relationships between them. A relationship is identified by a three-digit code. The relationships between basic object types are defined in view T778V and should not be changed because they are extensively used. You can define your own relationships. The range AAA to ZZZ is reserved for relationships created by the customer. Relationships between most objects are reciprocal. If a job describes a position, then the position, in turn, is described by the job. These relationships are distinguished by the identification A or B. It is therefore, only necessary to create a relationship between two objects in one direction. The inverse relationship is automatically created by the system. There are certain types of objects, e.g. person, which are called external objects. These objects don't exist in infotype 1000. The relationship of other objects with external objects is one-sided. There is only one record in infotype 1001 for relationship between these two objects. This is only a technical distinction. There is no difference in the behavior of external objects and other objects.

## 11.3 IMPORTANT RELATIONSHIPS

| *Functional Consultant* | *User* | *Business Process Owner* | *Senior Management* | *My Rating* | *Understanding Level* |
|---|---|---|---|---|---|
| A | A | A | A | | |

### 11.3.1 An Organizational Unit Reports to Another Organizational Unit

- **An organizational unit "reports to" another organizational unit** — A 002

  Example: Finance "reports to" Administration

- **An organizational unit "is line supervisor of" another organizational unit** — B 002

  Example: Executive Board "is line supervisor of" Administration, Production, and Sales.

Organizational structure is created by relationships between superior organizational unit and subordinate organizational units. An organizational unit could have many subordinate organizational units, but has only one superior. A subordinate organizational unit can have further subordinate organizational units, thus creating a tree-like organizational structure. There is no limit to the number of levels in an organizational structure.

### 11.3.2 A Position Belongs to an Organizational Unit

- **A position "belongs to" an organizational unit** — A 003
- **An organizational unit "incorporates" a position** — B 003

In an organizational plan, positions belong to an organizational unit.

### 11.3.3 A Position is Described by a Job

- **A job "describes" a position.** — A 007
- **A position "is described by" a job** — B 007

In an organizational plan, a position is described by a job. Thereby, the position inherits the tasks of the job. A job may describe several positions and a position may be described by several jobs. A person or user may not hold a job, only a position.

### 11.3.4 A Person Holds a Position

- **A position is assigned to a person as the "holder"** — B 008
- **A person is the "holder" of a position** — A 008

In an organizational plan, a person holds a position and is thereby required to perform the tasks of the position. A position may be held by more than one person and a person may hold more than one position.

### 11.3.5 A Position is Chief of its Organizational Unit

- **A position "manages" an organizational unit** — A 012
- **An organizational unit "is managed by" a position** — B 012

In an organizational plan, a position may be the head of the organizational unit to which it belongs. All other positions in the organizational unit then report to him. This managerial role is often used in business processes, e.g. approving leave, travel, etc. It is also used for giving authorization to manager to see data of his subordinate employees.

### 11.3.6 A Position Reports to Another Position

- **A position "reports to" another position.** — A 002

  Example: The position Payroll Administrator "reports to" the Payroll Manager.
- **A position "is line supervisor of" another position** — B 002

  Example: The Payroll Manager "is line supervisor of" the Payroll Administrator.

By specifying chief of an organizational unit, you specify which position reports to whom. However, the requirements of some organizations may not be met by the above design. For example, if your organizational units are very large, you may have intermediate reporting positions. You can directly specify reporting between positions, thus creating a reporting structure. Reporting structure gives you more flexibility, but requires more effort, as it has to be maintained in addition to the organizational structure. You also have to ensure consistency between the two structures.

### 11.3.7 An Organizational Unit Incorporates a Cost Center

| | |
|---|---|
| • **An organizational unit "incorporates" a cost center** | **B 003** |

The cost incurred by an organizational unit may be charged to a cost center. This is represented by the above relationship. Note that there is no reverse relationship created between cost center and organizational unit. This is because cost center is an external object. You will not find a cost center in the table of objects HRP1000. However, it is just a question of what SAP stores and what it interprets. From a user's perspective, the relationship between cost center and organizational unit exists, regardless of whether it is stored or not.

## 11.4 RELATIONSHIPS (INFOTYPE 1001)

| *Functional Consultant* | *User* | *Business Process Owner* | *Senior Management* | *My Rating* | *Understanding Level* |
|---|---|---|---|---|---|
| A | A | A | A | | |

In SAP you specify relationships between objects to create structures. Thus, by specifying reporting relationship between higher level organizational units and lower level organizational units, you create organizational structure. By linking positions to organizational units in the organizational structure you create organizational plan. All these relationships are stored in infotype 1001. No matter which interface you use, you can create relationships. In transaction PP01, you can select infotype Relationships and click to see all the relationships of an object.

| | | |
|---|---|---|
| Organizational unit | ABC Consult | ABC Consultants |
| Planning Status | Active | |
| Relationships | 01 O 50015902 1 | |

| Start | End | R.. | R... | Relat.text | R.. | Rel'd object ID | Abbr. | % Rate |
|---|---|---|---|---|---|---|---|---|
| 02.12.2008 | 31.12.9999 | A | 011 | Cost cente | K | 00011100010100 | MUV - postin | 0.00 |
| 02.12.2008 | 31.12.9999 | B | 002 | Is line su | O | 50015903 | SAP Consult | 0.00 |
| 02.12.2008 | 31.12.9999 | B | 002 | Is line su | O | 50015904 | SAP Educaton | 0.00 |
| 02.12.2008 | 31.12.9999 | B | 003 | Incorporat | S | 50015968 | CEO | 0.00 |

You can select a line and see its details.

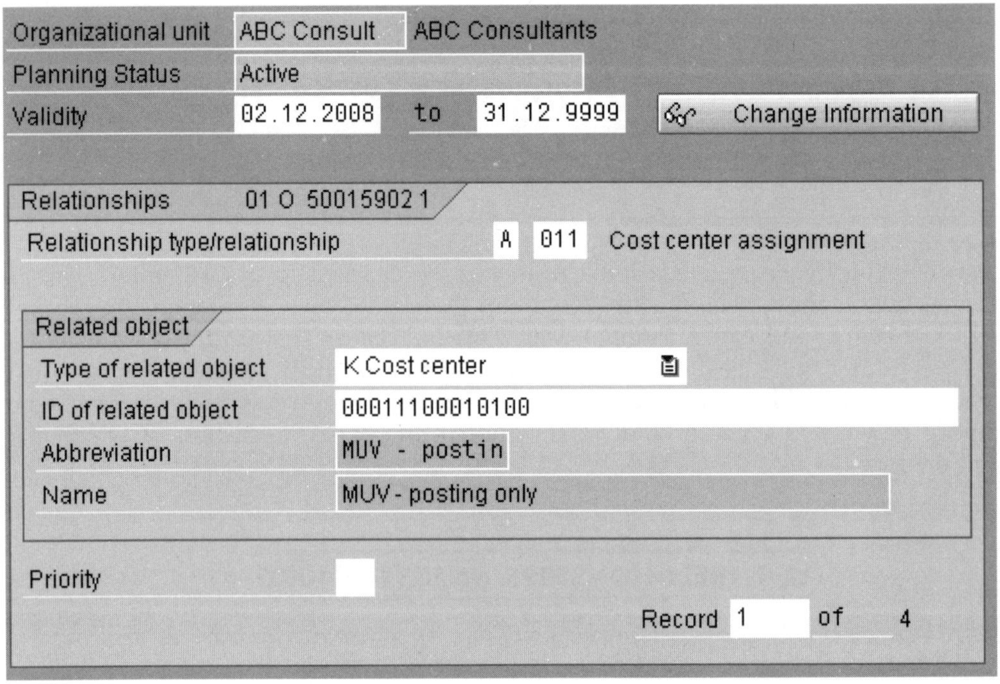


### *Object*

Object (organizational unit) whose relationship is being viewed or changed.

### *Planning status*

This field shows the planning status of the relationship, not of the object.

### *Validity*

An organizational unit can have one cost center up to certain date, and another after that date. This is stored using validity period of relationship. Similarly, a position may have one holder up to certain date and another holder after that date.

### *Change information*

If you click this icon, the system will show the user who created or last changed the record and the date when this was done.

### *Relationship type and relationship*

Objects relate to each other in different ways. The field 'relationship' identifies the nature of relationship, e.g. parent–child relationship. This relationship has two views, viz. 'X is parent of Y' and 'Y is child of X'. In SAP, each relationship is given a code and the two views are called type A and type B. While creating a relationship record, you should first specify the type of related object. It is then easier to select the relationship from a smaller list.

#### *Type, ID, abbreviation and name of related object*

This is the object with which the first object is related.

#### *Priority*

When multiple objects are located at the same hierarchical level of a structure, these must be ordered in a specific sequence from left-to-right (or from top-down). This is done by assigning priority values, where the value 1 is the highest (far left or top) and 99 the lowest priority (far right or bottom). If you specify no priority, the system places objects according to their object IDs.

## 11.5 PROPERTIES OF RELATIONSHIPS

| *Functional Consultant* | *User* | *Business Process Owner* | *Senior Management* | *My Rating* | *Understanding Level* |
|---|---|---|---|---|---|
| A | A | A | A | | |

### 11.5.1 Inheritance

Some relationships are inherited from the relationships of parent objects. Organizational units inherit the cost center assignment of their parent organizational unit in the absence of their own assignment. Positions inherit the tasks related to the job that describes them. Positions may also have direct relationships to tasks in addition to the inherited tasks.

### 11.5.2 Time Constraint

Time constraints are used by the system to guarantee the integrity of data. They ensure that the data is consistent and does not contradict each other. For example, an object can have only one name on a given day. It may have different names on different days but on a given day it must have only one name. Time constraints of infotypes are specified in table T777Z, where it can be defined at infotype level, infotype + subtype level, or infotype + subtype + object type level. For Relationships infotype 1001, time constraints are defined mostly at the level of type of relationship (subtype of infotype 1001). In exceptional cases, the time constraint may also depend on target object type and is defined in table T77ZR.

| *TC* | *Description* | *Explanation* | *Example* |
|---|---|---|---|
| 0 | May only exist once | Information must exist for the entire life cycle of the object and cannot be changed. | This time constraint is applicable only to infotype 1957. |
| 1 | Without gaps | Information must exist for the entire life cycle of the object but can be changed. | Infotype 1000 (Objects) has time constraint 1, as it must exist without gap. This time constraint is not applicable to any relationship. |
| 2 | With gaps | Information is optional but can exist only once within a user-defined period. | Infotype 1001, subtype A002 has time constraint 2. An organizational unit can report to only one organizational unit at a time, but there may be periods when it reports to none. |
| 3 | As often as required | Information is optional, and many data records can exist simultaneously within a user-defined period. | Infotype 1001, subtype B002 has time constraint 3. An organizational unit can be line supervisor of 0, 1, or more organizational units at the same time. |

### 11.5.3 Inverse Relationship

When a relationship is created, the inverse relationship is created by the system where applicable.

## 11.6 CLASSIFICATION OF RELATIONSHIPS

| *Functional Consultant* | *User* | *Business Process Owner* | *Senior Management* | *My Rating* | *Understanding Level* |
|---|---|---|---|---|---|
| A | X | X | X | | |

### 11.6.1 Hierarchical

Relationship between a higher level organizational unit and lower level organizational unit is hierarchical. In SAP, many relationships are hierarchical and often they are used to form multilevel hierarchies.

### 11.6.2 Lateral

In certain relationships one cannot say which of the two related objects is higher, e.g. the relationship between job and position. These relationships are called lateral relationships. Two jobs which are equivalent to each other also have a lateral relationship.

### 11.6.3 Unilateral

When you create a relationship between two objects, SAP stores two records in infotype 1001. First record links object X to Y, and the second record links object Y to X. This is done to facilitate the process of creating structures. Both the objects exist in infotype 1000. However, there are certain objects, which are not created in Organizational Management. Persons and cost centers are two examples. These are called external objects. For such objects, only one relationship record is kept. The relationship starting from an external object is not kept in infotype 1001. These relationships are called unilateral relationships.

## 11.7 ALLOWED RELATIONSHIPS

| *Functional Consultant* | *User* | *Business Process Owner* | *Senior Management* | *My Rating* | *Understanding Level* |
|---|---|---|---|---|---|
| A | B | C | X | | |

Certain relationships make sense only between certain object types. Therefore, SAP has specified which relationships are allowed between which object types. If you are creating a relationship record, you can display allowed relationship by choosing Extras ➢ Allowed relationships. Allowed relationships are stored in view T777E. The report RHRELAT0 (Allowed Relationships of Object Types) reports on the relationships permitted for an object type.

# CHAPTER 12

# Structures

## 12.1 STRUCTURE DEFINITION

| *Functional Consultant* | *User* | *Business Process Owner* | *Senior Management* | *My Rating* | *Understanding Level* |
|---|---|---|---|---|---|
| A | A | A | A | | |

An organization consists of organizational units, positions, persons, etc. These objects are related to each other to form various structures. SAP does not have separate database tables for each structure; that would limit SAP to only those structures for which it created database tables. Instead it has a flexible solution. It stores all objects in infotype 1000 (table HRP1000) and all relationships in infotype 1001 (table HRP1001). A structure uses some of these objects and some of these relationships in a certain way. These are defined in an evaluation path. Thus, using objects, relationships and evaluation paths, you can create unlimited number of structures.

## 12.2 EVALUATION PATH

| *Functional Consultant* | *User* | *Business Process Owner* | *Senior Management* | *My Rating* | *Understanding Level* |
|---|---|---|---|---|---|
| A | A | A | A | | |

You can maintain evaluation paths using transaction OOAW. The system first shows the list of evaluation paths.

| EvalPath | Info | Evaluation path text |
|---|---|---|
| A* | i | |
| A-S-O | i | Work center - position - org. unit / holder |
| A/B200_Q | i | Alternative qualifications |
| A001 | i | Is a subdivision of |

You can select an evaluation path and maintain its properties or create an evaluation path starting with Z.

| Evaluation Path | PLSTE | Position overview along organizational structure |
|---|---|---|

| No. | Obj.Type | A/B | Relat'ship | Relationship name | Priority | Rel.obj.type | Skip |
|---|---|---|---|---|---|---|---|
| 10 | O | B | 003 | Incorporates | * | S | ☐ |
| 20 | O | B | 002 | Is line supervisor of | * | O | ☐ |

The above evaluation path represents a pattern. You specify a starting organizational unit. According to the first line of the above evaluation path, all positions belonging to the starting organizational unit are found. Then, all organizational units reporting to the starting organizational unit are found. Thus, the first level structure of the starting organizational unit has organizational units and positions under it. The evaluation does not stop there. It is repeated for each organizational unit in the first level, giving the second level. This continues until there are no more organizational units in the last level.

The evaluation takes place in the sequence of number. The system matches the object type. Then it looks for relationship records where relationship (e.g. B003), priority and related object type matches. It selects all the objects found in the order of priority and goes to the next line of the evaluation path for each object. If skip is ticked, the next object is found, but the relationship is not displayed in the structure.

## 12.3 USING EVALUATION PATHS IN SAP PROGRAMS

| *Functional Consultant* | *User* | *Business Process Owner* | *Senior Management* | *My Rating* | *Understanding Level* |
|---|---|---|---|---|---|
| A | C | X | X | | |

SAP programs use the evaluation paths created by SAP. If you create your own evaluation paths which are slightly different from SAP's evaluation paths, you may want that evaluation path to be used instead. SAP lets you do this. Instead of hard-coding the evaluation path in the program, it picks them from view V_T77S0AW. If you want to use your own evaluation path, you can put it in this view, replacing SAP's entry, and the system will use the evaluation path specified by you.

| Group | Sem. abbr. | Description |
|---|---|---|
| PPWAY | A030 | Specialization |
| PPWAY | A605 | Appraisal Template |
| PPWAY | ALTQ | Alternative qualifications |
| PPWAY | ANFOR | Requirements of position, job, work center |

## 12.4 IMPORTANT STRUCTURES

| *Functional Consultant* | *User* | *Business Process Owner* | *Senior Management* | *My Rating* | *Understanding Level* |
|---|---|---|---|---|---|
| A | A | A | A | | |

### 12.4.1 Organizational Structure

***Evaluation path***

Evaluation Path | ORGEH | Organizational structure

| No. | Obj.Type | A/B | Relat'ship | Relationship name | Priority | Rel.obj.type | Skip |
|---|---|---|---|---|---|---|---|
| 10 | O | B | 002 | Is line supervisor of | * | O | ☐ |

***Structure***

You can see the organizational structure starting from the highest organizational unit, or starting from any other organizational unit (in all structures you specify the starting object). For the specified organizational unit, the next level organizational units are selected. Then for each organizational unit in the first level, next level organizational units are selected. This goes on until there are no more organizational units below the last level organizational units. In standard reporting, transaction S_AHR_61016493 uses evaluation path ORGEH to display the organizational structure.

**Plan Version:** 01
**Evaluation Path:** ORGEH (Organizational structure)
**Depth:** 0
**Status Vector:** 1
**Evaluation Period:** 01.01.1900 - 31.12.9999

| Object Description | Object abbr. | Object Type | Extended object ID |
|---|---|---|---|
| ▽ ABC Consultants Ltd. | ABC Consult | O | 50000075 |
| SAP Consulting | SAP Consult | O | 50000076 |
| SAP Education | SAP Educaton | O | 50000077 |

### 12.4.2 Organizational Structure with Positions

***Evaluation path***

Evaluation Path | PLSTE | Position overview along organizational structure

| No. | Obj.Type | A/B | Relat'ship | Relationship name | Priority | Rel.obj.type | Skip |
|---|---|---|---|---|---|---|---|
| 10 | O | B | 003 | Incorporates | * | S | ☐ |
| 20 | O | B | 002 | Is line supervisor of | * | O | ☐ |

***Structure***

This structure shows the complete organizational structure and positions under each organizational unit. In standard reporting, transaction S_AHR_61016494 uses evaluation path PLSTE to display the organizational structure with positions.

**Plan Version:** 01
**Evaluation Path:** PLSTE (Position overview along organizational structure)
**Depth:** 0
**Status Vector:** 1
**Evaluation Period:** 01.01.1900 - 31.12.9999

| Object Description | Object abbr. | O | Extended... | S | Start Date... | End Date... |
|---|---|---|---|---|---|---|
| ABC Consultants Ltd. | ABC Consult | O | 50000075 | 1 | 09.12.2008 | 31.12.9999 |
| Chief Executive Officer | CEO | S | 50000078 | 1 | 09.12.2008 | 31.12.9999 |
| SAP Consulting | SAP Consult | O | 50000076 | 1 | 09.12.2008 | 31.12.9999 |
| SAP HR Consultant | SAP HR | S | 50000079 | 1 | 09.12.2008 | 31.12.9999 |
| SAP FI/CO Consultant | SAP FI/CO | S | 50000080 | 1 | 09.12.2008 | 31.12.9999 |
| SAP MM Consultant | SAP MM | S | 50000081 | 1 | 09.12.2008 | 31.12.9999 |
| SAP PP Consultant | SAP PP | S | 50000082 | 1 | 09.12.2008 | 31.12.9999 |
| SAP PS Consultant | SAP PS | S | 50000083 | 1 | 09.12.2008 | 31.12.9999 |
| SAP PM Consultant | SAP PM | S | 50000084 | 1 | 09.12.2008 | 31.12.9999 |
| SAP Basis Consultant | SAP Basis | S | 50000085 | 1 | 09.12.2008 | 31.12.9999 |
| SAP ABAP Consultant | SAP ABAP | S | 50000086 | 1 | 09.12.2008 | 31.12.9999 |
| SAP Education | SAP Educaton | O | 50000077 | 1 | 09.12.2008 | 31.12.9999 |
| SAP Education Coordinator | SAP Edu Coor | S | 50000087 | 1 | 09.12.2008 | 31.12.9999 |

### 12.4.3 Organizational Structure with Positions and Persons

***Evaluation path***

| Evaluation Path | O-O-S-P | Staff assignments along organizational structure |
|---|---|---|

| No. | Obj.Type | A/B | Relat'ship | Relationship name | Priority | Rel.obj.type | Skip |
|---|---|---|---|---|---|---|---|
| 5 | O | B | 002 | Is line supervisor of | * | O | ☐ |
| 10 | O | B | 003 | Incorporates | * | S | ☐ |
| 20 | S | A | 008 | Holder | * | P | ☐ |

***Structure***

This structure shows the complete organizational structure with positions and persons under each organizational unit. You can use transaction S_AHR_61016528 with evaluation path O-O-S-P to display organizational structure with positions and persons.

**Plan Version:** 01
**Evaluation Path:** O-O-S-P (Staff assignments along organizational structure)
**Depth:** 0
**Status Vector:** 1
**Evaluation Period:** 01.01.1900 - 31.12.9999

| Object Description | Object abbr. | O | Extended ... | S | Start Date ... | End Date ... |
|---|---|---|---|---|---|---|
| ABC Consultants Ltd. | ABC Consult | O | 50000075 | 1 | 09.12.2008 | 31.12.9999 |
| SAP Consulting | SAP Consult | O | 50000076 | 1 | 09.12.2008 | 31.12.9999 |
| SAP Education | SAP Educaton | O | 50000077 | 1 | 09.12.2008 | 31.12.9999 |
| Chief Executive Officer | CEO | S | 50000078 | 1 | 09.12.2008 | 31.12.9999 |
| Agrawal Prem | Agrawal | P | 00121715 | 1 | 12.12.2008 | 31.12.9999 |

### 12.4.4 Organizational Structure with Persons

***Evaluation path***

| Evaluation Path | PERS-O | Persons along an organizational structure |
|---|---|---|

| No. | Obj.Type | A/B | Relat'ship | Relationship name | Priority | Rel.obj.type | Skip |
|---|---|---|---|---|---|---|---|
| 10 | O | B | 003 | Incorporates | * | S | ☑ |
| 20 | S | A | 008 | Holder | * | P | ☐ |
| 30 | O | B | 002 | Is line supervisor of | * | O | ☐ |

***Structure***

This structure shows the complete organizational structure and persons under each organizational unit. Note that the persons are attached to positions, but positions are omitted from display because skip checkbox is ticked. In standard reporting, transaction S_AHR_61016495 uses evaluation path PERS-O to display the organizational structure with persons.

**Plan Version:** 01
**Evaluation Path:** PERS-O (Persons along an organizational structure)
**Depth:** 0
**Status Vector:** 1
**Evaluation Period:** 01.01.1900 - 31.12.9999

| Object Description | Object abbr. | O | Extended ... | S | Start Date ... | End Date ... |
|---|---|---|---|---|---|---|
| ▽ ☐ ABC Consultants Ltd. | ABC Consult | O | 50000075 | 1 | 09.12.2008 | 31.12.9999 |
| Agrawal Prem | Agrawal | P | 00121715 | 1 | 12.12.2008 | 31.12.9999 |
| ▽ ☐ SAP Consulting | SAP Consult | O | 50000076 | 1 | 09.12.2008 | 31.12.9999 |
| Verma Abhishek | Verma | P | 00123459 | 1 | 01.01.2009 | 31.12.9999 |
| Mehta Ashish | Mehta | P | 00123460 | 1 | 01.01.2009 | 31.12.9999 |
| Yadav Raghunath | Yadav | P | 00123461 | 1 | 01.01.2009 | 31.12.9999 |
| Abhinav Desai | Abhinav | P | 00123462 | 1 | 01.01.2009 | 31.12.9999 |
| Sharma Vinod | Sharma | P | 00123463 | 1 | 01.01.2009 | 31.12.9999 |
| Sinha Alok | Sinha | P | 00123464 | 1 | 01.01.2009 | 31.12.9999 |
| Bansal Meenakshi | Bansal | P | 00123465 | 1 | 01.01.2009 | 31.12.9999 |
| ▽ ☐ SAP Education | SAP Educaton | O | 50000077 | 1 | 09.12.2008 | 31.12.9999 |
| Gupta Ranjana | Gupta | P | 00123466 | 1 | 01.01.2009 | 31.12.9999 |

## 12.4.5 Organizational Structure with Work Centers

Evaluation Path ARBP-O Work center assignment along organizational structure

| No. | Obj.Type | A/B | Relat'ship | Relationship name | Priority | Rel.obj.type | Skip |
|---|---|---|---|---|---|---|---|
| 10 | O | B | 003 | Incorporates | * | S | ☑ |
| 20 | O | B | 002 | Is line supervisor of | * | O | ☐ |
| 30 | S | B | 003 | Incorporates | * | A | ☐ |
| 40 | S | B | 002 | Is line supervisor of | * | S | ☑ |

***Structure***

This structure shows the complete organizational structure and work centers under each organizational unit. Note that the persons are attached to positions, but positions are omitted from display because skip checkbox is ticked. In standard reporting, transaction S_AHR_61016496 uses evaluation path ARBP-O to display the organizational structure with work centers. If there are positions reporting to positions within an organizational unit, their work centers are also displayed.

**Plan Version:** 01
**Evaluation Path:** ARBP-O (Work center assignment along organizational struct)
**Depth:** 0
**Status Vector:** 1
**Evaluation Period:** 01.01.1900 - 31.12.9999

| Object Description | Object abbr. | O | Extended... | S | Start Date... | End Date... |
|---|---|---|---|---|---|---|
| ABC Consultants Ltd. | ABC Consult | O | 50000075 | 1 | 09.12.2008 | 31.12.9999 |
| SAP Consulting | SAP Consult | O | 50000076 | 1 | 09.12.2008 | 31.12.9999 |
| SAP Consulting Work Center | SAP Cons Cen | A | 50000000 | 1 | 08.09.1995 | 31.12.9999 |
| SAP Education | SAP Educaton | O | 50000077 | 1 | 09.12.2008 | 31.12.9999 |

## 12.4.6 Reporting Structure without Persons

***Evaluation path***

Evaluation Path: ORGA — Supervisory and subordinate positions

| No. | Obj.Type | A/B | Relat'ship | Relationship name | Priority | Rel.obj.type | Skip |
|---|---|---|---|---|---|---|---|
| 10 | S | B | 002 | Is line supervisor of | * | S | ☐ |

***Structure***

This structure shows all position to position reporting. In standard reporting, transaction S_AHR_61016512 uses evaluation path ORGA to display the reporting structure.

**Plan Version:** 01
**Evaluation Path:** ORGA (Supervisory and subordinate positions)
**Depth:** 0
**Status Vector:** 1
**Evaluation Period:** 01.01.1900 - 31.12.9999

| Object Description | Object abbr. | O | Extended... | S | Start Date... | End Date... |
|---|---|---|---|---|---|---|
| SAP HR Consultant | SAP HR | S | 50000079 | 1 | 09.12.2008 | 31.12.9999 |
| SAP ABAP Consultant | SAP ABAP | S | 50000086 | 1 | 09.12.2008 | 31.12.9999 |

### 12.4.7 Reporting Structure with Persons

***Evaluation path***

Evaluation Path | ORGA-P | Supervisory and subordinate positions with person display

| No. | Obj.Type | A/B | Relat'ship | Relationship name | Priority | Rel.obj.type | Skip |
|---|---|---|---|---|---|---|---|
| 10 | S | A | 008 | Holder | * | P | ☐ |
| 20 | S | B | 002 | Is line supervisor of | * | S | ☐ |

***Structure***

This structure shows all position to position reporting along with holders of those positions. In standard reporting, transaction S_AHR_61016513 uses evaluation path ORGA-P to display the reporting structure.

**Plan Version:** 01
**Evaluation Path:** ORGA-P (Supervisory and subordinate positions with person)
**Depth:** 0
**Status Vector:** 1
**Evaluation Period:** 01.01.1900 - 31.12.9999

| Object Description | Object abbr. | O | Extended... | S | Start Date... | End Date... |
|---|---|---|---|---|---|---|
| SAP HR Consultant | SAP HR | S | 50000079 | 1 | 09.12.2008 | 31.12.9999 |
| SAP ABAP Consultant | SAP ABAP | S | 50000086 | 1 | 09.12.2008 | 31.12.9999 |
| Bansal Meenakshi | Bansal | P | 00123465 | 1 | 01.01.2009 | 31.12.9999 |

### 12.4.8 Activity Profile of Positions along Organizational Structure

***Evaluation path***

Evaluation Path | AUFGABEX | Activity profile of positions along organizational structure

| No. | Obj.Type | A/B | Relat'ship | Relationship name | Priority | Rel.obj.type | Skip |
|---|---|---|---|---|---|---|---|
| 10 | O | B | 003 | Incorporates | * | S | ☐ |
| 20 | O | B | 002 | Is line supervisor of | * | O | ☐ |
| 30 | S | B | 007 | Is described by | * | T | ☐ |
| 40 | S | B | 007 | Is described by | * | C | ☑ |
| 50 | S | B | 002 | Is line supervisor of | * | S | ☐ |
| 60 | C | B | 007 | Is described by | * | T | ☐ |
| 70 | T | B | 007 | Is described by | * | T | ☐ |

### *Structure*

This structure shows the organizational structure with positions and tasks. Tasks of the jobs associated with positions are also shown, but the jobs are not shown. If there are positions reporting to positions within an organizational unit, those positions and their tasks are also displayed. In standard reporting, transaction S_AHR_61016523 uses evaluation path AUFGABEX to show the tasks for positions along the organizational structure.

**Plan Version:** 01
**Evaluation Path:** AUFGABEX (Activity profile of positions along organizational
**Depth:** 0
**Status Vector:** 1
**Evaluation Period:** 01.01.1900 - 31.12.9999

| Object Description | Object abbr. | O | Extende... | S | Start Date... | End Date... |
|---|---|---|---|---|---|---|
| ABC Consultants Ltd. | ABC Consult | O | 50000075 | 1 | 09.12.2008 | 31.12.9999 |
| Chief Executive Officer | CEO | S | 50000078 | 1 | 09.12.2008 | 31.12.9999 |
| SAP Consulting | SAP Consult | O | 50000076 | 1 | 09.12.2008 | 31.12.9999 |
| SAP HR Consultant | SAP HR | S | 50000079 | 1 | 09.12.2008 | 31.12.9999 |
| Project preparation | Preparation | T | 50000097 | 1 | 10.12.2008 | 31.12.9999 |
| Hardware and software | Hard & So | T | 50000111 | 1 | 10.12.2008 | 31.12.9999 |
| Networking | Networking | T | 50000112 | 1 | 10.12.2008 | 31.12.9999 |
| Office space and facilitie | Office | T | 50000113 | 1 | 10.12.2008 | 31.12.9999 |
| Team building | Team | T | 50000114 | 1 | 10.12.2008 | 31.12.9999 |
| Blueprint | Blueprint | T | 50000098 | 1 | 10.12.2008 | 31.12.9999 |
| Study and document old | Old BP | T | 50000109 | 1 | 10.12.2008 | 31.12.9999 |
| Propose new business | New BP | T | 50000110 | 1 | 10.12.2008 | 31.12.9999 |
| Program development | Develop | T | 50000108 | 1 | 10.12.2008 | 31.12.9999 |
| Testing | Testing | T | 50000100 | 1 | 10.12.2008 | 31.12.9999 |
| Unit testing | Unit Test | T | 50000105 | 1 | 10.12.2008 | 31.12.9999 |
| Integration testing | Integ. test | T | 50000106 | 1 | 10.12.2008 | 31.12.9999 |
| Go live | Go Live | T | 50000101 | 1 | 10.12.2008 | 31.12.9999 |
| Data Preparation | Data Prepare | T | 50000103 | 1 | 10.12.2008 | 31.12.9999 |
| Data Upload | Data Upload | T | 50000104 | 1 | 10.12.2008 | 31.12.9999 |
| SAP ABAP Consultant | SAP ABAP | S | 50000086 | 1 | 09.12.2008 | 31.12.9999 |

### 12.4.9 Activity Profile of Positions with Persons along Organizational Structure

#### *Evaluation path*

Evaluation Path AUFGABEP Activity Profile of Positions with Persons Along Org. Structure

| No. | Obj.Type | A/B | Relat'ship | Relationship name | Priority | Rel.obj.type | Skip |
|---|---|---|---|---|---|---|---|
| 10 | O | B | 003 | Incorporates | * | S | ☐ |
| 20 | O | B | 002 | Is line supervisor of | * | O | ☐ |
| 30 | S | B | 007 | Is described by | * | T | ☐ |
| 40 | S | B | 007 | Is described by | * | C | ☑ |
| 50 | S | B | 002 | Is line supervisor of | * | S | ☐ |
| 60 | C | B | 007 | Is described by | * | T | ☐ |
| 70 | T | B | 007 | Is described by | * | T | ☐ |
| 80 | S | A | 008 | Holder | * | P | ☐ |

#### *Structure*

This structure is the same as above, except that the persons holding positions are also displayed. In standard reporting, transaction S_AHR_61016524 uses evaluation path AUFGABEP to show the tasks and persons for positions along the organizational structure.

**Plan Version:** 01
**Evaluation Path:** AUFGABEP (Activity Profile of Positions with Persons Along O
**Depth:** 0
**Status Vector:** 1
**Evaluation Period:** 01.01.1900 - 31.12.9999

| Object Description | Object abbr. | O | Extende... | S | Start Date... | End Date... |
|---|---|---|---|---|---|---|
| ABC Consultants Ltd. | ABC Consult | O | 50000075 | 1 | 09.12.2008 | 31.12.9999 |
| Chief Executive Officer | CEO | S | 50000078 | 1 | 09.12.2008 | 31.12.9999 |
| Agrawal Prem | Agrawal | P | 00121715 | 1 | 12.12.2008 | 31.12.9999 |
| SAP Consulting | SAP Consult | O | 50000076 | 1 | 09.12.2008 | 31.12.9999 |
| SAP HR Consultant | SAP HR | S | 50000079 | 1 | 09.12.2008 | 31.12.9999 |
| Project preparation | Preparation | T | 50000097 | 1 | 10.12.2008 | 31.12.9999 |
| Hardware and software | Hard & So | T | 50000111 | 1 | 10.12.2008 | 31.12.9999 |
| Networking | Networking | T | 50000112 | 1 | 10.12.2008 | 31.12.9999 |
| Office space and faciliti | Office | T | 50000113 | 1 | 10.12.2008 | 31.12.9999 |
| Team building | Team | T | 50000114 | 1 | 10.12.2008 | 31.12.9999 |
| Blueprint | Blueprint | T | 50000098 | 1 | 10.12.2008 | 31.12.9999 |
| Study and document olc | Old BP | T | 50000109 | 1 | 10.12.2008 | 31.12.9999 |
| Propose new business | New BP | T | 50000110 | 1 | 10.12.2008 | 31.12.9999 |
| Program development | Develop | T | 50000108 | 1 | 10.12.2008 | 31.12.9999 |
| Testing | Testing | T | 50000100 | 1 | 10.12.2008 | 31.12.9999 |
| Unit testing | Unit Test | T | 50000105 | 1 | 10.12.2008 | 31.12.9999 |
| Integration testing | Integ. test | T | 50000106 | 1 | 10.12.2008 | 31.12.9999 |
| Go live | Go Live | T | 50000101 | 1 | 10.12.2008 | 31.12.9999 |
| Data Preparation | Data Prepare | T | 50000103 | 1 | 10.12.2008 | 31.12.9999 |
| Data Upload | Data Upload | T | 50000104 | 1 | 10.12.2008 | 31.12.9999 |

## 12.5 STRUCTURE REPORTS

| Functional Consultant | User | Business Process Owner | Senior Management | My Rating | Understanding Level |
|---|---|---|---|---|---|
| A | A | A | A | | |

### *Displaying structures*

You can use transaction S_AHR_61016528 to display structures. You specify the evaluation path that determines the structure being shown.

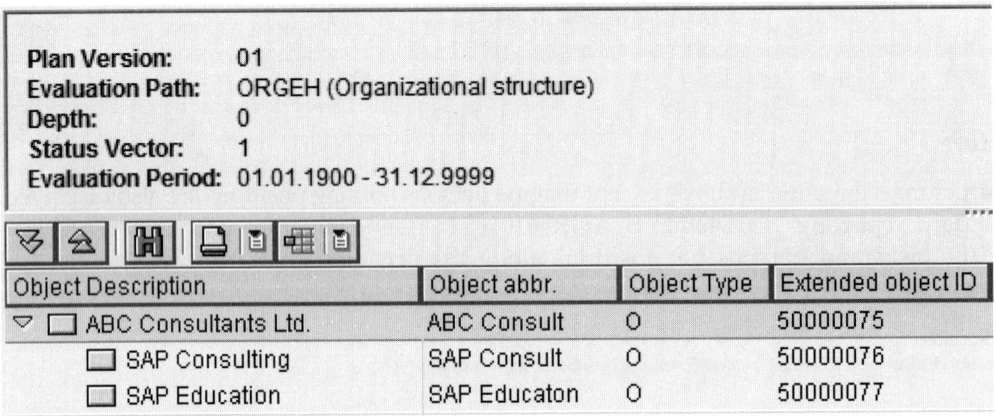


### *Structure navigation instrument*

You can use transaction S_AHR_61016529 to display objects in a structure by specifying the starting object and the evaluation path. The system shows all objects in the structure.

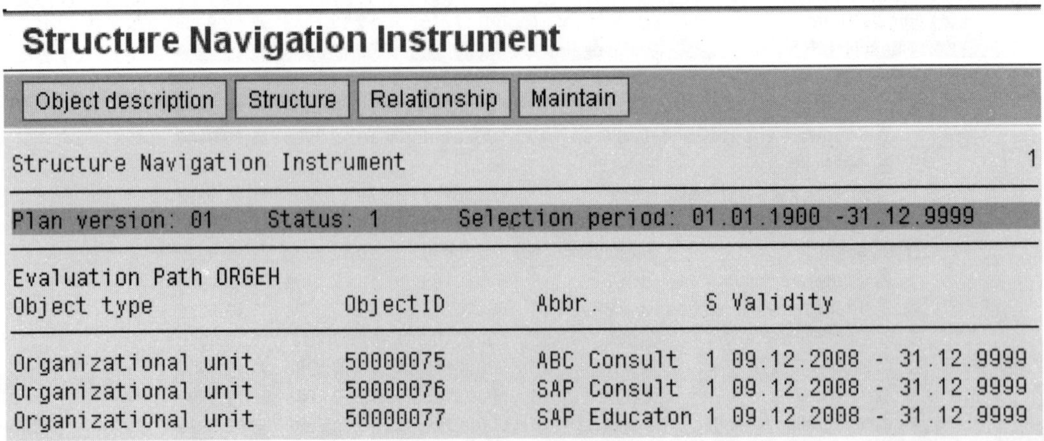

You can select an object and do the following.

| *Icon* | *Purpose* |
|---|---|
| Object description | You can display the selected object. |
| Structure | You specify the evaluation path and the system takes you to structure display/maintenance where you can maintain the structure. |
| Relationship | The system shows you all relationships of the object. You can select a line and perform all these functions for the related object. |
| Maintain | You can maintain the selected object. |

### *HR reporting via personnel planning structures*

You can run a Personnel Administration report for objects selected based on organizational plan using transaction RE_RHPNPSUB or S_AHR_61016533. In addition to the standard selection screen, the system gives the following additional fields on the selection screen.

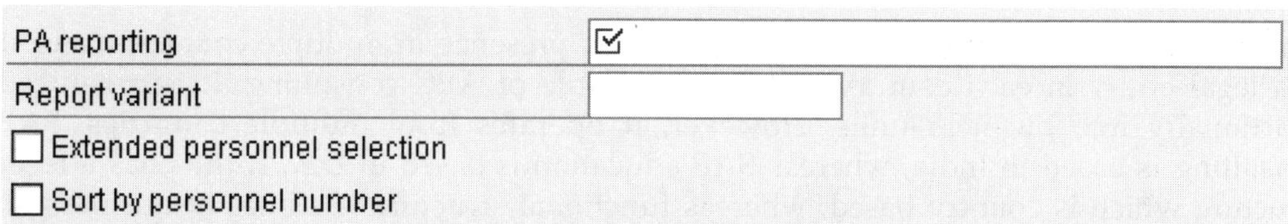


| *Selection parameter* | *Description* |
|---|---|
| PA reporting | Here you enter the report name you want to run. |
| Report variant | If you have saved a report variant, and you would like to run that variant, you specify that here. |
| Extended personnel selection | If you tick this checkbox, you can select from the parameters in Personnel Administration. |
| Sort by personnel number | If you tick this checkbox, you can sort the report by personnel number. |

## 12.6 MATRIX STRUCTURES

| *Functional Consultant* | *User* | *Business Process Owner* | *Senior Management* | *My Rating* | *Understanding Level* |
|---|---|---|---|---|---|
| A | A | A | A | | |

### 12.6.1 Purpose and Overview

An organizational plan is structured like a tree. You start with top level organizational unit, which has smaller organizational units. The smaller organizational units may in turn have still smaller organizational units and so on. There are positions which may belong to any of these organizational units. Then there are persons who occupy these positions.

HR practitioners have found difficulties with this concept of single position reporting. Should the finance manager of a plant report to the plant head, or should he report to the corporate finance manager? In such situations, many companies adopt dual reporting. Plant finance manager reports to the corporate finance manager functionally, and to the plant head administratively. This is called matrix organizational structure.

Similar situation may arise when a company has presence in multiple countries, and it is a legal entity in each country. Take the example of ABC consulting. It is organized functionally into business units. However, it operates from multiple countries. SAP consulting is based in India, whereas SAP education is based in U.K. It thus has a legal structure which is country based, whereas functional structure has lines of businesses. SAP supports matrix structures. Matrix structures have two dimensions. You create both the structures independently and then create relationship between objects of dimension 1 and objects of dimension 2.

### 12.6.2 Matrix Structure Definition

You can predefine your matrix structures in view T779M. Here you define both the dimensions and the relationship of objects in dimension 1 with objects in dimension 2. In each dimension, you specify the dimension name, the object type and the evaluation path.

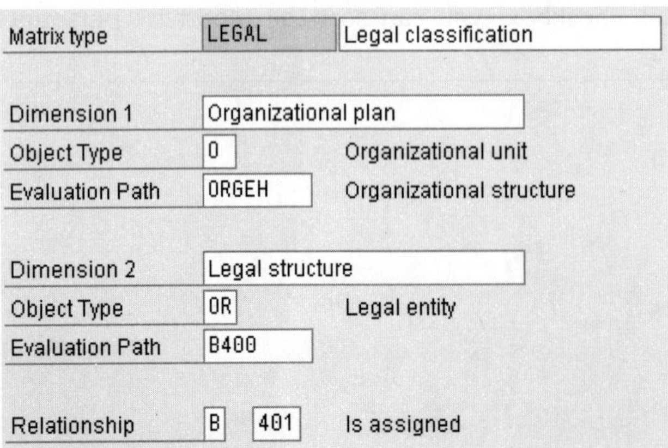

| | | | |
|---|---|---|---|
| Matrix type | LEGAL | | Legal classification |
| Dimension 1 | Organizational plan | | |
| Object Type | O | | Organizational unit |
| Evaluation Path | ORGEH | | Organizational structure |
| Dimension 2 | Legal structure | | |
| Object Type | OR | | Legal entity |
| Evaluation Path | B400 | | |
| Relationship | B | 401 | Is assigned |

### 12.6.3 Matrix Structure Creation

You create both the structures independently and then create relationship between objects of dimension 1 and objects of dimension 2. The matrix structure can be created or changed using transaction PPME and viewed using transaction PPMS. When you run transaction PPME, you get the following screen.

Here you can specify the matrix type. If you specify the matrix type, the system takes details of the two dimensions from view T779M. However, it is not mandatory. If you don't define the matrix structure here, you can directly input the parameters in standard selection. If you saved a variant while using this program earlier, you can specify that variant. In the selection screen, the system gives you a choice of three views.

***Structure dimension 1 view***

In structure dimension 1 view, the structure of dimension 1 is displayed. Dimension 2 objects are shown linked to dimension 1 structure. Dimension 2 structure is not shown.

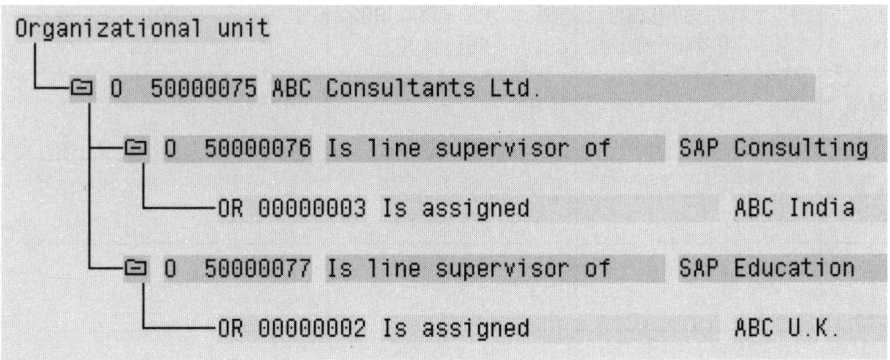

### *Structure dimension 2 view*

In structure dimension 2 view, the structure of dimension 2 is displayed. Dimension 1 objects are shown linked to dimension 2 structure. Dimension 1 structure is not shown.

```
Legal entity
 └─ OR 00000001 ABC World Wide
     ├─ OR 00000002 Is parent of          ABC U.K.
     │   └──O  50000077 Is assigned          SAP Education
     └─ OR 00000003 Is parent of          ABC India
         └──O  50000076 Is assigned          SAP Consulting
```

### *Matrix view*

In the matrix view, dimension 1 is shown as rows and dimension 2 as columns. Dark squares show the relationship between the two. You may switch on abbreviation (View ➢ Abbreviation on) to see the compact view of the matrix.

View: Organizational plan and Legal structure
Selection period: 05.03.2009 - 31.12.9999 Total number of columns: 3

| | 1 OR 00000001 ABC World | 2 OR 00000002 ABC U.K. | 3 OR 00000003 ABC India |
|---|---|---|---|
| 1 O 50000075 ABC Consult | □ | □ | □ |
| 2 O 50000076 SAP Consult | □ | □ | ■ |
| 3 O 50000077 SAP Educaton | □ | ■ | □ |

You can invert dimensions by clicking .

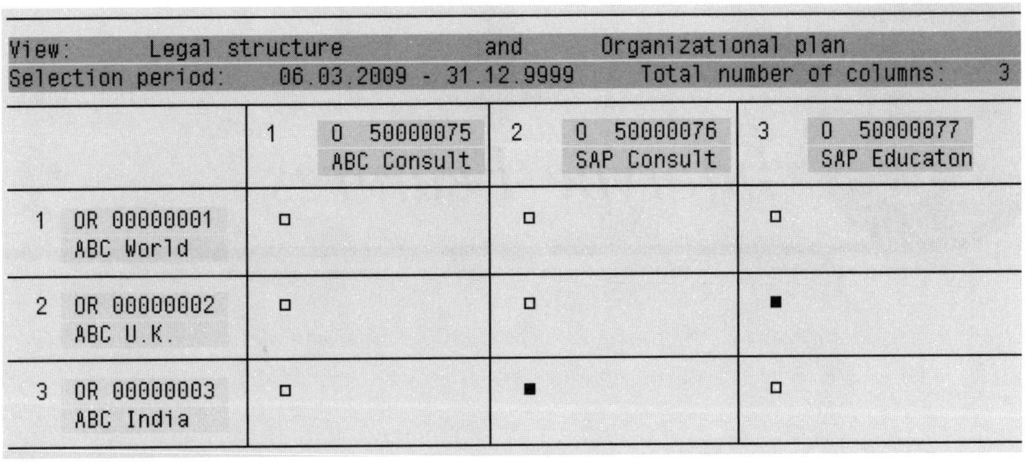


You can also show or hide additional object information such as the ID, the abbreviation, or the validity period. You can also create relationships by clicking the hollow squares.

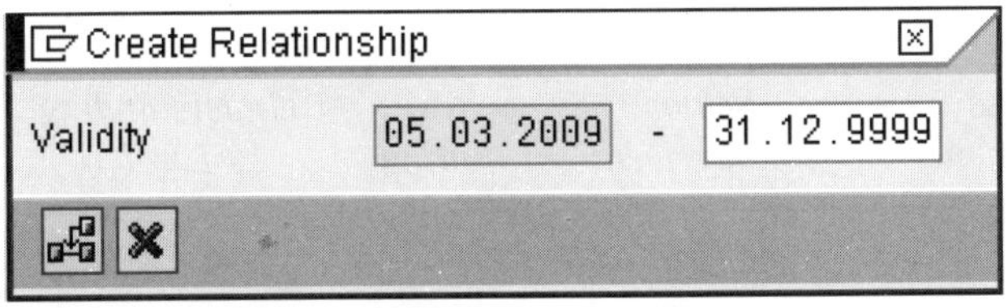


Similarly, you can delete a relationship by clicking a dark square.

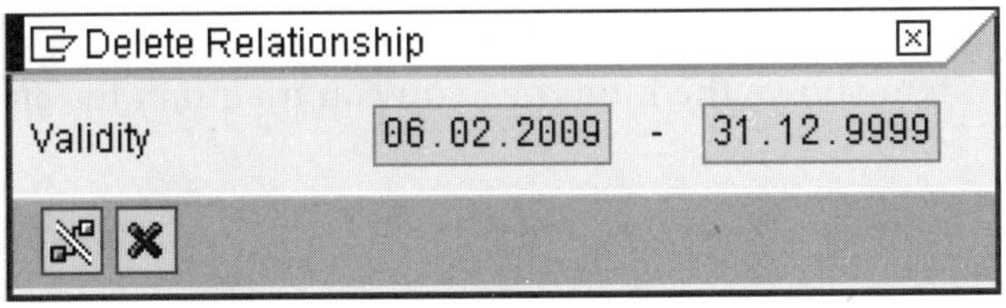


You can delimit a relationship by selecting a cell in the matrix (other than square), and clicking [icon].

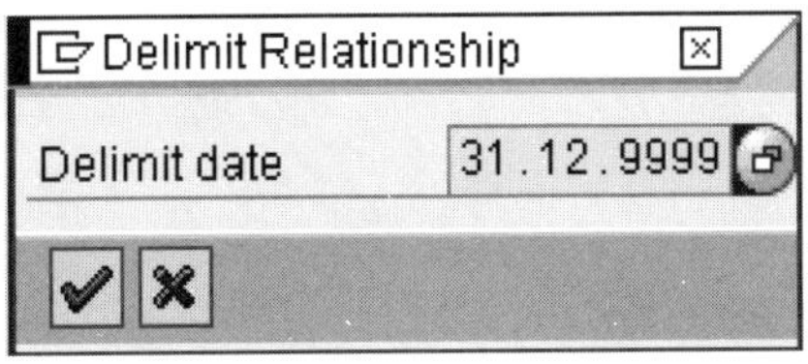

CHAPTER 13

# Infotype Features

## 13.1 INFOTYPES

| *Functional Consultant* | *User* | *Business Process Owner* | *Senior Management* | *My Rating* | *Understanding Level* |
|---|---|---|---|---|---|
| A | A | A | A | | |

It is not enough to create structures using objects and relationships. There is need to maintain information about objects. Information about objects is maintained in infotypes. Each infotype is a logical group of information. SAP provides a large number of infotypes. When you run transaction PP01, the system shows the infotypes you can maintain for an object.

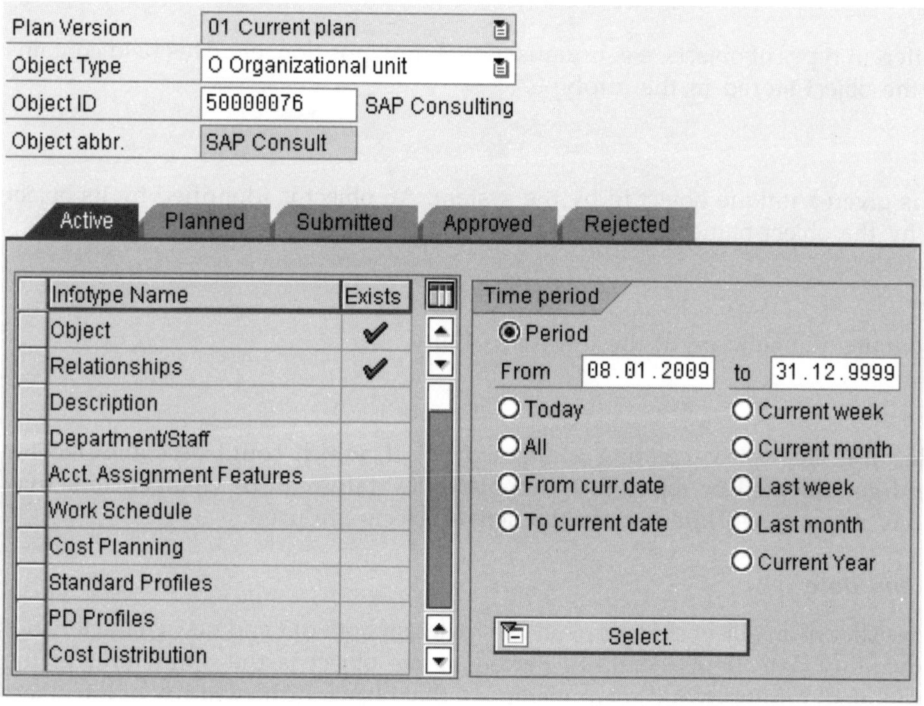


## 13.2 INFOTYPES COMMON STRUCTURE

| *Functional Consultant* | *User* | *Business Process Owner* | *Senior Management* | *My Rating* | *Understanding Level* |
|---|---|---|---|---|---|
| A | A | A | A | | |

Important infotypes are discussed in subsequent chapters. However, there are certain fields which are common to all infotypes. These will be discussed here to avoid repetition. Personnel planning infotypes are stored in HRPnnnn tables where nnnn is infotype number.

### *Client*

In a SAP server there may be multiple clients. When you logon to SAP, you specify the client. All the data you create in infotypes is stored with logon client in client field.

### *Plan version*

SAP lets you create alternative organizational plans using plan version. For each infotype record the plan version is stored in this field.

### *Object type*

There are different types of objects, e.g. organizational unit, position, etc. This field contains the type of the object stored in the infotype.

### *Object id*

Each object is given a unique object id by the system. An object is identified by its object id, and not by the object name.

### *Subtype*

This field contains the subtype of the infotype, if any.

### *Planning status*

SAP provides you facility for creating a planned object, which could be submitted for approval, and get accepted or rejected. If accepted, the status can be changed to active. For day to day use, e.g. workflow, only the active objects are used.

### *Start date, end date*

If the characteristics of an object changes, you can maintain both old and new characteristics using these validity date fields. Validity period of the object is the outer limit of the validity period of all infotypes and relationships of that object. If the validity of the object is delimited, validity of all its relationships and infotypes is also delimited.

### *Language key*

You can maintain object details in multiple languages.

### *Number of infotype record with same key*

If time constraint of an infotype permits multiple records to be held on the same day, this system generated field ensures uniqueness of the primary key.

### *Concatenation of object type and object id*

This field contains concatenation of object type and object id. This is only for operational ease of the SAP system.

### *Infotype*

Each database table contains data of only one infotype. This field contains that infotype number. This is also for operational ease of the SAP system.

### *Changed on*

The system automatically stores the date and time when an infotype record was created, or last changed.

### *User name*

The system automatically stores the name of the user who created, or last changed, an infotype record.

### *Reason*

If you specify the reason for changing an infotype record, that is stored in this field.

### *Historical record flag*

If you mark a record historical, it can be read but cannot be modified.

### *Text module for infotype*

This field contains the text module for the infotype, which contains more detailed description.

## 13.3 INFOTYPES ALLOWED FOR AN OBJECT TYPE

| *Functional Consultant* | *User* | *Business Process Owner* | *Senior Management* | *My Rating* | *Understanding Level* |
|---|---|---|---|---|---|
| A | A | A | A | | |

SAP has a large number of infotypes. For an object type only some of these make sense. Therefore, when you run transaction PP01, initially the system does not show any infotype. But when you select the object type, it shows all the infotypes which are allowed for that object type. Some of these infotypes are required in Organizational Management. Other infotypes are used for other functionalities of SAP. Infotypes which are allowed for an object type are stored in table T777I.

## 13.4 INFOTYPE TIME CONSTRAINT

| *Functional Consultant* | *User* | *Business Process Owner* | *Senior Management* | *My Rating* | *Understanding Level* |
|---|---|---|---|---|---|
| A | A | A | A | | |

Time constraints are used by the system to guarantee the integrity of data. They ensure that the data is consistent and does not contradict each other. For example, an object can have only one name on a given day. It may have different names on different days but on a given day it must have only one name. Time constraints of infotypes are specified in table T777Z, where it can be defined at infotype level, infotype + subtype level, or infotype + subtype + object type level. In exceptional cases, the time constraint may also depend on target object type and is defined in table T77ZR.

| *TC* | *Description* | *Explanation* | *Example* |
|---|---|---|---|
| 0 | May only exist once | Information must exist for the entire life cycle of the object and cannot be changed. | This time constraint is applicable only to infotype 1957. |
| 1 | Without gaps | Information must exist for the entire life cycle of the object but can be changed. | Infotype 1000 (Objects) has time constraint 1, as it must exist without gap. |
| 2 | With gaps | Information is optional but can exist only once within a user-defined period. | Infotype 1002 (Description) has time constraint 2. During different periods you may have different descriptions and for some period you may have none, but you can not have more than one description at the same time. |
| 3 | As often as required | Information is optional, and many data records can exist simultaneously within a user-defined period. | Infotype 1006 (Restrictions) has time constraint 3. At any time, you may have 0, 1, or more restrictions. |

## 13.5 INFOTYPE TOOLS AND REPORTS

| *Functional Consultant* | *User* | *Business Process Owner* | *Senior Management* | *My Rating* | *Understanding Level* |
|---|---|---|---|---|---|
| A | A | A | A | | |

***Infotype maintenance***

You can run transaction S_AHR_61016531 or PSO3 to display and maintain infotypes.

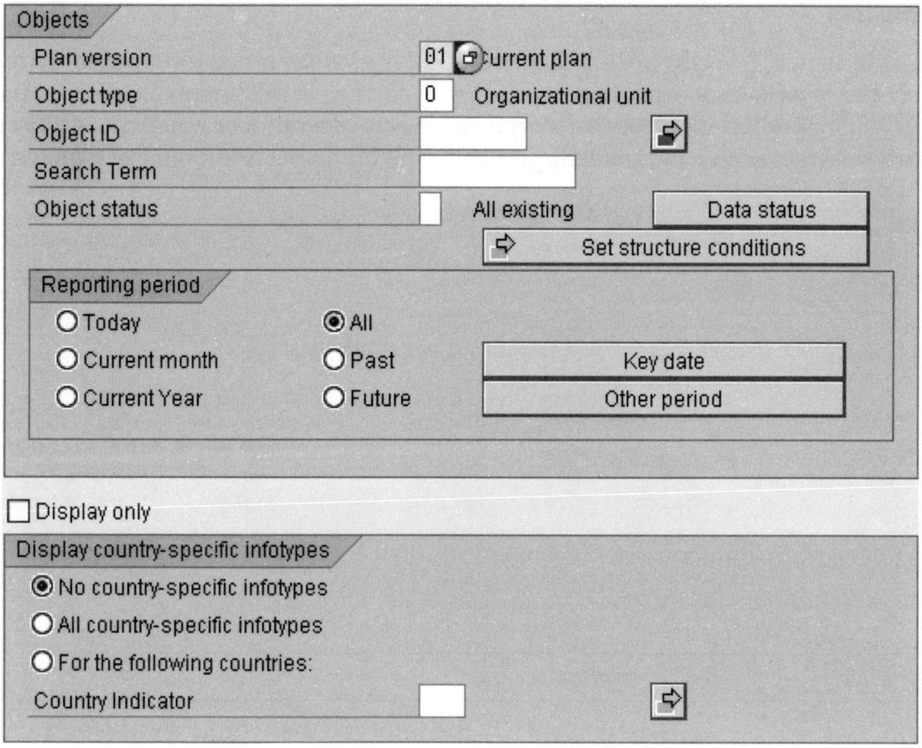


You can specify whether country-specific infotypes are to be displayed or not. If you specify an object, it calls transaction PP01 or PP01_DISP. If you do not specify the object, or specify a number of objects, it shows you the infotypes maintained for each object.

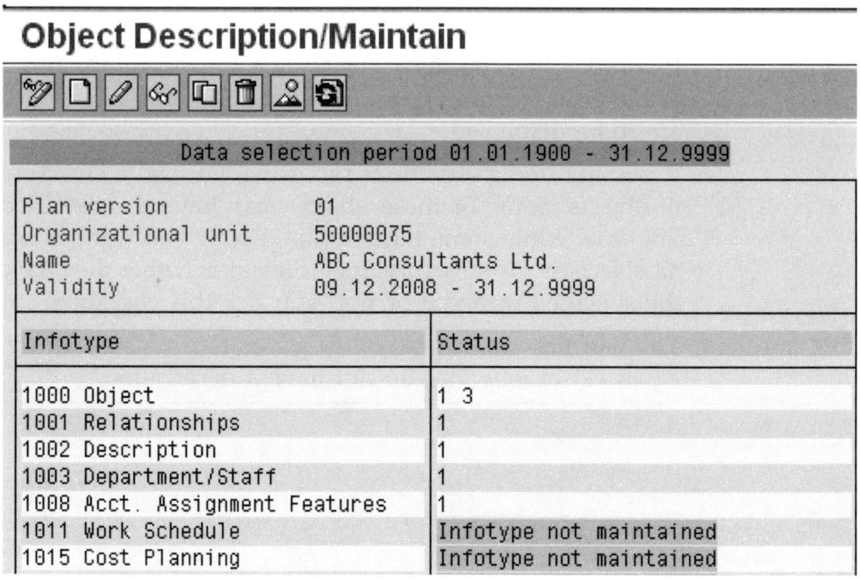

### *Infotype reporting*

You can use transaction S_AHR_61016532 or RE_RHINFAW0 to report on any infotype. You can select the objects structurally by specifying a starting object and evaluation path. Alternatively you may select all objects of a type, or objects in a number range. In addition to the standard selection screen parameters, you enter the following additional parameters.

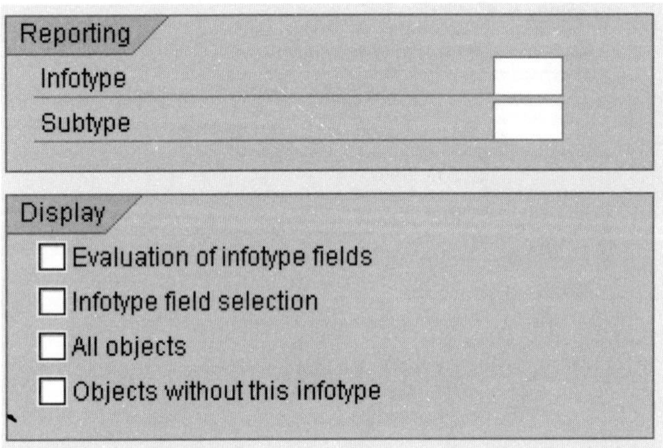


| *Selection parameter* | *Description* |
|---|---|
| Infotype | Here you specify the infotype that you wish to report on. Infotype must be entered. |
| Subtype | If you wish to report on a particular subtype, enter that. If subtype field is blank, all subtypes are reported. |
| Evaluation of infotype fields | If you do not tick this checkbox, the values of the fields are not displayed. |
| Infotype field selection | If you tick this checkbox, the system shows you the fields available in the infotype and you can select the fields which are to be displayed. |
| All objects | If you are doing structural reporting, you get a structure of objects. Some of these objects may have the specified infotype, while some may not have it. If you want to see all objects in the structure, regardless of whether they have the specified infotype or not, you tick this checkbox. |
| Objects without this infotype | You can tick this checkbox to generate a reverse report, e.g. a list of jobs that do not have a description. |

The selected infotypes are displayed.

**Plan version:** 01
**Key date:** 14.03.2009
**Infotype:** 1008
**Display:** With infotype only

| Object... | Object Name | Description |
|---|---|---|
| | ABC Consultants Ltd. | With 1 Acct. Assignment F |
| | Acct. Assignment Features | Company Code 0040 |
| | Acct. Assignment Features | Personnel Area PUNE |
| | Acct. Assignment Features | Personnel Subarea 0001 |
| | Acct. Assignment Features | Controlling Area 0040 |

### *Display infotypes*

You can use transaction RE_RHDESC10 to display infotypes. You specify a starting object and the evaluation path. The system shows you all the objects in the structure. You can select an object and display infotypes by clicking [Display Object Infotypes]. You can see the next infotype by pressing F3 or clicking .

### *Individual maintenance*

You can run transaction PSO4 to maintain a specific infotype from the list of objects displayed. An indicator beside the objects shows you whether the infotype has been maintained for them or not.

### *New end date*

You can run transaction RE_RHGRENZ4 to set a new delimitation date for the records found using the selection screen. It primarily serves to recreate or extend records that have been delimited in error. The records can be given a historical flag indicator so that they can no longer be modified using transaction PP01. You can also cancel this historical record. To access the correct selection of records, you must enter the old delimitation date. All records with the same end date as the delimitation date will be given the new delimitation date. All other records remain unchanged.

### *New start date*

You can run transaction RE_RHBEGDA0 to set a new start date for the records found using the selection screen. It primarily serves to correct the start date of records retrospectively. To access the correct selection of records, enter the old start date. All records with the old start date are given the new start date. All other records remain unchanged.

### *Translate*

You can run transaction RE_RHTRANS0 to translate language-dependent texts and all existing subtypes of the Object infotype (1000) and Description infotype (1002). Provided that the texts have been translated, they are displayed automatically in the appropriate logon language.

### *HR reporting via personnel planning structures*

You can run a Personnel Administration report for objects selected based on organizational plan using transaction RE_RHPNPSUB or S_AHR_61016533. In addition to the standard selection screen, the system gives the following additional fields on the selection screen.

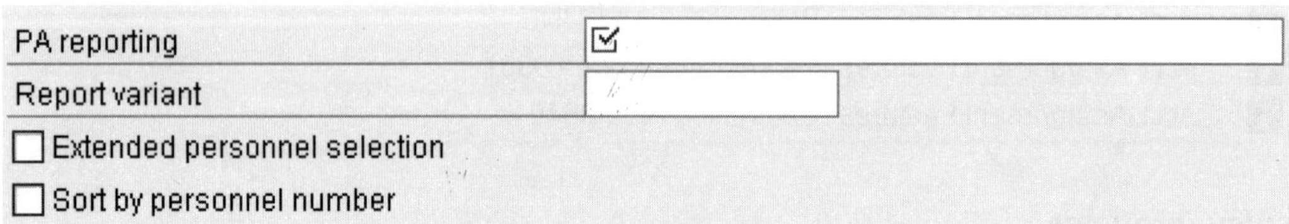


| *Selection parameter* | *Description* |
|---|---|
| PA reporting | Here you enter the report name you want to run. |
| Report variant | If you have saved a report variant, and you would like to run that variant, you specify that here. |
| Extended personnel selection | If you tick this checkbox, you can select from the parameters in Personnel Administration. |
| Sort by personnel number | If you tick this checkbox, you can sort the report by personnel number. |

CHAPTER 14

# Infotypes

## 14.1 DESCRIPTION

| *Functional Consultant* | *User* | *Business Process Owner* | *Senior Management* | *My Rating* | *Understanding Level* |
|---|---|---|---|---|---|
| A | A | A | A | | |

### 14.1.1 Description (Infotype 1002)

You may need to store descriptions of different objects. You may do so in infotype 1002. In transaction PP01, you select 'Description' and click Create. You will get the following screen.

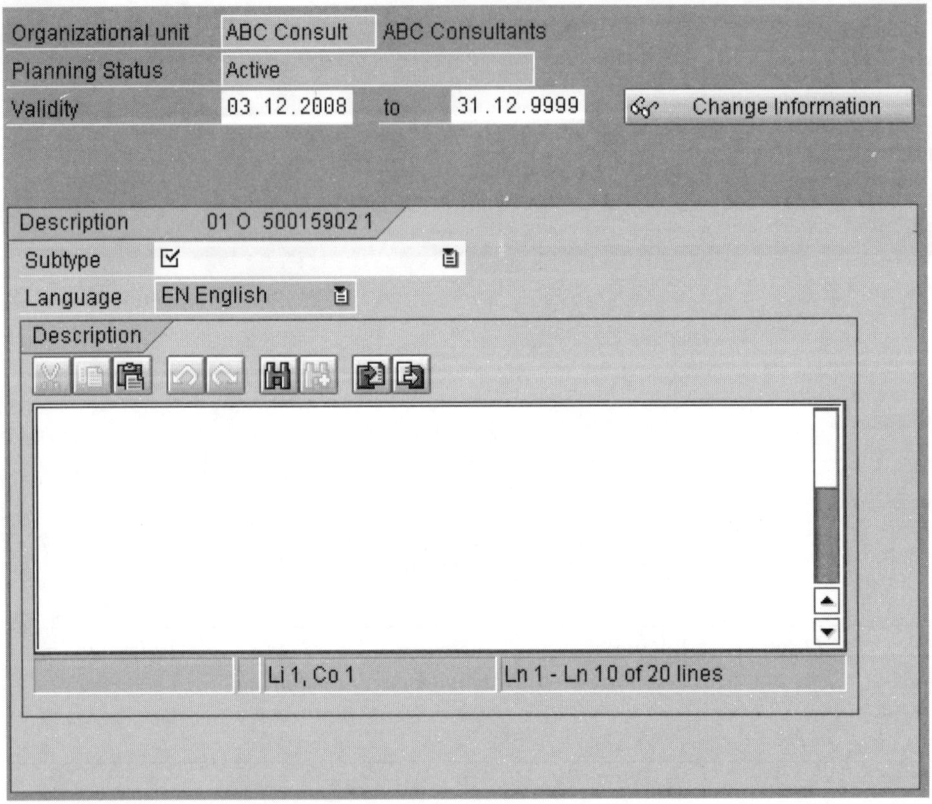


### *Object (organizational unit)*

Object whose description is being created, changed or displayed.

### *Planning status*

Planning status of the object description.

### *Validity*

An object can have one description up to a certain date, and another after that date. This is stored using validity period of description.

### *Change information*

If you click this icon, the system will show the user who created or last changed the record and the date on which it was done.

### *Subtype*

If you want to keep different types of descriptions for an object, you may do so by using different subtypes.

### *Language*

You can keep object descriptions in multiple languages. This field gets its value from the logon language.

### *Description*

Here you enter the object description. The information you store in this infotype is for reference only and cannot be reported on.

## 14.1.2 Types of Description

### *Purpose*

You can define the types of description you want. It is recommended that you don't delete the existing subtypes because they may be used in other modules, e.g. Training and Event Management.

### *IMG node*

SM30 ➢ V_778U

### *Screen*

| Inftyp. | Infotype Name | Subtyp | Subtype text |
|---|---|---|---|
| 1002 | Description | 0001 | General description |
| 1002 | Description | 0002 | Business event contents |
| 1002 | Description | 0003 | Notes |

### *Primary key*

Infotype + Subtype

## 14.1.3 Formatting of Description

When you create a description in infotype 1002, SAP gives you a blank text box in which you write your text.

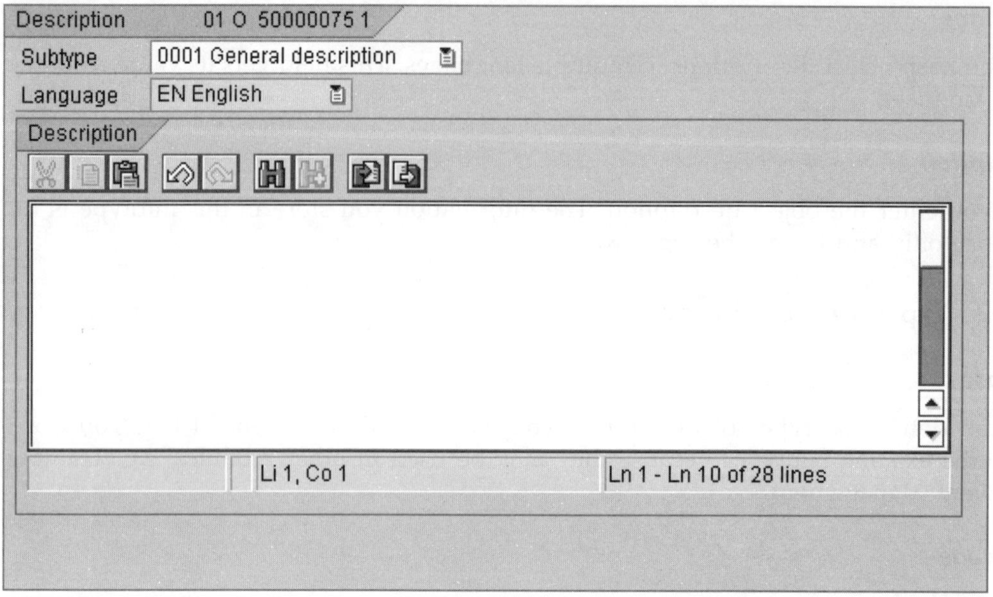


However, sometimes you may want the text to be formatted. SAP lets you define the subtypes for which you want the text to be formatted. For these subtypes, the screen looks as under. Here for each line, you can define the format.

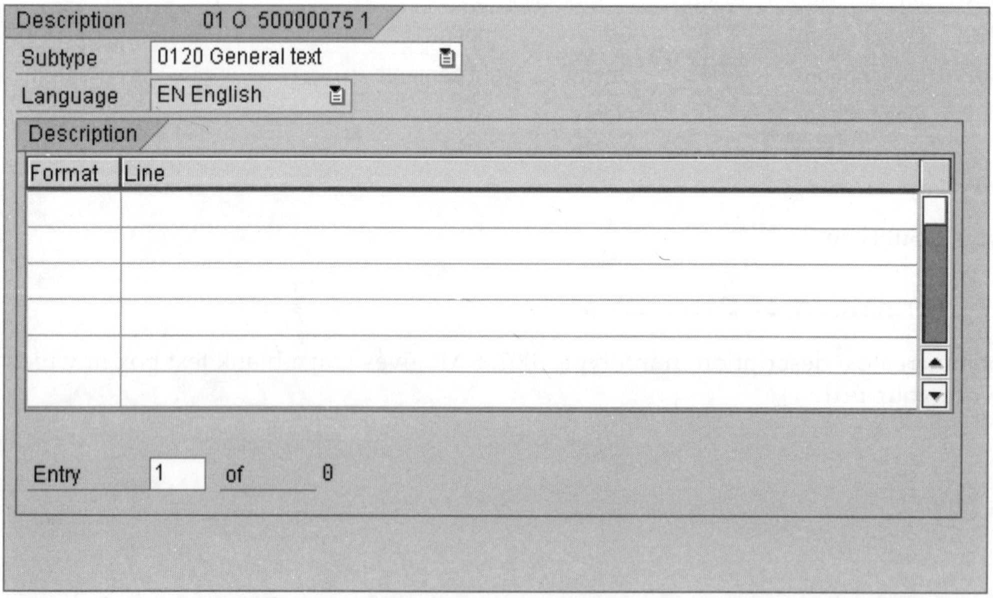

You can specify the subtypes for which you want the text to be formatted in view T772S.

| Subtyp | Subtype text |
|---|---|
| 0120 | General text |
| 0121 | Completion text |
| 0122 | Latest end text |
| 0123 | Requested end text |
| 0124 | Latest Start Text |

## 14.2 DEPARTMENT/STAFF

| *Functional Consultant* | *User* | *Business Process Owner* | *Senior Management* | *My Rating* | *Understanding Level* |
|---|---|---|---|---|---|
| A | A | B | B | | |

### 14.2.1 Department/Staff (Infotype 1003)

You can store department/staff indicator for an organizational unit or position in infotype 1003.

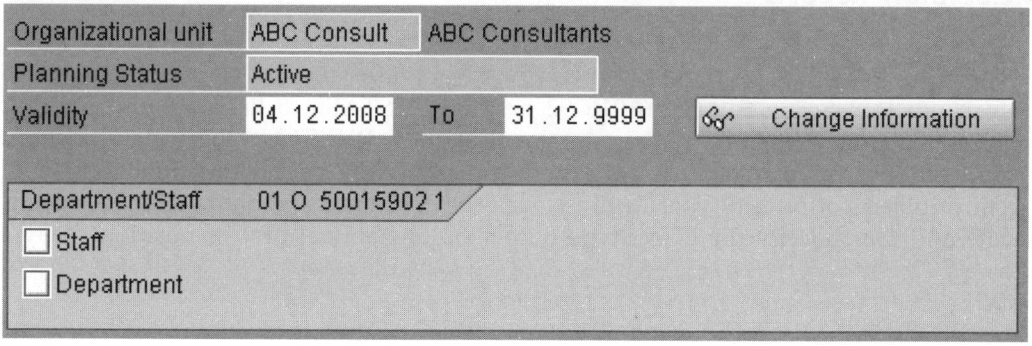


***Staff***

Some organizations differentiate between line functions and staff functions. If an organizational unit or position is a staff function, you can tick this checkbox. Positions or organizational units marked with a staff flag are shown in the graphic next to their respective superior nodes. Without a staff flag they are shown under the superior node.

### *Department*

When you hire an employee in Personnel Administration and assign him a position, the system also shows his organizational unit. However, some companies define certain organizational units as departments, while other organizational units are non-departments. In Personnel Administration the employees are shown only against departments. If you have such a scenario, you activate the department switch. Then you tick this checkbox for organizational units which are departments. In Personnel Administration when you assign a position to an employee, the system will show the organizational unit to which the position belongs. If that organizational unit is not a department, the system will find a superior organizational unit which is a department and show it.

## 14.2.2 Department Switch

You can use department flag in infotype 1003 to specify organizational units which are departments. If you don't want to maintain the department flag in infotype 1003, you set the department switch in table T77S0 to 0. In that case, the organizational unit directly above a position is its department. If you want to identify only certain organizational units as departments, then you set the switch to 1. In that case, the organizational unit with a department flag in infotype 1003 above a position is its department.

| Group | Sem.abbr. | Value abbr | Description |
|---|---|---|---|
| PPABT | PPABT | 0 | Switch: department |

## 14.2.3 Staff Reports

### *Staff functions for objects*

You can use transaction S_AHR_61016492 or RE_RHXSTAB0 to list staff functions for organizational units. Similarly, you can use transaction RE_RHXSTAB1 to list staff functions for all positions. You can also use both these transactions to report staff functions of all objects, or objects of certain type. To do so, tick the checkbox 'Standard selection screen', Execute and then specify the object type (either organizational unit or position).

## 14.3 CHARACTER

| *Functional Consultant* | *User* | *Business Process Owner* | *Senior Management* | *My Rating* | *Understanding Level* |
|---|---|---|---|---|---|
| B | C | C | C | | |

### 14.3.1 Character (Infotype 1004)

You can use infotype 1004 to specify the character of a task. In each box you can select one of the characteristics for the task. Infotype 1004 can also be maintained for work centers.

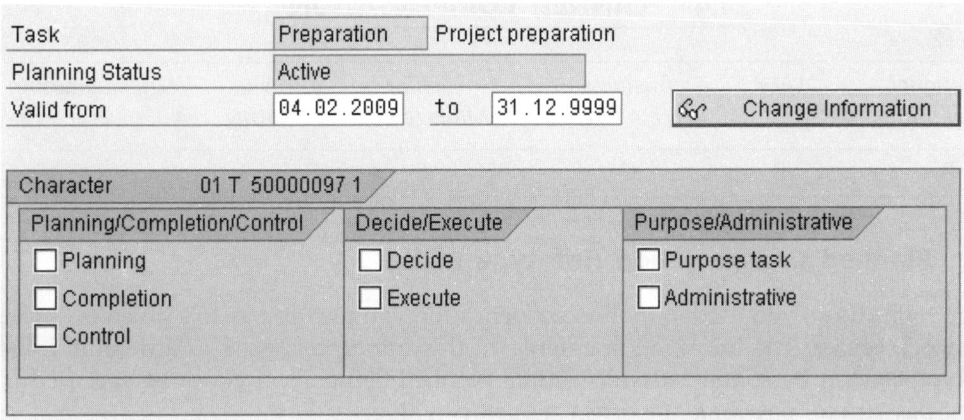


### 14.3.2 Character Reports

#### *Character of tasks in organizational structure*

You can run transaction S_AHR_61016525 to display tasks having character definition in infotype 1004. It uses evaluation path AUFGABEX to show the tasks in the organizational structure.

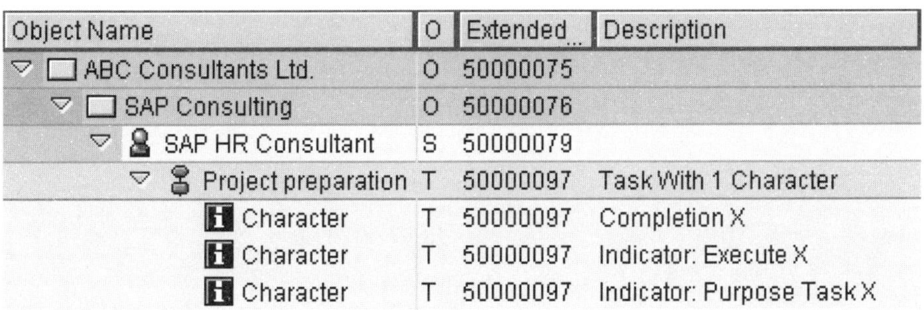

***Character of individual tasks***

You can run transaction S_AHR_61016526 to see the tasks for which infotype 1004 (Character) is maintained and its character attributes.

| Obj... | Object Name | Object ID | Description |
|---|---|---|---|
| | Project preparation | T 50000097 | With 1 Character |
| | Character | T 50000097 | Completion X |
| | Character | T 50000097 | Indicator: Execute X |
| | Character | T 50000097 | Indicator: Purpose Task X |

## 14.4 PLANNED COMPENSATION

| *Functional Consultant* | *User* | *Business Process Owner* | *Senior Management* | *My Rating* | *Understanding Level* |
|---|---|---|---|---|---|
| B | B | C | C | | |

### 14.4.1 Planned Compensation (Infotype 1005)

Infotype 1005 allows you to identify the compensation you plan to pay to a given position, job, or work center. The information entered in this infotype is used as a default value in infotype 0008 in Personnel Administration. Planned compensation can be specified in terms of pay grade, pay scale, or direct monetary value.

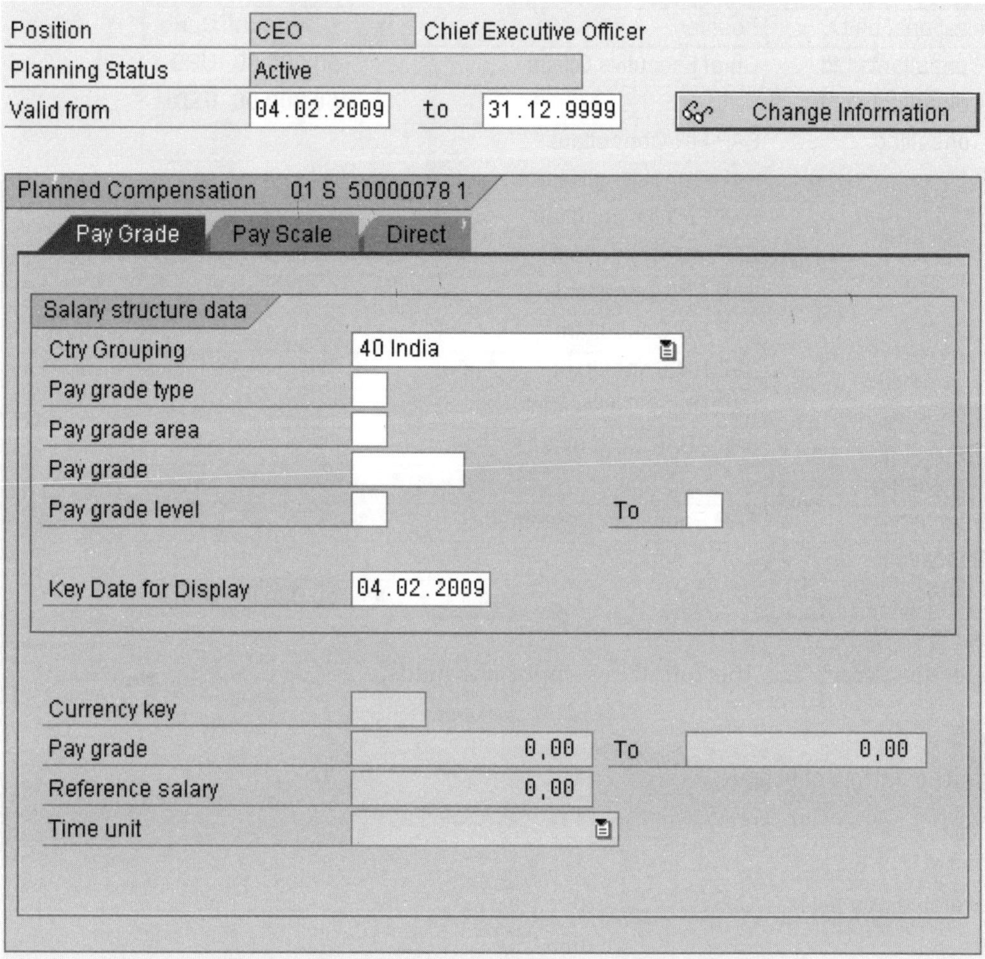


## 14.4.2 Planned Compensation Reports

***Planned labor costs***

You can run transaction S_AHR_61016517 or S_AHR_61016508 to see planned labor costs of an organizational unit in structural form.

| Organizational unit | Position | Σ | Amount | Curre... |
|---|---|---|---|---|
| ABC Consultants Ltd. | Chief Executive Officer | | 50.000,00 | USD |
| ABC Consultants Ltd. | | ▪ | **50.000,00** | **USD** |
| SAP Consulting | SAP HR Consultant | | | |
| | SAP Consulting Work Center | | | |
| | SAP FI/CO Consultant | | | |
| | SAP MM Consultant | | | |
| | SAP PP Consultant | | | |
| | SAP PS Consultant | | | |
| | SAP PM Consultant | | | |
| | SAP Basis Consultant | | | |
| | SAP ABAP Consultant | | | |
| SAP Consulting | | | | |
| SAP Education | SAP Education Coordinator | | | |
| SAP Education | | | | |
| | | ▪▪ | **50.000,00** | **USD** |

The selection screen has the following important fields.

| Controls | |
|---|---|
| Reporting along a structure | X |
| Values (1=mid,2=min,3=max) | 1 |
| Period | 1 |
| Conversion type as in TCURR | M |
| Currency | USD |

| *Selection parameter* | *Description* |
|---|---|
| Reporting along a structure | If you select this, the cost is reported for the entire organizational structure starting from the specified organizational unit, otherwise only for the specified organizational unit. |
| Values | Here you specify whether minimum, maximum or midpoint costs are to be reported. |
| Period | Here you specify whether planned costs are for a month or week, etc. |
| Conversion type | In case the reporting currency is different from the planned currency, the method of conversion to be used is specified here. |
| Currency | Here you specify the currency for reporting planned costs. |

## 14.5 RESTRICTIONS

| *Functional Consultant* | *User* | *Business Process Owner* | *Senior Management* | *My Rating* | *Understanding Level* |
|---|---|---|---|---|---|
| B | C | C | C | | |

### 14.5.1 Restrictions (Infotype 1006)

You can use infotype 1006 to record any restrictions applicable to employees who are assigned to a work center. For example, a work center that has no wheelchair access would be unsuitable for disabled employees. You can also specify the reason for the restriction. You can create an infotype 1006 record only for work centers.

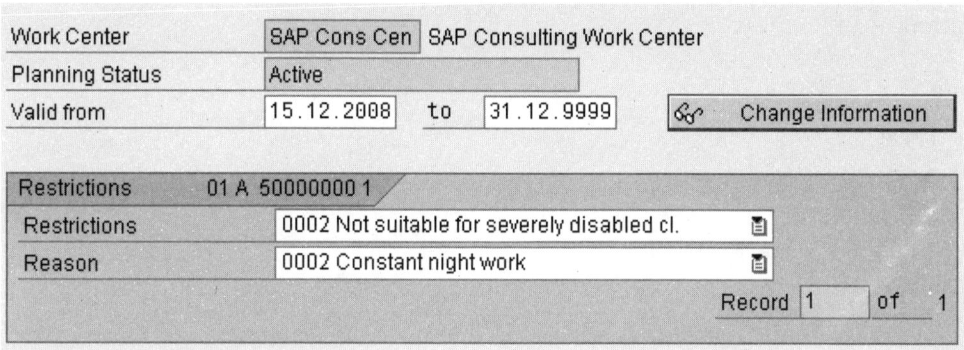


### 14.5.2 Restrictions Reports

#### *Work centers with restrictions along organizational structure*

You can run transaction RE_RHXIAW00 or S_AHR_61016518 to see work centers with restrictions along organizational structure. This report uses evaluation path ARBPLX. For this report to work, the work center must be linked to position.

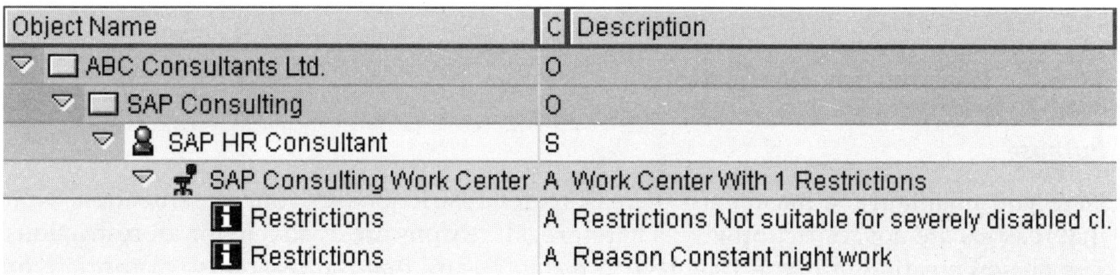

***Single work centers with restrictions***

You can run transaction RE_RHXIAW01 or S_AHR_61016519 to see restrictions on work centers.

| Obj... | Object Name | Object ID | Description |
|---|---|---|---|
| | SAP Consulting Work Cente | A 50000000 | With 1 Restrictions |
| | Restrictions | A 50000000 | Restrictions Not suitable for severely disabled cl. |
| | Restrictions | A 50000000 | Reason Constant night work |

## 14.5.3 Types of Restrictions

***Purpose***

Here you maintain the master list of restrictions applicable to all work centers in your organization.

***IMG node***

SM30 ➢ T778C

***Transaction***

S_AHR_61007156–Create Restrictions

***Screen***

| Res. | Restriction name |
|---|---|
| 0001 | Not suitable for female employees |
| 0002 | Not suitable for severely disabled cl. |
| 0003 | Not suitable for minors |

***Primary key***

Restrictions

## 14.5.4 Reasons for Restrictions

***Purpose***

Here you maintain the master list of reasons for restrictions in your organization. Note that reasons are not restrictionwise. Therefore, all reasons are available for all restrictions. The person creating infotype 1006 record has to ensure that the reason is appropriate for the restriction.

***IMG node***

SM30 ➢ T778X

***Transaction***

S_AHR_61003170–Create Justifications

***Screen***

| Reason | Reason name |
|---|---|
| 0001 | Exposure to X-rays |
| 0002 | Constant night work |
| 0003 | 10kg or more must often be lifted |
| 0004 | Piecework work center |

***Primary key***

Reason

## 14.6 VACANCY

| *Functional Consultant* | *User* | *Business Process Owner* | *Senior Management* | *My Rating* | *Understanding Level* |
|---|---|---|---|---|---|
| A | A | B | B | | |

### 14.6.1 Distinction between Unoccupied and Vacant Positions

One might consider every unoccupied position as vacant. In that case, whenever a position becomes unoccupied, it will be declared vacant and recruitment action will get triggered. Many companies don't want this to happen. They would like to review unoccupied positions, and declare them vacant selectively. Therefore, SAP provides a separate vacancy flag for positions. Thus, a position may be unoccupied, but not vacant. In a reverse scenario, you may declare an occupied position vacant so as to trigger recruitment action, because you are looking for a successor. Therefore, SAP allows vacancy flag for an occupied position.

### 14.6.2 Vacancy (Infotype 1007)

Vacancy flag is stored in infotype 1007. This infotype can be maintained only for positions. When the vacancy is filled, the system automatically changes the status of this infotype record. You can mark vacancy records as historical records, when you no longer need them—that is, once a position is filled. Historical records are maintained in the database, but cannot be changed or used in processing.

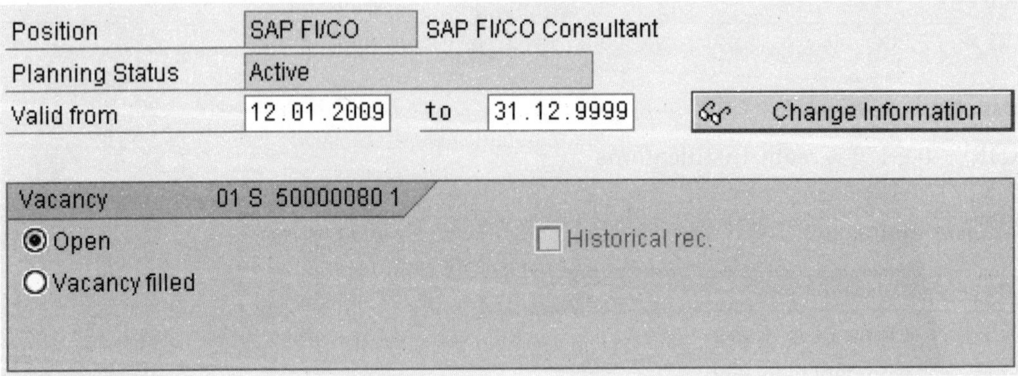


### 14.6.3 Use of Vacancy Flag

Vacancy information is used primarily to trigger recruitment action. It is also used in career and succession planning and personnel cost planning. SAP provides a report of vacant positions and another which lists occupied positions which are declared vacant. Refer to chapter 4.7 for details.

### 14.6.4 Vacant and Obsolete Positions

Positions cannot be flagged vacant and obsolete simultaneously. If a vacant position is flagged as obsolete, the vacancy is delimited at the start of the validity of the obsolete flag (minus one day).

### 14.6.5 Activation of Vacancy Infotype

System Switch (from Table T77S0)

| Group | Sem. abbr. | Value abbr. | Description |
|---|---|---|---|
| PPVAC | PPVAC | 1 | Switch for defining a vacancy |
| PPVAC | PREF | | 'X': dialog for personnel officer |
| PPVAC | VACWF | | Vacancy workflow on = X, Vacancy dialog box = ' ' |

| *Group* | *Sem. abbr.* | *Explanation* |
|---|---|---|
| PPVAC | PPVAC | If your company considers every unfilled position vacant, you maintain value 0 here. In such a case, infotype 1007 cannot be maintained. If you want to distinguish between unfilled and vacant positions, you maintain value 1 here, and maintain infotype 1007 for the positions you want to fill. If integration with the Recruitment component is active, data on vacancies (that is, positions marked as vacant in infotype 1007) is transferred to Personnel Administration table T750X. When you create infotype 1007 records, you can enter the additional information required by table T750X. Vacant positions are available in Recruitment for recruitment action. When a vacant position is filled by a new employee, vacancy infotype is delimited. |
| PPVAC | PREF | If this switch is set to 'X', when you create a vacancy, the system will ask you to enter the personnel officer and line manager responsible. However, in the Organization and Staffing interface, the system does not ask you to enter the personnel officer or line manager, regardless of the value you entered for this switch. |
| PPVAC | VACWF | When an employee leaves a position, vacancy needs to be created. Similarly, when an employee occupies a position, vacancy needs to be delimited. If this switch is blank, the system pops up a dialog box asking the user to confirm these actions. If this switch has value 'X', the system creates an event which triggers a workflow, and these questions are put to the chief of the organizational unit in which the position has become occupied or unoccupied. |

## 14.7 ACCOUNT ASSIGNMENT

| *Functional Consultant* | *User* | *Business Process Owner* | *Senior Management* | *My Rating* | *Understanding Level* |
|---|---|---|---|---|---|
| A | A | B | B | | |

### 14.7.1 Account Assignment Features (Infotype 1008)

You can maintain the following account assignments for organizational units and positions. Account assignments are inherited by lower level organizational units and positions. If integration with Personnel Administration is active, this infotype provides values for the classification of employees in the personnel structure. These values may be personnel areas, personnel subareas or business areas. If the data you enter differs from the default values, a warning message appears.

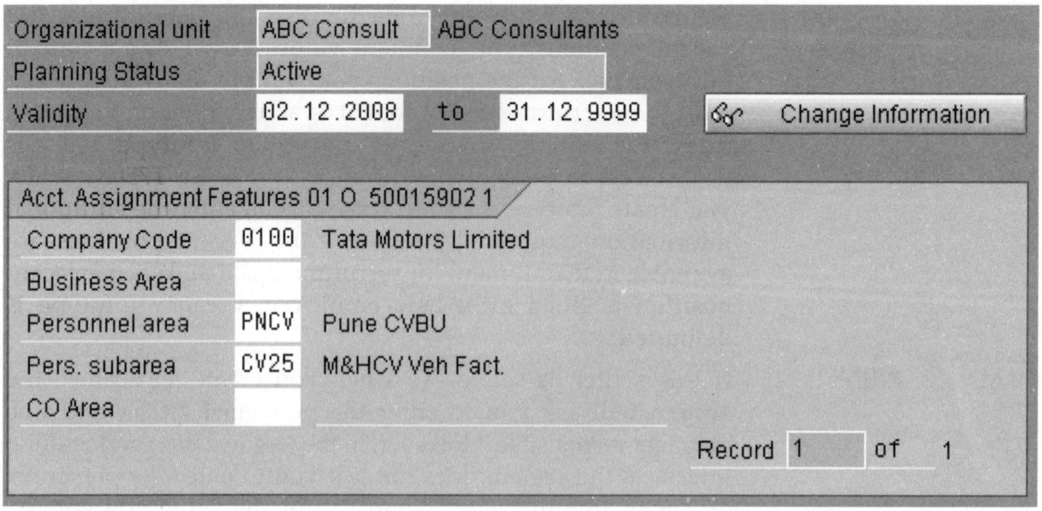


### *Company code*

Here you can specify the company code of an organizational unit. Company code is inherited by lower level organizational units. It is inherited by positions if position inheritance switch is active. The inherited values cannot be changed.

### *Business area*

Here you can specify the business area of an organizational unit. If you have specified the cost center, you must select the business area to which the cost center belongs. Business area is inherited by lower level organizational units. It is inherited by positions if position inheritance switch is active. You can change the inherited business area.

### *Personnel area and personnel subarea*

Here you can specify the personnel area and personnel subarea of an organizational unit. Personnel area and personnel subarea is inherited by lower level organizational units. It is inherited by positions if position inheritance switch is active. You can change the inherited personnel area and personnel subarea.

### *Controlling area*

An organizational plan must be entirely within one controlling area. You should specify the controlling area of the root organizational unit. All objects will inherit it from there. Controlling area cannot be changed for any object. If you have specified the cost center of an organizational unit, you should leave this field blank as the controlling area is already specified along with cost center.

***Enterprise organization***

You can specify the controlling areas for which enterprise organization is active in view V_TKA06_CC (Controlling ➢ Cost Center Accounting ➢ Enterprise Organization ➢ Enter Settings for Enterprise Organization).

| CO area | Name | Ent. org. active |
|---|---|---|
| ZA01 | Kostenrechnungskreis ZA01 | ☑ |

Enterprise organization is based on the organizational plan in HR, and contains additional functions and organizational units specific to accounting. It integrates the HR organizational plan, the cost center standard hierarchy and the Profit center standard hierarchy. If the enterprise organization is active for a controlling area, the HR organizational structure is maintained through transaction KEO1 (Controlling ➢ Cost Center Accounting ➢ Enterprise Organization ➢ Create Enterprise Organization). The account assignment of the organizational unit is specified here and not in the HR organizational structure.

### 14.7.2 Inheritance of Account Assignment by Positions

If you want positions to inherit controlling area, company code, and business area from their respective organizational units, you set the following switch to 'X' in view V_T77S0SC.

| Group | Sem. abbr. | Value abbr. | Description |
|---|---|---|---|
| PPOM | INHS | | Inheritance of acc. ass. features by positions |

### 14.7.3 Default Value for Controlling Area

A cost center is always specified along with a controlling area. When you create relationships between cost centers and positions or organizational units, the controlling area given here will be used as default.

| Group | Sem.abbr. | Value abbr | Description |
|---|---|---|---|
| PPINT | PPINT | 0040 | Default value for controlling area |

## 14.8 HEALTH EXAMINATIONS

| *Functional Consultant* | *User* | *Business Process Owner* | *Senior Management* | *My Rating* | *Understanding Level* |
|---|---|---|---|---|---|
| B | B | C | C | | |

### 14.8.1 Health Examinations (Infotype 1009)

Some of your work centers may be hazardous and you may want employees working there to undergo periodic health examinations. You can maintain such health examinations in infotype 1009. There may also be work centers where persons with certain health conditions are not permitted. For example, persons who have had TB may be excluded from work centers where food is handled. You can maintain this data in health exclusions. Information on both these conditions is maintained in infotype 1009. Infotype 1009 is maintained only for work centers.

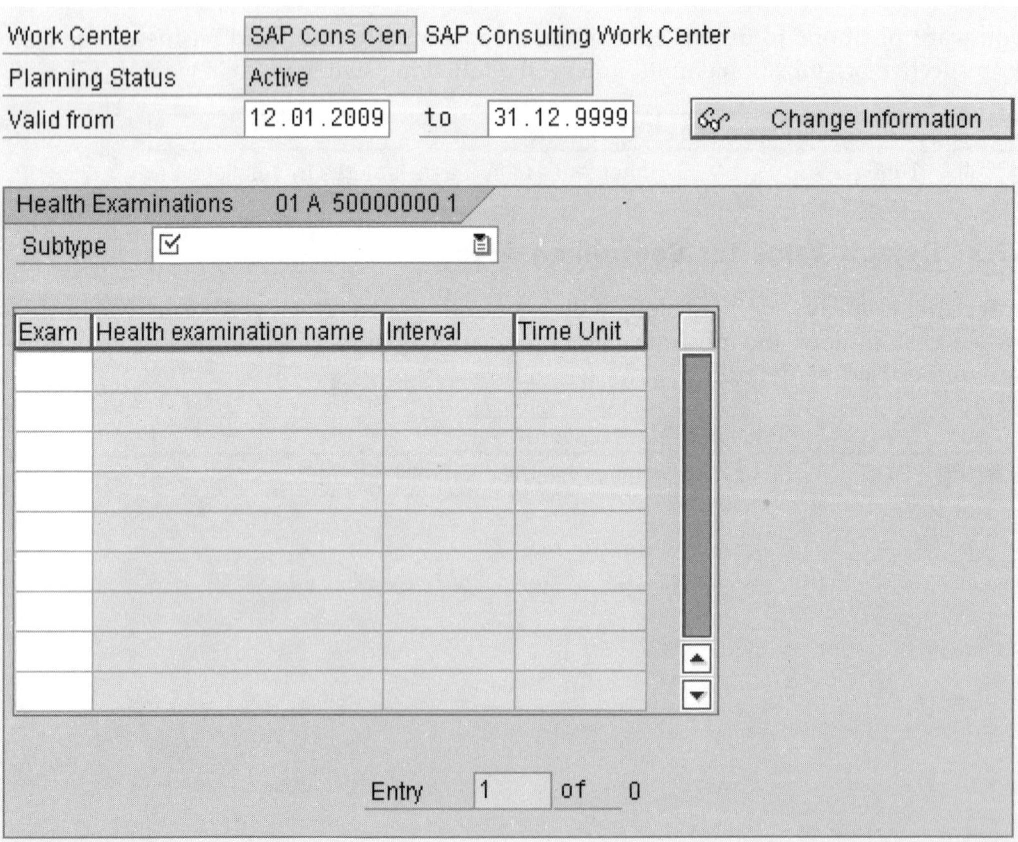

## 14.8.2 Health Examinations Reports

### *Work centers requiring health examinations in an organization*

You can run transaction RE_RHXIAW02 or S_AHR_61016520 to see work centers with health examinations and exclusions along organizational structure. This report uses evaluation path ARBPLX. For this report to work, the work center must be linked to position.

| Object Name | C | Description |
|---|---|---|
| ▽ ABC Consultants Ltd. | O | |
| ▽ SAP Consulting | O | |
| ▽ SAP HR Consultant | S | |
| ▽ SAP Consulting Work Center | A | Work Center With 1 Health Examinations |
| Health examinations | A | Examination Type Eye test |

### *Single work centers requiring health examinations*

You can run transaction RE_RHXIAW03 or S_AHR_61016521 to see health examinations and exclusions for work centers.

| Obj... | Object Name | Object ID | Description |
|---|---|---|---|
| | SAP Consulting Work Cente | A 50000000 | With 1 Health Examination |
| | Health examinations | A 50000000 | Examination Type Eye test |

## 14.8.3 Health Examinations Type

### *Purpose*

Here you maintain the master lists of health exclusions and health examinations. You can also specify the frequency of health examinations.

### *IMG node*

SM30 ➢ T778G

### *Transaction*

S_AHR_61003603–Create Health Promotion Measures

***Screen***

| STy. | Subtype text | Exam. type | Health examination name |
|---|---|---|---|
| 0001 | Health exclusions | 0001 | TB |
| 0002 | Health examinations | 0001 | Silicosis |
| 0002 | Health examinations | 0002 | Asbestos |
| 0002 | Health examinations | 0003 | Eye test |

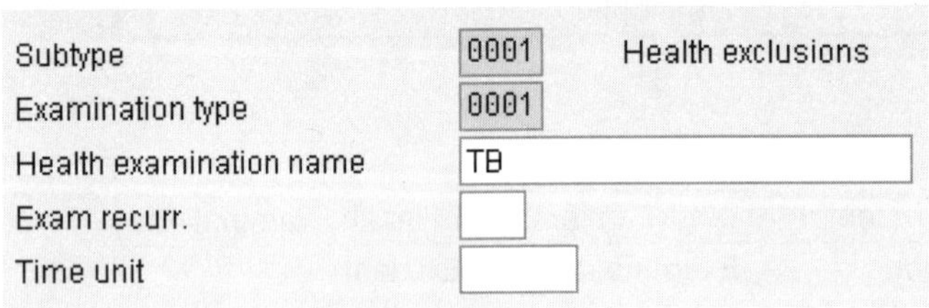


***Primary key***

Subtype + Examination Type

## 14.9 AUTHORITIES/RESOURCES

| *Functional Consultant* | *User* | *Business Process Owner* | *Senior Management* | *My Rating* | *Understanding Level* |
|---|---|---|---|---|---|
| B | C | C | C | | |

### 14.9.1 Authorities/Resources (Infotype 1010)

In infotype 1010 you can maintain the authority granted to a position. You can also maintain the technical resources available to a position. You can also maintain infotype 1010 for work centers.

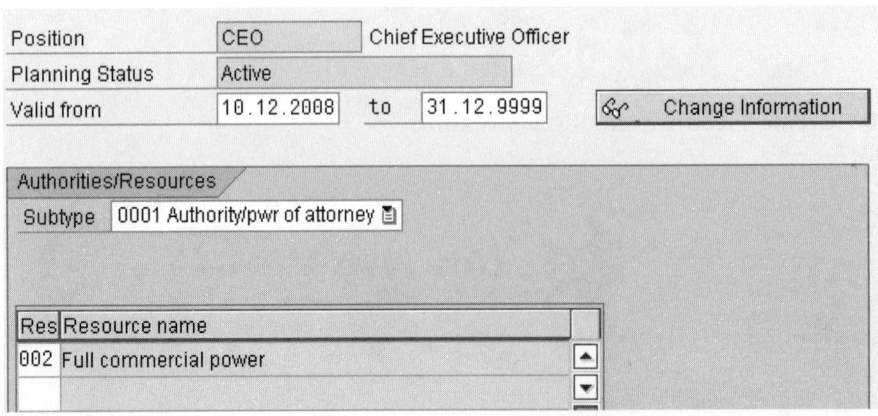

### 14.9.2 Authorities/Resources Reports

You can run transaction RE_RHXHFMT0, S_AHR_61016507 or S_AHR_61016516 to see authorities and resources for a position or for all positions directly belonging to an organizational unit. Authorities and resources may be maintained directly for positions. Alternatively, authorities and resources may be maintained for work centers which are linked to positions. The evaluation path used in the report is ARBPL. This evaluation path does not take you down the organizational structure.

```
Authorities and Resources

Plan version: 01    Status: 1       Selection period: 01.01.1900 -31.12.9999

O 50000075 ABC Consultants Ltd.
  S 50000078 Chief Executive Officer
      Authority/pwr of attorney
         Full commercial power
```

If you want to see authorities and resources along organizational structure, you should use evaluation path ARBPLX.

```
Authorities and Resources

Plan version: 01    Status: 1       Selection period: 01.01.1900 -31.12.9999

O 50000075 ABC Consultants Ltd.
  S 50000078 Chief Executive Officer
      Authority/pwr of attorney
         Full commercial power
  O 50000076 SAP Consulting
    S 50000079 SAP HR Consultant

      A 50000000 SAP Consulting Work Center
        Authority/pwr of attorney
           Limited commercial power
```

### 14.9.3 Authorities/Resources Type

***Purpose***

Here you maintain the master list of authorities and technical resources in your organization. You can use them in infotype 1010 to specify the authority of positions and resources available. You can also maintain infotype 1010 for work centers.

***IMG node***

SM30 ➢ T778W

***Transaction***

S_AHR_61007150–Create Authorities/Resources

***Screen***

| Subtyp | Subtype text | Resources | Resource name |
|---|---|---|---|
| 0001 | Authority/pwr of attorney | 001 | Limited commercial power |
| 0001 | Authority/pwr of attorney | 002 | Full commercial power |
| 0001 | Authority/pwr of attorney | 003 | Purchases up to DM 50,000 |
| 0002 | Technical resources | 001 | Computer monitor |
| 0002 | Technical resources | 002 | PC workstation |
| 0002 | Technical resources | 003 | CNC lathe 51367 |

***Primary key***

Subtype + Resources

## 14.10 WORK SCHEDULE

| *Functional Consultant* | *User* | *Business Process Owner* | *Senior Management* | *My Rating* | *Understanding Level* |
|---|---|---|---|---|---|
| B | B | C | C | | |

### 14.10.1 Work Schedule (Infotype 1011)

You can define planned working times for your organizational units, positions, or work centers in order to store the projected volume of work per object. If a position is to be reoccupied, you can, for example, compare the planned working time stored for the position with the planned working time stored for the employee in infotype 0007. In this way, you can avoid unwanted inconsistencies. The work schedule is only used as a reference in Organizational Management and does not affect payroll accounting. Work schedules are reported in staff assignment report (transaction S_AHR_61016503). You can create more complex work schedules using the Workforce Planning component.

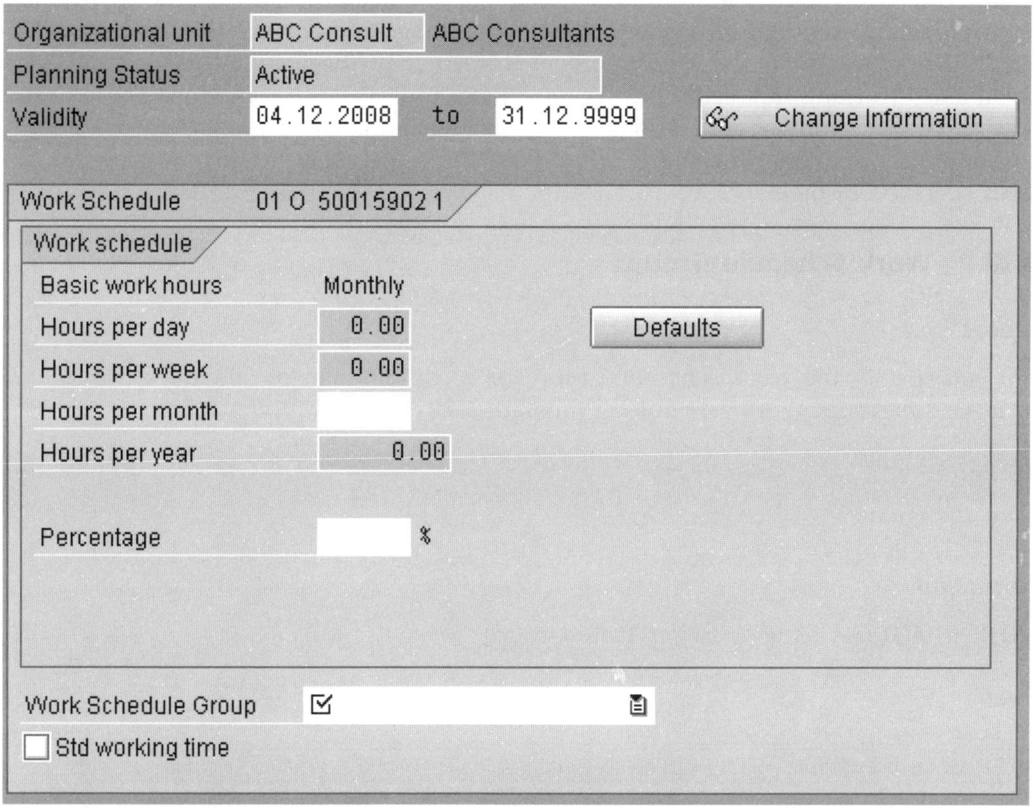


### *Hours per day/week/month/year*

You can specify working hours for a day, a week, a month, or a year.

### *Percentage*

Instead of directly specify working hours, you can specify a percentage which will be multiplied to default working hours to determine working hours.

### *Work schedule group*

Within an organizational unit there may be employees of different categories. If you want to have different working time for different categories of employees, you can create different work schedule groups based on employee groups and employee subgroups and assign different working times for different work schedule groups.

### *Standard working time*

If the working time of an organizational unit is to be inherited by its subordinate organizational units and positions, you tick this checkbox. The inherited value may be overridden by specifying the working time for the subordinate objects. If there is no working time specified for a position, the system will check if working time is specified for the organizational unit to which the position belongs and whether standard working time field is checked for the organizational unit. If both these conditions are met, the system takes working time from the organizational unit. If these conditions are not met, the system goes up further, until it finds an organizational unit which meets these conditions. If no organizational unit meets this condition, the system takes the time from global values specified in table T77S0.

## 14.10.2 Work Schedule Groups

***Purpose***

Here you specify the work schedule group for a combination of employee group and employee subgroup. Work schedule groups are subtypes of infotype 1011.

***IMG node***

SM30 ➢ T77WT

***Transaction***

S_AHR_61003187–Create Working Time Groups

***Screen***

| EEGrp | Employee group | ESgrp | Employee subgroup | WSGp | Work schedule group |
|---|---|---|---|---|---|
| * | All person groups | ** | All person subgroups | ALL | All work schedule group |
| 1 | Permanent | 10 | Hourly wage earner | 0002 | Hourly Paid Employees |
| 1 | Permanent | 11 | Incentive wage/hour | 0002 | Hourly Paid Employees |
| 1 | Permanent | 20 | Monthly wage earner | 0002 | Hourly Paid Employees |
| 1 | Permanent | 30 | Salaried staff | 0001 | Salaried employees |
| 1 | Permanent | 31 | Senior staff | 0001 | Salaried employees |
| 1 | Permanent | 32 | Non-PS staff | 0001 | Salaried employees |

***Primary key***

Employee Group + Employee Subgroup

## 14.10.3 Work Schedule Rule Values

***Purpose***

Here you specify the working time details which apply to all positions in the organization; unless a more specific assignment exists. However, it is recommended that rather than creating a working time for the whole enterprise, you create an infotype 1011 record for the root organizational unit and allow the value to be passed down the hierarchy. This will let you override the values wherever required. Also, if working hours change, you will be able to see both old and new values. This will not be possible if you maintain working hours here.

***IMG node***

SM30 ➢ T77S0

***Screen***

System Switch (from Table T77S0)

| Group | Sem. abbr. | Value abbr. | Description |
|---|---|---|---|
| WORKT | DAILY | 800 | Average working time per day |
| WORKT | DAYMT | 2170 | Average number of working days per month |
| WORKT | DAYWK | 500 | Average number of working days per week |
| WORKT | DAYYR | 26000 | Average number of working days per year |
| WORKT | DECNO | 2 | Number of decimal places for default working time |
| WORKT | FTEP | | Calculation of value for FTE |
| WORKT | FTEQ | | Quota planning in FTEs |
| WORKT | MAXHR | 2400 | Maximum values for working hours per day |
| WORKT | MINHR | 100 | Minimum values for working hours per day |
| WORKT | PATHA | WRKT_AO | Evaluation path: work center / organizational unit |
| WORKT | PATHO | WRKT_O | Evaluation path: org.unit / org.unit |
| WORKT | PATHS | WRKT_SO | Evaluation path: position / organizational unit |
| WORKT | PERCK | M | Type of working hours check |

## 14.11 EMPLOYEE GROUP/SUBGROUP

| *Functional Consultant* | *User* | *Business Process Owner* | *Senior Management* | *My Rating* | *Understanding Level* |
|---|---|---|---|---|---|
| B | B | C | C | | |

### 14.11.1 Employee Group/Subgroup (Infotype 1013)

You can use infotype 1013 to assign employee group and employee subgroup to a position, work center, or budget structure element. If you create this infotype for a position, and assign the position to a person in Personnel Administration, the system suggests the employee group and the employee subgroup, if integration is active. If you enter a different employee group or subgroup, a warning message appears. Also, assigning a position to an employee group/subgroup allows the system to determine the work schedule group and the relevant working time in infotype 1011.

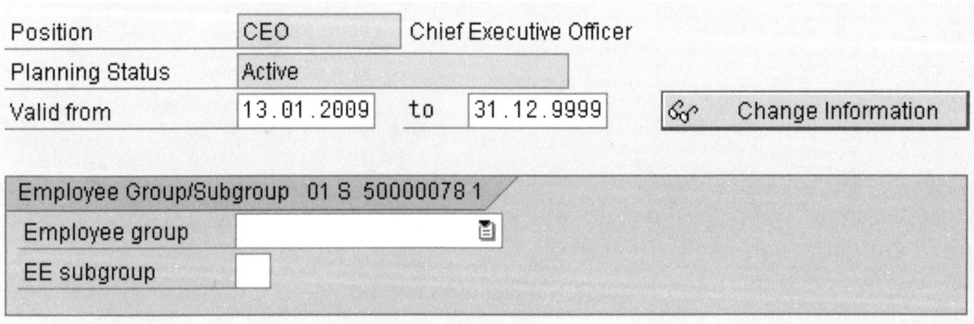


Master lists of employee groups and employee subgroups are defined in Personnel Administration. If you are using Organizational Management, but not Personnel Administration, and want to use this infotype, you have to define these master lists.

## 14.12 OBSOLETE

| *Functional Consultant* | *User* | *Business Process Owner* | *Senior Management* | *My Rating* | *Understanding Level* |
|---|---|---|---|---|---|
| A | A | B | B | | |

### 14.12.1 Obsolete (Infotype 1014)

Positions that are no longer required as a result of reorganization, but are still occupied can be flagged as obsolete in infotype 1014. This enables you to recognize instantly if any action is required, e.g. searching for new activities for the holders of such positions. When an obsolete position becomes unoccupied, recruitment action is not triggered, the system asks you to delimit the validity period of the obsolete position. Positions flagged as obsolete cannot be set to vacant and therefore recruitment action cannot be triggered. Obsolete positions cannot be reoccupied. This infotype is used mainly for positions, although you can use it for work centers as well.

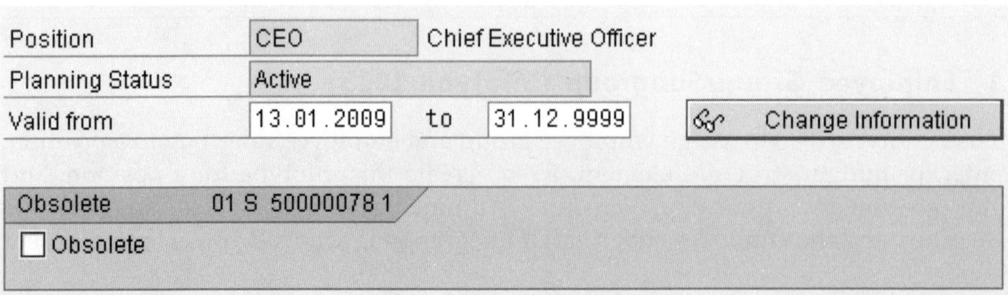

## 14.13 COST DISTRIBUTION

| *Functional Consultant* | *User* | *Business Process Owner* | *Senior Management* | *My Rating* | *Understanding Level* |
|---|---|---|---|---|---|
| A | A | A | A | | |

### 14.13.1 Cost Distribution (Infotype 1018)

Costs incurred by an organizational object are usually written to the cost center directly assigned to the object (master cost center) or the cost center inherited by the object from a superior object. However, sometimes you wish to distribute costs to more than one cost center. You can do so using infotype 1018. You can distribute the costs to multiple cost centers by specifying a percentage for each. You can even charge costs to orders and projects (WBS elements). If the percentages add to less than 100, the balance cost is charged to the master cost center of the object. Subordinate organizational objects within an organizational unit (positions, work centers) inherit cost distribution, if they have not been assigned their own master cost center or cost distribution. You can create this infotype for organizational units, positions and work centers. Distribution of employee costs may also be specified in infotype 0027 in Personnel Administration. If infotype 0027 exists, costs are distributed based on infotype 0027. If infotype 0027 does not exist, costs are distributed according to infotype 1018. Cost distribution to additional cost centers is simulated as external relationship A014 in reports.

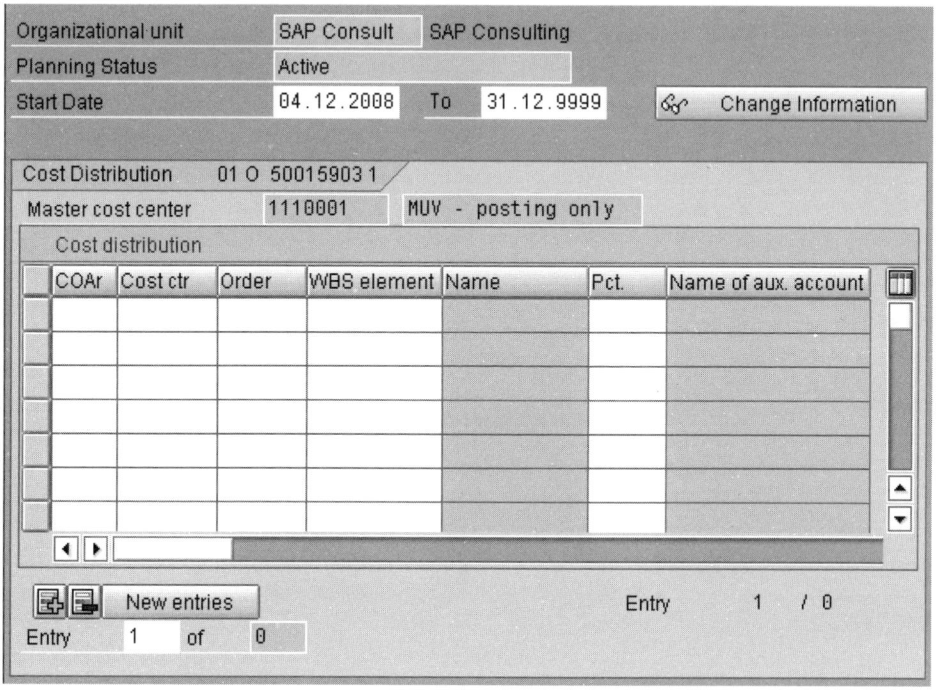

### 14.13.2 Cost Distribution Integration

For cost distribution to work, integration between organizational management and Personnel Administration (PLOGI ORGA) and the integration of cost distribution (PLOGI COSTD) should be active in view T77S0. Also the integration plan version should be specified.

| Group | Sem.abbr. | Value abbr | Description |
|---|---|---|---|
| PLOGI | COSTD | X | Integration of Cost Distribution PersAdm/OrgManag |
| PLOGI | ORGA | X | Integration Switch: Organizational Assignment |
| PLOGI | PLOGI | 01 | Integration Plan Version / Active Plan Version |

## 14.14 QUOTA PLANNING

| *Functional Consultant* | *User* | *Business Process Owner* | *Senior Management* | *My Rating* | *Understanding Level* |
|---|---|---|---|---|---|
| B | C | C | X | | |

### 14.14.1 Quota Planning (Infotype 1019)

You may do quota planning for an organizational unit in transaction PPOME. Quota planning can also be done in Manager Self-Service. That data is stored in infotype 1019. It stores number of positions or FTEs (Full-time Equivalents) for each job for an organizational unit, for a planning type (budget type) and for a validity period.

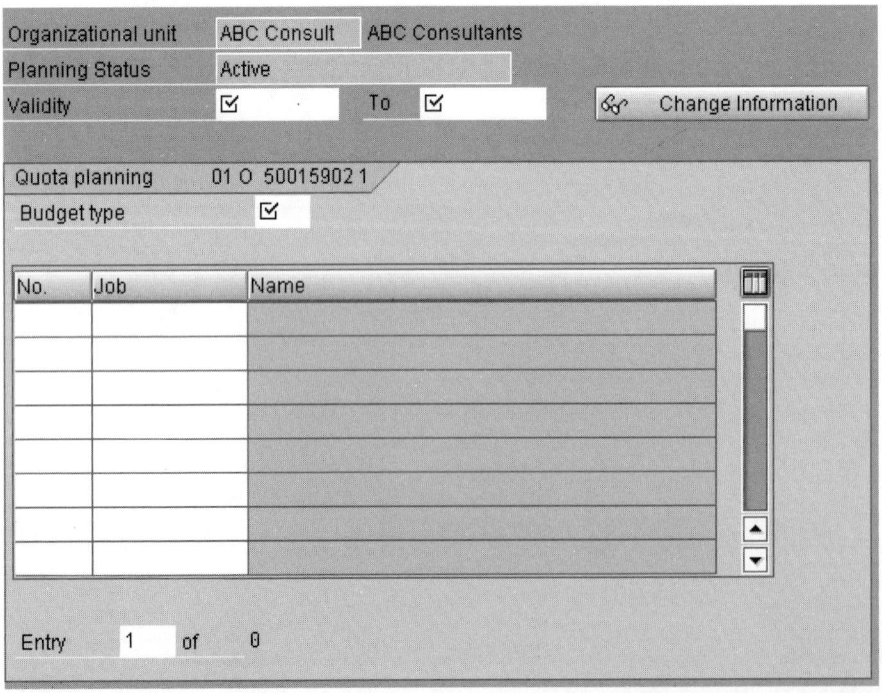

### 14.14.2 Generation of Positions for Quota Planning

After quota planning, if the planned positions are more than actual positions, you need to generate positions. On the other hand if the planned positions are less than actual positions, you need to reduce positions. You can do this using transaction S_PH0_48000084. If the positions are to be generated, the system generates them and displays the list. If the positions are to be reduced, it shows the number to be reduced and lists the positions from which you can select (List ➢ Reduction). Alternatively, you can tick the checkbox 'Automatic reduction' and the system reduces the FTE value of all positions in the required proportion.

### 14.14.3 Quota Planning Type

#### *Purpose*

If you have different types of quota planning, e.g. first planning, second planning, etc. you set that up here. You can choose from these in the 'Budget type' field in the expert mode and 'Planning type' field in the organization and staffing mode.

#### *IMG node*

SM30 ➢ V_778U

#### *Screen*

| Inftyp. | Infotype Name | Subtyp | Subtype text |
|---|---|---|---|
| 1019 | Quota planning | * | |
| 1019 | Quota planning | 0001 | First planning |
| 1019 | Quota planning | 0002 | Second planning |

#### *Primary key*

Infotype + Subtype

### 14.14.4 Planning Type and Periods

#### *Purpose*

Quota planning may take place in several iterations, e.g. first planning, second planning, etc. For each planning type, you specify the planning period, default time interval, and which planning type is currently being worked on in the planning process.

#### *IMG node*

SM30 ➢ T77POSBUD

***Screen***

| STy. | Current... | Total | Time int. | Start date | End Date |
|---|---|---|---|---|---|
| 0001 | ☑ | ☐ | M | 01.01.2009 | 31.12.2009 |

***Primary key***

Subtype

***Subtype***

This field contains the planning type for which you are specifying the planning period.

***Current planning***

A planning type is selected for each round of planning; that is, the system determines whether this is the first round of planning, or the second, etc. The user can only plan using the planning type flagged as current in this table. Only one planning type should be ticked in this table.

***Total***

***Time interval***

During quota planning, the planning period is divided into multiple time intervals of the size specified here. For example, if you have a planning period of one year, and time interval of one month, you can plan the manpower for each of the twelve months. When you are performing quota planning for an organizational unit, this is the default interval which can be changed.

***Start date and end date***

These fields contain the planning period for a planning type.

### 14.14.5 Calculation in Full-time Equivalents (FTE)

***Full-time equivalents***

You can do quota planning either in terms of number of positions, or in terms of number of full-time equivalents, FTEs. When you do quota planning in terms of FTEs, you consider the working time of position and the working time of the organizational unit to determine how many FTEs the position fills. Alternatively, you determine it on the basis of the staffing percentage of the position in conjunction with the capacity utilization level of the employee (person).

| Group | Sem.abbr. | Value abbr | Description |
|---|---|---|---|
| WORKT | FTEP | | Calculation of value for FTE |
| WORKT | FTEQ | | Quota planning in FTEs |

| *Group* | *Sem. abbr.* | *Explanation* |
|---|---|---|
| WORKT | FTEQ | If you set this switch to 'X', you are specifying that you want to carry out quota planning using FTEs rather than positions. In this case, in quota planning you can use FTEs with up to two places after the decimal point. |
| WORKT | FTEP | If this switch is blank, you compute FTEs considering the working time of position and the working time of the organizational unit.<br>➢ FTE of position = Working time (infotype 1011) of position/ working time of organizational unit.<br>➢ If working time of position is not maintained, FTE = 1.<br>If this switch is 'X', you compute FTE on the basis of the staffing percentage of the position in conjunction with the capacity utilization level of the employee (person).<br>➢ If the position is un-staffed, or staffed by a user, the value of the FTE is 0.<br>➢ If the position is staffed by an employee (person), the value of the FTE is the product of the staffing percentage (A/B 008 relationship between S and P) and the capacity utilization level (stored in infotype 0008 of Personnel Administration), where 100% corresponds to the value 1. |

### 14.14.6 Quota Planning Tools

***Copying the current required positions into a planning type***

When you do quota planning for a future period, you may like to copy the current plan and then modify. You can use transaction S_PH0_48000086 to create a future plan based on the current plan.

***Copying quota planning into another planning type***

If you have done the first round of quota planning, and now want to do the second round, it will save effort to copy the first round's plan in the second round's plan and modify. You can do so using transaction S_PH0_48000087. The target planning type must be the planning type marked as active, since it is only here that the current plan figures can be entered. Before copying the quota planning data of a particular organizational unit, the system deletes any existing records relating to that organizational unit which are already in the target planning type.

***Delete unoccupied positions on key date***

If you have unoccupied positions and you think they may not be needed, you can run transaction S_PH0_48000088 to delimit or delete them from the specified deletion date. The system does the following:

- Unoccupied positions whose object validity period starts before the deletion date are delimited.
- Unoccupied positions that exist from exactly the deletion date are deleted.
- Unoccupied positions whose object validity period does not begin until after the deletion date are neither delimited nor deleted. They remain unchanged.

| OT | Organiz... | Object name | OT | Position | Object name | Status |
|---|---|---|---|---|---|---|
| O | 50000075 | ABC Consult | S | 50000078 | Chief Executive Officer | Position was not deleted, beca |
| O | 50000076 | SAP Consulting | S | 50000079 | SAP HR Consultant | Position was not deleted, beca |
| O | | | S | 50000080 | SAP FI/CO Consultant | Position delimited on key date |
| O | | | S | 50000081 | SAP MM Consultant | Position delimited on key date |
| O | | | S | 50000082 | SAP PP Consultant | Position delimited on key date |
| O | | | S | 50000083 | SAP PS Consultant | Position delimited on key date |
| O | | | S | 50000084 | SAP PM Consultant | Position delimited on key date |
| O | | | S | 50000085 | SAP Basis Consultant | Position delimited on key date |
| O | | | S | 50000086 | SAP ABAP Consultant | Position delimited on key date |
| O | 50000077 | SAP Education | S | 50000087 | SAP Education Coordir | Position delimited on key date |

***Freeze planned quota***

When businesses face tough times, they often respond by putting their growth plans on hold and freezing quotas until a certain date. You can do that using transaction S_PH0_48000085. The current quota is used to overwrite quotas until the specified period. Quotas beyond the specified period remain unchanged.

## 14.15 ADDRESS

| *Functional Consultant* | *User* | *Business Process Owner* | *Senior Management* | *My Rating* | *Understanding Level* |
|---|---|---|---|---|---|
| A | A | B | C | | |

### 14.15.1 Address (Infotype 1028)

In infotype 1028, you can maintain addresses of organizational objects, e.g. organizational units, positions, work centers.

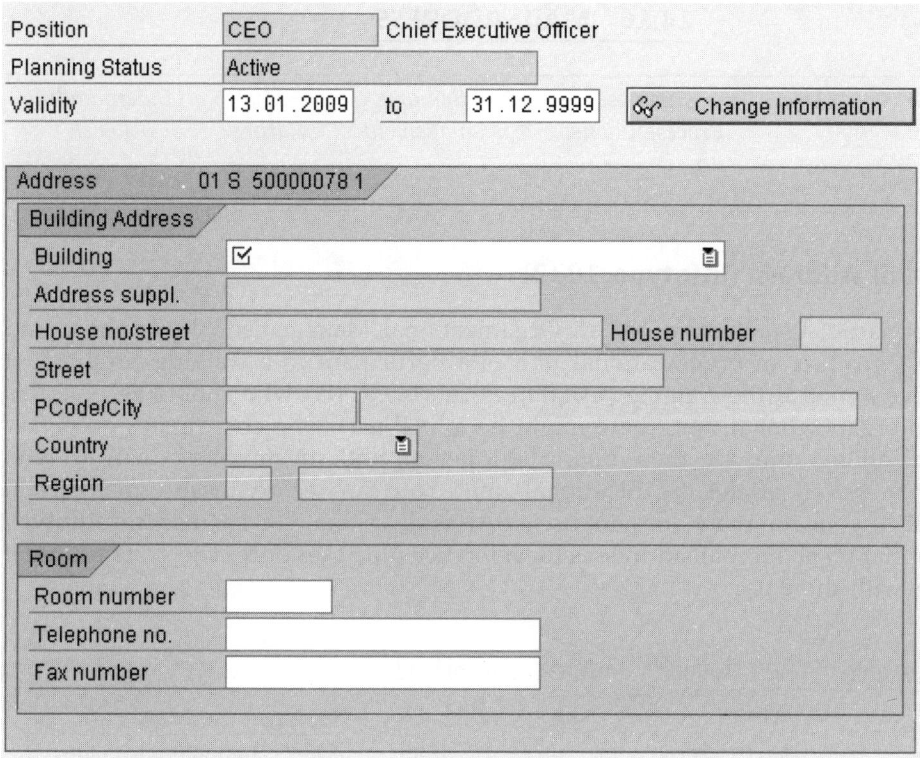


## 14.15.2 Buildings

You can maintain addresses of your different buildings using transaction S_AHR_61003172 or S_AHR_61011843. You may also do so using transaction SM30 ➢ T777A. Building addresses are used in infotype 1028.

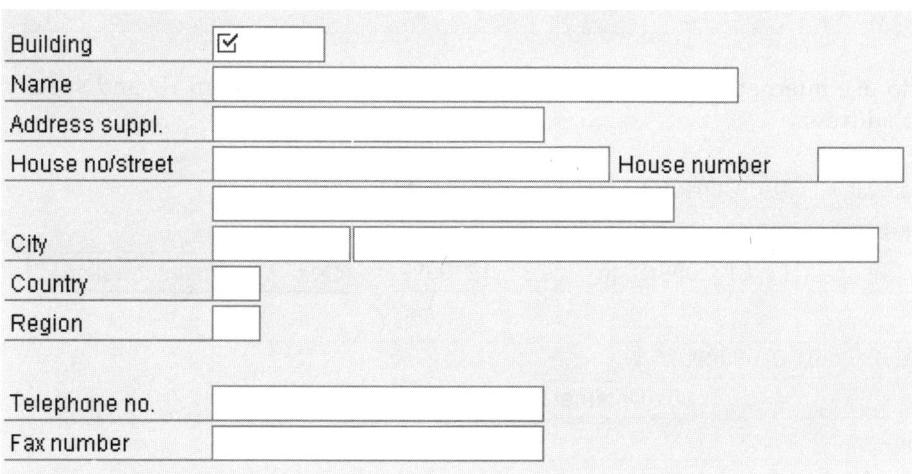

## 14.16 MAIL ADDRESS

| *Functional Consultant* | *User* | *Business Process Owner* | *Senior Management* | *My Rating* | *Understanding Level* |
|---|---|---|---|---|---|
| A | A | B | C | | |

### 14.16.1 Mail Address (Infotype 1032)

This infotype is not usually required in Organizational Management. In Training and Event Management, if an organizational unit is a participant in a training program, it should receive a mail if the training program is cancelled. But who should receive this mail? For an organizational unit, there might be a SAP user who coordinates on behalf of the organizational unit. Or, there might be a person with an internet e-mail id, who coordinates on behalf of the organizational unit. You can record these e-mail ids in infotype 1032. If your company does not use a SAP mail system, you can use this infotype to store information about mail addresses for reference purposes only. The system cannot do anything with the data.

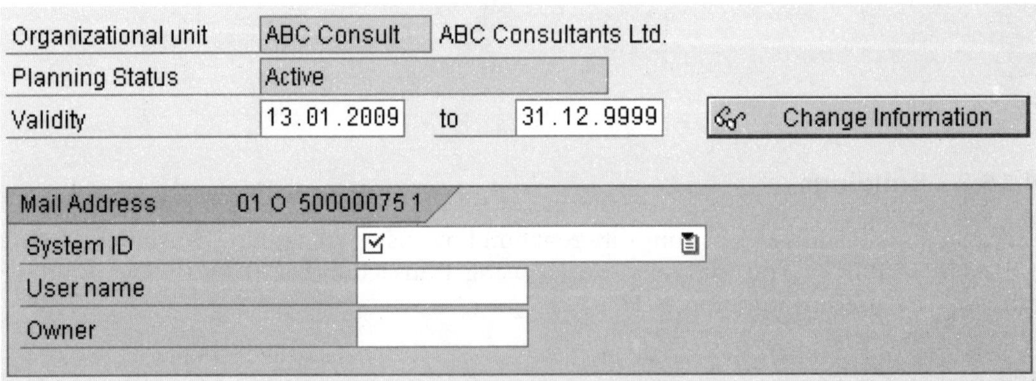


If you want to use internet mail, you specify Internet Mail in the system ID and specify only internet address.

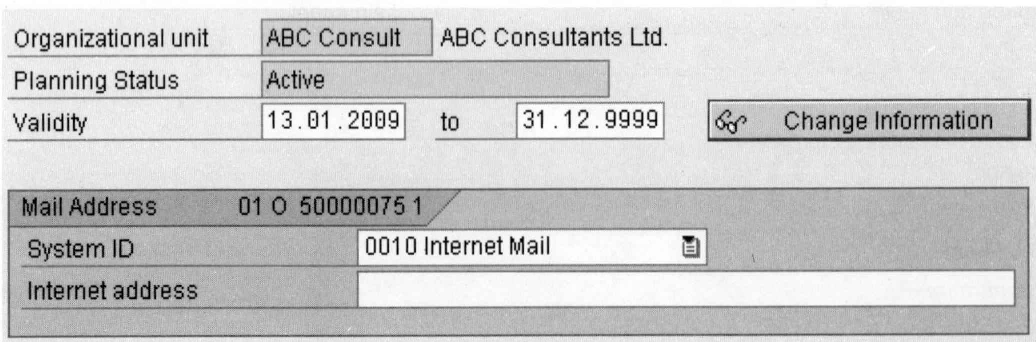

# Chapter 15 Plan Version

## 15.1 PLAN VERSION CONCEPT

| *Functional Consultant* | *User* | *Business Process Owner* | *Senior Management* | *My Rating* | *Understanding Level* |
|---|---|---|---|---|---|
| A | A | A | A | | |

Normally you would have an organizational plan, which reflects your current organization and is actively used. This plan may change with time to reflect your changing organization.

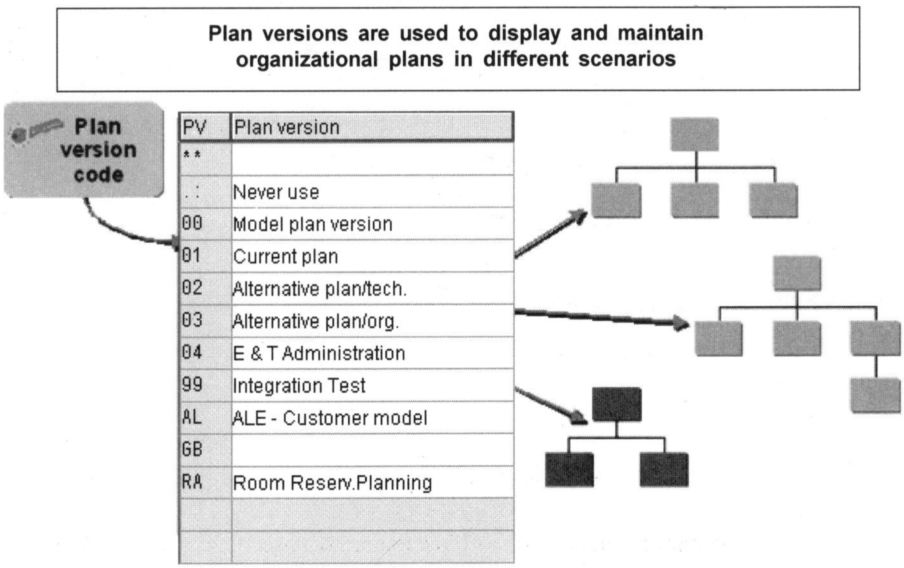

Sometimes companies plan a major reorganization. They will like to draw up one or more alternate plans without disturbing the current organizational plan. They will like to compare, discuss and decide what the organizational plan will be in future. Finally, they will like to implement the new organizational plan. In SAP, you don't have to do this planning on paper. You can create the alternate plans on the system without disturbing the current and active plan. You do so using multiple plan versions. You can discuss multiple plan versions, compare them, and decide the plan version that will represent your future organization. Finally, you implement the new plan. You may do this by copying the proposed plan in the current and active plan, or you may change the plan version of your active plan.

If you are not reorganizing and therefore creating alternate organizational plans, you don't need to worry about plan versions. By default the plan version is set to 01 (current plan) and the same plan is integrated with Personnel Administration.

However, if you are creating an alternate plan, you set the plan version to the alternate plan version and create the organizational plan in that plan version. You can also copy your current organizational plan in the alternate plan version and modify it.

## 15.2 MAINTAINING PLAN VERSION

| *Functional Consultant* | *User* | *Business Process Owner* | *Senior Management* | *My Rating* | *Understanding Level* |
|---|---|---|---|---|---|
| A | A | B | C | | |

You can maintain your own plan versions in table T778P.

| PV | Plan version | Active | Current |
|---|---|---|---|
| ** | | ☐ | ☐ |
| .: | Never use | ☐ | ☐ |
| 00 | Model plan version | ☐ | ☐ |
| 01 | Current plan | ☑ | ☑ |
| 02 | Alternative plan/tech. | ☐ | ☐ |
| 03 | Alternative plan/org. | ☐ | ☐ |
| 04 | E & T Administration | ☐ | ☐ |
| 99 | Integration Test | ☐ | ☐ |
| AL | ALE - Customer model | ☐ | ☐ |
| GB | | ☐ | ☐ |
| RA | Room Reserv.Planning | ☐ | ☐ |

## 15.3 SETTING PLAN VERSION

| *Functional Consultant* | *User* | *Business Process Owner* | *Senior Management* | *My Rating* | *Understanding Level* |
|---|---|---|---|---|---|
| A | A | B | C | | |

You can run transaction PSO0 or PSV4 to set plan version. Once you set the plan version, any objects and relationships you create will be created in that plan version. You can also set plan version in the Organization and Staffing interface by choosing Settings ➢ Plan version ➢ Alternative, or Settings ➢ Plan version ➢ Active employee.

## 15.4 ACTIVE PLAN VERSION

| *Functional Consultant* | *User* | *Business Process Owner* | *Senior Management* | *My Rating* | *Understanding Level* |
|---|---|---|---|---|---|
| A | A | B | C | | |

If there are multiple plan versions, the plan version which is integrated with Personnel Administration is specified in the following entry in view V_T77S0SC.

| Group | Sem. abbr. | Value abbr. | Description |
|---|---|---|---|
| PLOGI | PLOGI | 01 | Integration Plan Version / Active Plan Version |

## 15.5 NUMBER ASSIGNMENT FOR ALL PLAN VERSIONS

| *Functional Consultant* | *User* | *Business Process Owner* | *Senior Management* | *My Rating* | *Understanding Level* |
|---|---|---|---|---|---|
| A | B | B | C | | |

When you are going to use multiple plan versions, you may copy objects from one plan version to another. If you do so, should the objects be copied with same object numbers or with different object numbers? You specify your choice in the following entry in view V_T77S0.

| Group | Sem. abbr. | Value abbr. | Description |
|---|---|---|---|
| NUMRG | COMP | | Number assignment for all plan versions |

| *Value* | *Numbers are unique across* | *Copy behavior* | *Advantage* | *Disadvantage* |
|---|---|---|---|---|
| X | All plan versions | Copied objects are given new object numbers. | During copy, objects are not overwritten. | Organizational plans cannot be compared. |
| Blank | Within a plan version | Copied objects are given the same object numbers from which they are copied. | Organizational plans can be compared. | During copy, objects may be overwritten. |

## 15.6 COPYING PLAN VERSIONS

| *Functional Consultant* | *User* | *Business Process Owner* | *Senior Management* | *My Rating* | *Understanding Level* |
|---|---|---|---|---|---|
| A | B | C | X | | |

You can use transaction RE_RHCOPL00 to copy objects from one plan version to another. If you want to copy only certain infotypes and subtypes, you may specify that. You can also run this program in test mode.

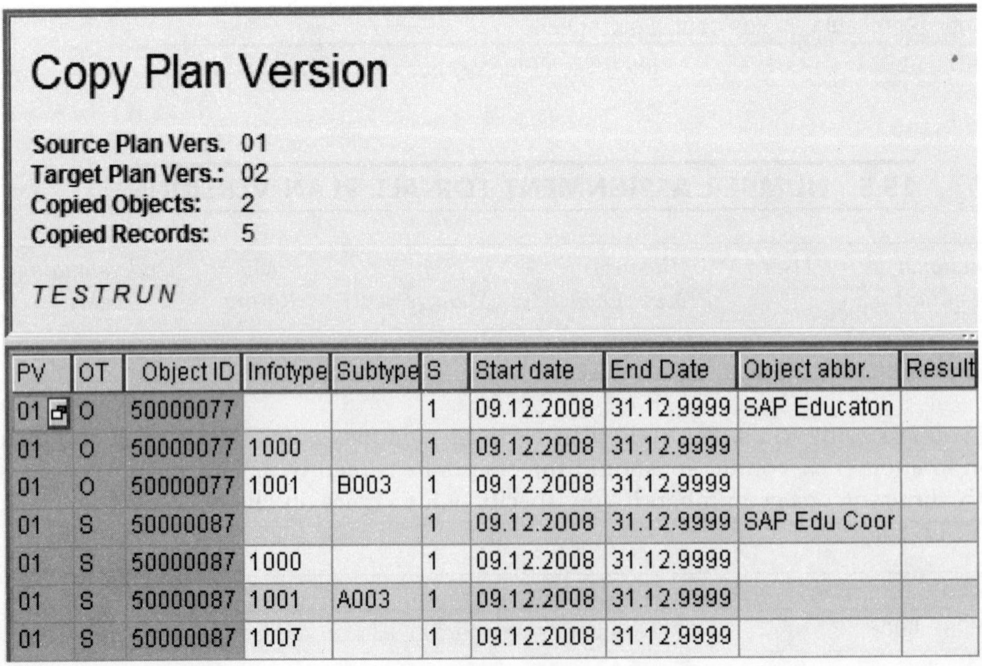
Copy Plan Version

Source Plan Vers. 01
Target Plan Vers.: 02
Copied Objects: 2
Copied Records: 5

TESTRUN

| PV | OT | Object ID | Infotype | Subtype | S | Start date | End Date | Object abbr. | Result |
|---|---|---|---|---|---|---|---|---|---|
| 01 | O | 50000077 | | | 1 | 09.12.2008 | 31.12.9999 | SAP Educaton | |
| 01 | O | 50000077 | 1000 | | 1 | 09.12.2008 | 31.12.9999 | | |
| 01 | O | 50000077 | 1001 | B003 | 1 | 09.12.2008 | 31.12.9999 | | |
| 01 | S | 50000087 | | | 1 | 09.12.2008 | 31.12.9999 | SAP Edu Coor | |
| 01 | S | 50000087 | 1000 | | 1 | 09.12.2008 | 31.12.9999 | | |
| 01 | S | 50000087 | 1001 | A003 | 1 | 09.12.2008 | 31.12.9999 | | |
| 01 | S | 50000087 | 1007 | | 1 | 09.12.2008 | 31.12.9999 | | |

## 15.7 COPYING STRUCTURES

| *Functional Consultant* | *User* | *Business Process Owner* | *Senior Management* | *My Rating* | *Understanding Level* |
|---|---|---|---|---|---|
| A | B | C | X | | |

You can run transaction RE_RHCOPYSTRUCT to copy structures from one plan version to another. It copies the structure specified in the selection screen to the specified plan version. All objects selected along the evaluation path are copied individually. All new object IDs are determined by internal number allocation. All infotypes and all relationships are copied for all the objects selected. The exception in this case is when a reverse relationship (in the direction of the object to be copied) has time constraint 2.

| OT | Object ID | Object abbr. | Object name | Infotype | STy. | S | Pr | Start date | End Date | Var.field |
|---|---|---|---|---|---|---|---|---|---|---|
| O | 1 | SAP Educatc | SAP Educatio | 1000 | | 1 | | 09.12.2008 | 31.12.9999 | E |
| O | 1 | SAP Educatc | SAP Educatio | 1001 | A002 | 1 | AB | 09.12.2008 | 31.12.9999 | O 50000075 |
| O | 1 | SAP Educatc | SAP Educatio | 1001 | B003 | 1 | | 09.12.2008 | 31.12.9999 | S 00000002 |
| S | 2 | SAP Edu Co | SAP Educatio | 1000 | | 1 | | 09.12.2008 | 31.12.9999 | E |
| S | 2 | SAP Edu Co | SAP Educatio | 1001 | A003 | 1 | | 09.12.2008 | 31.12.9999 | O 00000001 |
| S | 2 | SAP Edu Co | SAP Educatio | 1007 | | 1 | | 09.12.2008 | 31.12.9999 | |

## 15.8 COMPARING PLAN VERSIONS

| *Functional Consultant* | *User* | *Business Process Owner* | *Senior Management* | *My Rating* | *Understanding Level* |
|---|---|---|---|---|---|
| A | B | C | X | | |

You can use transaction RE_RHCOPLPT to compare plan versions and to copy structures from one plan version to another. It consists of two steps. In the first step the plan versions are compared, and in the second step the objects are copied.

### *Comparing plan versions*

You specify the objects or substructures that you want to compare in the selection screen. The system compares the selected objects and substructures in the source plan version with those in the target plan version. The result of this comparison is displayed on the next screen as a structural evaluation. A stoplight icon indicates the extent to which an object in the source plan version is compatible with an object in the target plan version, or whether it exists in both plan versions.

| | |
|---|---|
| Green | The object exists in both plan versions and is compatible with the selected evaluation path. |
| Yellow | The object exists in both plan versions and is partially compatible. |
| Red | The object only exists in the source plan version. |

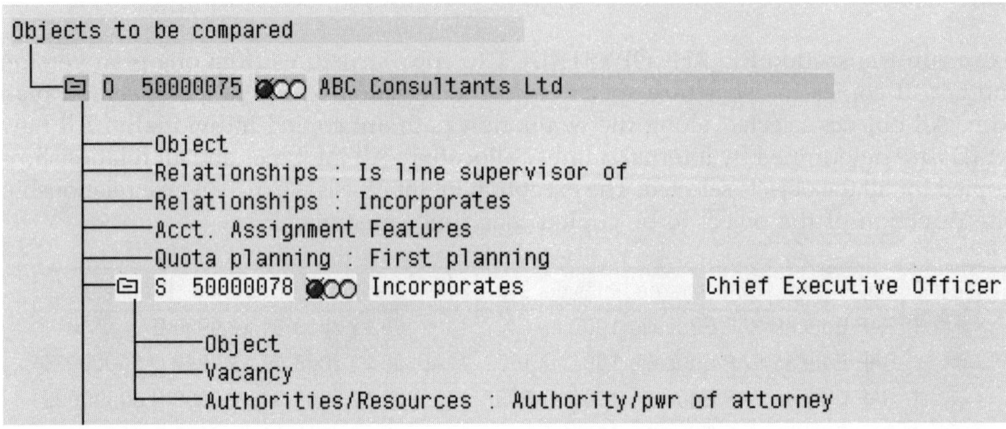


If you want to perform a more detailed comparison before copying the objects, you can display all infotypes of the selected object by choosing Goto ➢ Object description.

### *Copying objects*

You specify the objects you want to copy by selecting an area and clicking Transfer.

# CHAPTER 16 Planning Status

## 16.1 PLANNING STATUS

| *Functional Consultant* | *User* | *Business Process Owner* | *Senior Management* | *My Rating* | *Understanding Level* |
|---|---|---|---|---|---|
| A | A | A | A | | |

You can create all types of organizational objects using transaction PP01. When you run transaction PP01, you see the following screen. This screen shows tabs, e.g. Active, Planned, Submitted, etc. and you may have wondered what they are.

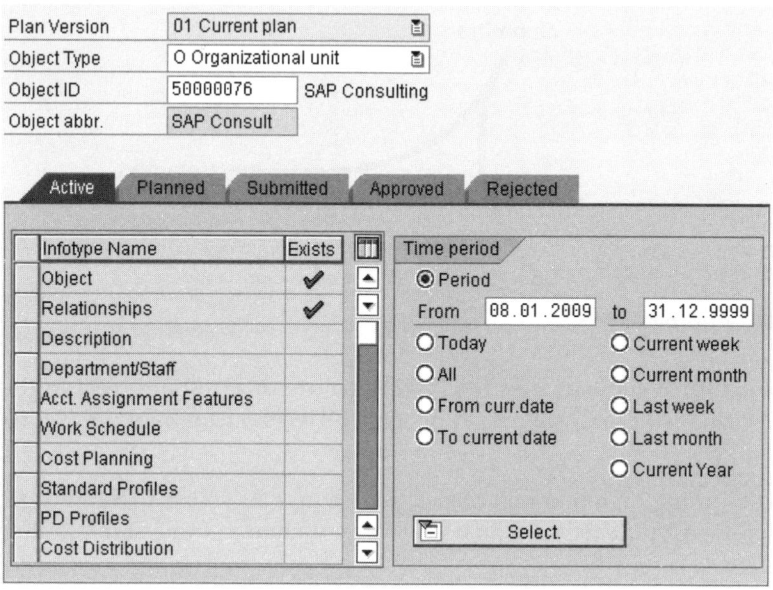

While creating your organizational objects, you can either create them directly in the Active status, or create them as Planned, and take them through an approval cycle. The planning status identifies the status of the object.

Objects with different status can appear in the same plan version. The active objects represent current operations in your organization, and the planned objects represent changes you plan to make, for example, adding a new department or a new position.

You must assign a status to every object and infotype record you create. However, you do not need to use all the statuses. If you are not using the planning cycle, you can directly create your organizational objects in the Active planning status. Most companies do just that.

## 16.2 PLANNING CYCLE

| *Functional Consultant* | *User* | *Business Process Owner* | *Senior Management* | *My Rating* | *Understanding Level* |
|---|---|---|---|---|---|
| A | A | A | A | | |

**The status feature allows the object to go through an approval cycle.**

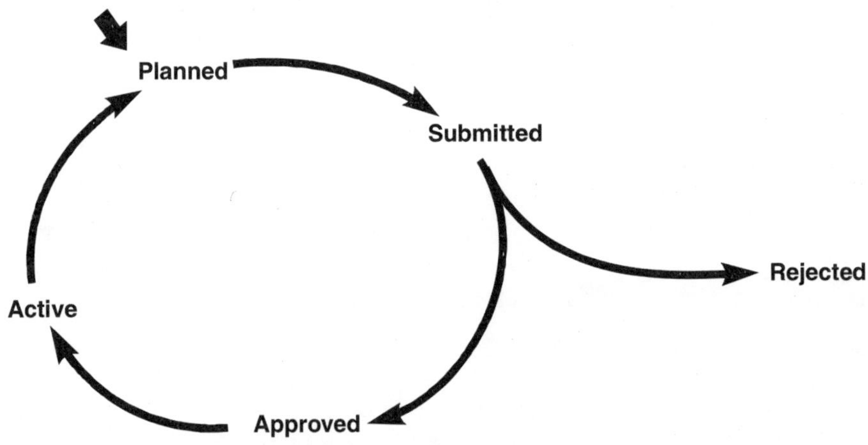


If you decide to follow the approval cycle, you first create an organizational object in the Planned status. Planned status is actually work-in-progress. Decision makers don't look at planned objects.

Once you have completed working on a planned object, you change its status to Submitted. Submitted objects are reviewed by decision makers, who may change their status either to Approved, or to Rejected.

Once an object is approved, you may change its status to Active. Objects in Active status are in current use. You may also create objects in Active status directly.

If an object is Rejected, you may either discard it, or change its status to Planned, and work further on it.

| *Status* | *Description* |
|---|---|
| Planned | Indicates that an object is proposed or anticipated, but not currently operable. You can create, change, display, delimit, delete and list the planned objects. |
| Submitted | Indicates that an object has been submitted for review and subsequent approval/rejection. You cannot create objects with submitted status. Nor can you make changes. |
| Approved | Indicates that an object, previously submitted for review, is accepted or authorized. By changing the status to active, you can edit the object (create, change, display, delimit, delete and list). |
| Rejected | Indicates that an object is rejected or turned down. You can only display objects with rejected status. However, you can change the status to planned so that you can work with the object again. |
| Active | Indicates that an object is currently operable. You can create, change, display, delimit, delete and list the active objects. |

## 16.3 PLANNING STATUS IN OM INTERFACES

| *Functional Consultant* | *User* | *Business Process Owner* | *Senior Management* | *My Rating* | *Understanding Level* |
|---|---|---|---|---|---|
| A | A | B | C | | |

| *Interface* | *Specifying planning status* |
|---|---|
| Organization and Staffing | All infotypes are created in the Active planning status only. |
| General Structures | All infotypes are created in the Active planning status only. |
| Simple Maintenance | All infotypes are created in the Active planning status only. |
| Expert Mode | You select the tab in which you create the infotype. Each tab corresponds to a planning status. |
| Structural Graphics | In transaction S_AHR_61016530 you specify the planning status on the selection screen. |
| Actions | You specify the planning status on the selection screen. |

## 16.4 CHANGING PLANNING STATUS

| *Functional Consultant* | *User* | *Business Process Owner* | *Senior Management* | *My Rating* | *Understanding Level* |
|---|---|---|---|---|---|
| A | A | B | C | | |

There are two ways in which you can change the status applied to objects and infotype records in the organizational plan.

### *Change status in expert mode*

You can change planning status of an infotype in the expert mode transactions, e.g. PP01. You go to the appropriate tab, select the record whose planning status you want to change and choose Edit ➢ Status change.

### *Change object status report*

You can use transaction RE_RHAKTI00 to change the status of one or more objects and their infotypes. You specify the change in planning status you want to make.

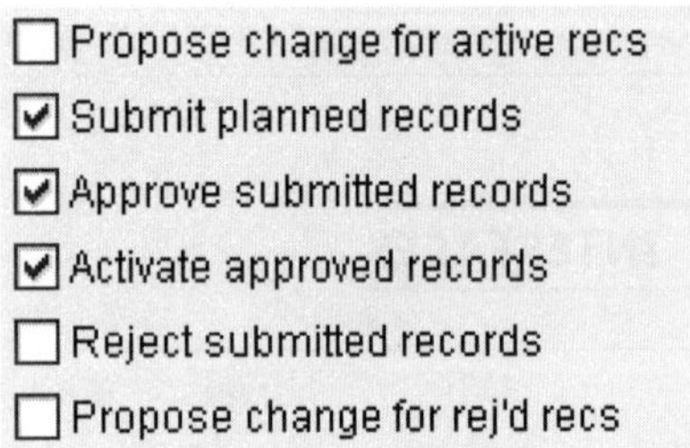


The status of the infotype record is changed as specified. If you propose change for an active or rejected infotype record, a copy of the infotype record is created in planned status while the active or rejected record remains unchanged. In all other cases, planning status of the record is changed.

In transaction PP01, you can change the planning status of one infotype record at a time, whereas by using this report, you can change the planning status of a number of objects and their infotypes at the same time. Also, by ticking multiple checkboxes, you can run all the steps in one execution. For example, you can move an object directly from the 'planned' to 'active' status if you tick the checkboxes as shown in the screenshot above.

## 16.5 FUNCTIONS PERMITTED IN PLANNING STATUS

| *Functional Consultant* | *User* | *Business Process Owner* | *Senior Management* | *My Rating* | *Understanding Level* |
|---|---|---|---|---|---|
| A | B | C | X | | |

Depending on the planning status of an infotype (including object and relationship infotypes), SAP lets you perform certain functions. These are specified in table T777F (Function Code Assignment to Planning Status). These are summarized below. You will notice that the functions which are restricted are the functions which should not be logically performed on an infotype in that planning status. For example, only an approved record can be activated, or only a submitted record can be approved.

| *Active* | *Planned* | *Submitted* | *Approved* | *Rejected* |
|---|---|---|---|---|
| | | | Activate | |
| | | Approve | | |
| Change | Change | | | |
| Create | Create | | | |
| Delete | Delete | | | |
| Delimit | | | | |
| Display | Display | Display | Display | Display |
| List display | List display | List display | List display | List display |
| List display with change | List display with change | | | |
| Propose change | | | | Propose change |
| | | Reject | Reject | |
| | Submit | | | |

CHAPTER 17

# Authorizations

## 17.1 AUTHORIZATION CONCEPTS

| Functional Consultant | User | Business Process Owner | Senior Management | My Rating | Understanding Level |
|---|---|---|---|---|---|
| A | A | A | A | | |

### 17.1.1 Authorization Objects

***Creating a test role***

The best way to understand how SAP controls authorizations is to create a test role using transaction PFCG. After creating the role, you go to 'menu' tab, and add a transaction, e.g. PA20. You then go to 'Authorizations' tab, and click 'Change Authorization Data'. You will see the following screen.

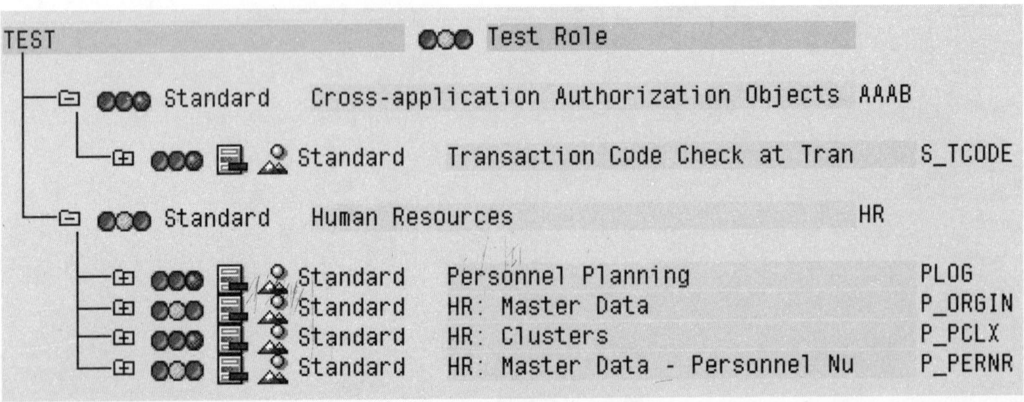

### *Object classes*

The 'Test Role' has two object classes, namely AAAB and HR.

### *Authorization objects*

The 'Test Role' has five authorization objects. Expand the authorization object P_ORGIN.

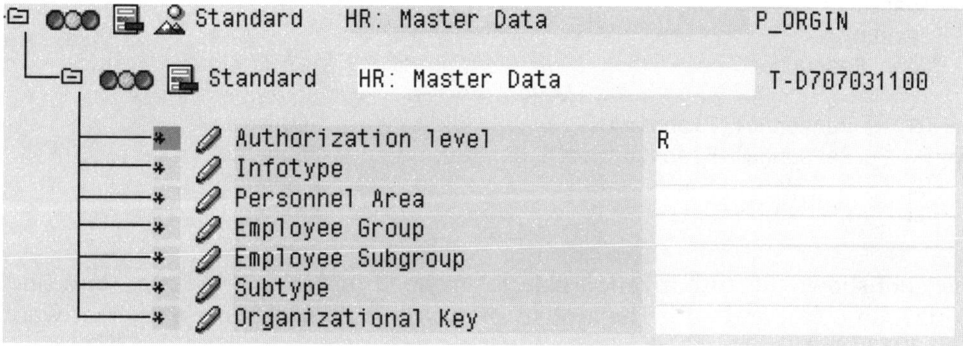


### *Authorization fields*

The screenshot above shows authorization fields in one authorization object. An authorization object groups up to ten authorization fields that are checked in an AND relationship. In this object you specify the authorization given to a role (or profile), which will become the authorization for one or more users through assignment of the role to users. In this object, you specify the following:

- For which infotype and subtype, the user has authorization.
- For which personnel area, employee group and employee subgroup, the user has authorization.
- If you use organizational key, for which organizational key, the user has authorization.
- What is the level of authorization, e.g. display or change?

If a user tries to create an infotype 0001 record for a person, the system will check whether the user has authorization for each field above. If any of the tests fail, the user will not be able to carry out the action. In other words, the final result is determined by applying AND operation to the result of all tests within an authorization object.

### *Multiple copies of the same authorization object*

But what would you do if you want to give display authorization for infotype 0001 and change authorization for infotype 0002? You can do that by creating two authorization objects in the same role, one for each infotype. If the user satisfies any one authorization object fully, he will be able to perform the transaction.

***Adding an authorization object manually***

You can add an authorization object manually. If you don't know the technical name of the organization object, you click Selection criteria. It opens the following screen.

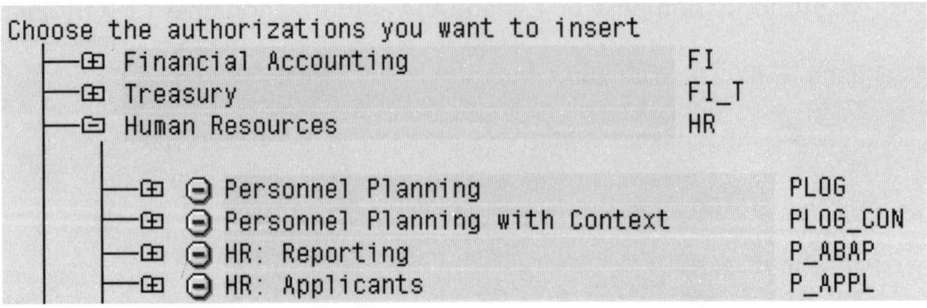


This screenshot shows the authorization objects, grouped under object classes. You find the authorization object and add. The system shows the authorization objects that were manually added, and those, which were added by the system.

***Default authorization objects and values***

When you generated authorization profile, the system automatically added certain authorization objects, and in some cases, it also put values for the fields. SAP has created these defaults, but you can change the default settings if you want. You are advised not to do so, unless you have adequate mastery over the subject.

***Authorization objects for infotypes***

You have seen an authorization object of type P_ORGIN. This can be used to control authorization for infotypes. There are also other authorization objects, e.g. P_ORGXX, which can be used to control authorization for infotypes. If you wish to give infotype authorization based on administrator, rather than PA, EG and ESG, you can use authorization object P_ORGXX. Similarly, if you want to use structural authorization, you can use authorization object P_ORGINCON. SAP provides a large number of authorization objects, which you can use to control different activities in SAP.

***Authorization objects for personnel planning***

For personnel planning infotypes you use authorization objects PLOG or PLOG_CON.

## 17.1.2 Structural Authorizations

For infotypes, you can control authorizations based on personnel area, employee group and employee subgroup in authorization object P_ORGIN. However, there is often a need to control authorization based on organizational structure. SAP meets this requirement through structural authorizations.

To maintain structural authorizations, you first maintain authorization profiles. This topic is discussed in detail, later in this chapter. Then, you use authorization object P_ORGINCON, in place of P_ORGIN. In P_ORGINCON, there is an additional field, 'Authorization Profile'. You attach the authorization profile created earlier to this field. In this way you will give authorization only for a specified part of organizational structure. If you are using structural authorizations, usually you do not restrict based on personnel area, employee group and employee subgroup.

### 17.1.3 Authorizations for User's Own Data

In Employee Self-Service (ESS), an employee may see, or update his own data, but he should not see data of other employees. To meet this requirement, SAP provides an authorization object P_PERNR. Also, you may want that while HR administrators update data for everyone else, they should not be able to update their own data. Even this requirement can be met through authorization object P_PERNR. The link between a user and his personnel number is maintained in infotype 0105, subtype 0001.

### 17.1.4 Roles and Profiles

You can create a role using transaction PFCG. You can also create a menu for a role. This is displayed in user menu of all users, who are assigned that role.

If you go to authorizations tab, and click 'Change authorization data', SAP proposes a set of authorization objects, along with their default values. You fill up the missing values, and check whether the proposed values are okay. If necessary, you may change them. Finally when you save them, all authorization objects should be green, as only those authorization objects are effective.

You can also see all users who have been granted the role. If 'User comparison' button on the user tab is not green, click it. Otherwise, the authorizations may not work correctly.

### 17.1.5 Authorization for User

You can use transaction SU01 to assign roles to users. You can assign him one or more roles, which govern user authorization in SAP. You can also specify a reference user, whose authorizations will be available to the current user. You can also assign a user one or more profiles, which also grant him authorization in SAP.

### 17.1.6 Authorization for Organizational Units and Positions

The work done by a person depends on his position in the organization. It therefore makes sense to give authorization to positions which may be inherited by the persons holding those positions. SAP supports this. It provides infotype 1016 through which you can assign profiles to positions. The holder of the position will then inherit the authorization. When he logs onto the system using a user id, the system will determine his personnel number from infotype 0105, subtype 0001, and give him the authorization granted to the position he holds.

Through infotype 1016 you can also give authorization to an organizational unit, which will then be available to all positions in the organizational unit. You can also give authorization to a job, which will be available to all positions which are linked to that job. You can also give authorization to a task, which will be available to all jobs which contain that task and all positions which perform that task. Infotype 1016 can be used only for normal authorization profiles. If you want to assign a structural authorization profile to positions, organizational units, etc. you may use infotype 1017.

### 17.1.7 Change Log

#### *Change log for personnel planning infotypes*

You may want to record change to critical data so that it can be reviewed periodically and is also available for audit. You can specify the data for which change log is to be maintained in view T77CDOC_CUST.

#### *Change log for personnel administration infotypes*

You can activate the change document in the Implementation Guide (IMG) for Personnel Management under Personnel Administration ➢ Tools ➢ Revision ➢ Set up change document. For more information about the change document, see the documentation of this IMG activity.

The change document has nothing to do with the authorization check. It does not prevent unauthorized users from accessing data. Rather it logs attempts made by unauthorized users to access data. You can evaluate the changes using the RPUAUD00 report (Logged Changes in Infotype Data).

### 17.1.8 Customer Enhancements

SAP lets you implement your own logic for authorization checks.

| *BadI* | *Use* |
|---|---|
| HRPAD00AUTH_CHECK | You can use this BadI to replace the standard SAP authorization checks completely. As soon as an implementation for this BadI is active, all HR master data authorization checks are stopped and checks only in the activated implementation are performed. |
| HRBAS00_STRUAUTH | You can use this BadI to replace structural authorization checks. |
| HRBAS00_GET_PROFL | If you use this BadI, you do not have to maintain the structural profiles in table T77UA (User Authorizations). |

### 17.1.9 Troubleshooting Authorization Problems

When a user faces authorization failure, you need to know what authorization he required, and what authorization he had. This is displayed by executing transaction SU53 immediately after authorization failure.

## 17.2 AUTHORIZATION MAIN SWITCHES

| *Functional Consultant* | *User* | *Business Process Owner* | *Senior Management* | *My Rating* | *Understanding Level* |
|---|---|---|---|---|---|
| A | B | C | X | | |

### 17.2.1 Purpose

SAP provides you a lot of choices in authorization control. These are exercised through switches explained in this chapter.

### 17.2.2 IMG Node

SM30 ➢ V_T77S0 (Group name AUTSW)

### 17.2.3 Screen

| Group | Sem. abbr. | Value abbr. | Description |
|---|---|---|---|
| AUTSW | ADAYS | 15 | HR: Tolerance Time for Authorization Check |
| AUTSW | APPRO | 0 | HR: Test Procedures |
| AUTSW | DFCON | 1 | HR: Default Position (Context) |
| AUTSW | INCON | 0 | HR: Master Data (Context) |
| AUTSW | NNCON | 0 | HR:Customer-Specific Authorization Check (Context) |
| AUTSW | NNNNN | 0 | HR: Customer-Specific Authorization Check |
| AUTSW | ORGIN | 1 | HR: Master Data |
| AUTSW | ORGPD | 0 | HR: Structural Authorization Check |
| AUTSW | ORGXX | 0 | HR: Master Data - Extended Check |
| AUTSW | PERNR | 1 | HR: Master Data - Personnel Number Check |
| AUTSW | XXCON | 0 | HR: Master Data - Enhanced Check (Context) |

### 17.2.4 Authorization Switches

| *Switch* | *Explanation* |
|---|---|
| ADAYS | If an HR administrator changes the organizational assignment of a person, and he has no authorization for the new area where the employee now belongs, he will not be able to see the record he has created. This can cause problems. Here you can specify the number of calendar days, for which the administrator can see the record he created, even though he does not have authorization for employee's new area. |
| APPRO | You set this switch to 1 if you want to implement infotype 0130, test procedures. Test procedures can be used if certain entries are to be checked centrally and should not be changeable after the check without further action. |
| DFCON | See the explanation in switch ORGPD. |
| INCON | This switch determines whether authorization object P_ORGINCON is used in the authorization check. |
| NNCON | This switch determines whether customer-specific authorization object P_NNNNNCON is used for authorization check. Note that this is not a standard authorization object. |
| NNNNN | This switch determines whether customer-specific authorization object P_NNNNN is used for authorization check. Note that this is not a standard authorization object. You have to create the authorization object first. |
| ORGIN | This switch determines whether authorization object P_ORGIN is used for authorization check. Alternatively you could use P_ORGXX or P_ORGINCON. |
| ORGPD | Structural authorizations can be implemented in two ways; by using P_ORGINCON object, or by assigning a profile to user in table T77UA. If you are using P_ORGINCON method, you use switch DFCON. If you are using T77UA method, you use switch ORGPD. These switches determine whether structural authorization check is on, and what is its behavior.<br><br>In structural authorization, a user has authorization for an organizational unit. The organizational unit has positions. The positions are linked to persons in infotype 0001. This is the link to determine whether a user has authorization for a personnel number or not.<br><br>However, sometimes you use default positions. In that case the above link will not work. You have the following options:<br><br>1 SAP Unit Checked (Initial ➢ No Authorization)<br>2 SAP Unit Not Checked (No Authorization)<br>3 SAP Unit Checked (Initial ➢ Authorization)<br>4 SAP Unit Not Checked (Authorization)<br><br>In options 1 and 3, employee's organizational unit in infotype 0001 is checked. If the organizational unit exists, it determines whether the user |

| Switch | Explanation |
|---|---|
| | is authorized or not. However, if the organizational unit does not exist, in option 3 the user is authorized, and in option 1 he is not authorized.<br>In options 2 and 4, the employee's organizational unit is not checked at all. In option 4 the user is authorized, and in option 2 he is not authorized. |
| ORGXX | This switch determines whether authorization object P_ORGXX is used for authorization check. You use this object if you want to check authorization of administrators. |
| PERNR | This switch determines whether authorization object P_PERNR is used for authorization check. You can use this object to permit, or deny, the user to see/change his own data. |
| XXCON | This switch determines whether authorization object P_ORGXXCON is used in the authorization check. |

## 17.3 AUTHORIZATION OBJECTS FOR TRANSACTIONS

| *Functional Consultant* | *User* | *Business Process Owner* | *Senior Management* | *My Rating* | *Understanding Level* |
|---|---|---|---|---|---|
| A | B | C | X | | |

### 17.3.1 Purpose and Overview

When you add a transaction in menu of a role and generate authorization profile, the system proposes the authorization objects, and in some cases default values. These are defined here, and you can change them if you wish.

The objects shown under C are checked, and objects shown under CM are both checked and maintained, i.e. inserted in the profile when you add a transaction to a role. You can add or delete an object. You can change between U, N, C and CM, simply by clicking the point of your choice. These are just like radio buttons. You can maintain default values of the fields, which will appear when the object is inserted.

### 17.3.2 Transaction

SU24 – Authorization Object Check under Transactions

### 17.3.3 Screen

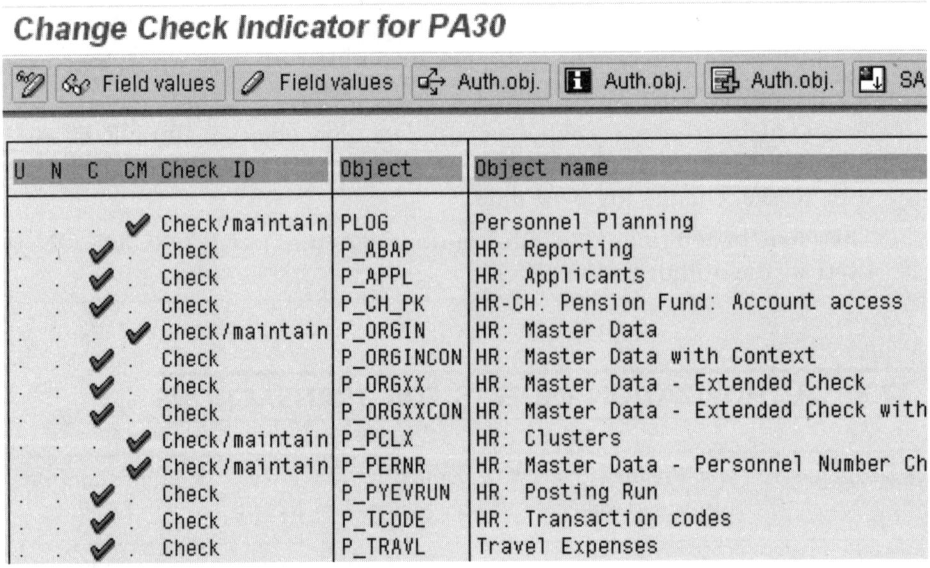


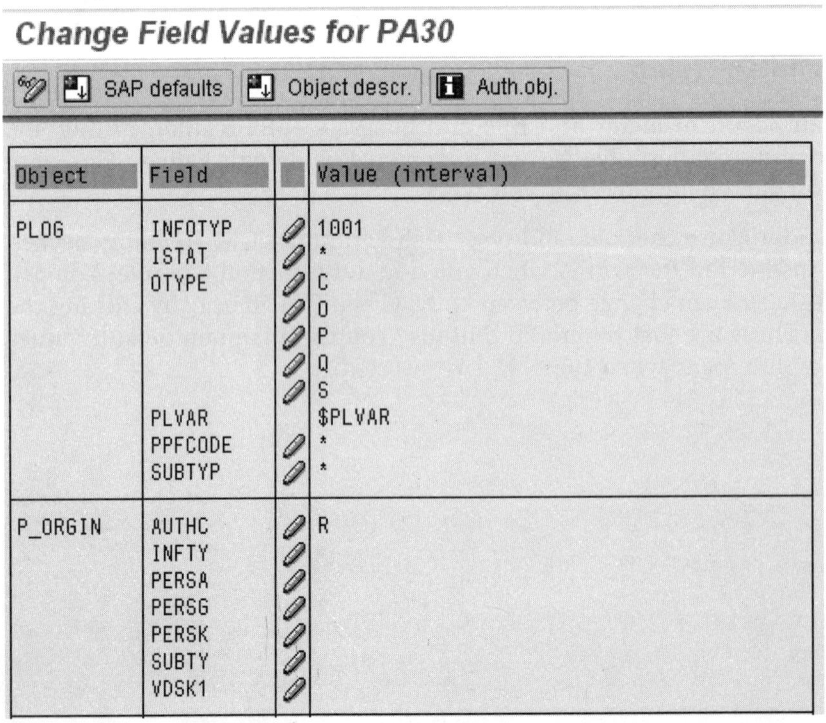

## 17.4 AUTHORIZATION PROFILES

| *Functional Consultant* | *User* | *Business Process Owner* | *Senior Management* | *My Rating* | *Understanding Level* |
|---|---|---|---|---|---|
| A | B | B | C | | |

### 17.4.1 Purpose

Here you maintain the master list of structural authorization profiles. These are either assigned to users in view T77UA, or assigned to the profile field in authorization object P_ORGINCON.

### 17.4.2 IMG Node

SM34 ➢ T77PQ (table T77PQ)

### 17.4.3 Transaction

S_AHR_61003751—Define Authorization Profiles
OOSP—Authorization Profiles
S_AHR_61011912—Maintain Authorization Profiles
S_AHR_61007222—Define Authorization Profiles

### 17.4.4 Screen

| Authoriz. profile | Auth.profile name | Info |
|---|---|---|
| ALL | ALL | i |
| ALL_01 | ALL_01 | i |
| ALL_02 | ALL_02 | i |
| ALL_03 | ALL_03 | i |
| ALL_04 | ALL_04 | i |

### 17.4.5 Primary Key

Authorization Profile

## 17.5 AUTHORIZATION PROFILE DEFINITION

| *Functional Consultant* | *User* | *Business Process Owner* | *Senior Management* | *My Rating* | *Understanding Level* |
|---|---|---|---|---|---|
| A | B | B | C | | |

### 17.5.1 Purpose

You can give authorization to a user for a part of the organizational structure, which is identified by a starting object and an evaluation path. These parts of the organizational structure are defined as authorization profiles. Alternatively, you can use BadI HRBAS00_GET_PROFL to implement an alternative determination of structural profiles.

### 17.5.2 IMG Node

SM34 ➢ T77PQ (view T77PR)

### 17.5.3 Transaction

S_AHR_61003751—Define Authorization Profiles

### 17.5.4 Screen

| Au... | No. | Plan Vers. | Obj.Type | Object I | Maint. | Eval.path | Status... | Depth | Sign | Period | Function... |
|---|---|---|---|---|---|---|---|---|---|---|---|
| ALL | 0 | ** | * | | ☑ | | | | | | |

### 17.5.5 Primary Key

Authorization Profile + Sequence Number

### 17.5.6 Important Fields

#### *Authorization profile*

Here you enter the authorization profile being defined.

#### *Sequence number*

An authorization profile may consist of several structures or sub-trees. Each structure is identified by a sequence number.

#### *Plan version*

Here you specify the plan version for which the defined profile is valid. Note that plan version 01 is generally the active plan version.

### *Object type and object ID*

Here you specify the start object for the evaluation path.

### *Maintenance*

If you tick this field, a user can maintain (create/change) data. If this field is not ticked, he can only display data. This can further restrict the authorization granted to the user in activity field.

### *Evaluation path*

In structural authorizations, the authorization is for a part of structure. The part of structure is defined by a starting object and an evaluation path, which determines the structure. The evaluation path is specified here.

### *Status vector*

Status vector determines whether you want to take into account only active relationships or planned relationships as well.

### *Depth*

When you go down the evaluation path, there may be multiple levels. If you do not want to go beyond certain depth, you can specify that here.

### *Sign*

Your evaluation path takes you in a certain direction of structure. If you want to go in reverse direction, you enter a '–' here.

### *Period*

The structures have a validity period. If you want to see the structure as on a certain date, or period, you can specify that here.

### *Function module*

Although you can explicitly specify a starting object in structural profiles, you will end up creating one profile for each user, just because the starting object is different. SAP lets you specify a function module where you can logically determine the starting object for each user.

If a position is manager of an organizational unit (A012), you can use function module RH_GET_MANAGER_ASSIGNMENT which uses evaluation path MANASS or MANAS to determine the manager of an organizational unit. In this way, you need only one profile for all managers, instead of one profile for each manager.

SAP also provides a function module, RH_GET_ORG_ASSIGNMENT which uses evaluation path ORGASS or ORGAS. If you specify this function module in a profile, the starting object for a person is the organizational unit to which he belongs. For both these functionalities to work, user to person relationship must be maintained in infotype 0105.

## 17.6 AUTHORIZATION PROFILES TO USER ASSIGNMENT

| *Functional Consultant* | *User* | *Business Process Owner* | *Senior Management* | *My Rating* | *Understanding Level* |
|---|---|---|---|---|---|
| A | B | B | C | | |

### 17.6.1 Purpose and Overview

Here you can assign structural authorization profiles to users. A user's authorization is limited to the objects (ultimately employees) selected by these profiles. These profiles restrict the authorization a user is granted otherwise. A user can be assigned multiple authorization profiles, thereby giving him authorization for multiple groups of employees. However, his authorization for all the employees will be same. If you want a user to have different authorization for different groups of employees, e.g. display of organizational assignment for all employees but change of organizational assignment for his subordinates, this method cannot support it.

SAP has therefore introduced an authorization object P_ORGINCON, where you can assign an authorization profile to an authorization object, and thereby provide different authorizations to a user for different groups of employees. To enable that method, you do appropriate coding in HRBAS00_GET_PROFL Business Add-In (BAdI). Alternatively, you grant unrestricted authorization to the user in this table by giving him authorization profile 'ALL' and restrict him in authorization object P_ORGINCON as appropriate.

If there is no entry in this table for a user, he is granted authorization profile which is linked to the user SAP*. Thus, if you maintain an entry with 'SAP*' in user name field and 'ALL' in authorization profile field (This entry is there in the table by default), all users who are not present in this table will have unrestricted authorization. Their authorization will then be restricted only by the authorization object P_ORGINCON.

### 17.6.2 IMG Node

SM30 ➢ T77UA

### 17.6.3 Transaction

S_AHR_61003750—Assign Authorization Profiles
OOSB—Assign Authorization Profiles
S_AHR_61011911—Assign Authorization Profiles
S_AHR_61003942—Assign Authorization Profiles

### 17.6.4 Screen

| | User name | Auth.profile | Start date | End date | Exclusion | Display Objects |
|---|---|---|---|---|---|---|
| | SAP* | ALL | 01.01.1900 | 31.12.9999 | ☐ | i |

### 17.6.5 Primary Key

User Name + Authorization Profile + Start Date

## 17.7 PREFIX FOR BATCH INPUT SESSIONS

| *Functional Consultant* | *User* | *Business Process Owner* | *Senior Management* | *My Rating* | *Understanding Level* |
|---|---|---|---|---|---|
| B | C | X | X | | |

### 17.7.1 Purpose

When you run batch jobs, you may want to prevent users from seeing each other's job and printing the output of others. SAP provides an authorization object, S_BDC_MONI, where you can give authorization based on session name. You then need to name your sessions correctly so that unauthorized persons cannot view your session. In feature BIMAP, you can define a prefix based on program name, and thus control unauthorized viewing of batch jobs.

### 17.7.2 IMG Node

PE03 ➢ BIMAP

### 17.7.3 Screen

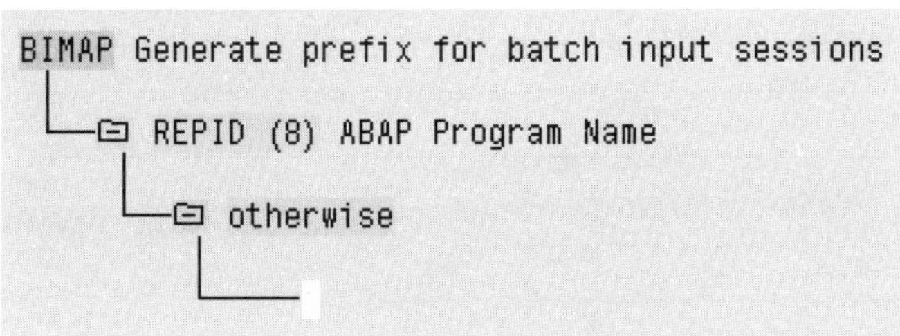


### 17.7.4 Fields for Decision-making

Transaction Code
Function Code
ABAP Program Name
User Name

Company Code
Personnel Area
Personnel Subarea
Country Grouping
Employee Time Management Status

### 17.7.5 Return Value

A prefix, which is inserted in front of the session name.

## 17.8 USER DATA IN SAP MEMORY

| *Functional Consultant* | *User* | *Business Process Owner* | *Senior Management* | *My Rating* | *Understanding Level* |
|---|---|---|---|---|---|
| B | B | C | C | | |

You can specify users for whom structural authorization data should be permanently stored in SAP memory in table T77UU. The main purpose of this function is to avoid performance problems for users with extensive authorization profiles.

| User name | Days | Gen.day |
|---|---|---|
| | | |
| | | |

## 17.9 AUTHORIZATION REPORTS

| *Functional Consultant* | *User* | *Business Process Owner* | *Senior Management* | *My Rating* | *Understanding Level* |
|---|---|---|---|---|---|
| B | C | C | C | | |

You can run transaction RE_RHAUTH00 to see authorization for a user or a profile.

| PV | OT | Object ID | Start date | End Date | M | Authoriz. profile | Exclusion |
|---|---|---|---|---|---|---|---|
| .: | | | | | X | ALL | |
| .: | A | | | | X | ALL | |
| .: | AC | | | | X | ALL | |
| .: | AG | | | | X | ALL | |
| .: | AP | | | | X | ALL | |

# Chapter 18 Organizational Management Integration

## 18.1 INTEGRATION WITH PERSONNEL ADMINISTRATION

| *Functional Consultant* | *User* | *Business Process Owner* | *Senior Management* | *My Rating* | *Understanding Level* |
|---|---|---|---|---|---|
| A | A | A | A | | |

### 18.1.1 Data Storage in Both OM and PA

***Dual storage***

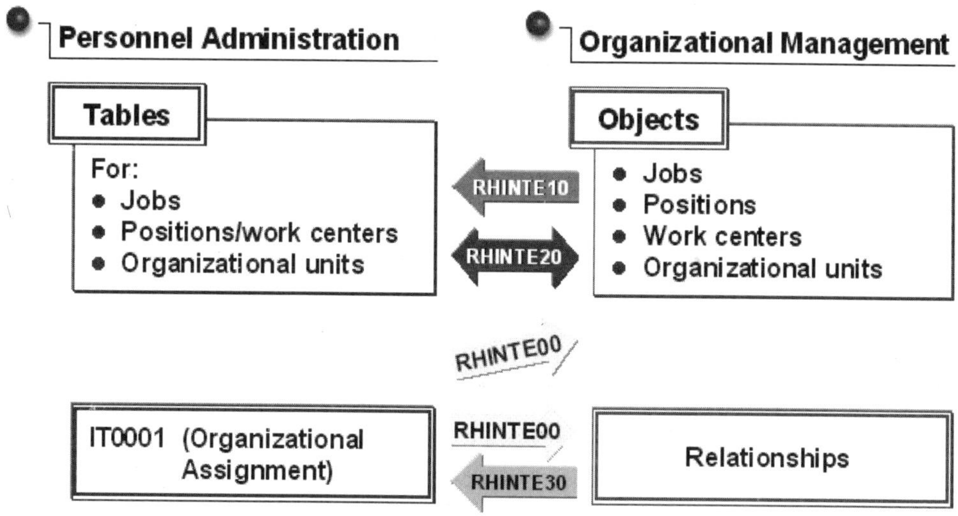

SAP keeps data about organizational units, positions, jobs, work centers, and relationship between position and person, in both Organizational Management and Personnel Administration. However, you don't have to enter the data twice. If integration between Organizational Management and Personnel Administration is active, when you create data in one, it is automatically created in the other. You generally create organizational units, positions, jobs and work centers in Organizational Management and this data is created in Personnel Administration automatically by the system. While hiring or transferring employees in Personnel Administration, you specify his position, and this data is created in Organizational Management automatically by the system. Entries created by the system are identified by value P in field MAINT. These entries cannot be deleted or changed.

| *Table description* | *Table name* |
|---|---|
| Jobs | T513, T513S |
| Positions/work centers | T528B, T528T |
| Organizational units | T527X |
| Organizational assignment | PA0001 |
| Objects | HRP1000 |
| Relationships | HRP1001 |

### *Data transfer*

SAP stores this data in two places because an organization may decide to implement only Organizational Management, or only Personnel Administration, instead of implementing both of them together. But if an organization, having implemented one module, wishes to implement the other module, it needs to transfer data to the other module. SAP provides a number of programs to do that as shown in the diagram on the previous page.

| *Program* | *Transaction* |
|---|---|
| RHINTE00 | OOPH |
| RHINTE10 | OOHP |
| RHINTE20 | OOPP, S_AHR_61003129 |
| RHINTE30 | OOHQ |

In order for the RHINTE reports to work correctly, SAP has created the following table entries which you must not change.

| *Table* | *Table name* | *Entry* |
|---|---|---|
| T77S0 | System Table | PLOGI PRELI |
| T77FC | PD Function Codes | INTE |
| T778A | Evaluation Paths | INTE-PS, INTEBACK, INTECHEK, INTEGRAT and INTE_OSP |

***Consistency check***

SAP also provides program RHINTECHECK to check consistency between Organizational Management and Personnel Administration.

## 18.1.2 OM PA Integration Switches

You determine the nature of integration between Organizational Management and Personnel Administration by maintaining integration switches in Personnel Management ➢ Organizational Management ➢ Integration ➢ Integration with Personnel Administration ➢ Set up Integration with Personnel Administration ➢ Basic Settings. Note that some of the switches, e.g. PLOGI PLOGI, are not displayed in this view. These switches are explained below:

| Group | Sem. abbr. | Value abbr. | Description |
|---|---|---|---|
| PLOGI | EVCCC | 02 | Master data action: company code change |
| PLOGI | EVCRE | X | Generate event with entry T77INT (action designat. |
| PLOGI | EVEGC | 02 | Master data action: employee subgroup change |
| PLOGI | EVENB | | Enhanced integration (X= on, Space= off) |
| PLOGI | EVPAC | 02 | Master data action for country reassignment |
| PLOGI | ORGA | X | Integration Switch: Organizational Assignment |
| PLOGI | PRELI | 99999999 | Integration: default position |
| PLOGI | PRELU | | Integration: PA update online or batch |
| PLOGI | TEXTC | | Integration: transfer short text of job |
| PLOGI | TEXTO | | Integration: transfer short text of org.unit |
| PLOGI | TEXTS | | Integration: transfer short text of position |
| PPABT | PPABT | 0 | Switch: department |
| PPINT | BTRTL | | Default value for personnel subarea |
| PPINT | PERSA | | Default value for personnel area |

***Basic integration***

| *Group* | *Sem.abbr.* | *Description* | *Explanation* |
|---|---|---|---|
| PLOGI | PLOGI | Integration Plan Version/ Active Plan Version | Since you can have multiple plan versions in Organizational Management, you need to specify integration plan version here, if integration is on. |
| PLOGI | ORGA | Integration Switch: Organizational Assignment | This is the main integration switch between Organizational Management and Personnel Administration. If integration between Organizational Management and Personnel Administration is on and you create the data in one, it is duplicated automatically in the other. |

| *Group* | *Sem.abbr.* | *Description* | *Explanation* |
|---|---|---|---|
| PLOGI | PRELI | Integration: default position | This position is used for those employees, for whom Organizational Management to Personnel Administration integration is not active. |
| PLOGI | PRELU | Integration: PA update online or batch | You can decide whether changes made in Organizational Management will be updated in Personnel Administration immediately or not. If they are to be updated in batch, use program RHINTE30. |
| PLOGI | SPLIT | Integration: New infotype 1 record at name change | Sometimes you could change description of jobs, positions or organizational units, without changing the objects themselves. Till some date, there is old description, after which there is new description. If you wish that the description is correctly shown in Personnel Administration, both before and after the date of change, then the Personnel Administration record needs to be split, otherwise it will show new description for the entire period. This choice is controlled by this integration switch. If this switch is set to 'X', and you change the description of jobs, positions or organizational units, new infotype 0001 records for the personnel numbers concerned are created on the date of change. |
| PLOGI | TEXTC | Integration: transfer short text of job | In Organizational Management, objects have a short text, and a long text. If this switch is blank, long text of the job is shown. If it is 'X', short text is shown. |
| PLOGI | TEXTD | Integration: Selection Date for OM Texts (IT0001) | If you do not create split when the Organizational Management text changes (PLOGI SPLIT), whether the Organizational Management text should be shown for the latest period or the earliest period is controlled by this. |
| PLOGI | TEXTO | Integration: transfer short text of org. unit | If this switch is blank, long text of the organizational unit is shown. If it is 'X', short text is shown. |
| PLOGI | TEXTS | Integration: transfer short text of position | If this switch is blank, long text of the position is shown. If it is 'X', short text is shown. |

### Cost distribution

| *Group* | *Sem.abbr.* | *Description* | *Explanation* |
|---|---|---|---|
| PLOGI | COSTD | Integration of Cost Distribution PersAdm/ OrgManag | You can activate integration between Organizational Management and Personnel Administration for cost distribution by setting the value of this switch to 'X'. |

### Department switch

| *Group* | *Sem.abbr.* | *Description* | *Explanation* |
|---|---|---|---|
| PPABT | PPABT | Switch: department | You set this switch to '1' if you want to identify organizational units which are departments using infotype 1003. |

### Default personnel area, subarea and cost center

| *Group* | *Sem.abbr.* | *Description* | *Explanation* |
|---|---|---|---|
| PPINT | BTRTL | Default value for personnel subarea | This value is used as the default value of personnel subarea if, for example, positions are reoccupied but do not have a record of infotype 1008 "Account Assignment Features". |
| PPINT | PERSA | Default value for personnel area | This value is used as the default value of personnel area if, for example, positions are reoccupied but do not have a record of infotype 1008 "Account Assignment Features". |
| PPINT | PPINT | Default value for controlling area | When you create relationships between cost centers and positions or organizational units in Organizational Management, the system requires that the controlling area be specified along with cost center. The value of this entry is used as the default value for the controlling area. |

***Enhanced integration***

| *Group* | *Sem.abbr.* | *Description* | *Explanation* |
|---|---|---|---|
| PLOGI | EVENB | Enhanced integration (X = on, Space = off) | If extended integration is set in this switch, you can move a person, position or organizational unit when these changes lead to a change in company code for the person concerned. Otherwise, you cannot. |
| PLOGI | EVCCC | Master data action: company code change | If a position is moved to another company code, the employee is locked (lock entry in table T77INT). A personnel action must then be executed for the employee concerned. This entry enables you to determine the action that is executed next for all employees who have changed company code and are flagged in table T77INT. |
| PLOGI | EVCRE | Generate event with entry T77INT (action designat.) | By setting this switch to 'X', you determine that an event is generated for employees who are flagged for an action in table T77INT. A workflow can then respond to this event. |
| PLOGI | EVEGC | Master data action: employee subgroup change | This entry is not relevant for customizing. |

### 18.1.3 Extent of OM–PA Integration

***Purpose***

Sometimes organizations do not wish to maintain organizational structure for all their employees. SAP permits you to maintain partial integration between Organizational Management and Personnel Administration. Through feature PLOGI, you can specify which groups of employees participate in integration, and which groups do not.

***IMG node***

PE03 ➢ PLOGI

***Screen***

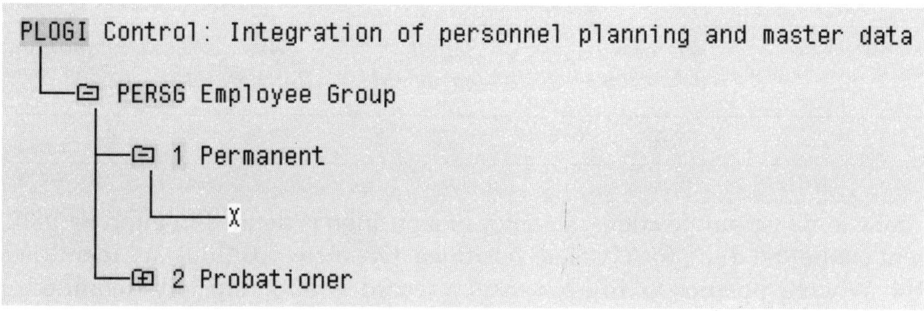


***Fields for decision-making***

Transaction Class for Data Storage
Country Grouping
Company Code
Personnel Area
Personnel Subarea
Employee Group
Employee Subgroup

***Return value***

| | |
|---|---|
| X | Integration on |
| Blank | Integration off |

## 18.1.4 Replace User

If you have users holding positions in the organizational plan, you can replace them with respective employees using transaction RE_RHREPL20. To do this, integration between Organizational Management and Personnel Administration should be active and relationship between user id and employee's personnel number should be maintained in infotype 0105, subtype 0001.

## 18.1.5 Validity Period of Persons to Organizational Management

In standard SAP the following employees are considered to be active:

- Employees with employment status 3 (Active).
- Employees with employment status 1 (Inactive), provided at least one record with employment status 3 (Active) exists for the employee, and the record with employment status 3 is earlier than the records with employment status 1.

Business Add-In HREIC_RETIREES enables you to override this SAP standard procedure to determine which employees are defined as active employees in your system. Employees with employment status 0 (Withdrawn) must not be interpreted as active, even with the help of this BAdI.

## 18.2 INTEGRATION WITH RECRUITMENT

| *Functional Consultant* | *User* | *Business Process Owner* | *Senior Management* | *My Rating* | *Understanding Level* |
|---|---|---|---|---|---|
| A | A | A | A | | |

Recruitment is done to fill vacant positions. Vacancy of a position is defined in infotype 1007. Also, recruitment cannot be done for obsolete positions. Obsolete positions are identified in infotype 1014. When a position is filled, vacancy record is automatically delimited.

## 18.3 INTEGRATION WITH WORKFLOW

| *Functional Consultant* | *User* | *Business Process Owner* | *Senior Management* | *My Rating* | *Understanding Level* |
|---|---|---|---|---|---|
| A | B | C | C | | |

### *Use of organizational management in workflow*

Workflow uses Organizational Management in two ways.

- Organizational management stores information on manager of a person, which is needed in processes supported by workflows, e.g. approval of leave, travel, etc. This information is frequently used by workflows.
- You can assign tasks to organizational units, positions, users, etc. which helps workflows in finding possible agents, etc.

### *Workflow for organizational change*

You can run transaction EXEORGCHEARM to do agent assignment and event linkage of this workflow.

| Application Co... | Application Component Description | Agent Assignment | Event Linkage |
|---|---|---|---|
| 01000008 | Execute Designated Personnel Action | Assign Agents | Activate event linking |

Possible agents must be specified for each task in order to define clearly the organizational responsibility for processing. Workflows can only be started in dialog by their possible agents. If a scenario requires that the relevant workflow be started in dialog, this workflow must be assigned to its possible agents. When you click Assign Agents, you get the following screen.

| Name | ID | General or Background ... | Task Version | Assigned as of | Assigned until |
|---|---|---|---|---|---|
| Execute | TG 01000008 | | | | |

You choose agent assignment ➢ Create, to create possible agents. You select the type of agent who will be performing the task.

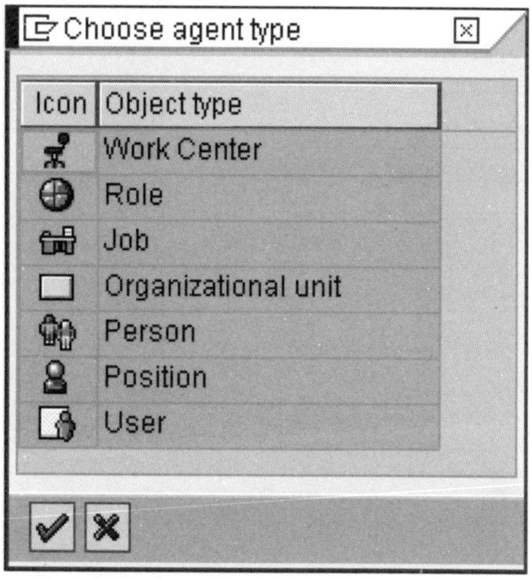


After you assign the possible agent, the system will show it.

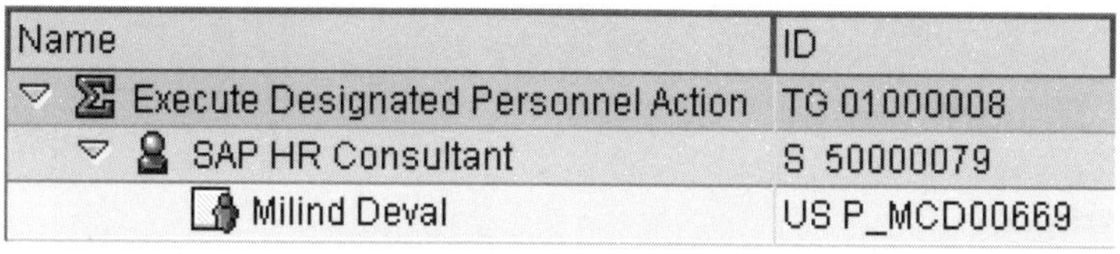


When you click Activate event linking, you get the following screen.

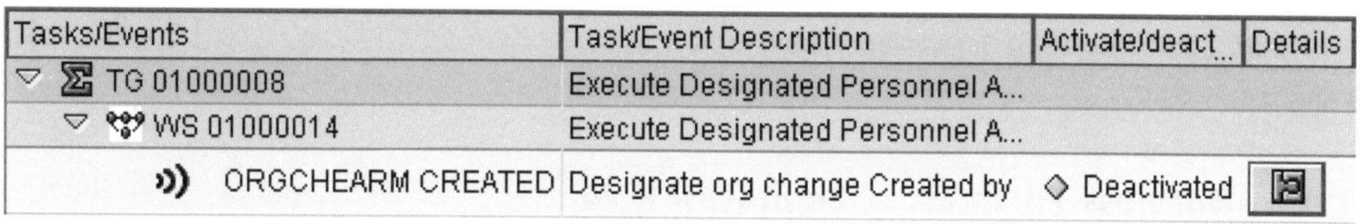


You can click detail view icon, tick event linkage activated checkbox and save. The event linkage is activated.

### *Workflow message about new employees*

You can run transaction WF_NEW_MAN to do agent assignment and event linkage of this workflow. You can assign possible agents and activate triggering event to workflow WS01200136 in the same way as described above.

## 18.4 INTEGRATION WITH SAP BUSINESS PARTNERS

| *Functional Consultant* | *User* | *Business Process Owner* | *Senior Management* | *My Rating* | *Understanding Level* |
|---|---|---|---|---|---|
| C | X | X | X | | |

### 18.4.1 Business Partners

SAP uses the concept of business partners in the following applications.

- SAP Supplier Relationship Management (SRM)
- SAP Customer Relationship Management (CRM)
- SAP E-Recruiting
- SAP Collaboration Projects (cProjects)
- SAP Strategic Enterprise Management (SAP SEM)
- SAP Internet Communication Manager (ICM)

Employees and organizational units are also considered business partners. Therefore, whenever an employee or organizational unit is created or changed, corresponding business partner must be created or changed. SAP provides a method of automating this process.

### 18.4.2 Business Partner Integration

#### *Business partner HR integration*

You activate integration between business partners and HR by setting this switch to 'X' in table T77S0.

| Group | Sem. abbr. | Value abbr. | Description |
|---|---|---|---|
| HRALX | HRAC | X | Activate HR Integration |

### 18.4.3 Business Partners in Employee Role

#### *Creating business partners automatically*

When an employee is created in the HR system, you may want a business partner in employee role to be created automatically. If this switch is OFF, business partner is not created. If it is CREATE, business partner is created when employee is created, but not changed when employee data changes. If it is ON, business partner is created and changed when an employee is created or changed. Data from infotypes 0002, 0006 (subtype 1) and 0105 (subtypes 0005, 0010 and 0020) are transferred.

| Group | Sem. abbr. | Value abbr. | Description |
|---|---|---|---|
| HRALX | PBPHR | ON | Employees Are Replicated from HR System |

### Replication of time recording (CATS) in the business partner

If you set this switch to 'X', the system replicates time recording (CATS) data in the business partner.

| Group | Sem. abbr. | Value abbr. | Description |
|---|---|---|---|
| HRALX | PCATS | | Integration P-BP for CATS Active |

### ALE distribution of inactive employees

If you set this switch to 'X', business partners are also generated for inactive employees.

| Group | Sem. abbr. | Value abbr. | Description |
|---|---|---|---|
| HRALX | PINAC | | Activate ALE Distribution of Inactive Employees |

### Import qualifications

If you set this switch to 'X', qualifications are written to the business partner.

| Group | Sem. abbr. | Value abbr. | Description |
|---|---|---|---|
| HRALX | PQUAL | | Import Qualifications |

### Number assignment of business partner

Here you specify the method of numbering business partners in employee role.

| Group | Sem. abbr. | Value abbr. | Description |
|---|---|---|---|
| HRALX | PNUMB | 1 | Number Assignment Business Partner (Employee) |

| *Value* | *Description* |
|---|---|
| 1 | A business partner number with internal number assignment is taken from the general number range of the business partner. |
| 2 | An individual number range interval exists for the business partner with the employee role. This interval must be indicated as an internal number assignment. A business partner grouping of the same name must have been created and specified in switch HRALX PSUBG. |
| 3 | The business partner in the employee role is to receive the same number as the corresponding employee. An individual number range interval must have been created with external number assignment. At the same time, you must also create a business partner grouping of the same name and specify in switch HRALX PSUBG. |

### *Subgroup of the number range interval*

This switch contains the subgroup of the number range interval for the business partner in the employee role.

| Group | Sem. abbr. | Value abbr. | Description |
|---|---|---|---|
| HRALX | PSUBG | | Business Partner Subgroup (Employees) |

## 18.4.4 Business Partners in Organizational Unit Role

### *Creating business partners automatically*

When an organizational unit is created in the HR system, you may want a business partner in organizational unit role to be created automatically. If this switch is OFF, business partner is not created. If it is CREATE, business partner is created when organizational unit is created, but not changed when organizational unit data changes. If it is ON, business partner is created and changed when an organizational unit is created or changed. Data from infotypes 1000, 1028 and 1032 are transferred.

| Group | Sem. abbr. | Value abbr. | Description |
|---|---|---|---|
| HRALX | OBPON | ON | Integraion O-BP Active |

### *Address necessary for business partner*

Integration with HR organizational units is used by Supplier Relationship Management (SRM). To enable integration with SRM, you must also ensure that the business partners in the organizational unit role have an address. If you set this switch to 'X', the system ensures that an address is available for business partners in organizational unit role.

| Group | Sem. abbr. | Value abbr. | Description |
|---|---|---|---|
| HRALX | OADRE | | Address Necessary for Business Partner? |

### *Standard address of business partners*

If an organizational unit does not have address, the system can take a standard address. Here you can specify the ID of the business partner that contains the standard address. This will always be used when creating business partners belonging to the organizational unit role if the relevant organizational units do not have an address of their own.

| Group | Sem. abbr. | Value abbr. | Description |
|---|---|---|---|
| HRALX | OADBP | | Business Partner of Standard Address |

### Business partner warnings

If you set this switch to 'X', all warnings are ignored when creating the business partner.

| Group | Sem. abbr. | Value abbr. | Description |
|---|---|---|---|
| HRALX | OBWIG | X | Ignore Business Partner Warnings |

### Number assignment of business partner

Here you specify the method of numbering business partners in organizational unit role.

| Group | Sem. abbr. | Value abbr. | Description |
|---|---|---|---|
| HRALX | ONUMB | 1 | Number Assignment Business Partner (Org. Unit) |

| *Value* | *Description* |
|---|---|
| 1 | A business partner number with internal number assignment is taken from the general number range of the business partner. |
| 2 | An individual number range interval exists for the business partner with the organizational unit role. This interval must be indicated as an internal number assignment. A business partner grouping of the same name must have been created and specified in switch HRALX OSUBG. |
| 3 | The business partner in the organizational unit role is to receive the same number as the corresponding organizational unit. An individual number range interval must have been created with external number assignment. At the same time, you must also create a business partner grouping of the same name and specify in switch HRALX OSUBG. |

### Subgroup of the number range interval

This switch contains the subgroup of the number range interval for the business partner in the organizational unit role.

| Group | Sem. abbr. | Value abbr. | Description |
|---|---|---|---|
| HRALX | OSUBG | | Subgroup of Business Partner (Organizational Unit) |

### 18.4.5 Data Synchronization

#### *Synchronizing HR and business partners data*

If your HR system already has employees or organizational units when you activate integration with business partners, you may want to create business partners for existing employees and organizational units. You may use report HRALXSYNC to run a consistency check for the integration of HR master data and organizational data with business partner data. If the business partner data is incomplete, you can also synchronize the data.

#### *Integration error in IDOC*

If this switch is activated, any errors that occur are entered in the relevant IDOC and the IDOC is set to incorrect.

| Group | Sem. abbr. | Value abbr. | Description |
|---|---|---|---|
| HRALX | MERID | X | Enter Integration Error in IDOC |

#### *Recipient of error message*

If there are errors in creating business partner, this switch determines who receives the error message.

| Group | Sem. abbr. | Value abbr. | Description |
|---|---|---|---|
| HRALX | MSGRE | 0 | Recipient of Error Message When Creating BP |

| *Value* | *Message sent to* |
|---|---|
| 0 | No workflow document is created and nobody, therefore, is informed about the incorrect settings. |
| 1 | A workflow document is created that is sent to the workflow administrator. |
| 2 | A workflow document is created that is sent to the user who is currently logged on. |
| 3 | A workflow document is created that is sent to the workflow administrator and the user who is currently logged on. |

### 18.4.6 Business Partner Integration in Separate Logical Systems

If your business partners and HR are in different systems, you have to set up ALE for data transfer. You may see SAP help on how to do this and other aspects that need to be considered.

### 18.4.7 Mapping of Marital Status Keys

***Purpose***

Here you define which marital status keys in Human Resources are to correspond to which marital status keys in SAP Business Partner.

***IMG node***

SM30 ➢ V_TB027HR_NEW

***Screen***

| | MarSt | MaritStat | Short name |
|---|---|---|---|
| | | | |
| | | | |

***Primary key***

Marital Status Key

### 18.4.8 Mapping of Form of Address Keys

***Purpose***

Here you define which form of address keys in Human Resources are to correspond to which form of address keys in SAP Business Partner.

***IMG node***

SM30 ➢ V_TSAD3HR_NEW

***Screen***

| | Title | Key | Title |
|---|---|---|---|
| | | | |
| | | | |

***Primary key***

Form-of-Address Key

# CHAPTER 19 Database Utilities and Dialog Control

## 19.1 DATABASE UTILITIES

| *Functional Consultant* | *User* | *Business Process Owner* | *Senior Management* | *My Rating* | *Understanding Level* |
|---|---|---|---|---|---|
| B | B | C | C | | |

### 19.1.1 Database Statistics

You can run transaction RE_RHDBST00 to see database statistics. In the summarized form, it shows table typewise number of records and storage in KB.

| Table type | Σ No. records | Σ Storage requirement in KB |
|---|---|---|
| Customer-specific infotypes (PLOG) | 0 | 0.000 |
| Primary data (HRPnnnn) | 2,111 | 682.734 |
| Secondary data (PLOGI, HRIADATANR, HRITABNR) | 4,447 | 302.664 |
| Table infotypes (HRTnnnn) | 1,691 | 865.411 |
| | **8,249** | **1,850.809** |

You can also see plan versionwise data.

| Plan Version | Table type | Σ No. records | Σ Storage re |
|---|---|---|---|
| 01 | Customer-specific infotypes (PLOG) | 0 | 0.000 |
| | Primary data (HRPnnnn) | 726 | 233.145 |
| | Secondary data (PLOGI, HRIADATANR, HRITABNR) | 2,306 | 158.722 |
| | Table infotypes (HRTnnnn) | 386 | 72.527 |
| 01 | | **3,418** | **464.394** |

You can also see tablewise data.

| Table type | Database table | Σ No. records | Σ Storage requirement in KB |
|---|---|---|---|
| Customer-specific infotypes (PLOG) | PLOG | 0 | 0.000 |
| Customer-specific infotypes (PLOG) | | ▪ **0** | ▪ **0.000** |
| Primary data (HRPnnnn) | HRP1000 | 424 | 207.760 |
| | HRP1001 | 226 | 81.586 |
| | HRP1002 | 5 | 1.260 |

You can also see plan versionwise tablewise data.

| Plan Version | Table type | Database table | Σ No. records | Σ Storage ... |
|---|---|---|---|---|
| .: | Customer-specific infotypes (PLOG) | PLOG | 0 | 0.000 |
| | Customer-specific infotypes (PLOG) | | ▪ **0** | ▪ **0.000** |
| | Primary data (HRPnnnn) | HRP1000 | 154 | 75.460 |
| | | HRP1001 | 43 | 15.523 |

### 19.1.2 Database Statistics–Number of Objects

You can run transaction RE_RHVSTA00 to see number of objects of each object type.

```
Plan versions        425      13 kb
  01 Current plan                   269   63.29 %      8 kb
    VC Criterion                     36    8.47 %      1 kb
    E  Course                        30    7.06 %      1 kb
    T  Task                          25    5.88 %      1 kb
    S  Position                      24    5.65 %      1 kb
    BK Criterion                     20    4.71 %      1 kb
    G  Resource                      17    4.00 %      1 kb
    D  Business event type           16    3.76 %      1 kb
```

### 19.1.3 Database Statistics–Number of Notes

You can run transaction RE_RHVSTA10 to see number of notes under each object type, infotype and subtype.

```
IDES-ALE: Production        1
  01 Current plan                    1  100.00 %
    D  Business event type             1  100.00 %
      1001 Relationships                  1  100.00 %
        A027 Has a prebooking for           1  100.00 %
```

### 19.1.4 Database Statistics–Number of Object Types per Infotype

You can run transaction RE_RHVSTA20 to see number of objects of each object type for a given infotype.

| | | | |
|---|---|---|---|
| IDES-ALE: Production | 1,166 | 210 kb | |
| 01 Current plan | 1,123 | 96.31 % | 202 kb |
| E Course | 240 | 20.58 % | 43 kb |
| G Resource | 132 | 11.32 % | 24 kb |
| O Organizational unit | 93 | 7.98 % | 17 kb |
| D Business event type | 82 | 7.03 % | 15 kb |
| S Position | 75 | 6.43 % | 13 kb |
| P Person | 58 | 4.97 % | 10 kb |

### 19.1.5 Database Statistics–Number of Infotypes

You can run transaction RE_RHVSTA30 to see statistics of all infotypes.

| | | |
|---|---|---|
| IDES-ALE: Production | 4,136 | 726 kb |
| 01 Current plan | 2,751 | 506 kb |
| 1001 Relationships | 1,123 | 202 kb |
| 1000 Object | 810 | 194 kb |
| 1217 Classification/Lock Ind. | 196 | 21 kb |
| 1211 WF Container Texts | 106 | 13 kb |
| 5022 Column/Cell Definition | 52 | 11 kb |
| 5020 Category Assignment | 52 | 7 kb |

### 19.1.6 Checking Consistency

You can run transaction RE_RHCHECK1 to perform the following checks.

- Do all infotypes of an object lie within the validity period of infotype 1000?
- Do all the objects exist that are referenced by relationships?
- Does a correct inverse relationship exist for every relationship?

| Error (number) | Plan... | Obj... | Object ID | Infoty. | Plan... | Subtyp | Var.field |
|---|---|---|---|---|---|---|---|
| ▽ Consistency of relationship( | | | | | | | |
| ALE administrator | .: | S | 50000000 | 1001 | 1 | A003 | O 00000001 |
| ALE administrator | .: | S | 50000000 | 1001 | 1 | B007 | TS00007988 |
| ▽ Data record's validity period not | | | | | | | |
| Create + send letter | .: | WS | 400019 | 1216 | 1 | | |
| Create + send letter | .: | WS | 400019 | 1211 | 1 | | E |
| Create + send letter | .: | WS | 400019 | 1211 | 1 | | D |
| Create + send letter | .: | WS | 400019 | 1210 | 1 | | |
| Create + send letter | .: | WS | 400019 | 1205 | 1 | | |
| Create + send letter | .: | WS | 400019 | 1205 | 1 | | |
| Create + send letter | .: | WS | 400019 | 1000 | 1 | | E |
| Create + send letter | .: | WS | 400019 | 1000 | 1 | | D |
| ▽ Validity/Status Related object( | | | | | | | |
| ALE administrator | .: | S | 50000000 | 1001 | 1 | B007 | TS00007988 |
| ALE administrator | .: | S | 50000000 | 1001 | 1 | A003 | O 00000001 |
| ALE administrator | 01 | S | 50000000 | 1001 | 1 | B007 | TS00007988 |

## 19.1.7 Checking Relationships

You can run transaction RE_RHCHECKV to display and create missing inverse relationships. If you tick the 'Automatic Without Display' checkbox, the system automatically creates all incorrect inverse relationships.

| PV | O | Object ID | S | Start date | End Date | A... | IT | S | Rel | S | Start date | End Date | Variation field |
|---|---|---|---|---|---|---|---|---|---|---|---|---|---|
| .: | S | 50000000 | 1 | 16.06.1995 | 31.12.9999 | ALI | 1001 | A | 003 | 1 | 16.06.1995 | 31.12.9999 | O 00000001 |
| .: | S | 50000000 | 1 | 16.06.1995 | 31.12.9999 | ALI | 1001 | B | 007 | 1 | 16.06.1995 | 31.12.9999 | TS00007988 |

## 19.1.8 Displaying Database Records

You can run transaction RE_RHRHAZ00 to display database records. You can select the objects by specifying an evaluation path and starting object. You can display specified infotypes and subtypes. You can also display data contents and the user who last changed the record.

| PV | OT | Object ID | Infotype | STy. | S | Start date | End Date | Var.field | RNo | H |
|---|---|---|---|---|---|---|---|---|---|---|
| 01 | O | 50000075 | 1000 | | 1 | 09.12.2008 | 15.12.2008 | E | | |
| 01 | O | 50000075 | 1000 | | 1 | 16.12.2008 | 31.12.9999 | E | | |
| 01 | O | 50000075 | 1000 | | 3 | 31.12.2008 | 31.12.9999 | E | | |
| 01 | O | 50000076 | 1000 | | 1 | 09.12.2008 | 31.12.9999 | E | | |

### 19.1.9 Deleting Database Records

You can use transaction RE_RHRHDL00 to delete objects and their infotypes. If you want you can lock the records instead of deleting. It is recommended that you first run this transaction in test mode and display objects and records which will be deleted. Only after you are sure of deleting the objects and records, you run transaction in update mode.

| PV | OT | Object ID | Infotype | Subtype | S | Start date | End Date | Abbr. | Result |
|---|---|---|---|---|---|---|---|---|---|
| 01 | O | 50000127 | | | 1 | 01.01.2008 | 31.12.9999 | ABC | |
| 01 | O | 50000127 | 1000 | | 1 | 01.01.2008 | 31.12.9999 | | |
| 01 | O | 50000127 | 1001 | B002 | 1 | 01.01.2008 | 31.12.9999 | | |
| 01 | O | 50000129 | 1001 | A002 | 1 | 01.01.2008 | 31.12.9999 | | |
| 01 | O | 50000127 | 1001 | B002 | 1 | 01.01.2008 | 31.12.9999 | | |
| 01 | O | 50000130 | 1001 | A002 | 1 | 01.01.2008 | 31.12.9999 | | |
| 01 | O | 50000127 | 1001 | B003 | 1 | 01.01.2008 | 31.12.9999 | | |
| 01 | S | 50000131 | 1001 | A003 | 1 | 01.01.2008 | 31.12.9999 | | |
| 01 | O | 50000127 | 1001 | B012 | 1 | 01.01.2008 | 31.12.9999 | | |
| 01 | S | 50000131 | 1001 | A012 | 1 | 01.01.2008 | 31.12.9999 | | |

### 19.1.10 Deleting Database Records with List

Transaction RE_RHRHDL00 does not let you select the records you want to delete. This functionality is provided by transaction RE_RHRHDC00. This transaction lists all infotype records it finds. You can delete them by selecting individual records and choosing the Delete function. However, you cannot use this program to delete records with time constraint 1, such as infotype 1000 (Object). If you need to delete such records, you have to use transaction RE_RHRHDL00 or transaction PP01.

| | Pl... | O | Object ID | Infotype | Subtype | P | Start date | End Date | Cha... | L... | Variable field |
|---|---|---|---|---|---|---|---|---|---|---|---|
| | 01 | O | 50000127 | 1000 | | 1 | 01.01.2008 | 31.12.9999 | 23.12. | P_ | ABC ABC |
| | 01 | O | 50000127 | 1001 | B002 | 1 | 01.01.2008 | 31.12.9999 | 23.12. | P_ | O 50000129 |
| | 01 | O | 50000127 | 1001 | B002 | 1 | 01.01.2008 | 31.12.9999 | 23.12. | P_ | O 50000130 |
| | 01 | O | 50000127 | 1001 | B003 | 1 | 01.01.2008 | 31.12.9999 | 23.12. | P_ | S 50000131 |
| | 0 | O | 50000127 | 1001 | B012 | 1 | 01.01.2008 | 31.12.9999 | 23.12. | P_ | S 50000131 |

### 19.1.11 Installation Consistency Check

You can run transaction OOCH to check consistency of data.

| Overview | Numb |
|---|---|
| Test: Table T777D/Infotypes | 657 |
| Check: Consistency of relationships | 54 |
| Check: subtypes in table T778U | 5 |
| Check: integration between Personnel Planning and Pers. Admin | 2 |
| Check: table T77AD/additional data | 34 |

## 19.2 SEQUENCE OF LANGUAGES AVAILABLE

| *Functional Consultant* | *User* | *Business Process Owner* | *Senior Management* | *My Rating* | *Understanding Level* |
|---|---|---|---|---|---|
| A | B | C | X | | |

### 19.2.1 Purpose

If you are using multiple languages and information is not available in your logon language, the system shows it in another language. The language is selected from this table in the order of sequence.

### 19.2.2 IMG Node

SM30 ➢ T778L

### 19.2.3 Screen

| Sequence | Lang. | Language |
|---|---|---|
| 01 | DE | German |
| 02 | EN | English |
| 03 | ES | Spanish |
| 04 | NL | Dutch |
| 05 | FR | French |
| 06 | IT | Italian |

### 19.2.4 Primary Key

Sequence Indicator

## 19.3 SEARCH FUNCTION SETTINGS

| *Functional Consultant* | *User* | *Business Process Owner* | *Senior Management* | *My Rating* | *Understanding Level* |
|---|---|---|---|---|---|
| B | C | X | X | | |

### 19.3.1 Purpose

Here you can determine the behavior of the search function that is used to find objects in Organizational Management, Training and Event Management, etc.

### 19.3.2 IMG Node

SM30 ➢ V_T77S0SC

### 19.3.3 Screen

| Group | Sem. abbr. | Value abbr. | Description |
|---|---|---|---|
| SEARK | GENER | 0 | Search Function: Warning for Generic Search |
| SEARK | LMODE | 1 | Language for search function |
| SEARK | NOAHQ | | Hide Free Search for People/Applicants |
| SEARK | NSTR1 | | Structure search: Object type not unlinked |
| SEARK | NSTR2 | | Structure search: Object type not unlinked |
| SEARK | NSTR3 | | Structure search: Object type not unlinked |
| SEARK | NSTR4 | | Structure search: Object type not unlinked |
| SEARK | NSTR5 | | Structure search: Object type not unlinked |

### 19.3.4 Primary Key

Group Name + Semantic Abbreviation

### 19.3.5 Important Fields

| *Group* | *Sem. abbr.* | *Explanation* |
|---|---|---|
| SEARK | GENER | This switch controls whether or not a confirmation prompt is displayed before the user executes a generic search of all data in a plan version. If the value is 1, confirmation prompt is displayed. If the value is 0, no prompt is displayed. It is recommended to set the value of this switch to 1 to prevent searches from being carried out for all objects. |
| SEARK | LMODE | This switch controls how the database search for objects is performed. Value 0 specifies that the search is only performed in the logon language. Value 1 specifies that the search is performed first in the logon language. If the system finds no object in the logon language, it continues to search in the languages listed in table T778L (Supported Languages) in the order in which the languages are ranked until it finds an object. It is recommended that you use this value. Value 2 specifies that the system always searches in all languages. This setting can be time consuming. |
| SEARK | NOAHQ | This switch determines whether the free search is hidden or displayed in input help for persons and applicants. If the switch has the value blank, the system displays the free search. If the switch has the value 'X', the free search is hidden. |
| SEARK | SMODE | This switch determines whether the possible entries help supports all search options such as the search function, the structure search and the standard matchcode (value 1), or only the option that the system stored from the first use of the function per user and per object type (value 0). |

## 19.4 PARAMETERS FOR STAFFING SCHEDULE

| *Functional Consultant* | *User* | *Business Process Owner* | *Senior Management* | *My Rating* | *Understanding Level* |
|---|---|---|---|---|---|
| B | C | X | X | | |

### 19.4.1 Purpose

Staff Assignments report is available in old version (program RHSBES10) and new version (program RHSBES00, transaction S_AHR_61016503). Both these reports call four evaluation paths which are specified here. Also, the old report calls three function modules which are specified here. In case you want to change the behavior of these reports, you can make a change here.

### 19.4.2 IMG Node

SM30 ➢ V_T77S0SC

### 19.4.3 Screen

| Group | Sem. abbr. | Value abbr. | Description |
|---|---|---|---|
| SBES | LIST | RH_SBES_LI | Staff Assignments Output |
| SBES | PERS | RH_SBES_PA | Additional Data on Persons in Staff Assignments |
| SBES | P_EXT | O-S-PEXT | Evaluation Path for Enhanced Staff Assignment |
| SBES | P_NOR | O-S-PNOR | Evaluation Path for Staff Assignment |
| SBES | P_O-O | ORGEH | Evaluation Path for Organizational Structure |
| SBES | P_S-S | S-S | Evaluation Path for Reporting Structure |
| SBES | TOPL | RH_SBES_TP | Header for Staff Assignments |

### 19.4.4 Primary Key

Group Name + Semantic Abbreviation

## 19.5 CUSTOMER ENHANCEMENTS (USER EXITS)

| *Functional Consultant* | *User* | *Business Process Owner* | *Senior Management* | *My Rating* | *Understanding Level* |
|---|---|---|---|---|---|
| B | C | X | X | | |

### 19.5.1 Purpose

SAP provides you a number of user exits which you can use to enhance customer functionality. You can implement enhancements RHGB0001, RHGP0001 and RHSI0001 with their components.

| *Enhancement* | *Component* | *Description* |
|---|---|---|
| RHGB0001 | SAPLRHGB+CUS | Additional info on/off |
| | SAPLRHGC+CUS | Additional info on/off |
| | EXIT_SAPLRHGB_001 | Further info on/off |
| | EXIT_SAPLRHGB_002 | Fill text for customer-specific field |
| | EXIT_SAPLRHGB_003 | Fill header for customer-specific field |
| RHGP0001 | SAPLRHGP+CUS | Additional info on/off |
| | EXIT_SAPLRHGP_001 | Further info on/off |
| | EXIT_SAPLRHGP_002 | Fill text for customer-specific field |
| | EXIT_SAPLRHGP_003 | Fill header for customer-specific field |
| RHSI0001 | SAPLRHSI+CUS | Additional info on/off |

### 19.5.2 IMG Node

Personnel Management ➢ Organizational Management ➢ Dialog Control ➢ Customer Enhancements (User Exits)

## 19.6 SETTINGS FOR SIMPLE MAINTENANCE

| *Functional Consultant* | *User* | *Business Process Owner* | *Senior Management* | *My Rating* | *Understanding Level* |
|---|---|---|---|---|---|
| A | B | C | C | | |

### 19.6.1 Purpose

Here you make settings for Simple Maintenance Interface.

### 19.6.2 IMG Node

SM30 ➢ V_T77S0SC

### 19.6.3 Screen

| Group | Sem. abbr. | Value abbr. | Description |
|---|---|---|---|
| PPOM | EXTCK | X | Switch error message delimit/delete object |
| PPOM | LEPER | | Manager info: ' '= key date, 'X'= period |

### 19.6.4 Primary Key

Group Name + Semantic Abbreviation

### 19.6.5 Important Fields

| *Group* | *Sem. abbr.* | *Explanation* |
|---|---|---|
| PPOM | EXTCK | If an organizational unit has positions and you delimit or delete the organizational unit, the position's assignment to the organizational unit will also get delimited. If your company wants the assignment of the subordinate objects to be delimited or deleted automatically, you keep this switch blank. But if your company wants to give error message so that de-assignment of subordinate objects is done explicitly before delimiting or deleting a superior object, you set this switch to 'X'. This setting is for Simple Maintenance only. |
| PPOM | LEPER | If you leave this switch blank, only the current (key date) chief or the next future chief of an organizational unit is displayed. If you set it to 'X', then all chiefs of an organizational unit are displayed. |

# CHAPTER 20 Data Transfer

## 20.1 TRANSPORT CONNECTION

| *Functional Consultant* | *User* | *Business Process Owner* | *Senior Management* | *My Rating* | *Understanding Level* |
|---|---|---|---|---|---|
| B | C | X | X | | |

### 20.1.1 Purpose

Here you specify whether you want the system to create transport request when you create, change or delete personnel planning objects in the customizing client.

### 20.1.2 IMG Node

SM30 ➢ V_T77S0SC

### 20.1.3 Screen

| Group | Sem. abbr. | Value abbr. | Description |
|---|---|---|---|
| TRSP | CORR | X | Transport Switch (X = No Transport) |
| TRSP | STOBJ | PDST_LSO | Redefinition: Standard Transport Object |
| TRSP | WFOBJ | PDWS_LSO | Redefinition: Workflow Transport Object |

### 20.1.4 Important Fields

| *Group* | *Sem. abbr.* | *Value* | *Explanation* |
|---|---|---|---|
| TRSP | CORR | Blank | Automatic transport connection is activated. Whenever you create, change, or delete objects, a dialog box always appears asking you to assign the object to a transport request or to create a new request. |
| TRSP | CORR | X | Automatic transport connection is deactivated. You have to transport the changed objects yourself. You can do so using transaction RE_RHMOVE30 (Manual Transport). You have to enter the objects to be transported yourself, which means that you have to ensure that all changed objects have been transported. |
| TRSP | CORR | T | Transport is via object lock (repair flag). If you decide to use the object lock option, there is no automatic query regarding a transport request. However, you can use the report RHMOVE50 (Transport of objects using object lock) to transport any objects that were changed. |

## 20.2 LOCKING INFOTYPES FOR IMPORT

| *Functional Consultant* | *User* | *Business Process Owner* | *Senior Management* | *My Rating* | *Understanding Level* |
|---|---|---|---|---|---|
| B | C | X | X | | |

### 20.2.1 Purpose

Here you can specify the object type, infotype and subtype which are not to be imported. This can be used to prevent the data from being accidentally overwritten.

### 20.2.2 IMG Node

SM30 ➢ T77TR

### 20.2.3 Screen

| OT | IT | STy. |
|---|---|---|
| | | |
| | | |

### 20.2.4 Primary Key

Object Type + Infotype + Subtype

## 20.3 MANUAL TRANSPORT

| *Functional Consultant* | *User* | *Business Process Owner* | *Senior Management* | *My Rating* | *Understanding Level* |
|---|---|---|---|---|---|
| B | C | X | X | | |

### 20.3.1 Purpose

If you want to transport the personnel planning objects you create in customizing client, you can do so using automatic transport, manual transport, or transport via object lock. If you choose manual transport option, you use this program to create the manual transport. The program creates a customizing request which can be transported like any other customizing request. The starting object and the evaluation path you specify determine the objects which are included in the customizing transport request.

### 20.3.2 Transaction

RE_RHMOVE30—Manual Transport Link

### 20.3.3 Selection Screen

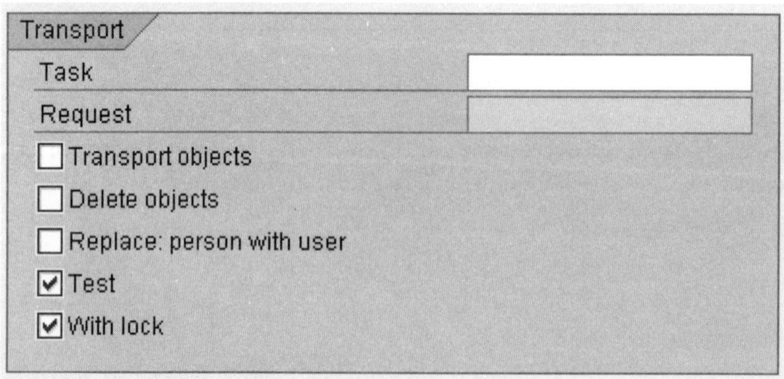


### 20.3.4 Functionality

The system transports the object infotype 1000 records and their dependent infotype records, e.g. infotype 1001. However, you can set an import lock using customizing in the target system. By doing so, you determine which infotypes are transported. Certain objects are not stored in infotype 1000. These objects such as cost centers or persons are called external objects and they are not transported.

When relationships of an object are imported, the relationships in the target system can only be created if the related object exists. This is true only for non-external objects. A relationship to the external object is always created. That is, the system does not first check that the external object exists. Thus, the system may create relationship records for external objects that do not exist.

If you specify that the objects be deleted, they are deleted from the source system. They are also deleted from the target system if they exist before importing them from the source system.

If you don't have employees in the target system, while transferring data, you can replace persons with users using their link in infotype 0105.

You can run the program in test mode.

## 20.4 DATA TRANSFER THROUGH SEQUENTIAL FILES

| *Functional Consultant* | *User* | *Business Process Owner* | *Senior Management* | *My Rating* | *Understanding Level* |
|---|---|---|---|---|---|
| B | C | X | X | | |

### 20.4.1 Create Sequential File

You can run transaction OOMV to create a sequential file of organizational management data in your SAP system.

| PV | OT | Object ID | Infotype | Subtype | S | Pr | Start date | End Date | Variation field | RNo |
|---|---|---|---|---|---|---|---|---|---|---|
| 01 | O | 50000075 | 1000 | | 1 | | 09.12.2008 | 15.12.2008 | E | |
| 01 | O | 50000075 | 1000 | | 1 | | 16.12.2008 | 31.12.9999 | E | |
| 01 | O | 50000075 | 1000 | | 3 | | 31.12.2008 | 31.12.9999 | E | |
| 01 | O | 50000076 | 1000 | | 1 | | 09.12.2008 | 31.12.9999 | E | |

### 20.4.2 Edit Sequential File

You can edit the sequential file generated in the previous step using transaction OOMW. You can select a row and click . The system lets you edit the data.

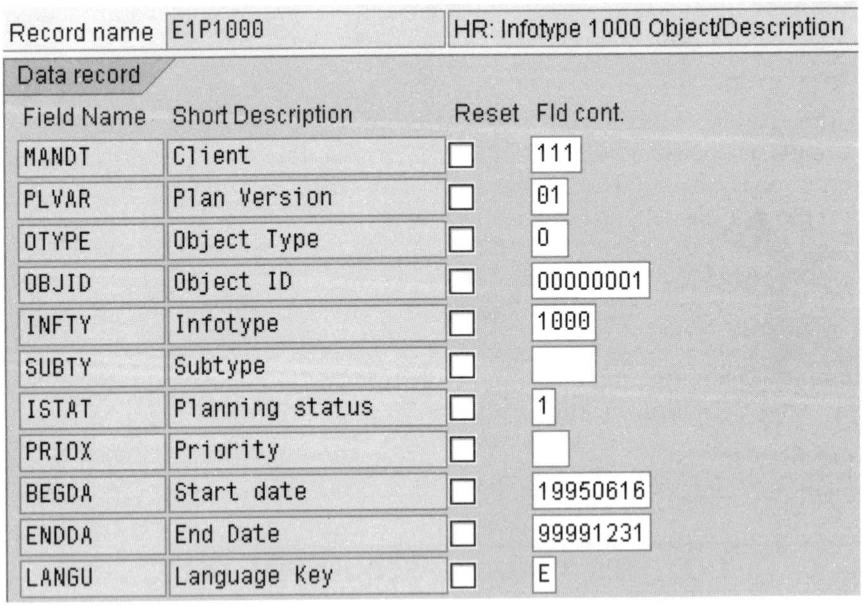


After making the required change you click Transfer data.

### 20.4.3 Load Sequential File

The sequential file generated and edited in the above steps is loaded in SAP using transaction OODT. You can specify the client, so that data file created in one client can be loaded into another client.

## 20.5 DATA DISTRIBUTION USING ALE

| *Functional Consultant* | *User* | *Business Process Owner* | *Senior Management* | *My Rating* | *Understanding Level* |
|---|---|---|---|---|---|
| B | C | X | X | | |

### 20.5.1 Distribute Master Data

If you have multiple SAP servers, you can maintain data on one server and distribute it to the other servers using ALE. Configuration of ALE is done using transaction SALE and distribution is done using transaction PFAL.

### 20.5.2 Display ALE Change Pointers

To distribute changes after a complete transport, you can use change pointers. You can run transaction RE_RHALECPS to display change pointers.

### 20.5.3 Evaluate ALE Change Pointers

You can run transaction RE_RHALESMD to evaluate change pointers. This program creates IDOCs based on the change pointers for HR organizational data and HR master data that have been written since the specified date and time. It then dispatches them to the receiving systems. If change pointers have been processed already, they are processed again. The receiving systems are determined on the basis of the distribution model for this message type.

## 20.6 DATA EXTRACTION

| *Functional Consultant* | *User* | *Business Process Owner* | *Senior Management* | *My Rating* | *Understanding Level* |
|---|---|---|---|---|---|
| B | C | X | X | | |

### 20.6.1 Scenarios

In view T77SCEN_AW you can define scenarios. Scenario ORGC with evaluation path ORGCHART is used in organizational management to extract data.

| Scenario | Eval.path |
|---|---|
| MDT0 | ORGCHART |
| ORGC | ORGCHART |
| PPOM | ORGCHART |

### 20.6.2 Assignment of Queries to Scenarios

The evaluation path assigned to a scenario gives only basic data about the objects. If you want additional data, you need to specify a query in view T77SCENQY. This query can be different for different object types. You specify user group along with the query to uniquely identify it.

| Scenario | Obj. type | User group | Query |
|---|---|---|---|
| MDT1 | C | | SY000000000145 |
| MDT1 | O | | ORGUNIT_TEST |
| MDT1 | P | | SY000000000187 |
| MDT1 | S | | SY000000000139 |
| MDT2 | O | /SAPQUERY/HO | ORGUNIT_DATA |
| MDT2 | P | /SAPQUERY/HO | PERSON_DATA |
| MDT2 | S | /SAPQUERY/HO | POSITION_DATA |
| ORGC | O | /SAPQUERY/HO | ORGUNIT_DATA |
| ORGC | P | /SAPQUERY/HO | PERSON_DATA |
| ORGC | S | /SAPQUERY/HO | POSITION_DATA |

# CHAPTER 21 Organization and Staffing Interface Customizing

When you run transactions PPOSE, PPOME or PPOCE, you get a user interface. This user interface can be customized to your requirements.

## 21.1 TAB PAGES

| *Functional Consultant* | *User* | *Business Process Owner* | *Senior Management* | *My Rating* | *Understanding Level* |
|---|---|---|---|---|---|
| C | X | X | X | | |

### 21.1.1 Functionality

In Organization and Staffing interface, you see tab pages. You can do the following so that they are as per your requirement.

| *What to do* | *How to do* | *Chapter* |
|---|---|---|
| Create your own tab page | Create new tab page in table T77OMTABS | 21.1.3 |
| Change name of a tab page | Change name of a tab page in view T77OCTABST | 21.1.3 |
| Add your tab page for an object type | Add a tab page in view T77OCTABUS | 21.1.5 |
| Hide a tab page | Hide a tab page in view T77OCTABUS | 21.1.5 |

| *What to do* | *How to do* | *Chapter* |
|---|---|---|
| Change name of a tab page dynamically depending on the object type | Call a function module to return tab page name for an object type in view T77OCTABUS | 21.1.5 |
| Change icon of an object type | Call a function module to return icon for an object type in view T77OCTABUS | 21.1.5 |
| Change sequence of tab pages | Change sequence of tab pages in view T77OCTABUS | 21.1.5 |
| Define your own service and its attributes for newly created object | For newly created object define your own service in T77OBJSER and its attributes in view T77OMATGT | 21.1.6 |
| Define your own request and assign it to an object type for use in structural overview | Define your own request in T77OMREGIS and assign it to an object type in T77OMIA_C for use in structural overview | 21.1.7 |

## 21.1.2 Dialog Structure

In order to make the changes listed in chapter 21.1.1, you can run transaction OOFRAMEWORKCUST. You will see the following screen. Against each line the table name is given. You may make the changes in them. Note that these tables are cross-client. Some of these tables have a corresponding customer table. You may modify them using transaction SM30.

| *Dialog structure* | *Cross-client view* | *Client-specific view* | *Chapter* |
|---|---|---|---|
| Dialog Structure | | | |
| Tab Page Definition | T77OMTABS | T77OCTABST | 21.1.3 |
| Definition Service | T77OBJSER | | 21.1.6 |
| Attribute Service | T77OMATGT | | 21.1.6 |
| Scenario Group Definition | T77OMSCENF | | 21.1.4 |
| Scenario Definition (Hierarchy Framework) | T77OMFRAS | | 21.1.4 |
| Attribute Scenario | T77OMFRAM | | 21.1.4 |
| Icon Legend | T77OMICON | | 21.1.4 |
| Tab Page in Scenario for each Object Type | T77OMTABUS | T77OCTABUS | 21.1.5 |
| Request Definition | T77OMREGIS | | 21.1.7 |
| Request in Scenario for each Object Type | T77OMIA | T77OMIA_C | 21.1.7 |

### 21.1.3 Tab Pages

#### *Tab page id*

Tab pages display information about the selected object in detail area. In order to customize tab pages, you need to know their ids. You can display the tab page id by adding parameter OM_TABTYPE_DISPLAY with value 'X' in System ➢ User Profile ➢ Own Data ➢ Parameters. When you do so, the tab page name will be followed by tab page id Basic data BASIS_O .

#### *Tab pages (cross-client)*

Tab pages are defined in table T77OMTABS. If forecast time logic is active, you can switch between the period view and key date view on the tab page. If the tab page is for a single infotype, you tick the checkbox infotype-specific, and specify the infotype. In this way you can add any infotype as a tab page and display in Organization and Staffing.

Tab Page Definition

| Tab Page | Description | Forecast time log. active | Infotype-specific | Infotype |
|---|---|---|---|---|
| BASIS_O | Basic data | ☑ | ☐ | |
| BASIS_P | Basic data | ☑ | ☐ | |
| BASIS_S | Basic data | ☑ | ☐ | |
| BASIS_T | Basic data | ☑ | ☐ | |
| BASIS_TG | Basic data | ☑ | ☐ | |
| BASIS_US | Basic data | ☑ | ☐ | |
| COMPS | Tax codes | ☐ | ☐ | |
| COSTDIST | Cost distribution | ☐ | ☐ | |
| EO_OBJ | Object information | ☐ | ☐ | |
| HEADC_EX | Quota Planning | ☐ | ☐ | |
| HEADC_MB | Max Budget | ☐ | ☐ | |
| HEADC_O | Quota Planning | ☐ | ☐ | |
| HIERARCH | Hierarchy | ☑ | ☐ | |
| IT0783 | Job Index | ☑ | ☐ | |
| IT0792 | Org. Additional Dat | ☐ | ☑ | 0792 |
| IT1000 | Name | ☐ | ☑ | 1000 |
| IT1002 | Description | ☐ | ☑ | 1002 |
| IT1003 | Department/staff | ☐ | ☑ | 1003 |

While you may add your own tab pages here, it is recommended that you do not change the characteristics of SAP provided tab pages. If you want to change the text on a tab page, you may do so in view T77OCTABST, which is client dependent and your changes will not be overwritten by SAP.

### *Tab page texts (client-specific)*

Although you can change tab page name in table T77OMTABS, it is recommended that you don't do so. Table T77OMTABS is a cross-client table and there is a risk that your change may be overwritten by SAP in client 000, which would affect all clients. You may change the tab page name in view T77OCTABST, which is client dependent.

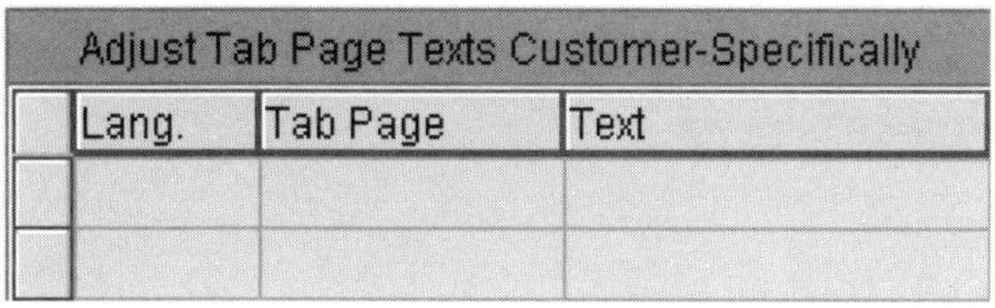


## 21.1.4 Scenario

SAP uses hierarchy framework for multiple purposes. Organization and Staffing is scenario OME0.

### *Scenario definition (cross-client)*

Scenarios are defined in table T77OMFRAS.

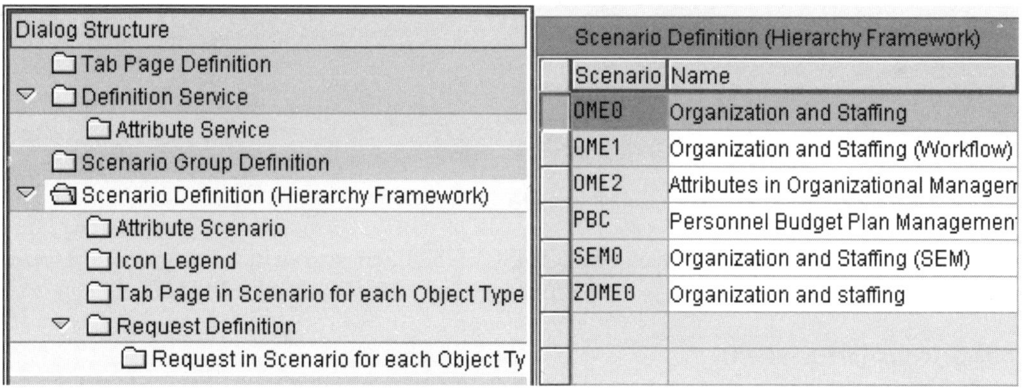


### *Scenario attributes (cross-client)*

The attributes of a scenario are defined in view T77OMFRAM. The attributes of scenario OME0 can be seen in the following screenshot. You can see that transactions PPOSE, PPOME and PPOCE are linked to scenario OME0. These are predefined by SAP, and you don't need to do anything.

| Scenario | OME0 |
|---|---|

**Attribute Scenario**

| | |
|---|---|
| Scenario group | ORGMANAGEMENT |
| Object manager scenario | OME000 |
| Transation code: Display | PPOSE |
| Transaction code: Change | PPOME |
| Transaction code: Create | PPOCE |
| Enhanced authorization | OM_ADDITIONAL_AUTHORITY_CHECK |
| Time-dependent | I Time Interval |
| ☐ No Undo/Redo | |
| Status object | OMST |
| Time object | STTI |
| Initialize framework | NF_GET_INIT_EVENT_WORKPLACE |
| Initialize object manager | NF_GET_INIT_EVENT_OBJMANAGER |
| Plan version | POP |
| Selection date | OM_DATE |
| Unsaved steps | 10 |

### *Scenario groups (cross-client)*

Scenario groups are defined in view T77OMSCENF. Each scenario belongs to a group. Organization and Staffing belongs to scenaıio group ORGMANAGEMENT.

### *Scenario icons (cross-client)*

Icons linked to a scenario are specified in table T77OMICON.

**Icon Legend**

| Scenario | Icon | Icon text |
|---|---|---|
| OME0 | | Chief |
| OME0 | | Vacant position |
| OME0 | | Unoccupied position |
| OME0 | | Obselete Position |
| OME0 | | Position with several holders |
| OME0 | | Object to be added |
| OME0 | | Object removed |

## 21.1.5 Tab Pages for Each Object Type

### *Tab pages for each object type (cross-client)*

For Organization and Staffing, the tab pages which are displayed for each object type is defined in view T77OMTABUS. For an object type, you can add a tab page, hide a tab page, and change the sequence of tab pages. If you don't want to display a tab page, you don't need to remove it; you just need to tick the 'Do not display' checkbox. You can define the function module for the icon to be displayed. If you want to change the tab name depending on object type, you can specify a function module for that.

Tab Page in Scenario for each Object Type

| Sce... | Obj... | Tab Page | Seq... | ReportName | Scr... | FM for icons | FM for text | Do Not Display |
|---|---|---|---|---|---|---|---|---|
| OME0 | O | ACCNTNG | 2 | SAPLRHOMDET | 0500 | RH_OM_DETAI | | ☐ |
| OME0 | O | ADDRESS | 3 | SAPLRHADDRE | 0400 | RH_OM_DETAI | | ☐ |
| OME0 | O | BASIS_O | 1 | SAPLRHOMDET | 0200 | RH_OM_DETAI | | ☐ |
| OME0 | O | COSTDIST | 3 | SAPLRHOMDET | 0501 | RH_OM_DETAI | | ☐ |
| OME0 | O | HEADC_EX | 6 | SAPLHROM_HC | 0810 | RH_OM_DETAI | | ☑ |
| OME0 | O | HEADC_MB | 6 | SAPLHROM_HC | 0810 | RH_OM_DETAI | | ☑ |
| OME0 | O | HEADC_O | 6 | SAPLRHOMDET | 0800 | RH_OM_DETAI | | ☐ |
| OME0 | O | IT1000 | 1 | | | | | ☑ |
| OME0 | O | IT1002 | 2 | | | | | ☑ |
| OME0 | O | IT1003 | 14 | | | | | ☑ |
| OME0 | O | IT1028 | 10 | | | | | ☑ |
| OME0 | O | IT1509GS | 15 | SAPLHRFPM_C | 0700 | HRFPM_DETAI | | ☐ |
| OME0 | O | IT1509GW | 15 | SAPLHRFPM_C | 0600 | HRFPM_DETAI | | ☐ |
| OME0 | O | TASKS | 15 | SAPLRHOMDET | 0401 | RH_OM_DETAI | | ☐ |
| OME0 | O | WORKTIME | 5 | SAPLRHOMDET | 0600 | RH_OM_DETAI | | ☐ |

### *Tab pages for each object type (client-specific)*

It is recommended that you don't make changes in table T77OMTABUS as it is a cross-client table and there is a possibility of your entries getting overwritten by SAP in client 000, which would affect all clients. Instead, you may make your changes in table T77OCTABUS, which has identical structure and which is client specific. The entry in table T77OCTABUS overrides the entry in table T77OMTABUS and is read with other entries in table T77OMTABUS.

### 21.1.6 Services

***Services (cross-client)***

Services of an interface object are defined in view T77OBJSER. They are used in the overview area.

| Interface object service | Object key |
|---|---|
| ACCOUNT ASSIGNMENT | GOWD |
| ACCOUNT ASSIGNMENT USAGE | GOWD |
| AGENT FOR TASK | GOWD |

***Attributes of services (cross-client)***

Attributes of services are defined in view T77OMATGT.

| | |
|---|---|
| Interface object service | ACCOUNT ASSIGNMENT |
| Object Type | * |

**Attribute Service**

| | |
|---|---|
| Selection | M Multiple selection |
| Evaluation Path | KOSTDIST |
| Technical depth | 2 |
| Column group | NF_GEN_OV |
| Header type | |

### 21.1.7 Requests

***Requests (cross-client)***

Requests are defined in table T77OMREGIS.

| Scenario | Hierarchy framework request | Name | Service for 1st ... | Service for 2nd ... | Tab Page |
|---|---|---|---|---|---|
| OMEO | ASSIGNMENT RULES (ORG) | Staffing Analy | ASSIGNMENT RL | DETAIL (GENER/ | |
| OMEO | DISPLAY_EMPTY_DETAIL_FR/ | | | DISPLAY_EMPTY_ | |

***Requests for object types (cross-client)***

Requests are linked to object types for each scenario in view T77OMIA.

| Scenario | Obj. type | Hierarchy framework request | Standard action |
|---|---|---|---|
| OMEO | O | ASSIGNMENT RULES (ORG) | ☐ |
| OMEO | S | ASSIGNMENT RULES (ORG) | ☐ |

***Requests for object types (client-specific)***

Customer-specific changes are in view T77OMIA_C which has the same structure as T77OMIA.

## 21.2 COLUMNS

| *Functional Consultant* | *User* | *Business Process Owner* | *Senior Management* | *My Rating* | *Understanding Level* |
|---|---|---|---|---|---|
| C | X | X | X | | |

### 21.2.1 Functionality

In the selection area and overview area of transaction PPOME, the system shows data about the objects in columns. These columns are defined and grouped in column groups and assigned to the selection area and the overview area. If you click  in the selection area or the overview area, you will see the associated column group and columns in it. You can hide or display these columns. You can also see the technical names of columns and column groups if you set parameter OM_ARRAYTYPE_DISPLAY to 'X'.

In Organization and Staffing interface, you can do the following.

| *What to do* | *How to do* | *Chapter* |
|---|---|---|
| Define your own column | Create new column in table T77COL | 21.2.3 |
| Add columns in a column group | Add columns in a column group in view T77ACOLC | 21.2.4 |
| Define your own column group | Define your own column group in table T77ARRAYTP | 21.2.4 |
| Define your own hierarchical column groups | Define your own hierarchical column groups in view T77HIERATC | 21.2.6 |
| Define your own column header type | Define your own column header type in view T77COLHTYP | 21.2.7 |
| Define your own column headers | Define your own column headers in view T77COLH_C | 21.2.7 |

### 21.2.2 Dialog Structure

In order to make the changes listed in chapter 21.2.1, you can run transaction OOCOLFRAMCUST. You will see the following screen. Against each line the table name is given. You may make the changes in them. Note that these tables are cross-client. Some of these tables have a corresponding customer table. You may modify them using transaction SM30.

| *Dialog structure* | *Cross-client view* | *Client-specific view* | *Chapter* |
|---|---|---|---|
| Dialog Structure | | | |
| Column Definition | T77COL | | 21.2.3 |
| Column Group Definition | T77ARRAYTP | | 21.2.4 |
| Columns in a Column Group | T77ACOL | T77ACOLC | 21.2.4 |
| Visibility of a Column | T77ACOLINI | T77ACOLC | 21.2.4 |
| Column/Object Type Assignment | T77COLOTYP | | 21.2.5 |
| Definition of a Hierarchical Column Group | T77HIERATP | T77HIERATC | 21.2.6 |
| Definition of Column Header Type | T77COLHTYP | | 21.2.7 |
| Redefine Column Header | T77COLHEAD | T77COLH_C | 21.2.7 |

### 21.2.3 Columns

***Columns (cross-client)***

If you want to add a new column, or modify the definition of an existing column, e.g. column heading, you can define it in table T77COL.

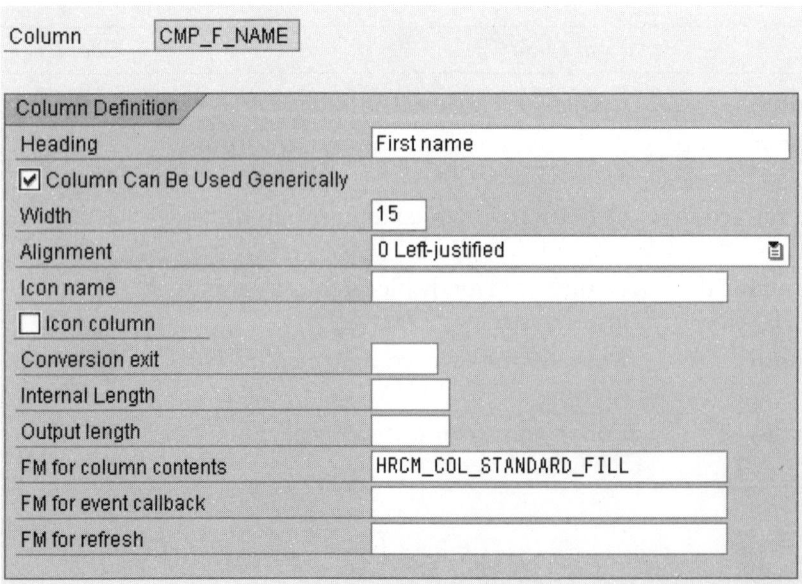

### 21.2.4 Column Groups

***Column groups (cross-client)***

You can define column groups in table T77ARRAYTP.

| Column group | Name | Query GUID | InfoSet |
|---|---|---|---|
| /ISDFPS/AGR | Column Roles in Org. Management | | |

***Columns in column group (cross-client)***

Columns are grouped in column groups in view T77ACOL.

| Column group | Column | Column fixed | Sequence | Coherence Relationship |
|---|---|---|---|---|
| /ISDFPS/AGR | /ISDF/ST_AGR | ☐ | 3 | |
| /ISDFPS/AGR | ORG_BEGDA | ☐ | 4 | OBEG |
| /ISDFPS/AGR | ORG_ENDDA | ☐ | 5 | OBEG |
| /ISDFPS/AGR | ORG_OBJID | ☐ | 1 | |
| /ISDFPS/AGR | ORG_RTEXT | ☐ | 99 | |
| /ISDFPS/AGR | ORG_SHORT | ☐ | 2 | |
| /ISDFPS/AGR | ORG_STEXT | ☐ | 88 | |
| /ISDFPS/AGR | ORG_VBEGDA | ☐ | 6 | VBEG |
| /ISDFPS/AGR | ORG_VENDDA | ☐ | 7 | VBEG |

***Visibility of a column (cross-client)***

Visibility of a column is defined in view T77ACOLINI.

| Column group | Column | Do Not Display | Hidden | Always visible |
|---|---|---|---|---|
| /ISDFPS/AGR | ORG_OBJID | ☐ | ☐ | ☐ |

***Columns in column group and visibility of a column (client-specific)***

If you want to make changes in columns in a column group, you do so in view T77ACOLC instead of views T77ACOL and T77ACOLINI, which are based on cross-client tables.

| Column group | Column | Column fixed | Position | Coheren... | Do Not Display | Hidden | Always visible |
|---|---|---|---|---|---|---|---|
| | | | | | | | |
| | | | | | | | |

## 21.2.5 Column/Object Type Assignment

### *Column/object type assignment (cross-client)*

Columns are assigned to object types in view T77COLOTYP.

| Column | Obj. type |
|---|---|
| ORG_JOB | C |
| ORG_ORG | O |

## 21.2.6 Hierarchical Column Group

### *Hierarchical column groups (cross-client)*

Hierarchical column groups are defined in view T77HIERATP.

| Column group | assigned column group | assigned column group |
|---|---|---|
| NF_GEN_OV_MANAG | NF_GEN_OV_ORG | NF_ORG_ORGUNIT |

### *Hierarchical column groups (client-specific)*

Customer changes are done in view T77HIERATC which has the same structure as view T77HIERATP.

## 21.2.7 Column Headers

### *Column header types (cross-client)*

Column header types are defined in view T77COLHTYP.

| Column header type |
|---|
| ORGSTRUC |

### *Column headers (cross-client)*

Column headers are defined in view T77COLHEAD.

| Lang. | Header type | Column | Heading |
|---|---|---|---|
| EN | ORGSTRUC | IM_NODE_ID | Organizational structure |
| FR | ORGSTRUC | IM_NODE_ID | Organigramme |

### *Column headers (client-specific)*

Customer modifications are made in view T77COLH_C.

| Language | Header type | Column | Column heading |
|---|---|---|---|
| | | | |
| | | | |

## 21.3 SEARCH NODES

| *Functional Consultant* | *User* | *Business Process Owner* | *Senior Management* | *My Rating* | *Understanding Level* |
|---|---|---|---|---|---|
| C | X | X | X | | |

### 21.3.1 Functionality

SAP has defined the object types which appear in the object manager. If you want to add your own object type, you can do so by running transaction OOOBJMANCUST, where you define search nodes. You also need to customize the overview area and the detail area.

You can do the following to customize the Organization and Staffing interface as per your requirement.

| *What to do* | *How to do* | *Chapter* |
|---|---|---|
| For the new object type you created, create a new search node | For the new object type you created, create a new search node in table T77FSEAN | 21.3.3 |
| For the new search node you created, define its properties, e.g. the order in which the new object will appear in the search area | For the new search node you created, define its properties in table T77CNODORD | 21.3.6 |
| For the new search node you created, define search tools | For the new search node you created, define search tools in view V77CSEAT | 21.3.6 |
| Define your own coherence relationship | Define your own coherence relationship in table T77FRIEND | 21.3.5 |
| Exclude nodes from search range | Exclude nodes from search range in view T77CNOD_EX | 21.3.6 |
| Exclude search tools from searching a search range | Exclude search tools from searching a search range in view T77CSEAT_E | 21.3.6 |

### 21.3.2 Dialog Structure

In order to make the changes listed in chapter 21.3.1, you can run transaction OOOBJMANCUST. You will see the following screen. Against each line the table name is given. You may make the changes in them. Note that these tables are cross-client. Some of these tables have a corresponding customer table. You may modify them using transaction SM30.

| *Dialog structure* | *Cross-client view* | *Client-specific view* | *Chapter* |
|---|---|---|---|
| Dialog Structure | | | |
| Definition of Search Node | T77FSEAN | | 21.3.3 |
| Definition of Search Tool | T77FSEAS | | 21.3.4 |
| Definition of Coherence Relationship | T77FRIEND | | 21.3.5 |
| ▽ Scenario Definition (Object Manager) | T77FOBJMAN | | 21.3.6 |
| Search Nodes | T77FNODORD | T77CNODORD | 21.3.6 |
| ▽ Search tool | T77FSEAT | V77CSEAT | 21.3.6 |
| Display Area (Column Group...) | T77FSEATGB | V77CSEAT | 21.3.6 |
| | | T77CNOD_EX | 21.3.6 |
| | | T77CSEAT_E | 21.3.6 |

### 21.3.3 Search Nodes

#### ***Search nodes (cross-client)***

Search nodes are defined in table T77FSEAN.

| Search Node Key | Name | Obj. type | Icon name |
|---|---|---|---|
| 0 | | 0 | |
| OBJ_HIST | Object history | | ICON_HISTORY |

### 21.3.4 Search Tools

#### ***Search tools (cross-client)***

Search tools are defined in table T77FSEAS.

| Search tool | Name | Searchtool type |
|---|---|---|
| CL_COINT_CP_EXTID_SINGLE | Individual External Object | GS General search tool |
| CL_COINT_CP_MESSAGESEL | Selection Variant Messages 1 | GS General search tool |

## 21.3.5 Coherence Relationships

### *Coherence relationships (cross-client)*

Coherence relationships are defined in table T77FRIEND.

| Coherence Relationship | Name |
|---|---|
| C_VAL | Validity period of job |
| IM_VDAT_EP | Relationship period program position |

## 21.3.6 Object Manager Scenarios

### *Object manager scenarios (cross-client)*

Object manager scenarios are defined in view T77FOBJMAN.

| Scenario | Selection |
|---|---|
| OME000 | M Multiple selection |
| OME001 | M Multiple selection |

### *Search nodes in a scenario (cross-client)*

Search nodes in a scenario are defined in table T77FNODORD.

| Scenario | Search Node Key | Name | Position | Column group | Header type |
|---|---|---|---|---|---|
| OME000 | BP | | 7 | | |
| OME000 | C | | 3 | | |
| OME000 | O | | 1 | | |
| OME000 | OBJ_HIST | | 99 | OBJ_HIST | |

### *Search nodes in a scenario (client-specific)*

Customer-specific changes are done in table T77CNODORD.

| Scenario | Search Node Key | Name | Position | Column group | Header type |
|---|---|---|---|---|---|
| | | | | | |
| | | | | | |

### *Excluding nodes from search range (client-specific)*

You can exclude nodes from search range in view T77CNOD_EX.

| Obj. Manager Scenario | Search Node Key |
|---|---|
| | |
| | |

### *Search tools in a scenario (cross-client)*

Search tools in a scenario are defined in table T77FSEAT.

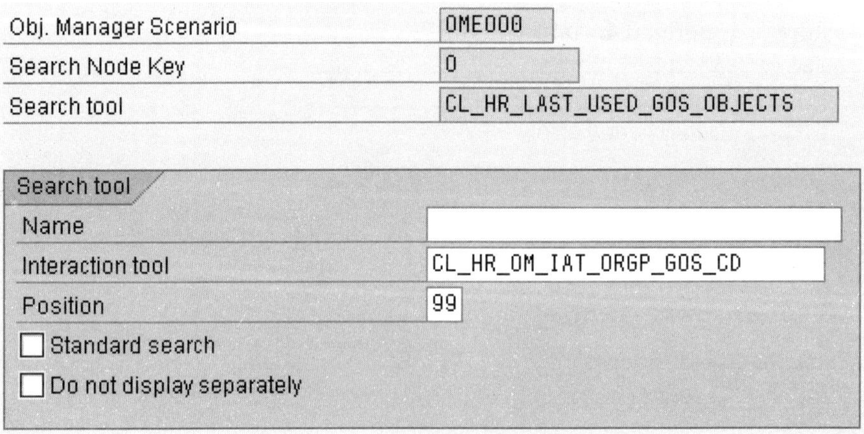


### *Column group for a search tool (cross-client)*

Column group for a search tool is defined in view T77FSEATGB.

| Scenario | Search Node Key | Search tool | Column group | Header ty... | Display... | Dynamic... |
|---|---|---|---|---|---|---|
| OME000 | 0 | CL_HR_LAS1 | OBJ_HIST |  | ☐ | ☐ |

### *Column group for a search tool in a scenario (client-specific)*

If you want to make changes in table T77FSEAT or view T77FSEATGB, you make changes in view V77CSEAT instead.

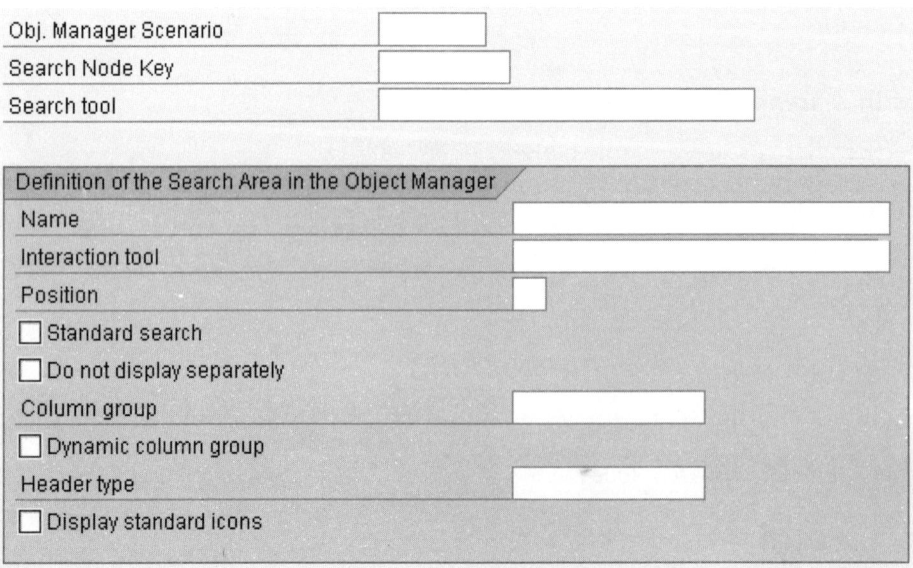

***Exclude search tools from search range (client-specific)***

If you want to exclude search tools from searching a search range, you can do so in view T77CSEAT_E.

| Scenario | Search Node Key | Search tool |
|---|---|---|
| | | |
| | | |

## 21.4 EXCLUDING INFOTYPES WHEN COPYING INTERNAL OBJECTS

| *Functional Consultant* | *User* | *Business Process Owner* | *Senior Management* | *My Rating* | *Understanding Level* |
|---|---|---|---|---|---|
| C | X | X | X | | |

### 21.4.1 Purpose

When you copy an object, its infotypes are also copied except for those specified in table T77ITEX. If you want to exclude more infotypes from getting copied, you can define them here.

### 21.4.2 IMG Node

SM30 ➢ T77ITEX_C

### 21.4.3 Screen

| Scenario | Obj. type | Infoty. | Subtyp | Type of related object |
|---|---|---|---|---|
| | | | | |
| | | | | |

### 21.4.4 Primary Key

Hierarchy Framework: Scenario + Object Type + Infotype + Subtype + Type of Related Object

## 21.5 BACKUP PROMPT

| *Functional Consultant* | *User* | *Business Process Owner* | *Senior Management* | *My Rating* | *Understanding Level* |
|---|---|---|---|---|---|
| C | X | X | X | | |

### 21.5.1 Purpose

In Organization and Staffing interface you can go on changing data in different tab pages in the detail area, or modify structures in the overview area. The data is saved only when you click the save icon. If your session gets interrupted due to some reason, your changes will be lost. In scenario OME0, you can specify the number of steps after which the system prompts you to save your data. The prompt is only a suggestion. You may save the data and continue to work, or you may continue to work without saving the data.

### 21.5.2 IMG Node

SM30 ➢ T77OMFRAMC

### 21.5.3 Screen

| Scenario | Maximum number of unsaved steps |
|---|---|
| OME0 | |

### 21.5.4 Primary Key

Hierarchy Framework: Scenario

## 21.6 ASSIGNMENT OF INFOSETS TO OBJECT TYPES

| *Functional Consultant* | *User* | *Business Process Owner* | *Senior Management* | *My Rating* | *Understanding Level* |
|---|---|---|---|---|---|
| C | X | X | X | | |

### 21.6.1 Purpose

Search functions for different object types are based on different infosets which are defined in table T77OMAHQ_FUNCARS.

| Scenario | Obj. type | InfoSet | Group |
|---|---|---|---|
| | O | /SAPQUERY/HR_XX_OM_O | PPOME_O |
| | P | /SAPQUERY/HR_XX_OM_P | PPOME_P |

If you add your own object types, and therefore need to change infoset linkage, you should not change the above view but create a record in the view given below.

### 21.6.2 IMG Node

SM30 ➢ T77OMAHQ_FUNCAR

### 21.6.3 Screen

| Scenario | Obj. type | InfoSet | Group |
|---|---|---|---|
| | | | |
| | | | |

### 21.6.4 Primary Key

Object Manager: Scenario + Object Type

CHAPTER 22

# Data Model

## 22.1 OBJECT TYPES

| *Functional Consultant* | *User* | *Business Process Owner* | *Senior Management* | *My Rating* | *Understanding Level* |
|---|---|---|---|---|---|
| A | B | C | C | | |

### 22.1.1 Purpose

SAP has defined the object types required for Organizational Management. If you need, you can also define your own object types. For example, if your company has cross-functional teams, you can create them as an object type. Employees of the company may be members or leaders of these teams. Object types created by you should be in the range of 01 to 99.

### 22.1.2 IMG Node

SM34 ➢ T7780 (view T778O)

### 22.1.3 Screen

| O | Object type text | OrgObj type | Icon name | BW ref. char. |
|---|---|---|---|---|
| * | | | | |
| A | Work Center | PDOTYPE_A | ICON_WORKPLACE | |
| AC | Rule | | ICON_ROLE | |
| AG | Role | | ICON_ACTIVITY_GROUP | |
| AP | Applicant | | ICON_EMPLOYEE | |

### 22.1.4 Primary Key

Object Type

## 22.2 ESSENTIAL RELATIONSHIPS

| *Functional Consultant* | *User* | *Business Process Owner* | *Senior Management* | *My Rating* | *Understanding Level* |
|---|---|---|---|---|---|
| C | X | X | X | | |

### 22.2.1 Purpose

Here you can define the relationship that should be proposed in the course of the structural authorization check.

### 22.2.2 IMG Node

SM34 ➢ T7780 (view T77SO)

### 22.2.3 Screen

| OT | Object type text | A/B | Rel | Relationship name | Rel.obj.type | Obj.type text |
|---|---|---|---|---|---|---|
| O | Organizational unit | A | 002 | Reports (line) to | O | Organizational unit |

Table T77SO contains only four entries.

| Object Type | Relationship | Relat'ship | Rel.obj.type |
|---|---|---|---|
| DE | B | 460 | P |
| O | A | 002 | O |
| Q | A | 030 | Q |
| S | A | 003 | O |

### 22.2.4 Primary Key

Object Type

## 22.3 EXTERNAL OBJECT TYPES

| *Functional Consultant* | *User* | *Business Process Owner* | *Senior Management* | *My Rating* | *Understanding Level* |
|---|---|---|---|---|---|
| C | X | X | X | | |

### 22.3.1 Purpose

This table contains the list of object types which are external. These objects are not created in Personnel Planning. For these object types, you must specify the interface program used to access these object types. For external objects, there is no record in infotype 1000. These objects exist only in infotype 1001. Person and cost center are examples of external object types.

### 22.3.2 IMG Node

SM34 ➢ T7780 (view T77EO)

### 22.3.3 Screen

| OT | Obj.type text | KeyStruct. | Screen | Inv.relat. | Interface | StdObjType | enh.exist. |
|---|---|---|---|---|---|---|---|
| P | | PKEYS | | ☑ | RHPREL00 | ☐ | ☑ |

### 22.3.4 Primary Key

Object Type

## 22.4 STRUCTURE SEARCH

| *Functional Consultant* | *User* | *Business Process Owner* | *Senior Management* | *My Rating* | *Understanding Level* |
|---|---|---|---|---|---|
| C | X | X | X | | |

### 22.4.1 Purpose

This table contains the evaluation path used for structural search of an object type.

### 22.4.2 IMG Node

SM34 ➢ T7780 (view T77OS)

### 22.4.3 Screen

Object Type | 0 | Organizational unit

| EvalPath | Evaluation path text | Status vec. | Key date | No Unrel. |
|---|---|---|---|---|
| ORGEH | Organizational structure | 1 | ☑ | ☐ |

### 22.4.4 Primary Key

Object Type + Sequence Number

## 22.5 OBJECT TYPE KEY

| *Functional Consultant* | *User* | *Business Process Owner* | *Senior Management* | *My Rating* | *Understanding Level* |
|---|---|---|---|---|---|
| C | X | X | X | | |

### 22.5.1 Purpose

If you have created new object types, change the value of the semantic abbreviation of each object type in the parameter group OTYPE, where necessary.

### 22.5.2 IMG Node

SM34 ➢ T7780 (view V_T77S0OT)

### 22.5.3 Screen

| Group | Sem. abbr | Value abbr | Text |
|---|---|---|---|
| OTYPE | ORGEH | O | Organizational unit |
| OTYPE | PARTN | PT | Contact person |
| OTYPE | PERNR | P | Person |
| OTYPE | PLSTE | S | Position |
| OTYPE | PTASK | T | Task |

### 22.5.4 Primary Key

Group Name + Semantic Abbreviation

## 22.6 TRANSACTIONS FOR MAINTAINING OBJECT TYPES

| *Functional Consultant* | *User* | *Business Process Owner* | *Senior Management* | *My Rating* | *Understanding Level* |
|---|---|---|---|---|---|
| C | X | X | X | | |

### 22.6.1 Purpose

You use different transactions to maintain different object types, e.g. PO10 to maintain organizational units and PO13 to maintain positions. These are specified in the parameter group TCODE in table T77S0.

### 22.6.2 IMG Node

SM34 ➢ T7780 (view V_T77S0OT)

### 22.6.3 Screen

| Group | Sem. abbr | Value abbr | Text |
|---|---|---|---|
| TCODE | P001 | A | Maintain Work Center |
| TCODE | P001D | A | Maintain Work Center |
| TCODE | P002 | B | Maintain training program |
| TCODE | P002D | B | Display training program |
| TCODE | P003 | C | Maintain Job |
| TCODE | P003D | C | Maintain Job |
| TCODE | P004 | D | Maintain business event type |
| TCODE | P004D | D | Display business event type |

### 22.6.4 Primary Key

Group Name + Semantic Abbreviation

## 22.7 INFOTYPES MASTER LIST

| *Functional Consultant* | *User* | *Business Process Owner* | *Senior Management* | *My Rating* | *Understanding Level* |
|---|---|---|---|---|---|
| A | B | C | C | | |

### 22.7.1 Purpose

This table contains the master list of infotypes.

### 22.7.2 IMG Node

SM34 ➢ T778T (view T778T)

### 22.7.3 Screen

| Inftyp. | Infotype Name |
|---|---|
| **** | |
| 1000 | Object |
| 1001 | Relationships |
| 1002 | Description |
| 1003 | Department/Staff |

### 22.7.4 Primary Key

Infotype

## 22.8 INFOTYPE TIME CONSTRAINTS

| *Functional Consultant* | *User* | *Business Process Owner* | *Senior Management* | *My Rating* | *Understanding Level* |
|---|---|---|---|---|---|
| A | B | C | C | | |

### 22.8.1 Purpose

Time constraints are used by the system to guarantee the integrity of data. They ensure that the data is consistent and does not contradict each other. For example, an object can have only one name on a given day. It may have different names on different days but on a given day it must have only one name. Time constraints of infotypes are specified in table T777Z, where it can be defined at infotype level, infotype + subtype level, or infotype + subtype + object type level. If object type is *, the time constraint applies to all object types. If subtype field is blank, then the time constraint applies to all subtypes. If there is another more specific record, which specifies the object type or subtype or both, that gets priority. In exceptional cases, the time constraint may also depend on target object type and is defined in table T77ZR.

| *TC* | *Description* | *Explanation* | *Example* |
|---|---|---|---|
| 0 | May only exist once | Information must exist for the entire life cycle of the object and cannot be changed. | This time constraint is applicable only to infotype 1957. |
| 1 | Without gaps | Information must exist for the entire life cycle of the object but can be changed. | Infotype 1000 (Objects) has time constraint 1, as it must exist without gap. |
| 2 | With gaps | Information is optional but can exist only once within a user-defined period. | Infotype 1002 (Description) has time constraint 2. During different periods you may have different descriptions and for some period you may have none, but you cannot have more than one description at the same time. |
| 3 | As often as required | Information is optional, and many data records can exist simultaneously within a user-defined period. | Infotype 1006 (Restrictions) has time constraint 3. At any time, you may have 0, 1, or more restrictions. |

### 22.8.2 IMG Node

SM34 ➢ T778T (view V_T777ZIT)
SM34 ➢ V_778U (view T777Z)

### 22.8.3 Screen

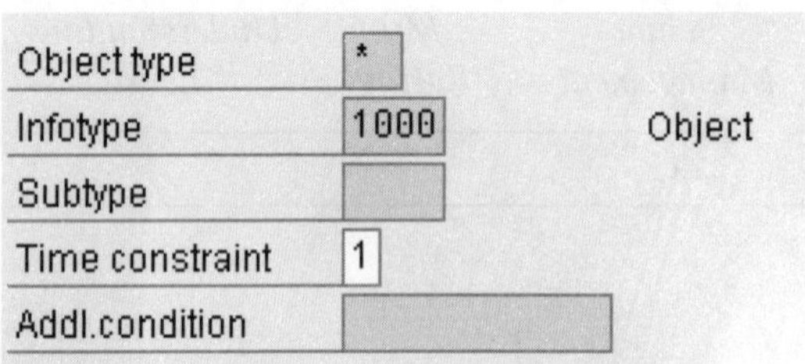


### 22.8.4 Primary Key

Object Type + Infotype + Subtype

## 22.9 OBJECT TYPES ALLOWED FOR AN INFOTYPE

| *Functional Consultant* | *User* | *Business Process Owner* | *Senior Management* | *My Rating* | *Understanding Level* |
|---|---|---|---|---|---|
| A | B | C | C | | |

### 22.9.1 Purpose

Here you define which object types are allowed for each infotype. When you specify an object type in transaction PP01, this table is used to show the infotypes which can be maintained for that object type.

### 22.9.2 IMG Node

SM34 ➢ T778T (view T777I)

### 22.9.3 Screen

| OT | Object type text | IT | Infotype Name | Alt.screen | No maintenance |
|---|---|---|---|---|---|
| O | Organizational unit | 1003 | Department/Staff | | ☐ |
| S | Position | 1003 | Department/Staff | | ☐ |

### 22.9.4 Primary Key

Object Type + Infotype + Subtype
Subtype column is blank for all entries. It is also not shown in the view.

## 22.10 SUBTYPES OF AN INFOTYPE

| *Functional Consultant* | *User* | *Business Process Owner* | *Senior Management* | *My Rating* | *Understanding Level* |
|---|---|---|---|---|---|
| A | B | C | C | | |

### 22.10.1 Purpose

Here you specify subtypes for each infotype.

### 22.10.2 IMG Node

SM34 ➢ V_778U (view V_778U)

### 22.10.3 Screen

| Inftyp. | Infotype Name | Subtyp | Subtype text |
|---|---|---|---|
| 1001 | Relationships | A* | |
| 1001 | Relationships | A001 | Is a subdivision of |
| 1001 | Relationships | A002 | Reports (line) to |
| 1001 | Relationships | A003 | Belongs to |

### 22.10.4 Primary Key

Infotype + Subtype

## 22.11 CUSTOMER-SPECIFIC SETTINGS FOR INFOTYPES

| *Functional Consultant* | *User* | *Business Process Owner* | *Senior Management* | *My Rating* | *Understanding Level* |
|---|---|---|---|---|---|
| C | X | X | X | | |

### 22.11.1 Purpose

In this table, you make customer-specific settings for infotypes.

### 22.11.2 IMG Node

SM30 ➢ T77CD

### 22.11.3 Screen

### 22.11.4 Primary Key

Infotype

### 22.11.5 Important Fields

#### *Infotype*

Infotype whose properties are being specified.

#### *Alternative screen number*

Here you specify the screen number of the single infotype screen if you are not using the standard screen 2000.

#### *Alternative list screen number*

Here you specify the screen number of the list screen for the infotype if you are not using the standard screen 3000.

#### *No maintenance*

Here you specify whether the infotype can be maintained in a standard transaction.

#### *Delete blank lines*

If you tick this checkbox, blank lines are deleted when you save the infotype.

#### *Sort entries*

If you tick this checkbox, the entries in table infotypes are sorted.

#### *Sort sequence*

Here you specify the sort sequence of the records.

| *Value* | *First sort field* | *First sort order* | *Next sort field* | *Next sort order* |
|---|---|---|---|---|
| Blank | Subtype | Ascending | From date | Descending |
| 1 | From date | Descending | Subtype | Ascending |
| 2 | Subtype | Ascending | From date | Ascending |
| 3 | From date | Ascending | Subtype | Ascending |

## 22.12 COUNTRY-SPECIFIC INFOTYPES

| *Functional Consultant* | *User* | *Business Process Owner* | *Senior Management* | *My Rating* | *Understanding Level* |
|---|---|---|---|---|---|
| C | X | X | X | | |

### 22.12.1 Purpose

Here you specify that an infotype is only relevant for a particular country or countries. This determines whether an infotype is displayed via country settings in basic transactions.

### 22.12.2 IMG Node

SM30 ➢ T77NI

### 22.12.3 Screen

| IT | Cty |
|---|---|
| 1511 | DE |
| 1514 | DE |
| 1600 | FR |
| 1601 | FR |
| 1610 | US |

### 22.12.4 Primary Key

Infotype + Country Key for Country – Specific Infotype

## 22.13 RELATIONSHIPS

| *Functional Consultant* | *User* | *Business Process Owner* | *Senior Management* | *My Rating* | *Understanding Level* |
|---|---|---|---|---|---|
| A | B | C | C | | |

### 22.13.1 Purpose

This table contains the list of relationships between objects. A relationship between objects X and Y have two views; from X to Y, and from Y to X. The text for both these views is specified here. If you want to create your own relationships, you may do so. The name of the relationship should comprise three characters and you should use only letters A to Z.

### 22.13.2 IMG Node

SM34 ➢ T778V (view T778V)

### 22.13.3 Screen

| Relat'ship | Relationship bottom up | Relationship top down |
|---|---|---|
| * | | |
| 001 | Is a subdivision of | Is subdivided into |
| 002 | Reports (line) to | Is line supervisor of |
| 003 | Belongs to | Incorporates |
| 004 | Is subordinate to (disc.) | Is disc.supervisor of |

### 22.13.4 Primary Key

Relationship Between Objects

## 22.14 RELATIONSHIP CHARACTERISTICS

| *Functional Consultant* | *User* | *Business Process Owner* | *Senior Management* | *My Rating* | *Understanding Level* |
|---|---|---|---|---|---|
| B | C | X | X | | |

### 22.14.1 Purpose

Here you can specify the checks that should be performed when relationship records are created.

### 22.14.2 IMG Node

SM34 ➢ T778V (view T77VA)

### 22.14.3 Screen

| A/B | Relat'ship | Relationship name | 100% check | Check work sch. | Check obsolete |
|---|---|---|---|---|---|
| A | 008 | Holder | | W | |
| B | 008 | Holder | W | | |

### 22.14.4 Primary Key

Relationship Specification + Relationship Between Objects

### 22.14.5 Important Fields

***A/B, relationship, relationship name***

The relationship, whose characteristics are being specified.

***100% check***

Here you can specify whether the 100% limit should be checked when percentages are entered for weighted relationships in infotype 1001. You specify whether the system should give error, issue warning, provide information, or perform no check.

***Check work schedule***

A position can have a work schedule in infotype 1011. A person can have a work schedule in infotype 0007. When a relationship between a position and a person is created, it is possible that the person has more working hours than those required by the position. Here you specify whether the system should give error, issue warning, provide information, or perform no check.

***Check obsolete***

Here you can specify the system reaction when relationships are entered or changed for positions or work centers which are declared obsolete in infotype 1014. The system can give error, issue warning, provide information, or perform no check.

## 22.15 ADDITIONAL DATA ON RELATIONSHIPS

| *Functional Consultant* | *User* | *Business Process Owner* | *Senior Management* | *My Rating* | *Understanding Level* |
|---|---|---|---|---|---|
| C | X | X | X | | |

### 22.15.1 Purpose

Here you can specify additional properties of relationships.

### 22.15.2 IMG Node

SM34 ➢ T778V (view T77AR)

### 22.15.3 Screen

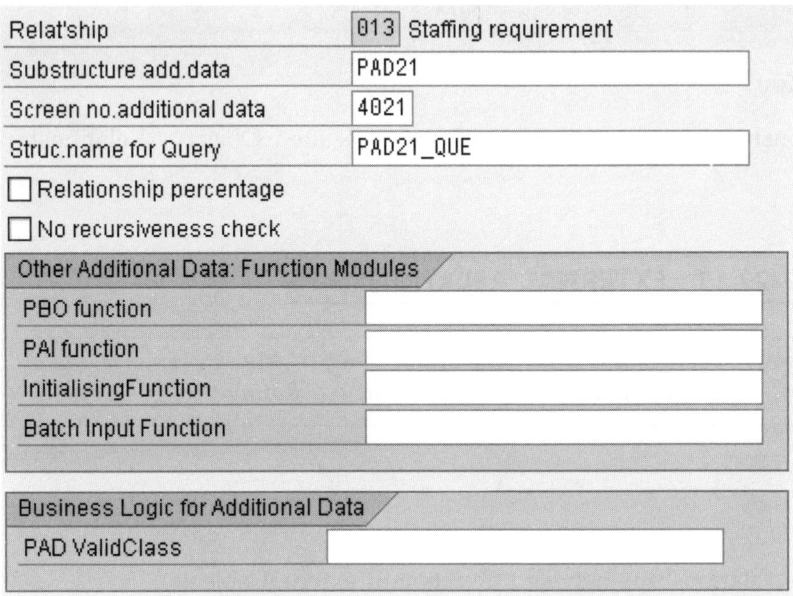


### 22.15.4 Primary Key

Relationship Between Objects

## 22.16 ALLOWED RELATIONSHIPS

| *Functional Consultant* | *User* | *Business Process Owner* | *Senior Management* | *My Rating* | *Understanding Level* |
|---|---|---|---|---|---|
| A | B | C | C | | |

### 22.16.1 Purpose

Relationships have a specific meaning and they make sense only between certain object types. This table contains the pair of objects between which a relationship is permitted.

### 22.16.2 IMG Node

SM34 ➢ T778V (view T777E)

### 22.16.3 Screen

| OT | Object type text | A/B | Rel | Relationship name | RelObjType | Not maint. |
|---|---|---|---|---|---|---|
| O | Organizational unit | A | 002 | Reports (line) to | O | ☐ |
| O | Organizational unit | B | 002 | Is line supervisor of | O | ☐ |
| S | Position | A | 002 | Reports (line) to | S | ☐ |
| S | Position | B | 002 | Is line supervisor of | S | ☐ |

### 22.16.4 Primary Key

Object Type + Relationship Between Objects + Type of Related Object + Relationship Specification

## 22.17 EXTERNAL RELATIONSHIPS

| *Functional Consultant* | *User* | *Business Process Owner* | *Senior Management* | *My Rating* | *Understanding Level* |
|---|---|---|---|---|---|
| C | X | X | X | | |

### 22.17.1 Purpose

This table contains the relationships between objects and external objects.

### 22.17.2 IMG Node

SM34 ➢ T778V (view T77EV)

### 22.17.3 Screen

| Obj.Type | A/B | Relat'ship | Acc. OType | Class Name | Program Name | Routine name |
|---|---|---|---|---|---|---|
| A | A | 014 | K | | SAPLRHCOSTC_READ | WORKPLACE_COSTCENTER_ |
| A | A | 014 | OD | | SAPLRHCOSTC_READ | WORKPLACE_COSTCENTER_ |
| A | A | 014 | PJ | | SAPLRHCOSTC_READ | WORKPLACE_COSTCENTER_ |
| K | B | 014 | A | | SAPLRHCOSTC_READ | COSTCENTER_DISTR_WORK |
| K | B | 014 | O | | SAPLRHCOSTC_READ | COSTCENTER_DISTR_ORGU |
| K | B | 014 | S | | SAPLRHCOSTC_READ | COSTCENTER_DISTR_POSI |

### 22.17.4 Primary Key

Object Type + Relationship Specification + Relationship Between Objects + Type of Related Object

## 22.18 RELATIONSHIP TIME CONSTRAINTS

| *Functional Consultant* | *User* | *Business Process Owner* | *Senior Management* | *My Rating* | *Understanding Level* |
|---|---|---|---|---|---|
| A | B | C | C | | |

### 22.18.1 Purpose

This view shows time constraints on relationships.

### 22.18.2 IMG Node

SM34 ➢ T778V (view V_T777ZVK)

### 22.18.3 Screen

| Obj.Type | IT | Infotype Name | STy. | Subty.text | TimeConstr |
|---|---|---|---|---|---|
| * | 1001 | Relationships | | | 2 |
| * | 1001 | Relationships | A003 | Belongs to | 3 |
| * | 1001 | Relationships | A030 | Is a specialization of | 2 |
| * | 1001 | Relationships | A031 | Requires | 3 |

### 22.18.4 Primary Key

Object Type + Infotype + Subtype

## 22.19 RELATIONSHIP ABBREVIATION

| *Functional Consultant* | *User* | *Business Process Owner* | *Senior Management* | *My Rating* | *Understanding Level* |
|---|---|---|---|---|---|
| B | C | X | X | | |

### 22.19.1 Purpose

If you want to change the name of a relationship, you may do so in parameter group PPREL in view V_T77S0VK.

### 22.19.2 IMG Node

SM34 ➢ T778V (view V_T77S0VK)

### 22.19.3 Screen

| Group | Sem. abbr. | Value abbr. | Description |
|---|---|---|---|
| PPREL | KOSTA | A011 | Cost center assignment |
| PPREL | LEADA | A012 | Manages... |
| PPREL | MATEV | A055 | Uses (for business event) |
| PPREL | MATNA | A054 | Uses (for attendee) |
| PPREL | NEEDA | A031 | Requires |

### 22.19.4 Primary Key

Group Name + Semantic Abbreviation

## 22.20 RELATIONSHIPS TIME CONSTRAINT DEPENDING ON TARGET OBJECT TYPE

| *Functional Consultant* | *User* | *Business Process Owner* | *Senior Management* | *My Rating* | *Understanding Level* |
|---|---|---|---|---|---|
| B | C | X | X | | |

### 22.20.1 Purpose

If the time constraint of a relationship depends on object types of related objects, you may specify that here.

### 22.20.2 IMG Node

SM30 ➢ T77ZR

### 22.20.3 Screen

| OT | IT | STy. | RO | T | Addl.co... |
|---|---|---|---|---|---|
| D | 1001 | A034 | AP | 3 | RELA034 |
| D | 1001 | A034 | H | 3 | RELA034 |
| D | 1001 | A034 | KI | 3 | RELA034 |

### 22.20.4 Primary Key

Object Type + Infotype + Subtype + Type of Related Object

## 22.21 RELATIONSHIPS UNTIL BIRTHDAY

| *Functional Consultant* | *User* | *Business Process Owner* | *Senior Management* | *My Rating* | *Understanding Level* |
|---|---|---|---|---|---|
| C | X | X | X | | |

### 22.21.1 Purpose

Usually relationship between two objects is within the validity period of the two objects. However, in case of persons and applicants, certain relationships can extend beyond the validity period of the related object. These are specified here.

### 22.21.2 IMG Node

SM30 ➢ T777BIRTH

### 22.21.3 Screen

| Obj. type | Rel.spec. | Relat'ship | RelObjType | Fr.birth | Till highd |
|---|---|---|---|---|---|
| AP | A bottom up | 032 | Q | ☑ | ☑ |
| AP | A bottom up | 038 | * | ☑ | ☑ |
| AP | A bottom up | 042 | * | ☑ | ☑ |
| AP | A bottom up | 043 | * | ☑ | ☑ |
| P | A bottom up | 032 | Q | ☑ | ☐ |
| P | A bottom up | 038 | * | ☑ | ☑ |

### 22.21.4 Primary Key

Object Type + Relationship Specification + Relationship Between Objects + Type of Related Object

# *Personnel Development*

CHAPTER 23

# Qualifications Catalog

## 23.1 QUALIFICATIONS AND REQUIREMENTS

| *Functional Consultant* | *User* | *Business Process Owner* | *Senior Management* | *My Rating* | *Understanding Level* |
|---|---|---|---|---|---|
| A | A | A | A | | |

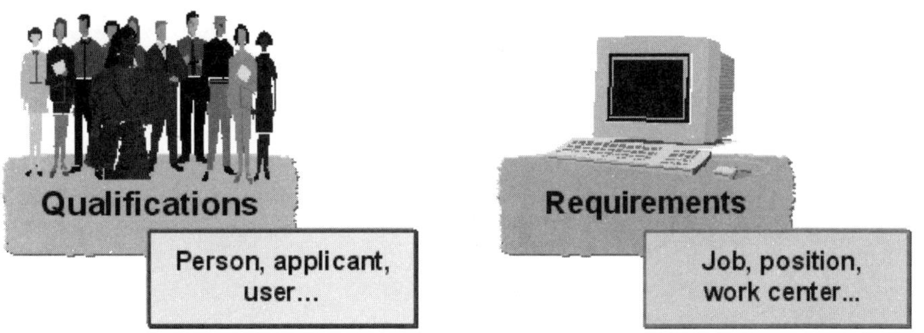


**The term "qualifications" refers to skills, abilities or knowledge that a person, applicant, user (and so on) possesses.**

**The term "requirements" refers to the skills, abilities or knowledge that are required for a job, position, task (and so on).**

People in an organization need competencies (skill, knowledge, or ability) to perform the work assigned to them. The organization needs to know which competencies are required for which position and which competencies are available with its employees and applicants, so that it can find the right candidates for the positions in the organization. SAP uses the term qualification to mean competency or skill, and not educational qualification. In this book, the terms qualification, competency and skill are used interchangeably.

***Finding suitable person for a position***

One of the key activities of a Human Resource department is to find suitable person for a position. How do you determine suitability of a person for a position? By comparing competencies required for a position with competencies that a person has. Competencies (called qualifications in SAP) are the common parameters on which persons and positions are compared and suitability of persons for positions determined.

## 23.2 QUALIFICATIONS CATALOG

| *Functional Consultant* | *User* | *Business Process Owner* | *Senior Management* | *My Rating* | *Understanding Level* |
|---|---|---|---|---|---|
| A | A | A | A | | |

### 23.2.1 Qualifications Catalog

The master list of competencies required by the organization is maintained in qualifications catalog using transaction OOQA or S_AHR_61003929 and displayed using transaction PPQD. The qualifications catalog is not a straight list of qualifications. It is a tree-like structure, in which similar qualifications are grouped together in qualification groups and qualification groups are further grouped in larger qualification groups. You can drill down the qualifications catalog to find the qualification you are looking for.

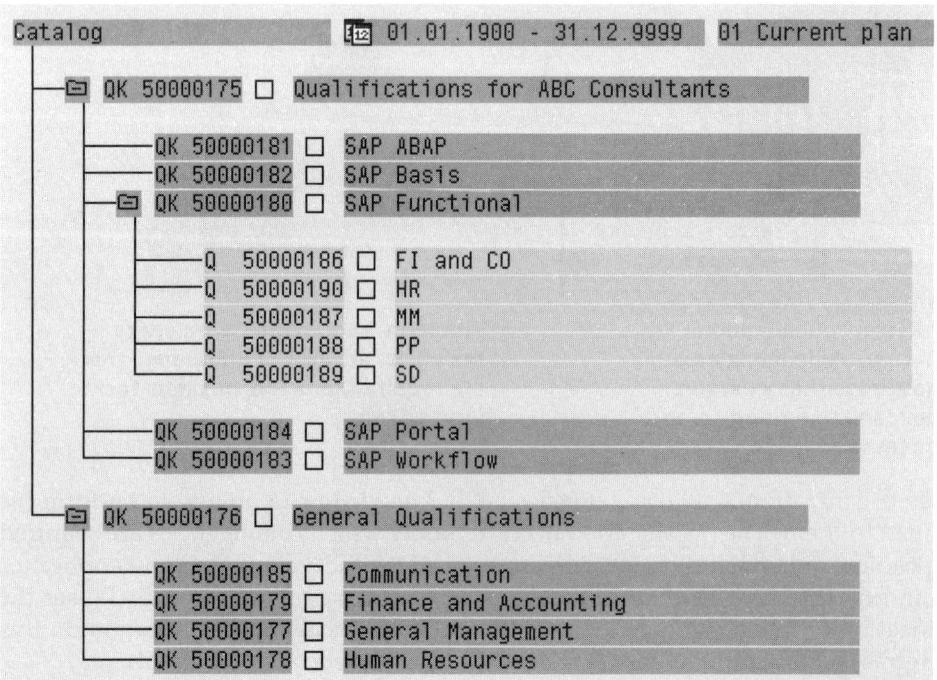

When you run transaction OOQA for the first time, you get a blank qualifications catalog.

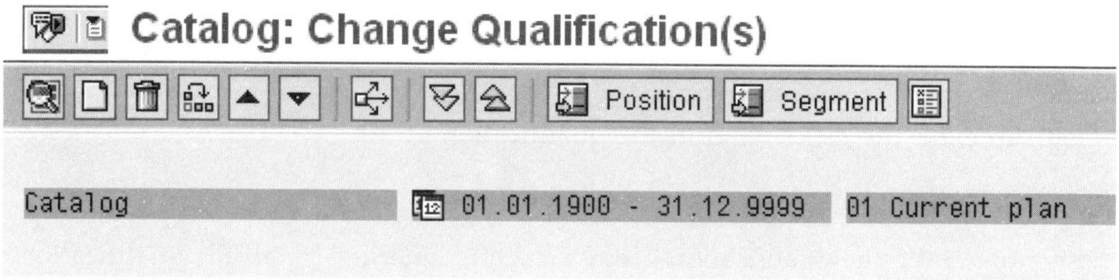


### 23.2.2 Qualification Group

Qualification groups are groups of qualifications. You create a qualification group by clicking , which gives you the following screen.

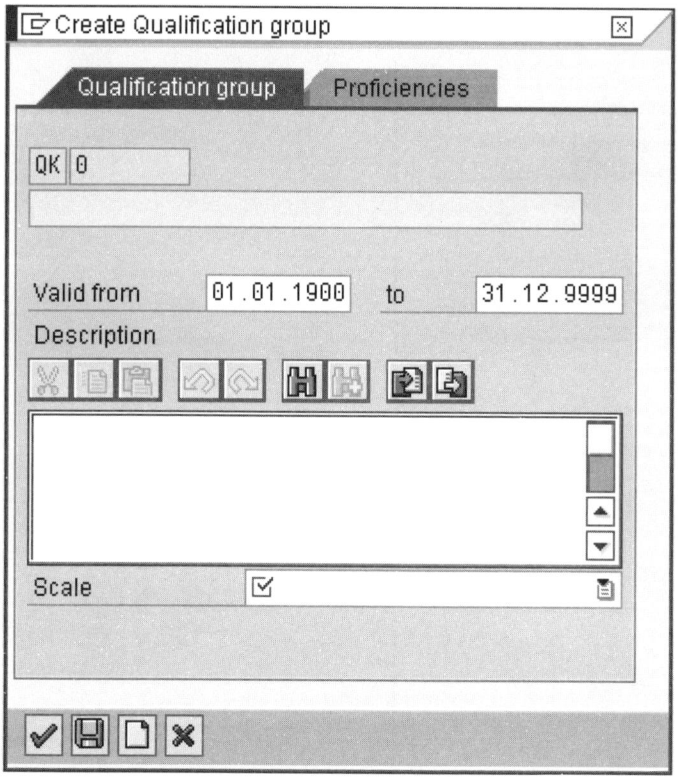


***Abbreviation and name***

A qualification group has an abbreviation and a name which helps the users to find the qualification they are looking for.

***Validity period***

Here you can enter the validity period of the qualification group.

***Description***

Here you can enter the description of the qualification group.

***Scale***

You assign a scale to the qualification group which is inherited by all the qualifications and qualification groups belonging to that qualification group. The inherited scale can be changed for a qualification group, but not for qualifications. You cannot have different scales for different qualifications in a qualification group. Choosing the right scale is very important. If necessary, create your own scale so that the proficiencies are easily and correctly understood.

***Proficiencies***

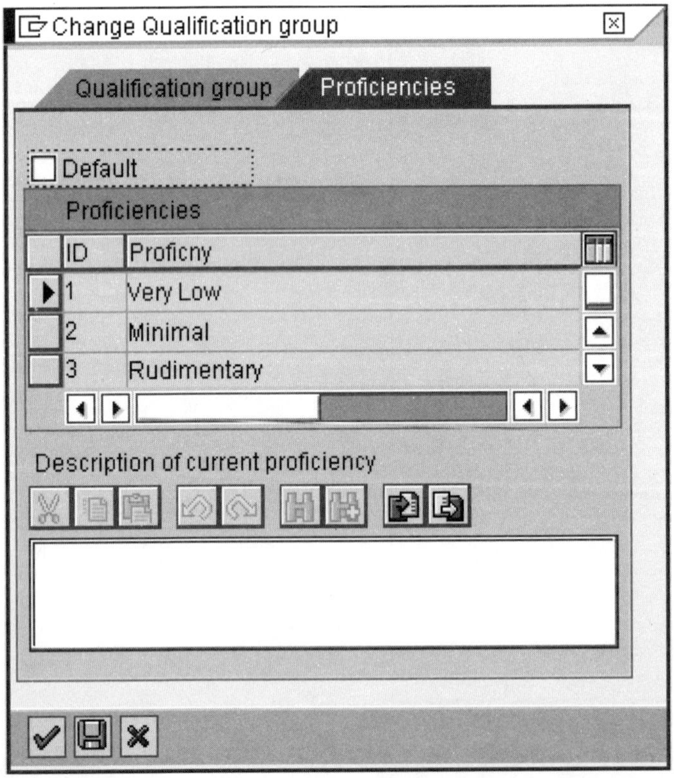


You can either use default proficiency descriptions, or remove the tick from the Default checkbox and enter your own description for all proficiency levels.

### 23.2.3 Qualifications

You create qualifications under qualification groups. Select the qualification group and click . The system asks you whether you want to create a qualification group or a qualification. Choose qualification.

***Qualification***

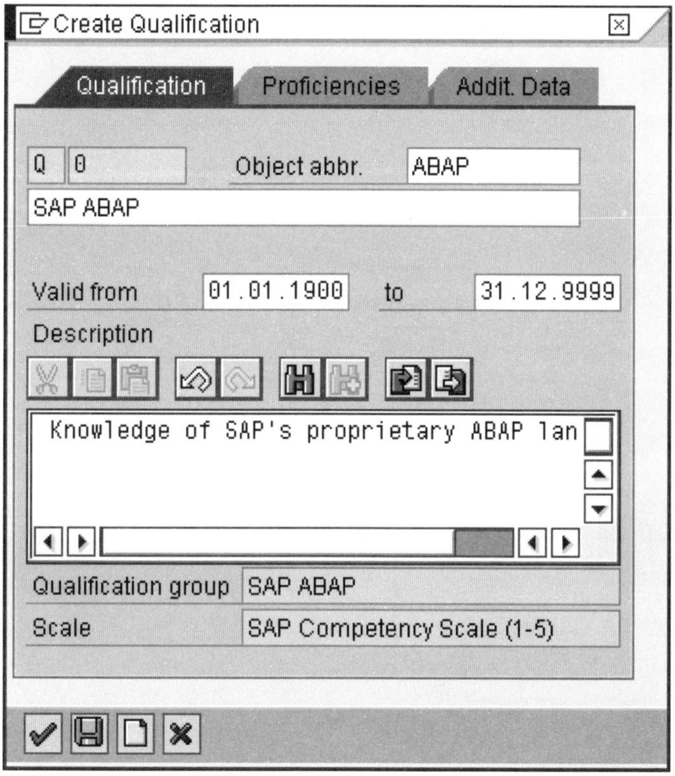


***Abbreviation and name***

A qualification has an abbreviation and a name which describes in short what the qualification is all about.

***Validity period***

You can specify a validity period for qualifications. This validity information enables you to show that certain qualifications, e.g. licenses, expire and have to be renewed at regular intervals. The validity determines the relationship period. If you assign a qualification to a person and the qualification has validity, the qualification is automatically deleted from the person's subprofile when the validity period expires.

You can run the Expired Qualifications report for a specific organizational unit and evaluation period. This report generates a list of the employees in the organizational unit whose qualifications has expired, or will expire, in the period specified. This information is based on the validity defined for the qualifications in question in the qualifications catalog.

It is also possible to use a workflow to monitor qualifications with limited validity. The standard system contains a standard workflow that can be adapted to specific customer requirements. The relevant person (the responsible course instructor, the employee's supervisor, and so on) is then informed that the qualifications in question are about to expire.

### *Description*

Here you can describe the qualification in more detail.

### *Scale*

Note that you cannot change the scale of a qualification because you cannot have different scales for different qualifications in a qualification group.

### *Proficiencies*

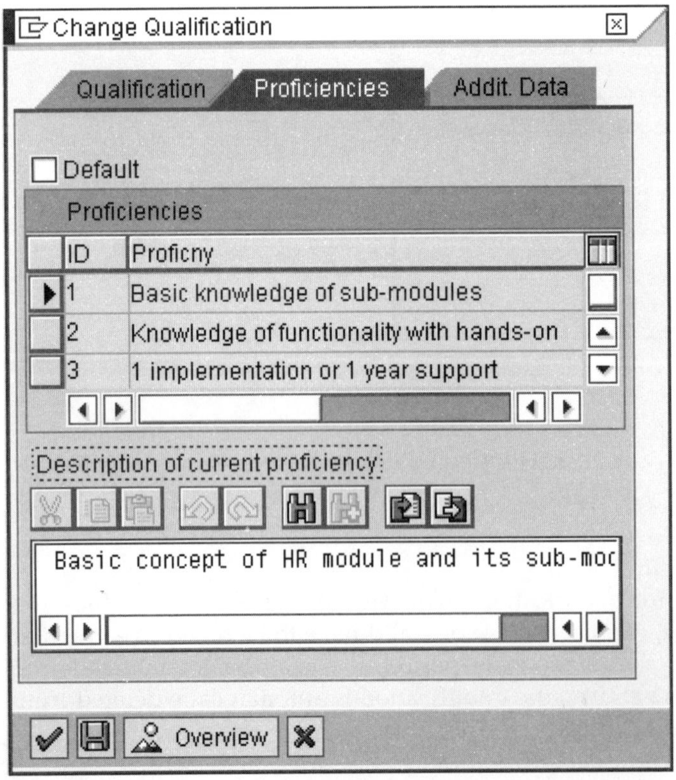

When you specify that a position requires a qualification, you also specify the level of that qualification required, by choosing a value from the scale. When you create the scale you can describe the proficiency. When you assign the scale to a qualification, these are inherited. You can also change the description of the proficiency for a qualification to make it more appropriate. In the Proficiencies tab, remove the tick from the Default checkbox and enter the description for each value of proficiency. If the Default checkbox is ticked, you will see the default description, instead of your custom description for all values of proficiency.

### *Additional data*

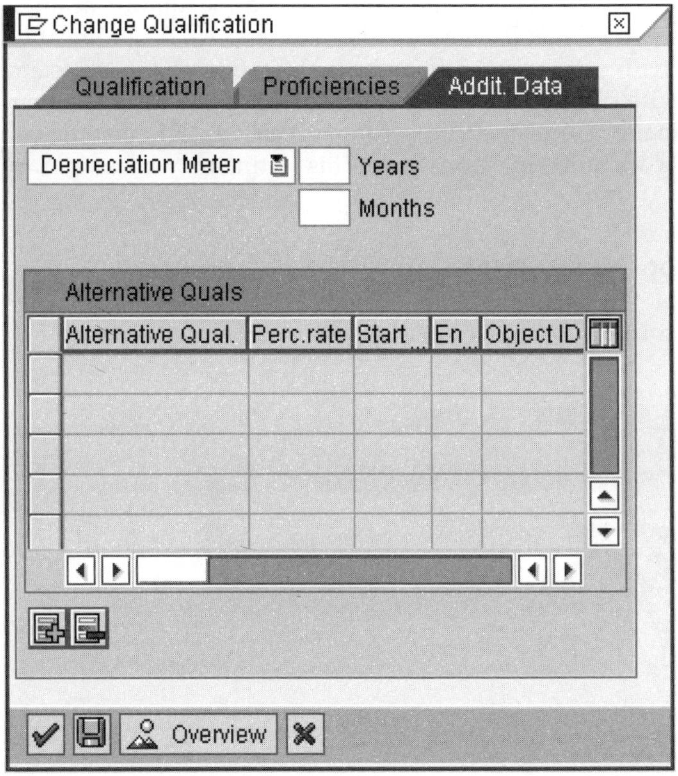


### *Depreciation meter*

Sometimes you lose a competency if you don't use it. You can specify this as a depreciation meter for the qualification. If a qualification with depreciation meter is assigned to a person, there are two possible scenarios.

- ➢ If the person's position requires that qualification, the person's proficiency remains unchanged.
- ➢ If the person's position does not require that qualification, the person's proficiency decreases exponentially. It becomes half in the period specified in the depreciation meter.

The proficiency stored in the database does not change. It is computed during comparison of qualifications with requirements. Even at that time you can make a user-specific setting specifying that the depreciation meter should not be included in evaluations in transaction PPUP. This setting may be temporary or permanent.

### *Alternative qualifications*

For a qualification, you can specify one or more alternative qualifications in the additional data tab. You can store alternative qualifications for a qualification by clicking . If the alternative qualification is not a full replacement of the qualification, but a partial one, you can specify a percentage. You can also specify the validity period of the alternative qualification. The relationship between qualification and alternative qualification is bi-directional (if A is an alternative to B, then B is also an alternative to A). A qualification can only be defined as an alternative to another if both qualifications have the same proficiency scale. Qualifications with different scales cannot be compared with each other. In transaction PPUP, you can make a user-specific setting specifying whether or not alternative qualifications should be included in evaluations. This setting may be temporary or permanent.

## 23.2.4 Qualifications Catalog Menu Items

### *Structuring the qualifications catalog*

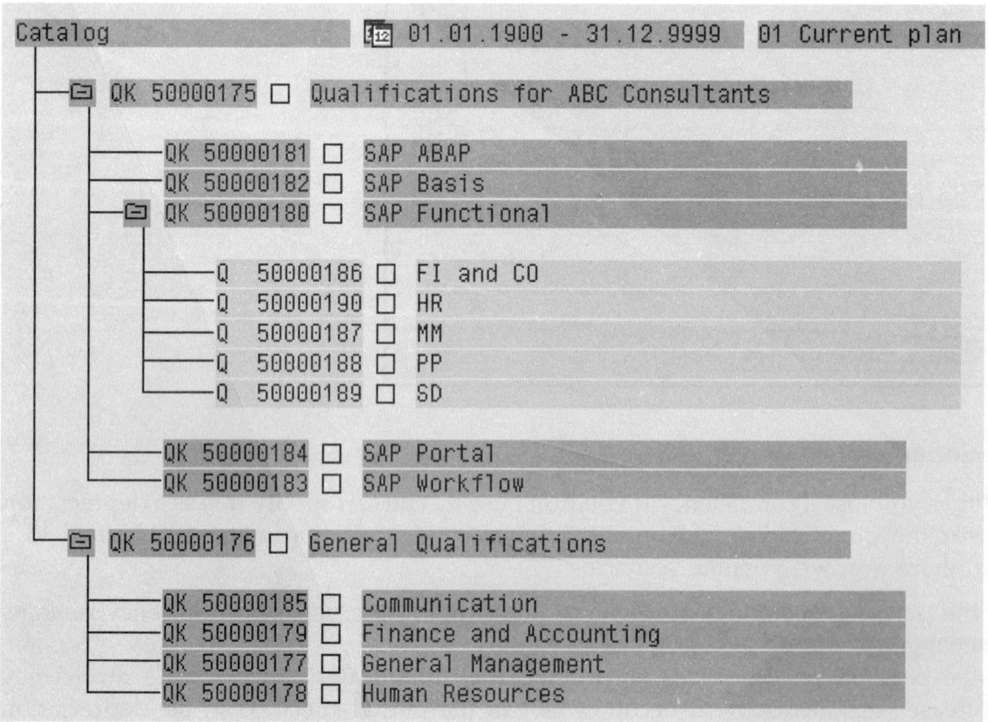

You would notice that SAP sorts the qualifications catalog alphabetically. However, you can use ▲ ▼ to change the order in which the qualifications catalog is structured. You can use the expand and collapse buttons to expand or collapse the qualifications catalog or any of its branches.

### *Overview of a qualification*

You may click Overview to see the overview of a qualification.

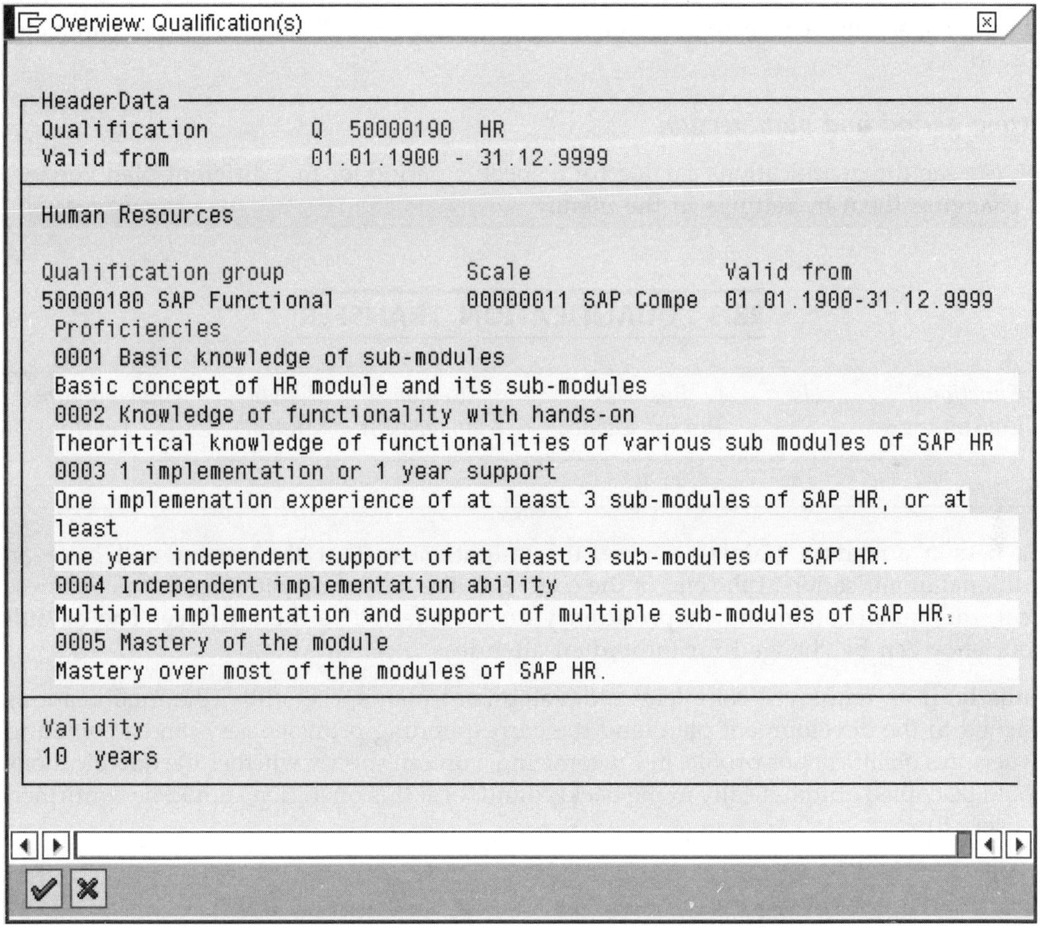


### *Where-used list*

If you select a qualification or qualification group and choose Entry ➢ Where-Used List, the system shows the relationship between that qualification, or qualification group, and all other objects.

### *Translation*

You can translate the entries in your qualifications catalog and their corresponding descriptions by choosing Entry ➢ Translate. This enables you to use the qualification catalog in different languages.

### *Abbreviation on*

You can switch abbreviation on by choosing View ➢ Abbreviation on. For this functionality to work, you should set switch QUALI SHORT to 'X'. You can further specify that abbreviation should be on by default for a user by setting second character of user parameter POK to 'X'.

### *Setting period and plan version*

You can see the qualifications catalog for a specific period, or in a different plan version, by changing them in Settings in the menu.

## 23.3 QUALIFICATION TRANSFER

| *Functional Consultant* | *User* | *Business Process Owner* | *Senior Management* | *My Rating* | *Understanding Level* |
|---|---|---|---|---|---|
| A | A | B | C | | |

If a person attends a training course, this might mean that the person will have an additional qualification at the end of the course. In the follow-up activities to the business event, this qualification and its proficiency are transferred to the attendee. The default proficiency can be changed for individual attendees.

Similarly, if an employee completes a development plan successfully, the qualifications assigned to the development plan (and the corresponding proficiencies) can be copied to the person's qualifications profile. In Customizing, you can specify whether the qualifications should be copied automatically in the background, or if this operation should be confirmed by users first.

## 23.4 FINDING OBJECTS FOR QUALIFICATIONS

| *Functional Consultant* | *User* | *Business Process Owner* | *Senior Management* | *My Rating* | *Understanding Level* |
|---|---|---|---|---|---|
| A | A | B | C | | |

### 23.4.1 Purpose

You can use the Find Objects for Qualifications report to search for persons (applicants, etc.) who have specific qualifications. You can also specify that a specific proficiency is required for each individual qualification. You can restrict your selection further by entering further selection criteria. You can use business add-in HRPDV00QSEARCH0001 to provide more selection options for the "Find Objects for Qualifications" function. This means that you can restrict the objects to be selected even further.

### 23.4.2 Transaction

PPPE_SEARCH_FOR_Q Find Objects for Qualifications

### 23.4.3 Selection Screen

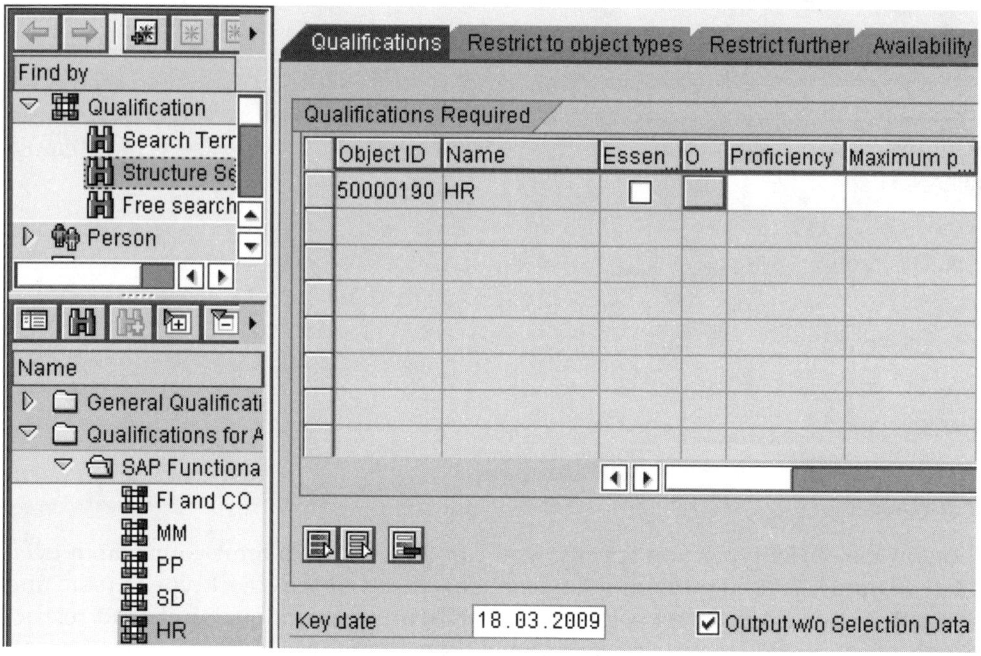

### *Search and selection area*

When you specify the qualifications for which you are trying to find objects, you can select qualifications individually from the qualifications catalog and/or you can take the qualifications/requirements profiles of objects of your choice and adapt them to your needs.

### *Qualifications*

In the Qualifications tab, you can have multiple qualifications. You can add qualifications by transferring from selection area. You can select a qualification and click delete icon to delete the selected qualification. When you specify the proficiencies you are looking for, you can enter individual values or value ranges. Furthermore, by setting the Essential requirement flag for a qualification, you can specify whether the object you are looking for must have the qualification in question. If you set the Essential requirement flag for a qualification, then only objects with at least this qualification are selected.

### *Restrict to object types*

You can limit your search to objects of specific object types. For example, you might wish to restrict your search to employees (object type P), or to applicants (object type AP). The search result is filtered to have only these object types.

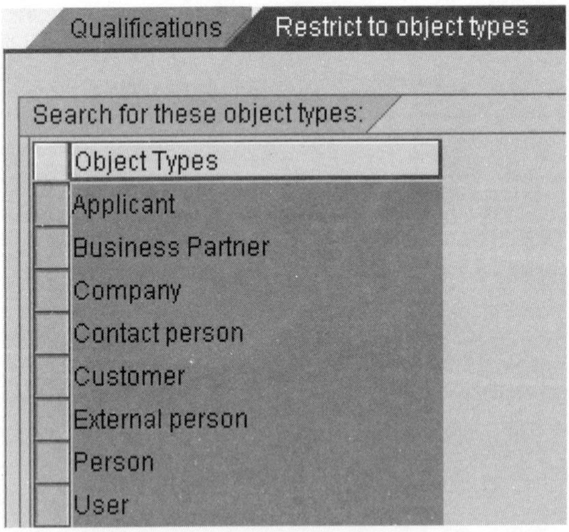


### *Restrict further*

Depending on the object types you specify, you can then go on to limit your search even further. For example, you might limit your search to objects of the object type Person, and then specify that the persons must belong to a particular organizational units and restrict the selection even further to specific personnel areas, employee subgroups, and so on (infotype data). The ad hoc query is the basis for defining these selection criteria by selecting fields. The objects that meet your criteria are inserted in the list in this tab and the search is restricted to these objects.

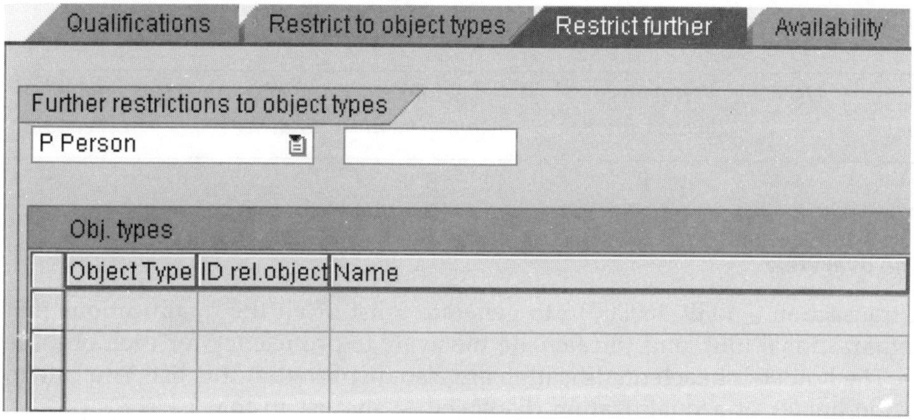


***Availability***

In addition, you can use the criteria availability when searching for persons with qualifications (object type P). This is checked via the interface with Time Management. The resulting hit list of persons is restricted to persons that are available for a certain number of days (entered in Planning days) in the planning period.

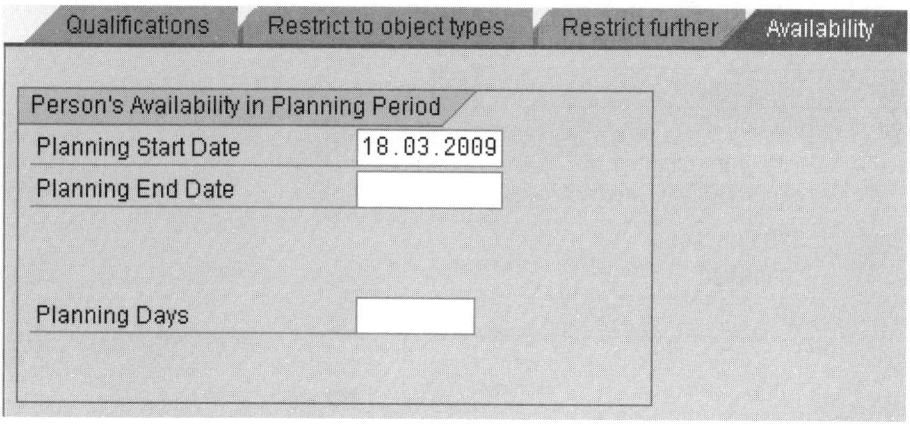


## 23.4.4 Output

The list generated by the report contains the objects that BOTH have the qualifications and proficiencies specified AND also fulfill the other selection criteria. Planning objects with alternative qualifications are also listed if you have specified this in the user-specific settings (transaction PPUP).

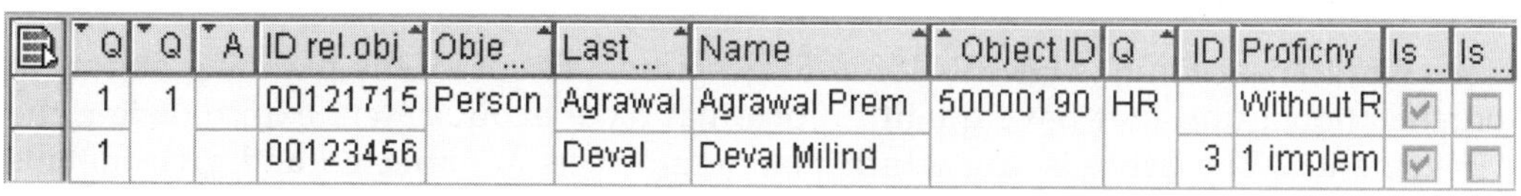

| Q | Q | A | ID rel.obj | Obje... | Last... | Name | Object ID | Q | ID | Proficny | Is... | Is... |
|---|---|---|---|---|---|---|---|---|---|---|---|---|
| 1 | 1 | | 00121715 | Person | Agrawal | Agrawal Prem | 50000190 | HR | | Without R | ☑ | ☐ |
| 1 | | | 00123456 | | Deval | Deval Milind | | | 3 | 1 implem | ☑ | ☐ |

## 23.5 QUALIFICATION REPORTS

| *Functional Consultant* | *User* | *Business Process Owner* | *Senior Management* | *My Rating* | *Understanding Level* |
|---|---|---|---|---|---|
| A | A | B | B | | |

### *Qualifications overview*

You can run transaction S_PH9_46000016 to generate a list of all the qualifications that exist in an organizational unit, and to calculate the average proficiency for each of these qualifications. The holders of each qualification are also displayed in this list. You can go directly from the holder of a qualification displayed in the list to that person's profile. You might use this report to get an insight into the ability of an organizational unit. This report gives a list output.

| ID rel.obj | Org... | Obj... | Qu... | Obje... | Q | Q | Avera... | Aver... | ID of r... | Last... | Name | Pr... | Profic... |
|---|---|---|---|---|---|---|---|---|---|---|---|---|---|
| 50000075 | ABC C( | 5000 | SAP F | 50000' | HR | 1 | 1.000 | Basic k | 001217 | Agrawa | Agrawa | | Withou' |
| 50000075 | | 5000 | | 50000' | MM | 1 | 1.000 | | 001217 | Agrawa | Agrawa | | Withou' |

You can also select and display a line in a more convenient form.

| Group description | Cell Content |
|---|---|
| ID of related object | 50000075 |
| Organizational unit | ABC Consultants Ltd. |
| Object ID | 50000180 |
| Qualification group | SAP Functional |
| Object ID | 50000190 |
| Qualification | HR |
| Qualification fulfilled | 1 |
| Average | 1.000 |
| Average proficiency | Basic knowledge of sub-modules |
| ID of related object | 00121715 |
| Last Name | Agrawal |
| Name | Agrawal Prem |
| Proficiency text | Without Rating |

### *Expired qualifications*

You can run transaction S_AHR_61015536 to generate a list of all the planning objects in an organizational unit that have qualifications that have expired/will expire during the specified period. The list tells you which planning objects are affected and gives details of the qualifications and their validity periods. You can also generate training proposals that are suitable for refreshing/renewing the qualifications in question.

| O | ID of relat... | Object name | O | ID of relat... | L... | Name | Object ID | Qu... | Start date | End Date |
|---|---|---|---|---|---|---|---|---|---|---|
| O | 50000075 | ABC Consult | P | 00121715 | Ag | Agrawal | 50000190 | HR | 16.02.2009 | 15.02.2019 |

You can choose between a planning object view and a qualification view. In the planning object view, each planning object is listed along with the qualifications it has that are about to expire. In the qualification view, each qualification about to expire is listed along with the planning objects that are affected. You can go directly from each planning object to the transaction for displaying its profile and to the transaction for career planning.

***Maintained qualifications***

You can run transaction HRPDV00REPORT0001 to generate a list of all qualifications maintained in the system.

| Q | Q | ID rel.obj | Organizational unit | ID of related ... | Name | Changed on |
|---|---|---|---|---|---|---|
| 0 | | 50000075 | ABC Consultants Ltd. | P_MCD00669 | Milind Deval | 16.02.2009 |
| 2 | X | 50000075 | | 00121715 | Agrawal Prem | 16.02.2009 |

***List of alternative qualifications***

You can run transaction S_PH9_46000022 to generate a list of all qualifications for which alternative qualifications have been defined. The replacement percentages are also displayed in the list.

| Object ID | Qualification | Object ID | Alternative Qualification | Perc.rate | Start date | End Date |
|---|---|---|---|---|---|---|

## 23.6 SCALES

| *Functional Consultant* | *User* | *Business Process Owner* | *Senior Management* | *My Rating* | *Understanding Level* |
|---|---|---|---|---|---|
| A | A | B | B | | |

### 23.6.1 Scale

Scales are used to determine levels of qualifications. Different qualifications are measured in different ways, i.e. on different scales. A scale is assigned to a qualification group and applies to all qualifications in that qualification group. There are different types of scales, e.g. quality scales, quantity scales, etc. Only quality scales can be assigned to qualification groups, and thereby qualifications. Scales are maintained using transaction SM34 ➢ VC_T77SK.

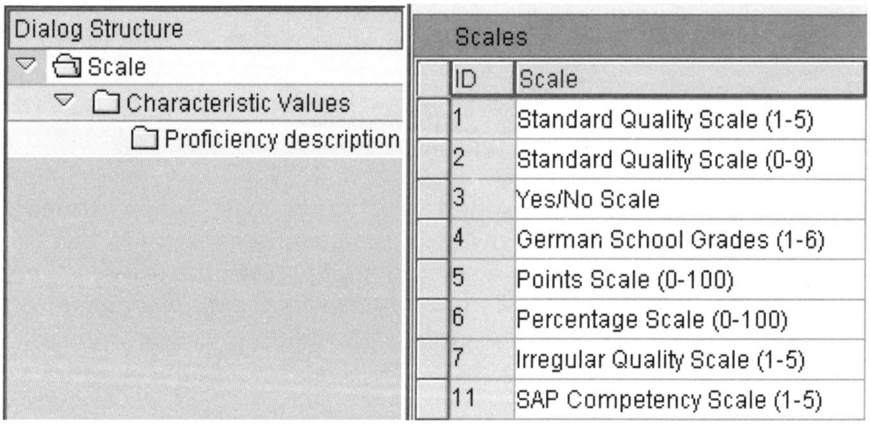


## 23.6.2 Proficiency

Each quality scale has multiple levels of proficiencies. Proficiencies have a numeric id and a text. The numeric id value is used for determining suitability. If a person has a qualification at level 4, and the position requires it at level 5, he is 80% suitable. The proficiency text, along with proficiency description, helps you determine the proficiency of a qualification required for a position or available with a person.

You must define proficiencies in ascending order (that is, the proficiency with the highest value in the ID field must be the highest (best) proficiency of a qualification). The lowest proficiency must have the value 1; all subsequent proficiencies must be numbered consecutively. You cannot use proficiency 0 for rating qualifications or requirements; instead you would delete that qualification or requirement.

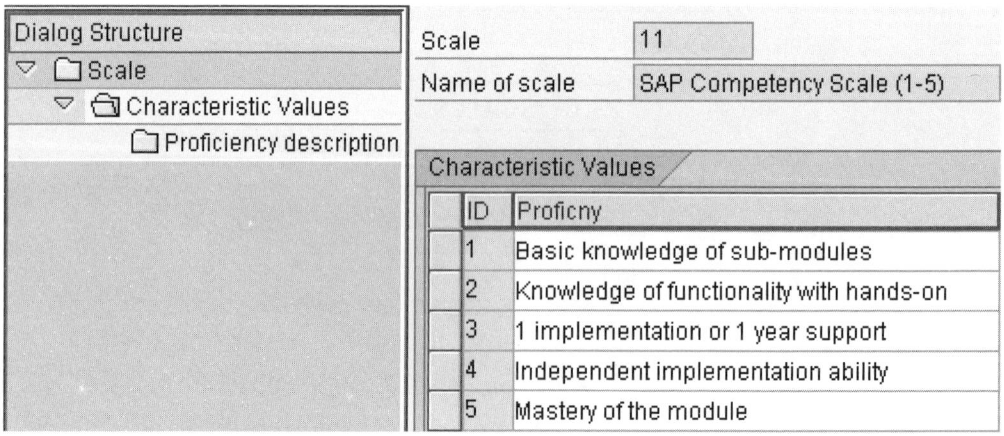

## 23.6.3 Proficiency Description

Proficiency descriptions enhance the understanding provided by proficiency texts. To determine a person's competence, you can compare it with different proficiency descriptions and find the description which best represents his competence, thereby determining his proficiency.

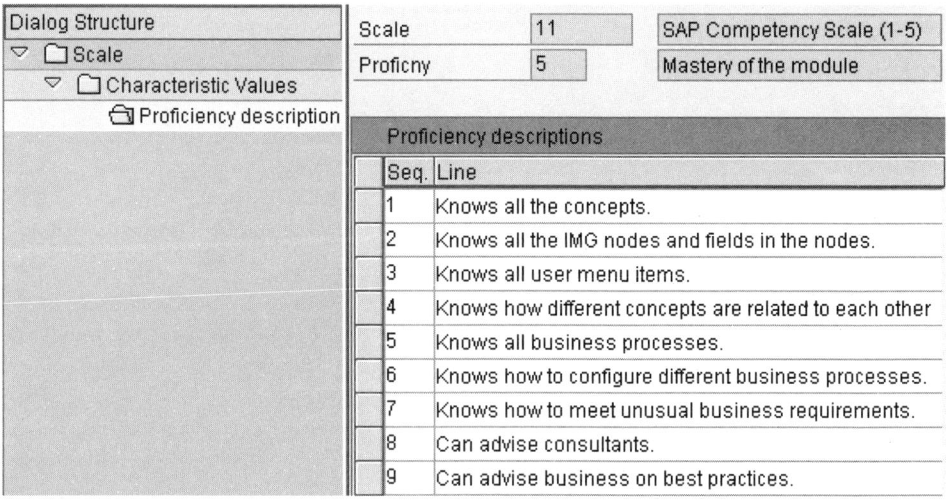


Proficiency descriptions are inherited by qualification groups and qualifications. However, if you can write a better description of proficiency for a qualification group or qualification, you are allowed to do so. In the proficiency tab of qualification group or qualification, if you tick the 'Default' checkbox, you see the inherited proficiency description.

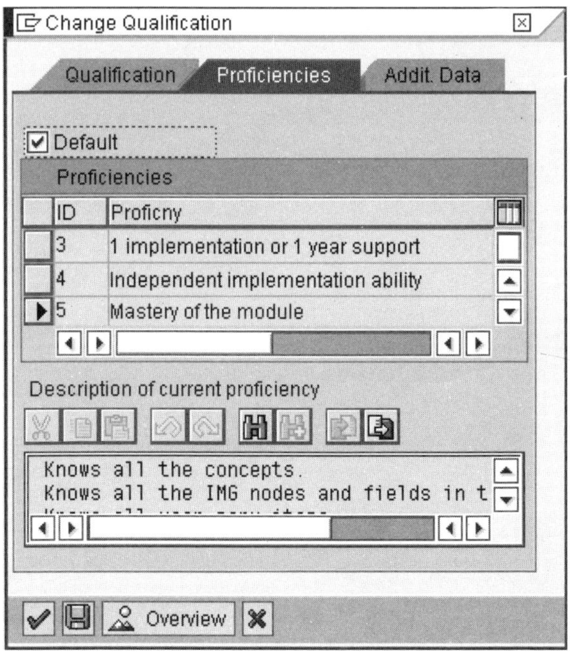

However, if you remove the tick from the 'Default' checkbox, you get blank space to write proficiency description which better represents the proficiency of that particular qualification or qualification group.

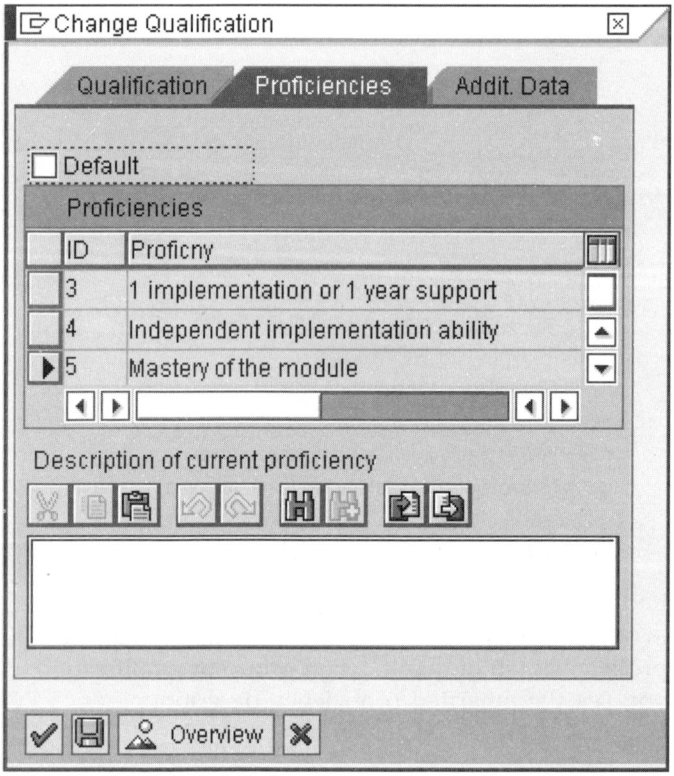

## 23.7 QUALIFICATION CONTROL PARAMETERS

| *Functional Consultant* | *User* | *Business Process Owner* | *Senior Management* | *My Rating* | *Understanding Level* |
|---|---|---|---|---|---|
| A | A | B | C | | |

### 23.7.1 Purpose

Here you specify various parameters related to qualifications that control system behavior.

### 23.7.2 IMG Node

SM30 ➢ V_T77S0SC

### 23.7.3 Screen

| Group | Sem. abbr. | Value abbr. | Description |
|---|---|---|---|
| QUALI | ESSST | | ESS: initial skills group for profile maintenance |

| Group | Sem. abbr. | Value abbr. | Description |
|---|---|---|---|
| QUALI | MAXEN | 20 | Maximum number of entries in the hit list |
| QUALI | OVERQ | 1 | Valuation of over-qualification |
| QUALI | QBUSE | | Use qualifications bundle |
| QUALI | QPROZ | 100.00 | Replacement percentage for alternative qual. |
| QUALI | SHORT | | Code in qualifications catalog |

### 23.7.4 Important Fields

| *Group* | *Sem.abbr.* | *Description* | *Explanation* |
|---|---|---|---|
| QUALI | ESSST | ESS: Initial skills group for profile maintenance | There is an ESS service which is used to edit the skills profile. Normally, it shows the entire qualifications catalog. However, if you want, you can restrict it to show only part of the tree instead of the whole. Here you can enter a qualification group. In ESS, this qualification group and the entire structure of qualifications catalog under it will be shown. If you do not enter a qualification group here, the ESS service displays the entire qualifications catalog for profile maintenance. |

| *Group* | *Sem.abbr.* | *Description* | *Explanation* |
|---|---|---|---|
| QUALI | MAXEN | Maximum number of entries in the hit list | This parameter specifies the maximum number of entries that appear at a time in the ranking lists of Career and Succession Planning. You can scroll to see more entries. |
| QUALI | OVERQ | Valuation of over-qualification | If a person has higher proficiency than requirement, it is called over-qualification and you can consider it in the following ways.<br>*Value* — *Meaning* — *Suitability*<br>–1 — Extra credit — > 100%<br>0 — Ignore — 100%<br>+1 — Penalize — < 100%<br>This setting can be changed at user level either temporarily or permanently. |
| QUALI | QBUSE | Use qualifications bundle | If you enter 'X' here, qualifications bundle is activated. For more information on qualification bundles and qualification blocks, see SAP help. |
| QUALI | QPROZ | Replacement percentage for alternative qual. | Here you specify the default replacement percentage that is proposed when you create alternative qualifications. |
| QUALI | SHORT | Code in qualifications catalog | Here you specify whether the abbreviation of an object in the qualifications catalog (qualification, qualification group) can be displayed. This setting affects all applications that use qualification objects except Appraisals. If the value for this setting is 'X', it is possible to display the abbreviation. You can display the abbreviation in the applications in question by choosing View ➢ Abbreviation on. You can set second character of user parameter POK to 'X' to specify whether the abbreviation should be displayed by default for a specific user. |

CHAPTER 24

# Profiles

## 24.1 PROFILES

| *Functional Consultant* | *User* | *Business Process Owner* | *Senior Management* | *My Rating* | *Understanding Level* |
|---|---|---|---|---|---|
| A | A | A | A | | |

An object, e.g. a person or a position, has a profile. You may run transaction PPPM to create or edit a profile and transaction PPPD to display it.

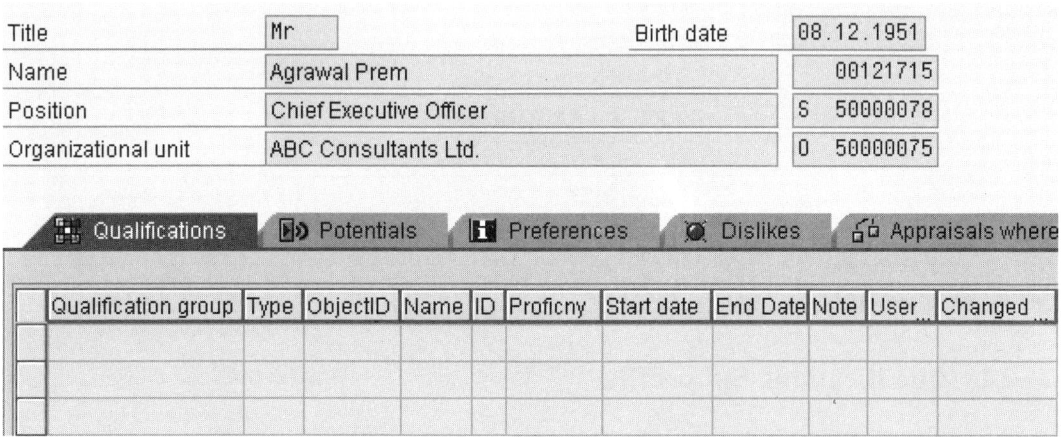


A profile consists of several subprofiles which are displayed as tab pages. You can use profile of a person to do profile matchup and career planning. Similarly you can use profile of a position to do profile matchup and succession planning. You can also display the entire profile on a single screen by choosing Goto ➢ Overall Profile (List).

```
HeaderData
Person                    P  00121715  Agrawal Prem
Valid from                12.12.2008 - 31.12.9999

Qualifications

OT ObjectID Qualification Group  S ID      Scale
OT ObjectID Qualification       Proficny             Period

QK 50000180 SAP Functional       00000011 SAP Competency Scale (1-5)
Q  50000190 HR                  0000Without Rating    16.02.2009 -15.02.2019
Q  50000187 MM                  0000Without Rating    16.02.2009 -Unlimited

Potentials

                                does not exist

Preferences

                                does not exist
```

You can see the same list by running transaction PEPP. In this program you can include multiple objects and these objects can be of different types. If you want you can also exclude certain subprofiles.

## 24.2 SUBPROFILES

| *Functional Consultant* | *User* | *Business Process Owner* | *Senior Management* | *My Rating* | *Understanding Level* |
|---|---|---|---|---|---|
| A | A | A | A | | |

### 24.2.1 Qualifications Subprofile

In the qualifications subprofile, you maintain qualifications possessed by a person. To create the qualifications subprofile of a person, you run transaction PPPM and select the person. In the qualifications tab, you click and select the qualification.

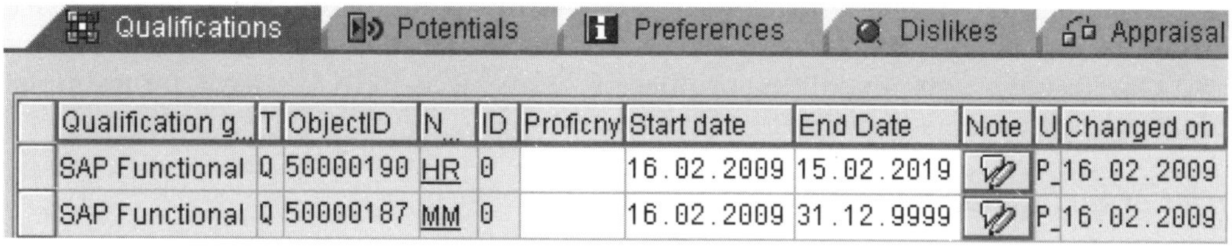

| Qualification g... | T | ObjectID | N... | ID | Proficny | Start date | End Date | Note | U | Changed on |
|---|---|---|---|---|---|---|---|---|---|---|
| SAP Functional | Q | 50000190 | HR | 0 | | 16.02.2009 | 15.02.2019 | | P_ | 16.02.2009 |
| SAP Functional | Q | 50000187 | MM | 0 | | 16.02.2009 | 31.12.9999 | | P_ | 16.02.2009 |

The system lets you enter proficiency, start date and end date. If a qualification has a validity period, its end date is restricted. You can also create a note for every qualification to keep additional details. The Qualifications subprofile can be assigned to person, external person, applicant, user, company and contact person.

### *Creating qualifications subprofile of several objects*

You can also create qualifications subprofile of several objects using transaction OOQM or S_AHR_61003917.

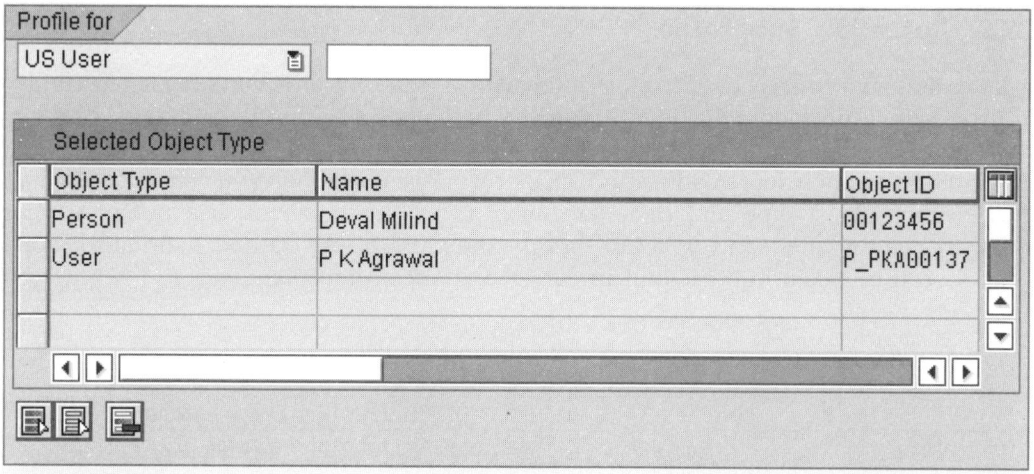

Profile for

US User

Selected Object Type

| Object Type | Name | Object ID |
|---|---|---|
| Person | Deval Milind | 00123456 |
| User | P K Agrawal | P_PKA00137 |

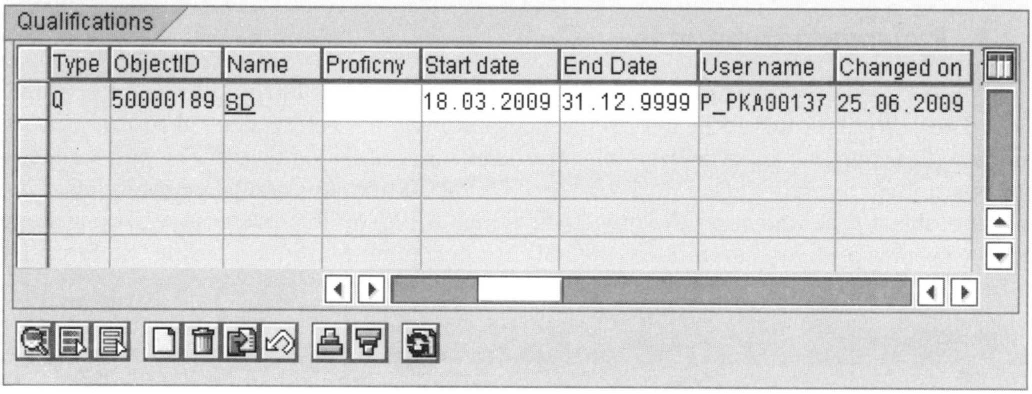

Qualifications

| Type | ObjectID | Name | Proficny | Start date | End Date | User name | Changed on |
|---|---|---|---|---|---|---|---|
| Q | 50000189 | SD | | 18.03.2009 | 31.12.9999 | P_PKA00137 | 25.06.2009 |

You can select all the objects which should possess the same qualifications, select those qualifications and choose Profiles ➢ Save. The qualifications are added to the profiles of selected objects. Later you can edit the profiles of these objects individually if, for example, you don't want the same proficiency for all the objects.

***Transfer of qualification***

If a person attends a training course, this might mean that the person will have an additional qualification at the end of the course. In the follow-up activities to the business event, this qualification and its proficiency are transferred to the attendee. The default proficiency can be changed for individual attendees.

Similarly, if an employee completes a development plan successfully, the qualifications assigned to the development plan (and the corresponding proficiencies) can be copied to the person's qualifications profile. In Customizing, you can specify whether the qualifications should be copied automatically in the background, or if this operation should be confirmed by users first.

## 24.2.2 Potentials Subprofile

The Potentials subprofile is used to store information regarding a person's future suitability and professional development. Identifying the potential of an employee gives a clearer direction to his development. A person, external person, applicant or user can have potential for a position, job, qualification, task or work center. When you create a potential, you select the object type and then the object for which a person has potential. The system creates the entry and you can modify the validity period and maintain a note. Potentials can be taken into account in career and succession planning.

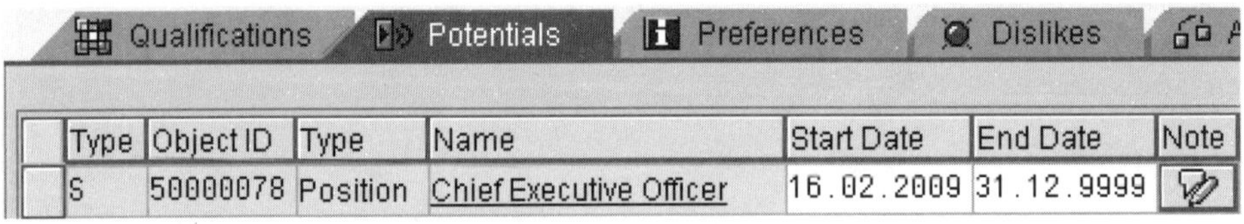


| Type | Object ID | Type | Name | Start Date | End Date | Note |
|---|---|---|---|---|---|---|
| S | 50000078 | Position | Chief Executive Officer | 16.02.2009 | 31.12.9999 | |

## 24.2.3 Preferences Subprofile

You should take a person's preferences into account while considering him for a position or job. These are maintained in the preferences subprofile. Preferences subprofile can be maintained for persons, external persons, applicants and users. They can have preferences for a position, job, qualification, task or work center. When you create a preference, you select the object type and then the object for which a person has preference. The system creates the entry and you can modify the validity period and maintain a note. Preferences can be taken into account in career and succession planning.

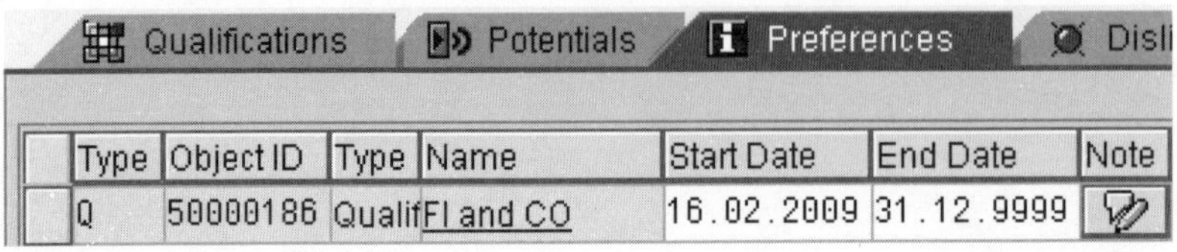


| Type | Object ID | Type | Name | Start Date | End Date | Note |
|---|---|---|---|---|---|---|
| Q | 50000186 | Qualif | FI and CO | 16.02.2009 | 31.12.9999 | |

### 24.2.4 Dislikes Subprofile

You should take a person's dislikes into account while considering him for a position or job. These are maintained in the dislikes subprofile. Dislikes subprofile can be maintained for persons, external persons, applicants and users. They can have dislikes for a position, job, qualification, task or work center. When you create a dislike, you select the object type and then the object for which a person has dislike. The system creates the entry and you can modify the validity period and maintain a note. Dislikes can be taken into account in career and succession planning by not selecting the objects for which a person has dislike.

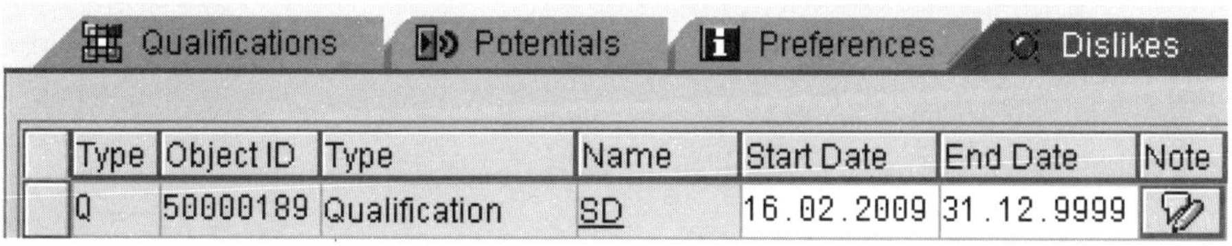


### 24.2.5 Requirements Subprofile

A position has a set of tasks which are performed by its holders. In order to perform those tasks competently, the holder of the position needs to have certain competencies or qualifications. These qualifications are the requirements of the position and are captured in requirements subprofile. If you edit profile of a position, you will see the requirements tab where you define the qualifications required for that position.

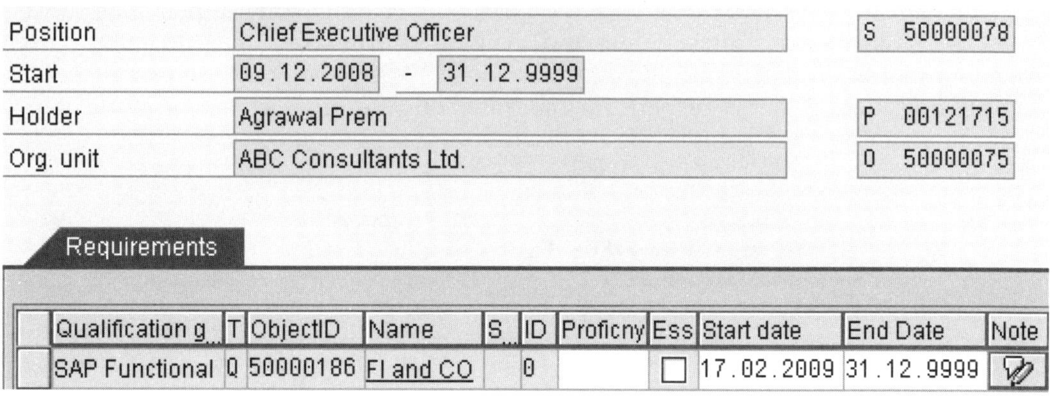


When you add a qualification to the requirements subprofile of a position, you can enter the proficiency level required, the period for which the qualification is required for the position (usually indefinitely) and write any other details in a note.

### *Essential requirements*

In addition to the above, you specify whether the requirement is essential or optional. This factor can be taken into account in profile matchups or during career and succession planning. In user settings (transaction PPUP), you may specify that the essential requirements must be met. When you search for persons who may hold a position, the system will pick up only those persons who possess essential qualifications required by the position.

### *Inherited requirements*

If you have defined requirements for a job, it is natural that positions which are based on that job should require those qualifications. Requirements of the job are shown as inherited requirements in positions which are based on that job. Requirements of tasks are also inherited by jobs, positions, and work centers to which that task is assigned.

Inherited requirements are identified by  in the status column. In the Requirements subprofile, you can click this icon in the Status field to go from the inherited requirement to the profile of the original object (i.e. the object that passed on the requirement).

Inherited requirements cannot be deleted from the subprofile. However, they can be assigned a different proficiency or even a different status. This is achieved by recreating the requirement in question for the object in the subprofile.

### *Copying requirements profiles to position holders*

During an implementation, you would create requirements profile for positions, and qualifications profile for their holders. Since the holders hold their positions because they are competent to hold them, it will save effort if the requirements of positions can be copied as qualifications of their holder and then edited to make required changes. SAP provides a tool to do that. You can run transaction OOQ5 to copy requirements profiles to position holders. When you perform this function, the proficiencies of any existing qualifications in persons' profiles are overwritten.

## 24.3 PROFILES FOR OBJECT TYPES

| *Functional Consultant* | *User* | *Business Process Owner* | *Senior Management* | *My Rating* | *Understanding Level* |
|---|---|---|---|---|---|
| A | A | A | A | | |

Profiles for different Object Types have different subprofiles in them. Some of these subprofiles have been discussed in the previous chapter. Subprofiles relating to Appraisal and Development plan are discussed in chapters dealing with them. Subprofiles of some object types are given below. For other object types they can be seen on the system.

### 24.3.1 Person

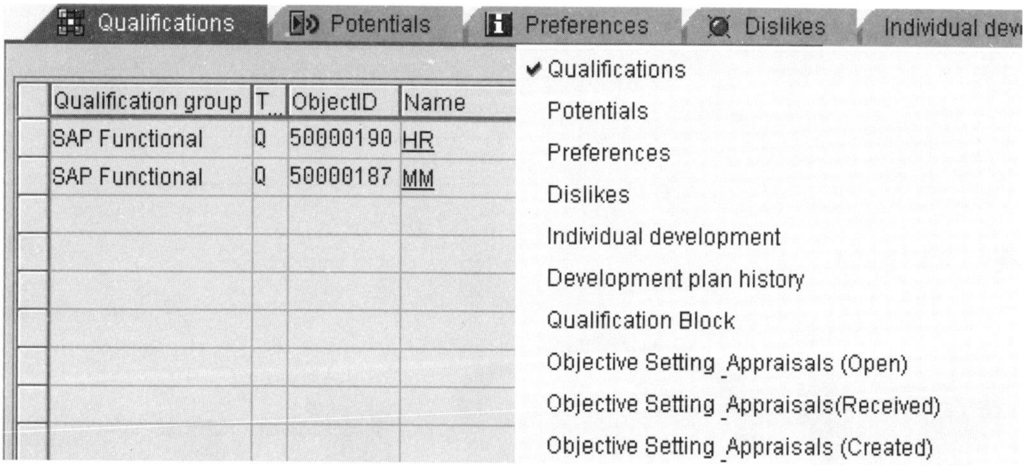


### 24.3.2 User

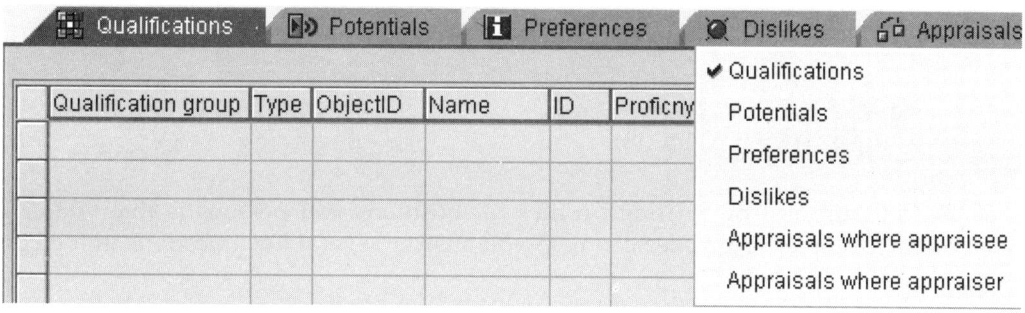


### 24.3.3 Position, Job, Task, Work Center

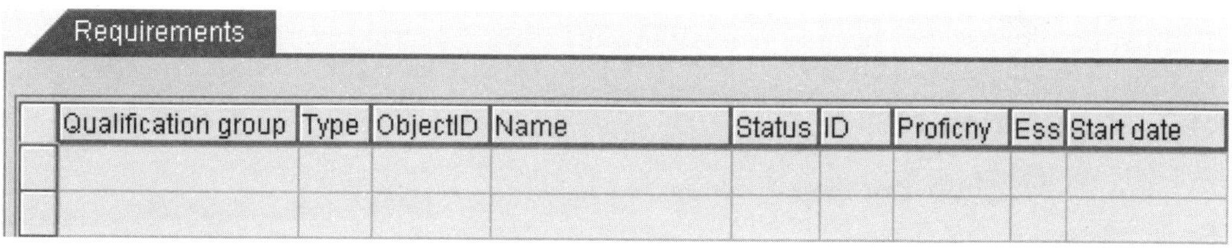

## 24.4 PROFILE MATCHUP

| *Functional Consultant* | *User* | *Business Process Owner* | *Senior Management* | *My Rating* | *Understanding Level* |
|---|---|---|---|---|---|
| A | A | A | A | | |

### 24.4.1 Purpose

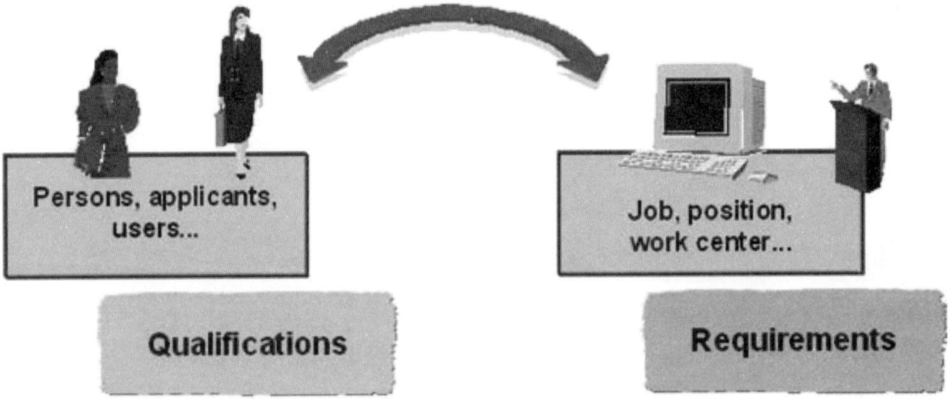


One of the key purposes of creating profiles for positions and persons is that you can compare them. Comparing profiles can help you answer several key questions in the HR practice.

- Who are the best employees/candidates for a position?
- Are the holders of positions in my organization competent enough to hold them? If not, what needs to be done to make them suitable for their current positions?
- What positions can an employee occupy in future (career planning)?
- Which employees can occupy a position in future (succession planning)?

### 24.4.2 Transaction

PEPM–Profile Matchup

### 24.4.3 Initial Screen

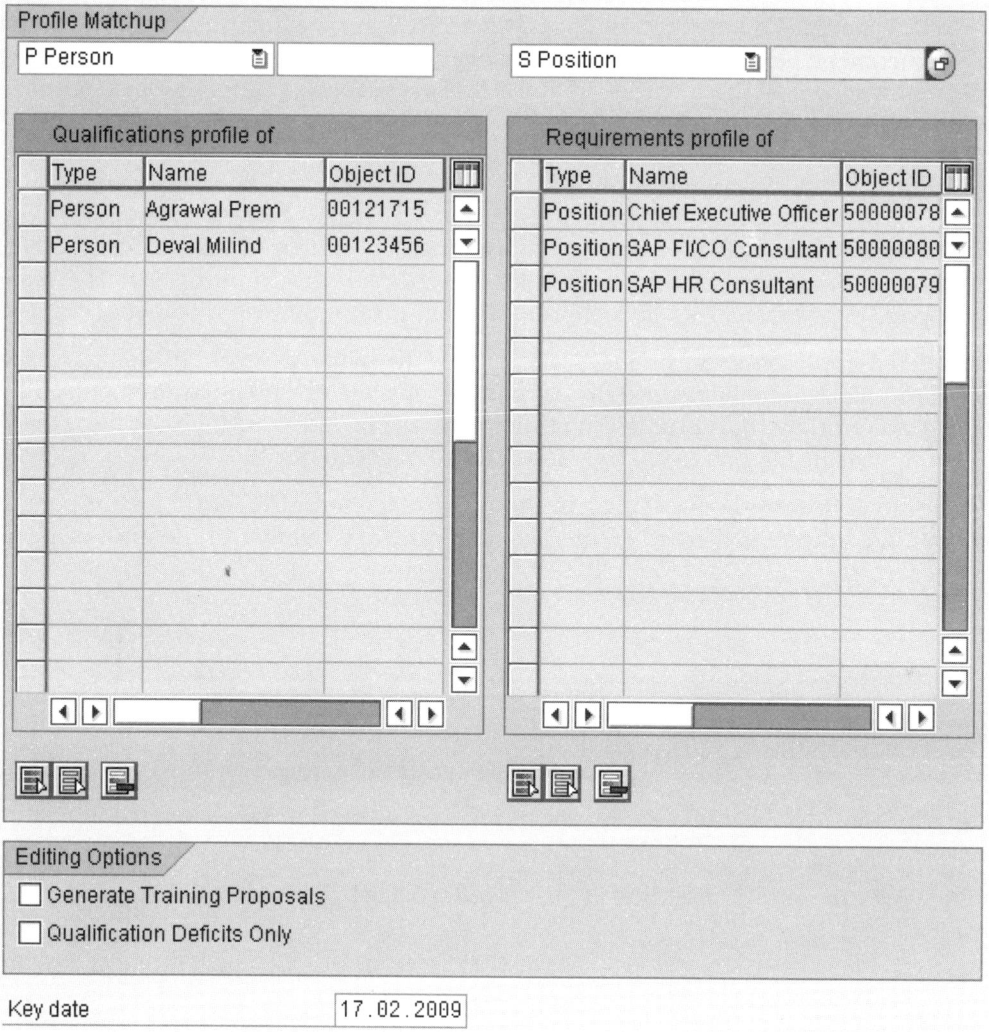


***Objects to be compared***

In the profile matchup screen you specify the objects which have requirements and the objects which have qualifications to meet those requirements. You can enter one or more objects on each side. The system compares each object on one side with every object on the other side, thus creating m into n comparisons.

***Generate training proposals***

If you tick this checkbox, training proposals are generated to cover the qualification deficit, provided that there are training courses which impart that qualification.

### *Qualification deficits only*

Profile matchup shows the comparison between requirements of a position and qualifications of a person. Sometimes a person may have a qualification which is not required by the position. Sometimes a person's qualification may meet or exceed the requirement. Normally, the comparison shows all these entries. If you tick this checkbox, then only those requirements which are not met are displayed.

## 24.4.4 Output

The proficiencies of requirements and qualifications are compared against each other. Requirements and qualifications are sorted by qualification group in the list. The scale and corresponding proficiencies of each qualification group are also displayed.

A standardized representation of the scale is used to make it easier to compare the qualifications with requirements visually. If requirements are essential requirements, they are flagged accordingly. If alternative qualifications are included in the matchup, these might also appear in the list. If so, they are flagged accordingly.

All qualifications that are not specified in the requirements profile, but which a person has anyway, are output at the end of the list. You can save this list to file and/or print it out.

### *ALV list*

| Q.group | Qualification | Ess... | Proficiency Required | Existing Proficiency | Diff... | Alt. Qual. |
|---|---|---|---|---|---|---|
| Communication | English language | ☑ | High | Do(es) Not Exist | 7- | |
| SAP Functional | HR | ☐ | Independent implem | 1 implementation o | 1- | |

### *List*

If you click [icon], the profile matchup is displayed as a list.

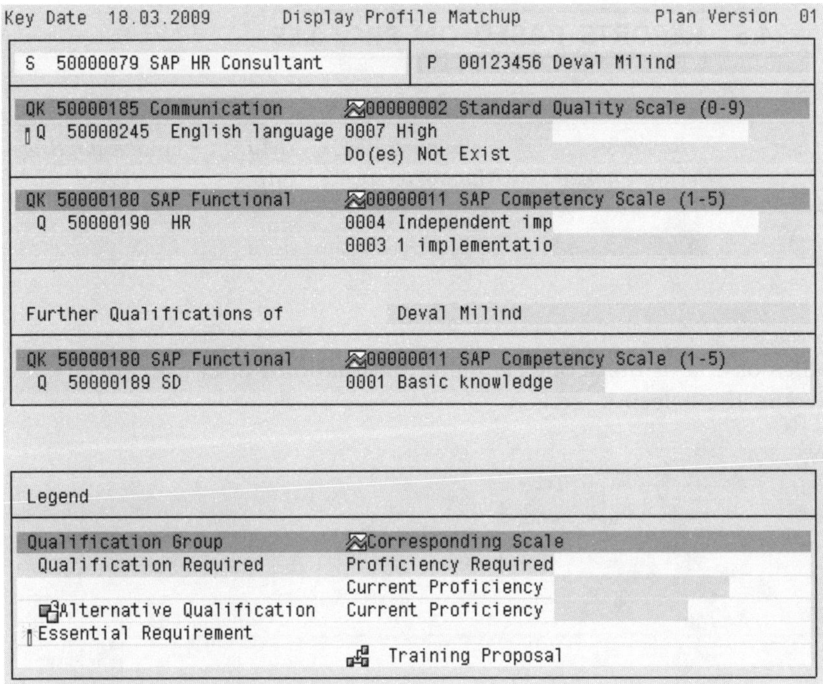


### *Graphic*

If you click [icon], the profile matchup is displayed as a graphic.

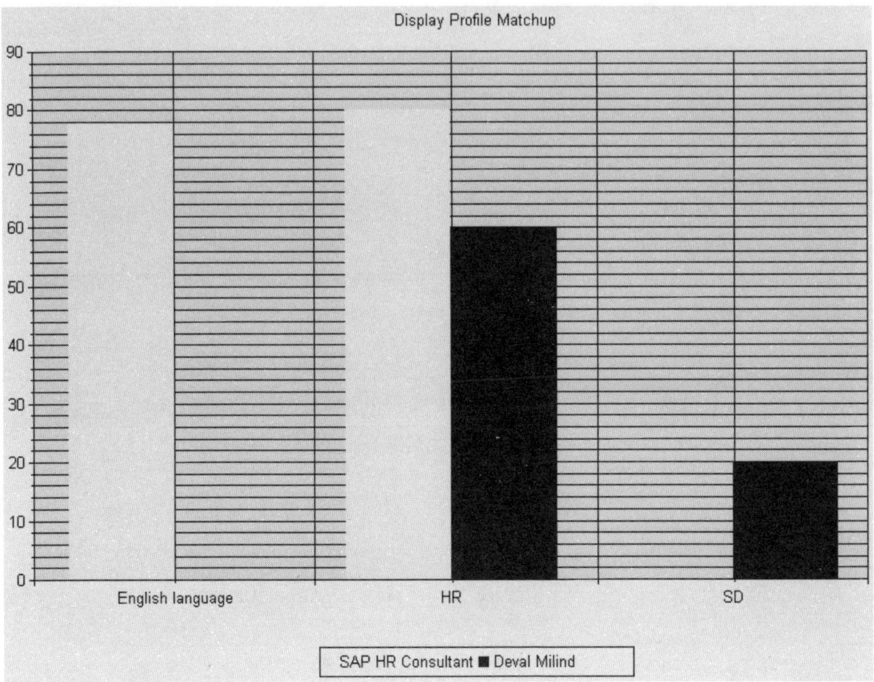

## 24.5 REPORTS BASED ON PROFILES

| *Functional Consultant* | *User* | *Business Process Owner* | *Senior Management* | *My Rating* | *Understanding Level* |
|---|---|---|---|---|---|
| A | A | A | A | | |

***Profile evaluation***

You can display profiles of one or more objects using transaction PEPP. You specify the objects and subprofiles in the selection screen.

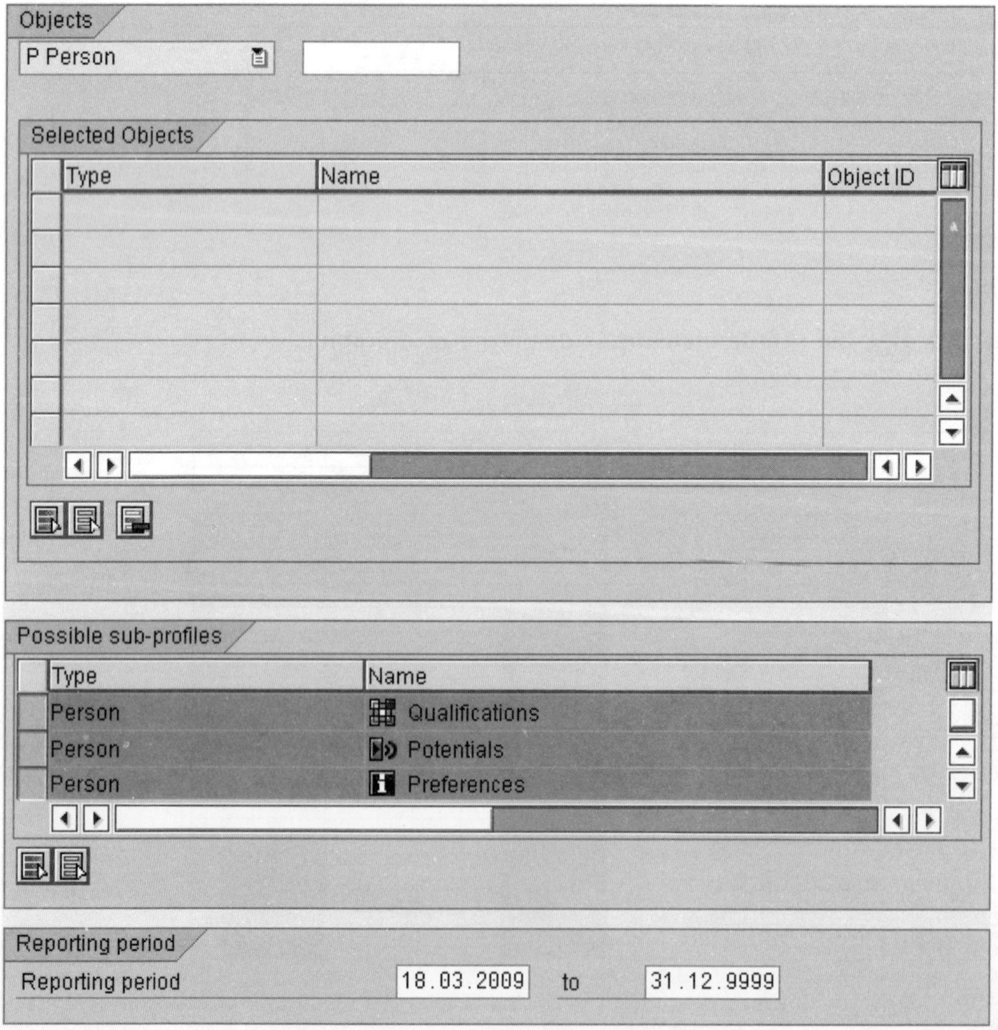

The output shows the profile of each selected object. The profile contains the selected subprofiles.

```
18.03.2009 - 31.12.9999              Profile                     01 Current plan

HeaderData
Person                   Agrawal Prem
ShortTxt                 Agrawal
Valid from               12.12.2008 - 31.12.9999

Qualifications

Qualification Group                  Scale
Qualification                     Proficny              Period

SAP Functional                     SAP Competency Scale (1-5)
HR                                Without Rating        16.02.2009 -15.02.2019
MM                                Without Rating        16.02.2009 -Unlimited

Potentials

                                  does not exist

Preferences

                                  does not exist

Dislikes

                                  does not exist
```

This graphic profile evaluation list gives you an overview of the profiles of persons, positions, and so on. You can specify which subprofiles you want to display for each object type.

This list displays general information for each object, and also information specific to the subprofiles you chose. For example, you can specify that you want to display the Qualifications and Potentials subprofiles for the object type Person. This means that the system will display qualifications and potentials (but no preferences or dislikes) for all the employees you specified.

A standardized scale representation is used to make it easier for you to compare different qualifications/requirements. You can save this list to a file and/or print it out.

### *Profiles for an organizational unit*

You can use transaction S_AHR_61015533 to display the subprofiles of all planning objects (positions, holders of positions, jobs that describe the positions, and so on) within a specific organizational unit. The system shows you all the objects. You can select the objects whose profiles you want to see. You can also limit your selection to specific subprofiles.

### *Profile matchup: positions/holders for an organizational unit*

If you want to know how well an organizational unit is manned, you will like to do the profile matchup of all its positions with the holders of those positions. You can do this using transaction S_AHR_61015532. This report compares the requirements of all the positions in one or more organizational units with the qualifications of the people who hold these positions. You can restrict your selection to situations involving qualification deficits. If Personnel Development is integrated with Training and Event Management, or if you also use the Development Plans component, you can also display suitable training proposals.

### *Objects without qualifications or requirements*

You may want to know if there are positions for which the requirement profile has not been maintained. Similarly, if there are any persons for whom the qualifications profile has not been maintained. You can get answer to these questions by running transaction S_PH9_46000019. This report generates a list of all the objects of a specific object type to which no qualifications or requirements have been assigned. You can go directly from an object in this list to profile maintenance to maintain the profile.

| PV | OT | Object ID | Object name |
|---|---|---|---|
| 01 | S | 50000086 | SAP ABAP Consultant |
| 01 | S | 50000085 | SAP Basis Consultant |
| 01 | S | 50000087 | SAP Education Coordinator |
| 01 | S | 50000080 | SAP FI/CO Consultant |
| 01 | S | 50000084 | SAP PM Consultant |
| 01 | S | 50000083 | SAP PS Consultant |

### *Objects with unevaluated qualifications or requirements*

For every qualification or requirement, you should specify proficiency. You would like to know if there are any objects for which proficiency has not been defined. You may use transaction S_PH9_46000018 to do that. This report generates a list of all the objects of a specific object type that have qualifications or requirements with the status Unevaluated. You can go directly from an object in this list (a person, for example) to profile maintenance.

| PV | OT | Object ID | Object name |
|---|---|---|---|
|  | S | 50000078 | Chief Executive Officer |

## 24.6 PERSONNEL DEVELOPMENT VIEW

| *Functional Consultant* | *User* | *Business Process Owner* | *Senior Management* | *My Rating* | *Understanding Level* |
|---|---|---|---|---|---|
| C | X | X | X | | |

### 24.6.1 Purpose

SAP has created various views including a Personnel Development view.

### 24.6.2 IMG Node

SM34 ➢ VC_T77PP_PROFILE (Table T77PP_VIEW)

### 24.6.3 Screen

| View | Name | Report |
|---|---|---|
| AE | Appraisals - employees | SAPLRHPA_WWW |
| AM | Appraisals - managers | SAPLRHPA_WWW |
| CP | Compensation management | |
| NQ | National Qualifications Framework (ZA) | |
| PD | Personnel development | SAPLRHPP |
| WP | Shift planning | SAPLRHPP |

### 24.6.4 Primary Key

Profile Maintenance – View of Profile Display

## 24.7 HEADERS

| *Functional Consultant* | *User* | *Business Process Owner* | *Senior Management* | *My Rating* | *Understanding Level* |
|---|---|---|---|---|---|
| C | X | X | X | | |

### 24.7.1 Purpose

Here you can define various headers. There may be more than one header for an object type. When headers are assigned to a view, e.g. Personnel Development view, there will be only one header for each object type.

### 24.7.2 IMG Node

SM34 ➢ VC_T77PP_PROFILE (View T77PP_HEAD)

### 24.7.3 Screen

| Obj. Type | Number | + | Report | Screen no. | Scr.Header |
|---|---|---|---|---|---|
| A | 1 | Work center | SAPLRHPP | 2000 | |
| AP | 1 | Applicant | SAPLRHPP | 2020 | 02 |
| BP | 1 | User | SAPLRHPP | 2000 | |
| C | 1 | Job | SAPLRHPP | 2000 | |
| H | 1 | External person | SAPLRHPP | 2000 | |
| KA | 1 | Capacity | SAPLRHPP | 2000 | |
| P | 1 | Person | SAPLRHPP | 2010 | 02 |
| P | 2 | Person | SAPRLHPP | 2010 | 00 |
| P | 3 | Person | | | 45 |
| PT | 1 | Partner | SAPLRHPP | 2000 | |
| QB | 1 | Qualification Block | SAPLRHPP | 2000 | |
| QP | 1 | Requirements profile (Logistics) | SAPLRHPP | 2000 | |
| S | 1 | Position | SAPLRHPP | 2030 | |
| SR | 1 | Planned staffing requirement | SAPLRHPP | 2000 | |
| T | 1 | Task | SAPLRHPP | 2000 | |
| U | 1 | Company | SAPLRHPP | 2000 | |
| US | 1 | User | SAPLRHPP | 2000 | |

### 24.7.4 Primary Key

Object Type + Two-digit Number

## 24.8 HEADERS FOR PD VIEW

| *Functional Consultant* | *User* | *Business Process Owner* | *Senior Management* | *My Rating* | *Understanding Level* |
|---|---|---|---|---|---|
| C | X | X | X | | |

### 24.8.1 Purpose

Here you assign headers to each object type in the PD view. These headers are displayed in profiles.

### 24.8.2 IMG Node

SM34 ➢ VC_T77PP_PROFILE (View V_T77PR_V_H)

### 24.8.3 Screen

View PD Personnel development

Header assignment

| Object Type | No | Name |
|---|---|---|
| A | 1 | Work center |
| AP | 1 | Applicant |
| BP | 1 | User |
| C | 1 | Job |
| H | 1 | External person |
| KA | 1 | Capacity |
| P | 1 | Person |
| QB | 1 | Qualification Block |
| QP | 1 | Requirements profile (Logistics) |
| S | 1 | Position |
| SR | 1 | Planned staffing requirement |
| T | 1 | Task |
| U | 1 | Company |
| US | 1 | User |

### 24.8.4 Primary Key

Profile Maintenance – View of Profile Display + Object Type

## 24.9 SUBPROFILES MASTER

| *Functional Consultant* | *User* | *Business Process Owner* | *Senior Management* | *My Rating* | *Understanding Level* |
|---|---|---|---|---|---|
| C | X | X | X | | |

### 24.9.1 Purpose

Here you can define various subprofiles.

### 24.9.2 IMG Node

SM34 ➢ VC_T77PP_PROFILE (Table T77PP_PART)

### 24.9.3 Screen

| No | Name | Report | Scr. | Icon |
|---|---|---|---|---|
| 1 | Qualifications | SAPLRHPP | 2101 | |
| 2 | Potentials | SAPLRHPP | 2200 | |
| 3 | Preferences | SAPLRHPP | 2300 | |
| 4 | Dislikes | SAPLRHPP | 2400 | |

### 24.9.4 Primary Key

Count Parameters

## 24.10 SUBPROFILE FOR AN OBJECT TYPE

| *Functional Consultant* | *User* | *Business Process Owner* | *Senior Management* | *My Rating* | *Understanding Level* |
|---|---|---|---|---|---|
| C | X | X | X | | |

### 24.10.1 Purpose

Here you specify which subprofiles will appear for an object and in what sequence. If you don't want a tab to appear in the profile of an object type, remove the tick from the Active checkbox.

### 24.10.2 IMG Node

SM34 ➢ VC_T77PP_PROFILE (View V_T77PR_V_H_P)

### 24.10.3 Screen

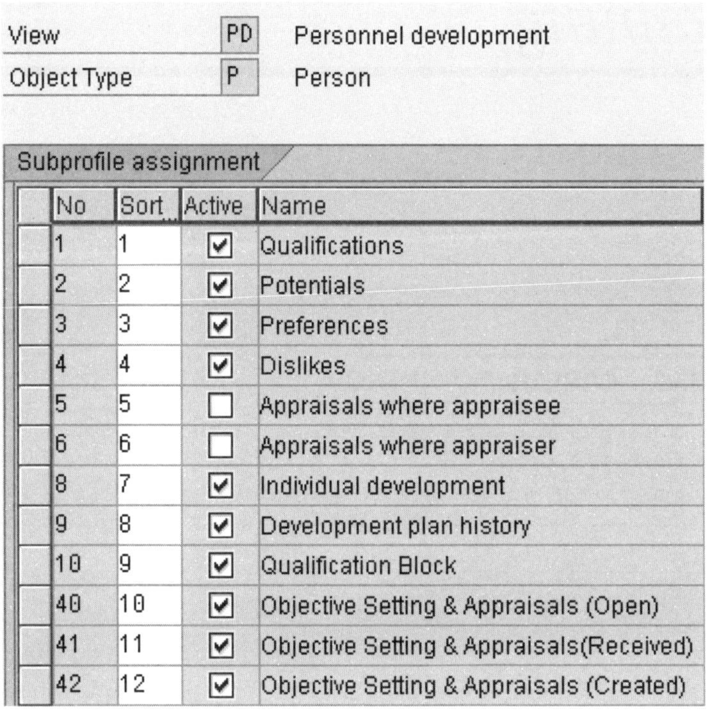

View: PD Personnel development

Object Type: P Person

Subprofile assignment

| No | Sort | Active | Name |
|---|---|---|---|
| 1 | 1 | ☑ | Qualifications |
| 2 | 2 | ☑ | Potentials |
| 3 | 3 | ☑ | Preferences |
| 4 | 4 | ☑ | Dislikes |
| 5 | 5 | ☐ | Appraisals where appraisee |
| 6 | 6 | ☐ | Appraisals where appraiser |
| 8 | 7 | ☑ | Individual development |
| 9 | 8 | ☑ | Development plan history |
| 10 | 9 | ☑ | Qualification Block |
| 40 | 10 | ☑ | Objective Setting & Appraisals (Open) |
| 41 | 11 | ☑ | Objective Setting & Appraisals(Received) |
| 42 | 12 | ☑ | Objective Setting & Appraisals (Created) |

### 24.10.4 Primary Key

Profile Maintenance – View of Profile Display + Object Type + Count Parameters

## 24.11 AUTHORIZATION CHECK FOR ACCESSING SUBPROFILES

| *Functional Consultant* | *User* | *Business Process Owner* | *Senior Management* | *My Rating* | *Understanding Level* |
|---|---|---|---|---|---|
| C | X | X | X | | |

You can use BAdI HRPDV00PROFILE0001 to run authorization checks when subprofiles are called up in display mode or change mode. These checks are run in addition to the structural authorization check.

# CHAPTER 25 Career and Succession Planning

## 25.1 CAREER PLANNING

| *Functional Consultant* | *User* | *Business Process Owner* | *Senior Management* | *My Rating* | *Understanding Level* |
|---|---|---|---|---|---|
| A | A | A | A | | |

### 25.1.1 Purpose

You plan careers of your employees so that employees can progress through organizational hierarchy, acquiring the skills required, contributing to the organization and remaining motivated. SAP lets you do the career planning considering employees' qualifications, potentials, preferences, dislikes, etc. These are called planning criteria.

### 25.1.2 Transaction

PPCP—Career Planning

### 25.1.3 Settings for Career Planning

When you do career planning, your settings which are done using transaction PPUP play an important role.

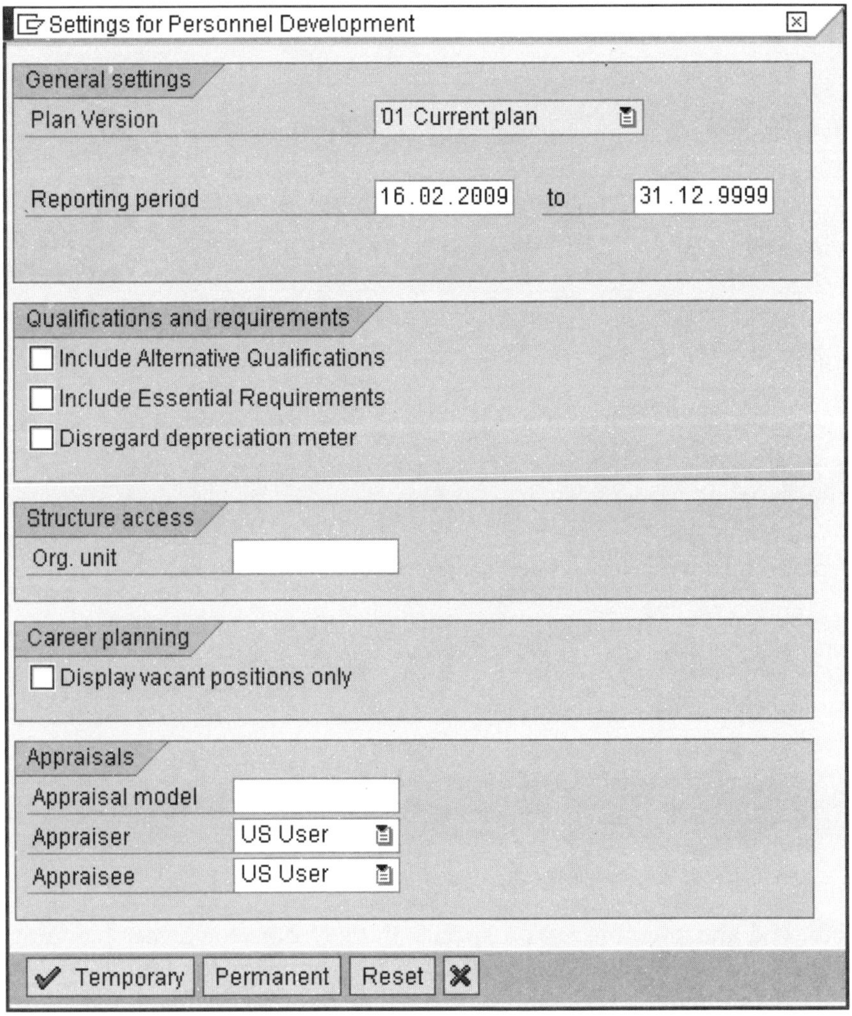


### *Display vacant positions only*

If you tick this checkbox, the system will only show vacant positions which are suitable for the career of an employee. This will exclude positions which are likely to fall vacant in future. Hence, you must be careful about selecting this checkbox.

### *Include essential requirements*

A position may have several requirements. In career and succession planning, if you insist that a person must have all the qualifications to be eligible for a position, you may severely restrict your options. On the other hand, you may not want to consider a person who does not have some of the essential competencies to succeed in the position, which you specify while defining requirements for a position. If you tick this checkbox, the system selects only those positions for which a person meets the essential requirements.

### 25.1.4 Initial Screen

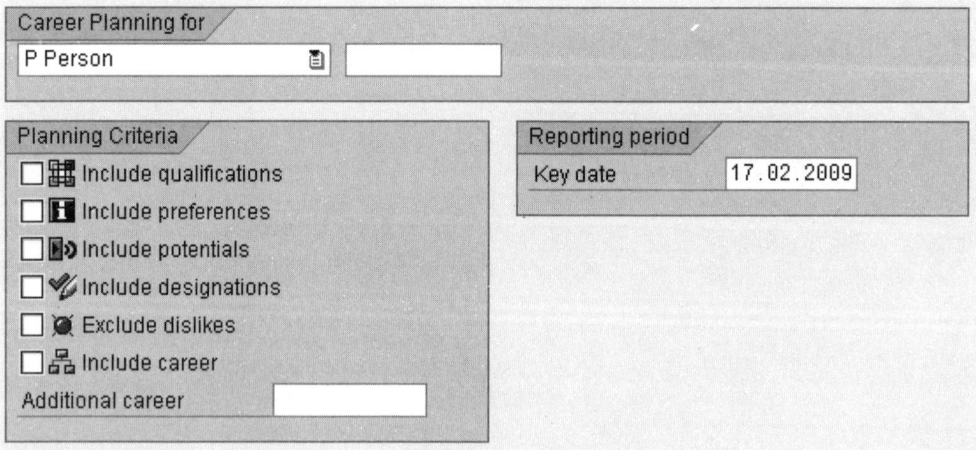


You can do career planning for various types of objects.

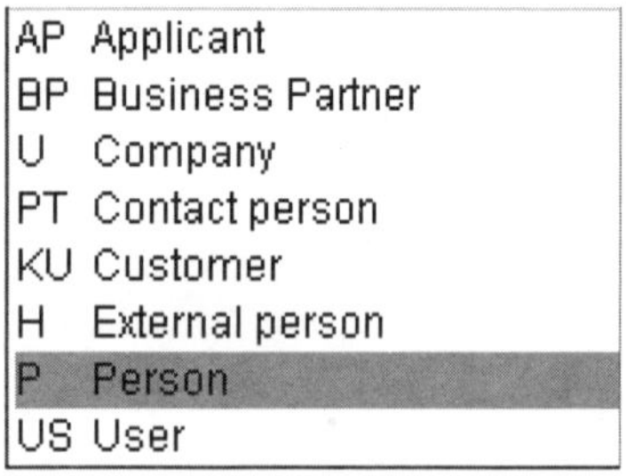


You select the object type and the object. You specify the key date for career planning. Career planning shows the objects which are suitable for a person (or the object) for whom you are doing career planning. The objects selected depend on the planning criteria you specify.

***Include qualifications***

If you use this planning criterion, then all objects that require even one qualification possessed by person will appear in the career plan. If you find that you are getting too many positions in the career plan, you may change the user settings to take essential requirements into account. The system will then show only those positions for which the employee meets all essential requirements.

***Include preferences***

If you tick this checkbox, the system includes the objects which are preferences of the person, in the career plan.

### *Include potentials*

If you tick this checkbox, the system includes all entries except qualifications from the Potentials subprofile of the person, in the career plan.

### *Include designations*

In an earlier career or succession planning exercise, you may have designated a person for certain positions. If you tick this checkbox, the system includes all positions or jobs for which the person is designated, in the career plan.

### *Exclude dislikes*

If a person has expressed dislike for certain positions, jobs, etc. these are excluded from the career plan. They are not shown under any planning criteria.

### *Include career*

The current position of a person may be in one or more career paths. Other objects in that career path are selected.

### *Additional career*

If you specifically specify a career, its career items are included in the career plan.

## 25.1.5 Career Plan

When you do career planning, the system shows positions and other objects under each planning criterion.

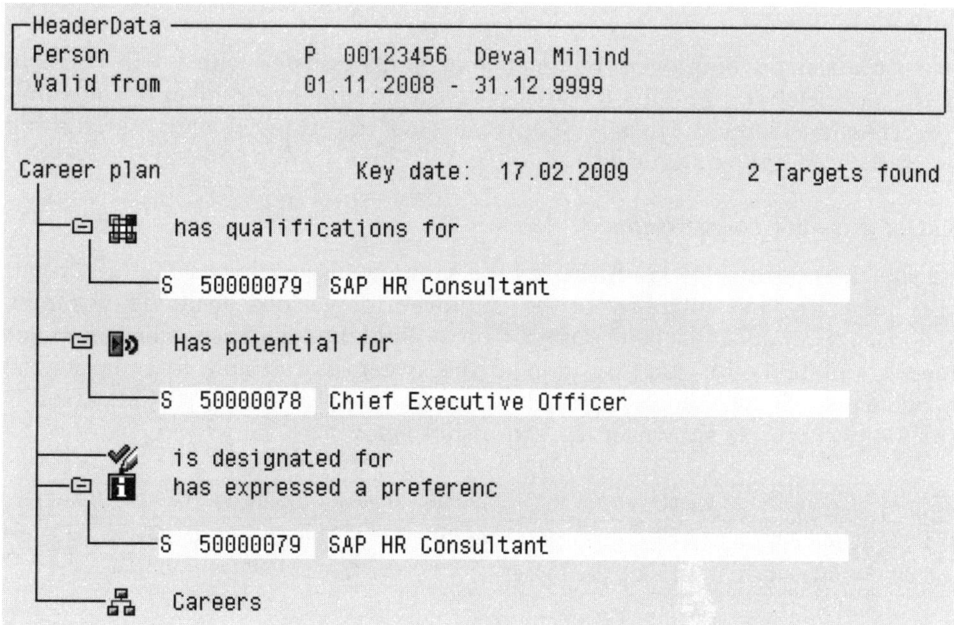

All the objects that fulfill a criterion are displayed under that criterion. An object may appear more than once under different criteria. The vacancy period of vacant positions is displayed.

### *Creating designation*

Out of the several positions displayed as possible career items for an employee, you decide the positions which will be in the employee's career path. You record your decision by selecting the position and choosing, Planning ➢ Create ➢ Designation. Thus, by designating the employee to one or more positions, both the employee and the management know which positions the employee is going to hold in future, and the employee's development plan can be prepared accordingly.

### *Deleting designation*

If you want to delete a designation created earlier, you may do so by selecting the position and choosing, Planning ➢ Delete ➢ Designation.

### *Creating preference/potential*

During career planning, apart from creating designation, you may create the employee's preference or potential. You may do so by selecting the position and choosing, Planning ➢ Create ➢ Preference/Potential.

### *Deleting preference/potential*

If you want to delete a preference/potential created earlier, you may do so by selecting the position and choosing, Planning ➢ Delete ➢ Preference/Potential.

### *Transferring an employee*

You can also transfer an employee, or enter a planned transfer which will come in effect on the specified date. You do so by selecting the position and choosing, Planning ➢ Transfer/Planned Transfer. You then enter the transfer date and staffing percentage in the dialog box and save.

### *Ranked list of possible career items*

If you find the classical display confusing as the same position appears multiple times and you do not know the suitability of the employee for various positions, you may switch the display to a ranked list by choosing, Goto ➢ Ranking List. The system computes the employee's suitability for each position. If the system is not able to compute the suitability percentage, it will show the suitability as 0% but still show that the person is suitable for the position (as shown in the screenshot below).

| | Suit... | To /% | OT | ID rel.obj | Object name | has qu... | Has po... | is desig... | has ex... | Careers |
|---|---|---|---|---|---|---|---|---|---|---|
| | | 75.00 | S | 50000079 | SAP HR Consultant | ☑ | ☐ | ☐ | ☑ | ☐ |
| | | 0.00 | S | 50000078 | Chief Executive Officer | ☐ | ☑ | ☐ | ☐ | ☐ |

### *Display profile*

You can display the profile of the selected object by choosing, Goto ➢ Profile.

### *Career path in graphic format*

The career plan shows the careers. If you want to see the career in graphic format, select the career and choose, Goto ➢ Career.

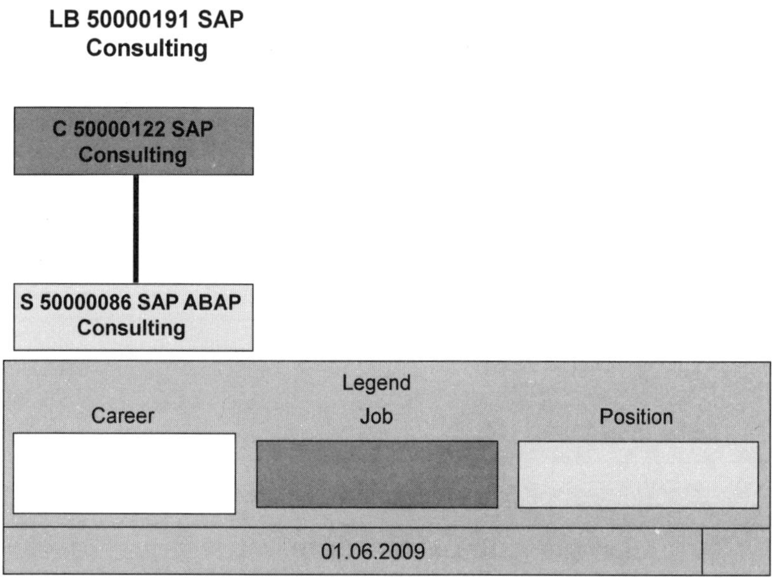


### *View options*

You can display/hide the object key by choosing, View ➢ Key on/Key off. You can display a compact or expanded view by choosing, View ➢ Switch Layout. You can display color legend by choosing, View ➢ Color Legend.

### 25.1.6 Profile Matchup

***Profile matchup***

You can select an object in the career plan or ranked list and see the profile matchup.

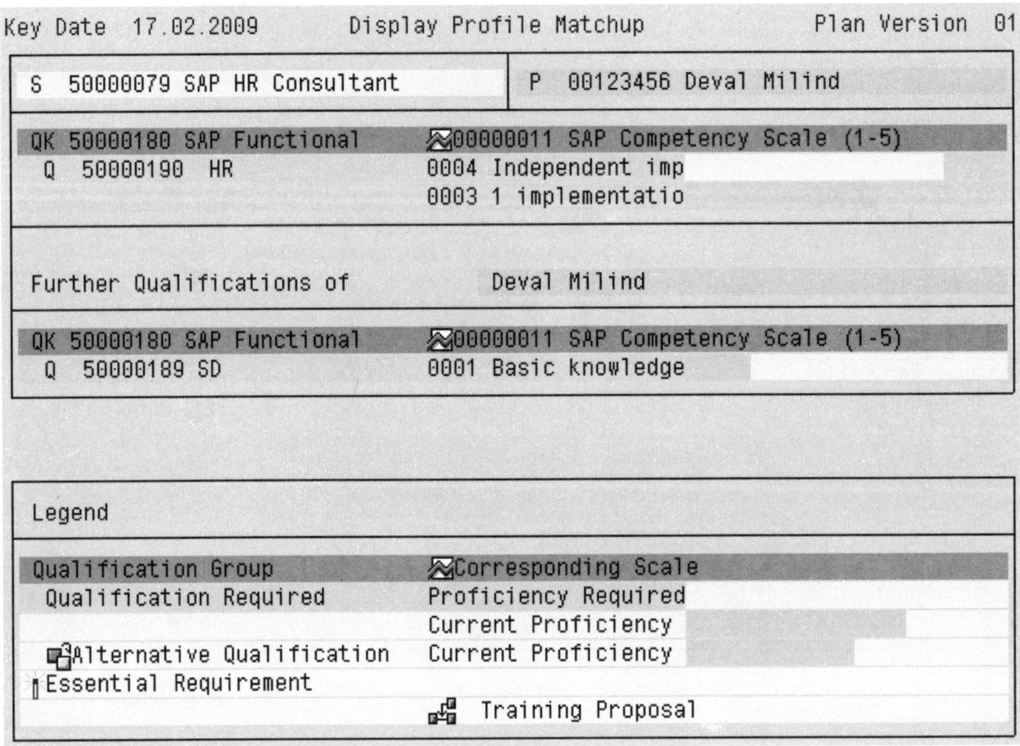

### *Profile matchup (all)*

You can also display profile matchup of the person with all the objects selected in career planning.

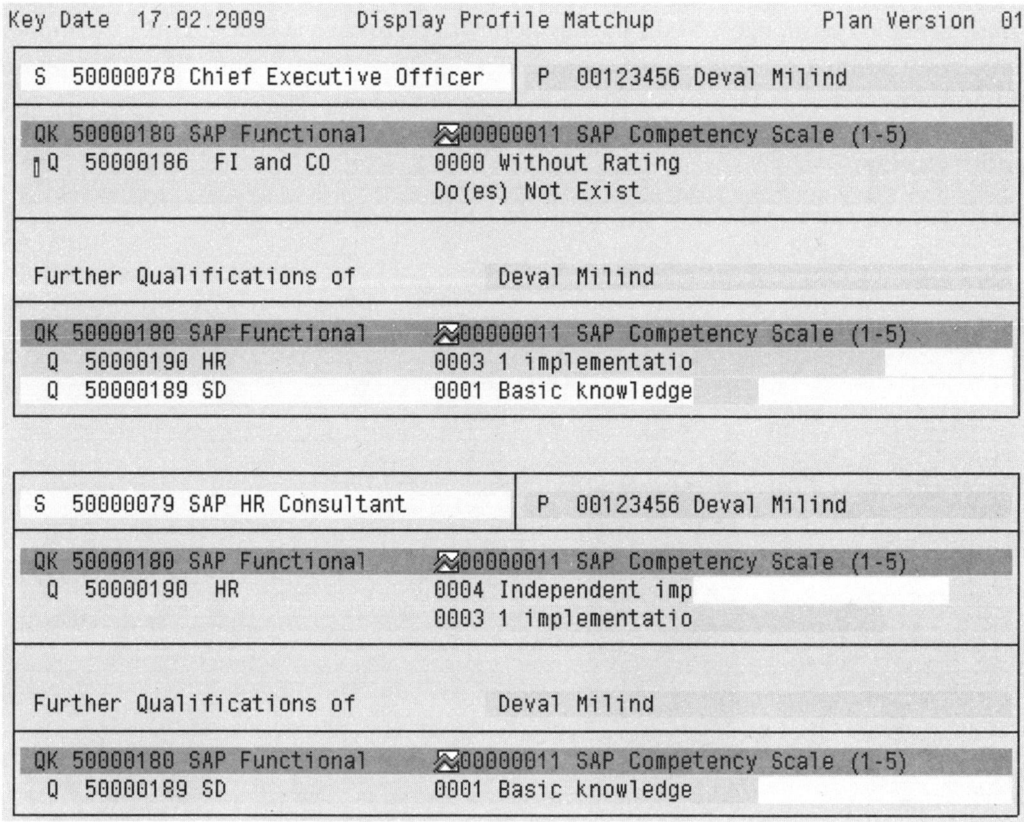


### *Displaying qualification deficit*

In the profile matchup screen, if you click [Editing Options], and choose 'Qualification Deficits only', the system will only show those requirements where there is a deficit.

### *Generating training proposals*

If a qualification does not meet a requirement and there is a training course or development plan that would impart the missing qualification, the system displays the training proposal icon and the name of the business event or development plan. To book the person on the business event in question, or to edit the development plan, choose Edit ➢ Further training. Alternatively, in the profile matchup screen, click Editing Options, and choose 'Generate Training Proposals'.

### *Graphic display*

You can see the profile matchup in a graphical form by clicking .

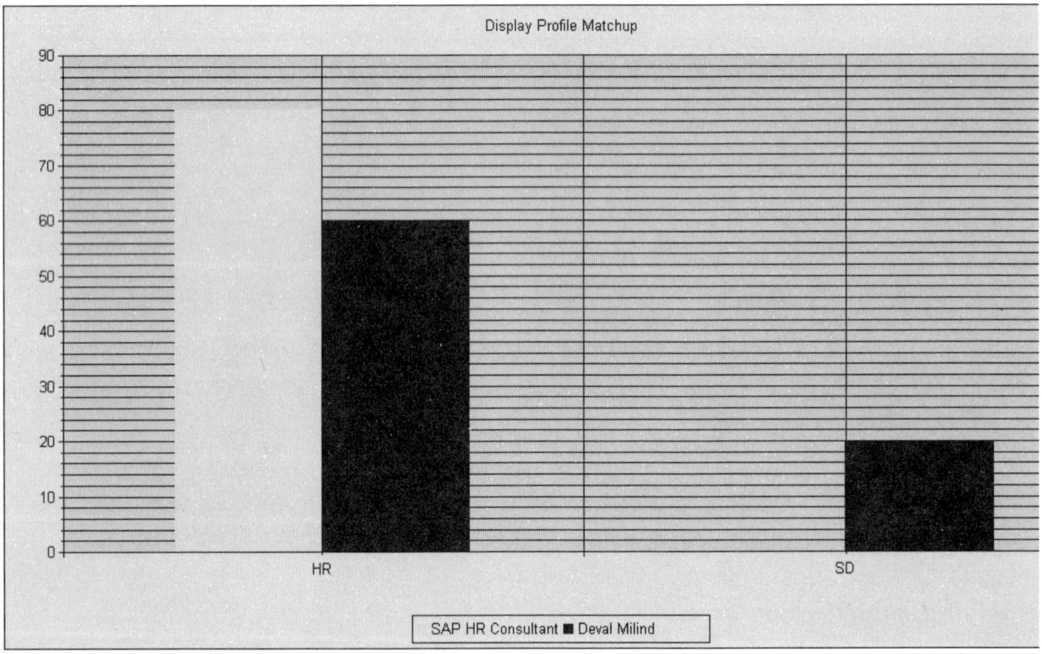


## 25.2 CAREERS

| *Functional Consultant* | *User* | *Business Process Owner* | *Senior Management* | *My Rating* | *Understanding Level* |
|---|---|---|---|---|---|
| A | B | C | C | | |

### 25.2.1 Purpose

Careers are non-person-specific paths within an organizational structure. They show the principal personnel development paths within your company. Careers can be used as a basis for career and succession planning.

### 25.2.2 Transaction

OOQ4—Career Maintenance
S_AHR_61007208—Edit Careers

### 25.2.3 Creating a Career

You can create careers using the create icon. The system gives you a dialog box, where you enter the name of the career and click the create icon.

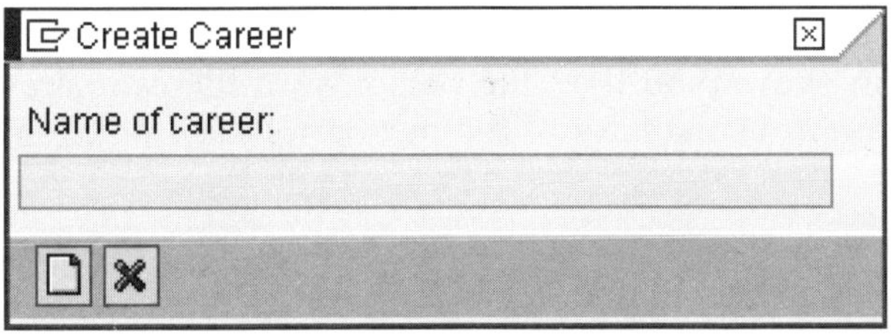


The system creates an object of type career. You then select the career and click the change icon. The system takes you to structural graphics.

### 25.2.4 Adding Career Items

Here you can add career items (jobs and positions) in the career. Careers can contain jobs and positions in any combination. You can depict vertical and horizontal movements within a career. The career items within a career are arranged in such a way that those lowest down in the hierarchy appear at the bottom of the career, and those higher up in the hierarchy appear at the top. Career items from the same hierarchy level appear beside each other.

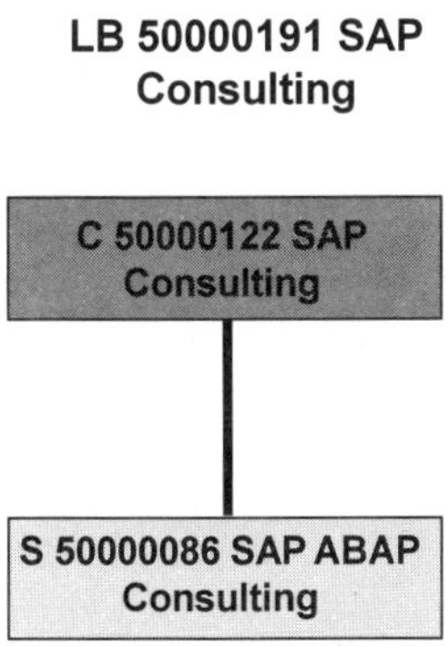


### 25.2.5 Career Reports

You can run transaction S_AHR_61015524 to see a list of careers.

| Object Type | Object ID | Object abbreviation | Object name |
|---|---|---|---|
| LB | 50000191 | SAP Consulti | SAP Consulting |

## 25.3 SUITABILITY

| *Functional Consultant* | *User* | *Business Process Owner* | *Senior Management* | *My Rating* | *Understanding Level* |
|---|---|---|---|---|---|
| A | B | C | C | | |

### *Suitability*

During career planning you compare profile of one person with profiles of multiple positions. For each position, the system shows you how the person's profile compares with the position's profile. It also determines suitability of the person for each position.

### *Suitability for a requirement item*

Suitability is computed for each requirement. Each requirement has a numeric proficiency value. If the person has that qualification, his qualification also has a numeric proficiency value. Suitability is computed as proficiency of the qualification divided by proficiency of the requirement.

### *Suitability in the case of over-qualification*

For a qualification, if the person's proficiency is higher than the proficiency of the requirement, what should be the suitability percentage? SAP gives you three choices. You may give the person extra credit, you may ignore over-qualification, or you may consider him less suitable because of over-qualification. This choice is captured in the following system switch in table T77S0.

| Group | Sem. abbr. | Value abbr. | Description |
|---|---|---|---|
| QUALI | OVERQ | 1 | Valuation of over-qualification |

### *Suitability in the case of alternative qualifications*

Some qualifications have alternative qualifications. If the person does not have the required qualification, but has an alternative qualification, that can be taken into account. In your user-specific setting (transaction PPUP), you specify ☐ Include Alternative Qualifications . If you tick this checkbox, alternative qualifications are taken into account. Alternative qualifications may have a replacement percentage, which is also taken into account in computing suitability.

Sometimes a person may have both the required qualification as well as alternative qualifications. In that case, the qualification which has better proficiency (after multiplying by the replacement percentage in case of alternative qualification) is considered.

### *Suitability in the case of depreciation meter*

Sometimes qualifications have depreciation meter. If the employee has a qualification, but is not using it because the position does not require it, it depreciates. While computing suitability, you can choose to disregard depreciation meter by ticking ☐ Disregard depreciation meter in user settings (transaction PPUP). If not disregarded, the person's qualification is depreciated, reducing his suitability.

### *Suitability percentage of a position for a person*

After computing suitability percentage for each requirement, it is averaged for all requirements. If certain requirements are flagged as essential requirements, and you have ticked ☐ Include Essential Requirements in user settings (transaction PPUP), a person is considered suitable only if he fulfils all essential requirements. Suitability percentage is shown in the ranked list of possible career items.

| Suit... | To /% | OT | ID rel.obj | Object name | has qu... | Has po... | is desig... | has ex... | Careers |
|---|---|---|---|---|---|---|---|---|---|
| | 75.00 | S | 50000079 | SAP HR Consultant | ☑ | ☐ | ☐ | ☑ | ☐ |
| | 0.00 | S | 50000078 | Chief Executive Officer | ☐ | ☑ | ☐ | ☐ | ☐ |

### *Suitability range*

Some companies discourage decision makers from taking suitability percentage literally. While they are useful for sorting ranking lists, the suitability percentage is calculated solely on the basis of system data, and cannot take all external factors into account. They define suitability ranges (range of suitability percentages). The decision makers then treat all positions in the same suitability range as equally suitable and consider external factors in making the final choice. You can define suitability ranges in view T77CS.

| Num... | From /... | To /% | ID |
|---|---|---|---|
| 1 | 50.00 | 0.00 | |
| 2 | 75.00 | 50.00 | △ |
| 3 | 100.00 | 75.00 | |
| 4 | 999.00 | 100.00 | |

If the system is set up to treat over-qualification as being positive (switch QUALI OVERQ), then it is possible to have a suitability percentage greater than 100%. If you specify an upper limit of 100% for your suitability ranges, then the system will display all objects with a suitability percentage greater than 100% in the highest suitability range. Alternatively, you can define a suitability range for over-qualification as shown above.

## 25.4 USER-SPECIFIC SETTINGS FOR PD

| *Functional Consultant* | *User* | *Business Process Owner* | *Senior Management* | *My Rating* | *Understanding Level* |
|---|---|---|---|---|---|
| A | B | C | C | | |

### 25.4.1 Purpose

You can make a number of user-specific settings. You can use these user-specific settings to override standard settings or to propose default values for specific fields. In Personnel Development, you can define the following user-specific settings.

### 25.4.2 Transaction

PPUP—User-Specific
In profiles, Settings ➢ User-specific

### 25.4.3 Screen

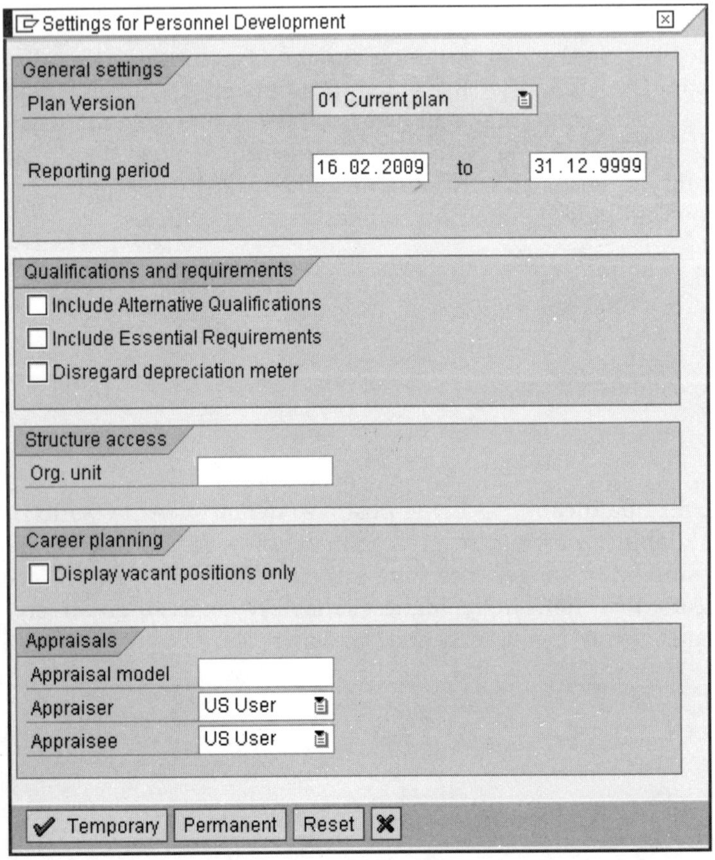

### 25.4.4 Important Fields

#### *Plan version*

If you always work a certain plan version you can specify that here. This plan version will be proposed automatically by the system at the relevant points.

#### *Reporting period*

By default, the start date is current system date and end date is 31.12.9999. These are proposed automatically by the system at the relevant points. You can change it if you want.

#### *Include alternative qualifications*

In career and succession planning you compute suitability percentage. If alternative qualifications are included, these are multiplied by the replacement percentage before the suitability percentage is calculated. If a person has both the qualification specified and a permissible alternative qualification, the qualification that gives the highest suitability percentage is taken.

#### *Include essential requirements*

A position may have several requirements. In career and succession planning, if you insist that a person must have all the qualifications to be eligible for a position, you may severely restrict your options. On the other hand, you may not want to consider a person who does not have some of the essential competencies to succeed in the position, which you specify while defining requirements for a position. If you tick this checkbox, the system selects only those positions for which a person meets the essential requirements. This setting does not affect the Find Objects for Qualifications search function.

#### *Disregard depreciation meter*

If a qualification has depreciation meter, a person's competency will decrease with time (provided that his current position does not require that qualification) and his suitability for a position requiring that qualification will reduce. If you don't want to depreciate the competencies, even though they are defined in the system, you may do so by ticking this checkbox.

#### *Organizational unit*

If you always work a certain organizational unit you can specify that here. If you specify a default organizational unit, you must also specify a plan version. This organizational unit will be proposed automatically by the system at the relevant points. If you do not specify an organizational unit here and you are chief of an organizational unit, that organizational unit is defaulted.

#### *Display vacant positions only*

If you tick this checkbox, the system will only show vacant positions which are suitable for the career of an employee. This will exclude positions which are likely to fall vacant in future. Hence, you must be careful about selecting this checkbox.

### *Appraisal model*

Here you specify the default appraisal model.

### *Appraiser*

Here you specify the object type of the appraiser.

### *Appraisee*

Here you specify the object type of the appraisee.

### *Temporary*

If you store the user settings temporarily, they only apply to the current terminal session. In this case, any permanent settings are overwritten temporarily.

### *Permanent*

If you store the user settings permanently, they apply to all future terminal sessions of the logged on user.

### *Reset*

If you have made temporary change in settings, and want to switch back to permanent settings, you click this icon.

## 25.4.5 Storage of Permanent User-Specific Settings

When you define permanent user-specific settings, you are in effect defining user parameters (System ➢ User Profile ➢ Own Data).

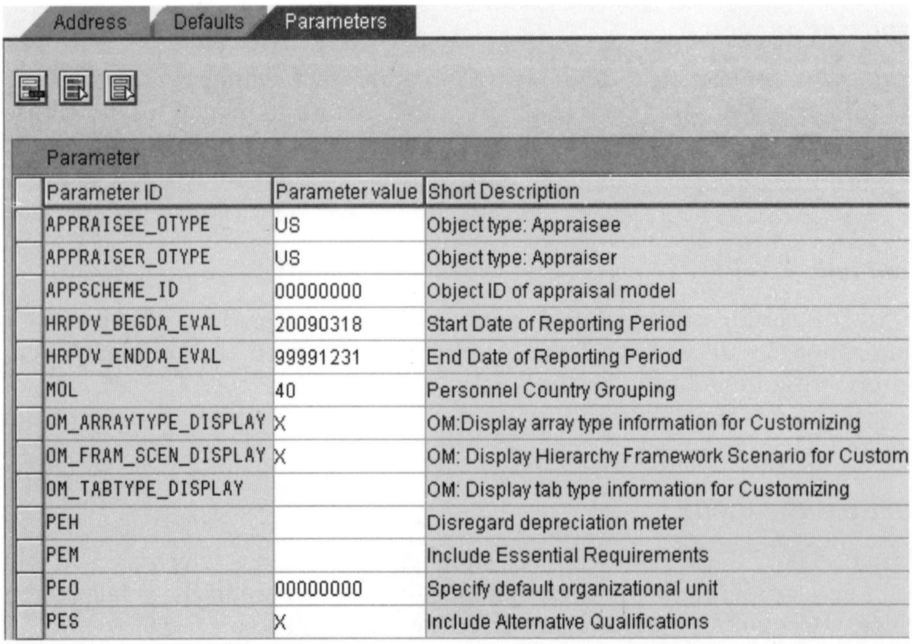


| Parameter ID | Parameter value | Short Description |
|---|---|---|
| APPRAISEE_OTYPE | US | Object type: Appraisee |
| APPRAISER_OTYPE | US | Object type: Appraiser |
| APPSCHEME_ID | 00000000 | Object ID of appraisal model |
| HRPDV_BEGDA_EVAL | 20090318 | Start Date of Reporting Period |
| HRPDV_ENDDA_EVAL | 99991231 | End Date of Reporting Period |
| MOL | 40 | Personnel Country Grouping |
| OM_ARRAYTYPE_DISPLAY | X | OM:Display array type information for Customizing |
| OM_FRAM_SCEN_DISPLAY | X | OM: Display Hierarchy Framework Scenario for Custom |
| OM_TABTYPE_DISPLAY | | OM: Display tab type information for Customizing |
| PEH | | Disregard depreciation meter |
| PEM | | Include Essential Requirements |
| PEO | 00000000 | Specify default organizational unit |
| PES | X | Include Alternative Qualifications |

### 25.4.6 User Parameters for Personnel Development

In addition to these user-specific settings, the following user parameters are also available for Personnel Development.

| *Parameter* | *Use* |
|---|---|
| HRPDV_OTYPE | You can use this parameter to specify a default standard object type for Personnel Development (does not apply to Appraisal Systems). This parameter overrides the standard setting, which is usually the object type User (exception: the standard default object type in Succession Planning is S for position). |
| HRPDV_SEARCH_OT YPES | You can use this parameter to define default object types when searching for objects for qualifications and requirements. You can specify multiple object types, each 2-character long without separators. If an object type is only one character, you leave second character blank. For example, <USP AP> represents user, person and applicant. |
| POK | You can use this parameter to switch on the display of the ID (of all displayed objects) and abbreviation (of qualifications objects) generally in Personnel Development. |

## 25.5 SUCCESSION PLANNING

| *Functional Consultant* | *User* | *Business Process Owner* | *Senior Management* | *My Rating* | *Understanding Level* |
|---|---|---|---|---|---|
| A | A | A | A | | |

### 25.5.1 Purpose

Succession planning is very similar to career planning. In career planning, the starting point is an employee, and you identify the positions he can hold. In succession planning, the starting point is a position, and you identify the persons who can hold that position. You do succession planning of a position to ensure smooth transition in a critical position. Apart from position, you can do succession planning for a job, task, work center, capacity and requirements profile. SAP lets you do the succession planning considering employees' qualifications, potentials, preferences and dislikes.

### 25.5.2 Transaction

PPSP—Succession Planning

### 25.5.3 Initial Screen

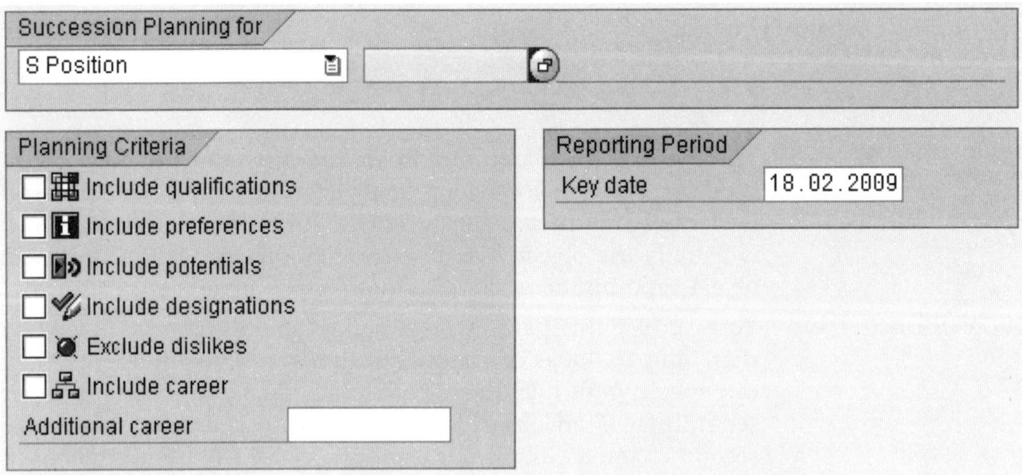


You can do succession planning for the types of objects given below.

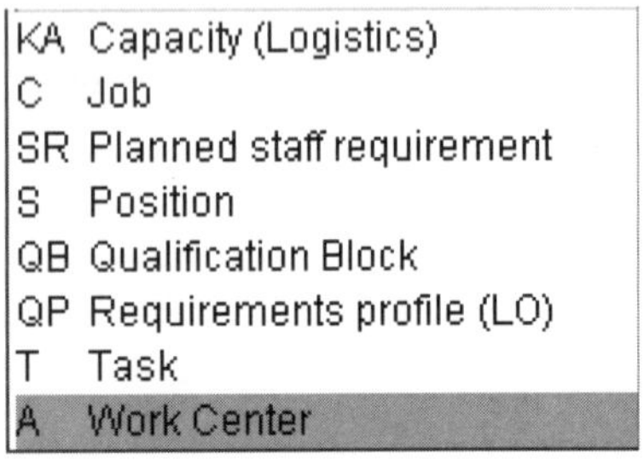


You select the object type and the object. You specify the key date for succession planning. Succession planning shows the objects which are suitable for a position (or the object) for which you are doing succession planning. The objects selected depend on the planning criteria you specify. The objects which are displayed when you select a planning criterion are discussed below.

#### *Include qualifications*

If you use this planning criterion, then all objects that possess even one qualification required by position will appear in the succession plan. If you find that you are getting too many persons in the succession plan, you may change the user settings to take essential requirements into account. The system will then show only those persons who meet all essential requirements.

#### *Include preferences*

If you tick this checkbox, the system includes all the persons who have shown preference for a position in the succession plan of that position.

### *Include potentials*

If you tick this checkbox, the system includes all the persons who have potential for a position in the succession plan of that position.

### *Include designations*

If you tick this checkbox, the system shows all persons who are designated for the position as possible successors.

### *Exclude dislikes*

If a person has expressed dislike for a position, for which succession planning is being done, then he is excluded from the list of possible successors.

### *Include career*

If the current position belongs to one or more career paths, then all positions in those career paths are selected and their holders are displayed.

### *Additional career*

All persons who hold a position in the specified career plan are displayed.

## 25.5.4 Succession Plan

When you run succession planning, the system shows the result as under:

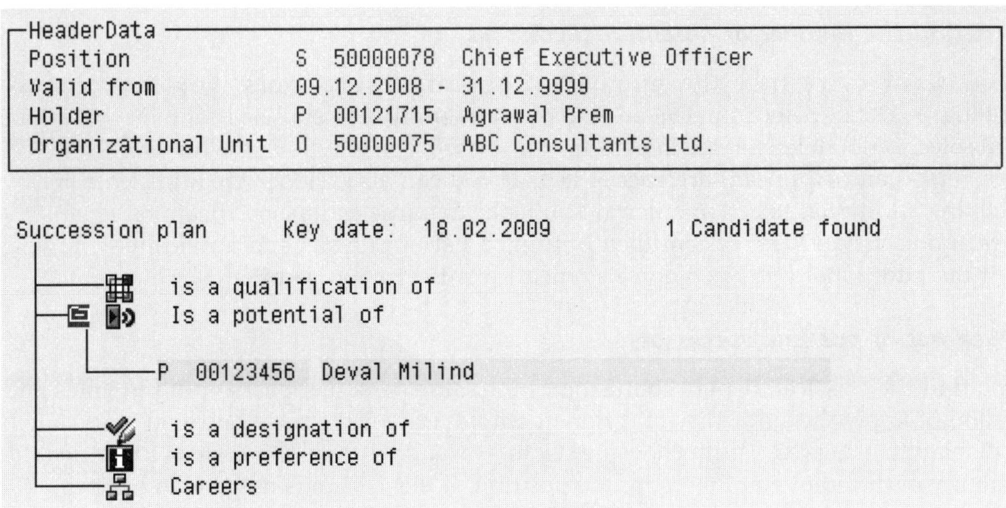


### *Creating designation*

Out of the several persons displayed as possible successors for a position, you decide the persons who will be successors for that position. You record your decision by selecting the person and choosing, Planning ➢ Create ➢ Designation. Thus, by designating one or more employees to the position, both the employee and the management know which employees are likely to hold the position in future, and the employees' development plan can be prepared accordingly.

### *Deleting designation*

If you want to delete a designation created earlier, you may do so by selecting the person and choosing, Planning ➢ Delete ➢ Designation.

### *Creating preference/potential*

During succession planning, apart from creating designation, you may create the employee's preference or potential. You do so by selecting the person and choosing, Planning ➢ Create ➢ Preference/Potential.

### *Deleting preference/potential*

If you want to delete a preference/potential created earlier, you may do so by selecting the person and choosing, Planning ➢ Delete ➢ Preference/Potential.

### *Transferring an employee*

You can also transfer an employee to a position, or enter a planned transfer which will come in effect on the specified date. You do so by selecting the person and choosing, Planning ➢ Transfer/Planned Transfer. You then enter the transfer date and staffing percentage in the dialog box and save.

### *Restricting the number of potential successors*

If you want to restrict the number of potential successors, you may choose Planning ➢ Detail Selection. The ad hoc query is used for detail selection. You can use detail selection to delete or retain objects of a specific object type in the hit list. The object types Person and Applicant are special in that you can also restrict the hit list further by specifying additional selection criteria. You make detail selection specifications separately for each object type. The system then outputs a list of persons and applicants who also fulfill the additional criteria. You can repeat detail selection as often as you want.

### *Ranked list of possible successors*

If you find the classical display confusing as the same person appears multiple times and you do not know the suitability of different employees for the positions, you may switch the display to a ranked list by choosing, Goto ➢ Ranking List. The system computes the suitability of different employees for the position. If the system is not able to compute the suitability percentage, it will show the suitability as 0%.

| | Suitable | Suit. | OT | ID rel.obj | Obj.name | has qual... | Has pot... | is desi... | has exp... | Careers |
|---|---|---|---|---|---|---|---|---|---|---|
| | | 0.00 | P | 00123456 | Deval Milind | ☐ | ☑ | ☐ | ☐ | ☐ |

### *Display profile*

You can display the profile of the selected object by choosing, Goto ➢ Profile.

### *Career path in graphic format*

The succession plan shows the careers. If you want to see the career in graphic format, select the career and choose Goto ➢ Career.

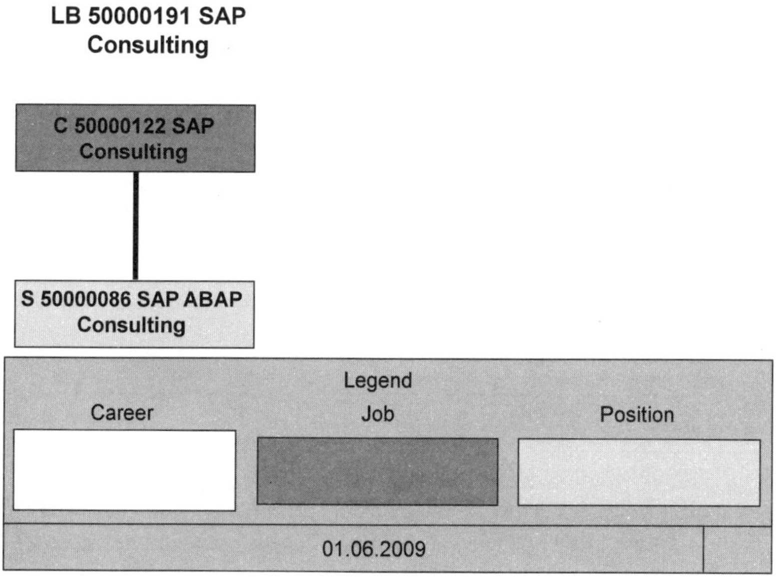


### *View options*

You can display/hide the object key by choosing, View ➢ Key on/Key off. You can display a compact, or expanded, view by choosing, View ➢ Switch Layout. You can display color legend by choosing, View ➢ Color Legend.

### 25.5.5 Profile Matchup

The profile matchup functionality in succession planning is similar to the profile matchup functionality in career planning.

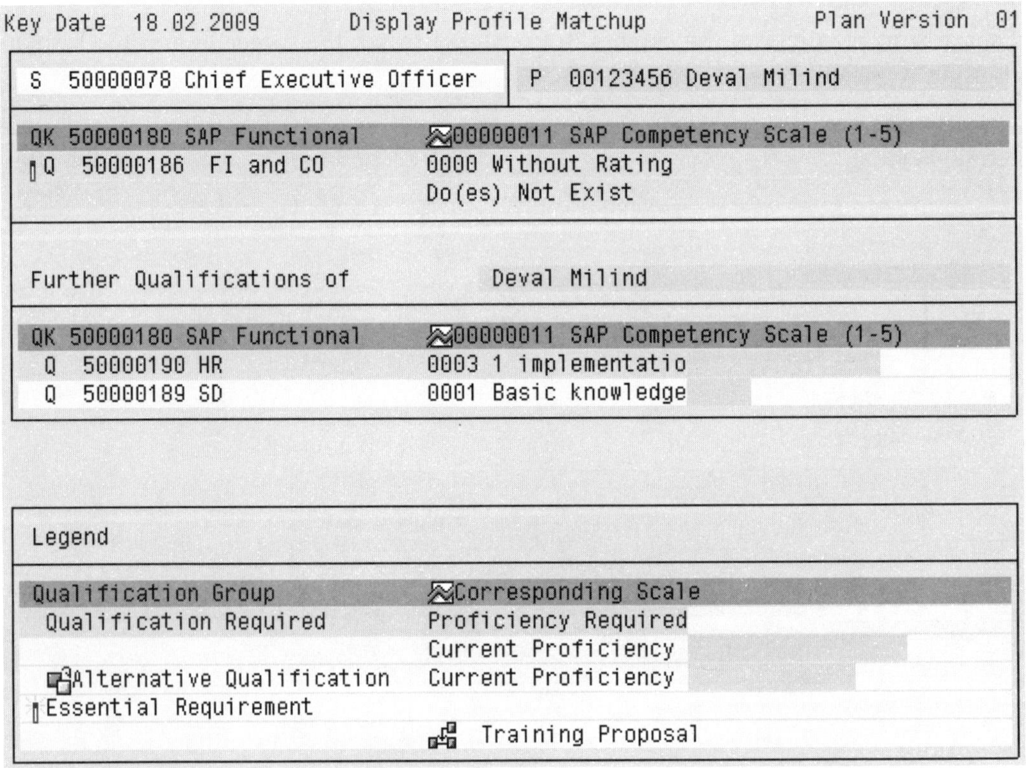


### 25.5.6 Succession Simulation

If an employee becomes successor for a position, the position that he is holding will become vacant and you will need to find a successor for it. This phenomenon will repeat until the successor does not leave behind a position, or you reach an obsolete position. You can perform succession simulation by choosing Planning ➢ Perform Simulation in the initial screen of succession planning. When the simulation is completed, the system displays a list of all positions that have to be re-staffed, and proposes suitable persons for these positions. You are also shown each person's suitability, and the planning criteria they fulfill.

When you simulate succession planning for a position or other object, the system always simulates the transfer of the person with the highest suitability. The system then works through a succession scenario for the new vacancy caused by this person. The simulation stops if a successor does not leave behind a position, or if a successor does not leave behind a position that requires re-staffing, or if it reaches an obsolete position.

### 25.5.7 Succession Overview

You can run transaction S_PH9_46000017 to see succession overview of an organizational unit. It displays an overview of the succession situation for all positions in an organizational unit. Potential successors are determined for every position on the basis of the planning criteria specified. The number of potential successors found is displayed for each planning criteria selected, and for all criteria as a whole. You can then go directly from here to a list of the potential successors found. The suitability of the best potential successor is always displayed in the succession overview. From here too you can go to a list of all potential successors. This list tells you how suitable each candidate is for the position in question.

# Chapter 26

# Development Plan

## 26.1 INDIVIDUAL DEVELOPMENT PLAN

| Functional Consultant | User | Business Process Owner | Senior Management | My Rating | Understanding Level |
|---|---|---|---|---|---|
| A | A | A | A | | |

### 26.1.1 Development Plan and Development Plan Items

***Individual development plan***

In order to develop your employees, you need to plan their development, and then execute the development plan. Individual development plan is a part of a person's profile.

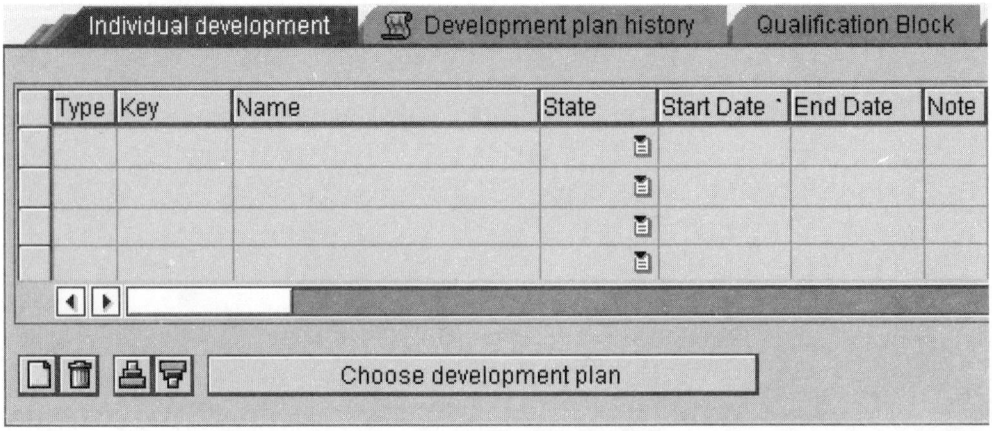

### *Development plan items*

A development plan contains development plan items, e.g. training, on-the-job training, job rotation, etc. A development plan item can be in different states, e.g. planned, completed, etc. It also has a period during which it is expected to be implemented. It is also possible for items to run in parallel to each other.

## 26.1.2 Individual Development Subprofile

### *Changing individual development plans*

You can run transaction PPDPIM or PPPM to change the profile of a person. You click the tab 'Individual development' to change the individual development plan of a person.

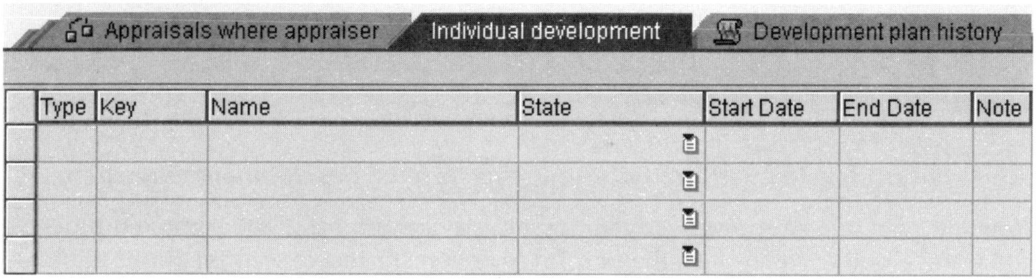


### *Creating development items*

Individual development subprofile is used to plan and manage an employee's individual development. Individual development may take place in many ways. The employee may be provided training, on-the-job training, job rotation, etc. When you create an individual development plan item, the system lets you choose from the following types of development plan items.

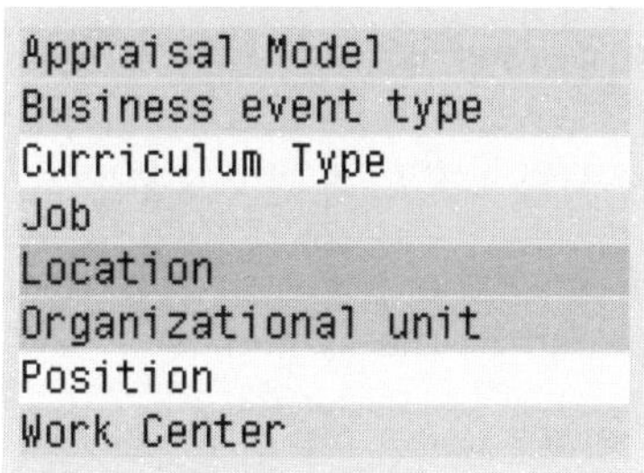


You first select the type of development plan item, and then the development plan item. When the record is inserted, you maintain the state (planned) and validity period. You can also keep notes.

### *Updating state*

Every item in an individual development plan has a state. When the item is created, the state is 'Planned'. When the employee starts working on an item, e.g. undergoing training or working in a position, etc. the state is changed to 'Current'. When the item is completed, e.g. completed working in a position, the state is changed to 'Completed'. If there is an evaluation to check whether the employee has completed the item successfully or not, e.g. a test at the end of a training program, the state may be changed either to 'Completed successfully', or to 'Completed unsuccessfully'. If the item is not carried out as planned, the state is changed to 'Not carried out'.

3 Completed<br>
5 Completed successfully<br>
4 Completed unsuccessfully<br>
2 Current<br>
6 Not carried out<br>
1 Planned

### *Linkage between development activity and the state of development plan item*

Development plan items represent development activity. If a position is in an employee's individual development plan and the employee is transferred to that position, the state of that development plan item should be changed to 'Current'. SAP supports this linkage in both ways. If the employee is transferred to the position, the state of the development plan item is automatically changed. Conversely, if the state of the development plan item is changed to 'Current', the employee is automatically transferred.

### *Triggering further processing steps*

When, in a development plan item, an object of a certain type achieves certain state, the system automatically triggers certain actions in the system.

- When the state of a position is changed to 'Current', the person is transferred to the specified position.
- When the state of a business event type is changed to 'Current', the person is booked to a business event of that type.
- When the state of an appraisal model is changed to 'Current', the 'perform appraisal function' is triggered. This processing needs to be activated in the system.

You can also make settings in Customizing to specify whether users have to confirm execution of a further processing module, or whether it should be executed entirely in the background.

### *Automatic state management*

You can assign and update the state of a development plan item manually. It is, however, possible to partially automate state management. You can specify that certain events should automatically trigger a change in the state of a development plan item.

- When appraisal process is completed, the state of the appraisal model is set to 'Completed'.
- When an employee is booked for a training program, the state of the development plan item of that business event type is set to 'Current'.
- When an employee completes the training program, the state of the development plan item of that business event type is set to 'Completed'.
- If an employee cancels his attendance for a training program, the state of the development plan item of that business event type is set to 'Planned'.
- If an employee's staffing assignment for a position is deleted, the state of the development plan item of that position is set to 'Not carried out'.
- When an employee is transferred to the position in his development plan item, the state of that item is set to 'Current'.
- When an employee is transferred out of the position in his development plan item, the state of that item is set to 'Completed'.

### *Automatic entry of training in individual development plan*

If you use the Training and Event Management functionality to book a person for a business event, this information can be written automatically to the individual development plan of the person.

### *Finding objects for a development plan item*

You can run transaction PPDPSPFS to find all objects for a development plan item in various states.

```
Evaluation period 01.01.1900 - 31.12.9999
Position          50000079 SAP HR Consultant

Is passed through by
```

| State of Development | Number of persons | | | |
|---|---|---|---|---|
| **RO ID of related object** | | **Person's name** | **Start Date** | **End Date** |
| Planned | 1 | | | |
| P 00123456 | | Deval Milind | 01.10.2009 | 31.12.2009 |
| Current | 0 | | | |
| Completed | 0 | | | |
| Completed unsuccessfully | 0 | | | |
| Completed successfully | 0 | | | |
| Not carried out | 0 | | | |

## 26.2 GENERAL DEVELOPMENT PLAN

| *Functional Consultant* | *User* | *Business Process Owner* | *Senior Management* | *My Rating* | *Understanding Level* |
|---|---|---|---|---|---|
| A | A | A | A | | |

### 26.2.1 General Development Plans

Individual development plans are development plans which are specific to individual employees. However, over a period of time you may observe certain patterns and may want to create general development plans which can be assigned to employees. SAP lets you do that. These general development plans also contain a set of development plan items. When you assign a general development plan to an employee, two things happen.

- The development plan appears in the 'Development plan history' subprofile of the employee.
- Development plan items are copied from the general development plan to the employee's individual development plan.

Subsequently, you complete both the individual development plan items in the 'Individual development' subprofile and the development plan in the 'Development plan history' subprofile. When you complete the development plan in the 'Development plan history' subprofile, qualifications associated with the development plan are assigned to the employee.

### 26.2.2 Copying a General Development Plan

You can run transaction PPDPIM to copy a general development plan into an individual development plan.

***Selection Screen***

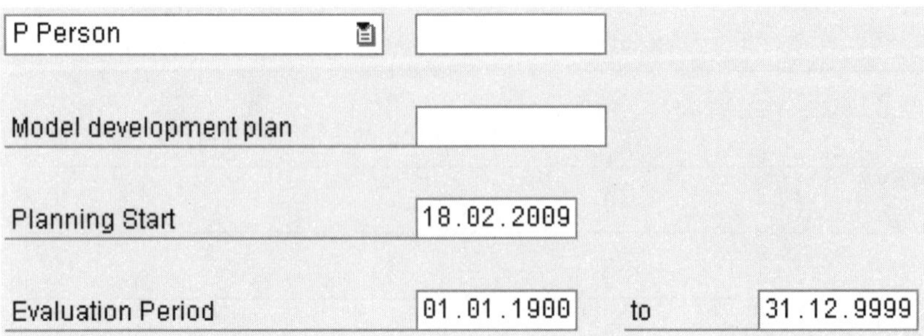


***Development plan for***

You can create individual development plan for a person or for a user. You select the object type and the object. However, the profile of object type user does not contain 'Individual development' and 'Development plan history' subprofiles. You may have to enable it in view cluster VC_T77PP_PROFILE.

### *Model development plan*

Here you specify the development plan you want to copy from. If you are not copying from a development plan, then you can create the individual development plan directly in the profile of the employee.

### *Planning start*

The individual development plan you create will be valid from the planning start date and will delimit any existing development plan.

### *Evaluation period*

You can specify the evaluation period to restrict the data displayed in an individual development plan to a specific period.

## 26.2.3 Copying Development Plan Items

### *General development plan sub-screen*

When you run transaction PPDPIM with a model development plan, the system shows all development plan items. You can either transfer all items, or only mandatory items, to the employee's individual development plan. You can also copy individual items in the general plan to the individual plan by double-clicking them.

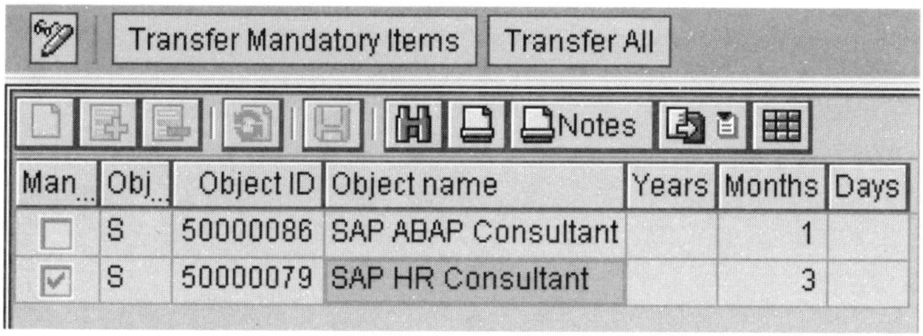


### *Individual development plan sub-screen*

When you copy development plan items, they get copied to the individual development plan of the employee which is in the right-half of the screen. Apart from development plan items, the development plan also gets assigned to the employee and shows in his 'Development plan history' subprofile. There it needs a state value, which you specify on the following screen.

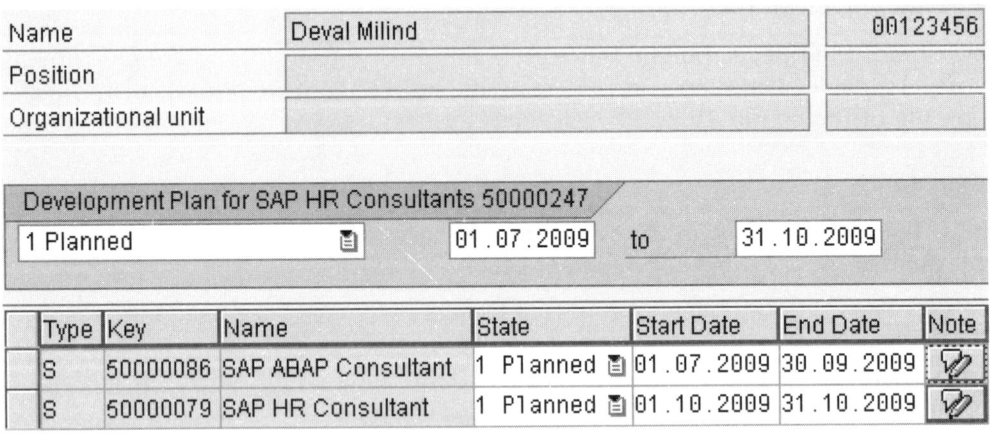


## 26.2.4 Development Plan History Subprofile

### *Development plan history subprofile*

You can run transaction PPPM to see the 'Development plan history' subprofile of a person which contains development plans assigned to him.

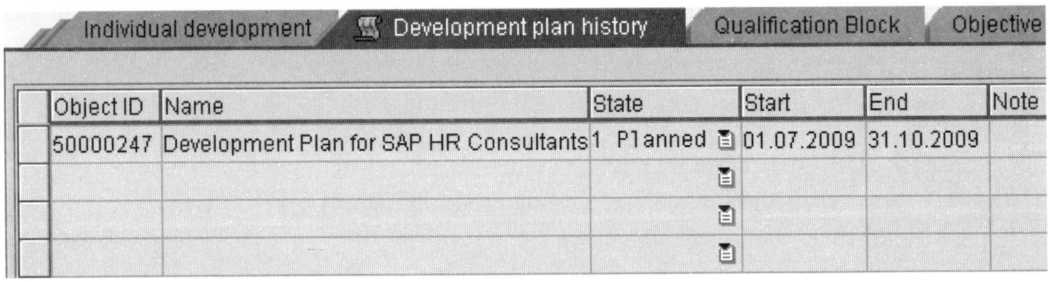


### *Creating development plan*

Development plans are assigned to a person by copying a development plan using transaction PPDPIM. You cannot insert a record in the Development plan history subprofile of a person. However, you can delete a development plan from the subprofile.

### *Updating state*

Every item in the development plan history has a state. When the item is created, the state is 'Planned'. When the employee starts working on a development plan the state is changed to 'Current'. When the development plan is completed, the state is changed to 'Completed'. If there is an evaluation to check whether the employee has completed the development plan successfully or not, the state may be changed either to 'Completed successfully', or to 'Completed unsuccessfully'. If the item is not carried out as planned, the state is changed to 'Not carried out'.

```
3 Completed
5 Completed successfully
4 Completed unsuccessfully
2 Current
6 Not carried out
1 Planned
```

### *Triggering further processing steps*

If the state 'Completed successfully' is assigned to a development plan in the 'Development plan history' subprofile, the qualifications imparted by the development plan are written to the person's qualifications subprofile. If the person already holds a qualification, only the proficiency of the qualification is updated provided that the new proficiency is higher than the existing one.

### *Finding objects for a development plan*

You can run transaction PPDPSPFP to find all objects for a development plan in various states.

Evaluation period 18.03.2009 - 31.12.9999
Development Plan 50000247 Development Plan for SAP HR Consultants

Is passed through by

| State of Development / RO ID of related object | Number of persons | Person's name | Start Date | End Date |
|---|---|---|---|---|
| Planned | 1 | | | |
| P 00123456 | | Deval Milind | 01.07.2009 | 31.10.2009 |
| Current | 0 | | | |
| Completed | 0 | | | |
| Completed unsuccessfull | 0 | | | |
| Completed successfully | 0 | | | |
| Not carried out | 0 | | | |

## 26.3 DEVELOPMENT PLAN CATALOG

| *Functional Consultant* | *User* | *Business Process Owner* | *Senior Management* | *My Rating* | *Understanding Level* |
|---|---|---|---|---|---|
| A | A | A | A | | |

### 26.3.1 Purpose

General development plans are listed in the development plan catalog. The development plan catalog is a multi-level hierarchy of development plan groups, which contain general development plans.

### 26.3.2 Transaction

OOEC—Change Development Plan Catalog
S_AHR_61007168—Edit Development Plan Catalog
PPDPCS—Display Development Plan Catalog

### 26.3.3 Development Plan Group

In the development plan catalog, when you click create, the system asks you whether you want to create a development plan group or a development plan. Usually you first create development plan groups. For a development plan group you specify a name, a description and a validity period.

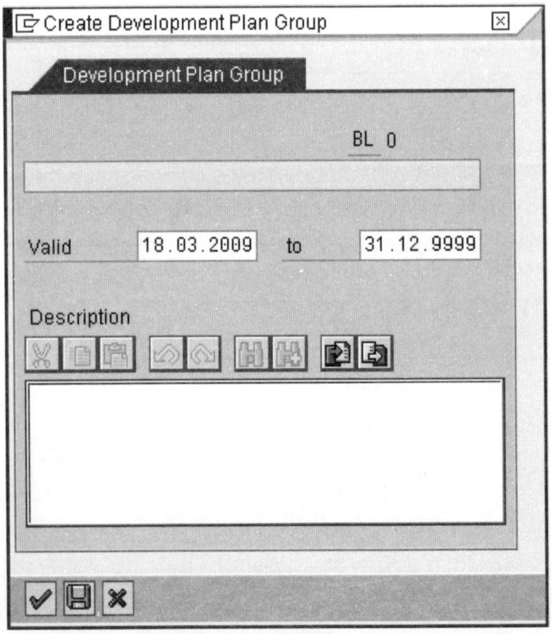

### 26.3.4 Development Plan

Having created the structure of the development plan catalog in the form of development plan groups, you create general development plans under the development plan group.

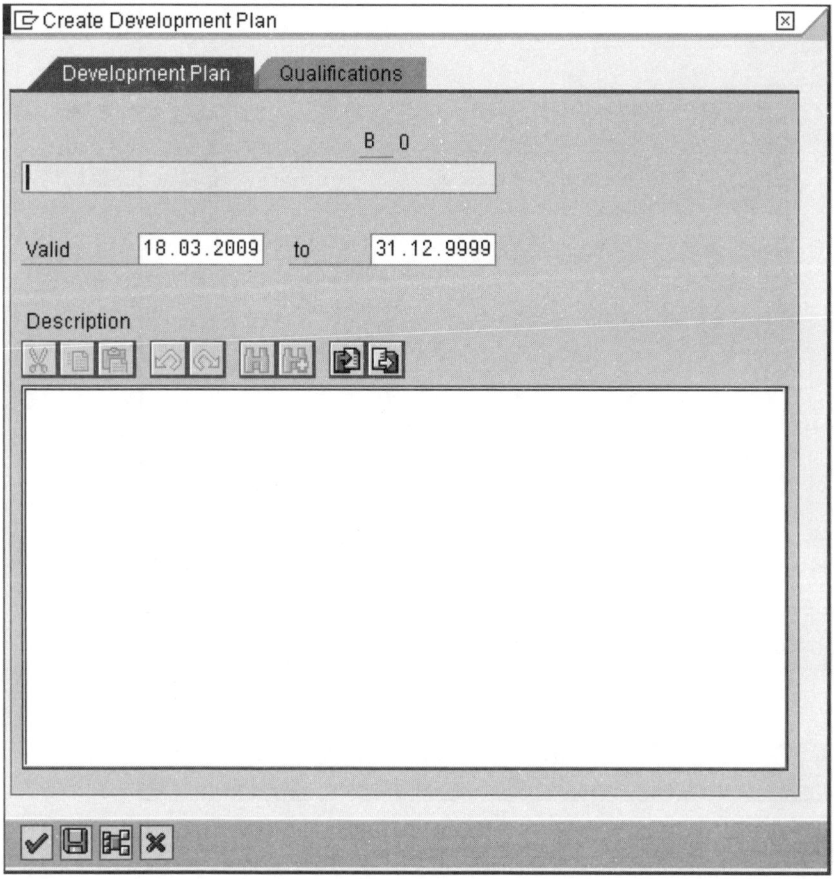


For a development plan also you specify a name, a description and a validity period. In addition, you can specify the qualifications which will be imparted if the development plan is completed, or completed successfully (in Development plan history subprofile).

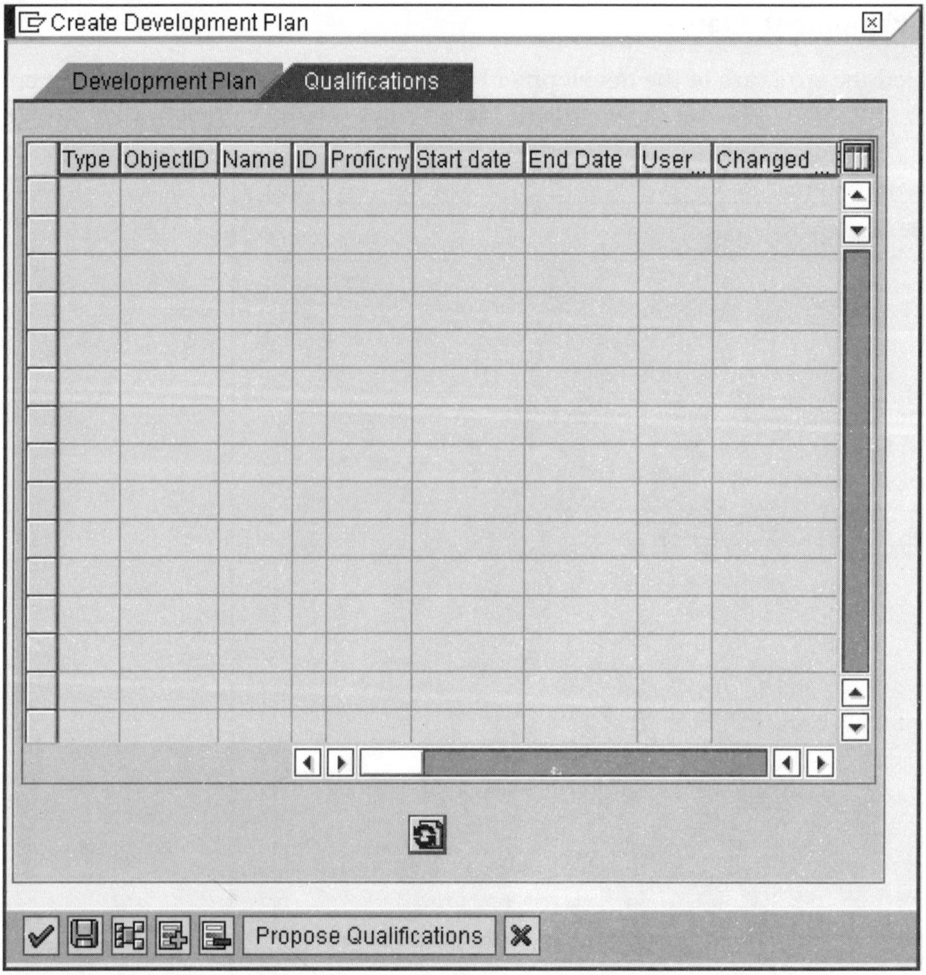


***Propose qualifications***

You can specify which qualifications should be imparted upon completion of a general development plan. You can have the system propose qualifications to help you here. In this case, the system proposes all the qualifications or requirements (including proficiencies) that are related to the individual items in the development plan. For example, if a position is a development plan item, and if it requires English (proficiency Good), then English (proficiency 'Good') will be proposed by the system as the qualification to be imparted upon completion of the development plan. You can change the list of qualifications proposed by the system, in other words, you can delete qualifications, or add more qualifications. You can also change the proficiencies proposed for the qualifications.

## 26.3.5 Development Plan Catalog

The development plan catalog shows the hierarchy of development plan groups and development plans.

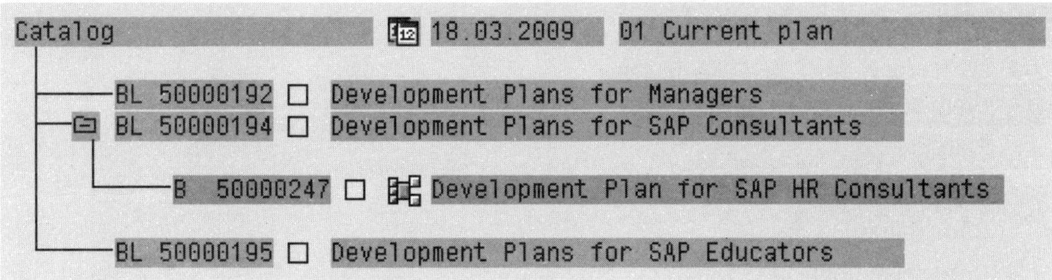


### 26.3.6 Development Plan Item

A development plan contains development plan items. You click [icon] to create items in the development plan. When you transfer development plan items from general development plan to individual development plan, you can specify whether you want to transfer only mandatory items or all items. Also, the system proposes an end date for the item in the individual development plan, computing it from the start date and the period specified here.

| Mandatory item | Obj.Type | Object ID | Object name | Years | Months | Days | Note | Details |
|---|---|---|---|---|---|---|---|---|
| ☑ | S | 50000079 | SAP HR Consultant | | 3 | | | |

## 26.4 DEVELOPMENT PLAN STATES

| *Functional Consultant* | *User* | *Business Process Owner* | *Senior Management* | *My Rating* | *Understanding Level* |
|---|---|---|---|---|---|
| A | B | B | C | | |

### 26.4.1 Purpose

The development plan items may have several states, e.g. planned, completed, etc. The state represents the current progress made in a development measure. States have to be assigned and updated manually for individual development plan items. In some cases, they may also be updated automatically. Here you define the master list of states you want to have in your organization.

### 26.4.2 IMG Node

SM30 ➢ T77BZ

### 26.4.3 Screen

| State | State of Development |
|---|---|
| 1 | Planned |
| 2 | Current |
| 3 | Completed |
| 4 | Completed unsuccessfully |
| 5 | Completed successfully |
| 6 | Not carried out |

### 26.4.4 Primary Key

State of Development Plan

## 26.5 PERMISSIBLE FURTHER PROCESSING

| *Functional Consultant* | *User* | *Business Process Owner* | *Senior Management* | *My Rating* | *Understanding Level* |
|---|---|---|---|---|---|
| A | B | C | C | | |

### 26.5.1 Purpose

When the state of a development plan item changes, the system can trigger further processing which is defined in view T77BX. Here you define the master list of further processing steps which will be available for selection in view T77BX.

### 26.5.2 IMG Node

SM30 ➢ T77FUNC

### 26.5.3 Screen

| Where-Used | Funct.Name | Short Text |
|---|---|---|
| DP Status | RHPQ_T77BX_ | "Add Qualifications Imparted by Development Plan" |
| DP Status | RHPQ_T77BX_ | Book attendance |
| DP Status | RHPQ_T77BX_ | Book attendance (in background) |
| DP Status | RHPQ_T77BX_ | Function "Assign Person as Holder of Position" |
| DP Status | RHPQ_T77BX_ | Function "Perform Appraisal" |

### 26.5.4 Primary Key

Type of Use for Function Module + Name of Function Module

## 26.6 FURTHER PROCESSING OF DEVELOPMENT PLAN ITEMS

| *Functional Consultant* | *User* | *Business Process Owner* | *Senior Management* | *My Rating* | *Understanding Level* |
|---|---|---|---|---|---|
| A | B | C | C | | |

### 26.6.1 Purpose

Here you can define the further processing steps that can be triggered when a certain state is assigned to a development plan item of a certain object type.

| *Object type* | *State* | *Further processing* |
|---|---|---|
| Development plan | Completed successfully | The qualifications imparted by the development plan are written to the person's qualifications profile. |
| Appraisal model | Current | Perform appraisal function can be triggered by function module RHPQ_T77BX_START_APPRAISAL. This function module is available, but the table does not contain this entry. |
| Business event type | Current | The standard entry calls function module RHPQ_T77BX_PARTICIPATION_INS which books the person for the business event of that type. If you want, you can call function module RHPQ_T77BX_PART_INS_NO_DIALOG, which books the person for the business event of that type without user confirmation. |
| Position | Current | The person is transferred to the specified position. |

The standard system contains the entries given above. However, you can also define further processing steps of your own. To help you do this, the standard system provides function module RHPQ_T77BX_INTERFACE_SAMPLE, which contains information on the interfaces, and can be used as a template to copy from.

### 26.6.2 IMG Node

SM30 ➢ T77BX

### 26.6.3 Screen

| OT | State | Further processing module |
|---|---|---|
| B | 5 | RHPQ_T77BX_ADD_QUALIS_OF_DPLAN |
| S | 2 | RHPQ_T77BX_SET_PERS_TO_POS |
| D | 2 | RHPQ_T77BX_PARTICIPATION_INS |

### 26.6.4 Primary Key

Object Type + State of Development Plan + Function Module for further Processing in Dev. Plan

### 26.6.5 Confirmation of Further Processing Step

SAP lets you specify whether users have to confirm execution of a further processing module, or whether it should be executed entirely in the background. If you enter the value 'X' for the following entry in table T77S0, the users will have to confirm the further processing step.

| Group | Sem. abbr. | Value abbr. | Description |
|---|---|---|---|
| DPLAN | CONFS | X | Individual planning: confirm further processing |

## 26.7 AUTOMATIC STATE MANAGEMENT

| *Functional Consultant* | *User* | *Business Process Owner* | *Senior Management* | *My Rating* | *Understanding Level* |
|---|---|---|---|---|---|
| A | B | C | C | | |

### 26.7.1 Purpose

In certain cases, it is possible for the system to automatically change the state of a development plan item on the basis of predefined events for particular object types. For example, a person is transferred to a position as a development measure and the state of the development plan item is set to Current. When the person has completed the development plan item, he is transferred to his original position. The transfer triggers the event S_OLD "Holder leaves position", and this sets the item in the person's individual development plan to Completed. Note that the change of state does not depend on the validity date of development plan items.

## 26.7.2 IMG Node

SM30 ➢ T77BW

## 26.7.3 Screen

| State key | Actv. | Original | Target st. | Text |
|---|---|---|---|---|
| APPR_HISTO | ☑ | | 3 | Create Historical Record for/Complete Appraisal |
| EVENT_BOOK | ☑ | 1 | 2 | Book Business Event Attendance |
| EVENT_FIN | ☑ | 2 | 3 | Business Event Follow-Up Processing |
| EVENT_STOR | ☑ | 2 | 1 | Cancel Business Event Attendance |
| S_DEL | ☑ | | 6 | Staffing assignment for position was deleted |
| S_NEW | ☑ | 1 | 2 | Position is restaffed |
| S_OLD | ☑ | 2 | 3 | Holder leaves position |

## 26.7.4 Primary Key

Development Plan: State Key

## 26.7.5 Important Fields

***State key and text***

In this field, you enter the event that is to trigger a change in the state of an item.

***Active***

If you do not wish to use certain events, do not delete them—deactivate them instead.

***Original state***

Here you enter the state that the item must have when the event occurs.

***Target state***

Here you enter the new state to be assigned to the item when the event occurs.

## 26.8 DISPLAY OF BUSINESS EVENTS IN INDIVIDUAL DEVELOPMENT PLANS

| *Functional Consultant* | *User* | *Business Process Owner* | *Senior Management* | *My Rating* | *Understanding Level* |
|---|---|---|---|---|---|
| A | B | C | C | | |

If you have an individual development plan for a person, he should be attending only those training programs which are in his individual development plan. But if he is booked for a training program, which is not in his individual development plan, what should the system do? If you want the system to show that training program in his individual development plan, you set the following switch in table T77S0 to 1. If you don't want the system to show the training programs which are not included in the individual development plan, you set this switch to 0.

| Group | Sem. abbr. | Value abbr. | Description |
|---|---|---|---|
| DPLAN | SIMU | 1 | Display bus. event part. in individ. develop. plan |

If the above switch is set to 1 and the business event for which the employee is booked is written in his development plan, what should be the state of that development plan item? You specify that state in the system switch given below.

| Group | Sem. abbr. | Value abbr. | Description |
|---|---|---|---|
| DPLAN | TSTAT | 3 | Individual planning:status after course attendance |

# CHAPTER 27

# Appraisals

## 27.1 APPRAISAL

| *Functional Consultant* | *User* | *Business Process Owner* | *Senior Management* | *My Rating* | *Understanding Level* |
|---|---|---|---|---|---|
| A | A | A | A | | |

SAP had an old 'Appraisal Systems', which has been replaced by 'Objective Setting and Appraisals'. Although the old system also works, this book deals only with the new system. You have to specify whether you want to use the old system or the new system in the following switch.

| Group | Sem.abbr. | Value abbr | Description |
|---|---|---|---|
| HAP00 | REPLA | A | Replace Old Appraisal System with New |

You can create appraisals in a person's profile using transaction PPPM. In subprofile for an object type (view V_T77PR_V_H_P, chapter 24.10), you should activate the subprofiles related to objective setting and appraisals which are for the new appraisal system and deactivate the subprofiles for the old appraisal system.

| | | |
|---|---|---|
| View | PD | Personnel development |
| Object Type | P | Person |

**Subprofile assignment**

| No | Sort | Active | Name |
|---|---|---|---|
| 1 | 1 | ☑ | Qualifications |
| 2 | 2 | ☑ | Potentials |
| 3 | 3 | ☑ | Preferences |
| 4 | 4 | ☑ | Dislikes |
| 5 | 5 | ☐ | Appraisals where appraisee |
| 6 | 6 | ☐ | Appraisals where appraiser |
| 8 | 7 | ☑ | Individual development |
| 9 | 8 | ☑ | Development plan history |
| 10 | 9 | ☑ | Qualification Block |
| 40 | 10 | ☑ | Objective Setting & Appraisals (Open) |
| 41 | 11 | ☑ | Objective Setting & Appraisals(Received) |
| 42 | 12 | ☑ | Objective Setting & Appraisals (Created) |

The Objective Setting and Appraisals (received) subprofile contains appraisals where the person was appraised. The Objective Setting and Appraisals (created) subprofile contains the appraisals where the person acted in the role of appraiser. You can also use this subprofile to create and edit appraisals.

You create appraisals using transaction APPCREATE or using transaction PPPM and selecting the tab 'Objective Setting & Appraisals (Open)'. Both transactions give the same user interface. When you run transaction PPPM, and select the tab 'Objective Setting & Appraisals (Open)', you will see the screen with all open appraisals. To create a new appraisal, you click and select the template you want to use for creating the appraisal.

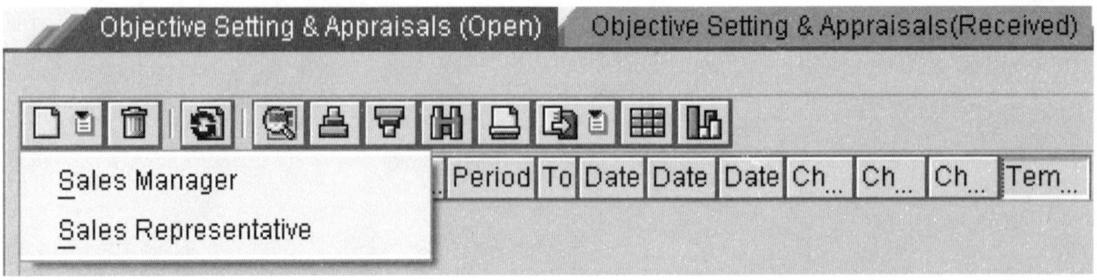

After selecting a template, you select the appraisee and the appraiser (during customizing the terms may have been changed to employee and manager, for example). You are in the preparation stage of the appraisal. You may like to save the data by clicking [End Preparation] and do objective setting later or proceed with [Set Objectives]. The system shows the appraisal form containing the header data and columns.

### *Header data*

| | | | |
|---|---|---|---|
| Objective Setting and Appr | Sales Manager | | |
| Appraisal Status | In Planning | | |
| Manager | Deval Milind | | |
| Employee | Kumar Ramesh | | |
| Reviewer | | | |
| Validity Period | 01.04.2008 | to | 31.03.2009 |
| Execution Period | | to | |
| Objective Setting Date | 25.02.2009 | | |
| Review Date | | | |

The header data contains the names of the appraisee and the appraiser. Validity period is the period for which appraisal is being done. Execution period is the period when appraisal will be done. If you do not wish some of these fields to be shown in the header, your consultant can hide them while defining the template.

### *Appraisal status*

During the appraisal process, at each stage the appraisal document has a status.

| Status / Substatus | Selected |
|---|---|
| In Preparation | ☑ |
| In Planning | ☑ |
| In Review | ☑ |
| ▽ In Process | ☑ |
| Part Appraisal in Process | ☐ |
| Completed | ☑ |
| Approved | ☑ |
| Closed Approved | ☑ |
| Rejected | ☑ |
| Closed Rejected | ☑ |

While defining the appraisal template, it is decided which status values are applicable to you and how the status is going to change.

### *Criteria*

The lower part of the template contains the criteria on which a person would be appraised. The criteria may be grouped in criteria groups, which may be grouped in further criteria groups. They are displayed in a numbered hierarchy. The system can be configured to display roman numbers or alphabet characters instead.

| Numbering | Element Name | Add Element | Delete Element |
|---|---|---|---|
| | Sales Manager | | |
| 1 | KPIs | | |
| 1.1 | Sales | | |
| 1.2 | New customers added | | |
| 1.3 | Enter a KPI | | |
| 2 | Company Initiatives | | |
| 2.1 | ISO 9000 | | |
| 2.2 | Six Sigma | | |
| 3 | Values & Personality | | |
| 3.1 | Excellence | | |
| 3.2 | Integrity | | |
| 3.3 | Communication | | |
| 3.4 | Leadership | | |

While defining the template, depending on your requirements, your consultant can specify whether a criterion can be deleted. If so, you will see the delete icon in the column 'Delete Element'. You can also add elements in certain criteria groups. In which criteria groups you can add criteria, and in which you can't, is defined by your consultant based on your requirements. These are displayed in the column 'Add Element'.

### *Scales*

Each criterion is evaluated on a scale defined in the template. The scales may be quantitative or qualitative. For qualitative scales you should ensure that the descriptions are meaningful for each criterion. If need be, get a scale defined for each criterion, rather than use scales with general descriptions. Also, even in qualitative scales, the values are numeric and they are used for computation. On a 1–5 qualitative scale, if actual is 1 and target is 5, the target is achieved 20%. Hence, you must ensure that the numbers assigned are representative.

### *Columns*

You set the target and enter actual values achieved for a criterion in columns. The columns are customized as per your requirement and typically include target, current value (actual achieved), final appraisal (actual/target), weighting of different criteria and weighted result (final appraisal multiplied by weighting). The scales on which these column values are measured are also displayed in separate columns. SAP also provides you facility to write notes. These are displayed as wherever notes are permitted.

| N... | Element Name | O... | Target | Curre... | C... | Final A... | Fi... | Weighting | W... | Weighted... |
|---|---|---|---|---|---|---|---|---|---|---|
| | Sales Manager | | | | | 77.60 | Perc | | | 77.600 |
| 1 | KPIs | | | | | 75.50 | Perc | 0.700 | | 52.850 |
| 1.1 | Sales | | 500.00 | 400.00 | | 80.00 | Perc | 80.00 | Perc | 6,400.000 |
| 1.2 | New customers added | | 20.000 | 10.000 | | 50.00 | Perc | 15.00 | Perc | 750.000 |
| 1.3 | Enter a KPI | | 10.000 | 8.000 | | 80.00 | Perc | 5.00 | Perc | 400.000 |
| 2 | Company Initiatives | | | | | 87.50 | Perc | 0.100 | | 8.750 |
| 2.1 | ISO 9000 | | 4 | 5 | | 100.00 | Perc | 1.00 | Perc | 100.000 |
| 2.2 | Six Sigma | | 4 | 3 | | 75.00 | Perc | 1.00 | Perc | 75.000 |
| 3 | Values & Personality | | | | | 80.00 | Perc | 0.200 | | 16.000 |
| 3.1 | Excellence | | 5 | 4 | | 80.00 | Perc | 1.00 | Perc | 80.000 |
| 3.2 | Integrity | | 5 | 4 | | 80.00 | Perc | 1.00 | Perc | 80.000 |
| 3.3 | Communication | | 5 | 3 | | 60.00 | Perc | 1.00 | Perc | 60.000 |
| 3.4 | Leadership | | 5 | 5 | | 100.00 | Perc | 1.00 | Perc | 100.000 |

In some of the columns, e.g. target, current value (actual), weighting (relative importance of criteria), you enter values. In some columns, e.g. final appraisal (actual/target), the value is computed. If for a criterion, computation is specified in a column but entry is also permitted, the system will compute the value which can be overwritten manually.

### *Status flow*

As the appraisal process progresses, the appraisal document goes through change of status. You may modify the appraisal using transaction PPPM or APPCHANGE. Depending on the status of the appraisal, the actions you perform would be different. Accordingly you will find different action icons on the screen, e.g. Complete.

## Appraisal Process and Status Processing

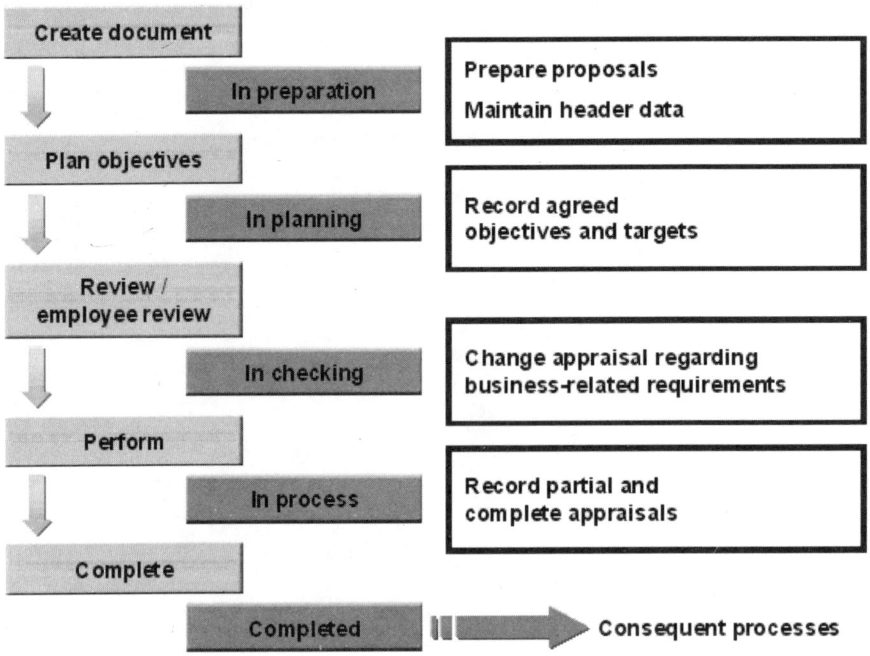


Further statuses can be added to the status specified above:

- Approved
- Rejected
- Finally approved
- Finally rejected

Further processing can be triggered using the workflow and can underlie an approval process, whereby, for instance, the employee accepts his or her own appraisal.

In this scenario, approval would trigger updation of qualifications, as well as adjustment of the compensation components.

### *Part appraisals*

You can have multiple part appraisals and a final appraisal based on the part appraisals.

### *Anonymous appraisals*

In the appraisal template, in processing tab, in template mode field, you can specify that appraisals are anonymous by choosing from the following options.

- Not anonymous
- Anonymous with registration
- Anonymous without registration
- Make anonymous when closing without registration
- Make anonymous when closing with registration

### *Workflow and appraisal subprofiles*

Appraisals may be implemented with or without workflow. If implemented without workflow, appraisals can be created in 'Objective Setting & Appraisals (Open)' tab of a person's profile. The appraisee sees the appraisals in 'Objective Setting & Appraisals (Received)' tab. Appraisers process them in 'Objective Setting & Appraisals (Created)' tab.

### *Appraisals related to training*

You can create appraisal templates for business events and attendees.

### *Appraisal approval*

A standard workflow is available for approving appraisals. Approval of appraisals is only possible with this workflow. Once an appraiser has held and completed an appraisal, the appraisal can be passed on to the appraisee for approval. The appraisee can view the appraisal, and decide whether he wishes to approve or reject the appraisal. If the appraisee rejects the appraisal, the appraisal is automatically put back in the status 'In process' so that the appraiser can review it.

### *Evaluate appraisal documents*

You can use transaction APPSEARCH to find appraisal documents as per the selection criteria you specify. You can display an appraisal document by clicking its hyperlink.

| N | App.Document Name | AppDoc... | Type | Name | Type | Appraisee | App. Stat |
|---|---|---|---|---|---|---|---|
| 1 | Sales Manager | Appraisal | Person | Deval Milind | Person | Kumar Ramesh | Completed |
| 1 | Business Event Appraisal | Appraisal | Person | Agrawal Prem | Course | SAP HR | Completed |
| 1 | Business Event Appraisal | Appraisal | Person | Agrawal Prem | Course | SAP HR | In Process |
| 1 | SAP HR Attendee Appraisal | Appraisal | Course | SAP HR | Person | Agrawal Prem | Completed |

## 27.2 APPRAISAL CATALOG

| *Functional Consultant* | *User* | *Business Process Owner* | *Senior Management* | *My Rating* | *Understanding Level* |
|---|---|---|---|---|---|
| A | A | A | A | | |

### *Appraisal customizing structure*

Appraisal documents are created based on the appraisal templates, which are defined by consultants according to customer requirements using transaction PHAP_CATALOG_PA, PPAD, OOAM or S_AHR_61003969. Appraisal customizing consists of the following nested elements.

Category group
- Category
  - Template
    - Criteria group
      - Criteria
      - Criteria
      - Criteria
    - Criteria group
    - Criteria group
  - Template

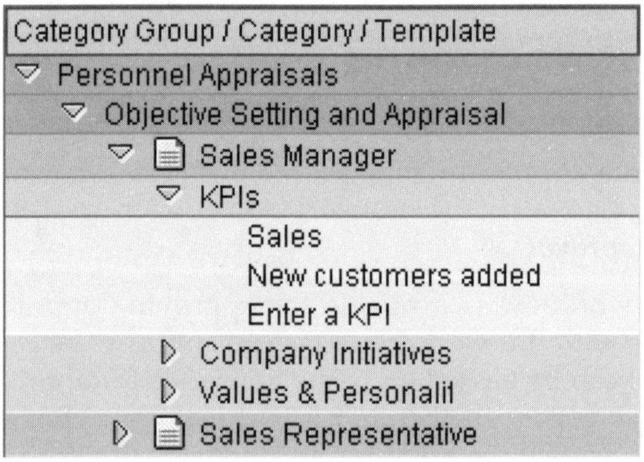


You can create different categories for different appraisal processes (for example, objective setting, 360 degree appraisals, standard appraisals, certificates of employment, and so on).

### *Category group, category*

Appraisal templates are grouped in categories, which are further grouped in category groups. Category groups are, in general, only created by System Administration. At the level of category group, the permissible object types are determined that are available in the forms. These object types are available for selection when you define participants in categories. Properties of category group and category apply to all appraisal templates under them. Category group and category can be used for authorization control, as these fields are available in authorization object P_HAP_DOC.

### *Template*

You create appraisal templates for groups of people who need to be appraised in a similar manner. For example, they may have the same set of criteria, and you may not want the participants in the appraisal process to delete any criteria. Planning of appraisal templates for an organization should be done very carefully. One strategy is to create few templates, each containing large number of criteria. In this scenario, the person setting the objectives will delete the criteria not applicable to the appraisee. Some organizations, on the other hand, may have well defined job roles and fixed set of criteria for each job role. These organizations may prefer to have well defined job role based appraisal templates. Template can be used for authorization control, as this field is available in authorization object P_HAP_DOC.

### *Criteria group*

Criteria are grouped in criteria groups, so that the appraisal document is well structured. Criteria groups can be grouped in further criteria groups creating a tree structure. Criteria numbering reflects this multi-level organization. Criteria groups can be sorted in the desired order and they can be given different weightings which are taken into account while computing final appraisal rating.

### *Criteria*

A person is appraised based on pre-defined criteria. Each criterion has a scale which may be quantitative or qualitative. For each criterion, final appraisal value is computed which is rolled up to generate the final appraisal of the person. Criteria can also be sorted and weighed. You can also use qualification or business event type as a criterion in the appraisal template. When you insert a node in a criteria group, you can choose to insert qualification or business event type.

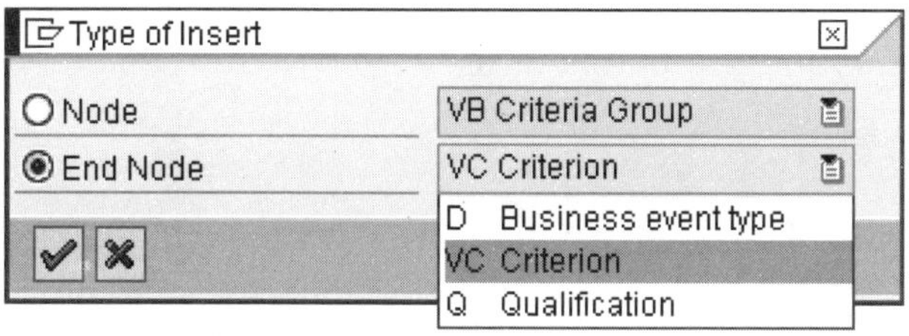


Since you can use qualification as an appraisal criterion, you can also use qualification group in place of criteria group.

### *Creating templates*

You can create appraisal templates in the following ways.

- Using example form
- Using wizard
- By uploading
- By creating manually

### *Releasing templates*

After defining a template, it is released. Only then it is available for the appraisal process. If you want to change a released template, you can cancel release, provided that it has not been used to create any appraisal document. You can archive templates that you no longer want, since these cannot be deleted.

### Using template versions

After an appraisal template has been used, you may need to modify it before next appraisal cycle. SAP does not permit modification of appraisal templates after they have been used. So, you have to archive it and create another one. SAP identifies the appraisal template by its object id, and not by its name. It is, therefore, possible to create another appraisal template whose name is the same as that of an existing template (the screenshot below has two templates using the same name, 'Sales Manager'). This will not create any problem for the users because they will see only released templates and not the archived templates. But it may present a problem to the maintenance persons, who would see two templates with the same name in customizing, without any visible sign that one is released and another is archived. You should avoid having two released appraisal templates with the same name, as the users will not know which template to use and may use the wrong one.

| Category Group / Category / Template | Element Key |
|---|---|
| ▽ Personnel Appraisals | |
| ▽ Objective Setting and Appraisal | |
| ▷ Sales Manager | VA 50000225 |
| ▷ Sales Manager | VA 50000241 |
| ▷ Sales Representative | VA 50000196 |

In order to avoid such confusion you may suffix the template name by version number (e.g. v1, v2 or 2008, 2009). Otherwise, maintenance persons have to know that if multiple appraisal templates have the same name, the last one is in use.

### Copying and inserting

If you are defining a number of templates, you may like to create them by copying and changing. SAP lets you copy template, criteria group and criteria to clipboard and insert from clipboard. When you copy template or criteria group to clipboard, the entire substructure gets copied, and when you insert, the entire substructure gets inserted. In this process a copy of all the objects is created. Increasing the objects in this manner is undesirable from the maintenance point of view. It is okay to copy and insert a criterion to create another criterion with similar attributes. But, don't copy and insert templates or criteria groups. Instead, create template or criteria group and add lower level objects by right-clicking and selecting Insert ➢ Existing Element.

### Where used

If you use an appraisal element in multiple templates, changing it will change its behavior in all the places where it is used. Therefore, before changing an appraisal element, right-click and select Where-Used List to determine whether it is safe to change an appraisal element or you should create a new one instead.

### Master template

If you are going to use multiple templates, it is better to maintain a master template in which you define all the criteria in appropriate criteria groups. Whenever you need a new criterion, you should define it in master template and use in other templates. This will prevent proliferation of criteria. You also need to standardize their attributes and behavior. Unless this is done, different individuals will define the same criterion in multiple ways. This will result in proliferation of criteria and other appraisal elements leading to a maintenance nightmare.

***Translation***

You can enter language-specific texts in multiple languages using translation function.

***Appraisal authorization***

You can control authorization of appraisal documents using authorization object P_HAP_DOC. In this authorization object, you can also specify authorization profile which restricts your authorization to the specified part of the organizational structure. If you use substitution of managers, you need to maintain the following entry in table T77S0. Then you can give different authorization to an employee for an area where he is a manager, and different authorization for area where he is substituting for the manager of that area.

| Group | Sem.abbr. | Value abbr | Description |
|---|---|---|---|
| HAP00 | AUTHO | | Activate Extended Authorization Check |

## 27.3 APPRAISAL CATEGORY GROUP

| *Functional Consultant* | *User* | *Business Process Owner* | *Senior Management* | *My Rating* | *Understanding Level* |
|---|---|---|---|---|---|
| A | X | X | X | | |

### 27.3.1 Allowed Object Types

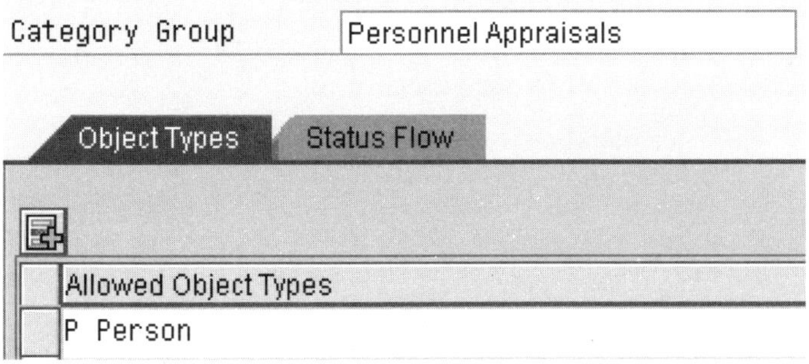


Here you can enter the type of objects that participate in the appraisal process. When you define participants at category level, you can choose from these object types.

### 27.3.2 Status

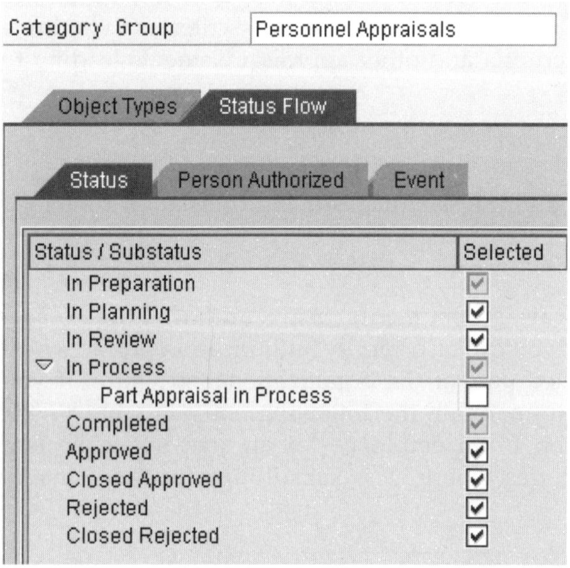


During the appraisal process, an appraisal can have different statuses. Here you specify the status values that will be available for selection. These may be further restricted at category level.

### 27.3.3 Person Authorized

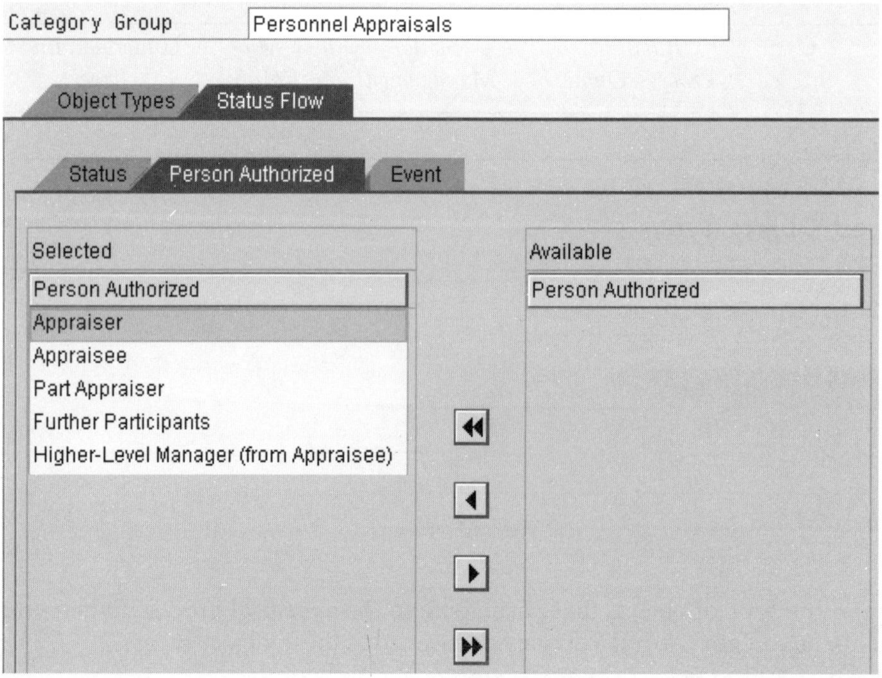

Here you specify the roles that persons are going to play in the appraisal process. For example, if you are not going to have part appraisals, you may not select 'Part Appraiser'. These may be further restricted at category level.

### 27.3.4 Event

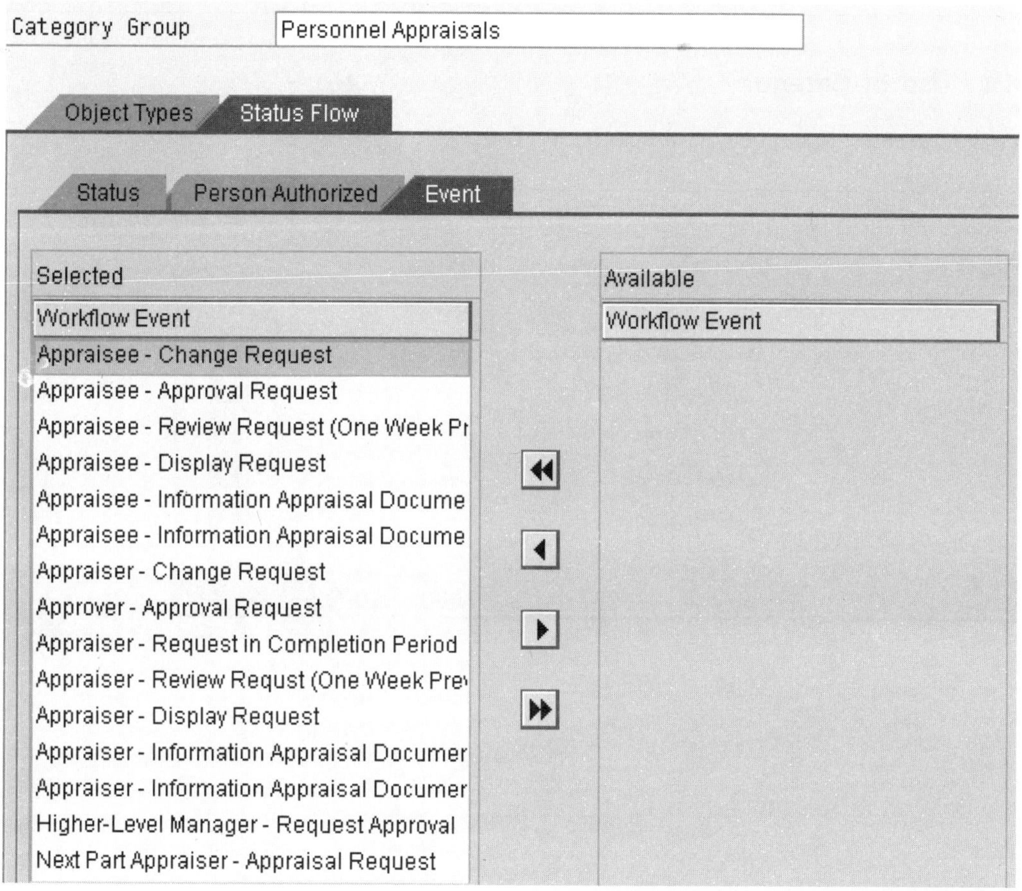


Here you specify the events that are applicable to your appraisal process when you use workflow. These may be further restricted at category level.

## 27.4 APPRAISAL CATEGORY

| *Functional Consultant* | *User* | *Business Process Owner* | *Senior Management* | *My Rating* | *Understanding Level* |
|---|---|---|---|---|---|
| A | X | X | X | | |

### 27.4.1 Use of Category

When you create a category, you specify its use.

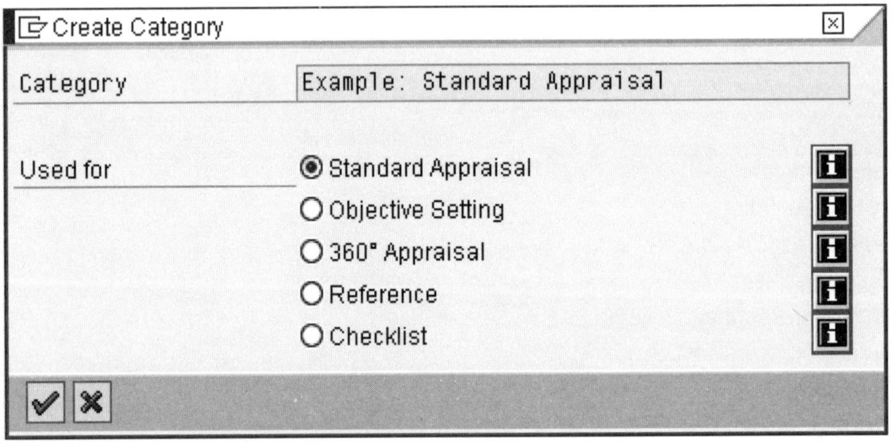

## 27.4.2 Participants

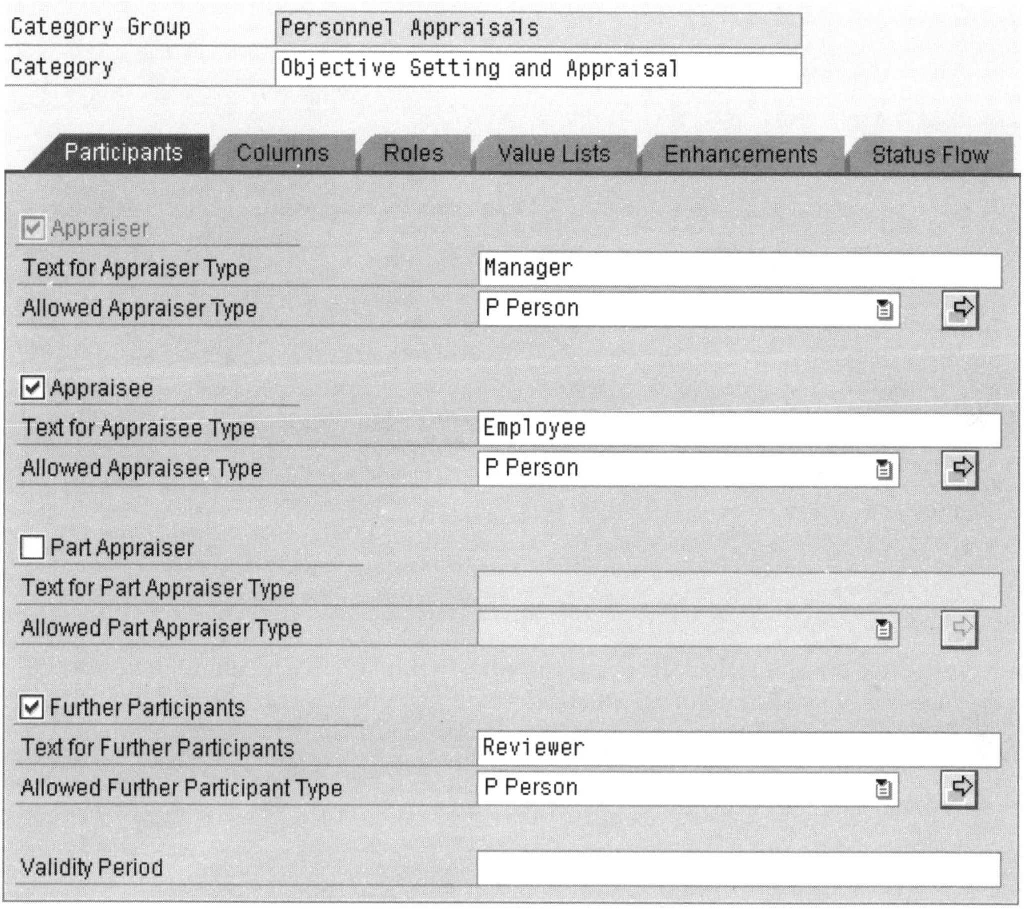


Here you specify the participants in the appraisal process, their object types and texts. If you would like to use the word employee in place of appraisee, or manager in place of appraiser, you may enter that here. Similarly, the appraisal header contains a field, validity period. If you do not like that term and would like to call it 'Appraisal Period', or 'Period Appraised', you may enter that here. If you do not specify any text, the system will use the text, 'Validity Period'. When an appraisal document is created, you specify the appraisee, the appraiser, etc. This information is displayed in the header of the appraisal document.

### 27.4.3 Columns

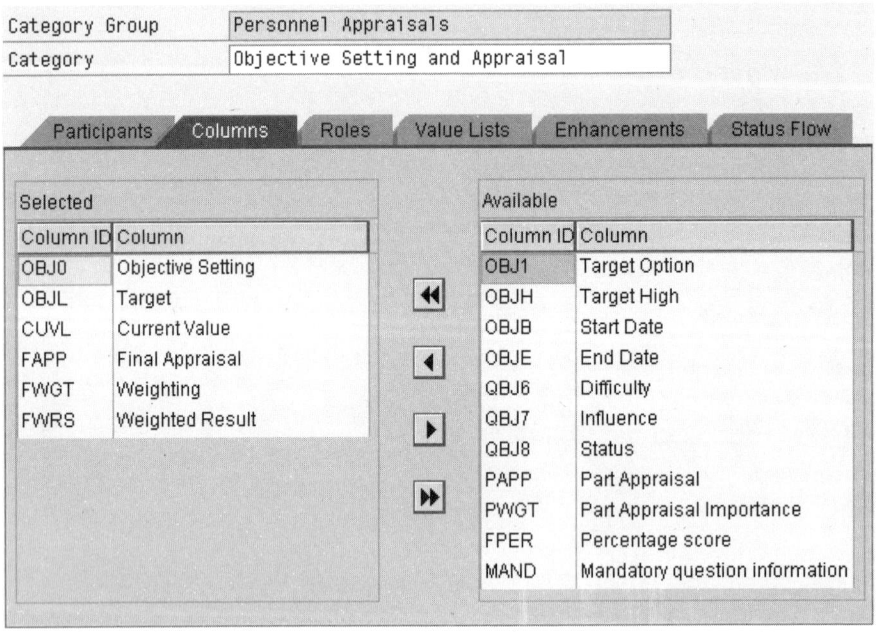


Here you specify the columns used in the appraisal template. Each column has a specific purpose. Customer-specific columns can be defined using transaction OOHAP_BASIC. In the template, you specify the columns that will appear in the appraisal document.

### 27.4.4 Roles

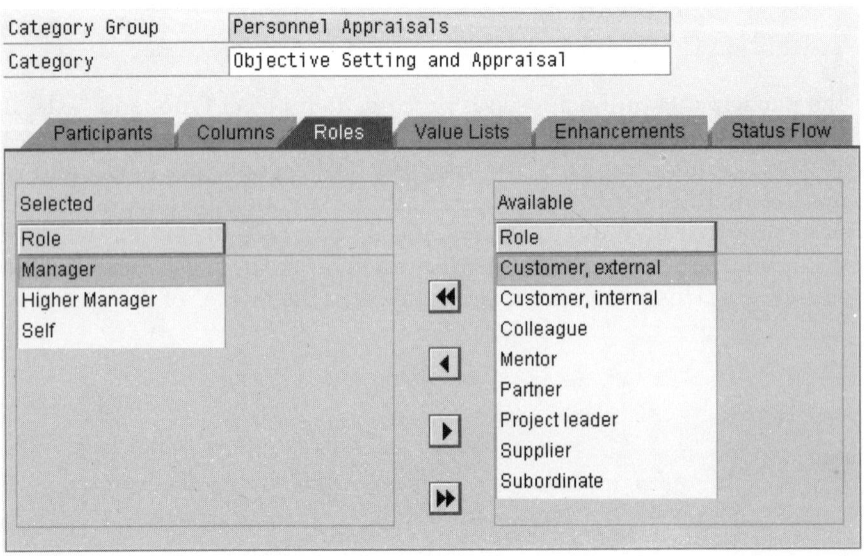

Here you specify the roles in the appraisal process. Customer-specific roles can be defined using transaction OOHAP_BASIC. Note that there is no link between the roles of Objective Setting and Appraisals and the role concept delivered by SAP.

### 27.4.5 Value Lists

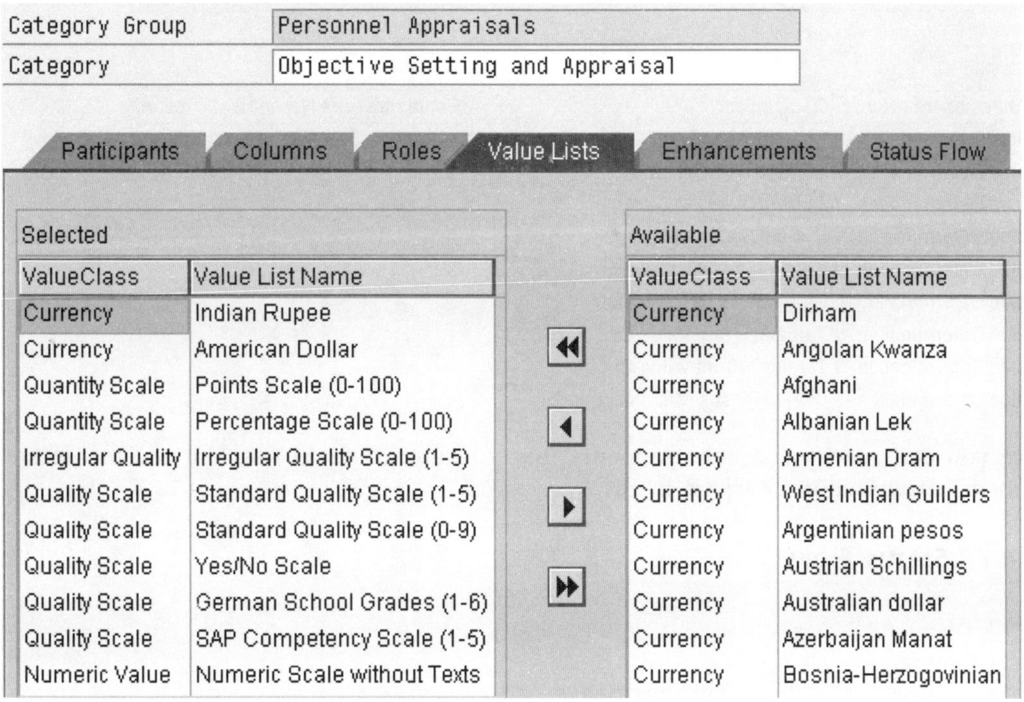


Here you specify the scales and currencies you are going to use. You may define scales using SM34 ➢ VC_T77SK. If you want to define any other type of value list, you may use transaction OOHAP_BASIC. In the template, value lists are associated with columns.

### 27.4.6 Enhancements

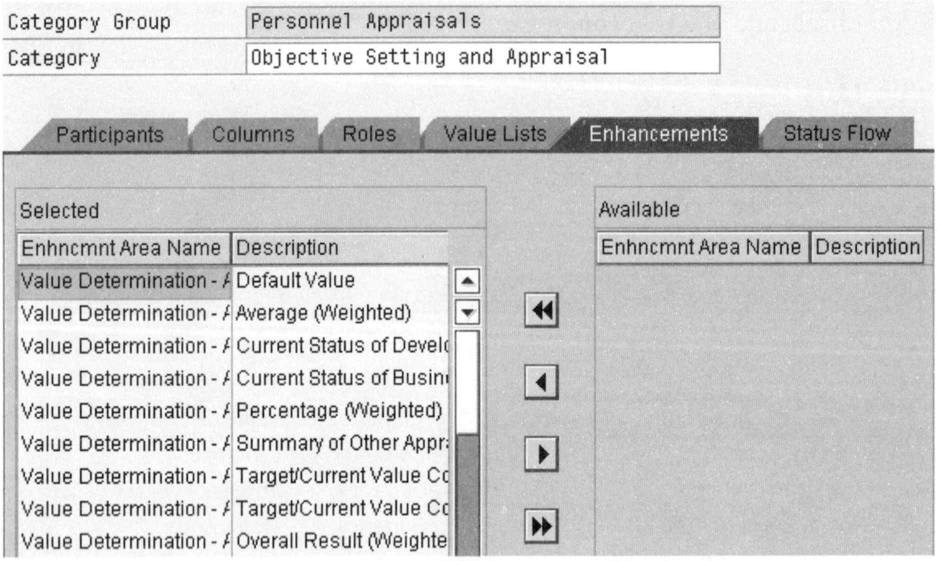


Here you can specify the enhancements that you are going to use. Enhancements are defined in transaction OOHAP_BASIC.

### 27.4.7 Status Flow

#### *Status*

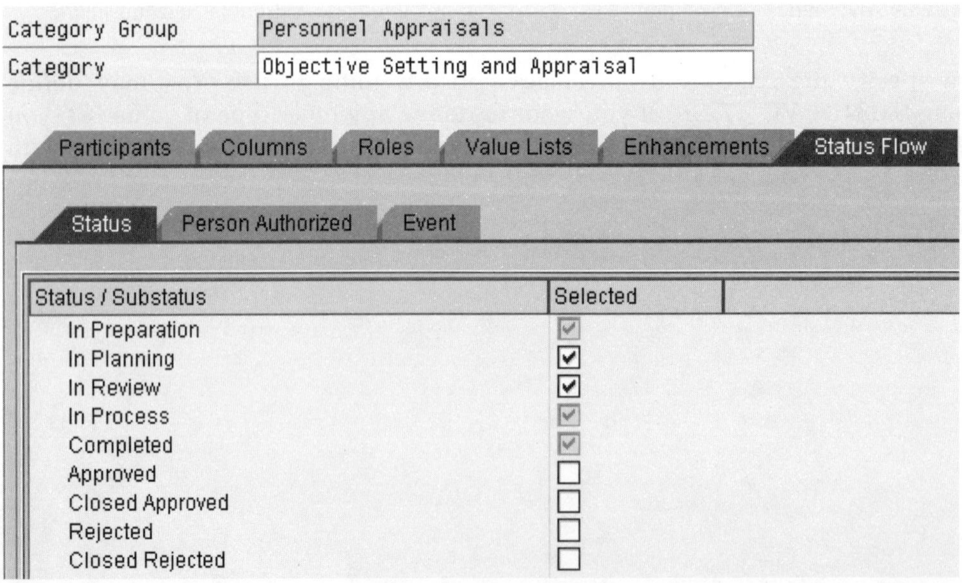


Here you can further restrict the status values used in the appraisal process for this category.

### *Persons authorized*

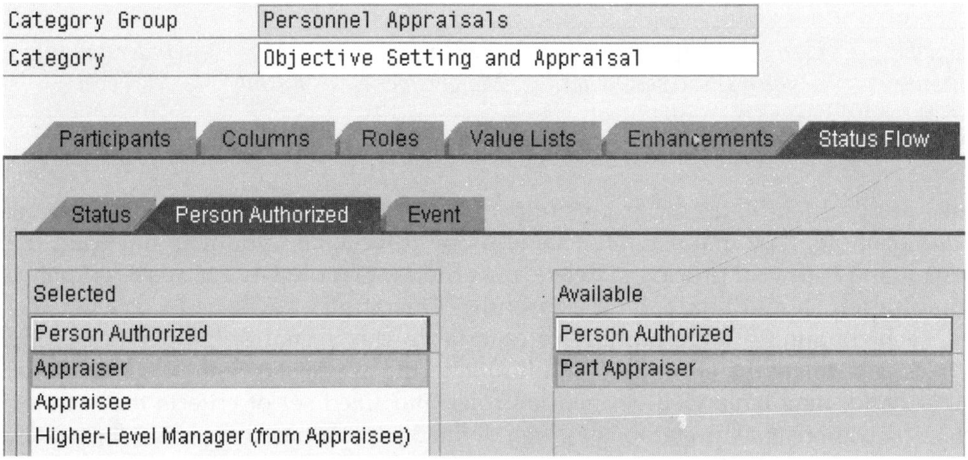


Here you can further restrict the authorized persons.

### *Event*

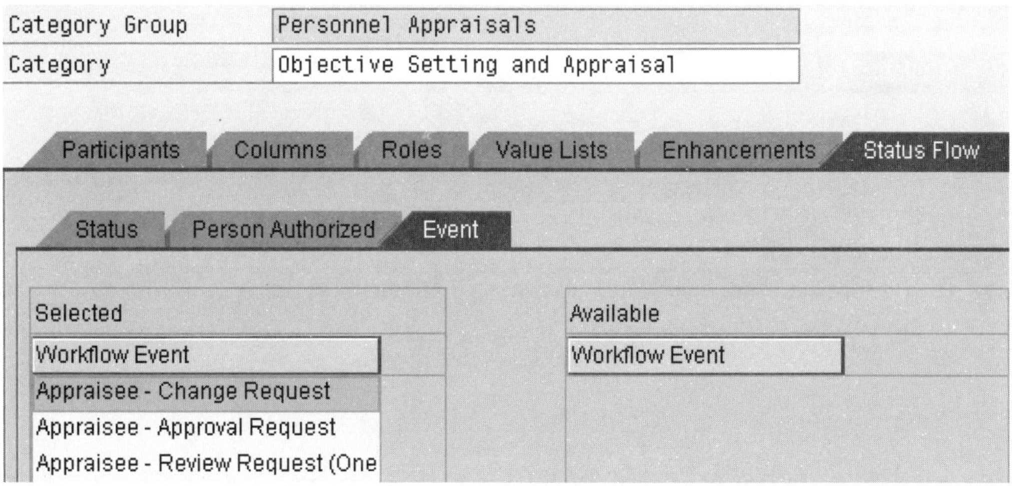


Here you can further restrict the workflow events.

## 27.5 APPRAISAL TEMPLATE

| *Functional Consultant* | *User* | *Business Process Owner* | *Senior Management* | *My Rating* | *Understanding Level* |
|---|---|---|---|---|---|
| A | X | X | X | | |

You create appraisal templates for groups of people who are to be appraised in a similar fashion. For example, they may have the same set of criteria, and you may not want the participants in the appraisal process to delete any criteria. Planning of appraisal templates for an organization should be done very carefully. One strategy will be to create a few templates, each containing large number of criteria. In this scenario, the person setting the objectives will delete the criteria not applicable to the appraisee. Some organizations, on the other hand, may have well defined job roles and fixed set of criteria for each job role. Such organizations may prefer to have well defined job role based appraisal templates. In such cases, you may like to create a master template to control creation of criteria. An appraisal template has a name. It belongs to a category group and category, whose properties apply to the appraisal template. An appraisal template has the following properties.

### 27.5.1 Description

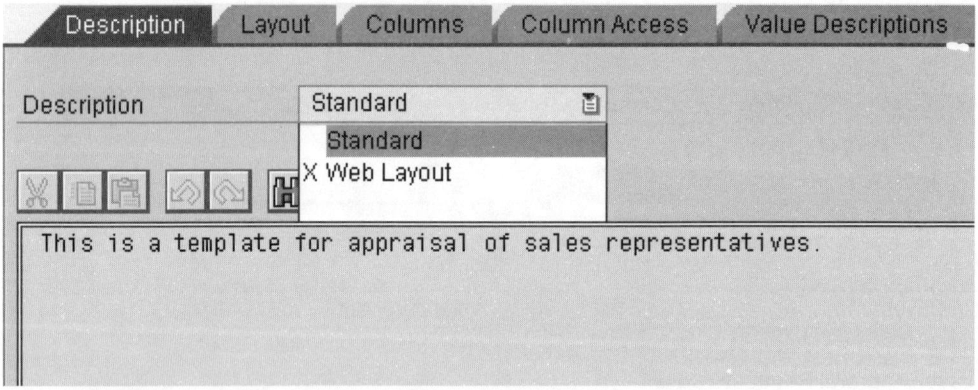


You can maintain both 'Standard' and 'Web Layout' descriptions of a template. Standard description is used in the ECC environment and web layout description is used in the web environment. Alternatively, you can maintain only 'Standard' description which is then used in both the environments.

## 27.5.2 Layout

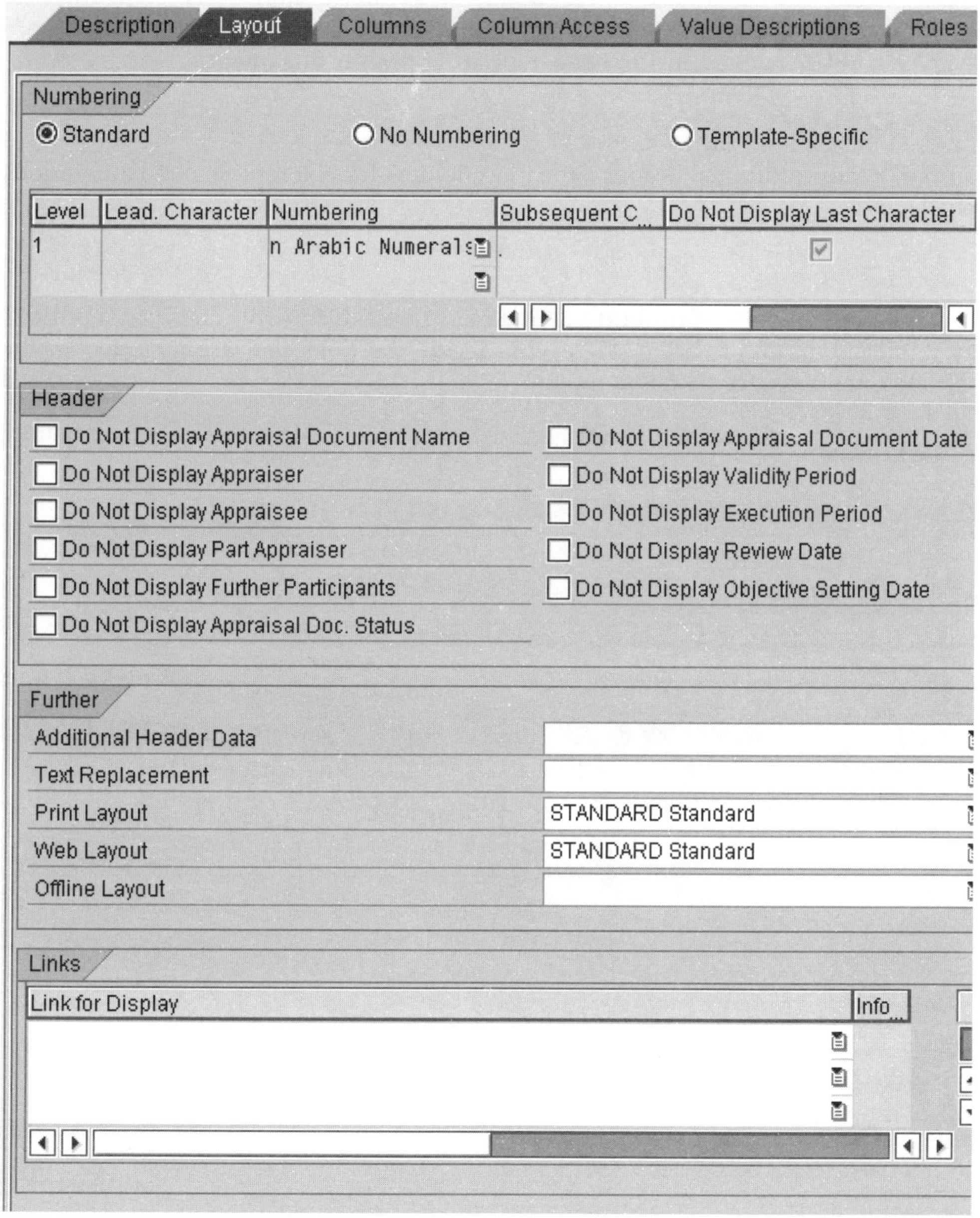


Here you define the layout of the appraisal document based on this template.

***Numbering***

An appraisal document has criteria which are grouped in one or more levels of criteria groups. These criteria are numbered. Here you can define the style of criteria numbering.

#### *Header*

An appraisal document has a header with a variety of information. Some companies do not want to display some of this data in the appraisal document. Here you can specify the data that is not displayed in the header of an appraisal document.

#### *Further*

Here you can specify additional header data, placeholders for text replacement and various document layouts.

#### *Links*

You can display a number of pushbuttons in an appraisal document. These pushbuttons are links to additional information. Here you decide the links that are included in the appraisal documents based on this template.

## 27.5.3 Columns

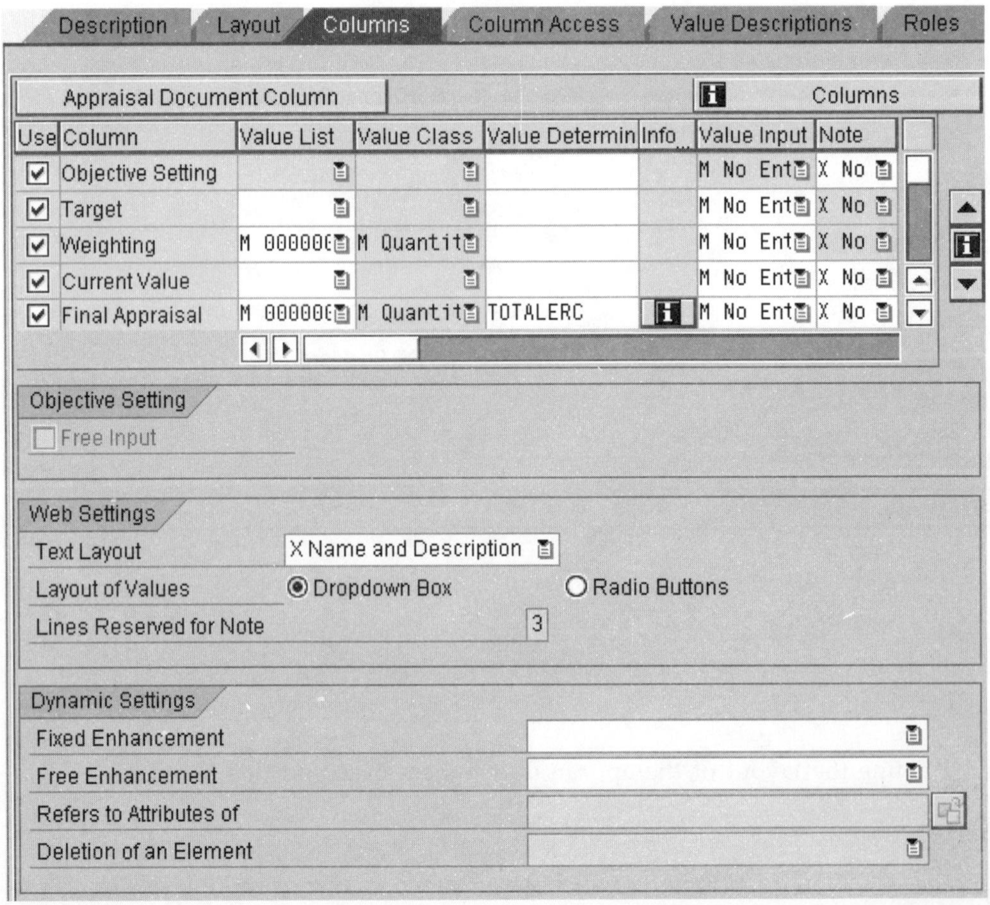

At the category level you define the columns that are available. Here you specify

- The columns that will appear in the appraisal document
- The sequence in which the columns will appear
- The value list for a column where applicable
- Value determination logic for a column where applicable
- Whether entry is optional, required, or not permitted
- Whether notes can be stored, for example, to explain the current/actual value

### 27.5.4 Column Access

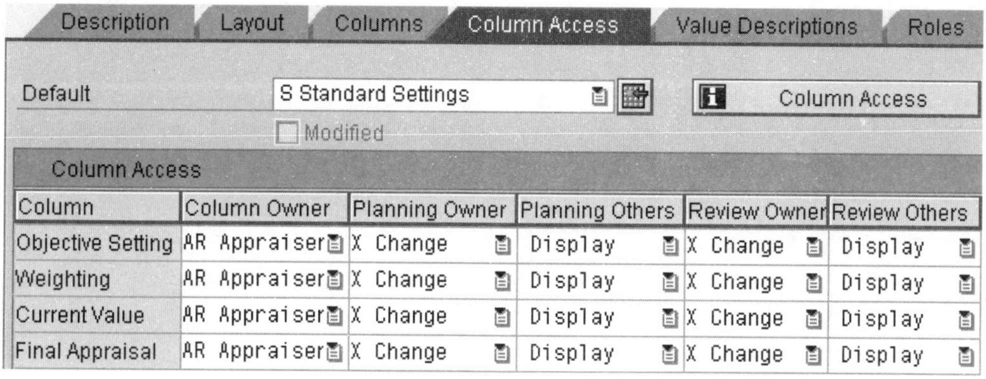


| Column | Column Owner | Planning Owner | Planning Others | Review Owner | Review Others |
|---|---|---|---|---|---|
| Objective Setting | AR Appraiser | X Change | Display | X Change | Display |
| Weighting | AR Appraiser | X Change | Display | X Change | Display |
| Current Value | AR Appraiser | X Change | Display | X Change | Display |
| Final Appraisal | AR Appraiser | X Change | Display | X Change | Display |

You can define which roles (for example, employees or managers) involved in the appraisal process can access which columns during a particular phase of the appraisal process. You can choose from various default settings, or specify your own. The roles involved in the appraisal process can either be the owner of a column, or another user (abbreviation: other). You can define the type of column access (for example, change access) for owners and others, for each process phase. During the runtime, the system checks the attribute assignment of the column access depending on the current status of the appraisal. As soon as an appraisal has the status completed or greater, the system always displays all columns.

### 27.5.5 Value Descriptions

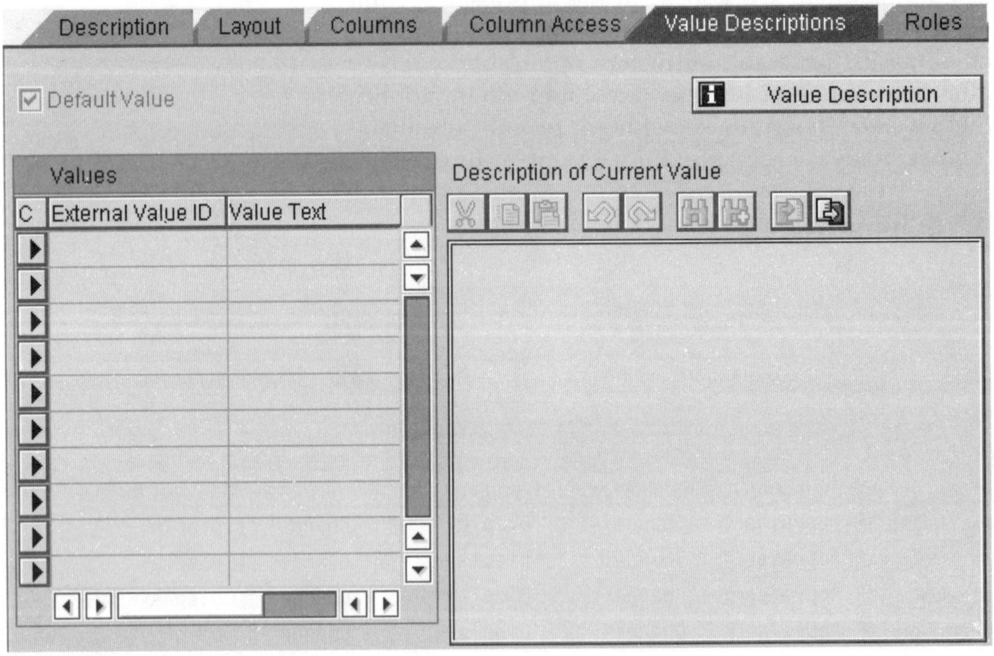


For the Final Appraisal column, you specify a value list. Here you can specify a description for each value in the value list.

### 27.5.6 Roles

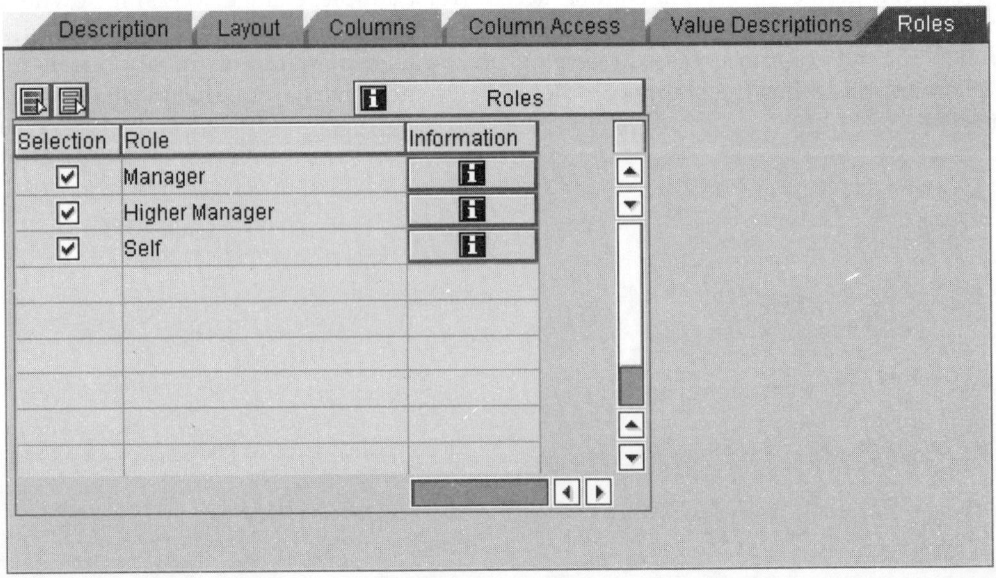

Roles reflect the relationship between the appraisee and other persons involved in the appraisal process. The roles are used for the following purposes.

| *Purpose* | *Description* |
|---|---|
| To prepare appraisal documents | For the proposal of the corresponding appraiser or appraisee. |
| To clarify the role of the part appraisers for the appraisee | A role can be assigned to part appraisers. You can allocate this role specifically in the SAP system, or the SAP system can determine it automatically. To determine a role, the system uses a BAdI implementation for the role in question (for example, it can determine the appraisee's manager via the chief position in an organizational structure). |
| To control access authorizations on element level (Subappraisals) | At criteria group and criteria level you can specify which role has authorization for which criteria or criteria group. Thus, managers and colleagues can appraise an employee on different criteria in the same template. |

### 27.5.7 Processing

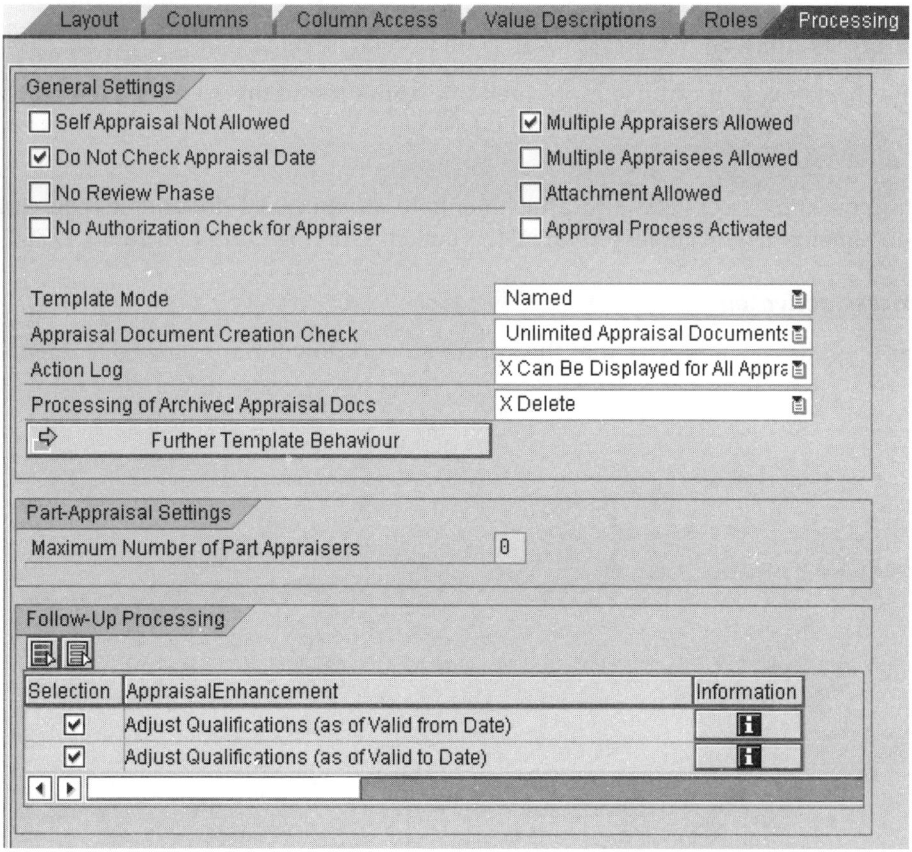

### *Self-appraisal not allowed*

If you tick this checkbox, a person cannot appraise himself, i.e. he cannot have the role of appraiser and appraisee at the same time.

### *Do not check appraisal date*

If you tick this checkbox, the system does not check the appraisal document date against the validity period of the appraisal document.

### *No review phase*

If you tick this checkbox, the status 'In Review' cannot be assigned to the appraisal document.

### *No authorization check for appraiser*

If you tick this checkbox, the system does not check an appraiser's authorizations when an appraisal document is called.

### *Multiple appraisers allowed*

If you tick this checkbox, you can use more than one appraiser in the appraisal document.

### *Multiple appraisees allowed*

If you tick this checkbox, you can use more than one appraisee in the appraisal template.

### *Attachment allowed*

If you tick this checkbox, users can add attachments to an appraisal document. You can only attach documents if you have activated the switch GENER OBJSV in table T77S0.

### *Approval process activated*

If you tick this checkbox, you specify that the approval workflow for appraisal documents is active.

### *Template mode*

You can specify one of the following modes for an appraisal template.

| *Mode* | *Description* | *Explanation* |
|---|---|---|
| Blank | Not anonymous | |
| R | Anonymous with registration | The administrator must register participants (appraisers). Only those participants, who are registered by an administrator, are authorized to participate. The administrator enters participants in a separate table so they are not associated with the actual appraisal document. |
| A | Anonymous without registration | Any user may participate in the appraisal. If the parameter 'Appraisal Document Creation Check' is set so that a participant may only participate in an appraisal once, an entry is still written to the anonymous registration table for these templates. This is to prevent participants from participating more than once. |
| C | Make anonymous when closing without registration | Users can temporarily store anonymous appraisal documents and continue editing them at a later point. The system only makes the template anonymous after users close the appraisal document so that users can no longer access it. |
| X | Make anonymous when closing with registration | The administrator must register participants (appraisers). Users can temporarily store anonymous appraisal documents and continue editing them at a later point. The system only makes the template anonymous after users close the appraisal document so that users can no longer access it. |

### *Appraisal document creation check*

Here you specify whether multiple appraisal documents can be created at the same time, or only one document can be created for an appraisee at a time. You may also specify that there can be one document per appraiser for an appraisee.

### *Action log*

You can specify that the action log is not activated, or is in summarized form, or is in detailed form. If created, the action log may be visible in the appraisal document, or it can only be analyzed using transaction SLG1.

### *Processing of archived appraisal docs*

Here you specify whether completed appraisal documents are reset or not, and deleted or not.

### *Further template behavior*

Here you can specify template enhancements for further behavior.

### *Maximum number of part appraisers*

If you have selected only the Part Appraiser (PAPP) and/or Importance Part Appraisal (PWGT) columns in an appraisal template, this is a 360° appraisal, and the system does not restrict the number of part appraisers allowed. If you select the Objective Setting (OBJ0) column or any other column, it is no longer a 360° appraisal, and the system restricts the number of part appraisers.

### *Follow-up processing*

These enhancements enable you to determine the functions that are available for users when they perform follow-up processing for an appraisal document. If an appraisal template contains qualifications, they can be transferred in the follow-up activities.

## 27.5.8 Status Flow

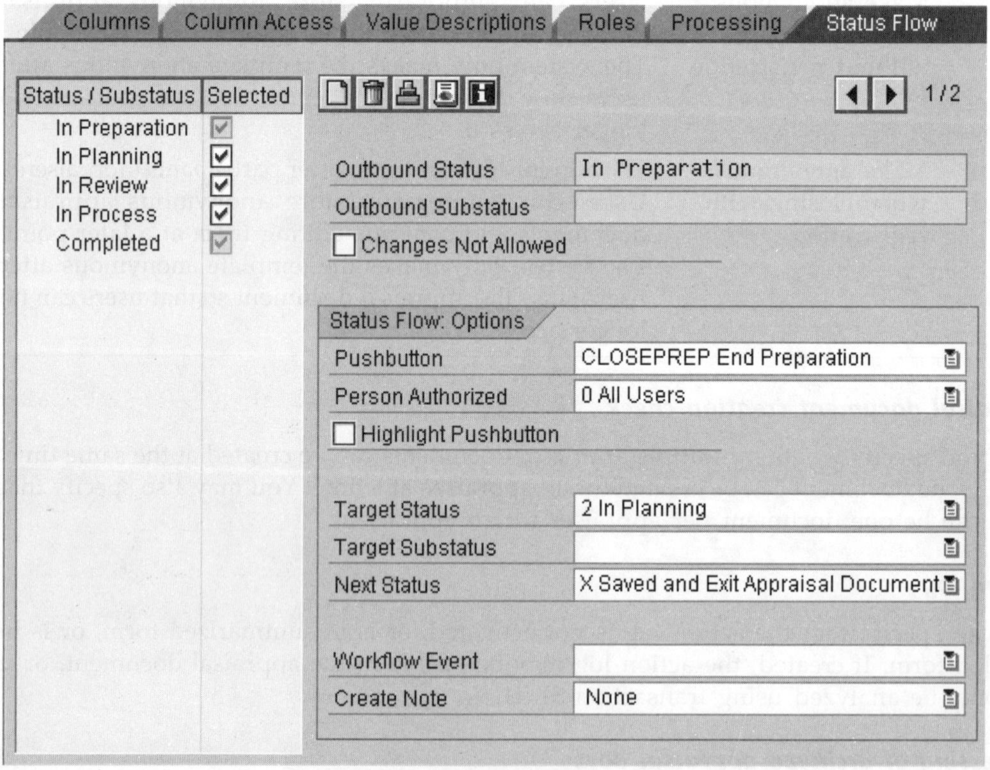


Here you specify the pushbuttons that will appear on the appraisal form depending on the status of the appraisal form. You can navigate to different buttons using the left and the right arrows in the top-right corner of the screen.

### Outbound status and substatus

When the status of the appraisal form matches the outbound status, the pushbuttons specified on this page are displayed on the appraisal form.

### Changes not allowed

This flag indicates that the appraisal document cannot be changed. It enables you to override the entries on the Column Access tab page. If according to an entry made on this tab page, change access is allowed for the appraisal document during a particular phase, the flag overrides this entry and the appraisal document can only be displayed. It makes more sense to set this flag for a substatus.

### Pushbutton

This is the pushbutton which is displayed on the appraisal form. There can be multiple pushbuttons for an outbound status and substatus. You navigate to different pushbuttons using .

### Person authorized

Here you specify the persons who are authorized to press the pushbutton.

### Highlight pushbutton

Here you specify that the pushbutton is highlighted and pressing Enter amounts to clicking the pushbutton. You should highlight only one pushbutton for an outbound status and substatus.

### Target status and substatus

Here you specify the status and substatus that the appraisal form will receive after the pushbutton is pressed.

### Next status

After saving the document, you can either exit the appraisal document, or change its status to display.

### Workflow event

Here you specify the workflow event that will be generated by the system to trigger the workflow.

### Create note

Here you can specify whether a note can be created, and if so, whether it is mandatory or optional.

## 27.6 APPRAISAL CRITERIA GROUP

| *Functional Consultant* | *User* | *Business Process Owner* | *Senior Management* | *My Rating* | *Understanding Level* |
|---|---|---|---|---|---|
| A | X | X | X | | |

### 27.6.1 Description

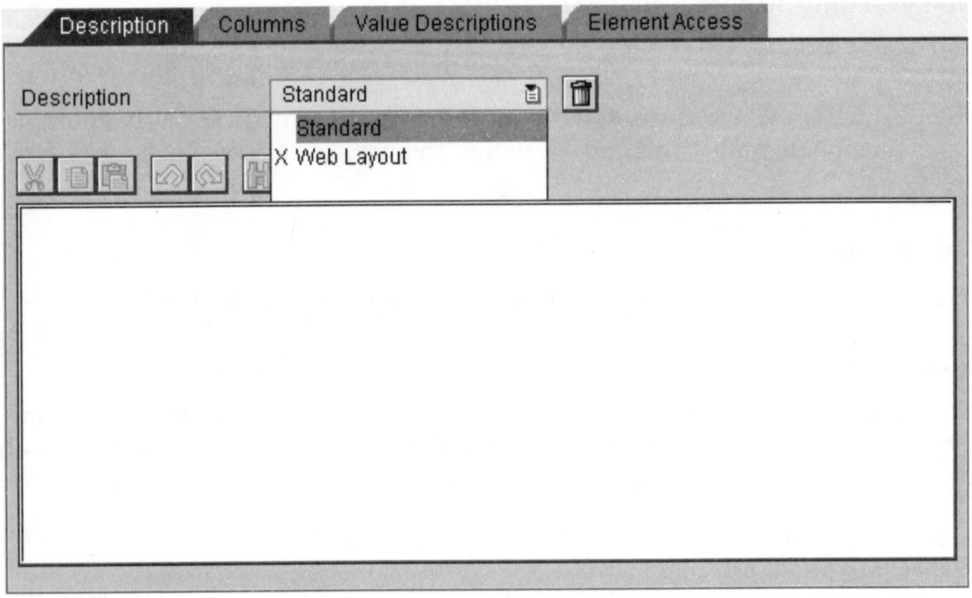


Here you can maintain descriptions of a criteria group.

## 27.6.2 Columns

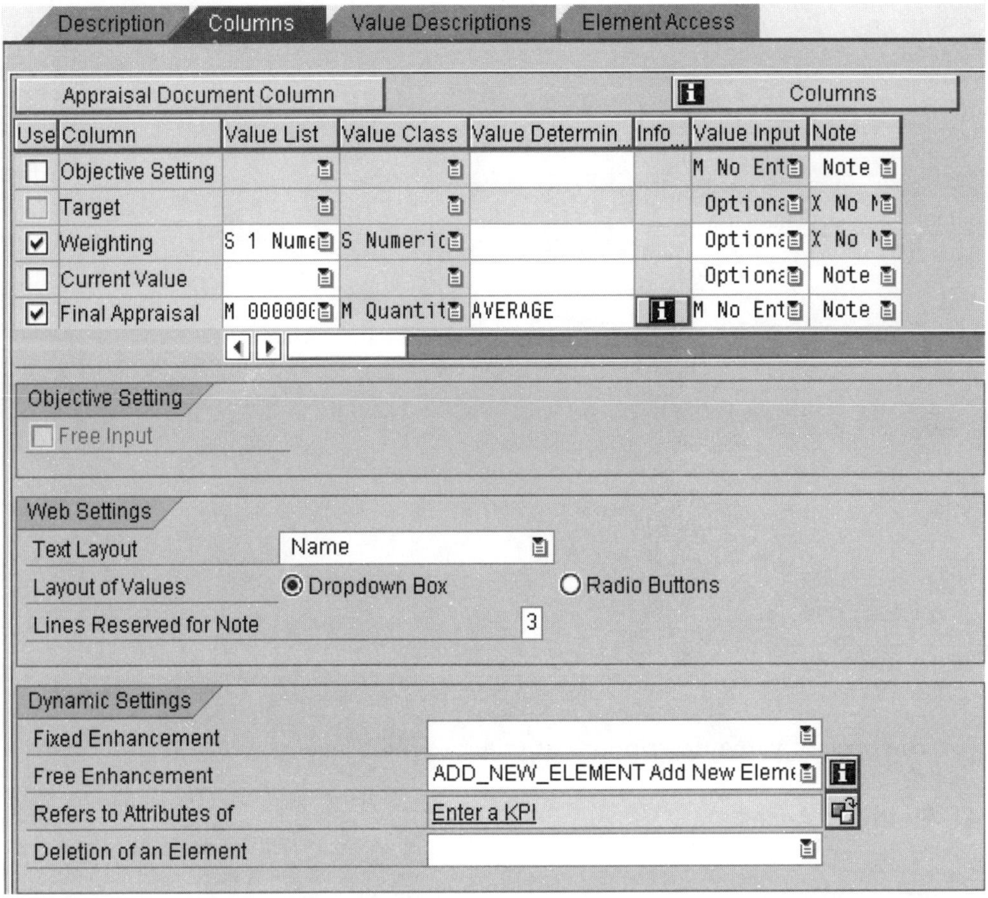


Here you can make changes in column properties at criteria group level. These will apply to all criteria under the criteria group.

### 27.6.3 Value Descriptions

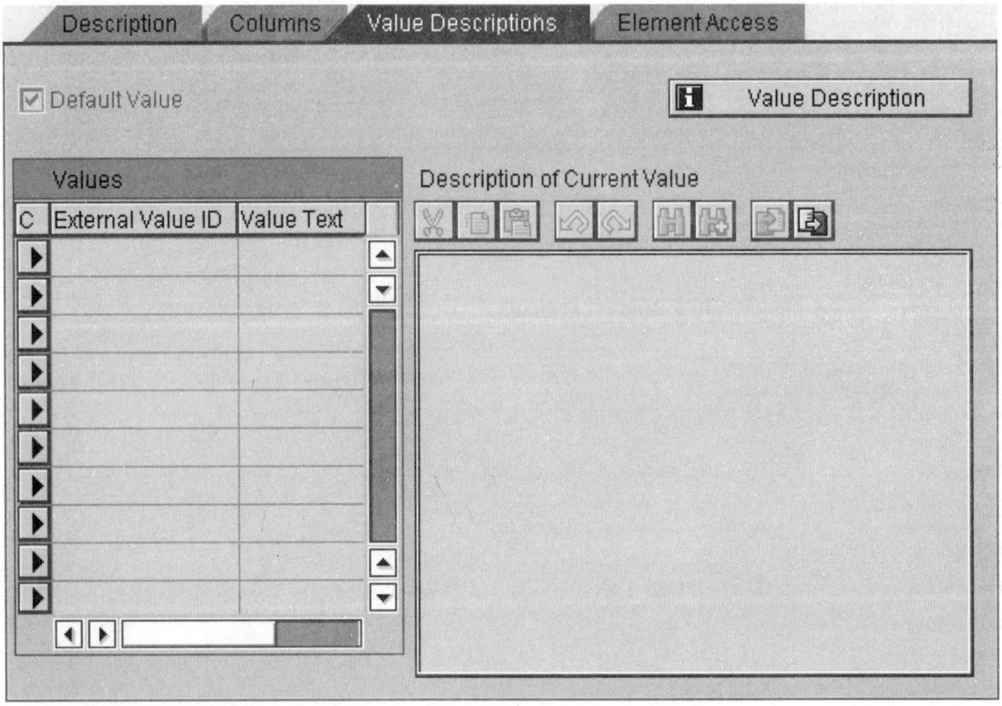


Here you can specify value descriptions at criteria group level.

### 27.6.4 Element Access

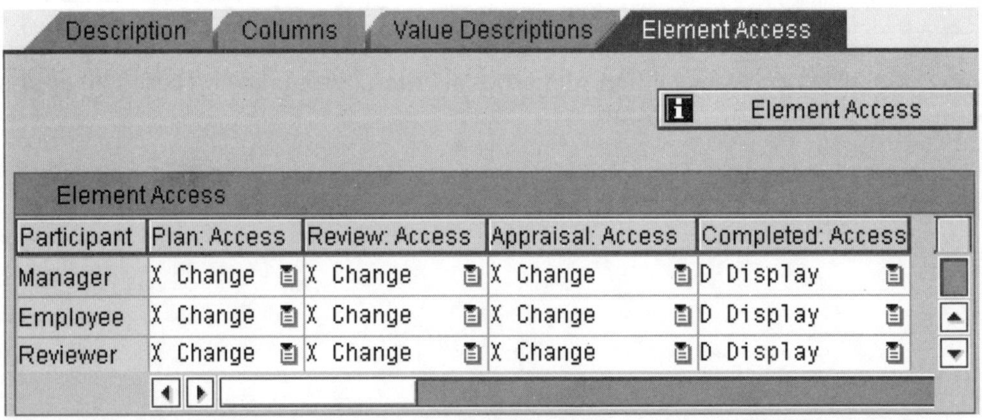


The system uses the settings on this tab page to control access to elements according to the individual participant and the participant's role in the appraisal process. These can be defined at criteria group level and further refined at criteria level.

## 27.7 APPRAISAL CRITERIA

| *Functional Consultant* | *User* | *Business Process Owner* | *Senior Management* | *My Rating* | *Understanding Level* |
|---|---|---|---|---|---|
| A | X | X | X | | |

### 27.7.1 Description

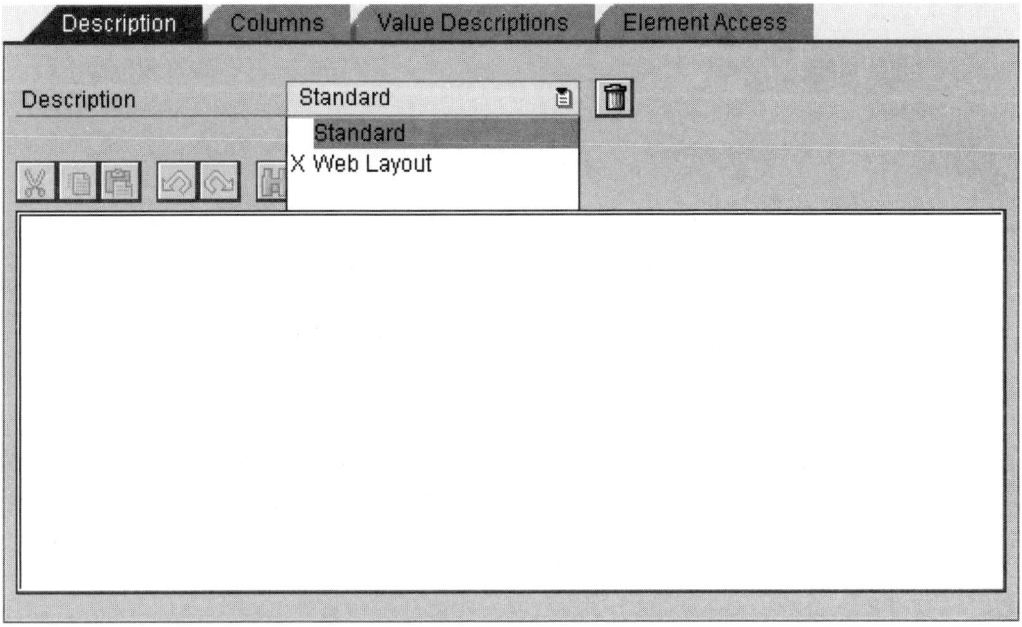


Here you can maintain descriptions of a criterion.

## 27.7.2 Columns

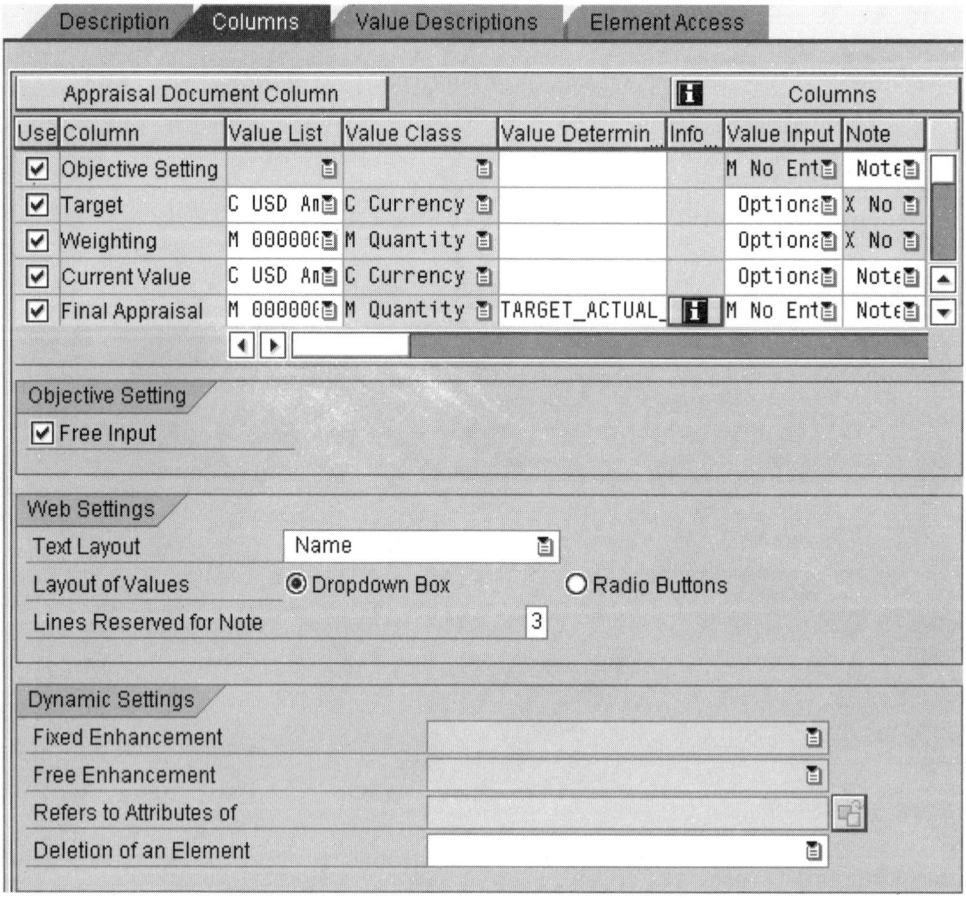


Here you can make changes in column properties at criterion level.

### 27.7.3 Value Descriptions

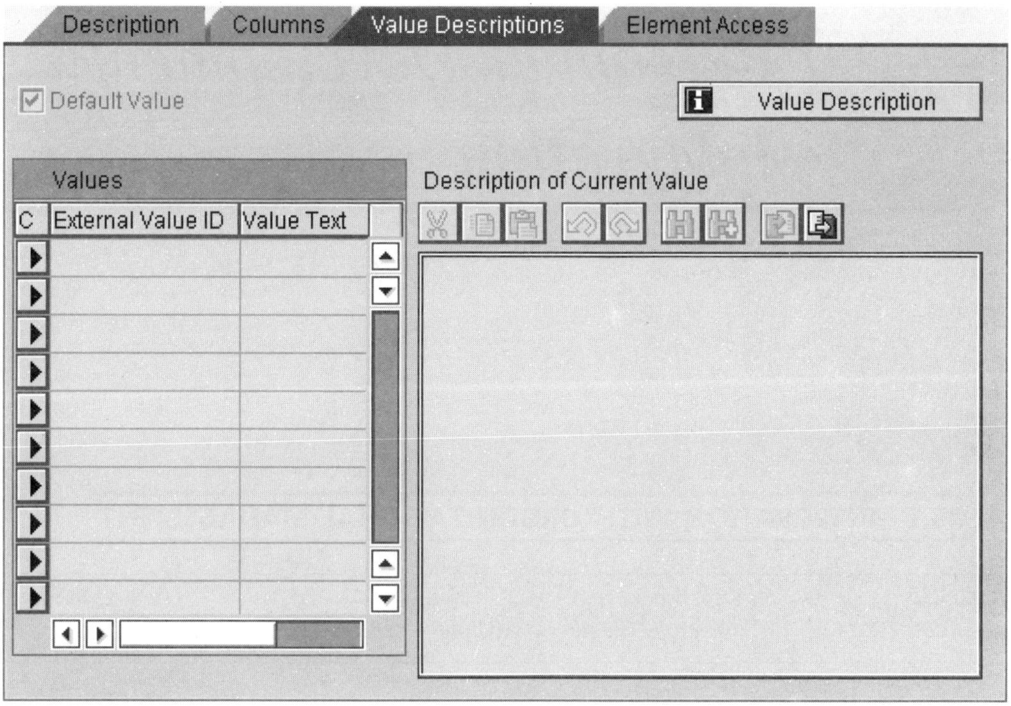


Here you can specify value descriptions at criterion level.

### 27.7.4 Element Access

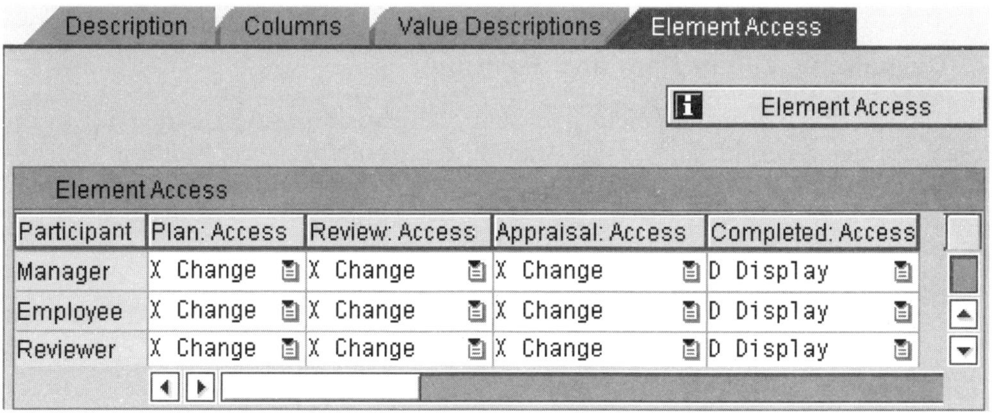


The system uses the settings on this tab page to control access to elements according to the individual participant and the participant's role in the appraisal process. These can be defined at criteria group level and further refined at criteria level.

# CHAPTER 28 Personnel Development Integration

## 28.1 INTEGRATION WITH ORGANIZATIONAL MANAGEMENT

| *Functional Consultant* | *User* | *Business Process Owner* | *Senior Management* | *My Rating* | *Understanding Level* |
|---|---|---|---|---|---|
| A | A | A | A | | |

### 28.1.1 Determining an Employee's Superior

Organizational structure is used for determining an employee's superior in appraisal workflow.

### 28.1.2 Development Plan Item and Position

Change in the status of a development plan item, which is a position, can result in the employee getting transferred. Conversely, transfer of an employee to a position, which is also a development plan item, can result in the change of status of the development plan item.

## 28.2 INTEGRATION WITH PERSONNEL ADMINISTRATION

| *Functional Consultant* | *User* | *Business Process Owner* | *Senior Management* | *My Rating* | *Understanding Level* |
|---|---|---|---|---|---|
| A | A | A | A | | |

### 28.2.1 Integration of Qualification

In Personnel Administration and Recruitment, you have the option either of using infotype 0024, or of using Personnel Development subprofiles to create qualifications. If you wish to manage qualifications in Personnel Development, you must activate the following integration switch by setting its value to '1 A032 Q'.

| Group | Sem. abbr. | Value abbr. | Description |
|---|---|---|---|
| PLOGI | QUALI | 0 A032 Q | Integration switch for qualifications |

If this integration switch is activated, and you use transaction PA30 (Maintain HR Master Data) to call up infotype 0024, you will go to the profile of the person in question. From here, you can then work through the tasks you wish to carry out. Integration will only take effect if an active plan version has been specified in switch PLOGI PLOGI.

### 28.2.2 Transfer of Qualification Data from PA to PD

While implementing Personnel Development, qualifications data stored in Personnel Administration can be transferred to Personnel Development. You use transaction OOQI to generate a batch input session with the appropriate qualifications and relationships. This batch input session is imported into the system by transaction OODT. Infotype 0024 records of the persons are deleted.

### 28.2.3 Integration of Appraisal

| Group | Sem. abbr. | Value abbr. | Description |
|---|---|---|---|
| PLOGI | APPRA | 0 | Integration switch for appraisal |

If integration between Personnel Administration and Appraisal is active (value 1 in the above switch), infotype 0025 in Personnel Administration shows appraisal data stored in Personnel Development.

### 28.2.4 Transfer of Appraisal Data from PA to PD

While implementing Personnel Development, appraisals data stored in Personnel Administration can be transferred to Personnel Development using transaction OOAI.

## 28.3 INTEGRATION WITH RECRUITMENT

| *Functional Consultant* | *User* | *Business Process Owner* | *Senior Management* | *My Rating* | *Understanding Level* |
|---|---|---|---|---|---|
| A | A | A | A | | |

### 28.3.1 Integration of Qualification

Refer to chapter 28.2.1.

### 28.3.2 Transfer of Qualification Data from Recruitment to PD

While implementing Personnel Development, qualifications data stored in Recruitment can be transferred to Personnel Development. You use transaction OOQB to generate a batch input session with the appropriate qualifications and relationships. This batch input session is imported into the system by transaction OODT. Infotype 0024 records of the applicants are deleted.

## 28.4 INTEGRATION WITH TRAINING AND EVENT MANAGEMENT

| *Functional Consultant* | *User* | *Business Process Owner* | *Senior Management* | *My Rating* | *Understanding Level* |
|---|---|---|---|---|---|
| A | A | A | A | | |

### 28.4.1 Training with Qualification

Qualifications can be prerequisites for business events. Training programs can impart qualifications. When a person completes a training program, this qualification can be added to his profile. Based on the qualification deficits in profile matchup, training programs can be proposed.

### 28.4.2 Training with Development Plan Item

Change in the status of a development plan item, which is a training program, can result in the employee being booked for the training program. Conversely, booking for a training program, which is also a development plan item, can result in the change of status of the development plan item.

### 28.4.3 Training with Appraisal

You can hold business event appraisals and attendee appraisals.

## 28.5 INTEGRATION WITH COMPENSATION MANAGEMENT

| *Functional Consultant* | *User* | *Business Process Owner* | *Senior Management* | *My Rating* | *Understanding Level* |
|---|---|---|---|---|---|
| A | A | A | A | | |

### 28.5.1 Appraisal with Compensation Management

When the appraisal is completed, the appraisal results can be passed on to compensation management.

## 28.6 INTEGRATION WITH STRATEGIC ENTERPRISE MANAGEMENT

| *Functional Consultant* | *User* | *Business Process Owner* | *Senior Management* | *My Rating* | *Understanding Level* |
|---|---|---|---|---|---|
| A | A | A | A | | |

### 28.6.1 Appraisal with Strategic Enterprise Management

The value from the SAP Strategic Enterprise Management Performance Matrix can be transferred to the individual appraisals in SAP HR. The descriptions from the Performance Matrix are displayed on the appraisal sheets and represent the individual objectives in more detail. Strategic Objectives can also be taken into account as individual objectives, whereby these are accepted in the appraisal documents of the individual employees.

If you want to integrate appraisals with SAP Strategic Enterprise Management you specify the RFC connection of the Strategic Enterprise Management system in the following switch.

| Group | Sem.abbr. | Value abbr | Description |
|---|---|---|---|
| HAP00 | RFCSE | | RFC Destination in SEM System |

# *Training and Event Management*

# CHAPTER 29

# Business Event Catalog

## 29.1 CONCEPTS

| *Functional Consultant* | *User* | *Business Process Owner* | *Senior Management* | *My Rating* | *Understanding Level* |
|---|---|---|---|---|---|
| A | A | A | A | | |

### *Business event*

In SAP, training programs are called business events. Business events have wider meaning and include, apart from training programs, conferences, seminars, conventions, etc. Business events are scheduled training programs. If a training program is held on multiple dates, each one is a separate business event. In this book, the terms 'training program' and 'business event' are used interchangeably.

### *Business event type*

Business event types are templates of business events. They have content, duration and instructors. Business events are created by copying these templates and specifying the dates on when they will be held.

### *Business event group*

Related or similar business event types are grouped in business event groups so that they can be easily found. Business event groups can be grouped in larger business event groups, thus creating a tree structure.

### *Business event catalog*

A company normally has a list of training programs it usually conducts. These are organized in a business event catalog. A business event catalog is a tree-like structure of business event groups which contain business event types.

### *Organizer*

A business event has an organizer. The organizer may either be an organizational unit or a company as can be seen by running transaction PSVQ to create organizer or transaction PSVO to change/display organizer.

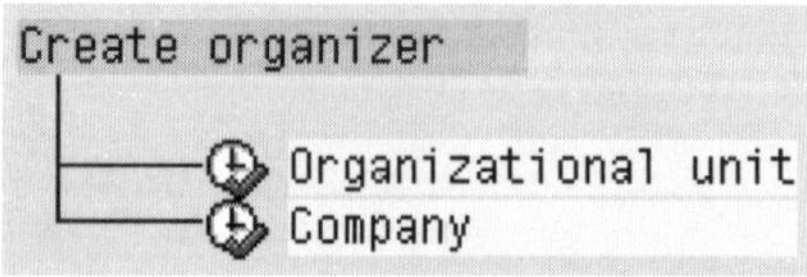


### *Instructors*

Instructors teach at business events. There may be internal instructors or external instructors. Internal instructors are employees of the company and are created in Personnel Administration. External instructors are created as external persons.

## 29.2 BUSINESS EVENT CATALOG

| *Functional Consultant* | *User* | *Business Process Owner* | *Senior Management* | *My Rating* | *Understanding Level* |
|---|---|---|---|---|---|
| A | A | A | A | | |

Before creating the business event catalog on the system, you first create it on paper. It is important to have clear unambiguous groupings of business event types. This task may require brainstorming by key stake holders, and may require a few iterations before it is completed. You then create the business event catalog on the system using transaction OOC3 or S_AHR_61011887. When you first run this transaction, you will see a blank business event catalog.

You select the top line (Current plan) and create an entry below it by choosing Object ➢ Create ➢ Create Level Lower. The system will give you the screen to create the business event group.

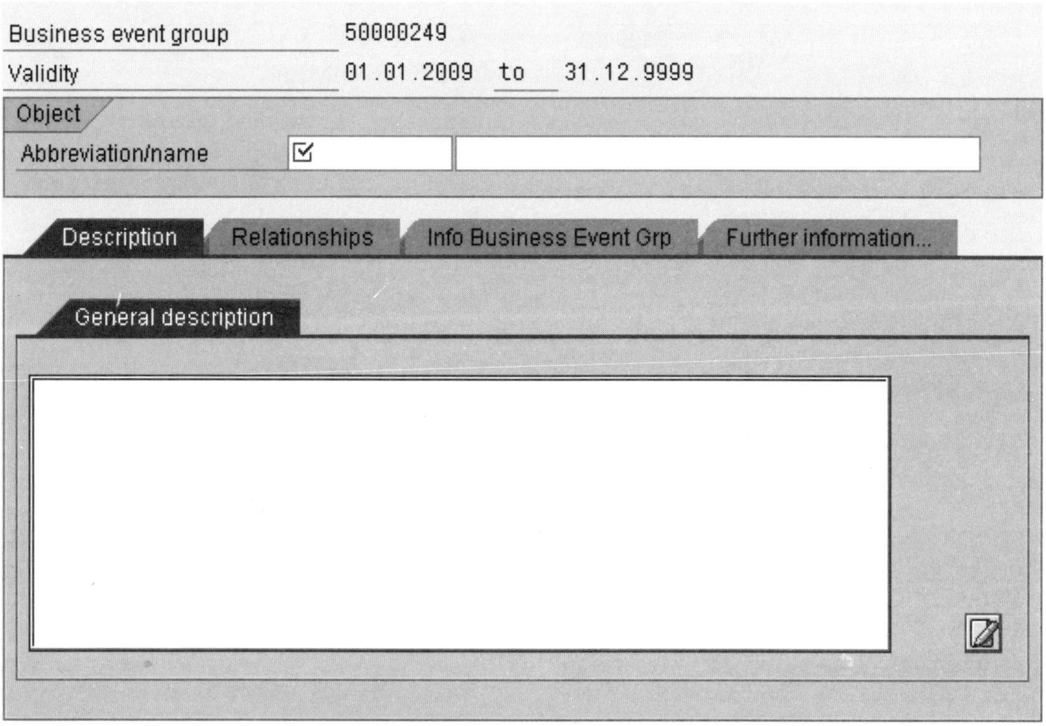


Enter the abbreviation and name. Take note of the validity period. The business event group you are creating will be valid for this period. Save your data; you can enter remaining data later. Create other top level business event groups in the same way.

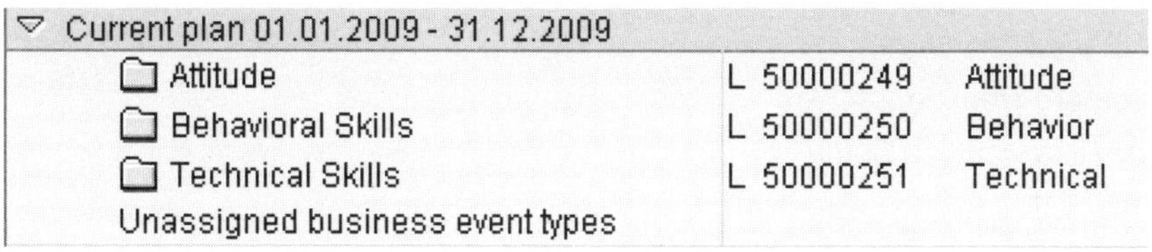

Having created the top level business event groups, create the next level business event groups by selecting the higher level business event group. The process is the same except that the system asks you whether you want to create business event group or business event type.

| Current plan 01.01.2009 - 31.12.2009 | | |
|---|---|---|
| Attitude | L 50000249 | Attitude |
| Behavioral Skills | L 50000250 | Behavior |
| Communication | L 50000252 | Communicaton |
| Creativity | L 50000253 | Creativity |
| Decision Making | L 50000254 | Decision Mkg |
| Leadership | L 50000255 | Leadership |
| Management | L 50000256 | Management |
| Technical Skills | L 50000251 | Technical |
| Computer Skills | L 50000257 | Computers |
| Microsoft | L 50000258 | Microsoft |
| SAP | L 50000259 | SAP |
| Unassigned business event types | | |

Now you create business event types under business event groups. The process is the same, except that now you choose business event type when the system asks you, and you choose 'Classroom Training' as the delivery method.

| Del. | Delivery Method |
|---|---|
| 0001 | Classroom Training |
| 0002 | Virtual Classroom Sessions |
| 0003 | Web-Based Training |
| 0004 | Online Test |
| 0006 | Static Web-Based Training |
| 0007 | External Web-Based Training |
| 0008 | External Classroom Training |
| 0009 | External Virtual Classroom Training |
| 0010 | External Online Test |
| 0011 | WBT in Classroom |

When you save, the system will ask you to enter capacity; do that. The business event type will get created. You can also create objects at the same level and objects by copying. In this manner, create the full business event catalog.

| Current plan 01.01.2009 - 31.12.2009 | | |
|---|---|---|
| Attitude | L 50000249 | Attitude |
| Positive Attitude | D 50000260 | +ve Attitude |
| Think Customer | D 50000261 | Customer |
| Behavioral Skills | L 50000250 | Behavior |
| Communication | L 50000252 | Communicaton |
| English | D 50000262 | English |
| German | D 50000263 | German |
| Japanese | D 50000264 | Japanese |
| Presentations | D 50000265 | Presentation |
| Creativity | L 50000253 | Creativity |
| Creativity and Problem Solving | D 50000266 | Creativity |
| Decision Making | L 50000254 | Decision Mkg |
| Decision Making Skills | D 50000267 | Decision Mkg |
| Leadership | L 50000255 | Leadership |
| Mentoring | D 50000268 | Mentoring |
| Management | L 50000256 | Management |
| Management By Objectives | D 50000269 | MBO |
| Time Management | D 50000270 | Time Mgmt |
| Technical Skills | L 50000251 | Technical |
| Computer Skills | L 50000257 | Computers |
| Microsoft | L 50000258 | Microsoft |
| Microsoft Word | D 50000272 | MS Word |
| Microsoft Excel | D 50000273 | MS Excel |
| SAP | L 50000259 | SAP |
| SAP HR | D 50000274 | SAP HR |
| SAP FI | D 50000275 | SAP FI |
| Unassigned business event types | | |
| Yoga | D 50000276 | Yoga |

## 29.3 BUSINESS EVENT TYPE RELATIONSHIPS

| *Functional Consultant* | *User* | *Business Process Owner* | *Senior Management* | *My Rating* | *Understanding Level* |
|---|---|---|---|---|---|
| A | A | A | A | | |

Business event catalog not only shows business event types organized in business event groups but also a number of relationships that business event types have with other objects.

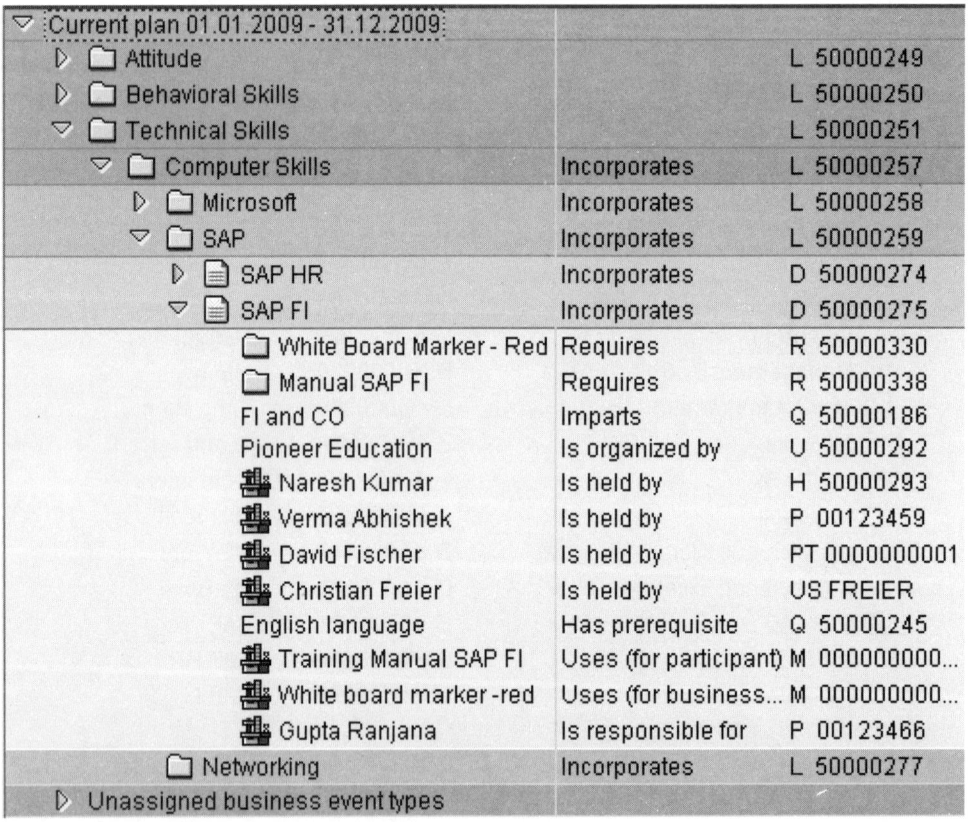

If you select a business event type, right-click and choose 'Create Lower Level', the system gives the following choices.

| S | Rel | RO | Relationship name | Object type text |
|---|---|---|---|---|
| A | 022 | R | Requires | Resource type |
| A | 028 | Q | Imparts | Qualification |
| A | 036 | U | Is organized by | Company |
| A | 026 | H | Is held by | External person |
| A | 026 | P | Is held by | Person |
| A | 026 | PT | Is held by | Contact person |
| A | 026 | US | Is held by | User |
| A | 029 | Q | Has prerequisite | Qualification |
| A | 054 | M | Uses (for participant) | Material |
| A | 055 | M | Uses (for business event) | Material |
| A | 090 | H | Is responsibility of | External person |
| A | 090 | P | Is responsibility of | Person |
| A | 090 | PT | Is responsibility of | Contact person |
| A | 090 | US | Is responsibility of | User |

All these relationships of a business event type are displayed in the business event catalog. It is recommended that you create these objects and their relationship with the business event type using appropriate transactions. Use the business event catalog to display these objects and check their correctness and completeness.

# CHAPTER 30 Business Event Group

## 30.1 BUSINESS EVENT GROUP

| *Functional Consultant* | *User* | *Business Process Owner* | *Senior Management* | *My Rating* | *Understanding Level* |
|---|---|---|---|---|---|
| A | A | A | A | | |

The purpose of business event groups is to classify business event types so that they can be easily found. Business event groups can also be grouped in larger business event groups, thus creating a tree structure called business event catalog.

## 30.2 BUSINESS EVENT GROUP CREATION AND DISPLAY

| *Functional Consultant* | *User* | *Business Process Owner* | *Senior Management* | *My Rating* | *Understanding Level* |
|---|---|---|---|---|---|
| A | A | A | A | | |

When you create a business event group in business event catalog or using transaction OOEG or S_AHR_61011889 you can enter all the data about it in tabs. Similarly, when you display a business event group, you can see the data in tabs.

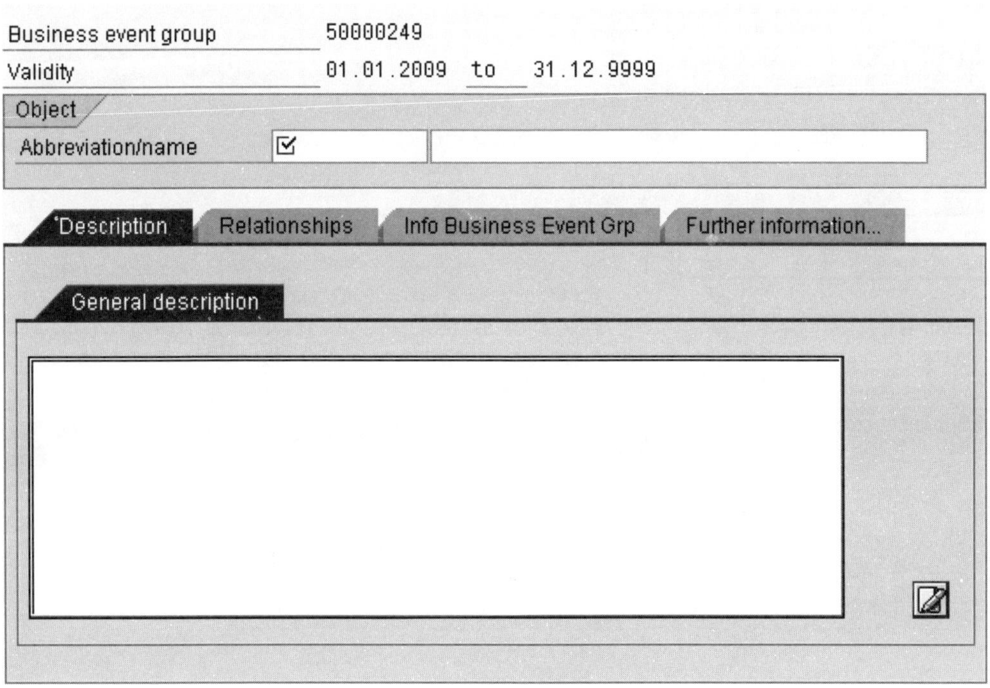

## 30.3 BUSINESS EVENT GROUP CHANGE

| *Functional Consultant* | *User* | *Business Process Owner* | *Senior Management* | *My Rating* | *Understanding Level* |
|---|---|---|---|---|---|
| A | A | A | A | | |

However, changing data about a business event group is possible only in the 'Maintain object' format. This should not bother you because both the formats capture the same data and store in the same place. Only the user interfaces are different.

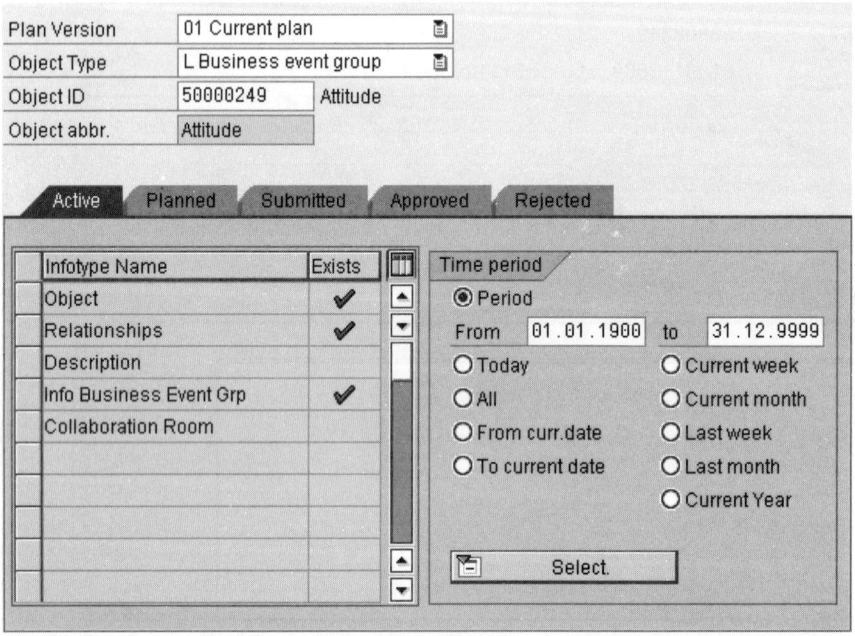

## 30.4 OBJECT

| Functional Consultant | User | Business Process Owner | Senior Management | My Rating | Understanding Level |
|---|---|---|---|---|---|
| A | A | B | C | | |

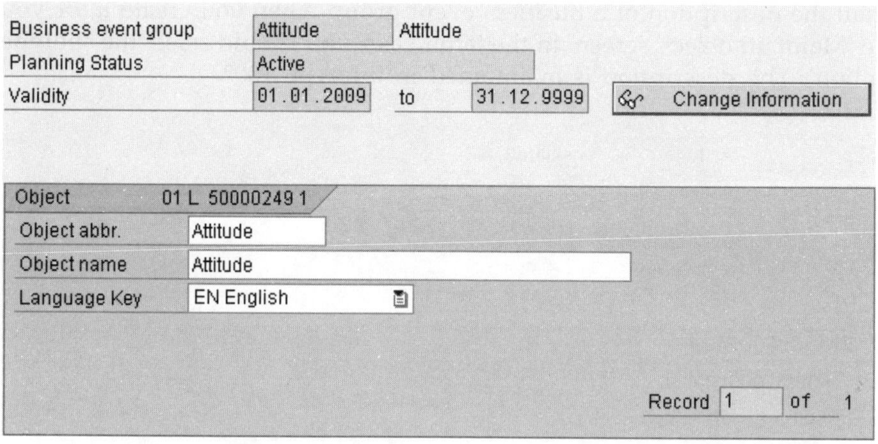


When you created the business event group by entering its abbreviation and name, the object infotype was created. Each object is identified by a unique eight-digit system generated numeric id. If you want to change the abbreviation or name of the business event group, you may do so. You can even have different names during different periods. You can also maintain the object abbreviation and name in different languages.

## 30.5 DESCRIPTION

| *Functional Consultant* | *User* | *Business Process Owner* | *Senior Management* | *My Rating* | *Understanding Level* |
|---|---|---|---|---|---|
| A | A | B | C | | |

You may maintain the description of a business event group when you create it, or you may do so in the 'Maintain object' screen. In the latter case, you should select the subtype 'General description'. The description is maintained in infotype 1002.

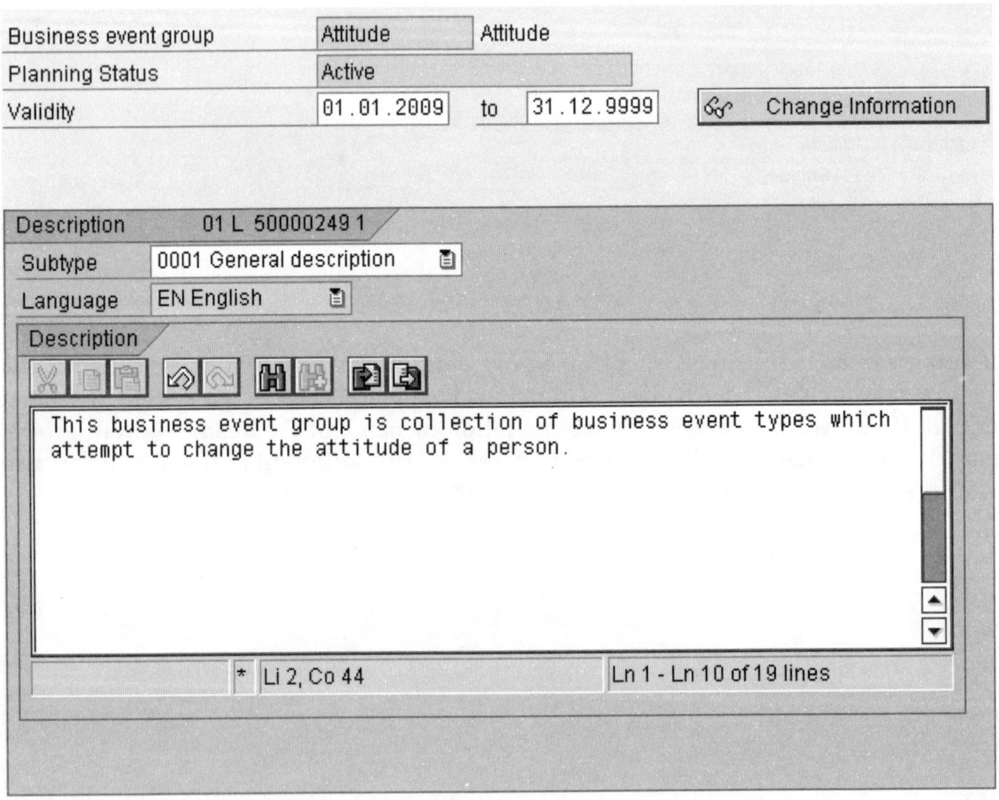

## 30.6 RELATIONSHIPS

| *Functional Consultant* | *User* | *Business Process Owner* | *Senior Management* | *My Rating* | *Understanding Level* |
|---|---|---|---|---|---|
| A | A | B | C | | |

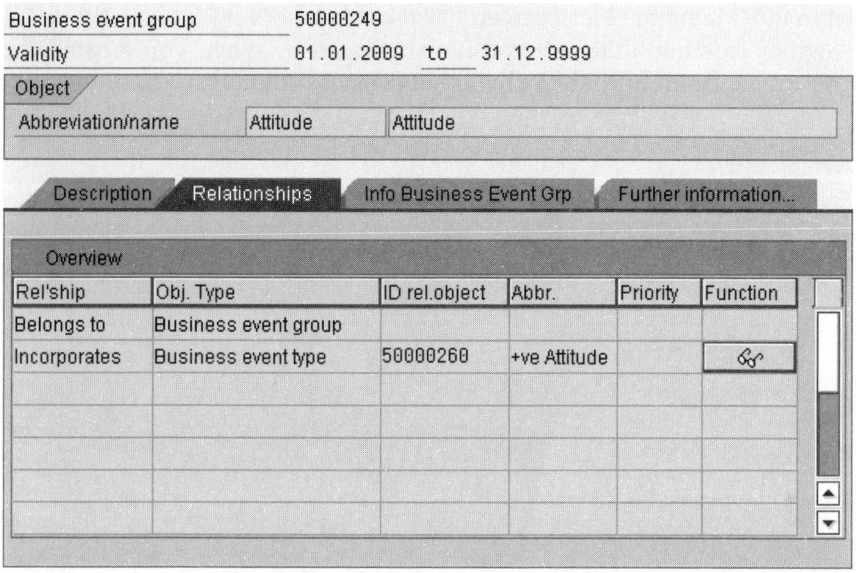


The Relationships tab shows the relationships that exist between the displayed object and all other objects. Although you never explicitly created a relationship, the system created it when you created business event type 'Positive Attitude' under business event group 'Attitude'. But, why does the screen not show the business event type 'Think Customer'? Click [button] and the system shows both the business event types. This is done to conserve space in the main display.

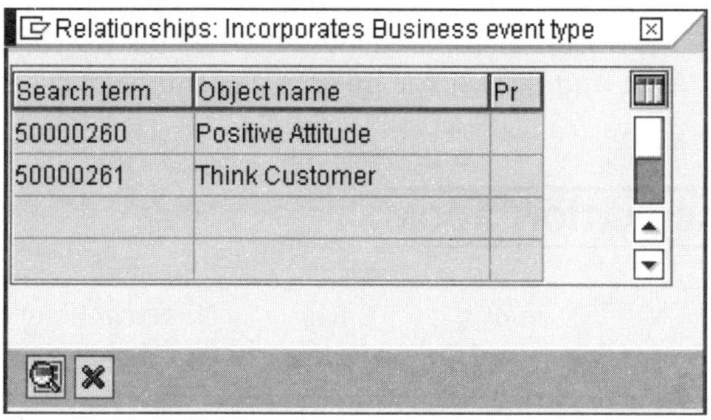


You don't always create relationships by creating new object under an object. If the object already exists, you can create relationship in the 'Maintain object' screen.

## 30.7 INFO BUSINESS EVENT GROUP

| *Functional Consultant* | *User* | *Business Process Owner* | *Senior Management* | *My Rating* | *Understanding Level* |
|---|---|---|---|---|---|
| A | B | C | X | | |

You may notice that in the 'Maintain object' screen 

, this infotype is shown as existing although you never created it. When you created the business event group, the system automatically created it with default value.

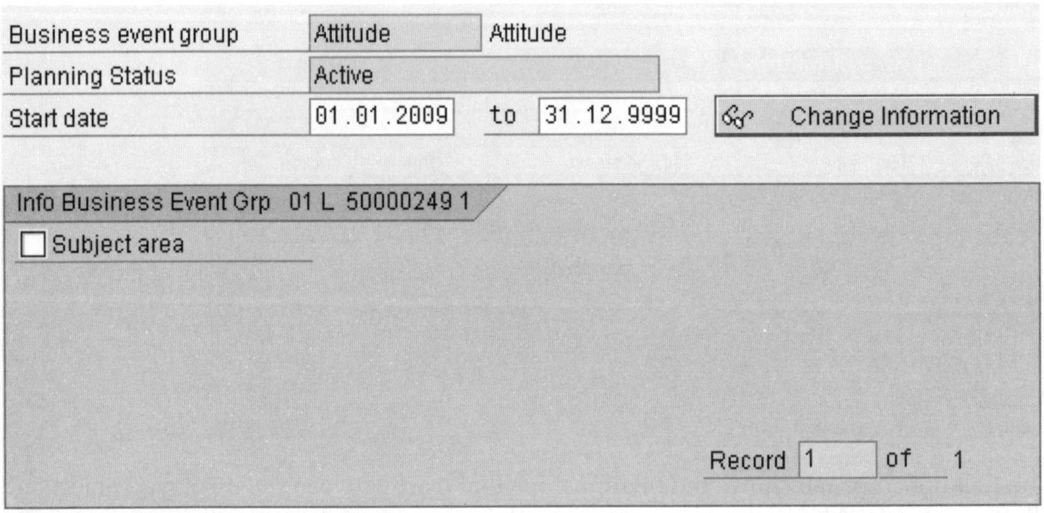


In this infotype you specify whether a business event group is displayed in the Training Center of the Employee Self-Service (ESS). If you select this indicator, the business event group will be displayed in the ESS under Subject Area. If you select a subject area, the system only searches for business events that belong to the specified subject area (business event group). If you do not select this indicator, the business event group will not be displayed in the ESS under Subject Area. Therefore, an employee will not be able to select this business event group in the Subject Area and search for business events in it.

## 30.8 COLLABORATION ROOM

| *Functional Consultant* | *User* | *Business Process Owner* | *Senior Management* | *My Rating* | *Understanding Level* |
|---|---|---|---|---|---|
| X | X | X | X | | |

This infotype is used in LSO.

CHAPTER 31

# Business Event Type

## 31.1 BUSINESS EVENT TYPE

| *Functional Consultant* | *User* | *Business Process Owner* | *Senior Management* | *My Rating* | *Understanding Level* |
|---|---|---|---|---|---|
| A | A | A | A | | |

Business event types are templates of business events. They have content, duration and instructors. Business events are created by copying these templates and specifying the dates on when they will be held.

## 31.2 OBJECT

| *Functional Consultant* | *User* | *Business Process Owner* | *Senior Management* | *My Rating* | *Understanding Level* |
|---|---|---|---|---|---|
| A | A | A | A | | |

When you create a business event type in business event catalog or using transaction OOET or S_AHR_61011888 you see the following screen.

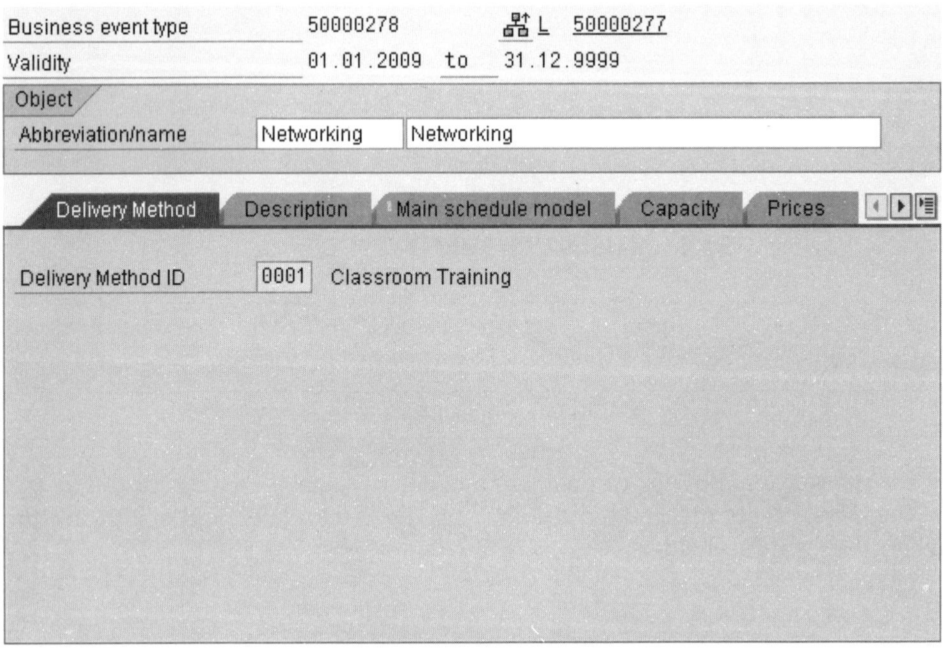


A business event type is an object. It has an object type (L), an object id and a validity period. This data is stored in infotype 1000. A business event type also has many properties which are shown in different tabs and stored in different infotypes. You can see all the tabs and navigate to them by clicking .

## 31.3 DELIVERY METHOD

| *Functional Consultant* | *User* | *Business Process Owner* | *Senior Management* | *My Rating* | *Understanding Level* |
|---|---|---|---|---|---|
| A | C | X | X | | |

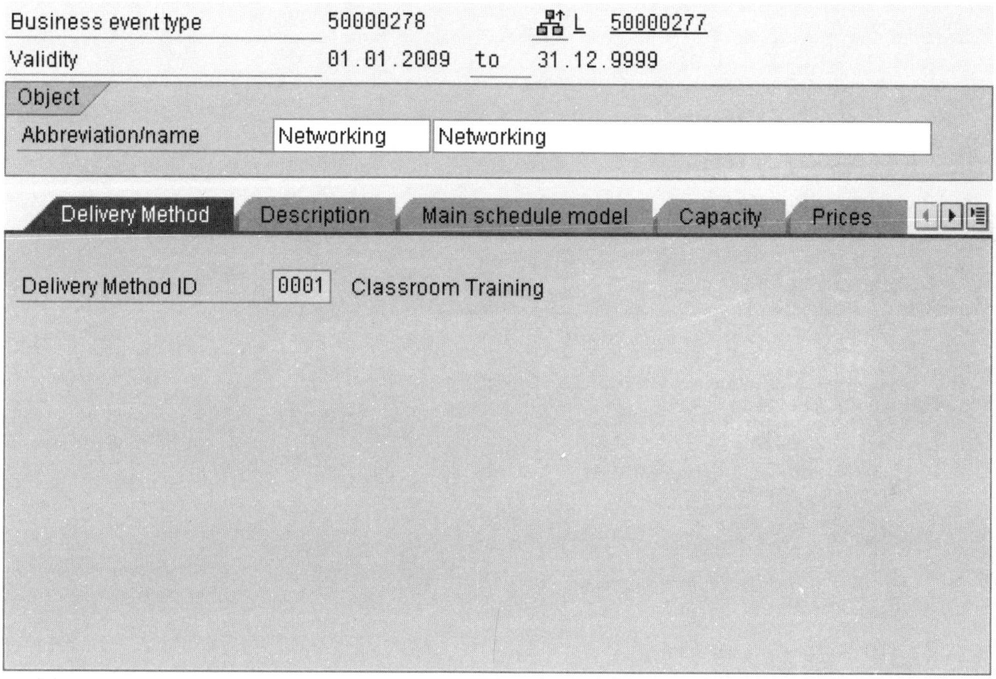


In the delivery method you specify how the training program is delivered. This attribute of a business event type has a lot of significance in Learning Solutions (LSO), which is the newer version of Training and Event Management. In Training and Event Management, the delivery method is 'Classroom Training'.

## 31.4 DESCRIPTION

| *Functional Consultant* | *User* | *Business Process Owner* | *Senior Management* | *My Rating* | *Understanding Level* |
|---|---|---|---|---|---|
| A | A | B | C | | |

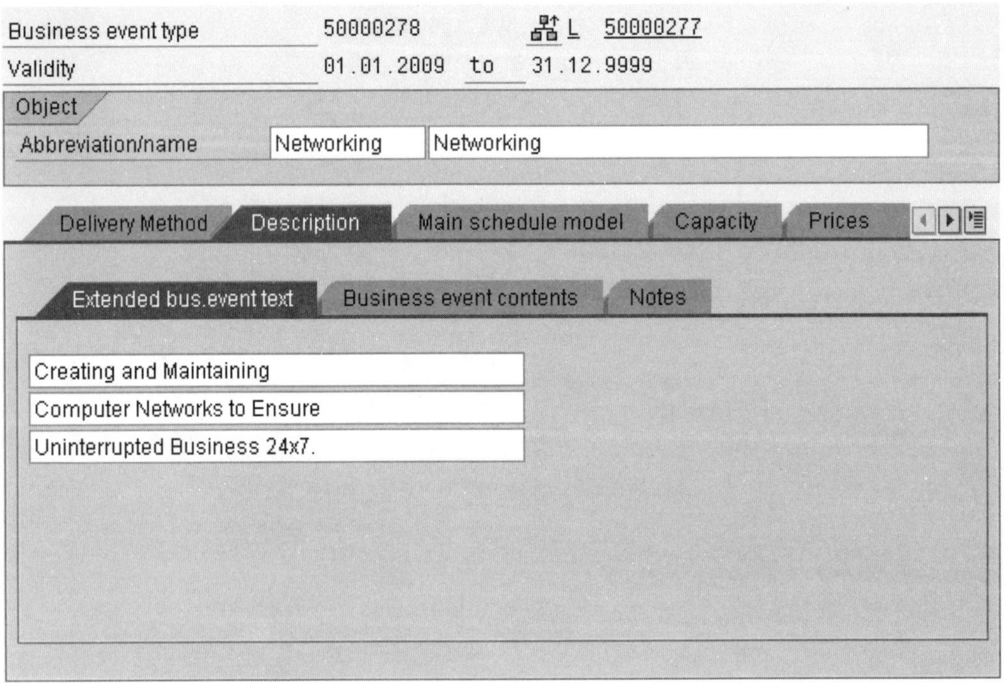


You can use extended business event text to maintain a longer name for the business event. In the business event contents you maintain the content of the business event. You can also maintain notes about the business event type. The descriptive texts you enter here can be included in the business event brochure and displayed in the ESS/Internet applications.

## 31.5 MAIN SCHEDULE MODEL

| *Functional Consultant* | *User* | *Business Process Owner* | *Senior Management* | *My Rating* | *Understanding Level* |
|---|---|---|---|---|---|
| A | A | B | C | | |

A training program has certain duration. You can define the duration for a business event type which is inherited by business events of that type. You can define this duration in three different ways. When you plan or create a business event date, you can copy the schedule model stored for the business event type and use it as the actual schedule for your business event.

### 31.5.1 Business Event Type without Pattern

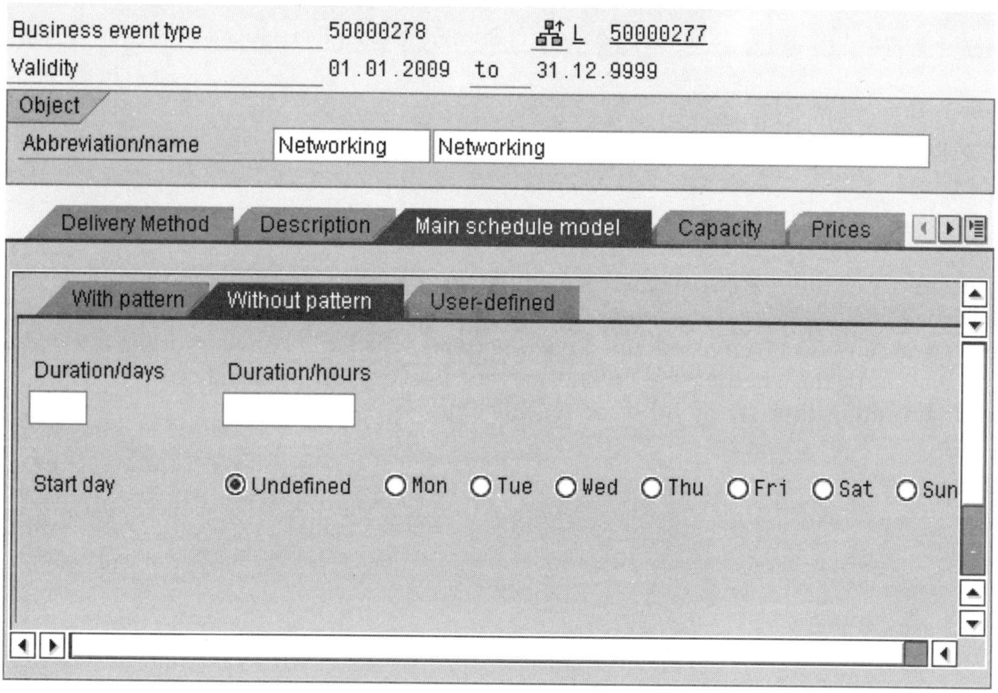


Even if you don't want to specify more details, you should at least specify the duration of business events of a type in number of hours and number of days. If business events of a type usually start on certain days, you can specify the start day. When you create or plan a business event date, the schedule without pattern becomes a generalized schedule.

### 31.5.2 Business Event Type with User-Defined Schedule

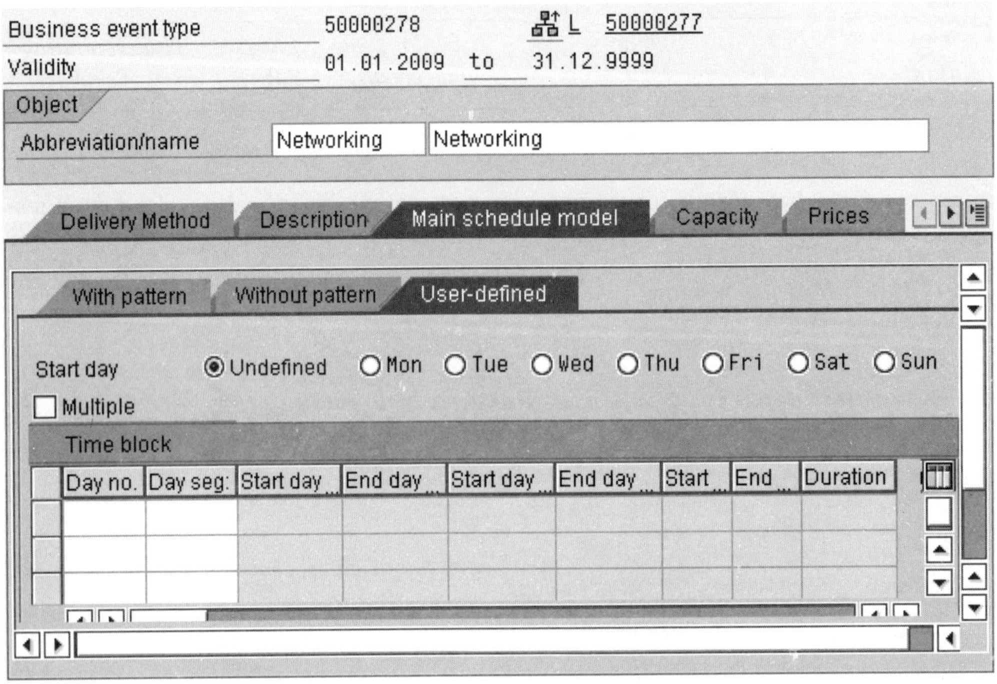


You can specify a more sophisticated schedule for a business event type in the User-defined tab. A business event may last several days, and in each day there may be several segments. You can select from predefined day segments which may have multiple intervals. You can also indicate whether the business event is a one-off occurrence or whether it will recur multiple times at monthly or weekly intervals.

### 31.5.3 Business Event Type with Pattern

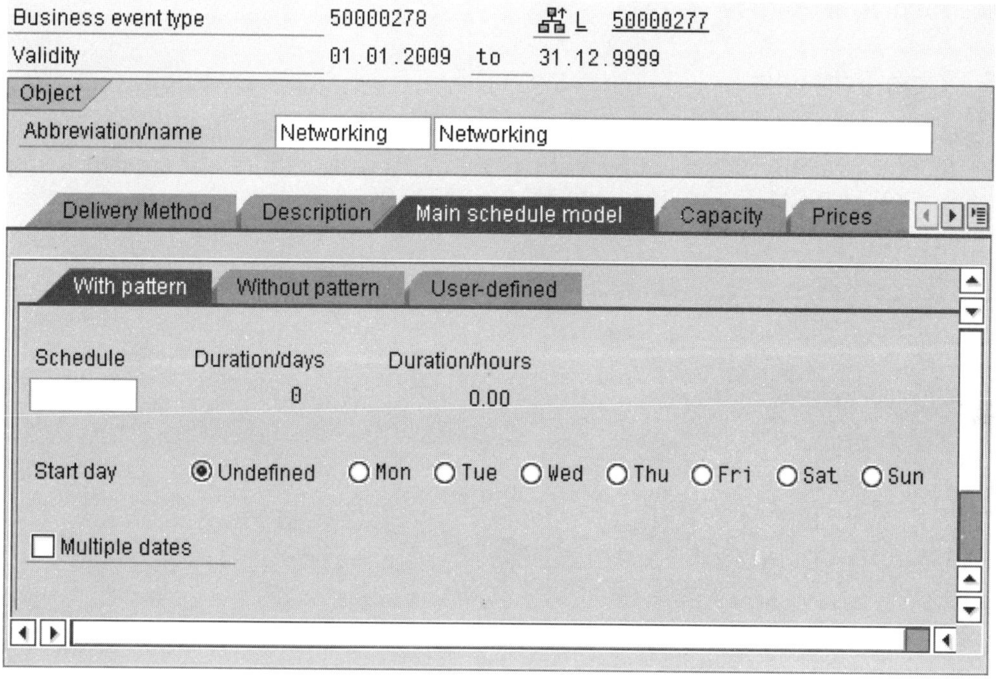


You use this method when you want to use predefined schedules. You specify the schedule and start day if any. You can also indicate whether the business event is a one-off occurrence or whether it will recur multiple times at monthly or weekly intervals.

### 31.5.4 Day Segment

| Day segment | Start 1 | End TB 1 | Start 2 | End TB 2 | Start 3 | End TB 3 | Duration |
|---|---|---|---|---|---|---|---|
| ABEND | 17:00:00 | 19:00:00 | 00:00:00 | 00:00:00 | 00:00:00 | 00:00:00 | 02:00:00 |
| FRUEH | 08:00:00 | 09:00:00 | 00:00:00 | 00:00:00 | 00:00:00 | 00:00:00 | 01:00:00 |
| NACHMITT | 13:00:00 | 17:00:00 | 00:00:00 | 00:00:00 | 00:00:00 | 00:00:00 | 04:00:00 |
| NORMAL | 09:00:00 | 17:00:00 | 00:00:00 | 00:00:00 | 00:00:00 | 00:00:00 | 08:00:00 |
| SPAET | 10:00:00 | 17:00:00 | 00:00:00 | 00:00:00 | 00:00:00 | 00:00:00 | 07:00:00 |
| SPMITTAG | 15:00:00 | 19:00:00 | 00:00:00 | 00:00:00 | 00:00:00 | 00:00:00 | 04:00:00 |
| VORMITT | 09:00:00 | 12:00:00 | 00:00:00 | 00:00:00 | 00:00:00 | 00:00:00 | 03:00:00 |

Day segments are parts of a day. They may consist of up to three time intervals. For example, if you normally have a morning session from 9:00 AM to 1:00 PM with a tea break from 11:00 to 11:15, you may define it as a day segment. Day segments are used when you specify a user-defined schedule for a business event type. They are also used in defining time schedules, which are used in defining schedules for business event types with pattern. You can create day segments and time schedules using transaction OOTM, S_AHR_61011844 or SM34 ➢ T77AM.

### 31.5.5 Time Schedule

If business events follow a time pattern, you can create these patterns called time schedules and use them repeatedly in schedules with pattern. Time schedules are created using transaction OOTM, S_AHR_61011844 or SM34 ➢ T77AM.

| Schedule | Name |
|---|---|
| ABEND | ABEND |
| DOPLWOCH | DOPLWOCH |
| FRUEH | FRUEH |
| HALB1 | HALB1 |
| HALB2 | HALB2 |
| MEETING1 | MEETING1 |
| MEETING2 | MEETING2 |
| WOCHE | WOCHE |
| X1 | X1 |

After defining the name of the schedule, you specify the time segments for each day of the schedule.

| Schedule | WOCHE |
|---|---|
| Name | WOCHE |

Day schedules

| Day no. | Day seg. |
|---|---|
| 1 | SPAET |
| 2 | NORMAL |
| 3 | NORMAL |
| 4 | NORMAL |
| 5 | VORMITT |

## 31.6 CAPACITY

| Functional Consultant | User | Business Process Owner | Senior Management | My Rating | Understanding Level |
|---|---|---|---|---|---|
| A | A | B | C | | |

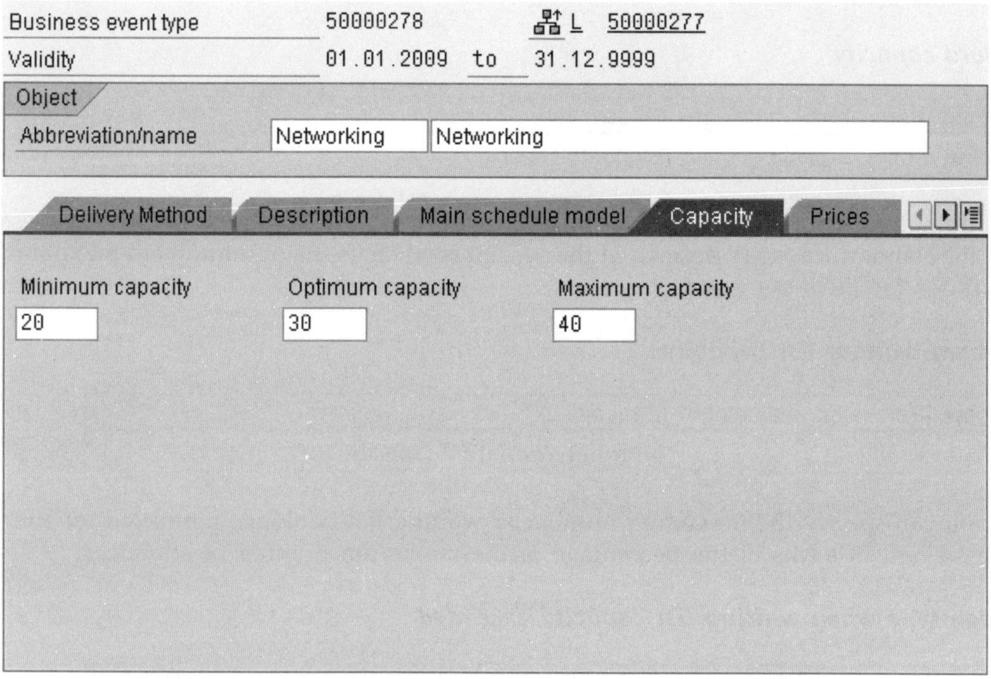


### *Minimum, optimum and maximum capacity*

In this tab, you specify the minimum, optimum and maximum number of attendees for business events of this type. When you firmly book a business event and booking is less than the minimum capacity, the system asks you whether you will like to cancel the business event.

### *Inheritance by business event*

When you create a business event, the capacity specified for the business event type is defaulted for the business event. However, you can change these capacity values for the business event.

### *Capacity of the room*

The capacity defined for a business event may be further restricted by the capacity of the room reserved for the business event.

### Capacity and booking priority

When booking is made, normal priority bookings can be made up to optimum capacity. Essential priority bookings can be made up to maximum capacity. Any bookings beyond maximum capacity are waiting list bookings.

### Filled capacity

Business events which are filled to different capacities are shown in different traffic light colors in the system.

### Standard capacity

| Group | Sem. abbr. | Value abbr. | Description |
|---|---|---|---|
| SEMIN | KAP | 99 | Standard capacity |

If you do not specify the capacity for the business event type, as well as for the business event, the standard capacity defined in the system is taken as the optimum and maximum capacity for the business event.

### Maximum waiting list capacity

| Group | Sem. abbr. | Value abbr. | Description |
|---|---|---|---|
| SEMIN | WKAPM | | Maximum waiting list capacity |

Here you can specify the maximum number of waiting list bookings permitted for each business event in terms of the percentage of the maximum number of attendees.

### Message type when waiting list capacity exceeded

| Group | Sem. abbr. | Value abbr. | Description |
|---|---|---|---|
| SEMIN | WKAPT | | Message Type When Waiting List Capacity Exceeded |

If a booking is made after the maximum waiting list capacity has been exceeded you can give an error, a warning, information, or no message.

## 31.7 PRICES

| *Functional Consultant* | *User* | *Business Process Owner* | *Senior Management* | *My Rating* | *Understanding Level* |
|---|---|---|---|---|---|
| A | A | B | C | | |

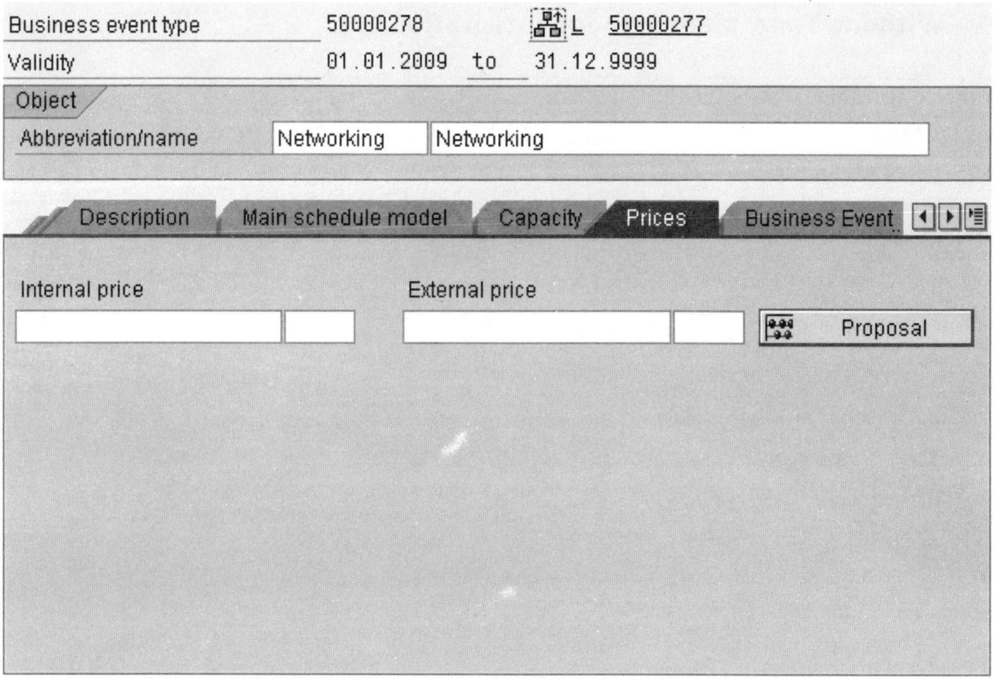


In this tab, you store an internal price for internal activity allocation and an external price for billing. You can use the option of the price proposal function to have the system calculate a suitable attendance price taking all the business event costs into consideration. Price proposal is discussed in detail in chapter 34.14.

## 31.8 BUSINESS EVENT TYPE INFO

| *Functional Consultant* | *User* | *Business Process Owner* | *Senior Management* | *My Rating* | *Understanding Level* |
|---|---|---|---|---|---|
| A | A | B | C | | |

### 31.8.1 Without Time Management Integration

| Group | Sem. abbr. | Value abbr. | Description |
|---|---|---|---|
| PLOGI | TIME | | Integration switch: Training and Event Mgmt/ Time |

When integration of Training and Event Management with Time Management is off, you see the following screen.

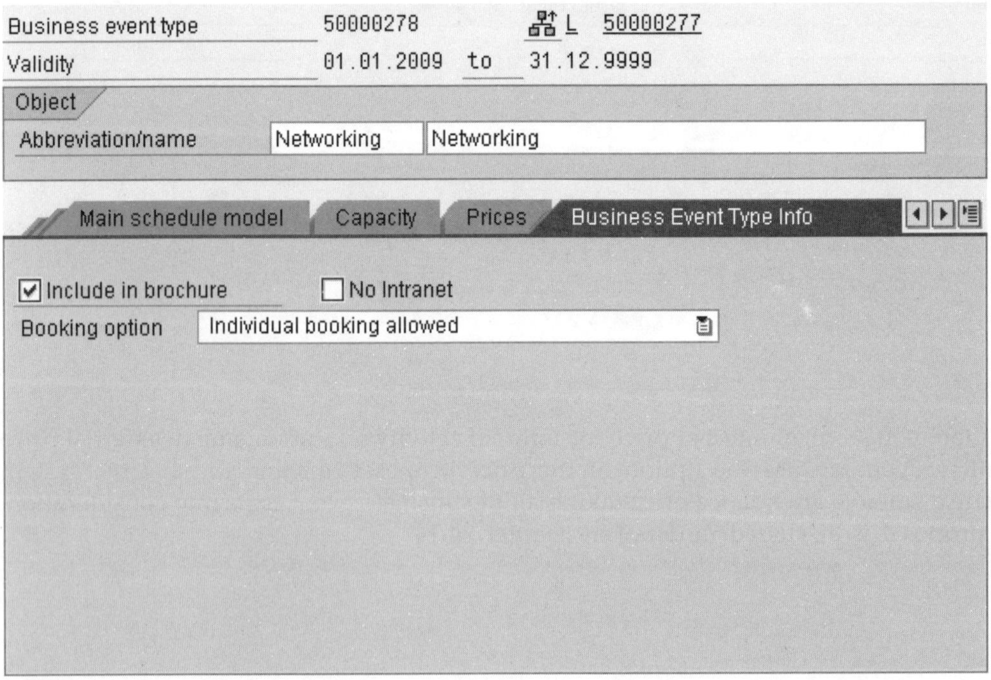


***Include in brochure***

If you tick this checkbox, the business event type is included in the business event brochure.

***No intranet***

You tick this checkbox if you do not want a business event type to be available in the Employee Self-Service.

### *Booking option*

In LSO there are curricula and certain business events can be booked only as a part of a curriculum. In Training and Event Management, you use the option 'Individual booking allowed'.

## 31.8.2 With Time Management Integration

| Group | Sem. abbr. | Value abbr. | Description |
|---|---|---|---|
| PLOGI | TIME | X | Integration switch: Training and Event Mgmt/ Time |

When integration of Training and Event Management with Time Management is on, attendance records are written to Time Management for instructors and attendees and availability checks are carried out. You can turn off these checks at business event type level in this tab. When integration is on you see the following screen.

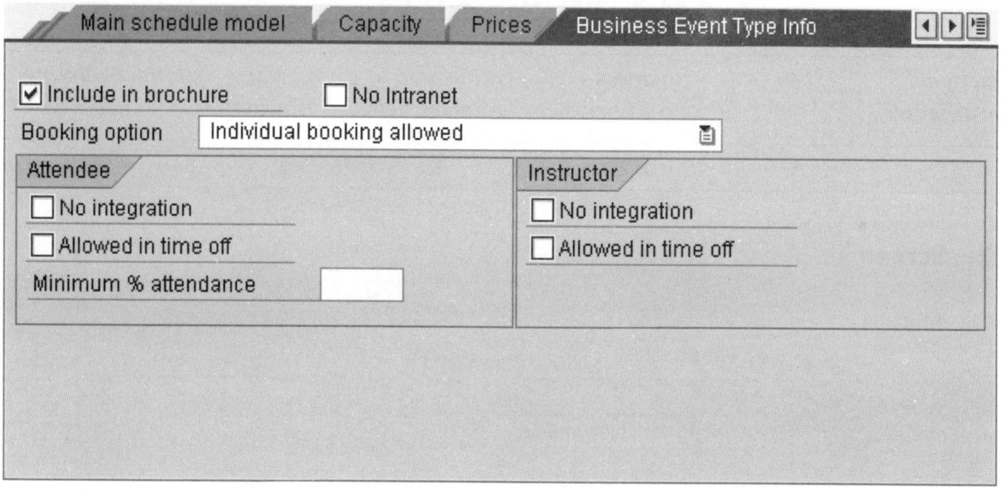


### *No integration*

If you tick this checkbox for a business event type, attendance records are not written to Time Management. No availability checks are carried out either.

### *Allowed in time off*

In view T77KA you can specify that an employee cannot be an attendee or an instructor on his off days. You can deactivate this check for a business event type in this field. If you do so, an employee can be an attendee or an instructor even on his off days as per shift plan. When an employee does so, an attendance record is not written for him and he does not get credit for working as an attendee or an instructor during time evaluation.

***Minimum % attendance***

If an employee attends a business event partly, would you say that he attended the business event or would you say that he did not? Here you can specify the minimum percentage which the employee must attend so that he is considered present for the business event. If you do not specify a value in this field for a business event type, the global value you specify in table T77S0 is taken.

| Group | Sem. abbr. | Value abbr. | Description |
|---|---|---|---|
| SEMIN | TIMEP | 100 | Minimum percentage attendance |

If you create absence records such that the attendance of the attendee falls below the minimum percentage, his booking for the business event is cancelled.

## 31.9 RELATIONSHIPS

| *Functional Consultant* | *User* | *Business Process Owner* | *Senior Management* | *My Rating* | *Understanding Level* |
|---|---|---|---|---|---|
| A | A | B | C | | |

### 31.9.1 Screen

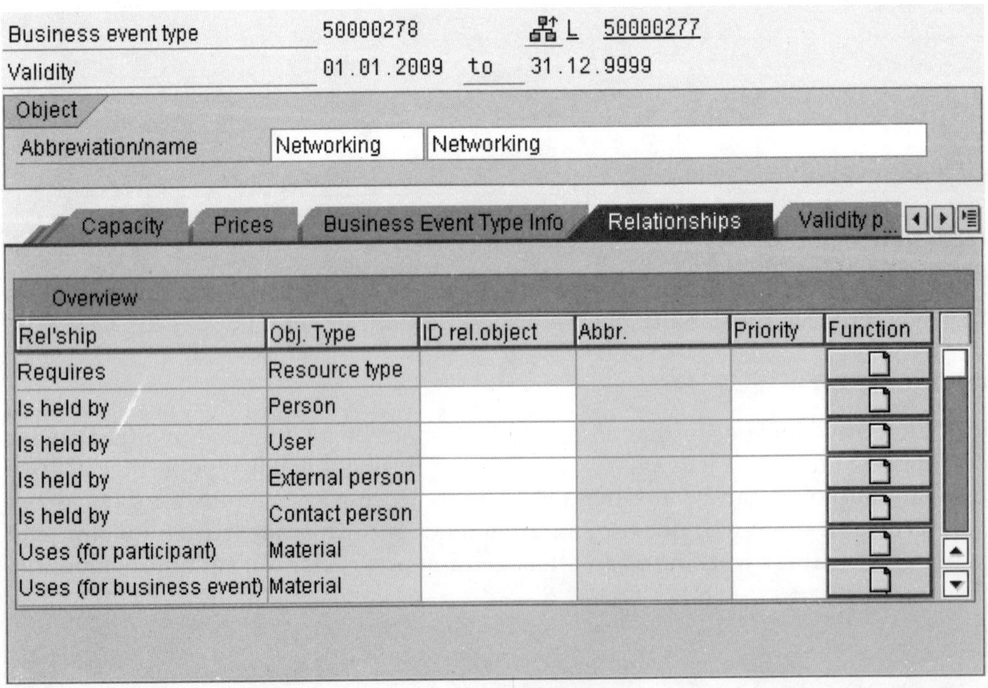

### 31.9.2 Allowed Relationships

If you click Allowed relationships, the system shows you all the relationships allowed with a business event type.

| | | |
|---|---|---|
| A\|003\|B | Belongs to | Development Plan |
| A\|003\|L | Belongs to | Business event group |
| A\|011\|K | Cost center assignment | Cost center |
| A\|022\|R | Requires | Resource type |
| A\|026\|H | Is held by | External person |
| A\|026\|P | Is held by | Person |
| A\|026\|PT | Is held by | Contact person |
| A\|026\|US | Is held by | User |
| A\|028\|Q | Imparts | Qualification |
| A\|029\|D | Has prerequisite | Business event type |
| B\|029\|D | Is prerequisite of | Business event type |
| A\|029\|DC | Has prerequisite | Curriculum Type |
| B\|029\|DC | Is prerequisite of | Curriculum Type |
| A\|029\|Q | Has prerequisite | Qualification |
| A\|033\|AC | Is planned for | Rule |
| A\|033\|C | Is planned for | Job |
| A\|034\|AP | Was participated in by | Applicant |
| A\|034\|H | Was participated in by | External person |
| A\|034\|KI | Was participated in by | Prospect |
| A\|034\|KU | Was participated in by | Customer |
| A\|034\|O | Was participated in by | Organizational unit |
| A\|034\|P | Was participated in by | Person |
| A\|034\|PT | Was participated in by | Contact person |
| A\|034\|U | Was participated in by | Company |
| A\|034\|US | Was participated in by | User |
| A\|036\|KI | Is organized by | Prospect |
| A\|036\|KU | Is organized by | Customer |
| A\|036\|O | Is organized by | Organizational unit |
| A\|036\|U | Is organized by | Company |
| B\|049\|P | Develops | Person |
| B\|049\|US | Develops | User |
| A\|054\|M | Uses (for participant) | Material |
| A\|055\|M | Uses (for business event) | Material |
| A\|057\|BS | Has particpnt aprsl model | Appraisal Model |
| A\|058\|BS | Has event apprsl model | Appraisal Model |
| A\|090\|H | Is responsibility of | External person |
| A\|090\|P | Is responsibility of | Person |
| A\|090\|PT | Is responsibility of | Contact person |
| A\|090\|US | Is responsibility of | User |
| A\|607\|VC | Is described by | Criterion |
| A\|608\|VA | Has appraisal template | Appraisal template |
| A\|615\|C | Mandatory for | Job |
| A\|615\|O | Mandatory for | Organizational unit |
| A\|615\|P | Mandatory for | Person |
| A\|615\|S | Mandatory for | Position |
| A\|712\|BG | Imparts | Criteria Group |
| A\|712\|BK | Imparts | Criterion |

### 31.9.3 Explanation of Relationships

You can maintain different types of relationships for a business event type. Their significance is explained below.

| *Code* | *Relationship* | *Object types* | *Explanation* |
|---|---|---|---|
| A003 | Belongs to | Development Plan | A business event type may belong to a development plan. A person undergoing a development plan is expected to attend a business event of this type. |
| A003 | Belongs to | Business event group | In the business event catalog, a business event type is shown under a business event group because of this relationship. Note that this relationship has time constraint 3. Therefore, it is possible to show a business event type under multiple business event groups at the same time. |
| A011 | Cost center assignment | Cost center | Here you specify the cost center to which the cost incurred by business events of this type is charged. |
| A022 | Requires | Resource type | You may have different types of resources, e.g. overhead projector. Each overhead projector is a resource with unique id. All overhead projectors are resources of type 'overhead projector'. A business event type requiring an overhead projector can use any one of the overhead projectors. Therefore, you specify a resource type which is required for a business event type. |
| A026 | Is held by | External person<br>Person<br>Contact person<br>User | You use this relationship to specify which instructors can hold business events of this type. The system proposes these during resource reservation. You can have multiple instructors for a business event type. |
| A028 | Imparts | Qualification | Here you specify the qualifications imparted by business events of this type. After an attendee successfully completes a business event, these qualifications are transferred to his profile in the follow-up activities. |
| A029 | Has prerequisite | Business event type<br>Curriculum Type<br>Qualification | You use this relationship to specify the prerequisites of a business event type. When an attendee is booked for a business event, the system ensures that he fulfils these requirements. |

| *Code* | *Relationship* | *Object types* | *Explanation* |
|---|---|---|---|
| B029 | Is prerequisite of | Business event type<br>Curriculum Type | You use this relationship to specify that this business event type is a prerequisite for another business event type. When an attendee is booked for a business event, the system ensures that he fulfils these requirements. |
| A033 | Is planned for | Rule<br>Job | Here you specify the target audience (persons holding a job) for business events of this type. Information regarding the target group at which a business event is aimed can be included in the business event brochure. A business event type may be planned for more than one job. |
| A034 | Was participated in by | Applicant<br>External person<br>Prospect<br>Customer<br>Organizational unit<br>Person<br>Contact person<br>Company<br>User | You can set up the system in such a way that when a business event is followed up (confirmed that it was held), the system can create this relationship between all its attendees and the business event type. |
| A036 | Is organized by | Prospect<br>Customer<br>Organizational unit<br>Company | You use this relationship to specify the organizer of business events of this type. You can have multiple organizers for a business event type. |
| B049 | Develops | Person<br>User | Business events of this type develop a person or a user. |
| A054 | Uses (for participant) | Material | You use this relationship to specify the material, e.g. training material, which is required for each participant. |
| A055 | Uses (for business event) | Material | You use this relationship to specify the material which is required for each business event. |
| A057 | Has particpnt aprsl model | Appraisal Model | Here you can specify the appraisal model for appraisal of participants. If an appraisal model is specified for a business event type, it overrides the global appraisal model for attendees. |
| A058 | Has event apprsl model | Appraisal Model | Here you can specify the appraisal model for appraisal of business events of this type. If an appraisal model is specified for a business event type, it overrides the global appraisal model for business event types. |

| *Code* | *Relationship* | *Object types* | *Explanation* |
|---|---|---|---|
| A090 | Is responsibility of | External person<br>Person<br>Contact person<br>User | Here you can specify the person who is responsible for doing administrative work for business events of this type. He corresponds with the attendees and instructors, provides resources and answers queries. |
| A607 | Is described by | Criterion | You can use a business event type as a criterion in Appraisal. You specify that here. |
| A608 | Has appraisal template | Appraisal template | Here you specify the appraisal template for a business event type. |
| A615 | Mandatory for | Job<br>Organizational unit<br>Person<br>Position | Here you can specify that a business event type is mandatory for the specified object. |
| A712 | Imparts | Criteria group<br>Criterion | If you attend business event of this type, you achieve this criteria or criteria group. |

## 31.10 VALIDITY PERIOD

| *Functional Consultant* | *User* | *Business Process Owner* | *Senior Management* | *My Rating* | *Understanding Level* |
|---|---|---|---|---|---|
| A | A | B | C | | |

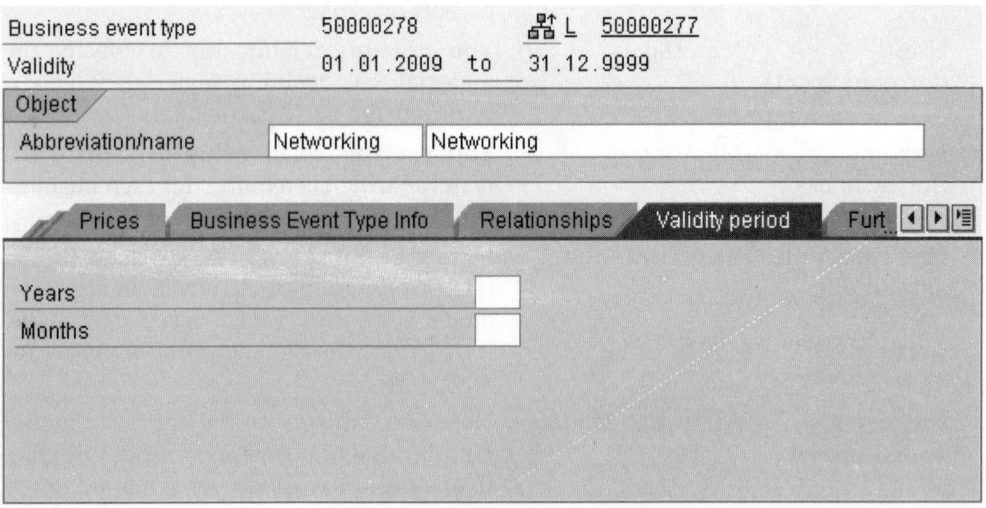

This infotype lets you define the validity for a business event type. After this period, attendance of business event of this type expires. If this business event type is a prerequisite of another business event type, that requirement is not fulfilled by an expired business event.

## 31.11 FURTHER INFORMATION

| *Functional Consultant* | *User* | *Business Process Owner* | *Senior Management* | *My Rating* | *Understanding Level* |
|---|---|---|---|---|---|
| C | C | C | C | | |

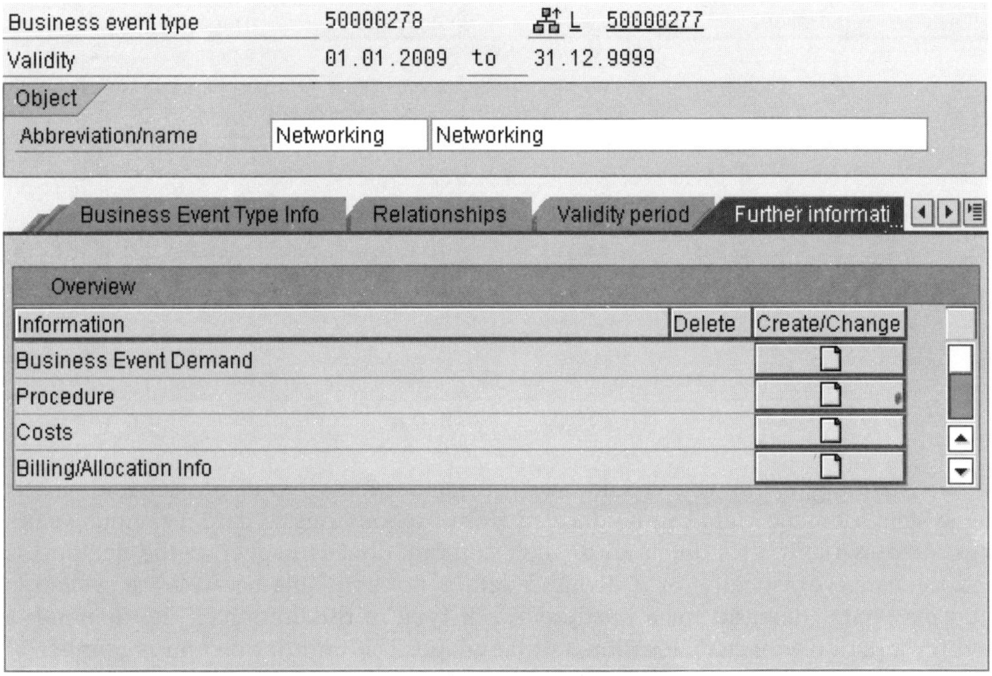


Through this tab of the business event type you can create, change or delete data in various infotypes. Each of these infotypes is discussed separately.

## 31.12 BUSINESS EVENT DEMAND

| *Functional Consultant* | *User* | *Business Process Owner* | *Senior Management* | *My Rating* | *Understanding Level* |
|---|---|---|---|---|---|
| A | A | B | C | | |

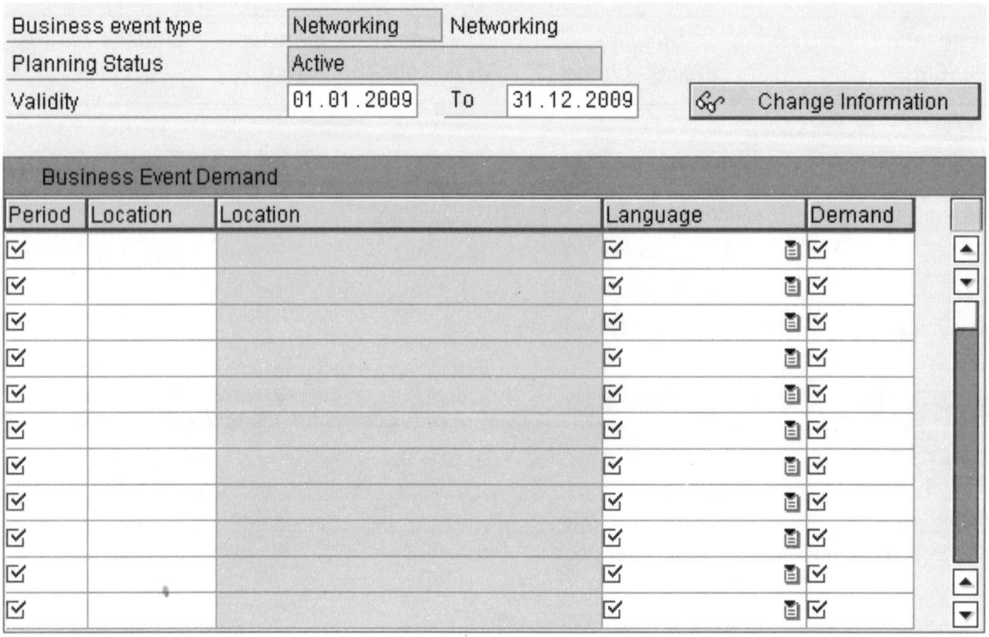


During the planning cycle, you would plan business events based on demand. In an ongoing system, demand data can be derived from prebookings to date, previous year's bookings, or previous year's demand, or their combination. However, if the demand is expected to change drastically, or if demand data is not available because the system is new, you may enter demand for a business event type in this infotype. The demand is specified for a period (quarter), location and language. The unit of demand is number of business events, and not number of attendees.

## 31.13 PROCEDURE

| *Functional Consultant* | *User* | *Business Process Owner* | *Senior Management* | *My Rating* | *Understanding Level* |
|---|---|---|---|---|---|
| A | A | A | B | | |

In view V_T77KV_1 you specify attendee-related checks before business event booking which apply to all business event types.

| AT | Attendee type | Booked for ... | Prbkg on same ... | Check prerequisite | Check qualification |
|---|---|---|---|---|---|
| H | External person | W | W | W | |
| P | Person | W | W | W | W |

Also, in view V_T77KV_2 you specify business event follow-up actions which apply to all business event types.

| AT | Attendee type | Transfer quals | Del. BE/A rel. | Rel.BE type/Att |
|---|---|---|---|---|
| H | External person | ☐ | ☐ | ☐ |
| P | Person | ☑ | ☐ | ☐ |

If you make an entry in the procedure tab for a business event type, you can override the above settings. This gives you more flexibility as your checks can be different for different business event types.

| | | | |
|---|---|---|---|
| Business event type | Networking | Networking | |
| Planning Status | Active | | |
| Validity | 01.01.2009 | to 31.12.9999 | Change Information |

Procedure 01 D 50000278 1

| AT | Attendee type | BookT | PrebT | ChPre | CheckQ | Quals | Del.BE/A | E/A rel |
|---|---|---|---|---|---|---|---|---|
| | | | | | | ☐ | ☐ | ☐ |
| | | | | | | ☐ | ☐ | ☐ |
| | | | | | | ☐ | ☐ | ☐ |
| | | | | | | ☐ | ☐ | ☐ |
| | | | | | | ☐ | ☐ | ☐ |
| | | | | | | ☐ | ☐ | ☐ |
| | | | | | | ☐ | ☐ | ☐ |
| | | | | | | ☐ | ☐ | ☐ |
| | | | | | | ☐ | ☐ | ☐ |
| | | | | | | ☐ | ☐ | ☐ |
| | | | | | | ☐ | ☐ | ☐ |
| | | | | | | ☐ | ☐ | ☐ |

#### *Attendee type*

You can have different checks for different attendee types.

#### *Check for bookings for the same business event type (BookT)*

When an attendee books for a business event, you may want to know if the attendee has already attended a business event of the same type or is already booked to attend such a business event. If yes, you may give an error (E), a warning (W), or a message (I). If you don't want to perform this check, you can leave this field blank.

#### *Check for prebookings on the same business event type (PrebT)*

When an attendee prebooks for a business event type, you may want to know if the attendee has already attended a business event of the same type or is already booked to attend such a business event. If yes, you may give an error (E), a warning (W), or a message (I). If you don't want to perform this check, you can leave this field blank.

#### *Check for prerequisite business event (ChPre)*

When an attendee books for a business event, you may want to know whether the attendee has attended the prerequisite business events. If yes, you may give an error (E), a warning (W), or a message (I). If you don't want to perform this check, you can leave this field blank.

#### *Check attendee's qualification (CheckQ)*

When an attendee books for a business event, you may want to know whether the attendee has the qualifications or alternative qualifications required to attend the business event. If yes, you may give an error (E), a warning (W), or a message (I). If you don't want to perform this check, you can leave this field blank.

#### *Transfer objectives to attendee as qualifications (Quals)*

A business event may impart a qualification. When an attendee attends a business event, he acquires that qualification. You may add the qualification to the attendee manually, or you may want the system to do it automatically. If you want the system to do it automatically, you tick this checkbox.

#### *Delete and create relationships (Del.BE/A, E/A rel)*

When an attendee books a business event, relationship 025 is created which says that the attendee takes part in the business event. When the business event has actually taken place (followed up), this relationship 025 is deleted and another relationship 034 is created which says that the attendee participated in the business event type. Relationship 034 was read by the system to determine whether the employee has attended prerequisite business event. However, now the system reads both relationships 025 and 034. Hence, the system will work equally well if relationship 025 was not deleted and relationship 034 was not created. If you choose to delete and create relationships, you should tick both these checkboxes; although it is recommended that you leave both these checkboxes blank.

## 31.14 COSTS

| *Functional Consultant* | *User* | *Business Process Owner* | *Senior Management* | *My Rating* | *Understanding Level* |
|---|---|---|---|---|---|
| A | A | A | B | | |

### 31.14.1 Cost Items

When you hold a business event you incur cost under various heads or items. You define these cost items using transaction OOKB or S_AHR_61011845 in table T77KB and specify which cost items are required for which business events. Cost items are required for cost transfer posting of business event costs, for internal activity allocation of instructors' costs (via resource type), and for determining a price proposal.

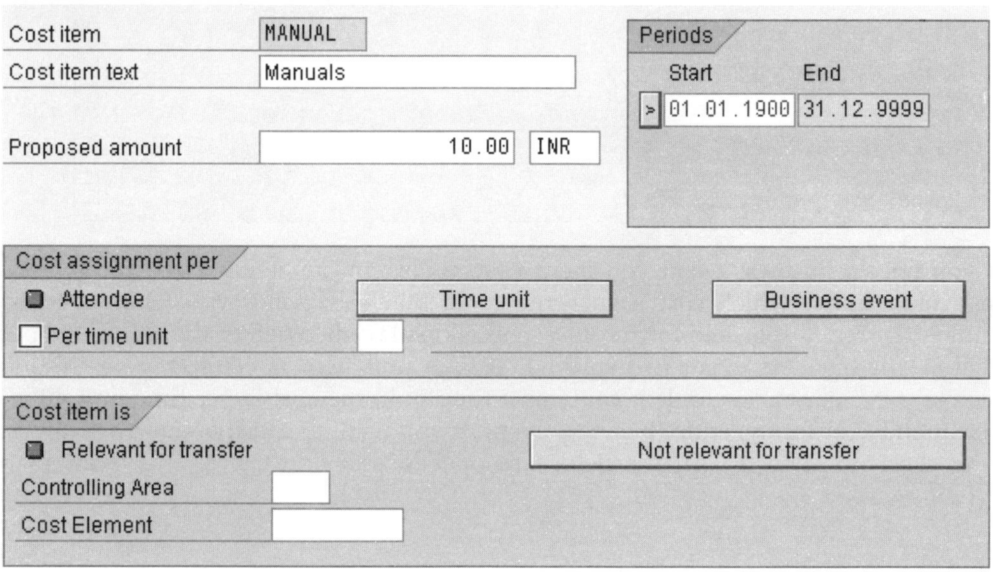


In the cost item you specify the proposed amount with currency. You also specify whether the amount is per business event, per time unit, per attendee or per attendee per time unit. You specify whether the cost item is relevant for cost transfer. If yes, the cost is transferred to which controlling area and cost element.

Cost may be incurred directly for a business event, or indirectly through use of a resource. You can store cost items for resource types, resources, business event types, and business events using the Costs infotype. If the same cost item is stored for a business event type and the corresponding business event, the system takes the value stored for the business event. Similarly, if the same cost item is stored for both resource type and resource, the value stored for the actual resource is taken.

### 31.14.2 Costs

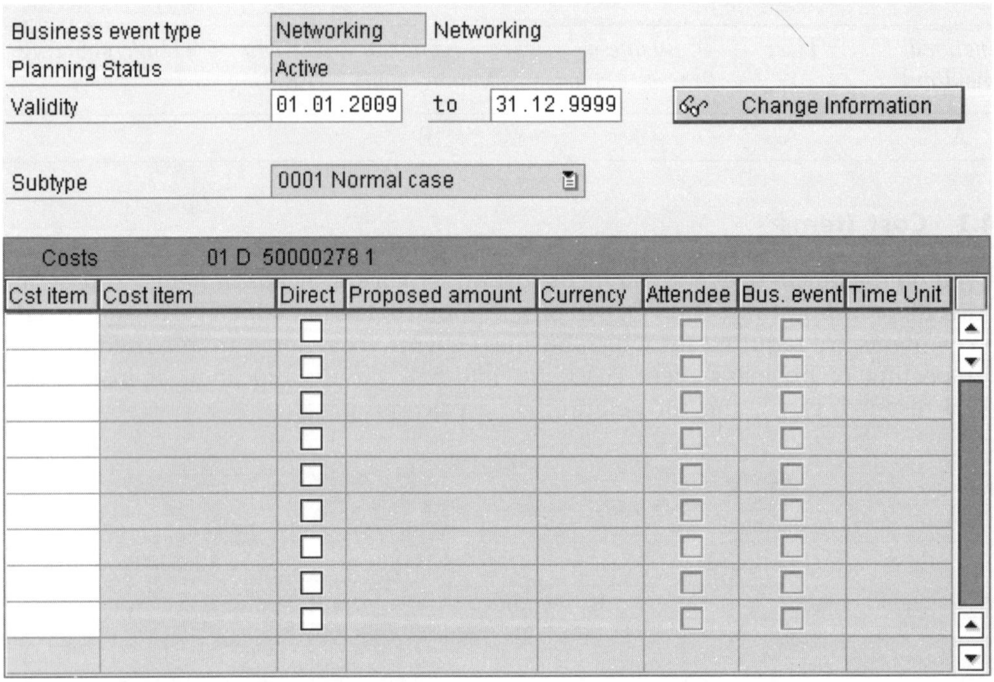


When you hold a business event you incur cost under various items. Here you specify the cost items under which cost is incurred for a business event type. The proposed amount and currency specified for the cost item is displayed. Whether the amount is per attendee or per business event is displayed. If time unit field is blank, the cost is per attendee or per business event. If it contains a time unit, the cost is per time unit either for each attendee or for the entire business event. If you want to specify your own values, click the checkbox 'Direct'. All the fields are opened and you can specify your own values.

## 31.15 BILLING/ALLOCATION INFO

| *Functional Consultant* | *User* | *Business Process Owner* | *Senior Management* | *My Rating* | *Understanding Level* |
|---|---|---|---|---|---|
| A | B | C | C | | |

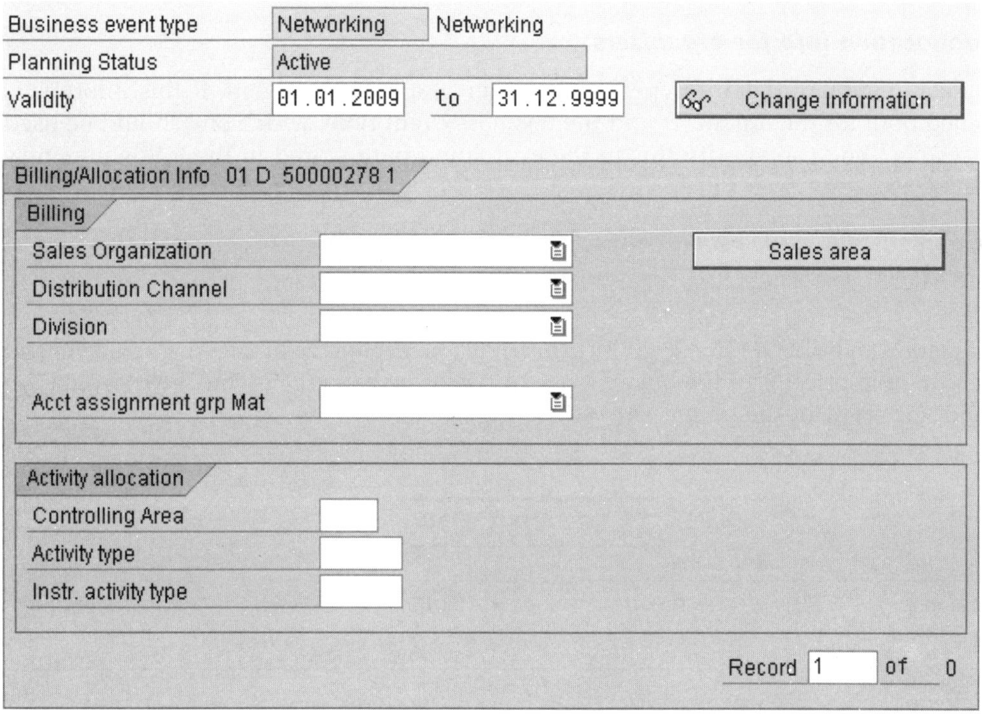


Details for billing and activity allocation are defined at global level. If you want to use different values for a business event type, you can specify them in this infotype.

### *Sales area*

In Sales and Distribution, you sell through a sales area, which comprises of sales organization, distribution channel and division. Your Sales and Distribution consultant will set up the sales areas you require. In this infotype, you will click the 'Sales area' icon and select the appropriate sales area. The system will populate the sales organization, distribution channel and division.

### *Account assignment group for materials*

The revenue from different types of materials you sell might go to different accounts. This is determined by the account assignment group for materials. Your Finance and Sales and Distribution consultants will decide the account assignment group for materials and you will choose from this list as per their guidance.

### *Activity allocation*

Whereas you bill your external customers using Sales and Distribution, you charge your internal customers using activity allocation. Activity allocation is done based on activity types. You can specify an activity type for attendees which will be used to charge your internal attendees. You can also specify an activity type for instructors which will be used to create credit for the work done by your instructors. You specify the controlling area in which both these activity allocations will take place.

### *Billing/allocation info for organizers*

You can also maintain this infotype for organizer of a business event. If this infotype is maintained both for the organizer and the business event type, which one should be used by the system? You can specify this in the evaluation path stored in the following entry in table T77S0.

| Group | Sem. abbr. | Value abbr. | Description |
|---|---|---|---|
| SEMIN | FLWAY | LSOFLWAY | Info determination for billing and allocation |

The evaluation path LSOFLWAY gives priority to the organizer of the business event. If you want to give priority to the business event type, you can create your own evaluation path, and specify it in the above entry.

## 31.16 WEB LINK

| *Functional Consultant* | *User* | *Business Process Owner* | *Senior Management* | *My Rating* | *Understanding Level* |
|---|---|---|---|---|---|
| A | B | C | C | | |

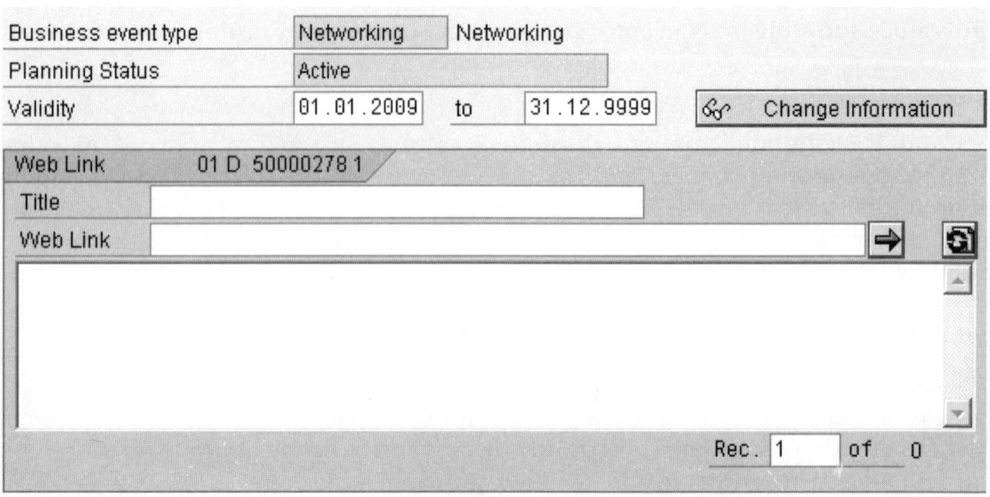

When you right-click a business event type in business event menu and some other dynamic menus, the system shows you 'Web link'.

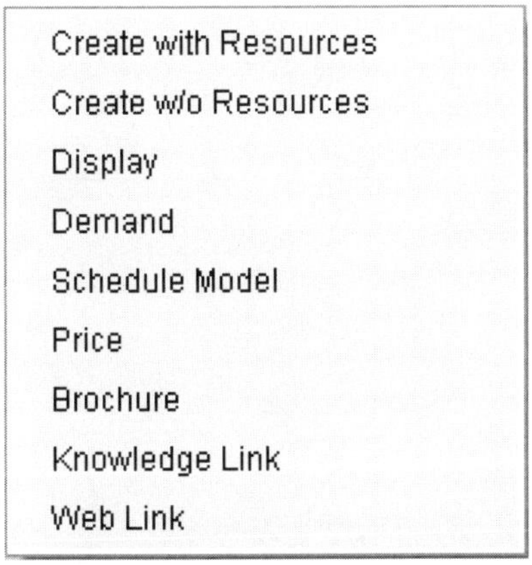


If you have created web links using this infotype, you can access them from there. If there is a single web link, it is opened directly. If there are multiple web links, the system displays them and you choose the one you want to see.

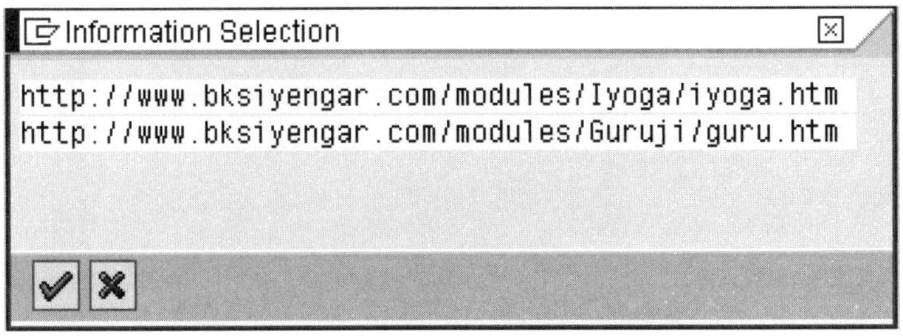

## 31.17 KNOWLEDGE LINK

| *Functional Consultant* | *User* | *Business Process Owner* | *Senior Management* | *My Rating* | *Understanding Level* |
|---|---|---|---|---|---|
| A | B | C | C | | |

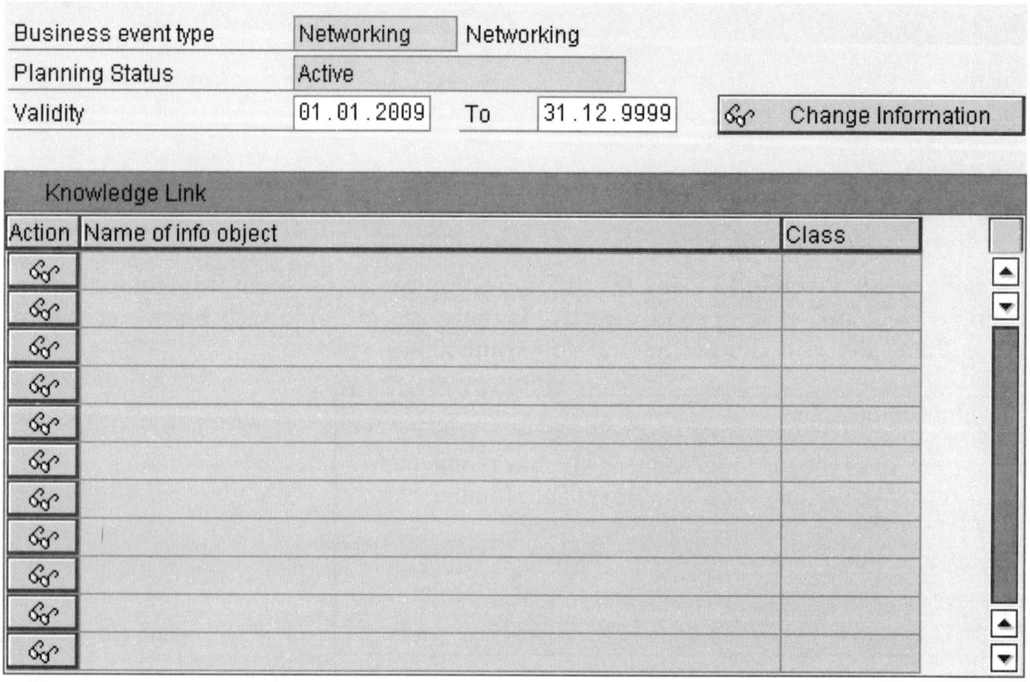


In SAP, there is a lot of knowledge, created by both SAP and you, which is stored in various places.

| Area | Description |
|---|---|
| ARCHLINK | ArchiveLink |
| BDS | Business Document Service |
| BW | Business Information Warehouse |
| CFF | Collaboration Folders |
| DATAARCH | Data Archiving |
| DMS | Document Management System |
| DMS2 | Document Management System |
| FILESYSTEM | File System |
| FOPC | MIC |
| HR_KW | Document Repository for HR Objects |
| HR_RU_PF | HR-RU: Pension Fund of Russia |
| ISM | Document Management in IS-M |
| IWBASAP | AcceleratedSAP |
| IWBHELP | Documentation |
| IWBMISC | Management |
| IWBNR3TRAN | Translation of non-R/3 texts |
| IWBPROJ | IMG document repository |
| IWBSOLAR | Solution Manager |
| IWBTRAIN | Training |
| IWB_EXTHLP | Extended help |

Some of this information may be useful for a business event. For example, you may have created a document in Solution Manager which may be useful in training your SAP users. SAP lets you store a link to these documents in a business event type. Note that most of these areas need RFC connection and you will need the help of your Basis consultant to know which ones are available. In addition, you need to know which documents are available where, so that you can choose an appropriate document to create a knowledge link. Once you create a knowledge link using Edit ➢ Insert Entry, you can access the document by clicking the knowledge link in this infotype for a business event or a business event type. You can also access the document in the Employee Self-Service.

## 31.18 WORKFLOW SETTINGS

| *Functional Consultant* | *User* | *Business Process Owner* | *Senior Management* | *My Rating* | *Understanding Level* |
|---|---|---|---|---|---|
| X | X | X | X | | |

This infotype is used in LSO.

## 31.19 COLLABORATION ROOM

| *Functional Consultant* | *User* | *Business Process Owner* | *Senior Management* | *My Rating* | *Understanding Level* |
|---|---|---|---|---|---|
| X | X | X | X | | |

This infotype is used in LSO.

## 31.20 FOLLOW-UP CONTROL OPTIONS

| *Functional Consultant* | *User* | *Business Process Owner* | *Senior Management* | *My Rating* | *Understanding Level* |
|---|---|---|---|---|---|
| X | X | X | X | | |

This infotype is used in LSO.

# Chapter 32 Dynamic Menus

## 32.1 DYNAMIC MENUS

| *Functional Consultant* | *User* | *Business Process Owner* | *Senior Management* | *My Rating* | *Understanding Level* |
|---|---|---|---|---|---|
| A | A | A | A | | |

### 32.1.1 Overview

Training and Event Management provides the following dynamic menus.

| *Menu* | *Chapter* |
|---|---|
| Master data catalog (Business event catalog) | 29.2 |
| Attendance menu | 36.3 |
| Business event menu | 34.2 |
| Information menu | 32.2 |
| Planning menu | 34.5 |
| Resource menu | 33.6 |
| Tool menu | 32.3 |

You can perform most of the functions in Training and Event Management through dynamic menus. The advantage of the dynamic menus is that you create data and access functions directly in the clearly structured environment of the business event hierarchy.

### 32.1.2 Navigation

There are two ways of navigating in dynamic menus. You can select an object and choose the function in the menu. Alternatively, you can right-click an object and choose the function. You can switch between the attendance menu, the information menu, and the business event menu as required. You always access the same level of the structure as the one you leave.

### 32.1.3 Substructure Access

If you want to access only a part of the business event catalog from a menu, you can do so by setting access.

***Set access***

You select a root object (business event group or business event type) from which you want to access the structure and choose . The display includes all objects underlying the root object you select. This access setting is valid until you delete it.

***Delete access***

You can revoke the access at any time by choosing . The entire business event catalog is displayed.

***General overview***

From within your own special access, you can choose to view the complete structure. Your access choice is not deleted when you do this.

### 32.1.4 Extended Search

You can search for different objects in dynamic menus. When you click , the system gives you the following dialog box, where you enter the search criteria.

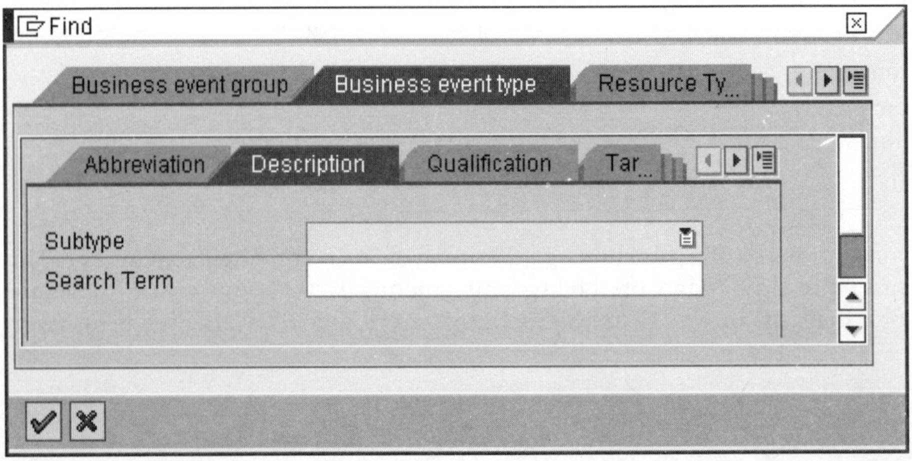

The search is not limited to the name or abbreviation of the object. You can even search the descriptions of business events. Similarly, you can search for business events which impart certain qualification. The menu structure need not be expanded when you start the search.

### 32.1.5 Planning Period

| Group | Sem. abbr. | Value abbr. | Description |
|---|---|---|---|
| SEMIN | PFORC | 360 | Planning period |

In dynamic menus, you specify a planning period. The setting above is used the first time the planning period is read in the dynamic menus (with the exception of the Planning menu). After this, the planning period is created user-specific. In addition, the value you enter here is used when you create a business event using transaction PV10 or PV11.

### 32.1.6 Virtual Business Event Group

| Group | Sem.abbr. | Value abbr | Description |
|---|---|---|---|
| SEMIN | LROOT | | General initial access to dynamic menus |

If you have too many business event groups and business event types at the top level, the system performance in dynamic menus may be affected. You can create a virtual business event group to which all top level business event groups and business event types belong using relationship B003, and enter the name of the virtual business event group here. This business event group will not be shown in the business event catalog and the system performance will considerably improve.

### 32.1.7 Additional Line in Dynamic Menus

| Group | Sem.abbr. | Value abbr | Description |
|---|---|---|---|
| SEMIN | MINFO | RH_MORINFO | Function module for output of additional info |

You use this entry to specify that an additional line is output under each node in the dynamic menus. The standard system contains the sample function module RH_MORINFO that you can copy and adapt to suit your requirements.

## 32.2 INFORMATION MENU

| *Functional Consultant* | *User* | *Business Process Owner* | *Senior Management* | *My Rating* | *Understanding Level* |
|---|---|---|---|---|---|
| A | A | B | C | | |

### 32.2.1 Purpose

Information menu provides an easy and organized method of accessing standard reports in Training and Event Management. You select a business event group, a business event type, a business event or an attendee and right-click. You choose the report category and then the report. The system runs the report taking the object you selected as parameter. If you want the system to run the report directly, without showing selection screen, check and if necessary correct the user-specific settings.

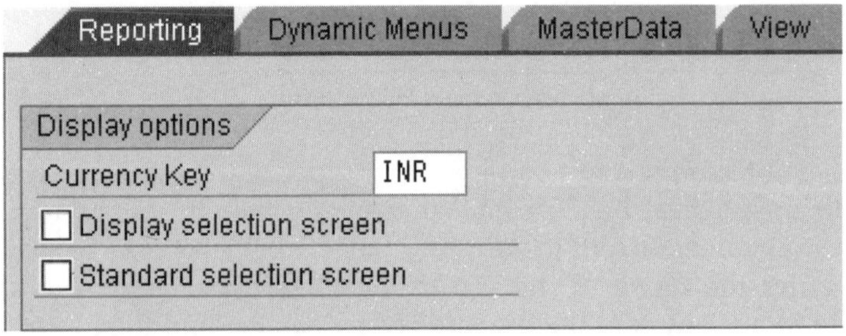


Traffic lights show whether the business event is full, accepting only essential bookings, or accepting normal bookings.

### 32.2.2 Transaction

PSV3—Information Menu

### 32.2.3 Navigation

Select an object and right-click (or go through menu).

### 32.2.4 Screen

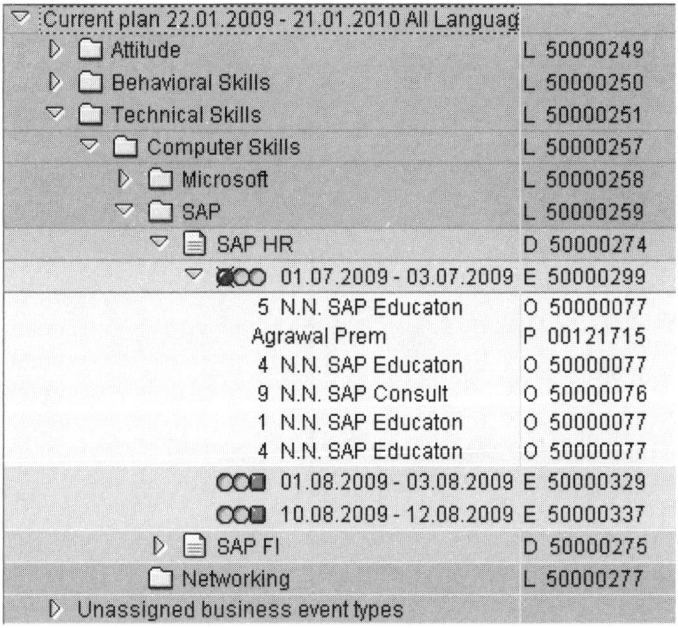


### 32.2.5 Information Menu: Attendance

You can run the following reports in the attendance menu.

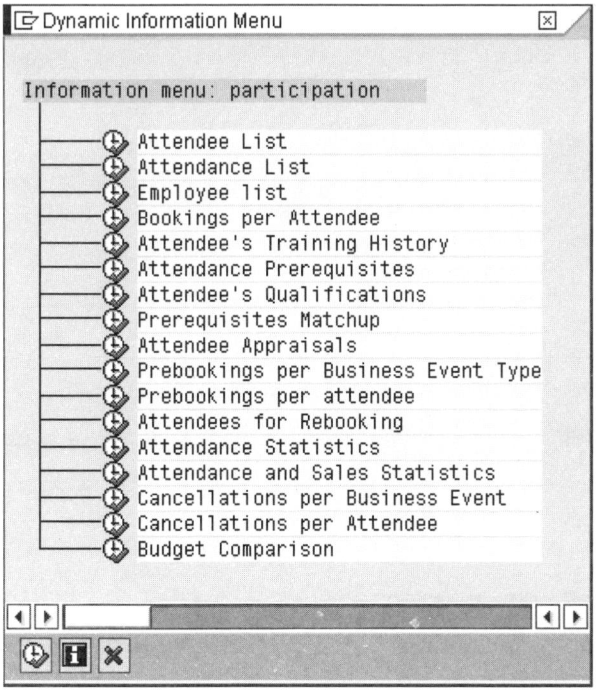

### 32.2.6 Information Menu: Business Events

You can run the following reports in the business events menu.

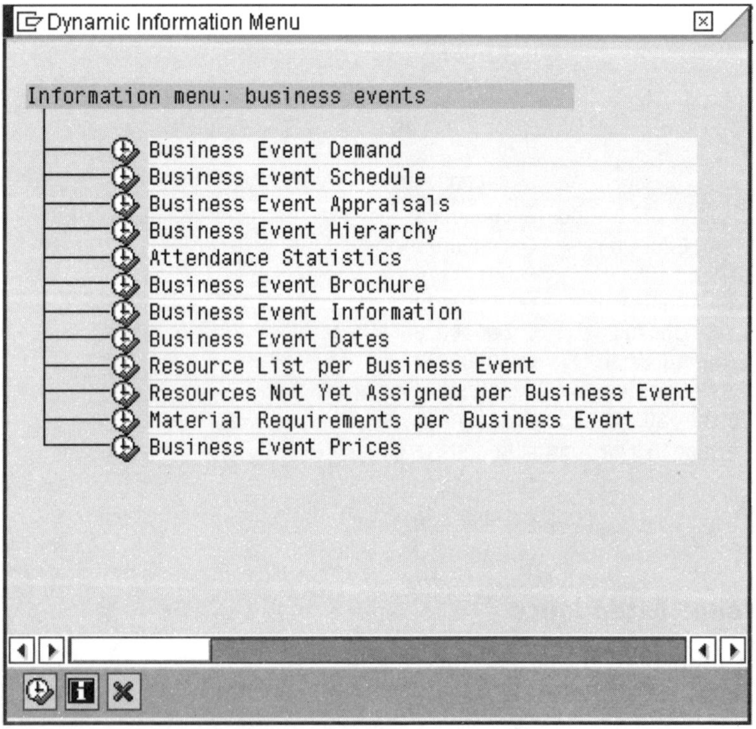


### 32.2.7 Information Menu: Resources

You can run the following reports in the resources menu.

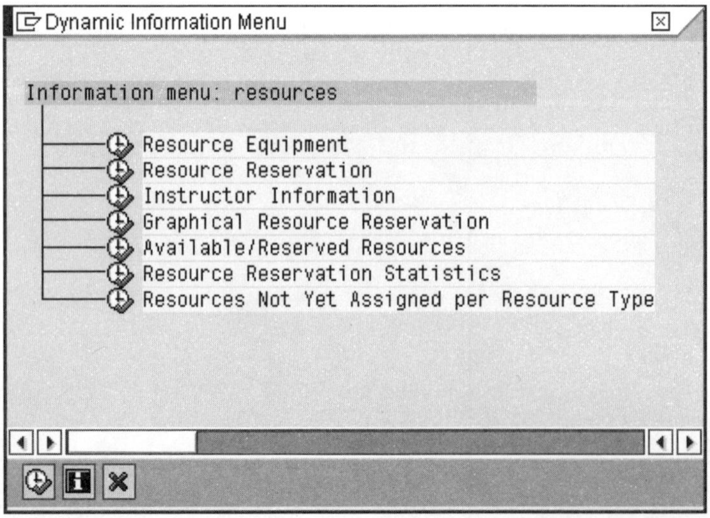

### 32.2.8 Integration of Customer-Specific Reports

The information menu you see above contains standard reports provided by SAP. You can add your own reports to the information menu using transaction PVDM.

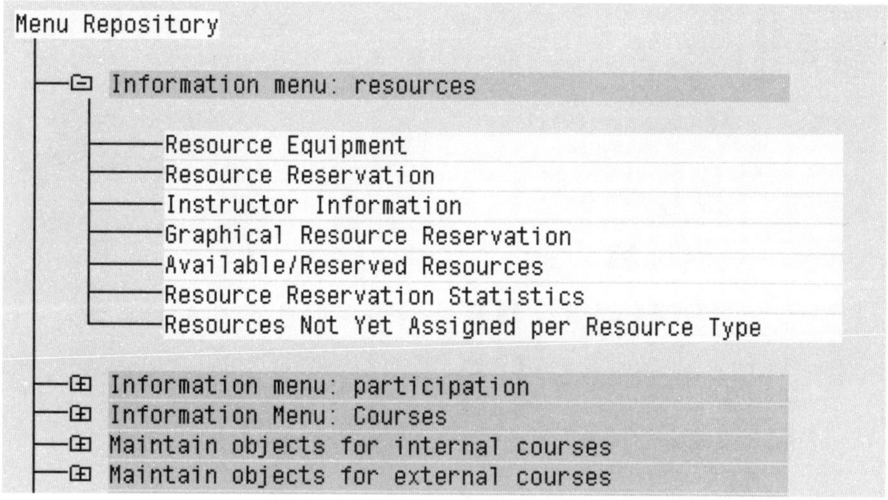


### 32.2.9 Ad Hoc Query

You can use transaction S_PH0_48000535 to query the Training and Event Management database and extract information as per your need.

## 32.3 TOOL MENU

| *Functional Consultant* | *User* | *Business Process Owner* | *Senior Management* | *My Rating* | *Understanding Level* |
|---|---|---|---|---|---|
| A | A | B | C | | |

### 32.3.1 Purpose

In the tool menu, you cannot create business event group, business event type or business event; but you can change all information about them. You can also translate language-dependent data, lock/unlock objects and maintain prices.

### 32.3.2 Transaction

PSVT—Tool Menu

### 32.3.3 Navigation

Select an object and right-click (or go through menu).

### 32.3.4 Screen

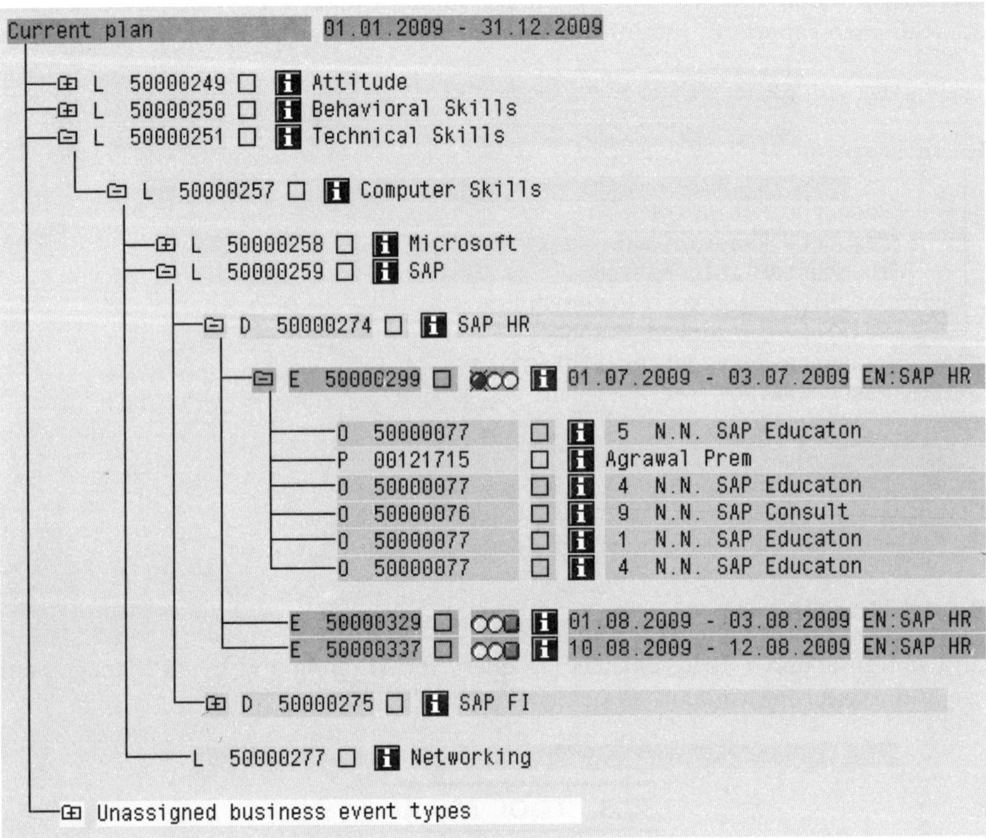


## 32.4 USER-SPECIFIC SETTINGS

| *Functional Consultant* | *User* | *Business Process Owner* | *Senior Management* | *My Rating* | *Understanding Level* |
|---|---|---|---|---|---|
| A | A | B | C | | |

### 32.4.1 Purpose

You can run transaction PSVI to make user-specific settings so that you see only that data in the dynamic menus which you want to see. For example, you may want to see only firmly booked business events, and not planned business events, because you don't want to book attendance for a business event about which there is uncertainty. But another user is keen on finding a business event whose dates suit him better, even though the organizers have not yet taken a final decision on it. These settings, as the name suggests, are user-specific. Each user's choice of access is retained even after the user logs off. You can also see and change user-specific settings in all the dynamic menus under Settings ➢ Change Settings.

## 32.4.2 Reporting

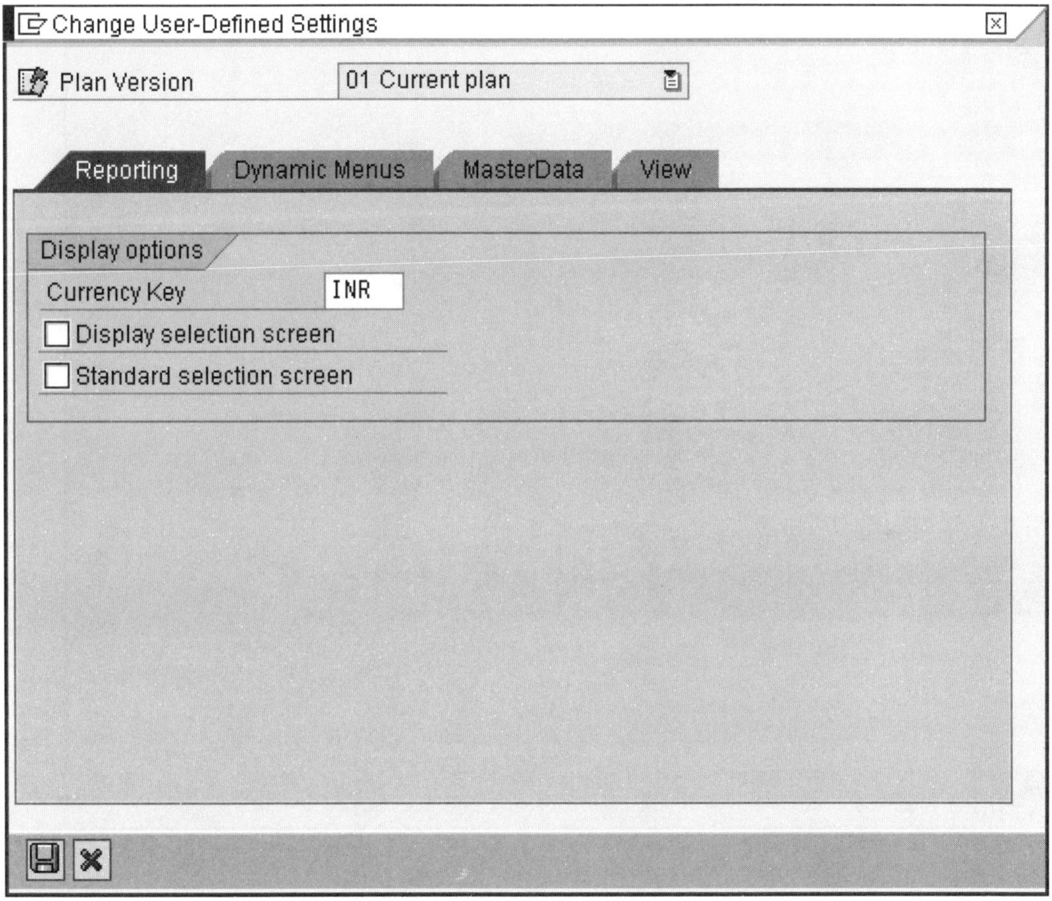


***Currency key***

All amount fields displayed in the dynamic menus are in this currency unless you specify some other currency in the report's selection screen.

***Display selection screen***

If you do not tick this checkbox, the report from dynamic menus is run directly without showing the selection screen. If you tick this checkbox, the selection screen is shown first.

***Standard selection screen***

If you tick this checkbox, the field 'Standard selection screen' on the selection screen of reports is selected by default.

### 32.4.3 Filter

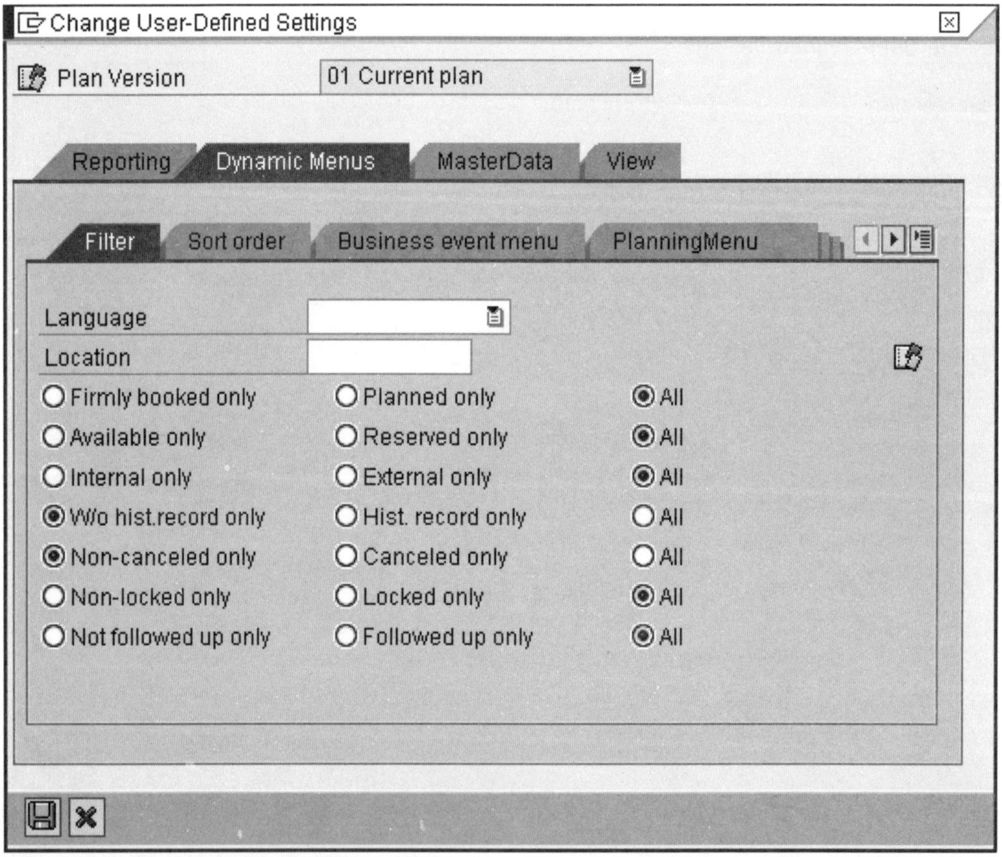


Here you can restrict the business events that are displayed in the dynamic menus by specifying a language, location, status, or business event attributes (such as internal or external). You should be careful with these settings because these settings will hide certain business events and you may wonder why you are not seeing certain business events. It will be worse if you don't even realize that you are not seeing certain business events. However, these settings are also a great boon if used properly. For example, the person in charge of the training function may want to see only locked business events and ask why they are locked and when they will be unlocked.

### 32.4.4 Sort Order

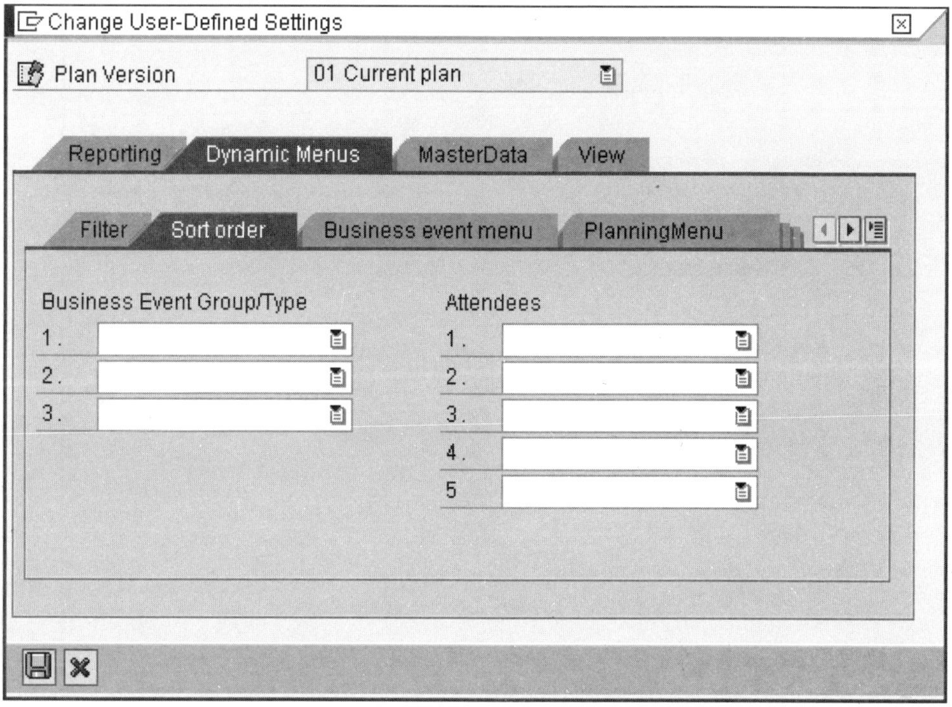


***Business event group/type***

In the first field you define how the business event groups and business event types are sorted. You can sort by the following fields.

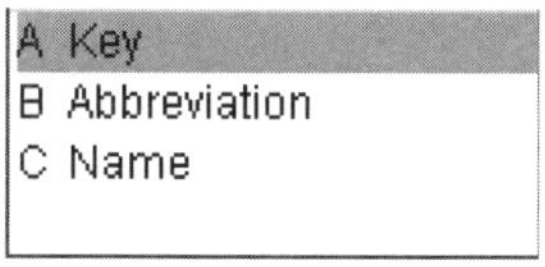


In case the sort key is identical, the sorting is done by the second field and if necessary by the third field.

***Attendees***

Attendees can similarly be sorted by the following fields.

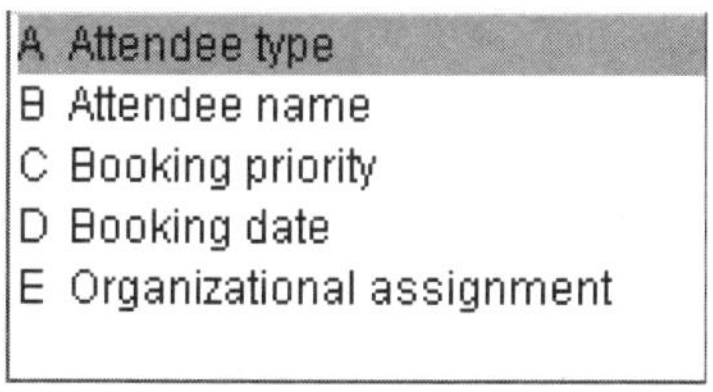


In case the sort key is identical, the sorting is done by the second field, third field and so on.

### 32.4.5 Business Event Menu

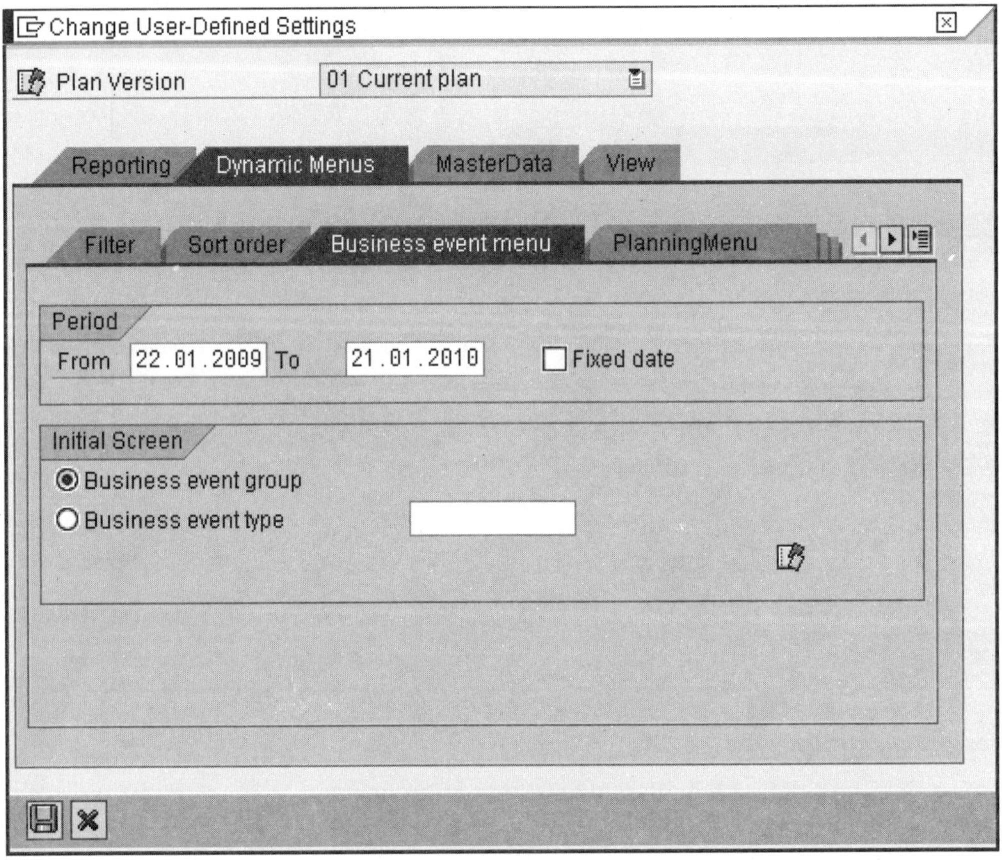


***Period***

You can enter a start and an end date here to determine the data selection period. If you select the option 'Fixed date', the dates you enter are retained. If you do not select this option, the start and end dates are moved forward by one day on a daily basis.

***Initial screen***

If you don't want to see the entire business event catalog in the business event menu, but only certain business event type, you can specify that here.

### 32.4.6 Planning Menu

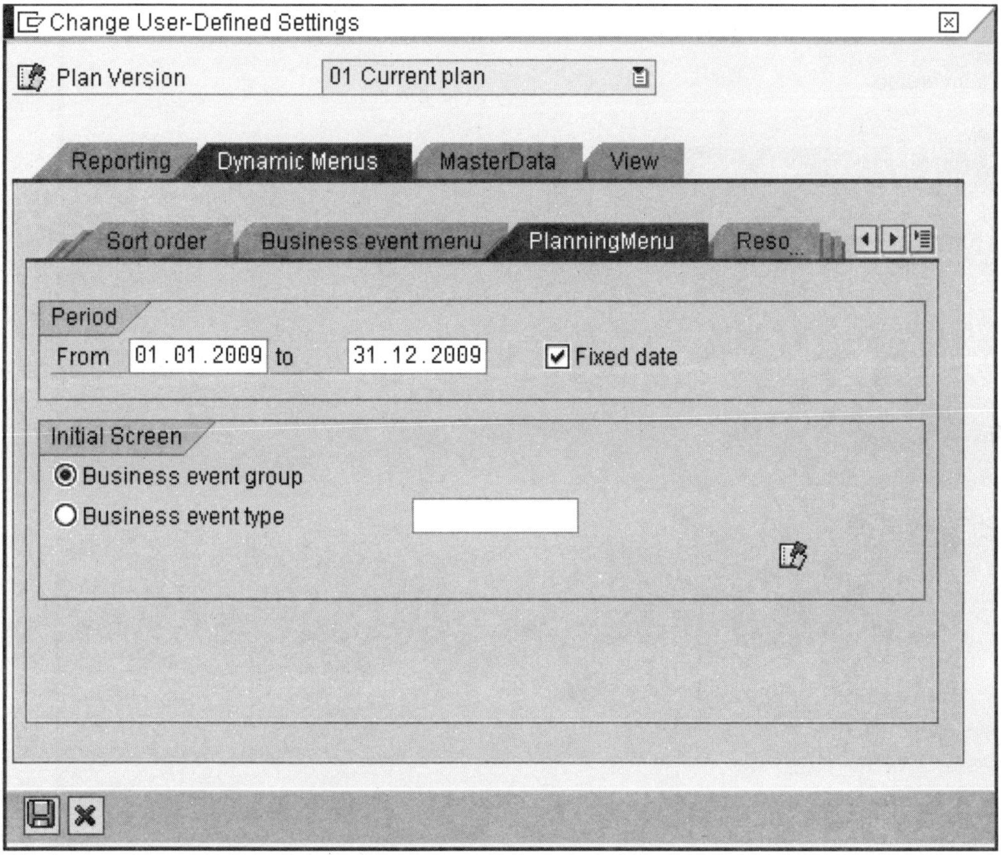


***Period***

You can enter a start and an end date here to determine the data selection period. If you select the option 'Fixed date', the dates you enter are retained. If you do not select this option, the start and end dates are moved forward by one day on a daily basis.

***Initial screen***

If you don't want to see the entire business event catalog in the planning menu, but only certain business event type, you can specify that here.

### 32.4.7 Resource Menu

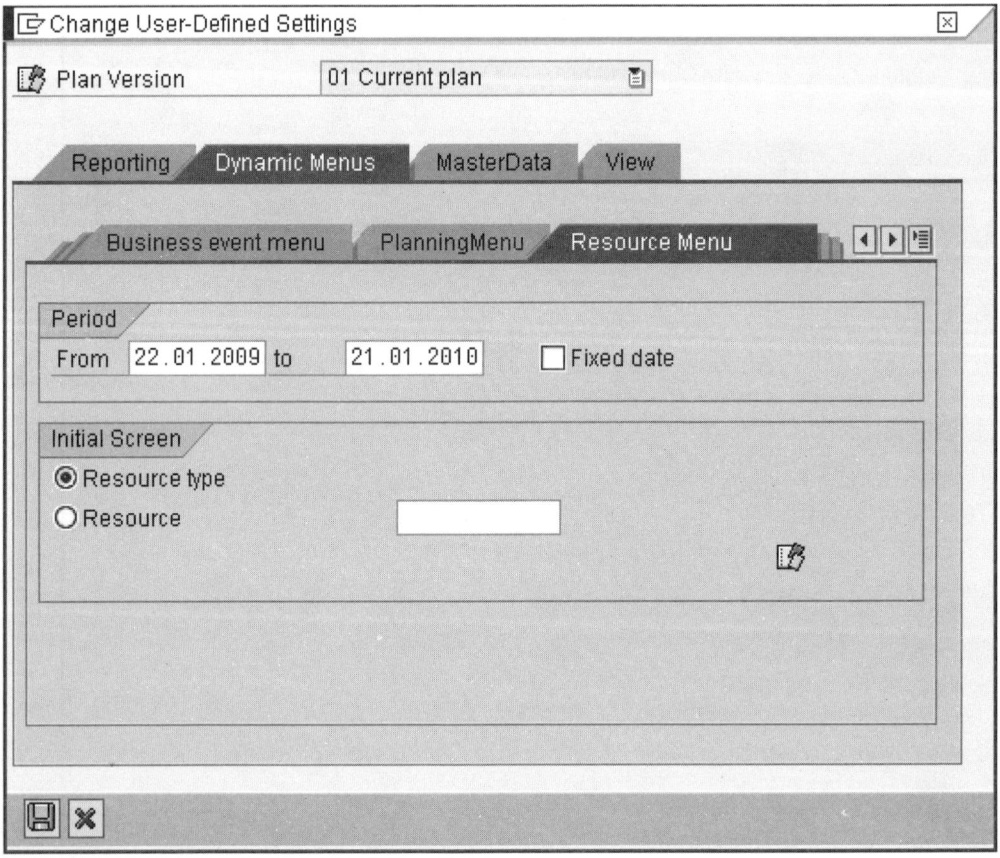


***Period***

You can enter a start and an end date here to determine the data selection period. If you select the option 'Fixed date', the dates you enter are retained. If you do not select this option, the start and end dates are moved forward by one day on a daily basis.

***Initial screen***

If you don't want to see all the resource types in the resource menu, but only certain resources, you can specify that here.

### 32.4.8 Tool Menu

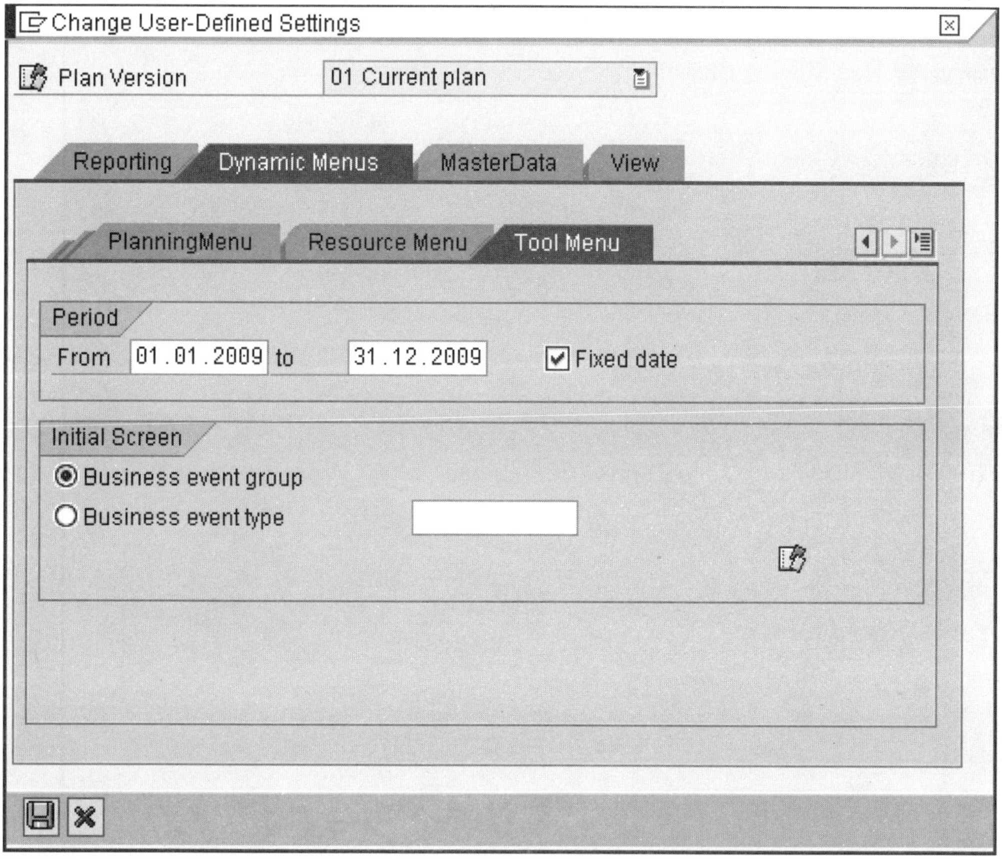


***Period***

You can enter a start and an end date here to determine the data selection period. If you select the option 'Fixed date', the dates you enter are retained. If you do not select this option, the start and end dates are moved forward by one day on a daily basis.

***Initial screen***

If you don't want to see the entire business event catalog in the tool menu, but only certain business event type, you can specify that here.

### 32.4.9 Master Data

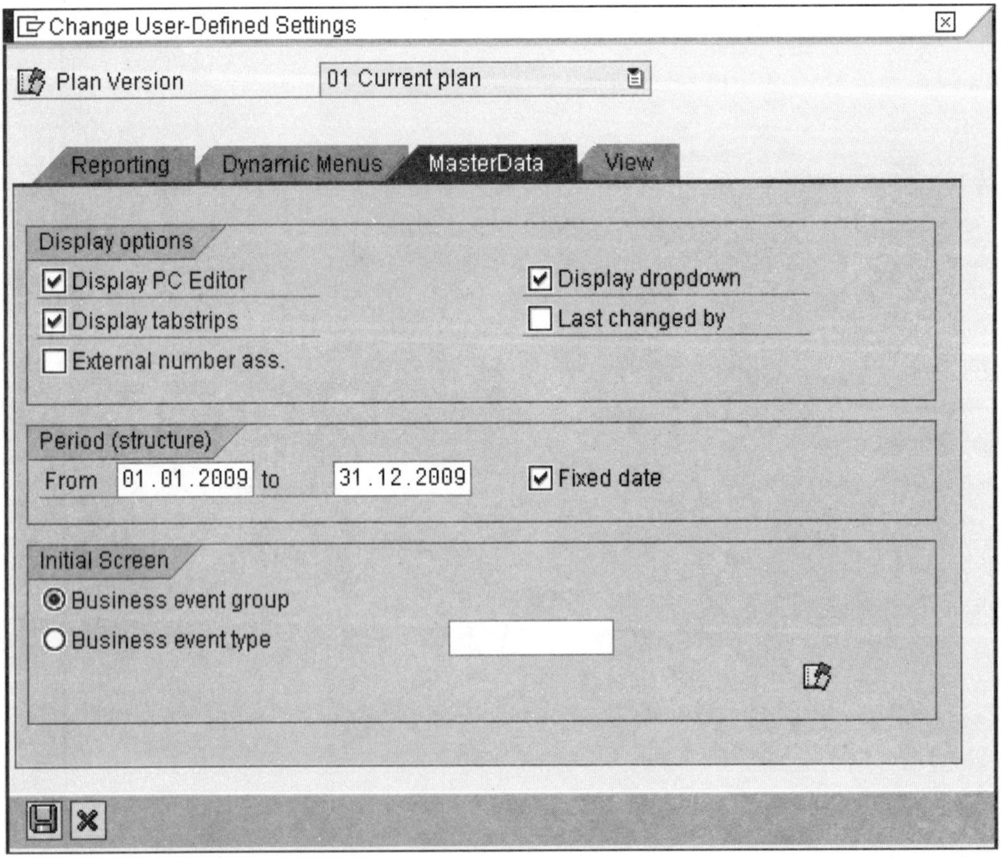


These settings are used for business event catalog.

#### *Display PC editor*

If you tick this checkbox, you can use a text editor for entering subtypes of the Description infotype. If you do not select the option, only a line editor is available.

#### *Display tabstrips*

When you select an object and choose Display, if this checkbox is ticked, the infotypes of the object are displayed as tab pages. If this checkbox is not ticked, the infotypes are displayed one below the other.

#### *External number assignment*

If you tick this checkbox, you can assign object IDs manually when you create new objects. Otherwise, the system uses internal number assignment.

### *Display dropdown*

If you tick this checkbox, possible entries help is available for input fields in the form of a dropdown list.

### *Last changed by*

If you tick this checkbox, data change information is automatically displayed.

### *Period*

You can enter a start and an end date here to determine the data selection period. If you select the option 'Fixed date', the dates you enter are retained. If you do not select this option, the start and end dates are moved forward by one day on a daily basis.

### *Initial screen*

If you don't want to see the entire business event catalog, but only certain business event type, you can specify that here.

## 32.4.10 View

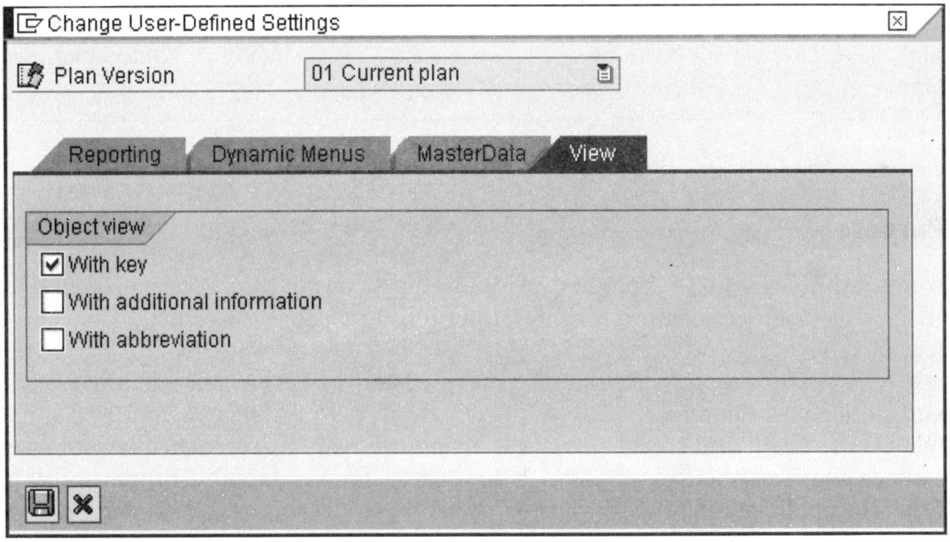


### *With key*

If you tick this checkbox, the object IDs and object type keys are displayed in the dynamic menus.

### *With additional information*

If you tick this checkbox, additional information is displayed in the dynamic menus.

### *With abbreviation*

If you tick this checkbox, the object short name is displayed in the dynamic menus.

CHAPTER 33

# Resources

## 33.1 RESOURCE TYPE

| *Functional Consultant* | *User* | *Business Process Owner* | *Senior Management* | *My Rating* | *Understanding Level* |
|---|---|---|---|---|---|
| A | A | A | B | | |

### 33.1.1 Purpose

Business events require resources. You may have different types of resources, e.g. overhead projector. Each overhead projector is a resource with unique id. All overhead projectors are resources of type 'overhead projector'. Resource types describe the general attributes of resources. A business event type requiring an overhead projector can use any one of the overhead projectors. Therefore, you specify a resource type which is required for a business event type. When you create a business event, the system automatically proposes resources, which you can then reserve for it depending on availability. Properties of a resource type stored in availability indicator apply to all resources of that type and cannot be changed for individual resources. Relationships, capacity and cost are defaulted for the resources but they can be changed for individual resources.

### 33.1.2 Transaction

S_AHR_61011886—Resource Type
OORT—Create Resource Type

### 33.1.3 Object

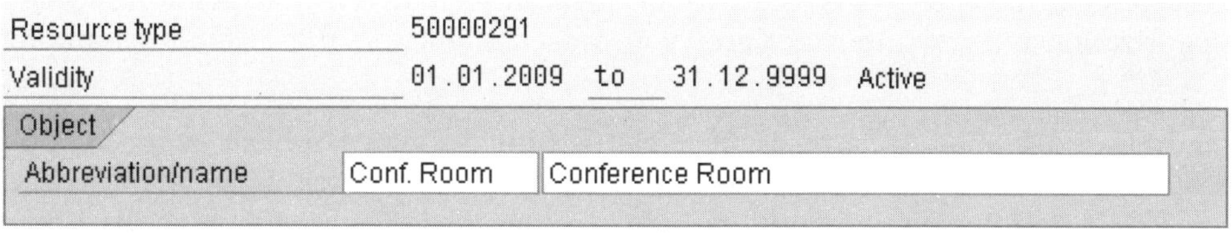


#### *Resource type id*

Each resource type is assigned a unique object id by the system.

#### *Validity*

You specify the validity period of the resource type.

#### *Abbreviation and name*

You specify the abbreviation and name of the resource type.

### 33.1.4 Availability Indicators

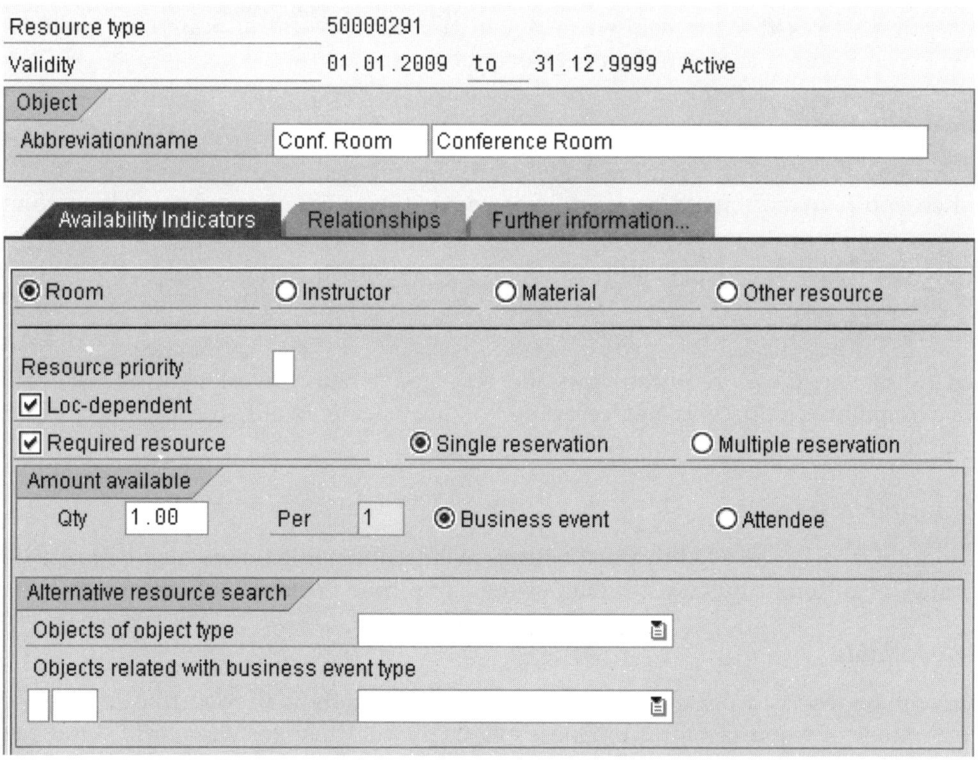

### *Room/instructor/material/other resource*

Resource types can be categorized into room, instructor, material and other resources. This categorization is very important and you must understand the differences among them.

For categories room and other resources, you create resources (object type G). You may create resources, e.g. conference rooms 1 to 3, classrooms 1 to 5, Overhead projectors 1 to 7, and personal computers 1 to 25. After these resources are created, you can reserve them for your business events. For rooms you can also maintain capacity which may restrict the capacity of a business event.

For category material, you do not create resources; instead you create material, e.g. Training manual SAP HR. You also specify which materials are required by which business event types. For a business event, you create material reservation or purchase requisition.

For category instructor also, you do not create resources. Instructors may be External persons, Persons, Contact persons or Users. Persons (employees) and Users should exist in the system in the normal course. You may create External persons or Contact persons if required. For a business event type, you specify instructors. For a business event you choose from the available instructors and reserve.

### *Resource priority*

Resource priority specifies the sequence in which resources are allocated to business events when you plan and create business events.

### *Location dependent*

If you are using locations in Training and Event Management, the system carries out a check when you plan and create business event dates to see whether location-dependent resources are available at the location you specify. You must set this indicator for resources of the type room that are only available in a certain location.

### *Required resource*

Resource types flagged as required must be reserved when you plan business event dates. If a required resource is not reserved for a business event, the business event cannot be held.

### *Single/multiple reservation*

Some resources may be reserved by one business event only, while others may be reserved by a number of different business events at the same time. You set this indicator here.

### *Amount available*

Resources can be reserved per event or per attendee. This data is needed to calculate the required number of resources for a business event. If two attendees share a PC, you can indicate 1 quantity per 2 attendees. The system will then calculate 5 PCs for 9 attendees.

### *Alternative resource search*

This function is used for resources of type material and instructor. It lets you specify a relationship or object type to be used by the system in the search for these resources. The system automatically defaults the relevant relationship depending on whether you are searching for a material or an instructor.

## 33.1.5 Relationships

### *Screen*

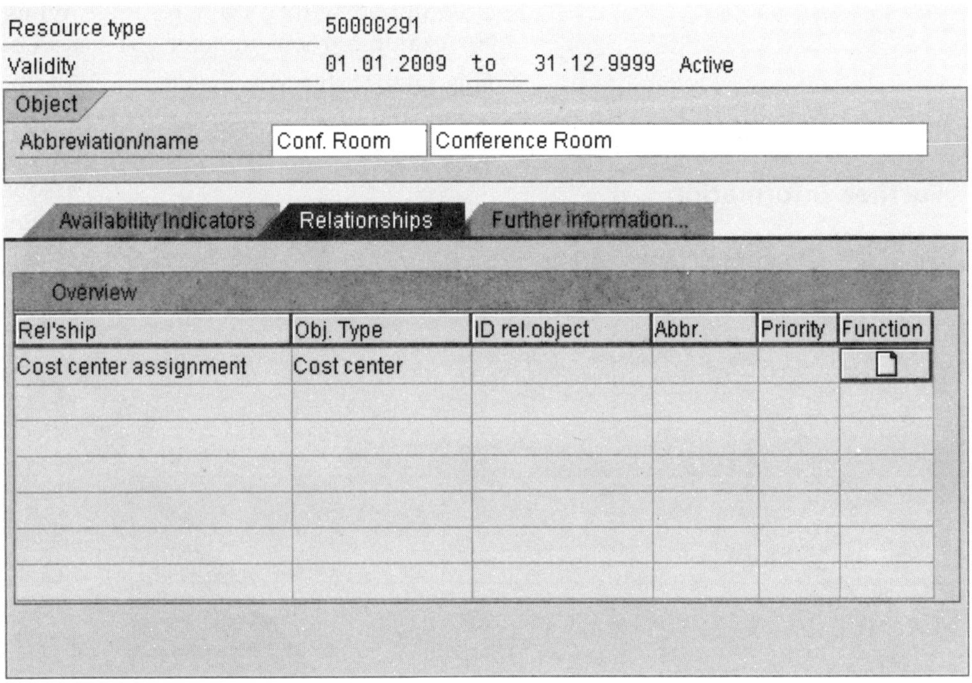


### *Allowed relationships*

| R'shp/OT | Relationship name | Object type text |
|---|---|---|
| A\|011\|K | Cost center assignment | Cost center |
| B\|020\|G | Is a generalization of | Resource |
| B\|021\|G | Is contained in | Resource |
| B\|022\|D | Is required by | Business event type |

***Explanation of relationships***

| *From* | *To* | *Relationship code* | *Relationship description* | *Explanation* |
|---|---|---|---|---|
| R | K | A011 | Cost center assignment | This relationship specifies the cost center for a resource type. |
| R | G | B020 | Is a generalization of | This relationship specifies that a resource is of a particular resource type. |
| R | G | B021 | Is contained in | This relationship specifies that the resource is equipped with certain resource types. For example, room number 101 has PCs. |
| R | D | B022 | Is required by | This relationship specifies that a resource type is required by a business event type. |

## 33.1.6 Further Information

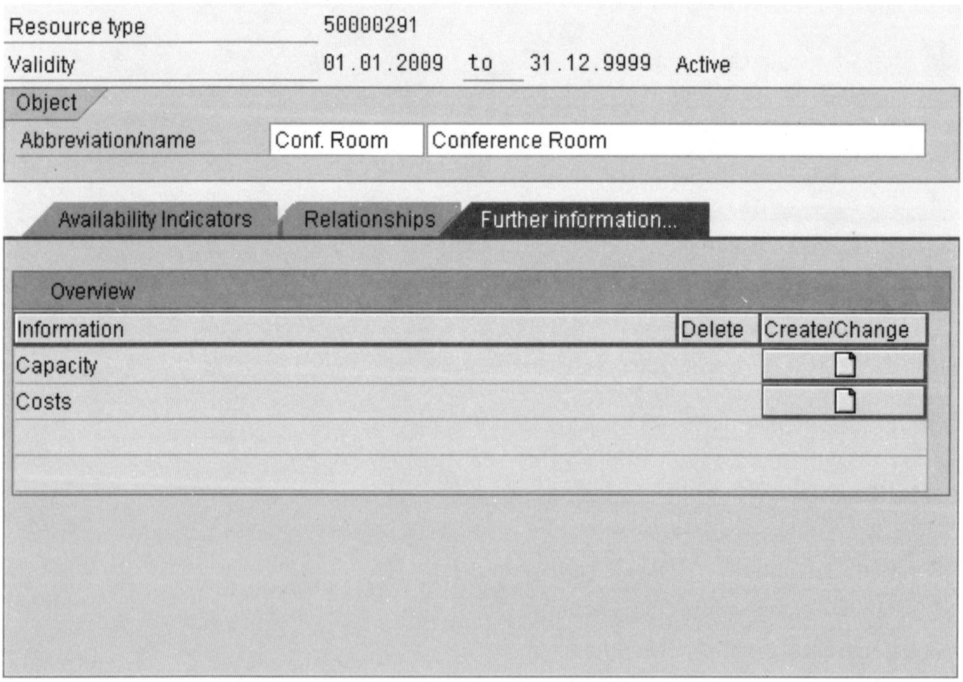


Through this tab of the resource type you can create, change or delete data in various infotypes. Each of these infotypes is discussed separately.

### 33.1.7 Capacity

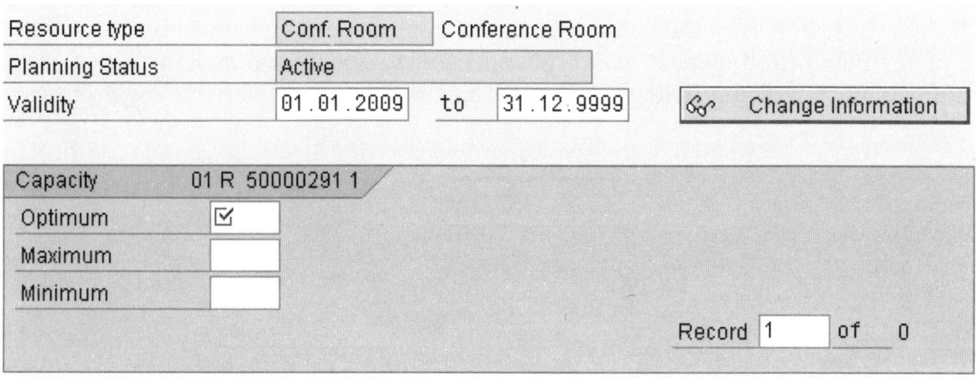


Capacity infotype is required only for rooms. Here you specify the optimum, maximum and minimum number of attendees who can be accommodated in the room. The capacity defined for a business event may be restricted by the capacity of the room reserved for the business event.

### 33.1.8 Costs

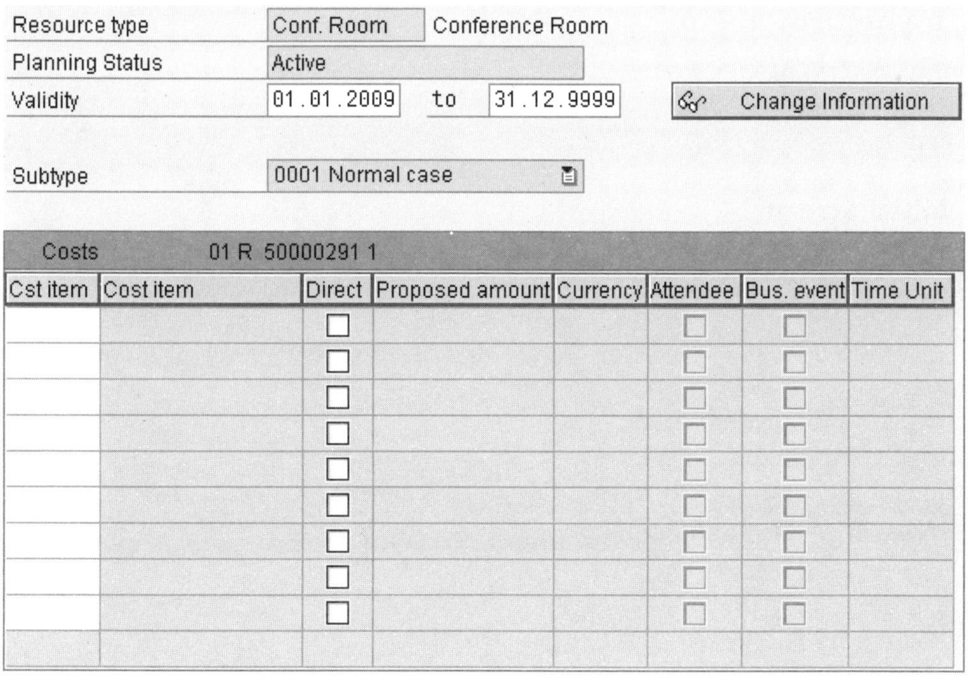


You can define cost for both resource type and resource. The cost of resource type is defaulted when you create a resource. The cost of a resource type as well as a resource is defined under various cost items. The proposed amount and currency specified for the cost item is displayed. Whether the proposed amount is per attendee or per business event is also displayed. If the time unit field is blank, the cost is either per attendee or per business event. If it contains a time unit, the cost is per time unit either for each attendee or for the entire business event. If you want to specify your own values, click the checkbox 'Direct'. All the fields are opened and you can specify your own values.

## 33.2 ROOM

| *Functional Consultant* | *User* | *Business Process Owner* | *Senior Management* | *My Rating* | *Understanding Level* |
|---|---|---|---|---|---|
| A | A | A | B | | |

### 33.2.1 Purpose

A room is a physical space in a building with an address and a room number or name. A room is a resource. First you create resource types, e.g. conference rooms, classrooms, interview rooms, etc. Then you create specific rooms, e.g. Classroom 101, etc.

### 33.2.2 Transaction

S_AHR_61011885—Room
OORA—Create Room
PO18—Room

### 33.2.3 Initial Screen

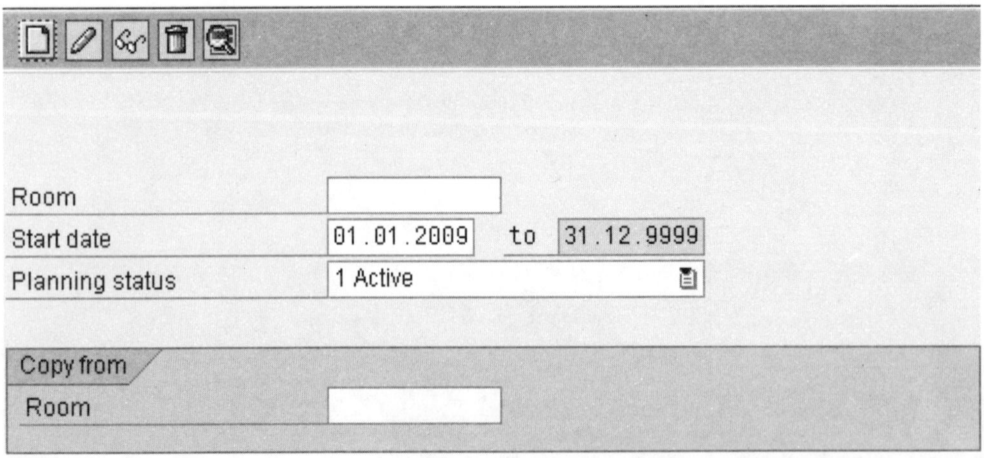


You can create a new room, modify details of an existing room, display details of a room, delete a room and create a room by copying from another room.

### 33.2.4 Object

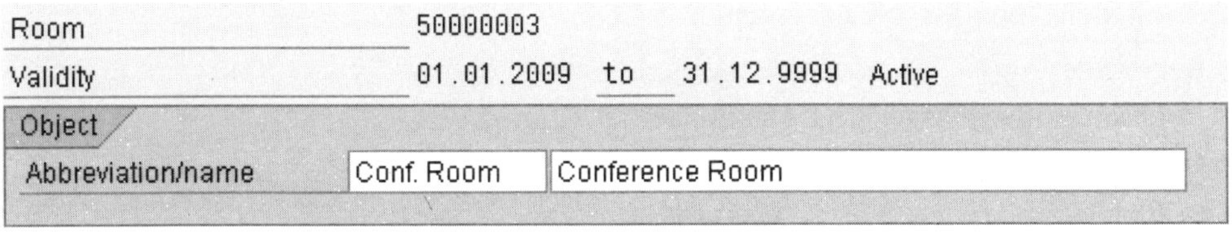
Room 50000003
Validity 01.01.2009 to 31.12.9999 Active
Object
Abbreviation/name Conf. Room Conference Room

#### *Resource id*

Each room is assigned a unique object id by the system.

#### *Validity*

You specify the validity period of the room.

#### *Abbreviation and name*

You specify the abbreviation and name of the room.

### 33.2.5 Relationships

#### *Screen*

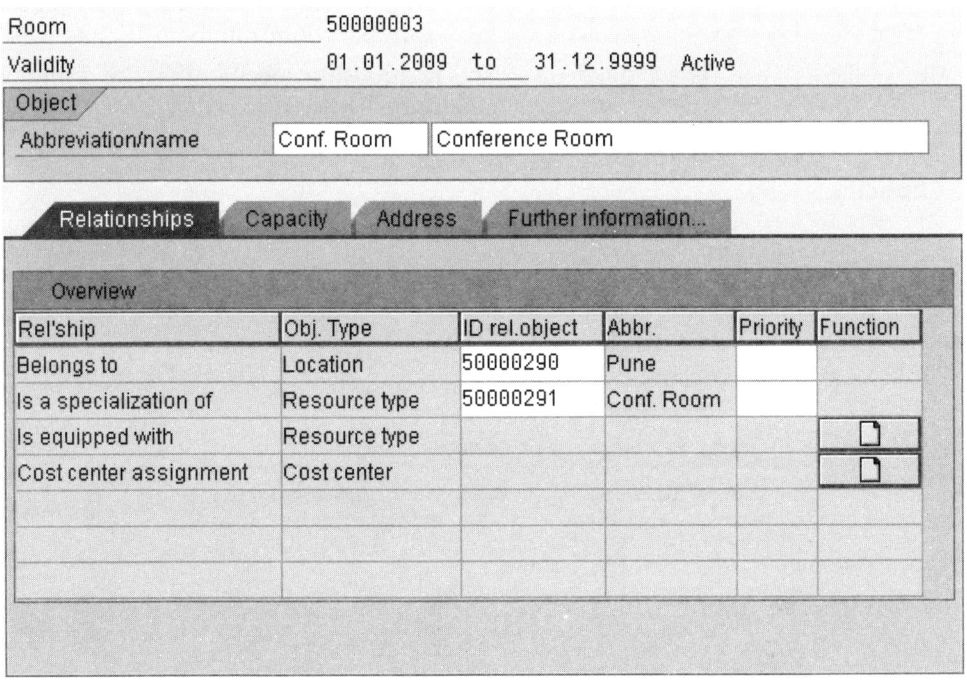
Room 50000003
Validity 01.01.2009 to 31.12.9999 Active
Object
Abbreviation/name Conf. Room Conference Room
Relationships | Capacity | Address | Further information...
Overview

| Rel'ship | Obj. Type | ID rel.object | Abbr. | Priority | Function |
|---|---|---|---|---|---|
| Belongs to | Location | 50000290 | Pune | | |
| Is a specialization of | Resource type | 50000291 | Conf. Room | | |
| Is equipped with | Resource type | | | | |
| Cost center assignment | Cost center | | | | |

***Allowed relationships***

| R'shp/OT | Relationship name | Object type t... |
|---|---|---|
| A\|003\|F | Belongs to | Location |
| A\|011\|K | Cost center assignment | Cost center |
| A\|020\|R | Is a specialization of | Resource type |
| A\|021\|R | Is equipped with | Resource type |
| B\|039\|VE | Is supplied by | Service |

***Explanation of relationships***

| *From* | *To* | *Relationship code* | *Relationship description* | *Explanation* |
|---|---|---|---|---|
| G | F | A003 | Belongs to | This relationship specifies that the resource belongs to a location. |
| G | K | A011 | Cost center assignment | This relationship specifies the cost center of a resource. |
| G | R | A020 | Is a specialization of | This relationship specifies that the resource is of a certain resource type. |
| G | R | A021 | Is equipped with | This relationship specifies that the resource is equipped with certain resource types. For example, room number 101 has PCs. |
| G | VE | B039 | Is supplied by | This relationship specifies that the resource is supplied by a service. |

## 33.2.6 Capacity

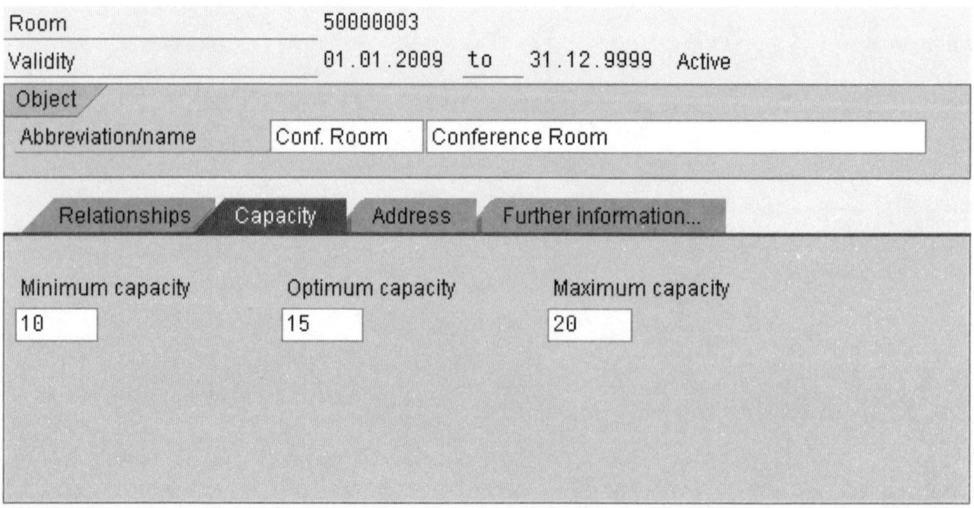

Capacity infotype is required only for rooms and not for other resources. Here you specify the optimum, maximum and minimum number of attendees who can be accommodated in the room. The capacity defined for a business event may be restricted by the capacity of the room reserved for the business event.

### 33.2.7 Address

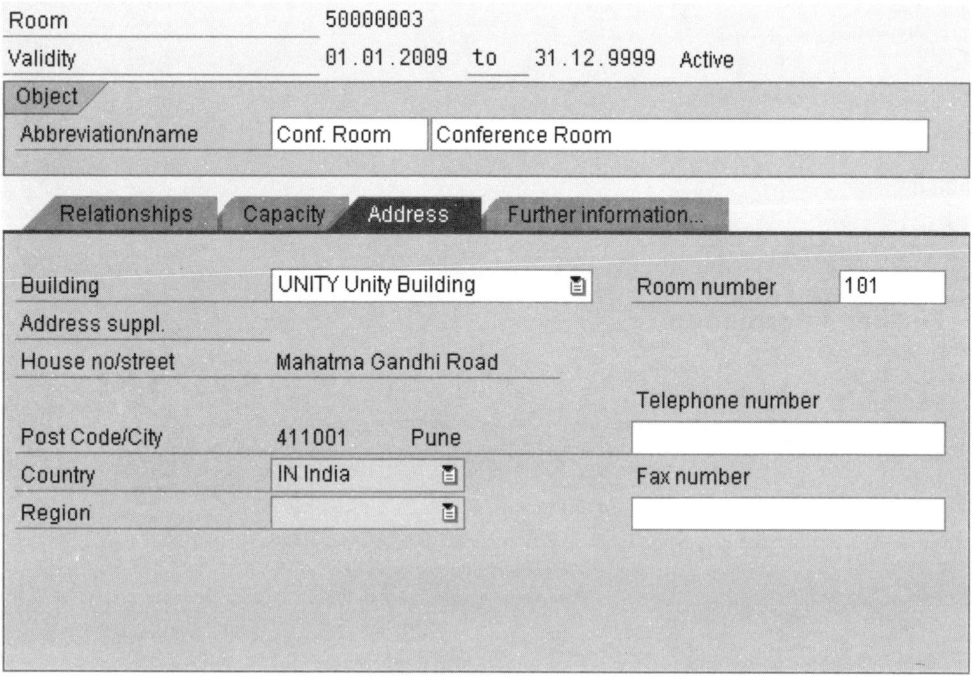


A room is a part of a building. Therefore, you need to define a building before you can define the address of a room.

#### *Building*

You can define buildings using transaction S_AHR_61011843. Building address is needed when you define rooms.

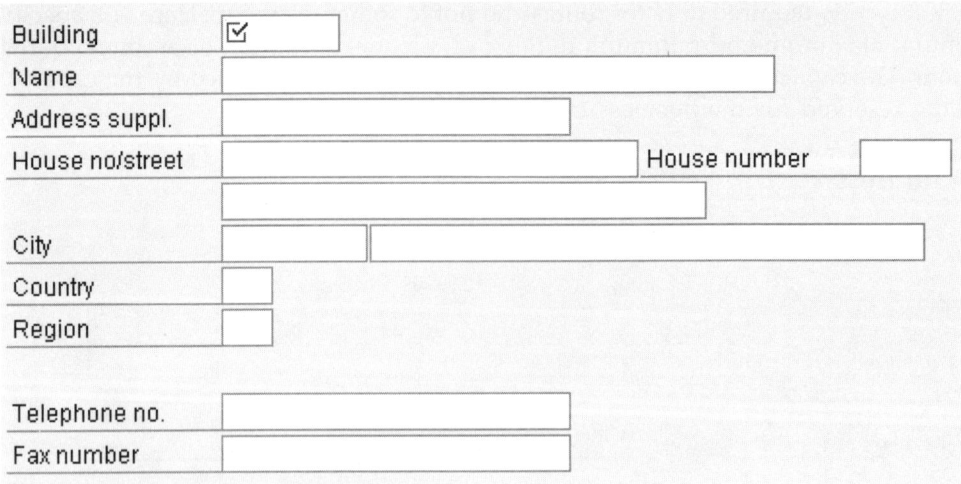


### 33.2.8 Further information

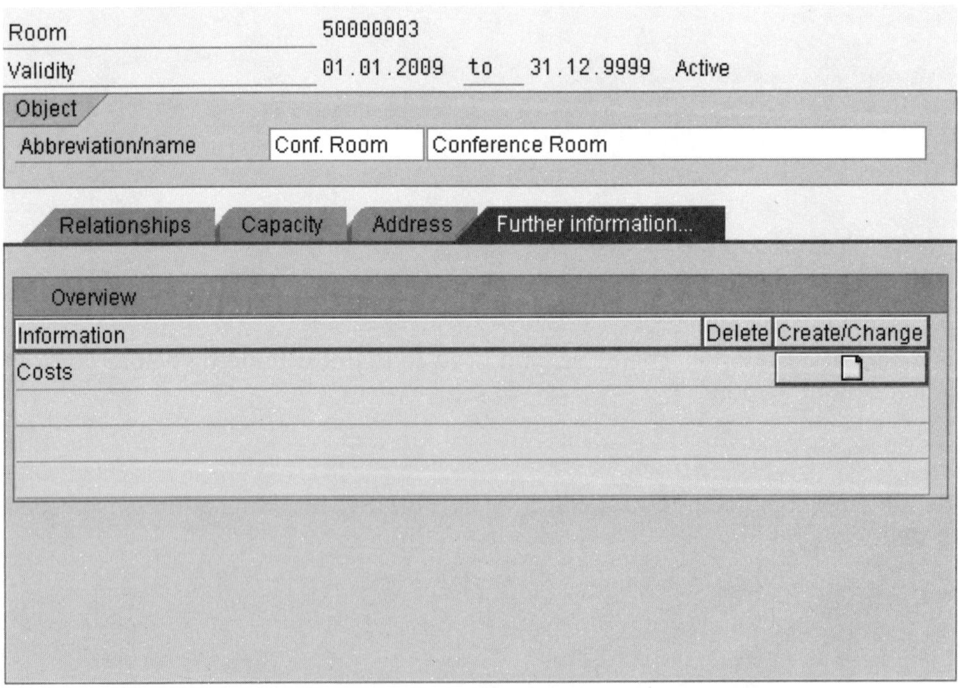


Through this tab you can maintain the cost details for a room.

### 33.2.9 Costs

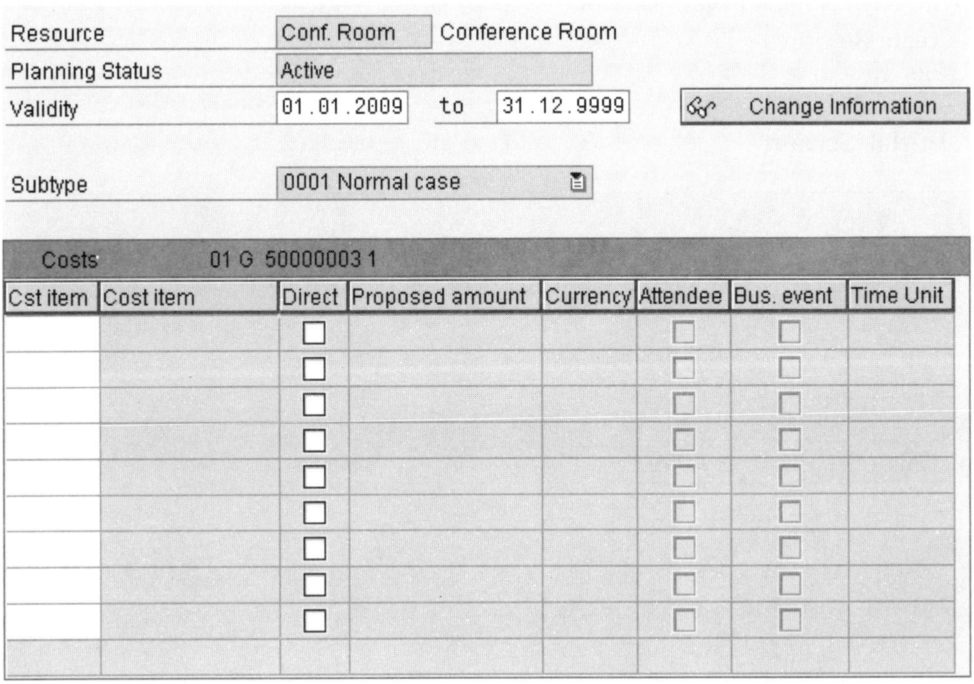


You can define cost for both resource type and resource. The cost of resource type is defaulted when you create a resource. The cost of a resource type as well as a resource is defined under various cost items. The proposed amount and currency specified for the cost item is displayed. Whether the proposed amount is per attendee or per business event is also displayed. If the time unit field is blank, the cost is either per attendee or per business event. If it contains a time unit, the cost is per time unit either for each attendee or for the entire business event. If you want to specify your own values, click the checkbox 'Direct'. All the fields are opened and you can specify your own values.

## 33.3 OTHER RESOURCE

| *Functional Consultant* | *User* | *Business Process Owner* | *Senior Management* | *My Rating* | *Understanding Level* |
|---|---|---|---|---|---|
| A | A | A | B | | |

### 33.3.1 Purpose

All resources other than room, external instructor and material are created under other resource. First you define the resource type, e.g. PC, and then you define individual resources, e.g. PC001.

### 33.3.2 Transaction

S_AHR_61011901—Other Resource
OORE—Create Resource
PO07—Other Resource

### 33.3.3 Initial Screen

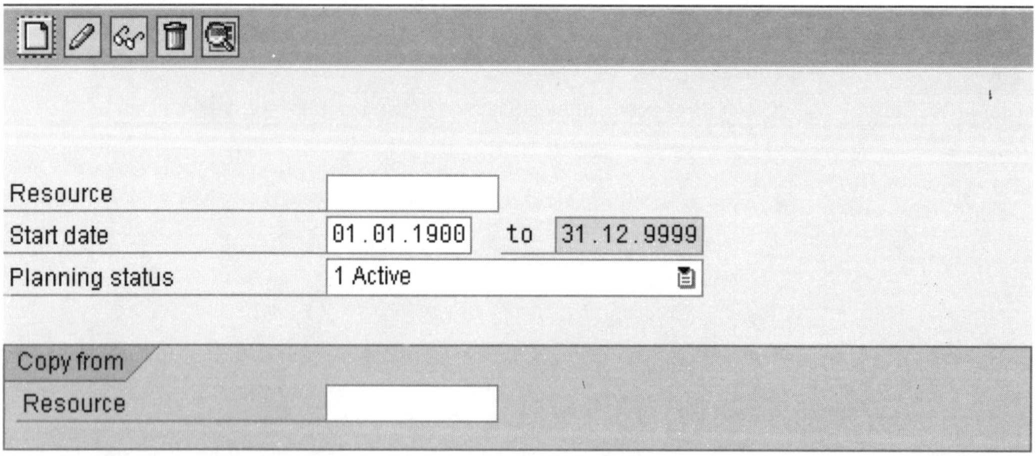


You can create a new resource, modify details of an existing resource, display details of a resource, delete a resource and create a resource by copying from another resource.

### 33.3.4 Object

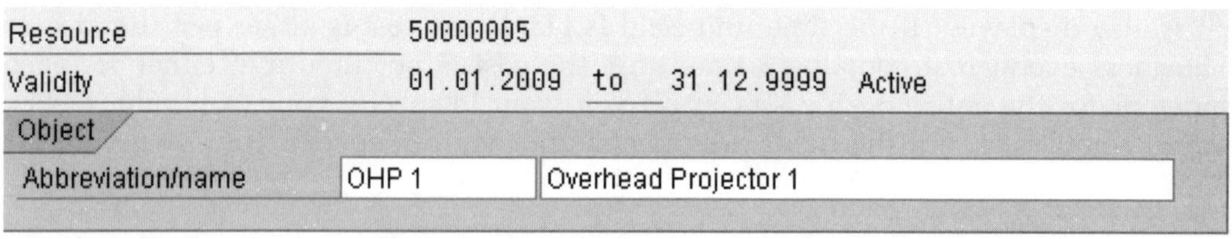


#### *Resource id*

Each resource is assigned a unique object id by the system.

#### *Validity*

You specify the validity period of the resource.

#### *Abbreviation and name*

You specify the abbreviation and name of the resource.

## 33.3.5 Relationships

### *Screen*

Resource 50000005

Validity 01.01.2009 to 31.12.9999 Active

Object

Abbreviation/name OHP 1 Overhead Projector 1

Relationships | Capacity | Further information...

Overview

| Rel'ship | Obj. Type | ID rel.object | Abbr. | Priority | Function |
|---|---|---|---|---|---|
| Is a specialization of | Resource type | 50000295 | OHP | | |
| Cost center assignment | Cost center | | | | |
| Belongs to | Location | 50000290 | Pune | | |

### *Allowed relationships*

| R'shp/OT | Relationship name | Object type t... |
|---|---|---|
| A\|003\|F | Belongs to | Location |
| A\|011\|K | Cost center assignment | Cost center |
| A\|020\|R | Is a specialization of | Resource type |
| A\|021\|R | Is equipped with | Resource type |
| B\|039\|VE | Is supplied by | Service |

***Explanation of relationships***

| *From* | *To* | *Relationship code* | *Relationship description* | *Explanation* |
|---|---|---|---|---|
| G | F | A003 | Belongs to | This relationship specifies that the resource belongs to a location. |
| G | K | A011 | Cost center assignment | This relationship specifies the cost center of a resource. |
| G | R | A020 | Is a speciali-zation of | This relationship specifies that the resource is of a certain resource type. |
| G | R | A021 | Is equipped with | This relationship specifies that the resource is equipped with certain resource types. For example, room number 101 has PCs. |
| G | VE | B039 | Is supplied by | This relationship specifies that the resource is supplied by a service. |

### 33.3.6 Capacity

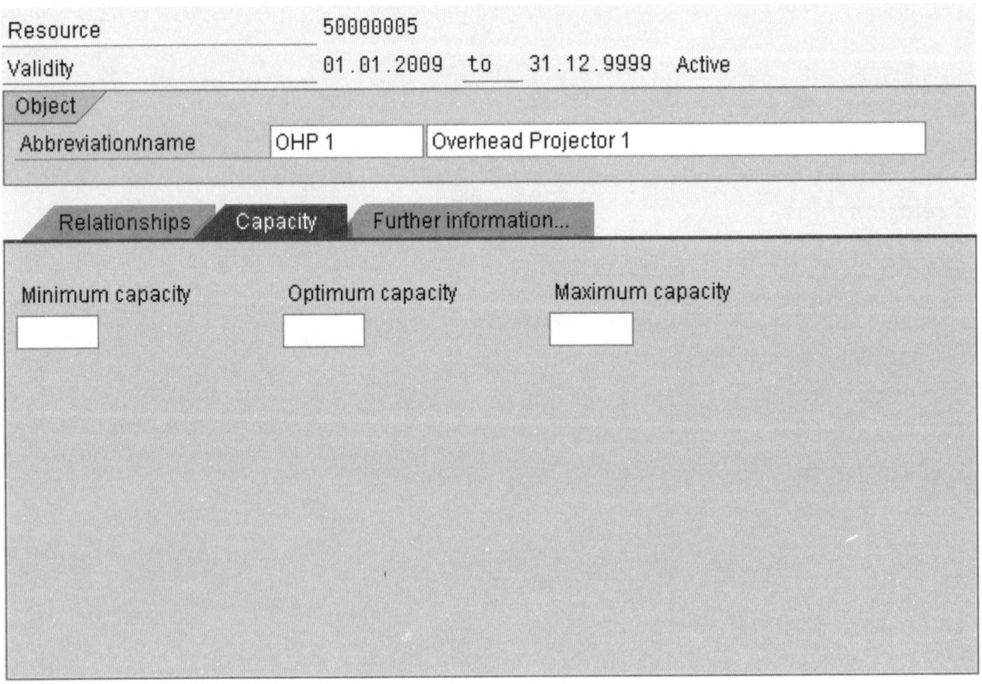


Certain types of resources may have capacity constraint. For example, if you have master–slave equipment for PCs, it may be able to connect to only a limited number of PCs.

### 33.3.7 Further Information

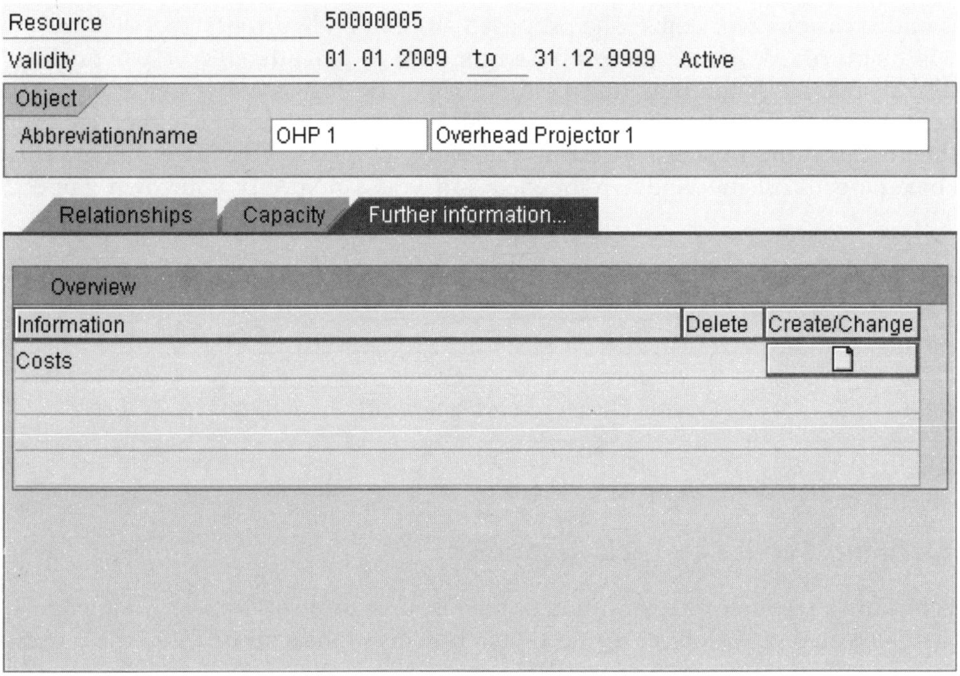


Through this tab you can maintain the cost details for a resource.

### 33.3.8 Costs

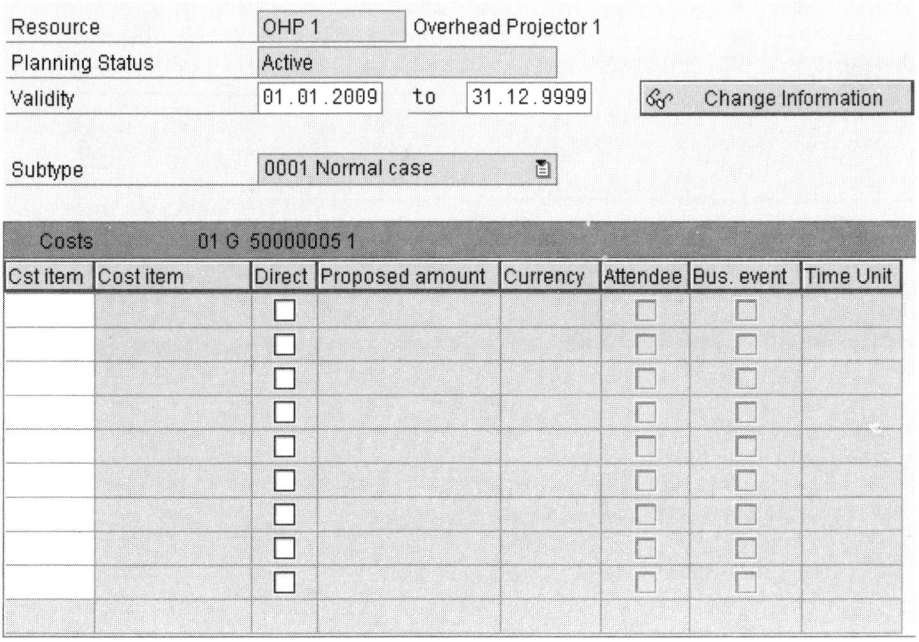

You can define cost for both resource type and resource. The cost of resource type is defaulted when you create a resource. The cost of a resource type as well as a resource is defined under various cost items. The proposed amount and currency specified for the cost item is displayed. Whether the proposed amount is per attendee or per business event is also displayed. If the time unit field is blank, the cost is either per attendee or per business event. If it contains a time unit, the cost is per time unit either for each attendee or for the entire business event. If you want to specify your own values, click the checkbox 'Direct'. All the fields are opened and you can specify your own values.

## 33.4 RESOURCE LOCKING

| *Functional Consultant* | *User* | *Business Process Owner* | *Senior Management* | *My Rating* | *Understanding Level* |
|---|---|---|---|---|---|
| A | A | B | C | | |

### 33.4.1 Defining Service to Lock Resources

SAP treats locking a resource as reservation of the resource by a service, e.g. Maintenance. This service is created as an object of the type VE using transaction PVV0.

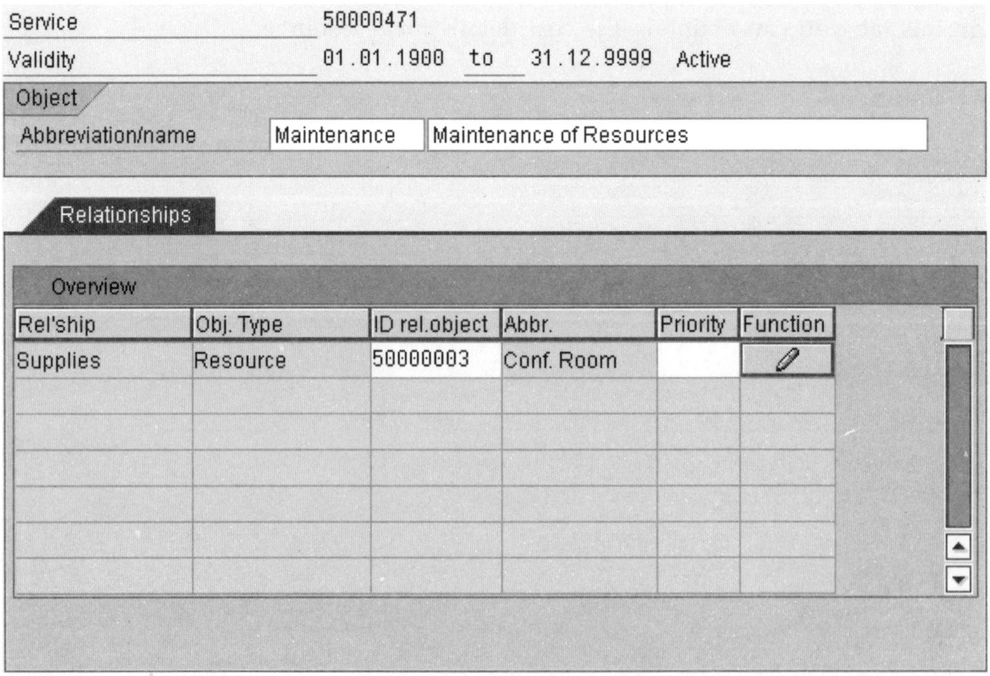

### 33.4.2 Assigning Service to Lock Resources

| Group | Sem. abbr. | Value abbr. | Description |
|---|---|---|---|
| SEMIN | ENQVE | 50000471 | Service for resource lock administration |

Here you specify the service which is used to lock resources.

### 33.4.3 Resource Locking

You can use transaction PVG2 to lock a resource for specified periods. The system shows the period for which the resource is reserved. When you lock a resource, the system creates a reservation (relationship 023) between the resource and the service. When you unlock a resource, the reservation is deleted.

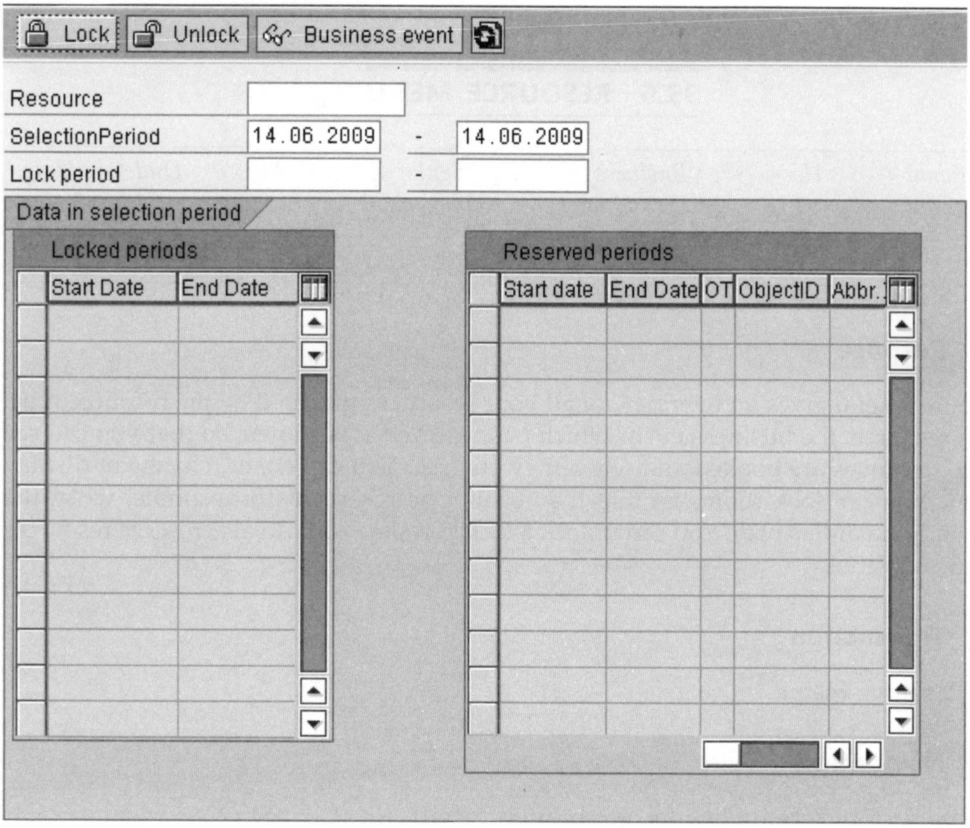

## 33.5 RESOURCE RESERVATION

| *Functional Consultant* | *User* | *Business Process Owner* | *Senior Management* | *My Rating* | *Understanding Level* |
|---|---|---|---|---|---|
| A | B | C | X | | |

You do resource reservation in business events. You can write a function module to directly access the resource reservation tables, for example, to delete or add reservations. You enter that user exit here.

| Group | Sem. abbr. | Value abbr. | Description |
|---|---|---|---|
| SEMIN | RESOC | RH_ALLOCAT | Customer enhancement for resource reservation |

## 33.6 RESOURCE MENU

| *Functional Consultant* | *User* | *Business Process Owner* | *Senior Management* | *My Rating* | *Understanding Level* |
|---|---|---|---|---|---|
| A | A | B | C | | |

### 33.6.1 Purpose

The resource menu gives an overview of all your resources grouped by the resource type. For each resource, the business event which has reserved it is shown, so that you can see when the resources are booked and when they are free. You can create, change or display resources. You can lock rooms so that they cannot be reserved (for example, when the room is under maintenance). You can unlock a locked room. You can also reserve resources for business events.

### 33.6.2 Transaction

PSVR—Resource Menu

### 33.6.3 Navigation

Select an object and right-click (or go through menu).

### 33.6.4 Screen

| | | |
|---|---|---|
| Current plan 22.01.2009 - 21.01.201 | | |
| Conference Room | | R 50000291 |
| Conference Room | | G 50000003 |
| 01.07.2009 - 03.07.2009 | Firmly Booked Internal Pune Camp | E 50000299 |
| Manual SAP FI | | R 50000338 |
| Training Manual SAP FI | | M 000000000000000019 |
| 05.07.2009 - 07.07.2009 | Firmly Booked Internal Pune Camp | E 50000339 |
| 11.07.2009 - 13.07.2009 | Firmly Booked Internal Pune Camp | E 50000340 |
| Manual SAP HR | | R 50000333 |
| Manual Yoga | | R 50000334 |
| Overhead Projector | | R 50000295 |
| Overhead Projector 1 | | G 50000005 |
| Personal Computer | | R 50000288 |
| Personnel Computer 1 | | G 50000006 |
| Personnel Computer 2 | | G 50000007 |
| Personnel Computer 3 | | G 50000008 |
| Personnel Computer 4 | | G 50000009 |
| Personnel Computer 5 | | G 50000010 |
| Personnel Computer 6 | | G 50000011 |
| Personnel Computer 7 | | G 50000012 |
| Personnel Computer 8 | | G 50000013 |
| Personnel Computer 9 | | G 50000014 |
| Personnel Computer 10 | | G 50000015 |

## 33.7 RESOURCE REPORTS

| *Functional Consultant* | *User* | *Business Process Owner* | *Senior Management* | *My Rating* | *Understanding Level* |
|---|---|---|---|---|---|
| A | A | B | B | | |

***Resource equipment***

You can run transaction S_AHR_61016224 to display the resources with which another resource (usually a room) is equipped. The report lists objects of type R (resource type) which are related with objects of type G (resource).

| Resource | Equipment | Start date | End date | Σ Number |
|---|---|---|---|---|
| Conference Room | Personal Computer | 01.01.2009 | 31.12.9999 | 10 |
| | | | | ■ **10** |

### *Instructor information*

You can run transaction S_PH0_48000096 to see reservation of one or more instructors.

| Res.type | Resource | Name | Start date | End date | Start Time | End time | Days | No. hours |
|---|---|---|---|---|---|---|---|---|
| SAP HR Instr | Naresh Kumar | SAP HR | 16.08.2009 | 18.08.2009 | 09:00:00 | 17:00:00 | 3 | 24.00 |
| SAP HR Instr | Naresh Kumar | SAP HR | 20.08.2009 | 22.08.2009 | 09:00:00 | 17:00:00 | 3 | 24.00 |
| SAP HR Instr | Naresh Kumar | SAP HR | 01.07.2009 | 03.07.2009 | 10:00:00 | 17:00:00 | 1 | 7.00 |
| SAP HR Instr | Naresh Kumar | SAP HR | 01.07.2009 | 03.07.2009 | 09:00:00 | 17:00:00 | 1 | 8.00 |
| SAP HR Instr | Naresh Kumar | SAP HR | 01.07.2009 | 03.07.2009 | 09:00:00 | 16:00:00 | 1 | 7.00 |

### *Resource reservation*

You can run transaction S_ALR_87014087 to generate a tabular display of the reservation of a selected resource type over a specified period of time. The report also displays any business events that have reserved the resource type. Depending on the period type you choose, the table is displayed in an hourly, daily or weekly period split.

22.06.2009 Resource Reservation 1

Resource Overhead Projector 1
Period 01.07.2009 - 05.07.2009

| Weekday<br>Date | | | Wednesday<br>01.07.09 | Thursday<br>02.07.09 | Friday<br>03.07.09 | Saturday<br>04.07.09 | Sunday<br>05.07.09<br>Day off |
|---|---|---|---|---|---|---|---|
| OHP 1 | | | SAP HR | SAP HR | SAP HR | | |

### *Graphical resource reservation*

You can run transaction S_PH9_46000441 to see resource reservation in graphical format.

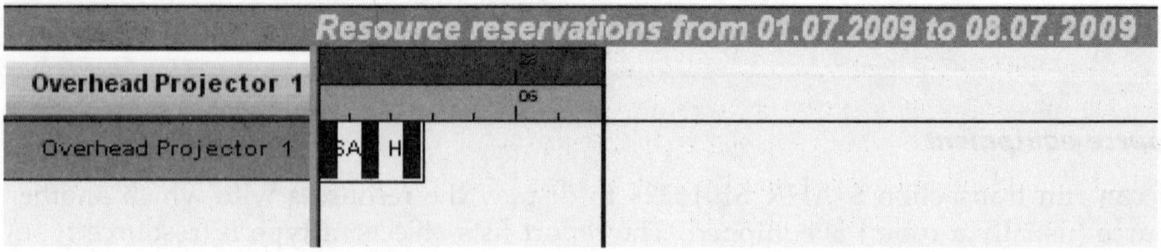

You can click a reservation to see its details.

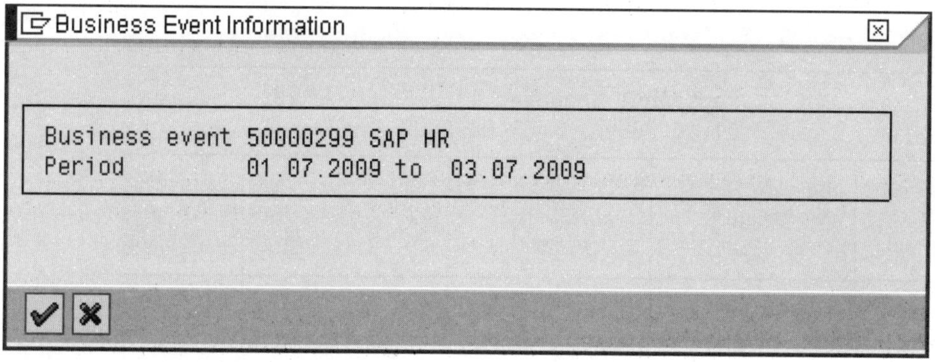


### *Available/reserved resources*

You can run transaction S_AHR_61016225 to display reserved and available resources of a specified resource type in a given period.

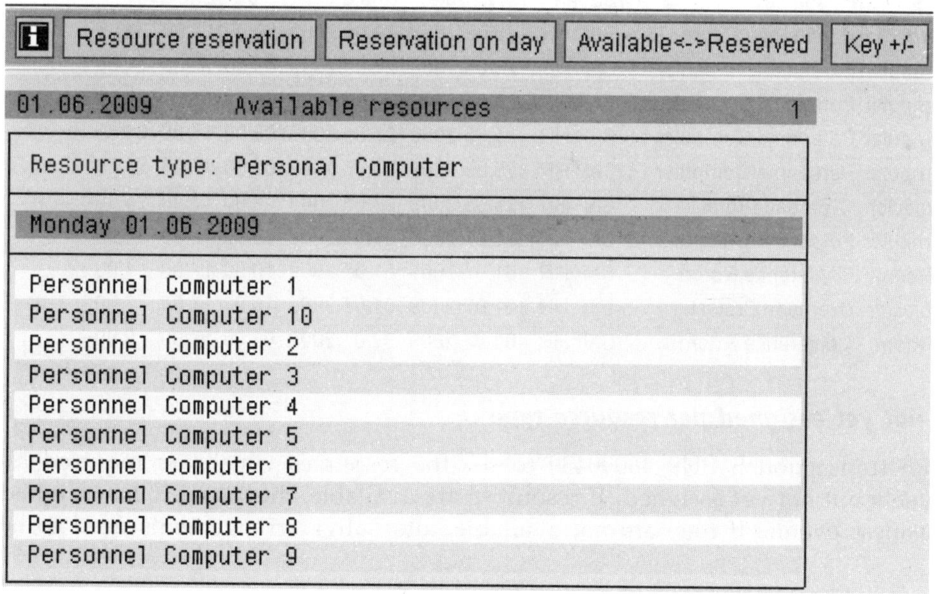


On the selection screen you specify whether you want to see available resources or reserved resources. You can also change from one to the other inside the report. The report displays available resources one day at a time. You can scroll down to see the availability/reservation for further days. You can select a resource and click Resource reservation to see the following view. There are also other views which you can explore.

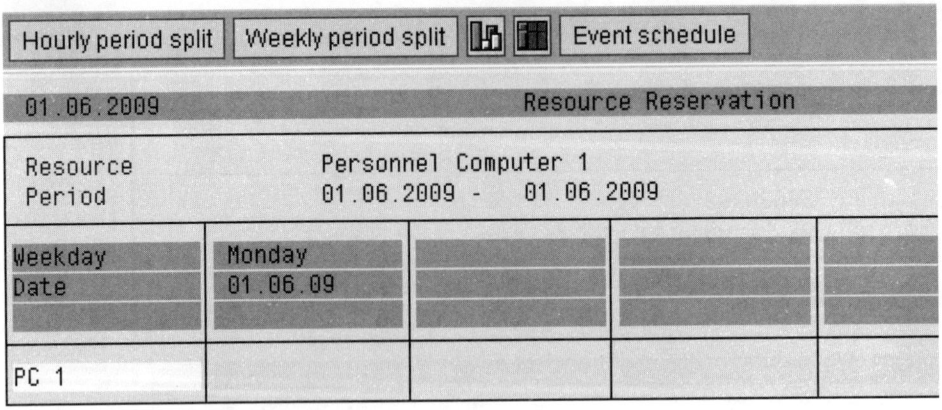


### *Resource reservation statistics*

You can run transaction S_PH9_46000440 to see reservation statistics of one or more resources over a period of time.

| Resource type | Resource | Busine... | Start date | End date | Start... | End... | Σ No. ... |
|---|---|---|---|---|---|---|---|
| Conference Room | Conference Room | SAP HR | 25.05.2009 | 27.05.2009 | 09:00 | 17:00 | 24.00 |
| Personal Computer | Personnel Computer 13 | SAP HR | 25.05.2009 | 27.05.2009 | 09:00 | 17:00 | 24.00 |
| Personal Computer | Personnel Computer 15 | SAP HR | 25.05.2009 | 27.05.2009 | 09:00 | 17:00 | 24.00 |
| Personal Computer | Personnel Computer 11 | SAP HR | 25.05.2009 | 27.05.2009 | 09:00 | 17:00 | 24.00 |
| Personal Computer | Personnel Computer 14 | SAP HR | 25.05.2009 | 27.05.2009 | 09:00 | 17:00 | 24.00 |
| Overhead Projector | Overhead Projector 1 | SAP HR | 25.05.2009 | 27.05.2009 | 09:00 | 17:00 | 24.00 |
| Personal Computer | Personnel Computer 12 | SAP HR | 25.05.2009 | 27.05.2009 | 09:00 | 17:00 | 24.00 |
| Conference Room | Conference Room | SAP HR | 01.07.2009 | 01.07.2009 | 10:00 | 17:00 | 7.00 |
| Overhead Projector | Overhead Projector 1 | SAP HR | 01.07.2009 | 01.07.2009 | 10:00 | 17:00 | 7.00 |
| Conference Room | Conference Room | SAP HR | 02.07.2009 | 02.07.2009 | 09:00 | 17:00 | 8.00 |

### *Resources not yet assigned per resource type*

You can run transaction S_PH9_46000439 to see the resources which are required by business events but not yet assigned. If resources are available, they need to be assigned to these business events. If they are not available, alternative arrangements need to be made.

| Resource type | Business event | Start date | End date | Start Time | End time | Σ No. hours |
|---|---|---|---|---|---|---|
| Personal Computer | SAP HR | 01.07.2009 | 01.07.2009 | 10:00:00 | 17:00:00 | 7.00 |
| Personal Computer | SAP HR | 02.07.2009 | 02.07.2009 | 09:00:00 | 17:00:00 | 8.00 |
| Personal Computer | SAP HR | 03.07.2009 | 03.07.2009 | 09:00:00 | 16:00:00 | 7.00 |
| | | | | | | ▪ **22.00** |

## 33.8 LOCATION

| *Functional Consultant* | *User* | *Business Process Owner* | *Senior Management* | *My Rating* | *Understanding Level* |
|---|---|---|---|---|---|
| A | A | B | B | | |

### 33.8.1 Purpose

There may be different locations where you conduct your business events. You can assign locations to both business events and location-dependent resources. The use of locations in Training and Event Management is optional. If you want to use location, you set the following switch in table T77S0 to 1. If you don't want to use locations, you set it to 0.

| Group | Sem. abbr. | Value abbr. | Description |
|---|---|---|---|
| SEMIN | ORT | 1 | Switch for business event locations |

### 33.8.2 Transaction

S_AHR_61011841—Location
OOLC—Location

### 33.8.3 Initial Screen

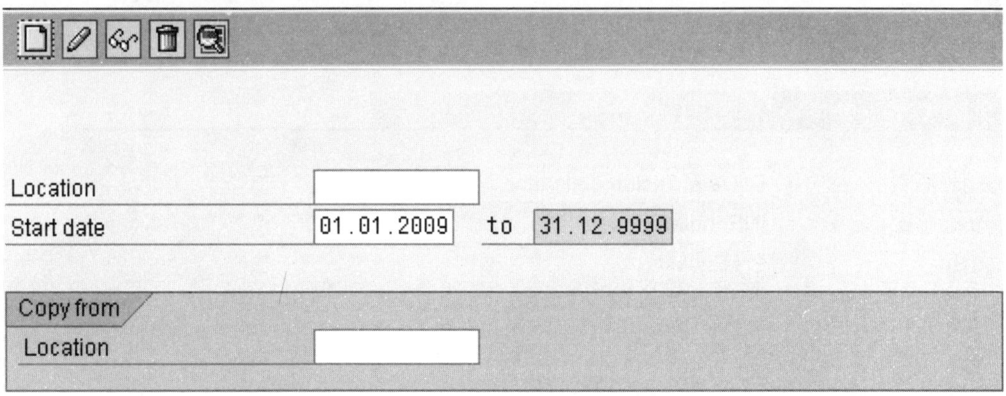


You can create, change, display or delete a location. You can also copy a location from another location.

### 33.8.4 Object

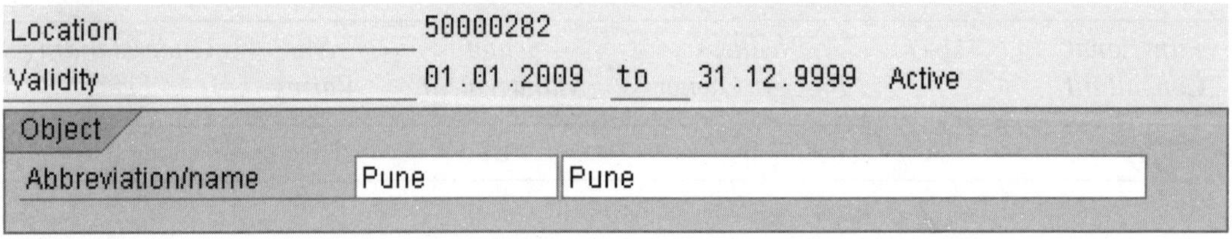


***Object id***

Each location is assigned a unique object id by the system.

***Validity***

You specify the validity period of the location.

***Abbreviation and name***

You specify the abbreviation and the name of the location.

### 33.8.5 Site-Dependent Info

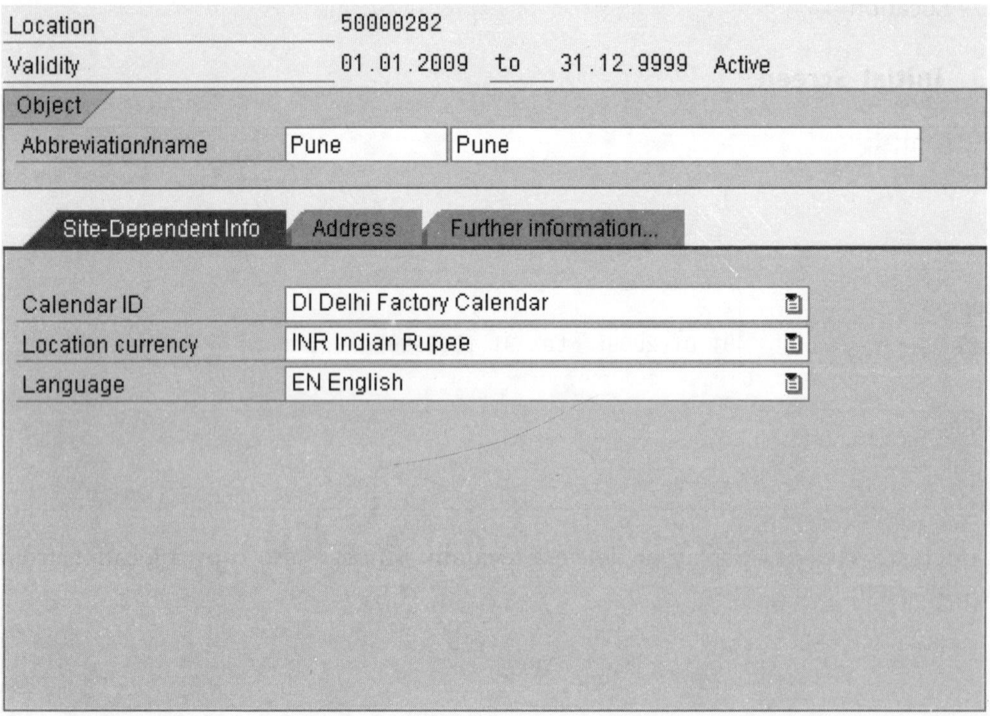

### *Default factory calendar*

Factory calendar is used to determine the off days of a location. If a factory calendar is not defined in the above infotype, the factory calendar defined in the following entry is taken.

| Group | Sem. abbr. | Value abbr. | Description |
|---|---|---|---|
| SEMIN | ORTCA | 01 | Default calendar ID |

### *Factory calendar*

Factory calendar can be defined using transaction OY05.

| ID | Calendar ID | Valid from | Valid to |
|---|---|---|---|
| DK | Factory calendar Denmark | 1995 | 2010 |
| E1 | Factory calendar Spain - Madrid | 1990 | 2098 |
| E2 | Factory calendar Spain - Catalonia | 1990 | 2098 |
| EL | Factory calendar France - Alsace | 1990 | 2005 |

### *Location currency*

Here you define the currency used at a location.

### *Language*

Here you define the language used at a location.

## 33.8.6 Address

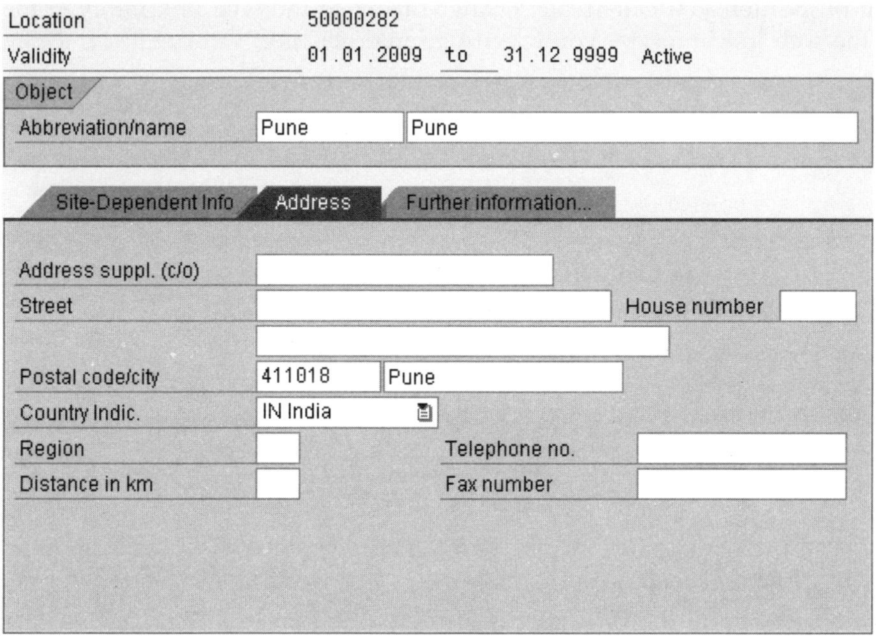


Here you define the address of a location.

### 33.8.7 Further Information

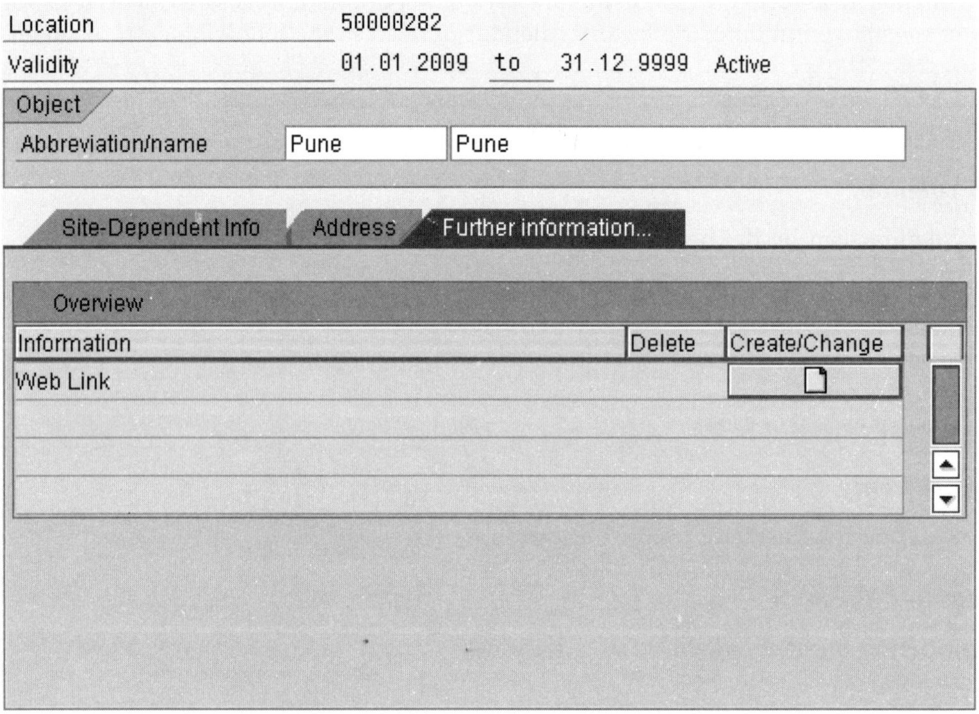


Through this tab of location you can create, change or delete the web link infotype for the location. In the web link infotype you specify an internet link.

CHAPTER 34

# Business Events

## 34.1 BUSINESS EVENTS

| *Functional Consultant* | *User* | *Business Process Owner* | *Senior Management* | *My Rating* | *Understanding Level* |
|---|---|---|---|---|---|
| A | A | A | A | | |

In SAP, training programs are called business events. Business events have wider meaning and include, apart from training programs, conferences, seminars, conventions, etc. Business events are scheduled training programs. If a training program is held on multiple dates, each one is a separate business event. A business event is a concrete entity. It has content which comes from business event type. It is scheduled to be held on specific dates. It is held at specific location in specific rooms. It has instructors who teach.

## 34.2 BUSINESS EVENT MENU

| *Functional Consultant* | *User* | *Business Process Owner* | *Senior Management* | *My Rating* | *Understanding Level* |
|---|---|---|---|---|---|
| A | A | A | A | | |

### 34.2.1 Purpose

In the business event menu, you can execute all the functions related to creating and editing business events. You can create business events with or without resources. You can change, firmly book, cancel, lock, unlock or follow-up a business event. You can do appraisal, price proposal, cost transfer posting, activity allocation, billing, budgeting and material procurement for a business event. You can display a variety of information about a business event. You can see business events under a business event type and attendees for a business event. But you cannot book attendees for a business event in this menu; you do that in the attendance menu. Traffic lights show whether the business event is full, accepting only essential bookings, or accepting normal bookings. You can switch between the business event menu, the attendance menu and the information menu as required. You always access the same level of the structure as the one you leave.

### 34.2.2 Transaction

PSV2—Business Event Menu

### 34.2.3 Navigation

Select an object and right-click (or go through menu).

### 34.2.4 Screen

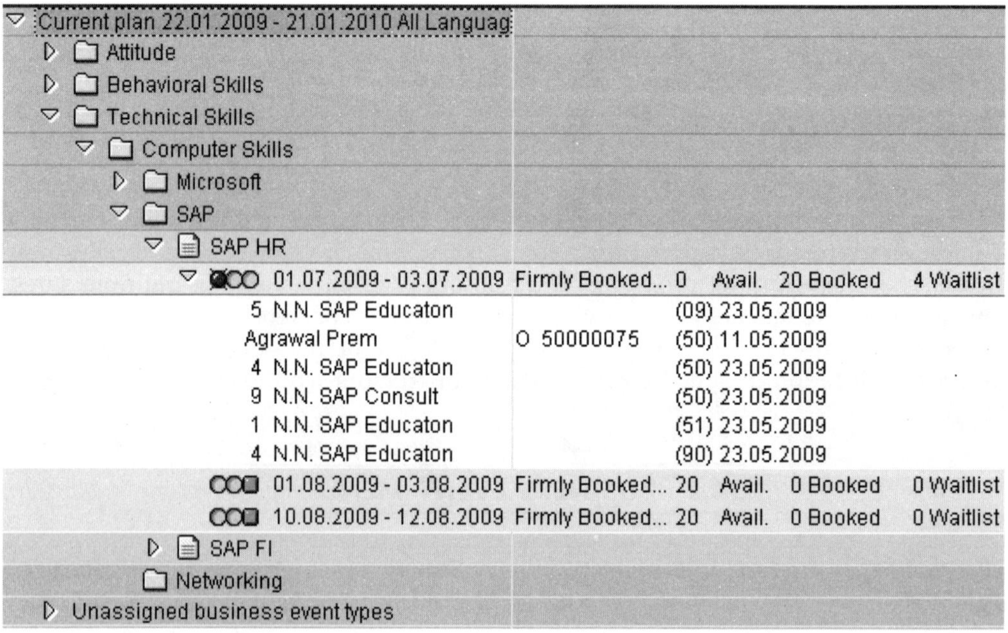

## 34.3 CREATING BUSINESS EVENT WITHOUT RESOURCES

| *Functional Consultant* | *User* | *Business Process Owner* | *Senior Management* | *My Rating* | *Understanding Level* |
|---|---|---|---|---|---|
| A | A | A | A | | |

### 34.3.1 Purpose

You create business event without resources when you are not using resource management.

### 34.3.2 Transaction

PSV2—Business Event Menu (Create w/o Resources)
PV11—Create without Resources

### 34.3.3 Business Event Menu

When you run transaction PSV2, the system shows you the business event catalog.

| Current plan 01.01.2009 - 31.12.2009 All Languages | | |
|---|---|---|
| Attitude | L 50000249 | Attitude |
| Positive Attitude | D 50000260 | +ve Attitude |
| Think Customer | D 50000261 | Customer |
| Behavioral Skills | L 50000250 | Behavior |
| Communication | L 50000252 | Communicaton |
| English | D 50000262 | English |
| German | D 50000263 | German |
| Japanese | D 50000264 | Japanese |
| Presentations | D 50000265 | Presentation |
| Creativity | L 50000253 | Creativity |
| Creativity and Problem Solving | D 50000266 | Creativity |
| Decision Making | L 50000254 | Decision Mkg |
| Decision Making Skills | D 50000267 | Decision Mkg |
| Leadership | L 50000255 | Leadership |
| Mentoring | D 50000268 | Mentoring |
| Management | L 50000256 | Management |
| Management By Objectives | D 50000269 | MBO |
| Time Management | D 50000270 | Time Mgmt |
| Technical Skills | L 50000251 | Technical |
| Computer Skills | L 50000257 | Computers |
| Microsoft | L 50000258 | Microsoft |
| Microsoft Word | D 50000272 | MS Word |
| Microsoft Excel | D 50000273 | MS Excel |
| SAP | L 50000259 | SAP |
| SAP HR | D 50000274 | SAP HR |
| SAP FI | D 50000275 | SAP FI |
| Networking | L 50000277 | Networking |
| Unassigned business event types | | |
| Yoga | D 50000276 | Yoga |

You select a business event type and create a business event either through menu (Business Event ➢ Dates ➢ Create ➢ Without Resources), or right-click and choose Create w/o Resources. The system gives you the following screen in which you enter the business event data.

### 34.3.4 Business Event without Resources

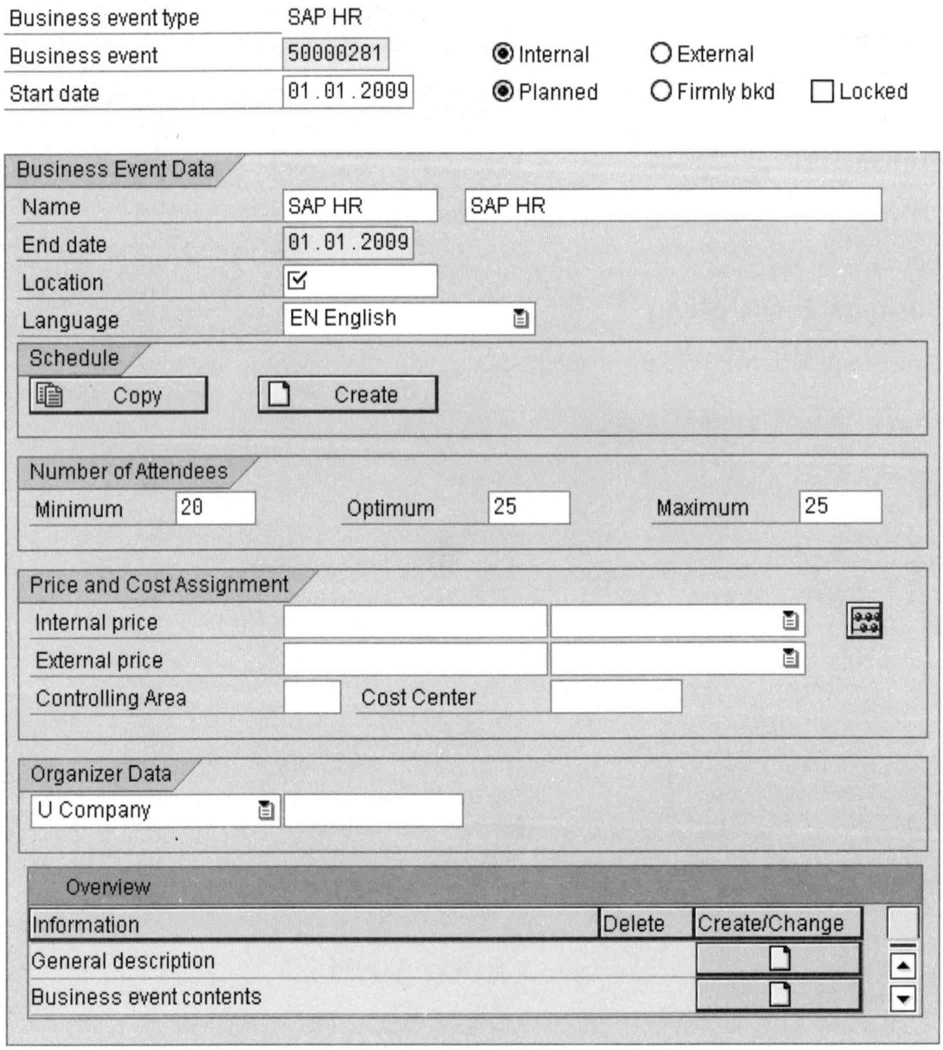


#### ***Business event type***

You always create a business event from a business event type. Most of the data you store for business event types is proposed as default values for the actual business events. You can overwrite this data as required. You only need to specify date, location and language at the business event level and do resource reservation.

### *Business event*

When you create a business event, the system gives it a unique id.

### *Start date*

The business event starts on this date.

### *Internal/external*

You can specify whether a business event is an internal event, or an external event.

### *Planned/firmly booked*

You should create the business event in planned status if you are not certain that it will actually take place. If you are certain that it will take place, you can create the business event in firmly booked status from the outset. When you create a business event in planned status, attendees booked for the business event receive provisional booking confirmation initially. Once you change the status to firmly booked, attendees receive definite confirmation of place. Business events created as planned have planning status Planned, and not Active. The relationship of the business event with business event type is also in the Planned status. Similarly, the relationship between a planned business event and its attendees is also in the Planned status.

### *Locked*

You can lock a business event to prevent attendees from booking it. When you want to allow bookings for the business event, you simply unlock it.

### *Name*

Abbreviation and name of the business event type is copied to the business event.

### *End date*

End date is determined from the start date and schedule.

### *Location*

You specify the location where the business event will be held.

### *Language*

You specify the language in which the business event will be held.

### *Schedule*

You can copy the schedule from the business event type, or you can create your own. The schedule can be with pattern, without pattern, or user-defined.

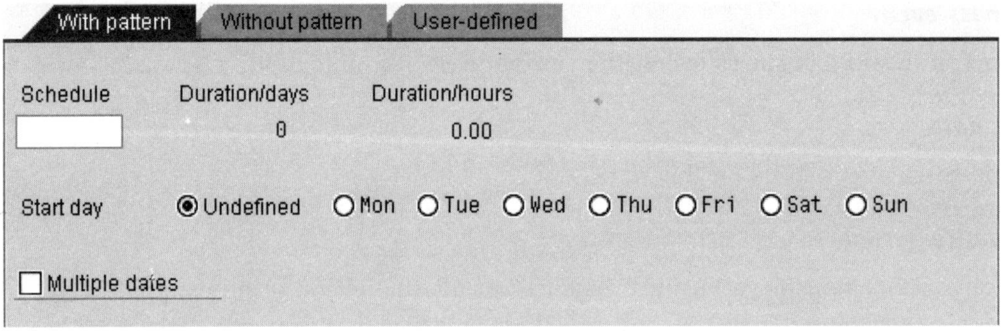


A schedule with pattern follows a predefined schedule which you specify.

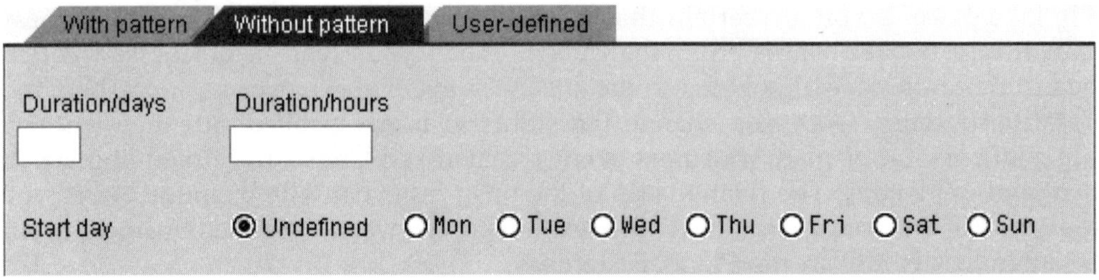


A schedule without pattern has only number of days and number of hours. You should not use a schedule without pattern for a business event because the attendees, the instructors and the organizers need to know the exact time when the business event would take place.

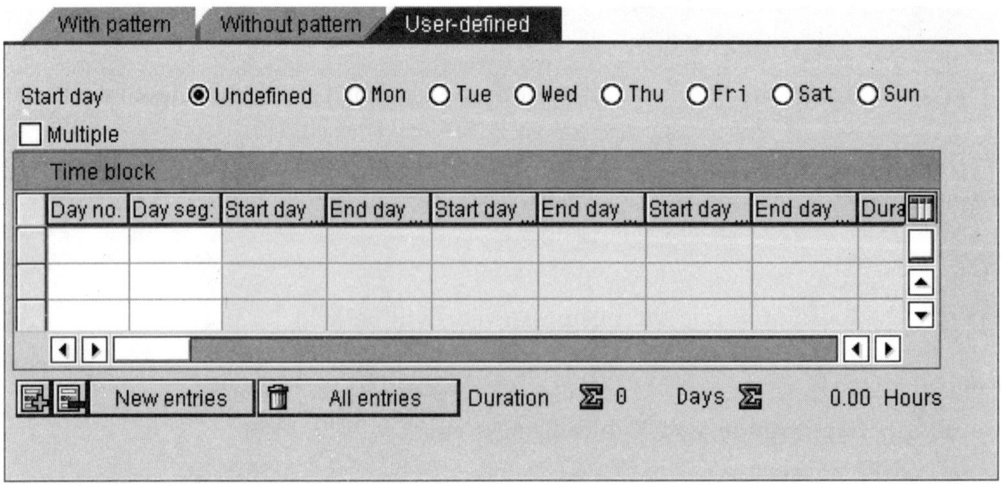


In user-defined schedule you define daywise segments.

***Number of attendees***

Minimum, optimum and maximum numbers of attendees are copied from the business event type. You may change these figures if you want.

***Internal and external prices with currencies***

Internal and external prices with currencies are copied from the business event type. You may change these figures if you want. If you click [icon], the system proposes price based on cost. The logic of proposing the price is explained in the price proposal report in chapter 34.14.

***Controlling area and cost center***

Controlling area and cost center are copied from the business event type. You may change them if you want.

***Organizer***

Organizer is copied from the business event type. You may change the organizer if you want.

***General description***

General description is copied from the business event type. You may change it if you want.

***Business event contents***

Business event content is copied from the business event type. You may change it if you want.

## 34.4 CREATING BUSINESS EVENT WITH RESOURCES

| *Functional Consultant* | *User* | *Business Process Owner* | *Senior Management* | *My Rating* | *Understanding Level* |
|---|---|---|---|---|---|
| A | A | A | A | | |

### 34.4.1 Purpose

You create business event with resources when you are using resource management.

### 34.4.2 Transaction

PSV2—Business Event Menu (Create with Resources)
PV10—Create with Resources

### 34.4.3 Business Event with Resources

When you create business events with resources using transaction PSV2, the system gives you the screen which is similar to the screen you get when you create business event without resources.

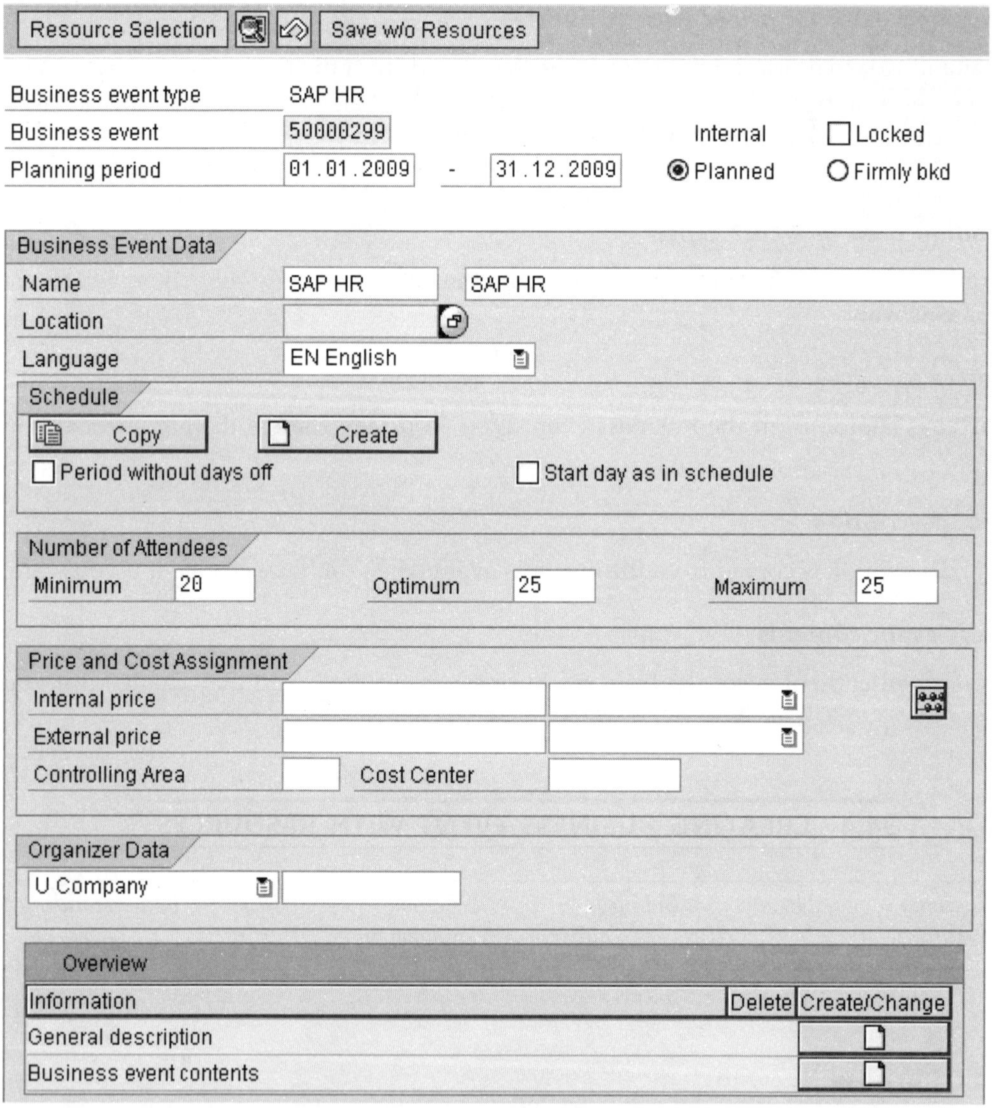


The key difference is in [Resource Selection], which lets you reserve resources. However, if you have not specified resource types which are required for the business event type, you will not get this icon. Instead you will get a message [Business event requires no resources]. Note that the attribute internal is automatically selected since you can only carry out resource reservation for internal events. After entering the details, you may either directly proceed with resource reservation or save the business event without resources. In the latter case, you select the business event, right-click and choose Change to do resource reservation.

### 34.4.4 Resource Reservation

***Resource requirement***

When you click the 'Resource Selection' icon, you see the following window which shows the resources required and their availability.

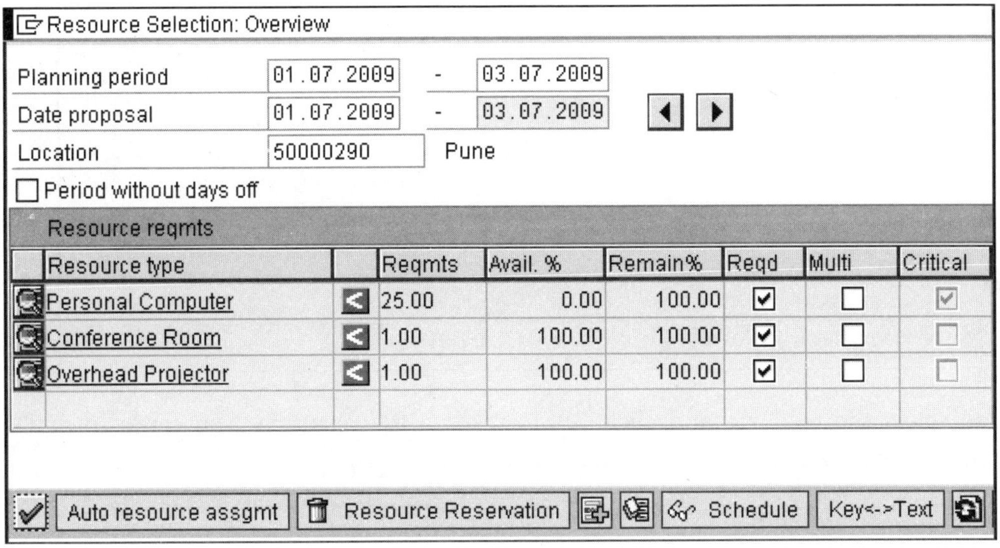


The system shows the requirement, availability % and % of resource not yet reserved. The checkbox 'Required' specifies that a resource is essential and must be reserved for the business event. The checkbox 'Multiple' specifies that a resource can be reserved by multiple business events at the same time. The checkbox 'Critical' specifies that the number of resources available is insufficient for the business event.

***Adding to resource requirement***

If your resource list is incomplete, you can add a resource type permanently by clicking or temporarily by clicking .

***Automatic resource assignment***

If you click Auto resource assgmt, the system will automatically assign the available resources. Only resources flagged as required are automatically allocated.

***Manual resource assignment***

To do manual assignment, you click . The system shows you all the resources of the resource type.

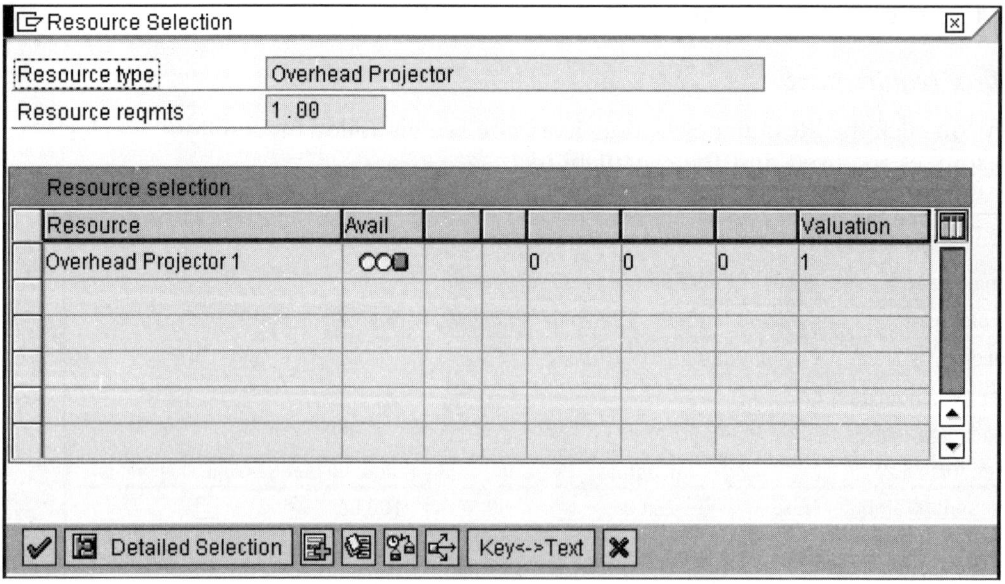


You can select the resource and click  to reserve the resource. You can also add a resource by clicking , or temporarily add by clicking .

### *Resource detail selection*

If you click  Detailed Selection  in the above screen, the system lets you reserve resources for specific time blocks within the business event schedule and thus, reserve different resources for individual time blocks. For each time block, you can click  and assign from the available resources.

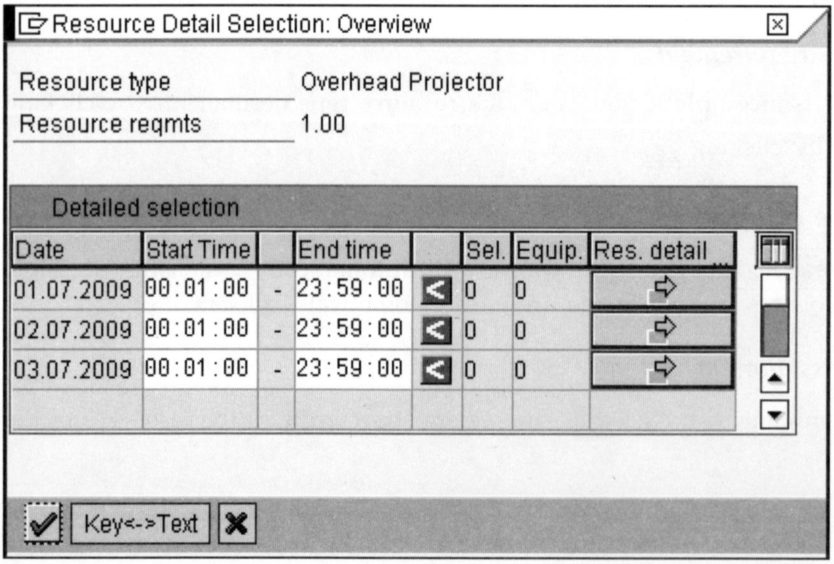

***Resource selection overview after resource assignment***

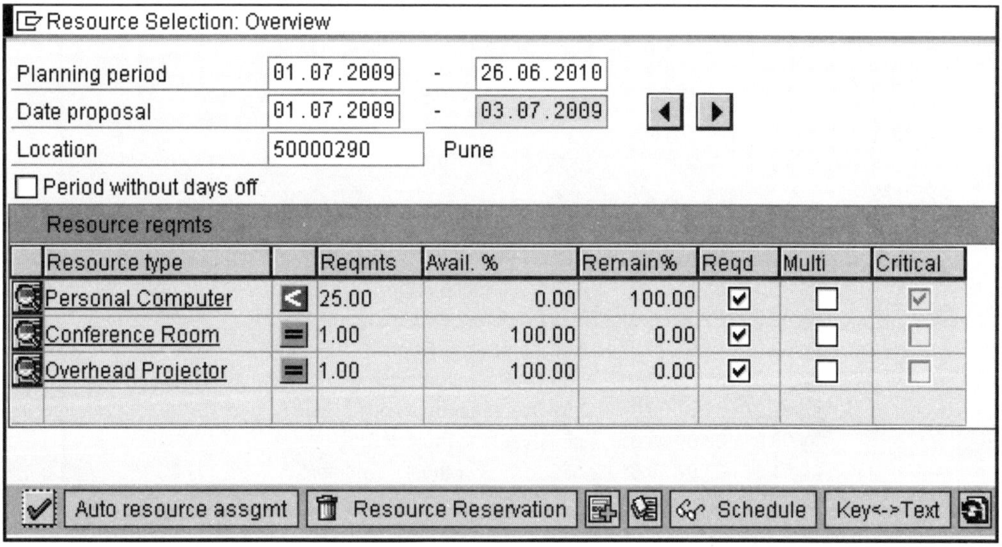


After resource assignment, the system shows the percentage availability of the resource. In case the requirement is fully met, it also shows it pictorially.

## 34.5 CREATING BUSINESS EVENTS THROUGH PLANNING

| *Functional Consultant* | *User* | *Business Process Owner* | *Senior Management* | *My Rating* | *Understanding Level* |
|---|---|---|---|---|---|
| A | A | B | C | | |

### 34.5.1 Purpose

If you routinely hold business events of a type, you can create multiple business events based on demand using the planning function, instead of manually creating them one by one. You can also use the planning menu to see the resource reservation for business events.

### 34.5.2 Transaction

PSVP—Planning Menu

### 34.5.3 Planning Menu

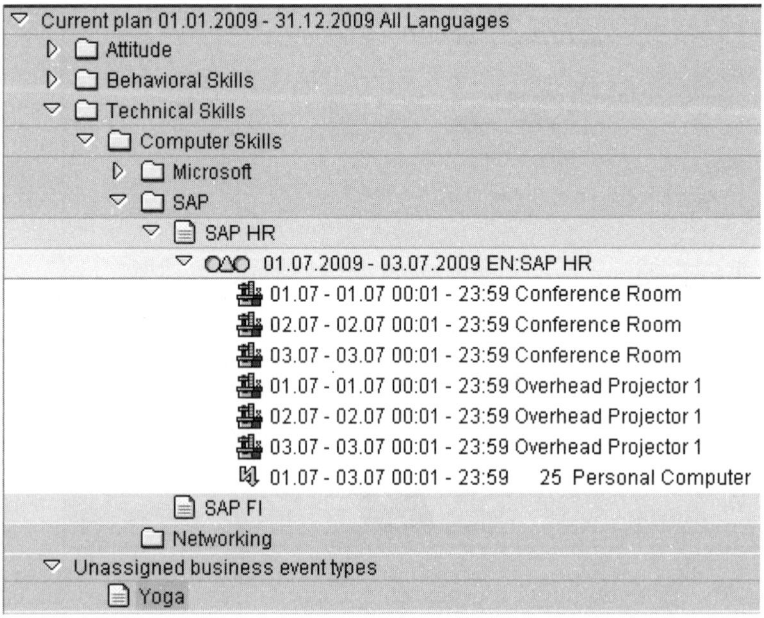


The system shows you the business event catalog with business events and the resources required for them.

### 34.5.4 Planning Screen

You select a business event type, right-click and choose 'Create Planning' to plan business events of that type. The system gives the following screen.

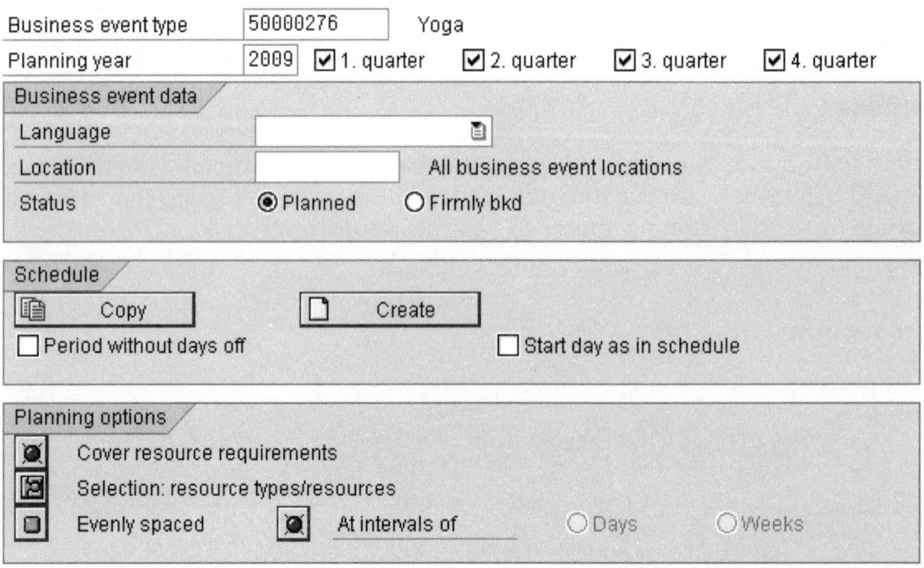

### *Planning year and quarters*

Here you specify the planning year and quarters you are planning for.

### *Language*

Here you specify the language in which the business event will be held. If you want to plan business events in multiple languages, leave it blank.

### *Location*

Here you specify the location where the business event will be held. If you want to plan business events at multiple locations, leave it blank.

### *Status*

Here you specify whether the business events will be created in the planned status or firmly booked status.

### *Schedule*

You also specify a time schedule for the business events either by copying the time schedule stored for the business event type or by creating a new one.

### *Period without days off*

If you tick this checkbox, the system proposes business event dates in such a way that there are no off days in a business event. The off days are taken from the factory calendar.

### *Start day as in schedule*

If you tick this checkbox, the system proposes business event dates that starts on the day specified in the time schedule.

### *Cover resource requirements*

If you click this icon, the system proposes business event dates in such a way that the resources flagged as required are actually available.

### *Selection: resource types/resources*

If you choose this function, the list of resource types required for the business event type is displayed and you can select the resource types that are required.

### *Business event spacing*

Here you specify whether the business events should be evenly spaced or that they should be planned at specified intervals.

### 34.5.5 Demand Determination

When you click Plan, the system lets you create demand if you have not already created it.

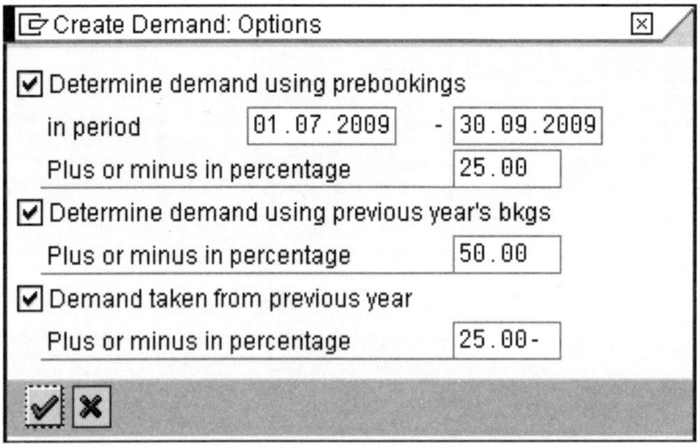


Based on your inputs, it gives you the demand. If you want, you can create your own entries. The unit of demand is number of business events, and not number of attendees.

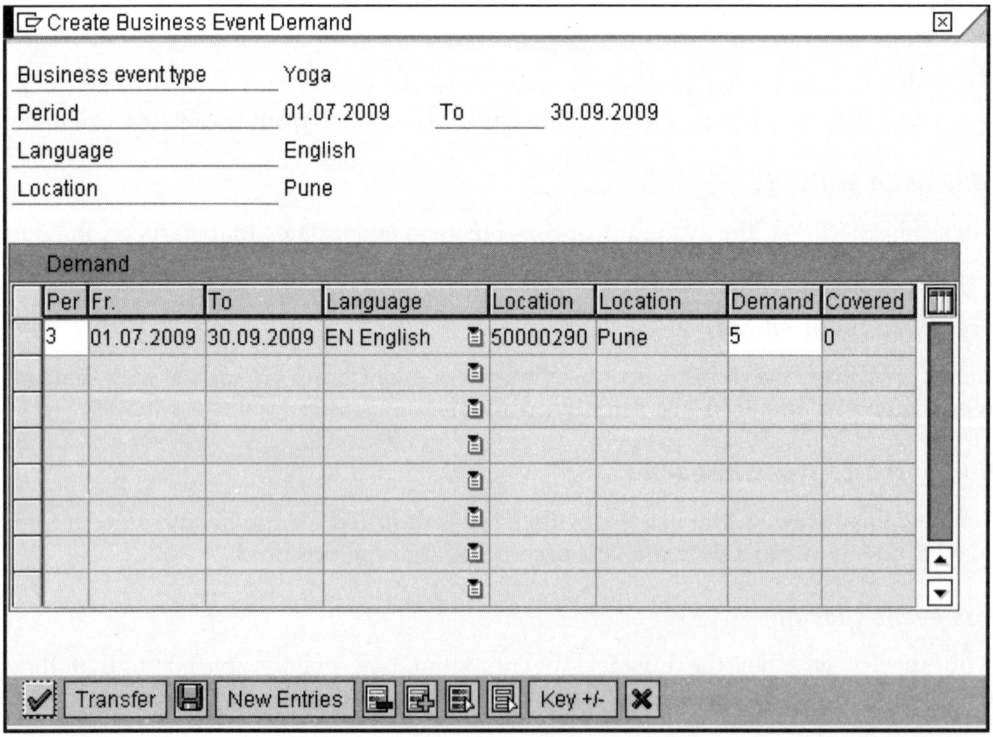


You select the entries and either transfer, or save. If you transfer an entry, it is used in the current planning process, but the demand infotype is not created.

### 34.5.6 Date Proposals

When you either save or transfer, the system determines and displays date proposals in the GANTT chart format.

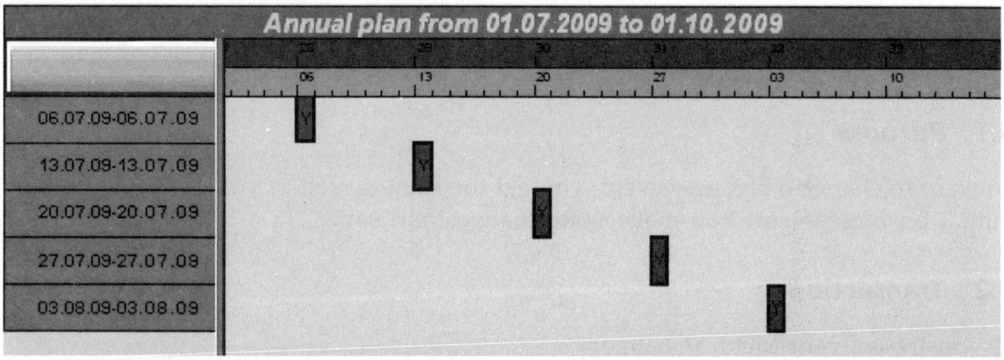


You can display and change the details of the planned business events by clicking the display or change icon.

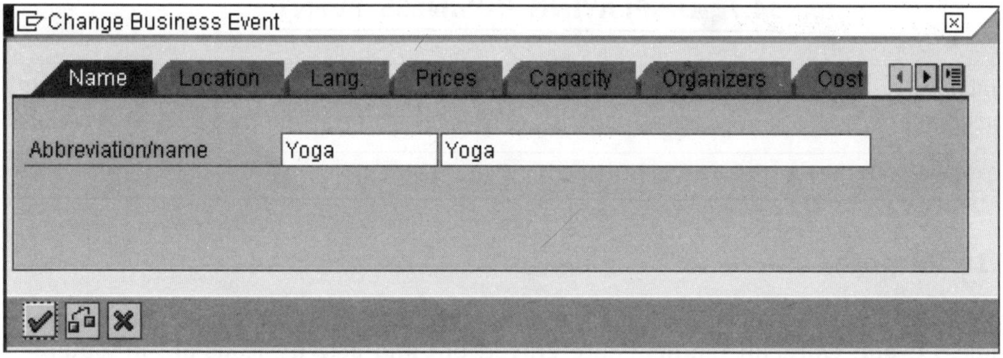


You can either copy a business event, delete a business event, move a business event, or change its schedule. When you change the schedule, you can change both date and time.

### 34.5.7 Business Event Creation

After you are satisfied, you can save the business events. This completes the business event planning exercise.

## 34.6 CHANGING BUSINESS EVENT

| *Functional Consultant* | *User* | *Business Process Owner* | *Senior Management* | *My Rating* | *Understanding Level* |
|---|---|---|---|---|---|
| A | A | B | C | | |

### 34.6.1 Purpose

If you want to change a business event, you get the same screen as you get when you are creating a business event. You make your changes and save.

### 34.6.2 Transaction

PSV2—Business Event Menu (Change)
PV1A—Change

## 34.7 DISPLAYING BUSINESS EVENT

| *Functional Consultant* | *User* | *Business Process Owner* | *Senior Management* | *My Rating* | *Understanding Level* |
|---|---|---|---|---|---|
| A | A | B | C | | |

### 34.7.1 Purpose

If you display a business event, you get the same screen as you get when you are changing a business event. Only, all the fields are grayed out and activity icons are missing.

### 34.7.2 Transaction

PV1B—Display

## 34.8 FIRMLY BOOKING BUSINESS EVENT

| *Functional Consultant* | *User* | *Business Process Owner* | *Senior Management* | *My Rating* | *Understanding Level* |
|---|---|---|---|---|---|
| A | A | B | B | | |

### 34.8.1 Purpose and Overview

#### *Planning status*

When you create a business event as firmly booked, it is stored in the objects table HRP1000 with planning status 1 (Active). In contrast, if you create a business event as planned, it is stored in the objects table with planning status 2 (Planned). Its relationship with the business event type also has status Planned. All bookings for a planned business event are also stored using status Planned. When you firmly book a business event, the planning status of the business event as well as all its relationships and infotypes is changed to Active.

#### *Attendee list changes*

When the business event is firmly booked, the attendee list is also revisited. If there were some cancellations, and the places were not given to waitlisted candidates, you now have the opportunity to do so. Also, if any waiting list remains, you can rebook them to other business events of the same type, leave them on the waiting list, or convert them into prebookings. You can also swap confirmed bookings with waitlisted bookings. Or, you may want to change the business event to increase its capacity.

#### *Communication*

When attendees booked a planned business event, they received communication confirming provisional booking. When the business event is firmly booked, attendees receive definite confirmation of place. So do instructors.

#### *Further options*

Firmly booking a business event is irrevocable, it cannot be undone. However, you can cancel the business event.

### 34.8.2 Transaction

PV12—Firmly Book/Cancel

### 34.8.3 Initial Screen

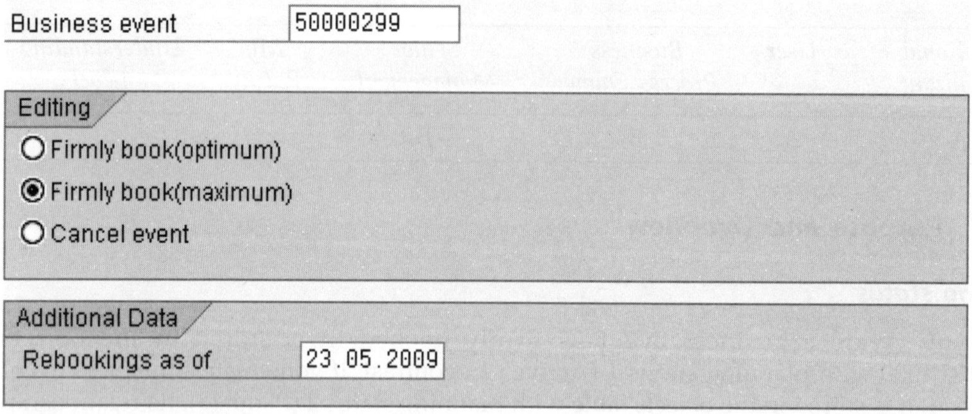


### 34.8.4 Bookings Less than Minimum Capacity

When you click Data Screen, if the bookings are less than the minimum capacity, the system asks you whether you will like to cancel the business event.

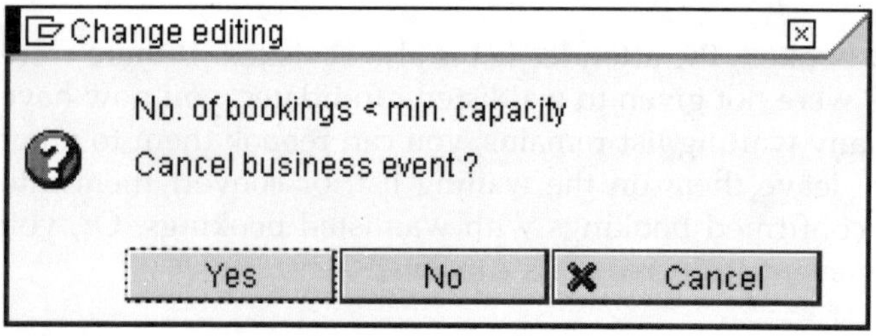


### 34.8.5 Data Screen

If there are enough bookings, or you choose not to cancel the business event, you get the following screen.

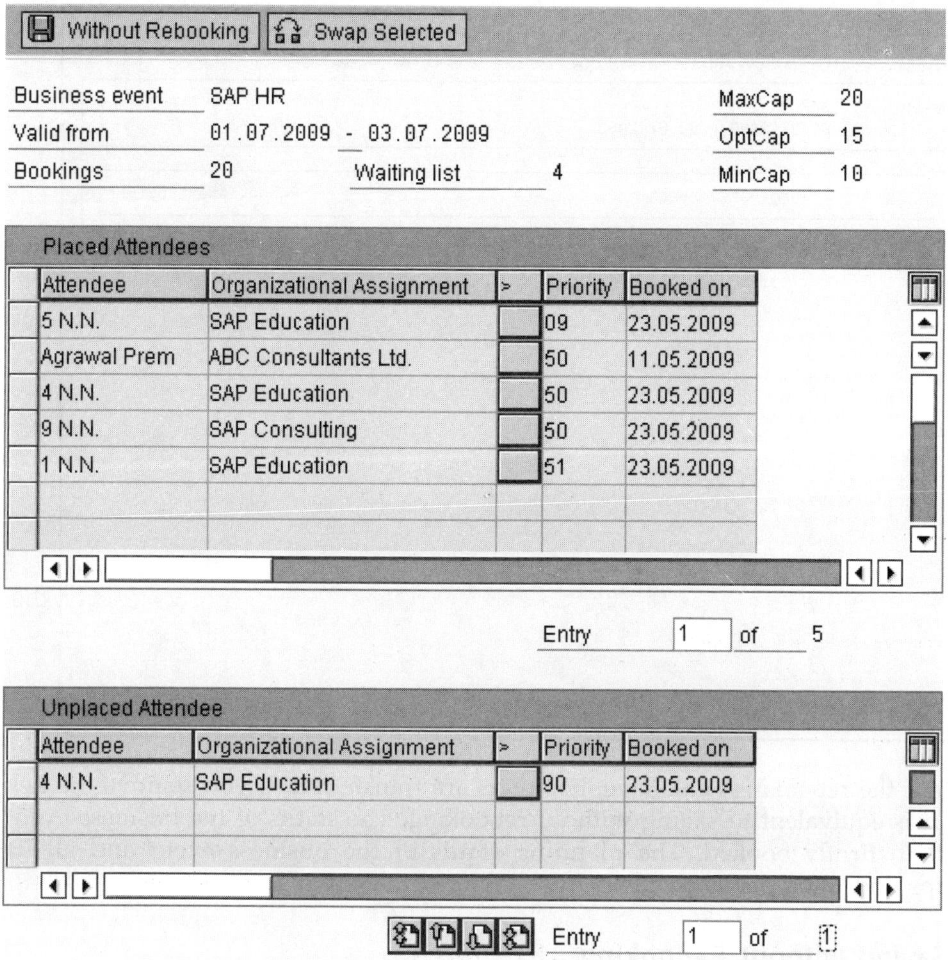


### 34.8.6 Swapping Attendees

The system automatically moves unplaced attendees to the placed attendees list. You can swap attendees by clicking Swap Selected.

### 34.8.7 Saving with Rebooking

If you save with rebooking, the system proposes the first business event after the 'Rebooking as of' date you specified in the initial screen.

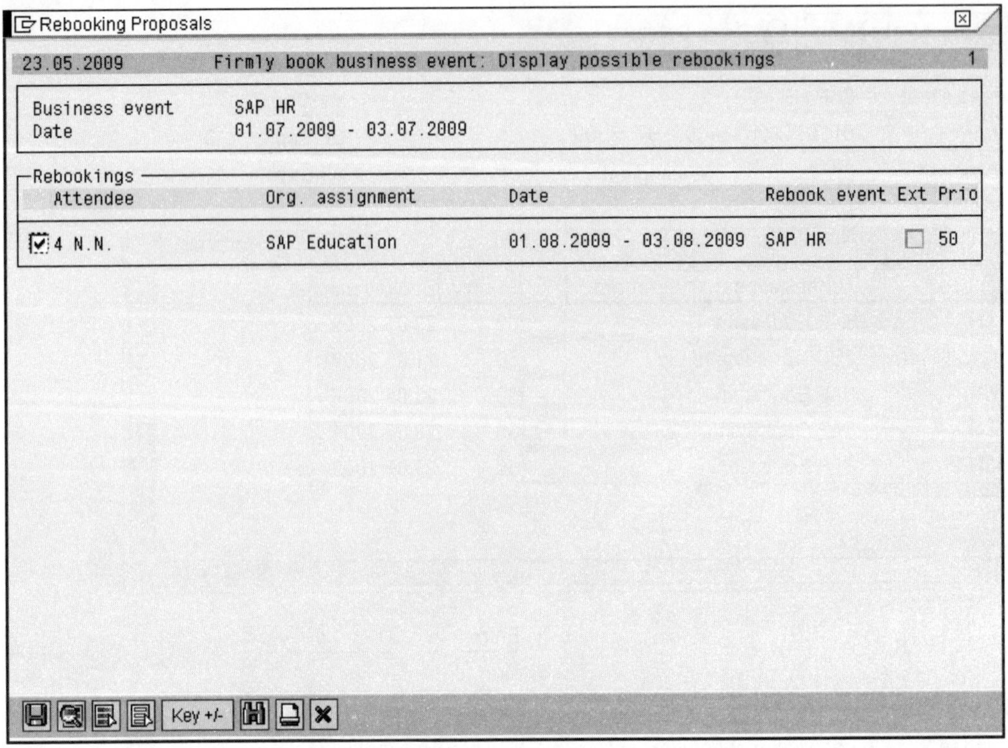


If you accept the rebookings and save, bookings are transferred. If you remove the tick and save, it is equivalent to saving without rebooking. The status of the business event is changed to firmly booked. The planning status of the business event and all its relationships and infotypes is changed from Planned to Active.

### 34.8.8 Saving without Rebooking

You can save without rebooking by clicking [Without Rebooking]. Unplaced attendees may remain on the waiting list, or may be moved to prebooking.

### 34.8.9 Waitlist Procedure

When you save without rebooking, unplaced attendees may remain on the waiting list, or may be moved to prebooking. This depends on the following setting in table T77S0.

| Group | Sem.abbr. | Value abbr | Description |
|---|---|---|---|
| SEMIN | FIXRV | 0 | Conversion of Unplaced Candidates to Prebookings |

If this switch is 0, unplaced attendances remain on the waiting list unless they are rebooked. If it is 1, unplaced attendances are cancelled and prebookings are created for them instead, leaving the waiting list empty.

### 34.8.10 Waitlist Procedure for a Business Event

You can also change this setting temporarily before firmly booking a business event by choosing Settings ➢ Waitlist Procedure. The system gives the following window, where you can change the setting temporarily.

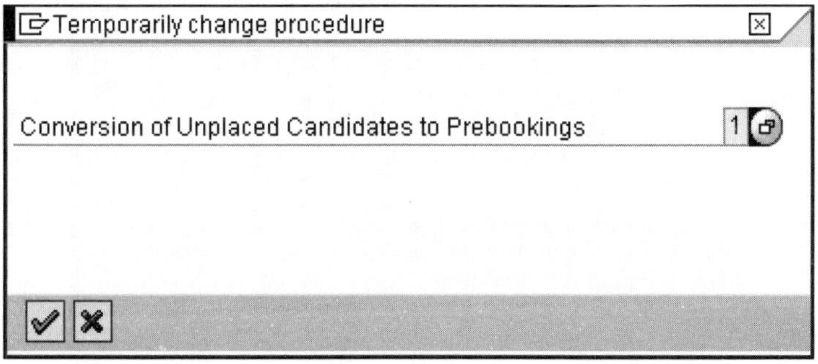


### 34.8.11 Attendee Notification for Rejection of Registration

If an attendee remains on the waiting list when the business event is firmly booked, he receives the following notification.

SAP Education

**Rejection of registration**

Date
May 23, 2009
Clerk
P_PKA00137
Telephone

Fax

Reference number (Please quote in enquiries)
E 50000299

Dear Sir or Madam,

We regret to inform you that your application for places on the business event

**SAP HR (SAP HR)**

from July 01, 2009 to July 03, 2009 has been rejected due to unexpectedly high demand.

We would ask you to contact us again to arrange for an alternative booking.

Yours faithfully,

Pioneer Education

## 34.8.12 Attendee Notification for Conversion to Prebooking

If an attendee is moved to prebooking when the business event is firmly booked, he receives the following notification.

SAP Consulting

**Rejection of registration / Prebooking**

Date
May 23, 2009
Clerk
P_PKA00137
Telephone

Fax

Reference number (Please quote in enquiries)
E 50000316

Dear Sir or Madam,

We regret to inform you that your registration for places on the business event

**Yoga (Yoga)**

from July 20, 2009 to July 20, 2009 has been rejected due to unexpectedly high demand.

Since there are no other business events of the same type available and/or the dates of the business events available are unsuitable, we have prebooked 19 places for you for the event type.

We look forward to contacting you again as soon as we are able to offer you other business events of the same business event type.

Yours faithfully,

## 34.9 CANCELLING BUSINESS EVENT

| *Functional Consultant* | *User* | *Business Process Owner* | *Senior Management* | *My Rating* | *Understanding Level* |
|---|---|---|---|---|---|
| A | A | B | B | | |

### 34.9.1 Purpose

Sometimes you may cancel a business event due to insufficient bookings, or other reasons. When you cancel a business event, reserved resources are released. You can rebook attendees for other business events. The system displays suitable alternatives where available. If attendees are not rebooked, they may be converted to prebookings depending on customizing setting. A delete flag is appended to the business event. Necessary correspondence is automatically generated. Cancelling a business event is irrevocable, it cannot be undone.

### 34.9.2 Transaction

PV12—Firmly Book/Cancel

### 34.9.3 Initial Screen

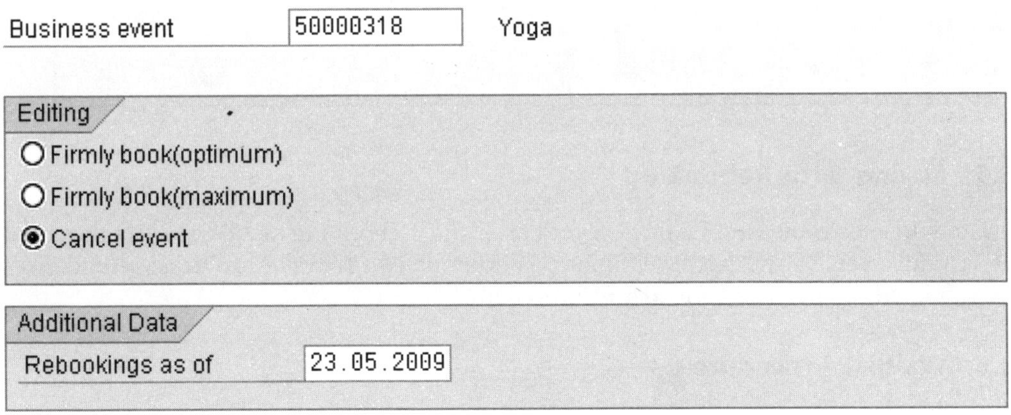

### 34.9.4 Rebooking Proposals

In the case of business event cancellation, the system takes you directly to rebooking proposals.

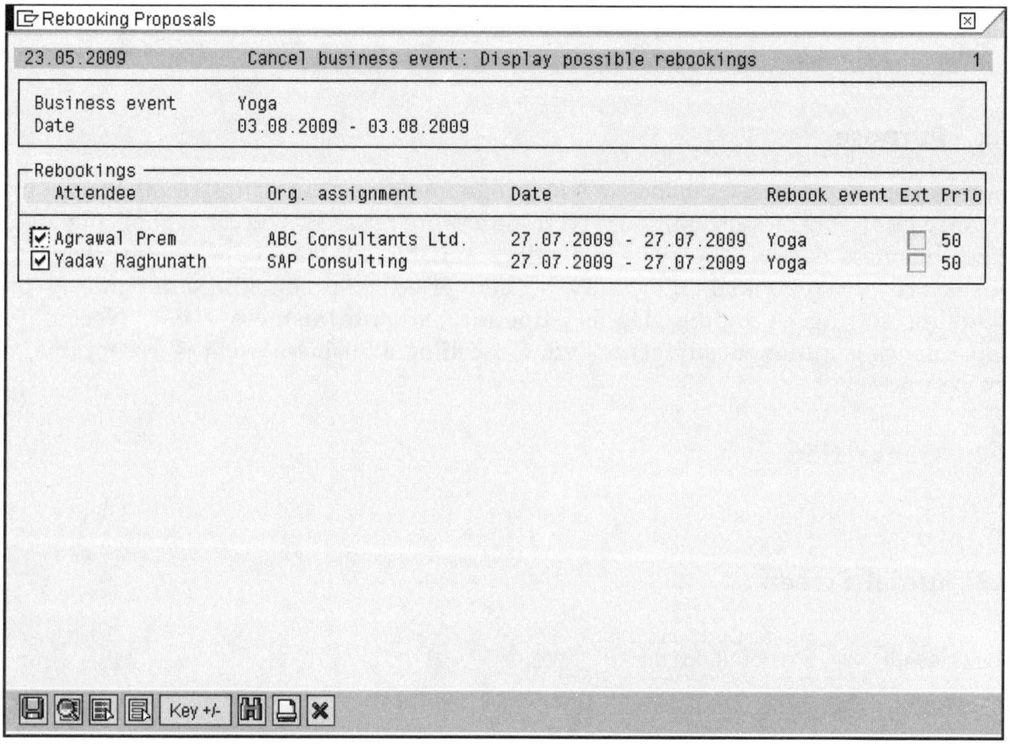


### 34.9.5 Saving with Rebooking

The system proposes the first business event after the 'Rebooking as of' date you specified in the initial screen. If you save, rebooking is done. If you remove the ticks, attendances may be deleted, or may be moved to prebooking.

### 34.9.6 Waitlist Procedure

When you save without rebooking, unplaced attendees may be moved to prebooking. This depends on the following setting in table T77S0.

| Group | Sem.abbr. | Value abbr | Description |
|---|---|---|---|
| SEMIN | FIXRV | 0 | Conversion of Unplaced Candidates to Prebookings |

If this switch is 0, unplaced attendances are lost unless they are rebooked. If it is 1, unplaced attendances are cancelled and prebookings are created for them instead, leaving the waiting list empty.

### 34.9.7 Waitlist Procedure for a Business Event

You can also change this setting temporarily before firmly booking a business event by choosing Settings ➢ Waitlist Procedure. The system gives the following window, where you can change the setting temporarily.

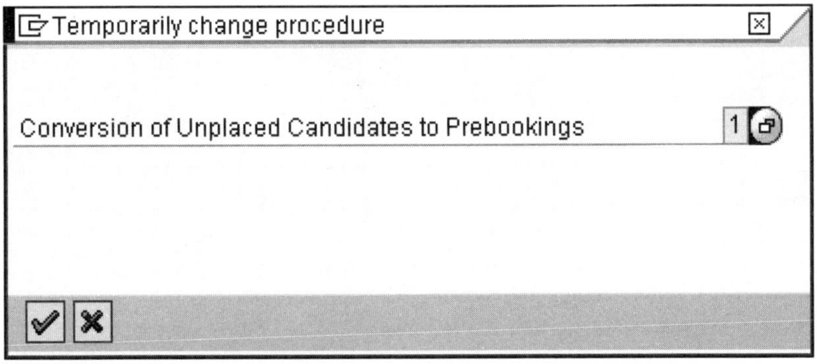


### 34.9.8 Cancellation Reasons

When you save, the system asks you for cancellation reason. Cancellation reasons are for information and analysis purpose only. You may or may not specify a cancellation reason.

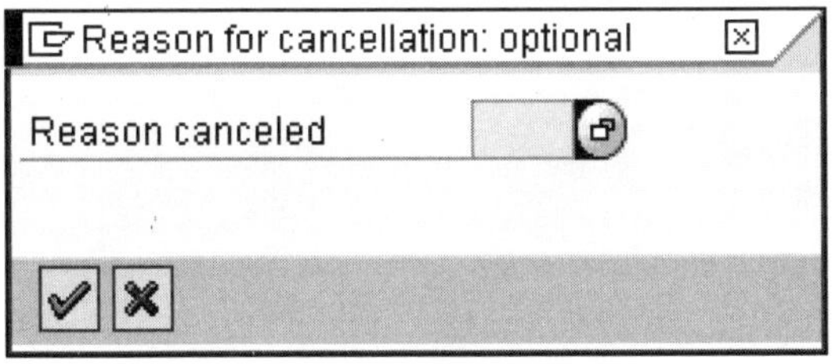


Cancellation reasons can be defined in view T77CR and can be used for information and analysis.

| Reas. | Reason for cancellation of event |
|---|---|
| | |
| | |
| | |

## 34.10 LOCKING/UNLOCKING BUSINESS EVENT

| *Functional Consultant* | *User* | *Business Process Owner* | *Senior Management* | *My Rating* | *Understanding Level* |
|---|---|---|---|---|---|
| A | A | B | B | | |

### 34.10.1 Purpose

You can lock a business event to prevent attendees from booking it. When you want to allow bookings for the business event, you simply unlock it. Locked business events may not show in the business event menu because in the dynamic menu settings, they are filtered out by default 

. You can change this setting to show all business events, but it may be confusing as the system does not show any distinguishing mark against the locked business events. If you want to view all locked business events, you may temporarily change this setting to 'Locked only'.

### 34.10.2 Locking/Unlocking a Business Event

In transaction PV14, you select the business event, choose lock/unlock radio button and save. The business event is locked/unlocked.

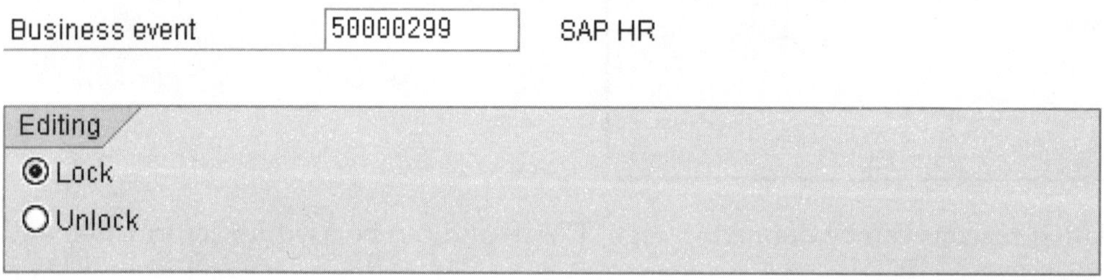


### 34.10.3 Locking/Unlocking in Business Event Menu

You can select a business event in the business event menu (transaction PV14), right-click, and choose Lock/Unlock. The business event is locked/unlocked.

### 34.10.4 Booking for Locked Business Events

Normally, a locked business event does not show in the attendance menu as it is filtered out. However, if you display it by removing filter, select it and right-click, you will find that you cannot book attendance for the business event.

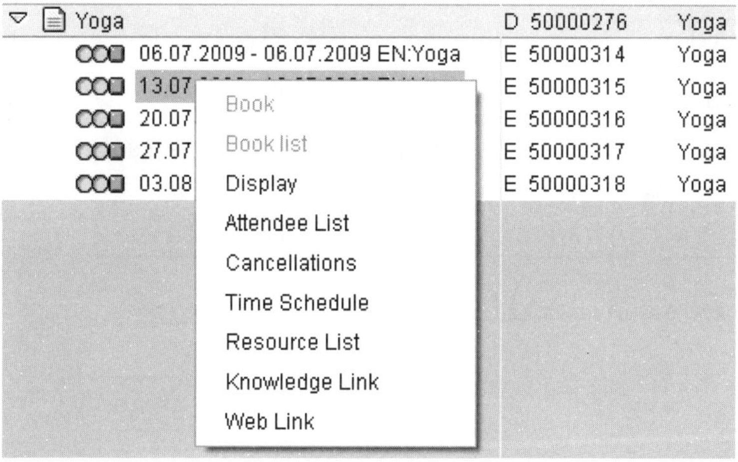


If you try to book attendee for a business event using transaction PV00, the locked business event does not show in the list of business events.

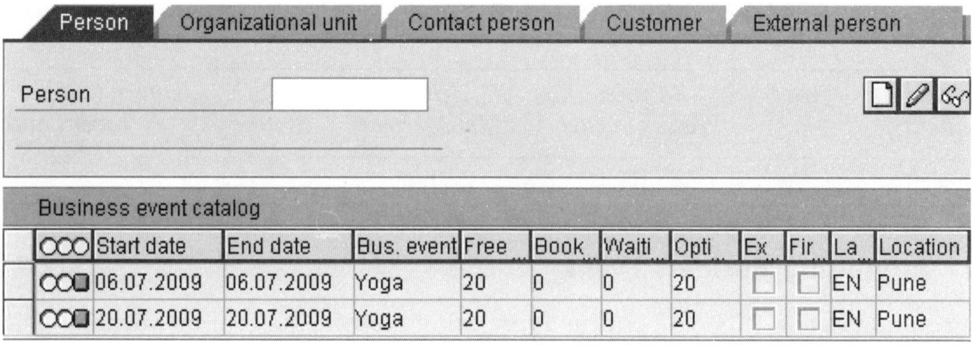


## 34.11 CONDUCTING BUSINESS EVENT

| *Functional Consultant* | *User* | *Business Process Owner* | *Senior Management* | *My Rating* | *Understanding Level* |
|---|---|---|---|---|---|
| A | A | B | B | | |

When you conduct a business event, you normally take signatures of the attendees. You can run transaction S_PH9_46000433 to generate attendance list for a business event. You can sort it by the organizational assignment or alphabetically. The attendees can sign the attendance list.

Org. assignment | Alphabetically

| 14.06.2009 | Business event attendance list | 1 |
|---|---|---|
| SAP HR | | from08.06.2009 - 10.06.2009 |
| | Business event language E | |
| | Please complete missing attendees' names in block letters | |
| **Attendees** | **Org. assignment** | **Signature** |
| Agrawal Prem | ABC Consultants Ltd. | |
| Kumar Ramesh | Component Factory | |
| Pande Geeta | PCB | |
| Yadav Raghunath | SAP Consulting | |

## 34.12 APPRAISING BUSINESS EVENT

| *Functional Consultant* | *User* | *Business Process Owner* | *Senior Management* | *My Rating* | *Understanding Level* |
|---|---|---|---|---|---|
| A | A | B | B | | |

### 34.12.1 Appraising Business Event

You can run transaction PV33 to perform appraisal of a business event by attendee. The system shows you the appraisal templates available for Training and Event Management. Appraisal templates are created by consultants using transaction OOAM as per your needs (Refer to chapter 27).

| ObjectID | Object abbr. | Object name | Start date | End Date |
|---|---|---|---|---|
| 50000443 | Business Eve | Business Event Appraisal | 01.01.1900 | 31.12.9999 |
| 50000459 | SAP HR Atten | SAP HR Attendee Appraisal | 01.01.1900 | 31.12.9999 |

You select the appropriate template. The system shows you the appraisal form. You enter the attendee, the business event, and the training period.

| | | |
|---|---|---|
| Appraisal Status | In Preparation | |
| Attendee | Agrawal Prem | |
| Training Program | SAP HR | |
| Training Period | 08.06.2009 | to 10.06.2009 |

Body Data

| Numbering | Element Name | Final Appraisal | Final Appraisal (Value Text) | Final... |
|---|---|---|---|---|
| | Business Event Appraisal | | | |
| 1 | Contents | | | |
| 1.1 | Relevance | | | |
| 1.2 | Sufficiency | | | |
| 2 | Training Material | | | |
| 2.1 | Availability | | | |
| 2.2 | Quality | | | |
| 3 | Instructor | | | |
| 3.1 | Knowledge | | | |
| 3.2 | Teaching Style | | | |
| 4 | Facilities | | | |
| 4.1 | Teaching Aids | | | |
| 4.2 | Food and Beverages | | | |

You then Execute the appraisal, enter the appraisal data and Complete it.

## 34.12.2 Business Event Appraisals Report

You can run transaction S_PH9_46000451 to see business event appraisals. You can filter appraisals based on appraisal template, appraisal status and period. The system shows you a list of appraisals meeting your selection criteria.

| N... | App.Document Name | AppDocType | Type | Name | Type | Appraisee | App. Stat |
|---|---|---|---|---|---|---|---|
| 1 | Business Event Appraisal | Appraisal Doc | Person | Agrawal Prem | Course | SAP HR | Completed |
| 1 | Business Event Appraisal | Appraisal Doc | Person | Agrawal Prem | Course | SAP HR | In Process |

You can select an appraisal document and display or change it. You can even create an appraisal document from this report. You can delete an appraisal document. You can change the status of a completed document to 'In process'.

## 34.13 FOLLOWING UP BUSINESS EVENT

| *Functional Consultant* | *User* | *Business Process Owner* | *Senior Management* | *My Rating* | *Understanding Level* |
|---|---|---|---|---|---|
| A | A | B | B | | |

### 34.13.1 Purpose

After a business event has been conducted, you need to update absenteeism as cancellations. You also need to do booking for attendees who turn up at the last moment. You then indicate to the system that the business event is over so that it can perform follow-up actions, e.g. printing attendance certificates. This is done by 'Following up' the business event. When a business event is followed up, the following activities take place.

- The correspondence linked to following up the business event is triggered. This may include printing certificate of attendance, which may be given to the participants.
- The business event may be marked historical. This means that no further changes can be made to the business event data.
- If the business event imparts a qualification, it may be updated for the attendees either manually or automatically.
- The relationship attendee takes part in the business event may be deleted and the relationship attendee participated in the business event type may be created.

### 34.13.2 Transaction

PV15—Follow-up

### 34.13.3 Selection Screen

Here you can specify whether you want to mark the business event historical. You can use transaction RE_RHGRENZ1 to remove the historical record flag from a business event.

### 34.13.4 Data Screen

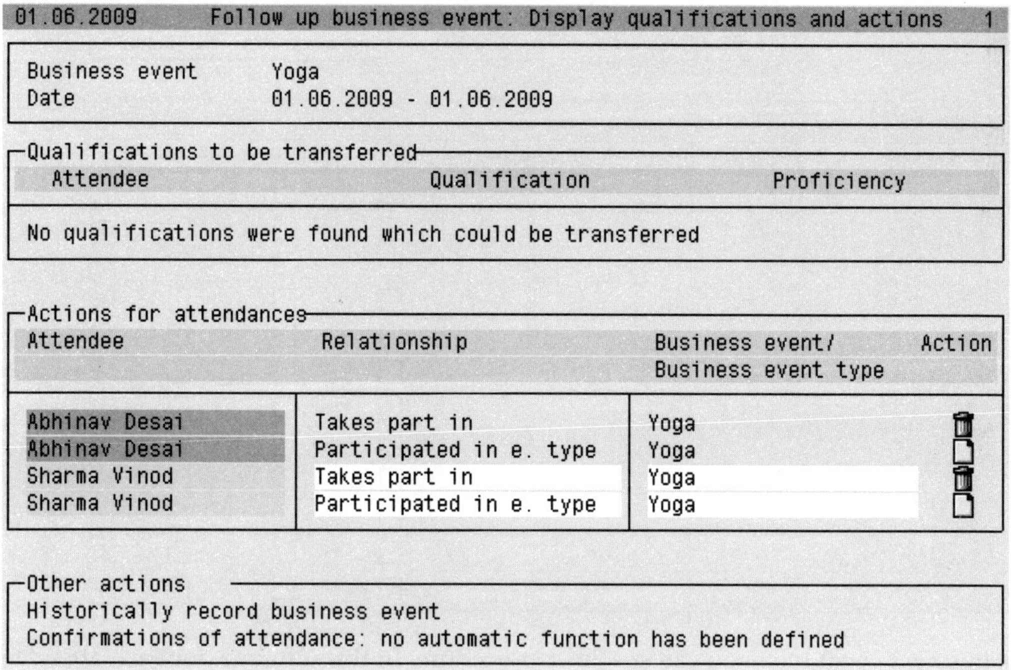


The system shows you the follow-up actions. You click the save icon to take the action. The system confirms that the actions have been taken.

### 34.13.5 Procedure

The follow-up actions can be set in the last three columns of the procedure infotype of the business event type. If the procedure infotype is not maintained for a business event type, global follow-up actions are taken.

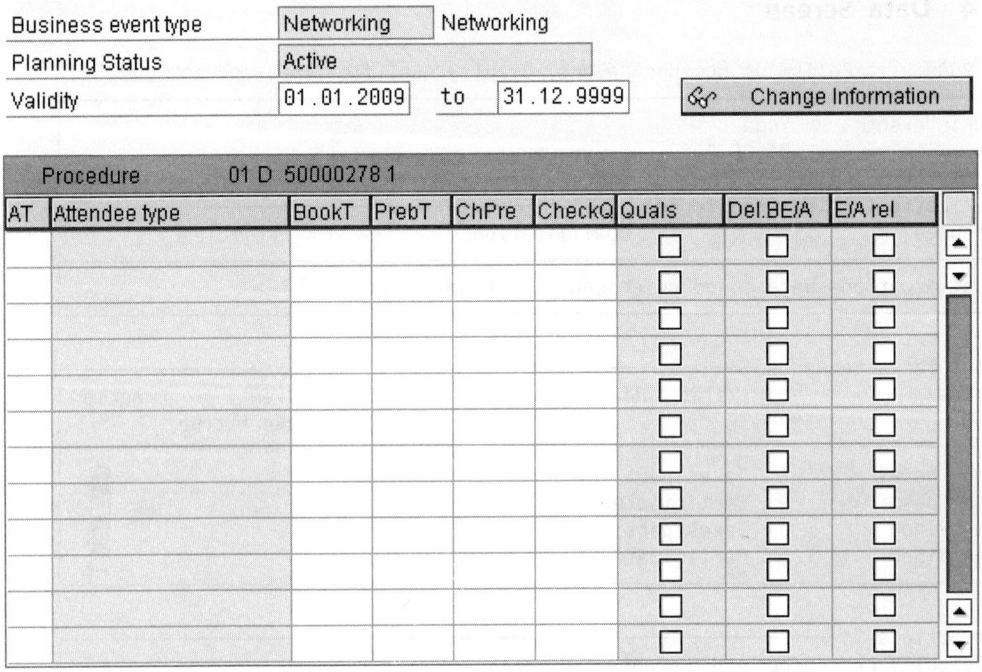


For a business event type you can specify a procedure. In this infotype, for each attendee type, you specify the following.

### *Transfer objectives to attendee as qualifications*

A business event may impart a qualification. When an attendee attends a business event, he acquires that qualification. You may add the qualification to the attendee manually, or you may want the system to do it automatically. If you want the system to do it automatically, you tick this checkbox.

### *Delete and create relationships*

When an attendee books a business event, relationship 025 is created which says that the attendee takes part in the business event. When the business event has actually taken place (followed up), this relationship 025 is deleted and another relationship 034 is created which says that the attendee participated in the business event type. Relationship 034 was read by the system to determine whether the employee has attended prerequisite business event. However, now the system reads both relationships 025 and 034. Hence, the system will work equally well if relationship 025 was not deleted and relationship 034 was not created. If you choose to delete and create relationships, you should tick both these checkboxes; although it is recommended that you leave both these checkboxes blank.

### 34.13.6 Global Follow-up Actions

In view V_T77KV_2 you specify business event follow-up actions which apply to all business event types. You can also specify them in procedure infotype of a business event type. If the procedure infotype exists for a business event type, the specification there gets a priority over global specification here.

| AT | Attendee type | Transfer quals | Del. BE/A rel. | Rel.BE type/Att |
|---|---|---|---|---|
| H | External person | ☐ | ☐ | ☐ |
| P | Person | ☑ | ☐ | ☐ |

## 34.14 BUSINESS EVENT REPORTS

| *Functional Consultant* | *User* | *Business Process Owner* | *Senior Management* | *My Rating* | *Understanding Level* |
|---|---|---|---|---|---|
| A | A | A | B | | |

#### *Attendee list*

You can run transaction S_PH9_46000434 to see the list of attendees for one or more business events. You can filter the business events selected based on period and location. You can filter the attendee list of selected business events by booking priority.

| Name ... | Start date | End date | Attendee Name | Σ Bookings | BP | Booking date | Σ Fee | Crcy | Notes |
|---|---|---|---|---|---|---|---|---|---|
| SAP HR | 08.06.2009 | 10.06.2009 | Agrawal Prem | 1 | 50 | 12.06.2009 | | | |
| SAP HR | 08.06.2009 | 10.06.2009 | Kumar Ramesh | 1 | 50 | 12.06.2009 | | | |
| SAP HR | 08.06.2009 | 10.06.2009 | Pande Geeta | 1 | 50 | 12.06.2009 | | | |
| SAP HR | 08.06.2009 | 10.06.2009 | Yadav Raghunath | 1 | 50 | 12.06.2009 | | | |
| | | | ▪ | 4 | | | | | |

#### *Attendance list*

You can run transaction S_PH9_46000433 to generate attendance list of a business event. You can sort the list alphabetically, or by organizational assignment. You can take signatures of attendees on an attendance list.

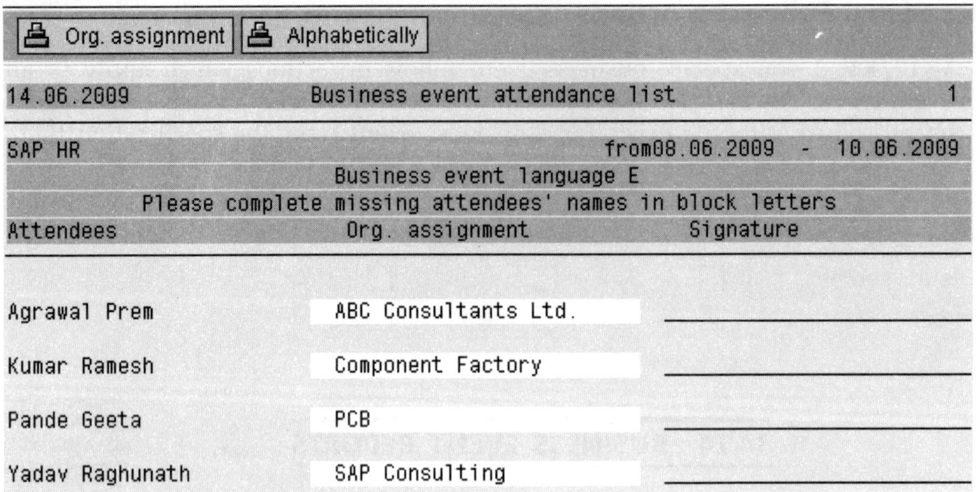


### *Price proposal*

You can run transaction PV1D to determine prices of one or more business events based on cost and to transfer it to infotype 1021. You may individually specify business events, or specify that business events belonging to a business event type or business event group within specified period be selected.

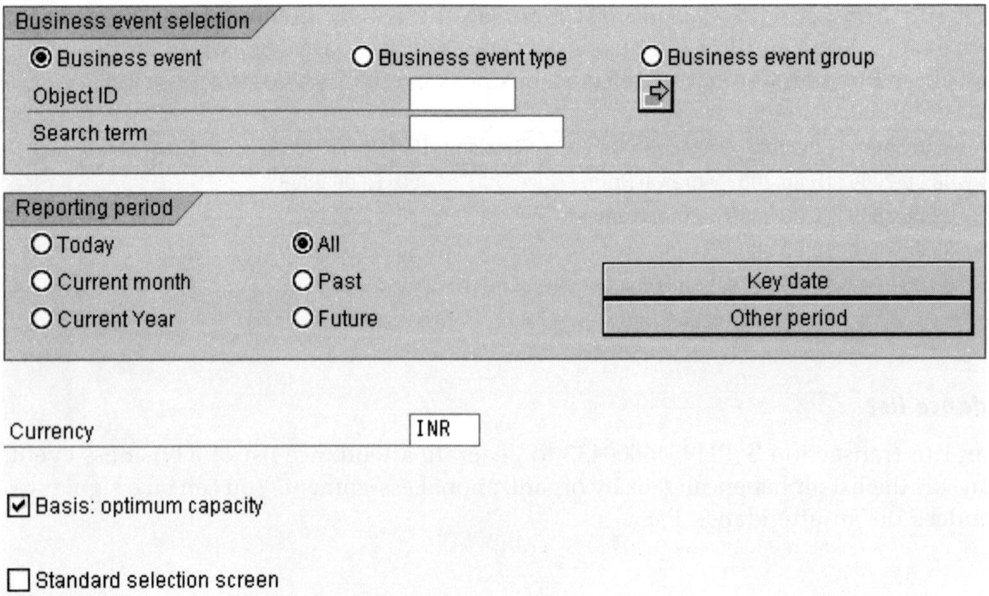


The price may be based on either optimum capacity or actual booking. The following items are added together to determine a price proposal:

- Cost items of business event (E).
- Cost items of business event type (D).

- ➢ Cost items of resources (G) reserved for the business event.
- ➢ Cost items of the resource types (R) related with the business event type.
- ➢ Cost items of the equipment (R) in the room reserved for the business event.

If the same cost items are maintained for both the business event and the business event type, the values stored for the business event itself are taken. The same applies to cost items stored for resource types and resources, the values stored for the actual resources are taken.

14.06.2009 Business event cost items 1

| Business event | SAP HR | | Internal |
|---|---|---|---|
| Date | 01.07.2009 - 03.07.2009 | | Firmly booked |

| Cost item / Cost origin | Status / Number | Amount | Cost elemen / Ref. unit |
|---|---|---|---|
| ☑ Depreciation | Active | 66.00 INR | 403000 |
| Overhead Projector 1 | 1 | | TIME |
| ☑ Electricity | Active | 71.50 INR | 403000 |
| Overhead Projector 1 | 1 | | TIME |
| ☑ Instructor Fee | Active | 2,200.00 INR | 403000 |
| Naresh Kumar | 1 | | TIME |
| ☑ Room Rent | Active | 2,200.00 INR | 403000 |
| Conference Room | 1 | | TIME |
| Total amount / capacity | | Σ 4,537.50 INR | / 15 |
| ☑ Propose as business event price | | 302.50 INR | |

### *Business event demand*

You can run transaction S_AHR_61016220 to display demand for a business event type. You can also create or change demand. You can call business event planning function from here.

Plan | Demand | Demand | Language +/- | Location +/- | Key +/-

Calendar year 2009 — Dmd = demand / cvd = demand covered

| Business event type | Location | Lng | Quarter 1. Dmd | 1. Cvd | 2. Dmd | 2. Cvd | 3. Dmd | 3. Cvd | 4. Dmd | 4. Cvd | Total Dmd | Total Cvd |
|---|---|---|---|---|---|---|---|---|---|---|---|---|
| SAP HR | No demand exists | | | | | | | | | | | |

### *Business event schedule*

You can run transaction S_PH9_46000438 to see the time schedule of a business event.

## Business Event Schedule

**Date** 01.07.2009 - 03.07.2009

**Business event** SAP HR

| DayNo./sch | Date | Day name | Start Time | End Time | Day off |
|---|---|---|---|---|---|
| 1 | 01.07.2009 | Wednesday | 10:00:00 | 17:00:00 | ☐ |
| 2 | 02.07.2009 | Thursday | 09:00:00 | 17:00:00 | ☐ |
| 3 | 03.07.2009 | Friday | 09:00:00 | 16:00:00 | ☐ |

### *Business event hierarchy*

You can run transaction S_AHR_61016217 to see the hierarchy of a business event group or business event type. You can also see business event brochure, prices and knowledge links of business events.

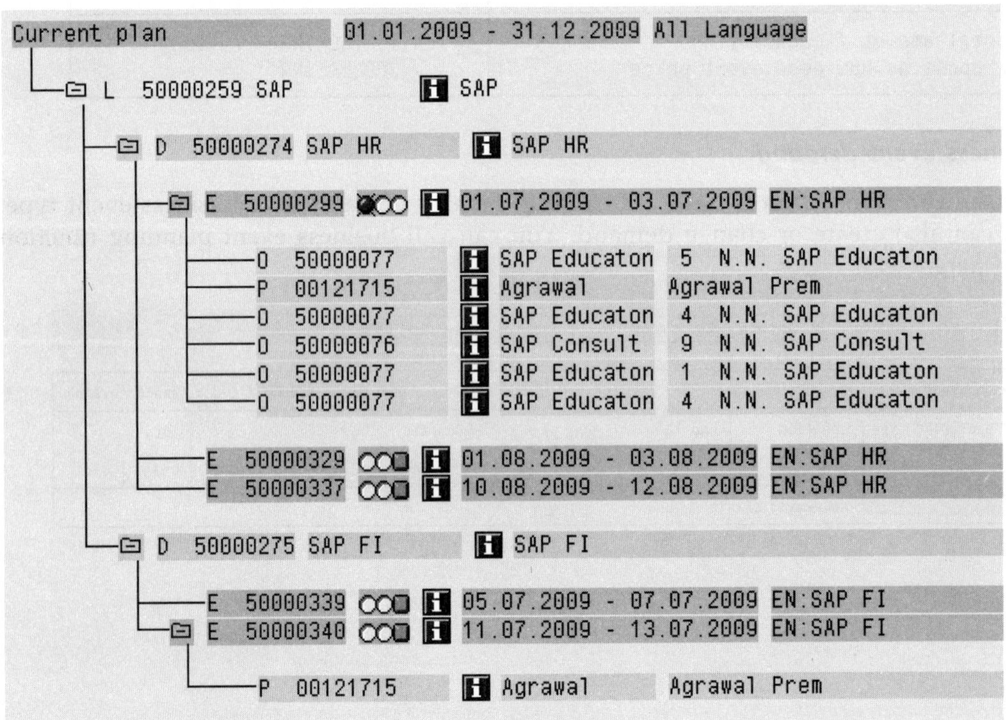

### *Attendance statistics*

You can run transaction S_ALR_87014085 to see the number of attendees and status of business events. You can select a business event and firmly book it, cancel it, or follow it up.

| Business event type | Business event | Start date | End date | L | ΣN... | ΣN | L | D | H | F | FB | Ext |
|---|---|---|---|---|---|---|---|---|---|---|---|---|
| SAP HR | SAP HR | 01.07.2009 | 03.07.2009 | EN | 20 | 4 | ☐ | ☐ | ☐ | ☐ | ☑ | ☐ |
| | | | | | ▪ 20 | ▪ 4 | | | | | | |

### *Business event brochure*

You can run transaction S_AHR_61016218 to generate business event brochure.

```
SAP HR        SAP HR                              (    0  Days )

Prerequisites
  do(es) not exist

Follow-up events
  do(es) not exist

Event contents
  do(es) not exist

Objectives
  do(es) not exist

Target group
  do(es) not exist

Notes on event
  do(es) not exist

Business event information
  do(es) not exist
```

You can use extended formatting options to decide which of these items are included in the business event brochure.

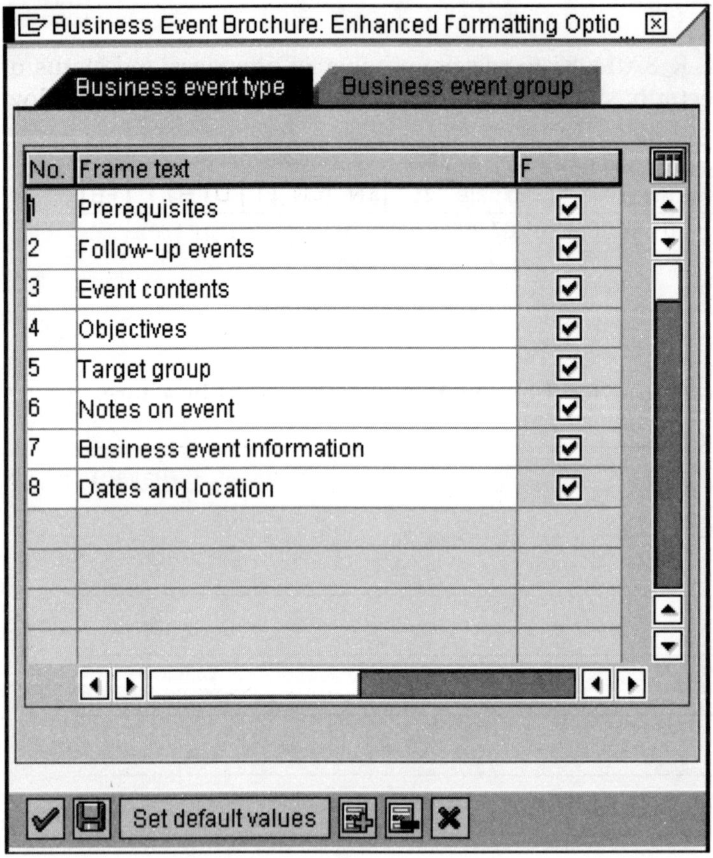


### *Business event information*

You can run transaction S_PH0_48000476 to display detailed information stored for business event dates such as event location, instructor, room, telephone number of room, event owner, availability of places on the business event, or duration of the business event.

| Bus. event | Start date | End date | L | Location | B | R | ΣN | ΣE | ΣN | ΣW | ΣD | ΣHo... | I... | L | H | D |
|---|---|---|---|---|---|---|---|---|---|---|---|---|---|---|---|---|
| SAP HR | 25.05.2009 | 27.05.2009 | EN | Pune Camp | UI | C( | 5 | 0 | 0 | 0 | 3 | 24.00 | | [ ] | [ ] | [ ] |
| SAP HR | 01.06.2009 | 03.06.2009 | EN | Pune Camp | | | 5 | 0 | 0 | 0 | 3 | 24.00 | | [ ] | [ ] | [ ] |
| SAP HR | 08.06.2009 | 10.06.2009 | EN | Pune Camp | | | 6 | 0 | 4 | 0 | 3 | 24.00 | | [ ] | [ ] | [ ] |
| SAP HR | 01.07.2009 | 03.07.2009 | EN | Pune Camp | UI | C( | 0 | 5 | 15 | 4 | 3 | 22.00 | Na | [ ] | [ ] | [ ] |
| SAP HR | 01.08.2009 | 03.08.2009 | EN | Pune Camp | UI | C( | 20 | 0 | 0 | 0 | 3 | 24.00 | | [ ] | [ ] | [ ] |
| SAP HR | 10.08.2009 | 12.08.2009 | EN | Pune Camp | | | 20 | 0 | 0 | 0 | 3 | 24.00 | | [ ] | [ ] | [ ] |
| SAP HR | 16.08.2009 | 18.08.2009 | EN | Pune Camp | | | 20 | 0 | 0 | 0 | 3 | 24.00 | | [ ] | [ ] | [x] |
| SAP HR | 16.08.2009 | 18.08.2009 | EN | Pune Camp | UI | C( | 15 | 0 | 0 | 0 | 3 | 24.00 | Na | [ ] | [ ] | [ ] |
| SAP HR | 20.08.2009 | 22.08.2009 | EN | Pune Camp | UI | C( | 15 | 0 | 0 | 0 | 3 | 24.00 | Na | [ ] | [ ] | [ ] |
| | | | | | | | ▪ 1 | ▪ 5 | ▪ 1 | ▪ 4 | ▪ 2 | ▪ 2... | | | | |

### *Business event dates*

You can run transaction S_AHR_61016219 to see business event dates of a business event type or a business event group.

| Business event type | Start date | End date | Location | Lang. | Business event | Σ No. |
|---|---|---|---|---|---|---|
| SAP HR | 01.07.2009 | 03.07.2009 | Pune Camp | EN | SAP HR | 1 |
| SAP HR | 01.08.2009 | 03.08.2009 | Pune Camp | EN | SAP HR | 1 |
| SAP HR | 10.08.2009 | 12.08.2009 | Pune Camp | EN | SAP HR | 1 |
| SAP FI | 05.07.2009 | 07.07.2009 | Pune Camp | EN | SAP FI | 1 |
| SAP FI | 11.07.2009 | 13.07.2009 | Pune Camp | EN | SAP FI | 1 |
| | | | | | | ▪ 5 |

### *Resource list per business event*

You can run transaction S_PH9_46000437 to see the resources reserved by one or more business events. Resources which are required and not reserved are shown as blank entries.

| Busin... | Resource type | Name Resource | Start date | End date | Start Time | End time | Σ No. ... |
|---|---|---|---|---|---|---|---|
| SAP HR | Conference Room | Conference Room | 01.07.2009 | 01.07.2009 | 10:00:00 | 17:00:00 | 7.00 |
| SAP HR | Conference Room | Conference Room | 02.07.2009 | 02.07.2009 | 09:00:00 | 17:00:00 | 8.00 |
| SAP HR | Conference Room | Conference Room | 03.07.2009 | 03.07.2009 | 09:00:00 | 16:00:00 | 7.00 |
| SAP HR | Overhead Projector | Overhead Projector 1 | 01.07.2009 | 01.07.2009 | 10:00:00 | 17:00:00 | 7.00 |
| SAP HR | Overhead Projector | Overhead Projector 1 | 02.07.2009 | 02.07.2009 | 09:00:00 | 17:00:00 | 8.00 |
| SAP HR | Overhead Projector | Overhead Projector 1 | 03.07.2009 | 03.07.2009 | 09:00:00 | 16:00:00 | 7.00 |
| SAP HR | SAP HR Instructor | Naresh Kumar | 01.07.2009 | 01.07.2009 | 10:00:00 | 17:00:00 | 7.00 |
| SAP HR | SAP HR Instructor | Naresh Kumar | 02.07.2009 | 02.07.2009 | 09:00:00 | 17:00:00 | 8.00 |
| SAP HR | SAP HR Instructor | Naresh Kumar | 03.07.2009 | 03.07.2009 | 09:00:00 | 16:00:00 | 7.00 |
| SAP HR | White Board Marker | White board marker - | 01.07.2009 | 01.07.2009 | 10:00:00 | 17:00:00 | 7.00 |
| SAP HR | White Board Marker | White board marker - | 02.07.2009 | 02.07.2009 | 09:00:00 | 17:00:00 | 8.00 |
| SAP HR | White Board Marker | White board marker - | 03.07.2009 | 03.07.2009 | 09:00:00 | 16:00:00 | 7.00 |
| SAP HR | | | | | 00:00:00 | 00:00:00 | 24.00 |
| SAP HR | | | | | 00:00:00 | 00:00:00 | 24.00 |
| SAP HR | | | | | 00:00:00 | 00:00:00 | 24.00 |
| | | | | | | | ▪ 16... |

### *Resources not yet assigned per business event*

You can run transaction S_PH9_46000436 to see resources not yet assigned for a business event.

| Business event | Resource type | Start date | End date | Start Time | End time | Σ No. hours |
|---|---|---|---|---|---|---|
| SAP HR | Personal Computer | 01.07.2009 | 01.07.2009 | 10:00:00 | 17:00:00 | 7.00 |
| SAP HR | Personal Computer | 02.07.2009 | 02.07.2009 | 09:00:00 | 17:00:00 | 8.00 |
| SAP HR | Personal Computer | 03.07.2009 | 03.07.2009 | 09:00:00 | 16:00:00 | 7.00 |
| | | | | | | ▪ 22.00 |

### *Material requirements per business event*

You can run transaction S_PH9_46000435 to see the material required for a business event. You can also select a material and reserve. If the material is available, it is reserved. If it is not available, a purchase requisition is generated.

| Busine... | Status | R | R | B | P | Start date | End date | B... | Material | Per att... | Per b... | Total |
|---|---|---|---|---|---|---|---|---|---|---|---|---|
| SAP HR | Firm bk | ■ | 2 | | | 01.07.2009 | 03.07.2009 | 20 | White board marker -red | 0 | 1 | 1 |

### *Business event prices*

You can run transaction S_AHR_61016221 to see prices of business event types. If you don't select one or more business event types, this report shows prices of all business event types. Note that this report does not show prices of business events which may be different from their respective business event types.

| Business event type | Internal prices | Currency | External prices | Currency |
|---|---|---|---|---|
| Positive Attitude | | | | |
| Think Customer | | | | |
| English | | | | |
| German | | | | |
| Japanese | | | | |
| Presentations | | | | |
| Creativity and Problem Solving | | | | |
| Decision Making Skills | | | | |
| Mentoring | | | | |
| Management By Objectives | | | | |
| Time Management | | | | |
| Microsoft Word | | | | |
| Microsoft Excel | | | | |
| SAP HR | | | | |
| SAP FI | | | | |
| Yoga | | | | |

# CHAPTER 35

# Attendee

## 35.1 TYPES OF ATTENDEES

| *Functional Consultant* | *User* | *Business Process Owner* | *Senior Management* | *My Rating* | *Understanding Level* |
|---|---|---|---|---|---|
| A | A | A | A | | |

A business event is attended by attendees. SAP supports various types of attendees as can be seen by running transaction PSV8 to create an attendee or transaction PSV9 to change/display an attendee.

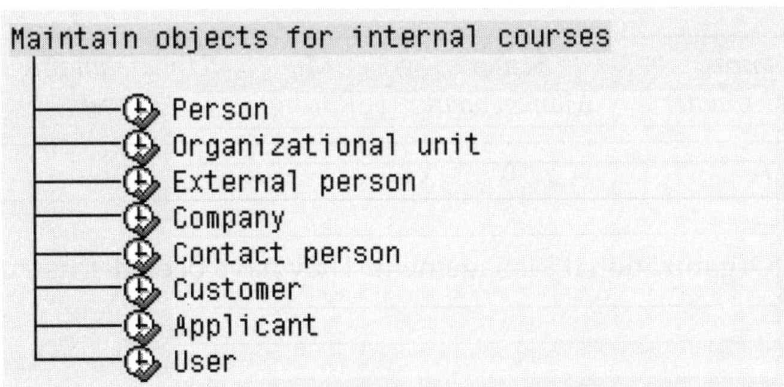


This is actually an area menu. Depending on the type of attendee, appropriate transaction is called.

## 35.2 INDIVIDUAL AND GROUP ATTENDEES

| *Functional Consultant* | *User* | *Business Process Owner* | *Senior Management* | *My Rating* | *Understanding Level* |
|---|---|---|---|---|---|
| A | A | A | A | | |

There are two types of attendees, namely individual attendees and group attendees. Person, external person, contact person, applicant and user are individual attendees, whereas organizational unit, company and customer are group attendees. In the case of group attendees, you can specify the number of persons who would attend a business event.

## 35.3 PERSON

| *Functional Consultant* | *User* | *Business Process Owner* | *Senior Management* | *My Rating* | *Understanding Level* |
|---|---|---|---|---|---|
| A | A | A | A | | |

A person is an employee of the company. He is created in the SAP system when he is hired in Personnel Administration.

## 35.4 ORGANIZATIONAL UNIT

| *Functional Consultant* | *User* | *Business Process Owner* | *Senior Management* | *My Rating* | *Understanding Level* |
|---|---|---|---|---|---|
| A | A | A | A | | |

Organizational units are created in Organizational Management. They have been discussed in chapter 3.

## 35.5 EXTERNAL PERSON/EXTERNAL INSTRUCTOR

| *Functional Consultant* | *User* | *Business Process Owner* | *Senior Management* | *My Rating* | *Understanding Level* |
|---|---|---|---|---|---|
| A | A | B | C | | |

### 35.5.1 Purpose

An external person is a person external to your organization. He may belong to a company, customer or prospect. External persons may be instructors or attendees. You maintain their name, relationship with the company, address and name format.

### 35.5.2 Transaction

PVH0—Create/Change External Instructor
S_AHR_61011893—External Instructor
OOER—Create External Instructor
PO19—External Instructor

### 35.5.3 Relationships

If you create an external person as attendee, you create a relationship between him and his company.

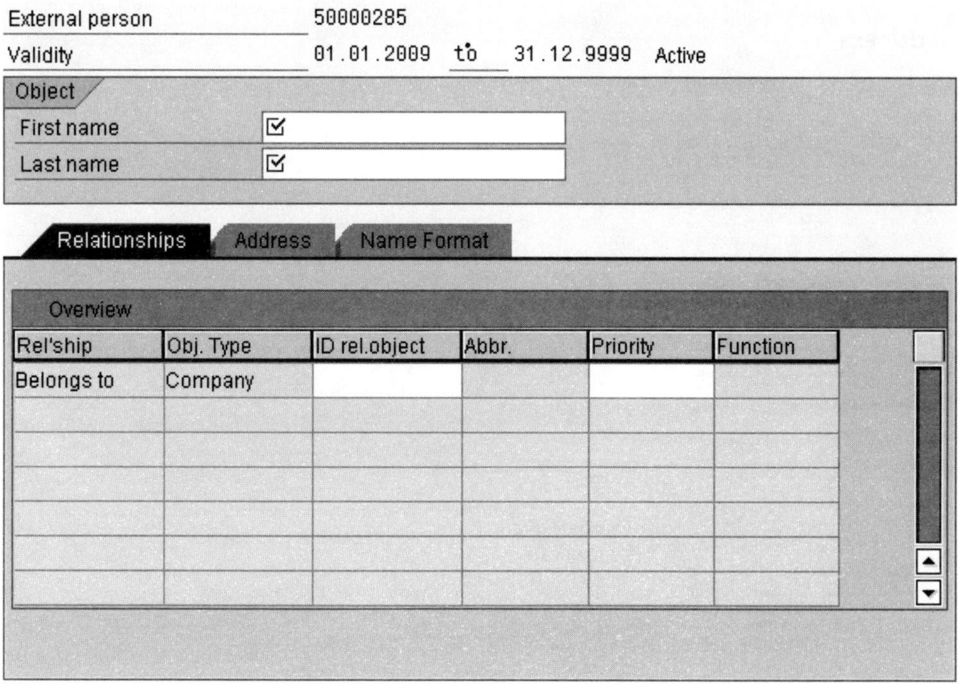

If, on the other hand, you create an external person as instructor, you not only create his relationship with the company but also with the business event type which he teaches. The relationship to a business event type is used to determine the instructors proposed to hold business events during resource selection. An external person may be instructor for more than one business event types. An external instructor may be reserved by a business event.

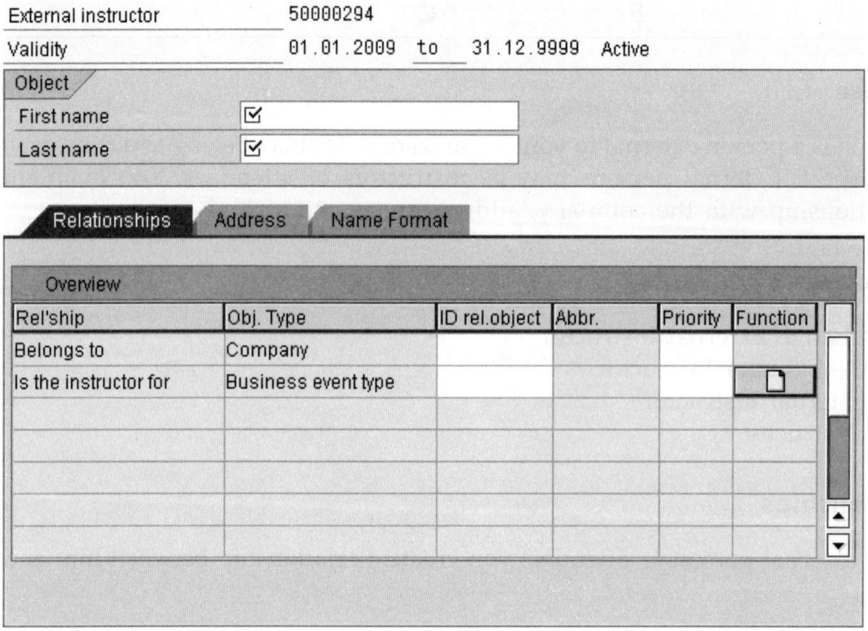


## 35.5.4 Address

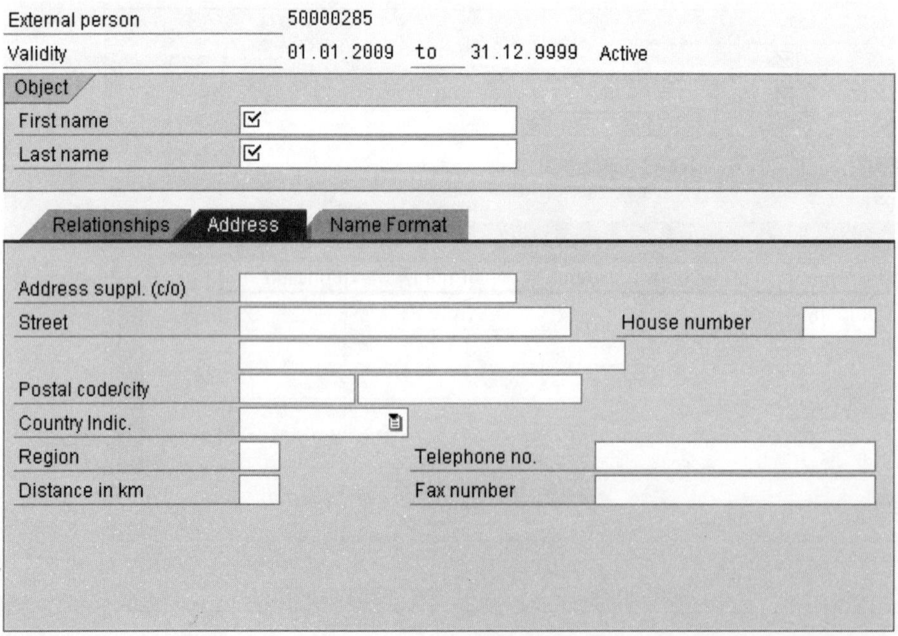

The system determines the business address of an external instructor using the company to which the instructor is assigned if the relationship, 'belongs to company' has been maintained. You can also maintain an address specifically for the instructor here.

### 35.5.5 Name Format

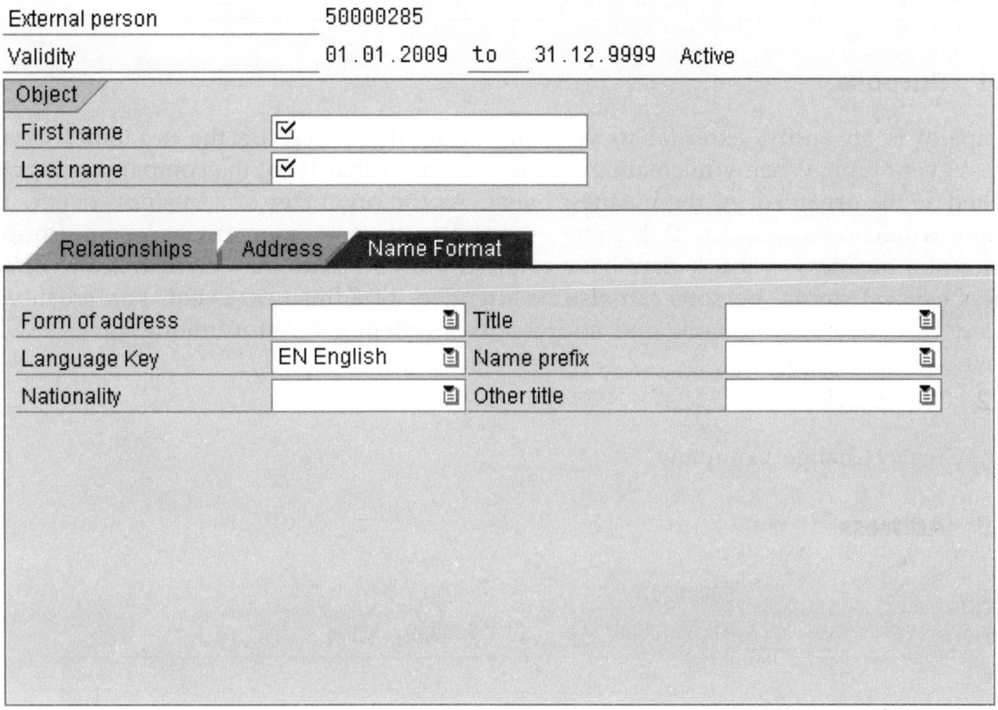


Here you can maintain the form of address, title, etc. for an external person.

## 35.6 COMPANY

| Functional Consultant | User | Business Process Owner | Senior Management | My Rating | Understanding Level |
|---|---|---|---|---|---|
| A | A | B | C | | |

### 35.6.1 Purpose

A company is an entity, external to your organization. It may be the organizer of a business event type. When you create a business event of that type, the company will get defaulted as the organizer of the business event. As the organizer of a business event, a company would correspond with business event attendees. A company can be a group attendee of a business event. It may have external persons, who may be instructors of a business event. External persons can also be attendees of a business event. You create a company by specifying its name and address. The system gives it a unique id.

### 35.6.2 Transaction

PVU0—Create/Change Company

### 35.6.3 Address

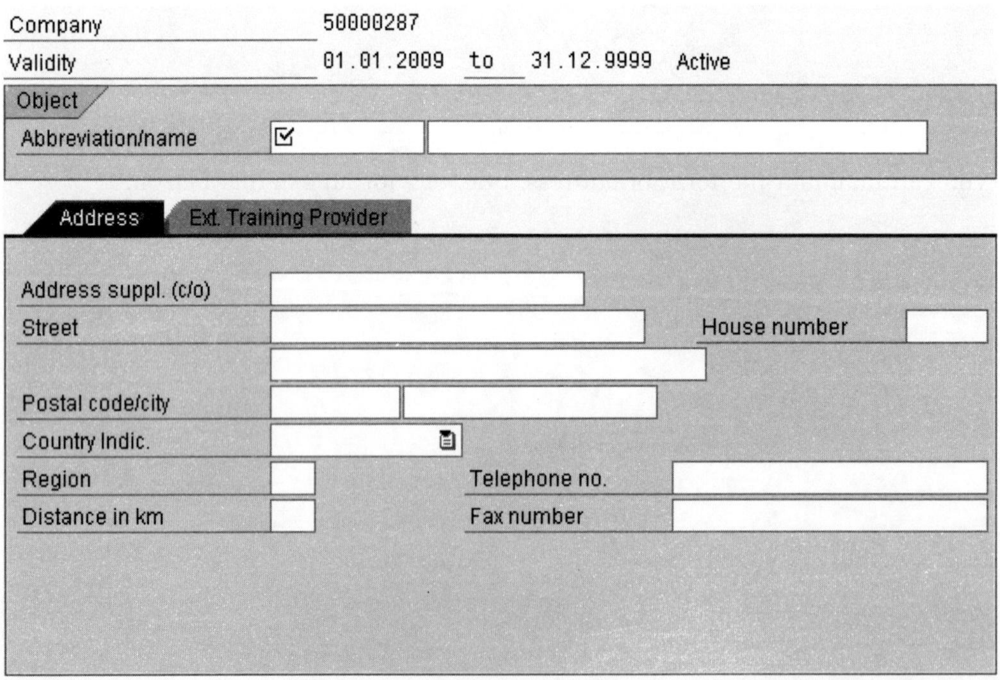

### 35.6.4 External Training Provider

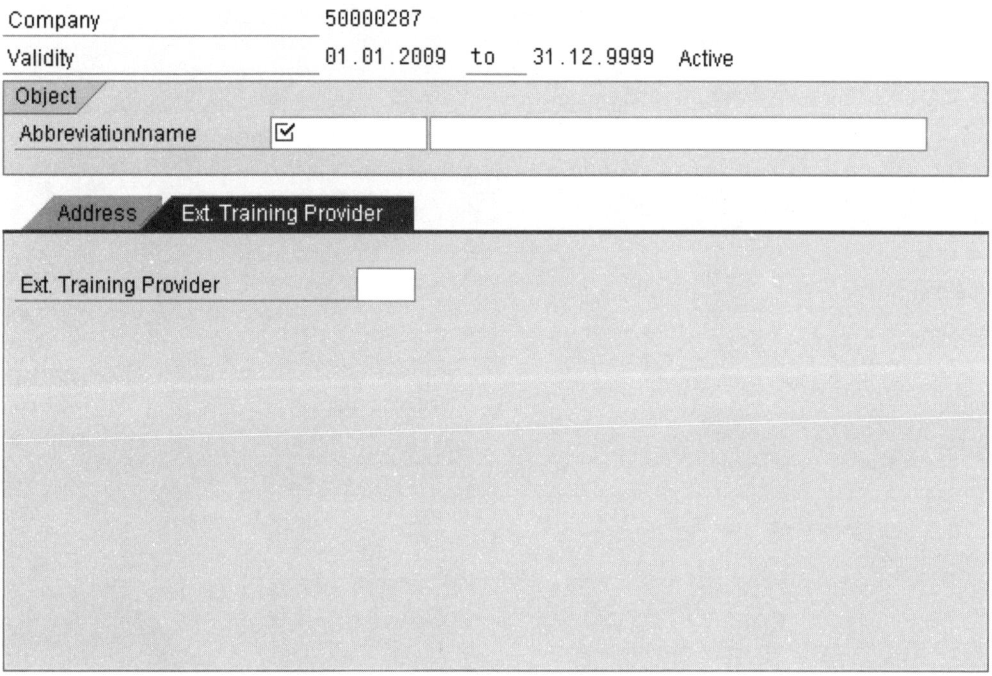


External training provider key is a unique key used in infotype 5043 in LSO.

## 35.7 CONTACT PERSON

| *Functional Consultant* | *User* | *Business Process Owner* | *Senior Management* | *My Rating* | *Understanding Level* |
|---|---|---|---|---|---|
| A | A | B | C | | |

### 35.7.1 Purpose

Contact persons belong to a customer. Contact persons may be instructors or attendees. Normally contact persons are created by your colleagues in the sales department.

### 35.7.2 Transaction

VAP1—Create Contact Person
VAP2—Change Contact Person

### 35.7.3 Screen

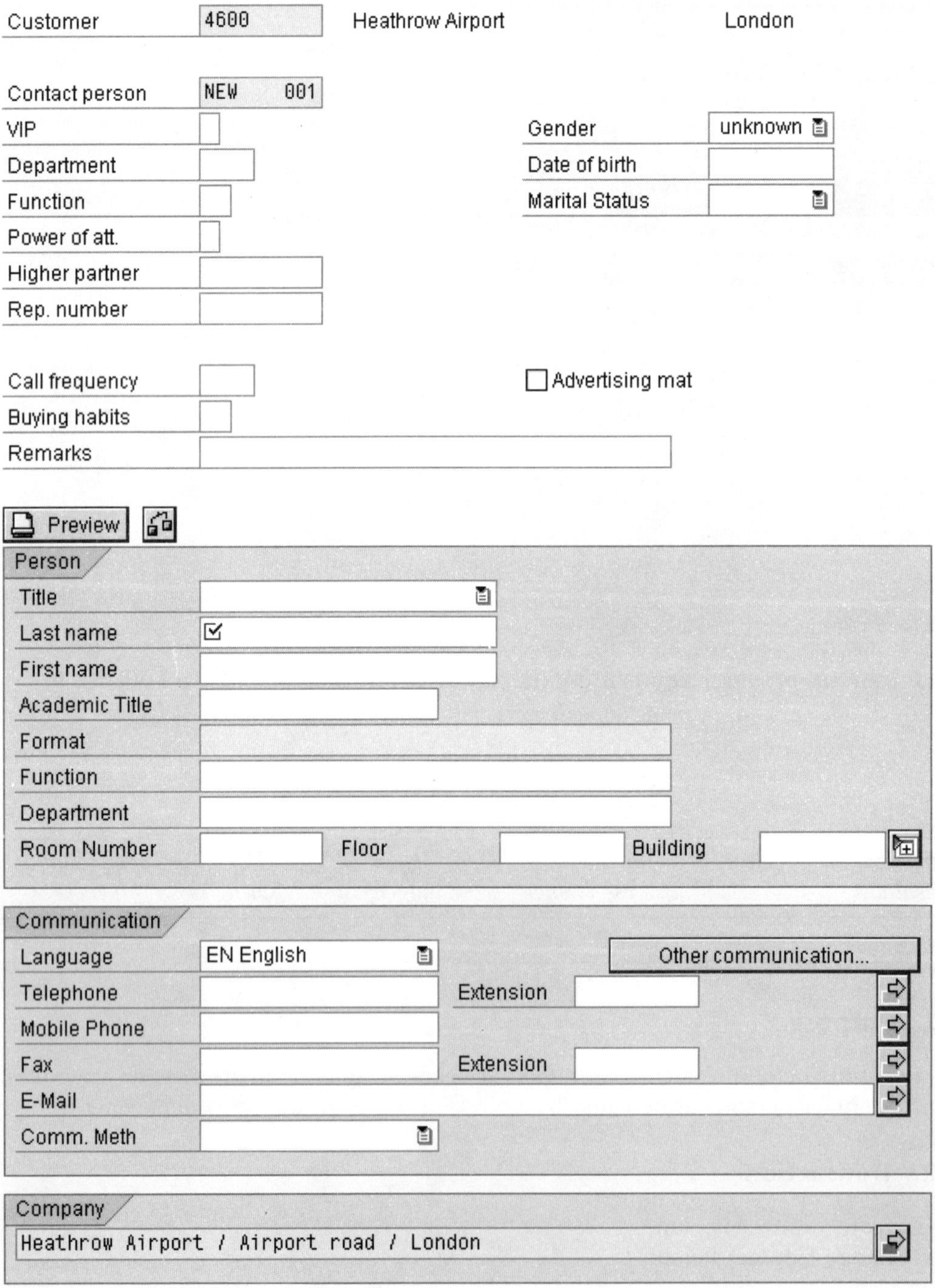
Customer
4600
Heathrow Airport
London
Contact person
NEW 001
VIP
Department
Function
Power of att.
Higher partner
Rep. number
Gender
unknown
Date of birth
Marital Status
Call frequency
Buying habits
Remarks
Advertising mat
Preview
Person
Title
Last name
First name
Academic Title
Format
Function
Department
Room Number
Floor
Building
Communication
Language
EN English
Other communication...
Telephone
Extension
Mobile Phone
Fax
Extension
E-Mail
Comm. Meth
Company
Heathrow Airport / Airport road / London

## 35.8 CUSTOMER

| *Functional Consultant* | *User* | *Business Process Owner* | *Senior Management* | *My Rating* | *Understanding Level* |
|---|---|---|---|---|---|
| A | A | B | C | | |

### 35.8.1 Purpose

Customers may be attendees in your business events. Normally, customers are created by your colleagues in the sales department.

### 35.8.2 Transaction

XD01—Create Customer (Centrally)
XD02—Change Customer (Centrally)

### 35.8.3 Screen

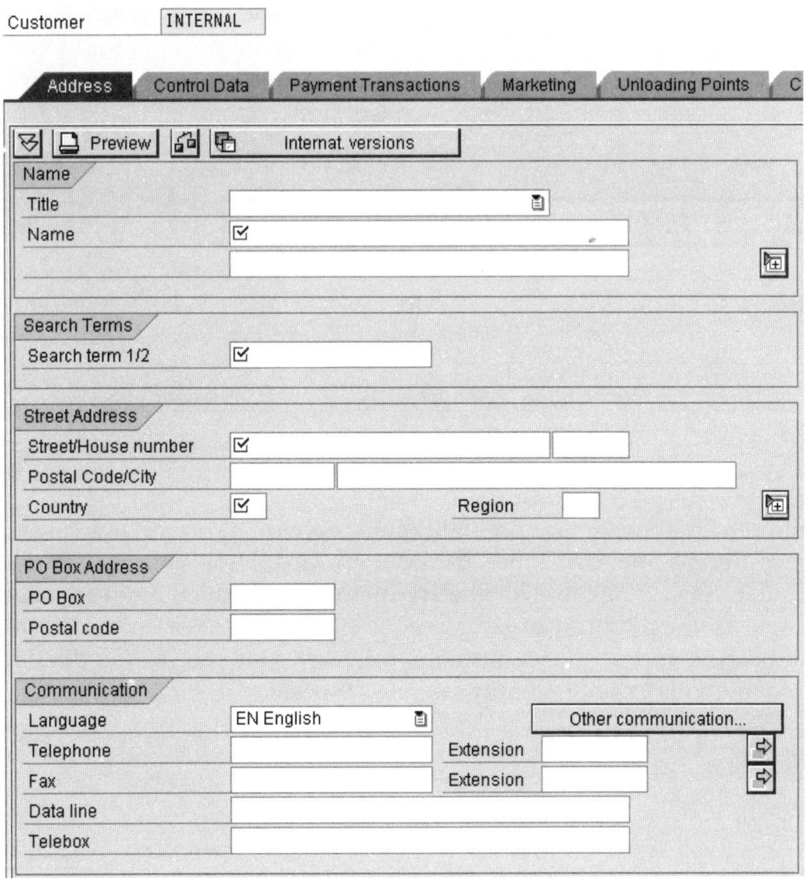

## 35.9 APPLICANT

| *Functional Consultant* | *User* | *Business Process Owner* | *Senior Management* | *My Rating* | *Understanding Level* |
|---|---|---|---|---|---|
| A | A | A | A | | |

Applicants are created in Recruitment. Applicants may be attendees in your business events.

## 35.10 USER

| *Functional Consultant* | *User* | *Business Process Owner* | *Senior Management* | *My Rating* | *Understanding Level* |
|---|---|---|---|---|---|
| A | A | A | A | | |

Every SAP system has users. Some of them may be your employees, whereas some may not be. You would identify employees by their personnel number in Training and Event Management. Users who are not employees may be attendees or instructors in Training and Event Management. Users are created by Basis consultants.

## 35.11 ATTENDEE TYPE CONTROL OPTIONS

| *Functional Consultant* | *User* | *Business Process Owner* | *Senior Management* | *My Rating* | *Understanding Level* |
|---|---|---|---|---|---|
| A | C | X | X | | |

### 35.11.1 Purpose

When you perform different functions, e.g. prebook, book, rebook, replace, and cancel, the system shows you different attendee types in different tabs. Here you specify the properties of each attendee type. You can also specify the order in which attendee type tabs appear. You can specify a maximum of six attendee types under Sort order in the number range of 01 to 06. The sort sequence function only lets you specify the display sequence; it does not enable you to hide certain attendee types.

### 35.11.2 IMG Node

SM30 ➢ V_T77R3_1

### 35.11.3 Overview Screen

| Typ | Participant Type | Sort order | OrgAss. | Organizational Assignment |
|---|---|---|---|---|
| AP | Applicant | | P-S-O | Direct organizational assignment of a person |
| H | External person | 05 | A003 | All relationships to A003 -> belongs to |
| KI | Prospect | | B003 | All relationships to B003 -> incorporates |
| KU | Customer | 04 | B003 | All relationships to B003 -> incorporates |
| O | Organizational unit | 02 | SBESX | Staff assignments along organizational structure |
| P | Person | 01 | P-S-O | Direct organizational assignment of a person |
| PT | Contact person | 03 | A003 | All relationships to A003 -> belongs to |
| U | Company | 06 | B003 | All relationships to B003 -> incorporates |
| US | User | | US-P-ORG | Users/persons in an organizational unit |

### 35.11.4 Details Screen

Attendee type: P — Person

☑ Individual attendee
☑ Internet attend.type

Org. assignment: P-S-O
FM Org. assignment:

**Billing and Allocation Information**

○ Billing   ◉ Activity allocation   ○ Free of charge

Cost center assignment:
FM:cost center assgn: RH_GET_KOSTL_P

### 35.11.5 Important Fields

#### *Attendee type*

You specify the control options for each attendee type.

#### *Individual attendee*

Certain attendees are individual attendees, e.g. person; whereas certain attendees are group attendees, e.g. organizational unit. In the case of group attendees, you specify the number of attendees. Here you specify whether the attendee type is an individual attendee.

### *Internet attendee type*

This setting determines, for example, whether the attendee type is included during user maintenance for internet applications.

### *Organizational assignment*

Here you specify the evaluation path used to determine an attendee's organizational assignment. For example, a person is linked to his organizational unit using evaluation path P-S-O, while an external person is linked to his company using evaluation path A003.

### *Function module–organizational assignment*

Instead of specifying an evaluation path, you can specify a function module used to determine the organizational assignment of an attendee.

### *Billing and allocation information*

You specify the settlement type (billing, activity allocation, or free of charge) used to settle costs for the attendee type. This settlement type is proposed as default when you use the function 'Book with Fee' for an attendee of this type.

### *Cost center assignment*

Cost center is required for activity allocation of attendance fees or cancellation fees. The value you enter here is proposed as default.

### *Function module–cost center assignment*

Instead of specifying a cost center, you can specify a function module used to determine the cost center assignment of an attendee.

# 36 Attendance

## 36.1 BOOKING PRIORITY

| *Functional Consultant* | *User* | *Business Process Owner* | *Senior Management* | *My Rating* | *Understanding Level* |
|---|---|---|---|---|---|
| A | A | A | B | | |

When booking a business event, you specify priority. Priority can be given a value from 00 to 99. 00 is the highest priority and 99 is the lowest priority.

| Group | Sem. abbr. | Value abbr. | Description |
|---|---|---|---|
| SEMIN | MAXMU | 09 | Maximum priority for essential booking |
| SEMIN | MINWL | 90 | Minimum priority for waiting-list booking |
| SEMIN | NPRIO | 50 | Default priority for normal booking |

Parameters MAXMU and MINWL divide the priority range in three intervals.

| *Booking type* | *Priority from* | *Priority to* | *Explanation* |
|---|---|---|---|
| Essential booking | 00 | Priority value in the parameter MAXMU | Essential booking can be booked up to maximum capacity. |
| Normal booking | Priority value in the parameter MAXMU + 1 | Priority value in the parameter MINWL – 1 | Normal booking can be booked up to optimum capacity. |
| Waiting list booking | Priority value in the parameter MINWL | 99 | |

Priority specified in parameter NPRIO is the default priority for normal booking. You must ensure that MAXMU < NPRIO < MINWL.

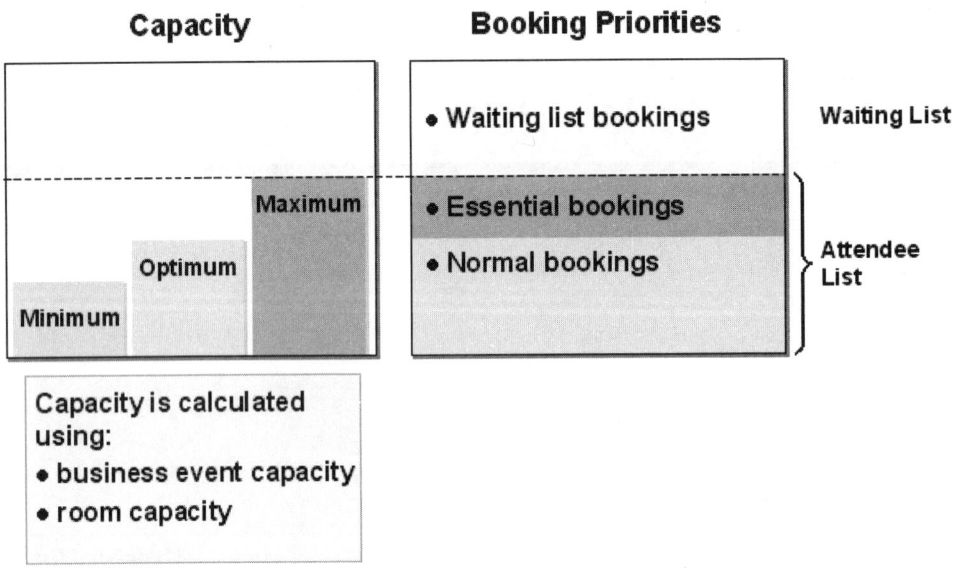


## 36.2 ATTENDEE CHECKS

| *Functional Consultant* | *User* | *Business Process Owner* | *Senior Management* | *My Rating* | *Understanding Level* |
|---|---|---|---|---|---|
| A | A | A | B | | |

### 36.2.1 Individual and Group Attendee Checks

When you book an attendee, the system performs several checks to ensure data integrity. The following checks are performed for both individual and group attendees.

- Existence check
- Availability check
- Capacity check

### 36.2.2 Individual Attendee Checks

The following checks are carried out for individual attendees.

- Is the attendee booked to attend another business event at the same time?
- Is the attendee reserved as instructor of a business event at the same time?

➢ Is the attendee booked for a business event of the same type?
➢ Is the attendee prebooked for a business event of the same type?
➢ Has the attendee attended the prerequisite business events?
➢ Does the attendee have the required qualifications?
➢ Are there attendance or absence records which are incompatible with business event attendance?

### 36.2.3 Attendance/Attendance Conflict

| Group | Sem. abbr. | Value abbr. | Description |
|---|---|---|---|
| SEMIN | TETEI | W | Message type for attendance/attendance conflict |

When you book attendees for business events, a check is performed to see if the attendee is already booked to attend another business event at the same time. Here, you can define whether the system should give error, warning, message, or perform no check.

### 36.2.4 Attendance/Instructor Conflict

| Group | Sem. abbr. | Value abbr. | Description |
|---|---|---|---|
| SEMIN | TEREF | E | Mess.type for attendance/instructor func. conflict |

When an attendance is booked, a check is performed to determine if the attendee is already booked as an instructor of a business event at the same time. Here, you can define whether the system should give error, warning, message, or perform no check.

### 36.2.5 Attendee Checks

In view V_T77KV_1 you can specify attendee-related checks before business event booking which apply to all business event types. These checks can be different for different attendee types. You can also specify these checks at business event type level in the procedure infotype, which get priority.

| AT | Attendee type | Booked for ... | Prbkg on same ... | Check prerequisite | Check qualification |
|---|---|---|---|---|---|
| H | External person | W | W | W | |
| P | Person | W | W | W | W |

#### *Booked for same type*

When an attendee books or prebooks for a business event, you may want to know if the attendee has already attended a business event of the same type or is already booked to attend such a business event. If yes, you may give an error (E), a warning (W), or a message (I). If you don't want to perform this check, you can leave this field blank.

### *Prebooking on same business event type*

When an attendee books or prebooks for a business event type, you may want to know if the attendee is already prebooked for this business event type. If yes, you may give an error (E), a warning (W), or a message (I). If you don't want to perform this check, you can leave this field blank.

### *Check prerequisite*

When an attendee books for a business event, you may want to know whether the attendee has attended the prerequisite business events. If yes, you may give an error (E), a warning (W), or a message (I). If you don't want to perform this check, you can leave this field blank.

### *Check qualification*

When an attendee books for a business event, you may want to know whether the attendee has the qualifications or alternative qualifications required to attend the business event. If yes, you may give an error (E), a warning (W), or a message (I). If you don't want to perform this check, you can leave this field blank.

## 36.2.6 Incompatible Attendance and Absence Types

### *Purpose*

If an employee is on leave, you may want that the system should not allow him to be booked as an attendee for a business event. You can build such checks here. When attendance is booked, or instructor reserved, the system carries out checks specified in this table. If the checks fail, attendance cannot be booked or instructor cannot be reserved.

### *IMG node*

SM30 ➢ T77KA

### *Screen*

| Event attendance type | Attendance type text | PS grpg | Att./Absence type | Att./abs. type text |
|---|---|---|---|---|
| A | Instructor function | 0 | $$$$ | Day off as per shift |
| A | Instructor function | 1 | 0100 | Leave |
| A | Instructor function | 1 | 0200 | Sickness with certificate |
| B | Event attendance | 0 | $$$$ | Day off as per shift |
| B | Event attendance | 1 | 0100 | Leave |
| B | Event attendance | 1 | 0200 | Sickness with certificate |

### *Incompatible attendance and absence types*

You specify the attendance/absence types when an employee cannot attend a business event. You also specify the attendance/absence types when an employee cannot be an instructor at a business event. You should replace the entries in this table with your own entries.

### *Check against day off*

If your company policy is that an employee cannot be an attendee or an instructor at a business event on his off days, you retain the entries with absence type $$$$; otherwise you delete them. If you retain these entries, a check is carried out against the employee's shift plan to ensure that he is not an attendee or an instructor on his off days.

If you specify that an employee cannot be an attendee or an instructor on his off days, you can deactivate this check for a business event type in infotype 'Business Event Type Info'. If you do so, business event attendance is allowed regardless of what is recorded in the shift plan.

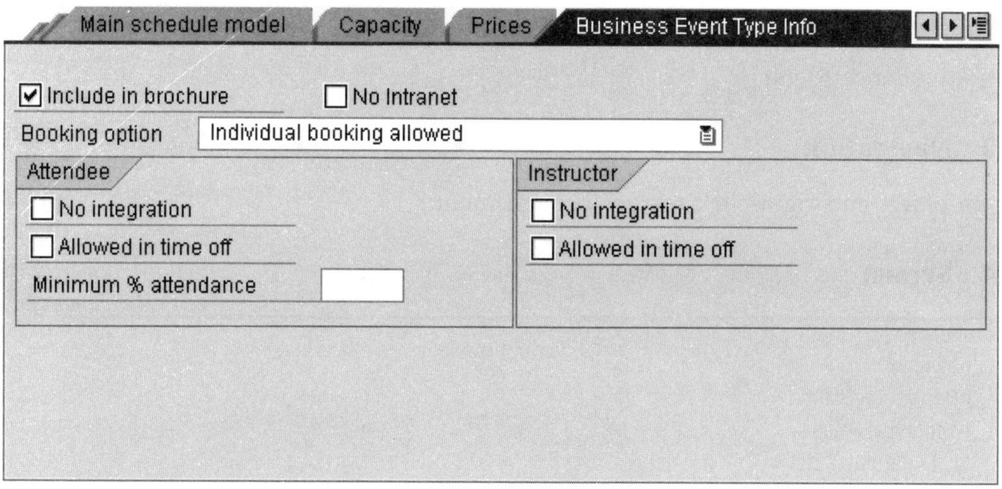


## 36.2.7 Additional Checks

In BAdI RHPV0001 you can build additional checks of attendance or business event data before an attendee is booked for a business event.

## 36.3 ATTENDANCE MENU

| *Functional Consultant* | *User* | *Business Process Owner* | *Senior Management* | *My Rating* | *Understanding Level* |
|---|---|---|---|---|---|
| A | A | A | B | | |

### 36.3.1 Purpose

In the attendance menu, you can execute all the functions related to booking activities. For business event groups, business event types and business events you cannot change information. For a business event type, you can prebook attendance. For a business event, you can book attendance. For an attendee, you can replace, rebook or cancel attendance. You can also do appraisals and correspondence. Traffic lights show whether the business event is full, accepting only essential bookings, or accepting normal bookings.

### 36.3.2 Transaction

PSV1—Attendance Menu

### 36.3.3 Navigation

Select an object and right-click (or go through menu).

### 36.3.4 Screen

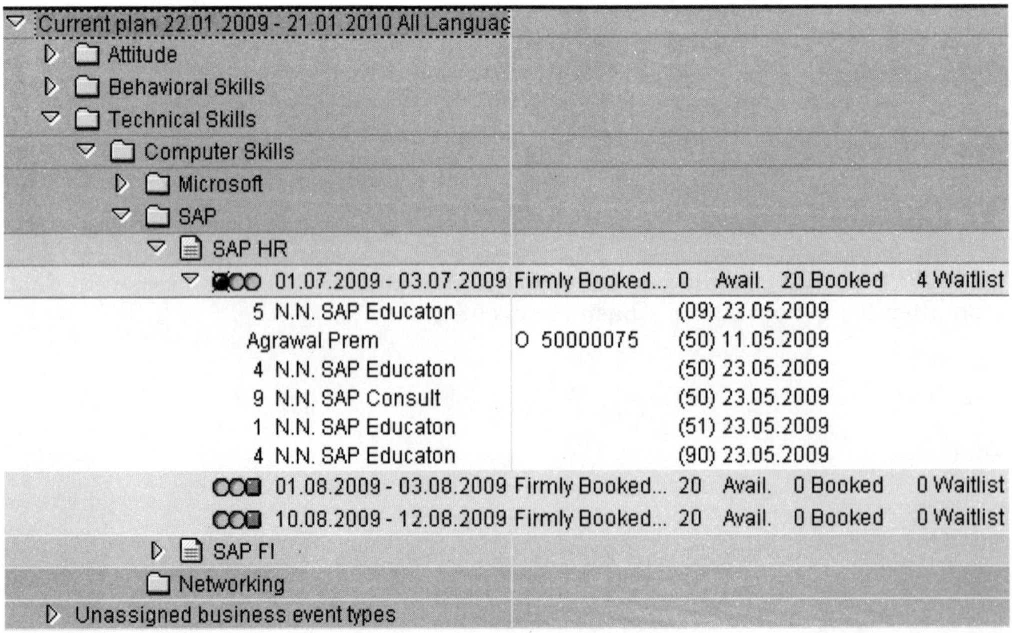

## 36.4 PREBOOKING ATTENDANCE

| *Functional Consultant* | *User* | *Business Process Owner* | *Senior Management* | *My Rating* | *Understanding Level* |
|---|---|---|---|---|---|
| A | A | A | B | | |

### 36.4.1 Prebooking

If you want to attend a business event of certain type but there are no business events, or the business event dates do not suit you, you can prebook attendance for a business event type.

### 36.4.2 Checking Business Events When Prebooking

Usually prebooking is done because there is no business event available during the period you want to attend. If a business event is available, you would like to be informed. You can set the following switch to 1 if you want the system to check whether a business event is available during the planning period and to give a message if a business event exists. If you don't want the system to give such a message, you set this switch to 0.

| Group | Sem. abbr. | Value abbr. | Description |
|---|---|---|---|
| SEMIN | OFFER | 1 | Read business event offer when prebooking |

### 36.4.3 Converting Prebookings to Bookings

You can display prebookings when booking attendance. You can convert prebookings to bookings when a suitable business event becomes available.

### 36.4.4 Planning Status of Prebookings

Prebooking is stored as a relationship between the business event type and the attendee. This relationship is in the Planned status, because prebooking is just a plan.

### 36.4.5 Prebooking Attendance

You can use transaction PV02 to prebook attendee for a business event type. For prebooking each type of attendee, there is a separate tab. For group attendees, you also specify the number of attendees. You can also write a note when you do prebooking.

***Prebooking individual attendance***

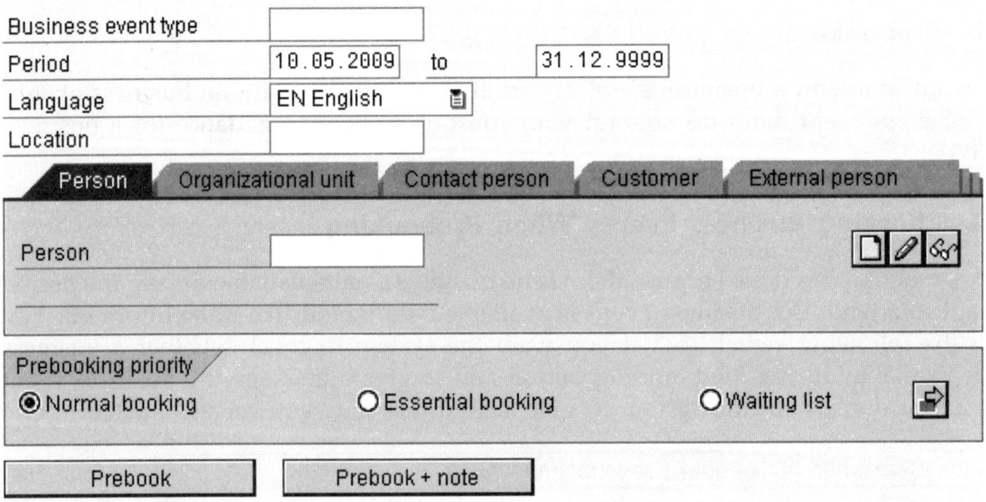


***Prebooking group attendance***

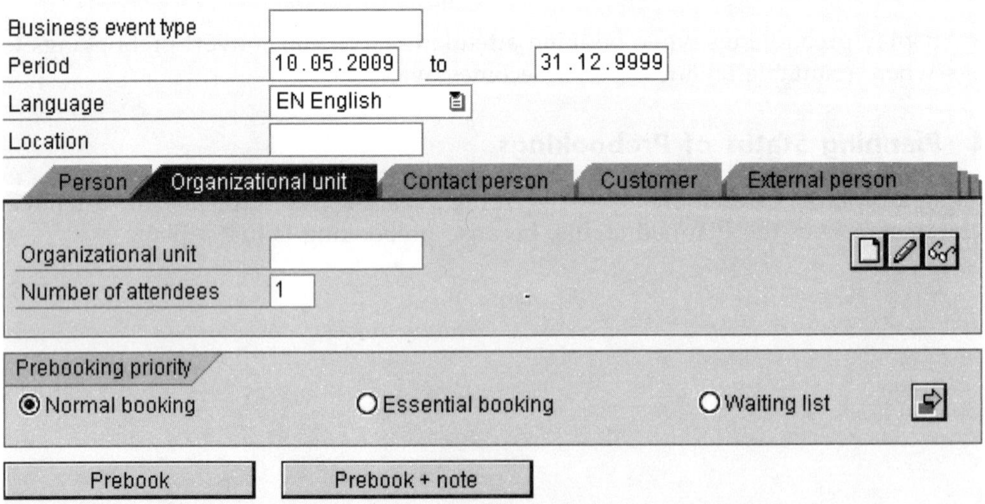

## 36.5 PREBOOKING ATTENDANCE LIST

| *Functional Consultant* | *User* | *Business Process Owner* | *Senior Management* | *My Rating* | *Understanding Level* |
|---|---|---|---|---|---|
| A | A | A | B | | |

You can run transaction PV06 to prebook attendee list for a business event type. You can create a prebooking list and save to prebook the whole list for a business event type.

### *Business event type screen*

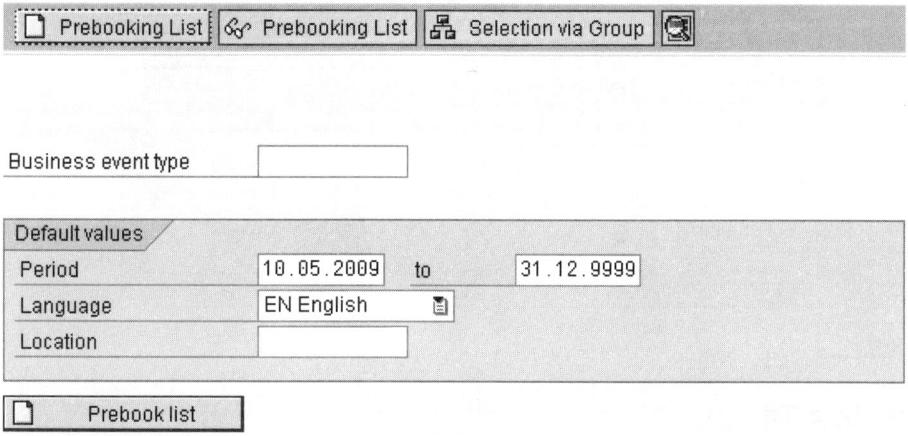


### *Attendee list*

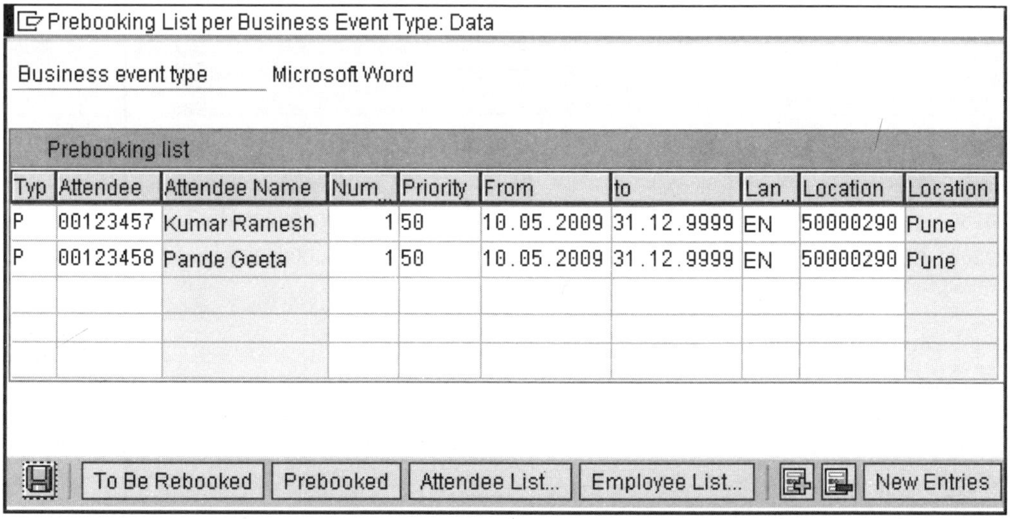


When you click save, prebooking of all attendees for the business event type takes place.

## 36.6 PREBOOKING ATTENDEE FOR BUSINESS EVENT TYPE LIST

| *Functional Consultant* | *User* | *Business Process Owner* | *Senior Management* | *My Rating* | *Understanding Level* |
|---|---|---|---|---|---|
| A | A | A | B | | |

You can run transaction PV16 to prebook attendee for business event type list.

***Attendee screen***

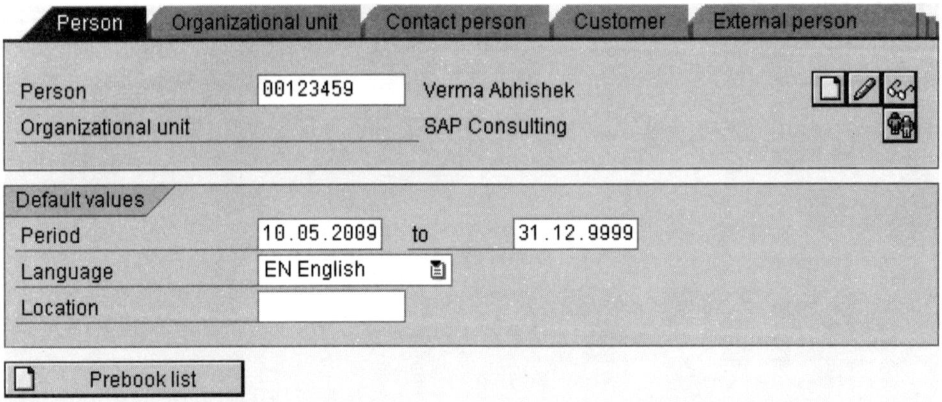


***Business event type list***

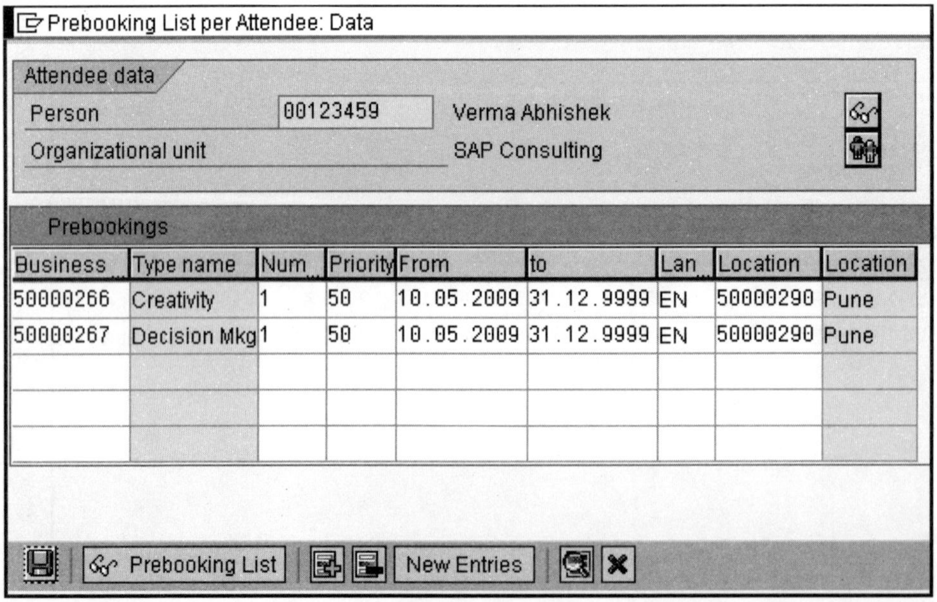


When you click save, prebooking of the attendee for all business event types takes place.

## 36.7 BOOKING ATTENDANCE

| *Functional Consultant* | *User* | *Business Process Owner* | *Senior Management* | *My Rating* | *Understanding Level* |
|---|---|---|---|---|---|
| A | A | A | B | | |

### 36.7.1 Booking Attendance

You can use transaction PV00 to book attendee for a business event type. For booking each type of attendee, there is a separate tab. For group attendees, you also specify the number of attendees. You can also charge a price to the internal or external customer for participation of an attendee in a business event.

### 36.7.2 Booking Individual Attendance

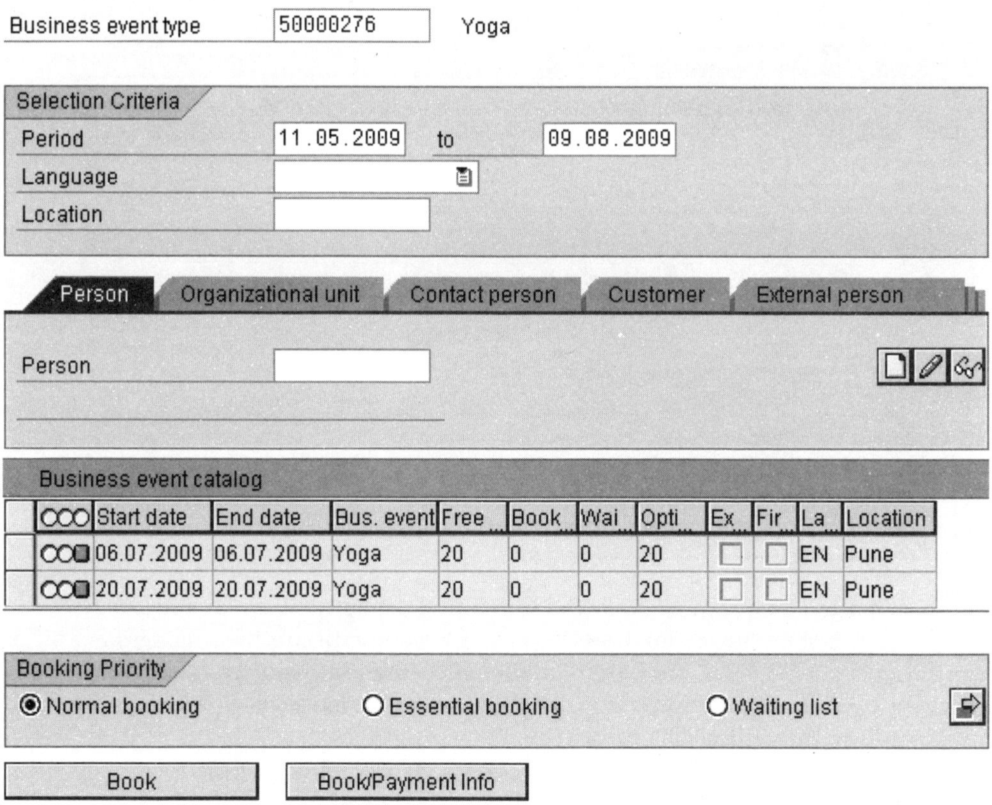


If you choose Book, the billing and allocation data stored for the attendee type is transferred automatically. For Book/Payment Info, refer to chapter 36.7.4.

In the above screen, the system shows you the period by default. This period is used to filter the business events shown in the screen, from which you can select the business event you want to book. The start date of this period is current date. The end date is determined from the start date and the following system setting.

| Group | Sem. abbr. | Value abbr. | Description |
|---|---|---|---|
| SEMIN | FORCA | 90 | Business event preview: period in days |

### 36.7.3 Booking Group Attendance

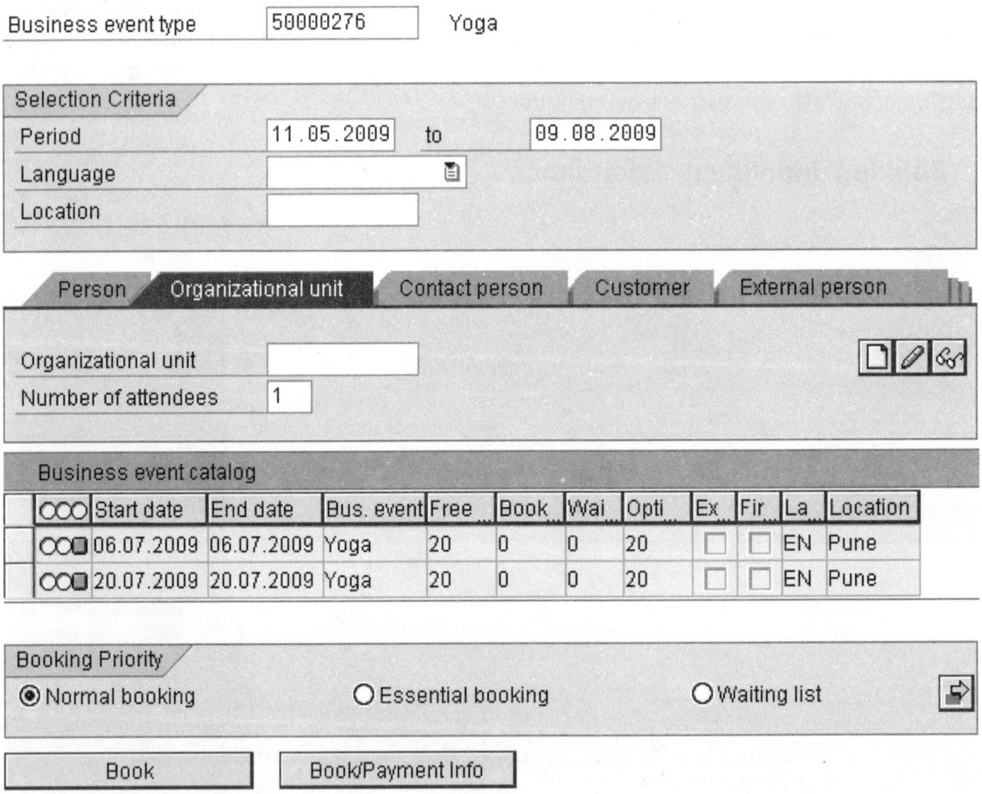


If the number of attendees is more than the remaining capacity of the business event, the booking is split. One booking is made with normal priority, filling the business event up to the optimum capacity. Next booking is made with essential priority which can fill the business event up to the maximum capacity. If the requirement is still not met, the third booking is made with waiting list priority.

### 36.7.4 Charging for Participation in Business Event

If you click Book/Payment Info, the system shows you the fees screen where you can specify whether the business event is free of charge, or it is to be billed to external party, or it is to be charged to internal customer using activity allocation.

### *Charge fee by default*

| Group | Sem. abbr. | Value abbr. | Description |
|---|---|---|---|
| SEMIN | CCOST | 0 | Switch for Special Event Costs for Bookings |

The system either defaults the fee, or defaults free of charge depending on the switch given above. If the value here is zero, all business events are free of charge by default. If the value is 1, the fee specified in the prices infotype is proposed by default. In either case, you can change the default value proposed by the system.

### *Cost maintenance*

| Group | Sem. abbr. | Value abbr. | Description |
|---|---|---|---|
| SEMIN | CCDCT | LSO_PRICES | Dialog Module Cost Maintenance for Bookings |

This entry contains the name of the function module that can be called at the time of booking or cancelling attendance in Training and Event Management. If the fee is to be charged by default, the function module specified here determines the assignment of settlement type (billing, activity allocation, free of charge).

### *Billing document*

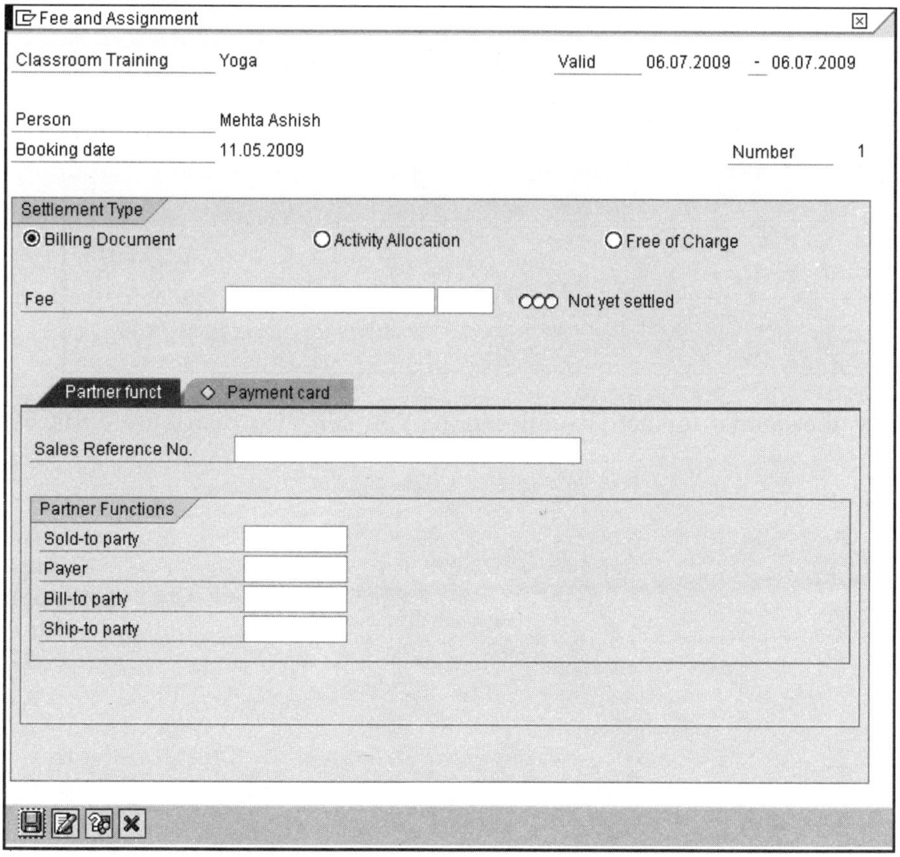


Here you specify the details for billing and card payment.

### *Activity allocation*

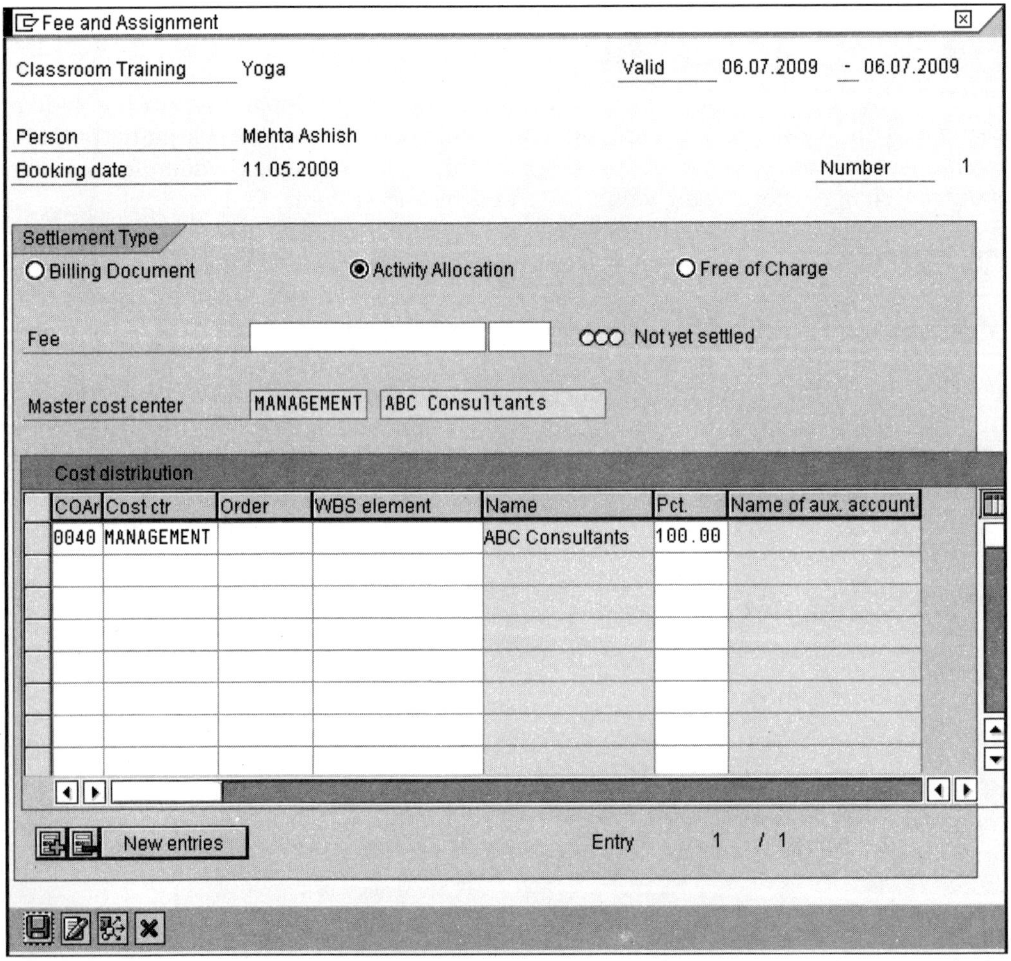


Here you specify the details for activity allocation. You can also distribute costs by selecting .

***Free of charge***

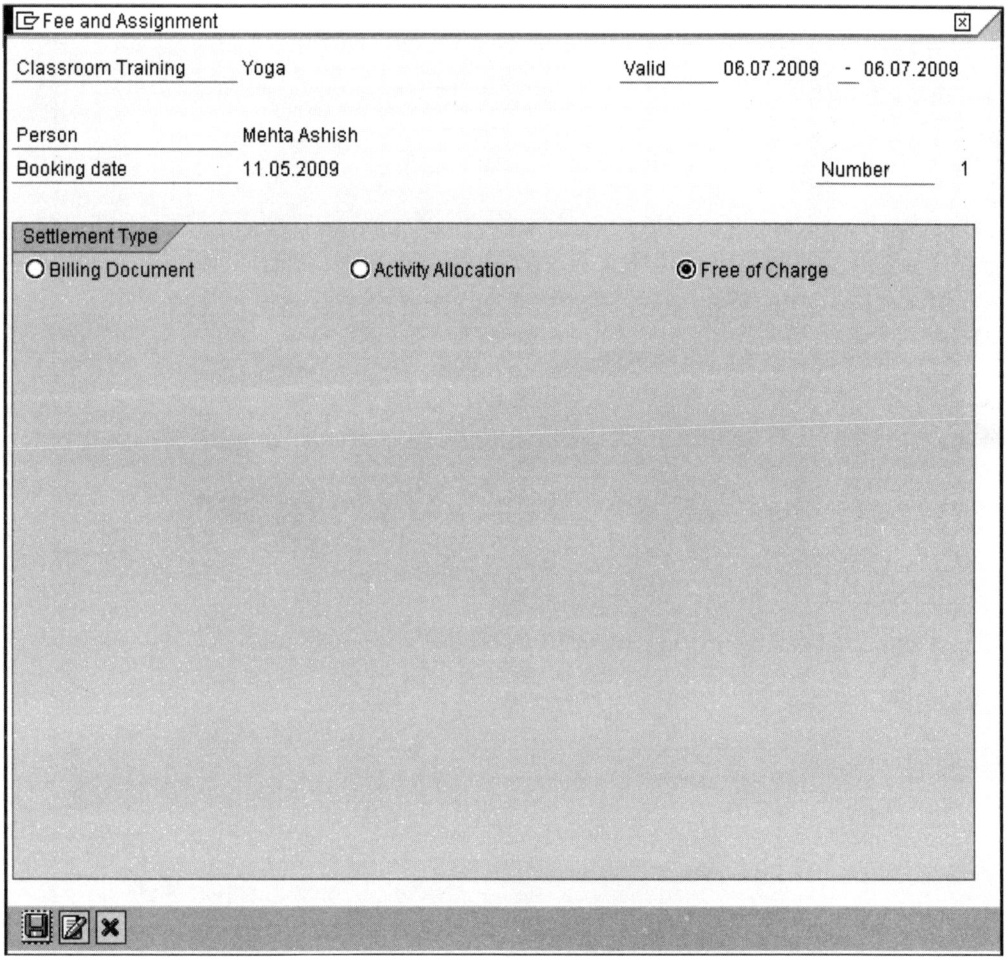


## 36.8 BOOKING ATTENDEE LIST

| *Functional Consultant* | *User* | *Business Process Owner* | *Senior Management* | *My Rating* | *Understanding Level* |
|---|---|---|---|---|---|
| A | A | A | B | | |

You can run transaction PV07 to book attendee list for a business event type. You can create a booking list and save to book the whole list for a business event type.

### *Business event screen*

Business event type 50000276 Yoga

Selection Criteria

| | | | |
|---|---|---|---|
| Period | 11.05.2009 | to | 09.08.2009 |
| Language | EN English | | |
| Location | | | |

Business event catalog

| | Start date | End date | Bus. event | Avail | Bookd | WaitL | Opt. | Ext | FB | La... | Location |
|---|---|---|---|---|---|---|---|---|---|---|---|
| | 06.07.2009 | 06.07.2009 | Yoga | 19 | 1 | 0 | 20 | ☐ | ☐ | EN | Pune |
| | 20.07.2009 | 20.07.2009 | Yoga | 20 | 0 | 0 | 20 | ☐ | ☐ | EN | Pune |
| | 27.07.2009 | 27.07.2009 | Yoga | 20 | 0 | 0 | 20 | ☐ | ☐ | EN | Pune |
| | 03.08.2009 | 03.08.2009 | Yoga | 20 | 0 | 0 | 20 | ☐ | ☐ | EN | Pune |

Attendee list

You select the business event you want to book the attendees for.

### *Attendee list*

Book Attendee List: Data

Business event type Yoga

Attendee list

| Typ | Attendee | Attendee Name | Organizational Assignment | Number | Priority | Fee |
|---|---|---|---|---|---|---|
| P | 00123461 | Yadav Raghunath | SAP Consulting | 1 | 50 | ☐ |
| P | 00123462 | Abhinav Desai | SAP Consulting | 1 | 50 | ☐ |

Business event data

| | Start date | End date | Bus. event | Avail | Bookd | WaitL | Opt. | Ext | FB | Lan... | Location |
|---|---|---|---|---|---|---|---|---|---|---|---|
| | 20.07.2009 | 20.07.2009 | Yoga | 20 | 0 | 0 | 20 | ☐ | ☐ | EN | Pune |

To Be Rebooked | Prebooked | Attendee List... | Employee List... | New Entries

The system shows the selected business event. When you save, all the attendees are booked for the business event.

## 36.9 BOOKING ATTENDEE FOR BUSINESS EVENT LIST

| *Functional Consultant* | *User* | *Business Process Owner* | *Senior Management* | *My Rating* | *Understanding Level* |
|---|---|---|---|---|---|
| A | A | A | B | | |

You can run transaction PV08 to book attendee for business event type list.

***Attendee screen***

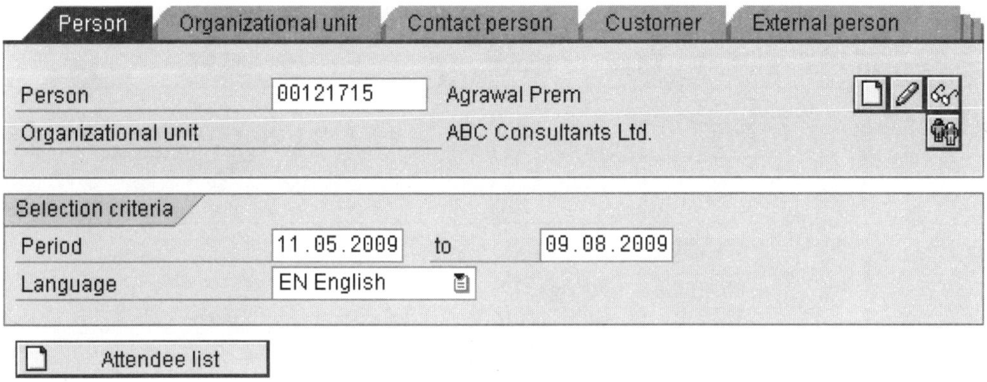


***Business event list***

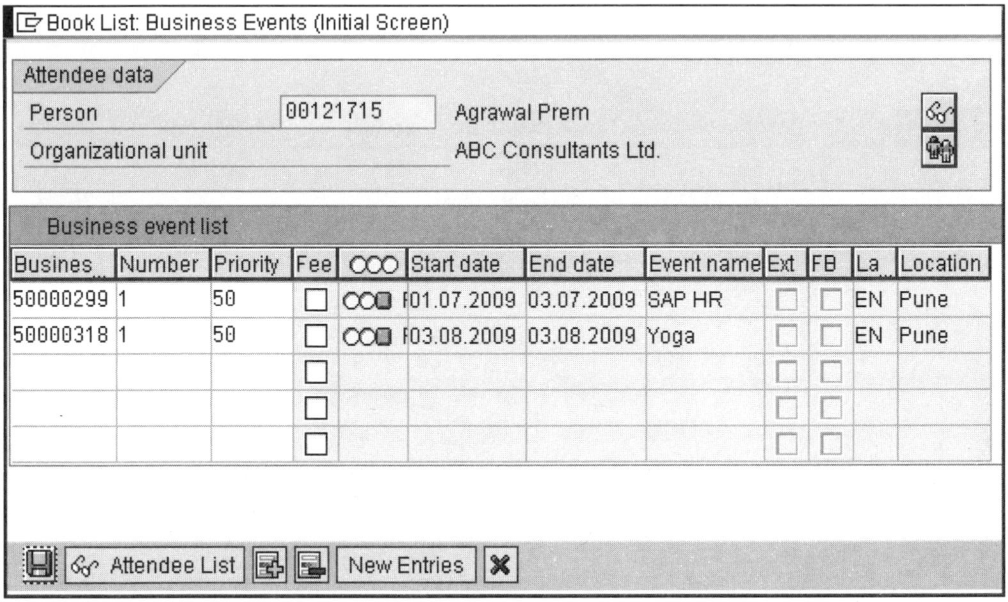


When you save, the attendee is booked for all business events.

## 36.10 REPLACING ATTENDANCE

| Functional Consultant | User | Business Process Owner | Senior Management | My Rating | Understanding Level |
|---|---|---|---|---|---|
| A | A | A | B | | |

### Attendee to be replaced

You can run transaction PV03 to replace one attendee by another. You can also replace a group of attendees. In the initial screen, you specify the attendees to be replaced.

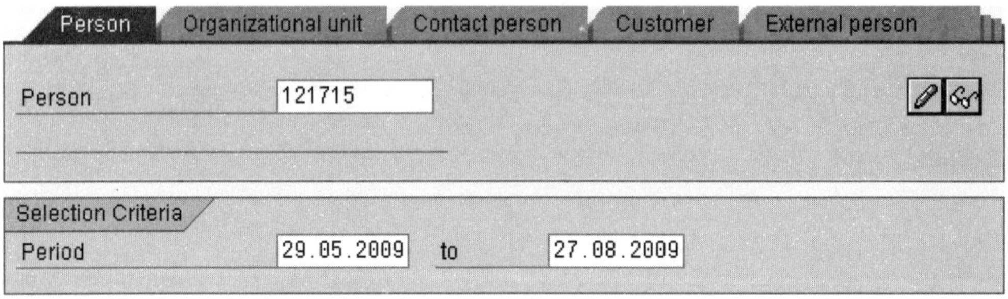


### Business event in which replaced

When you click Data Screen, the system shows the business events in which the attendee is booked in the specified period. You select the business event in which you want to replace the attendee.

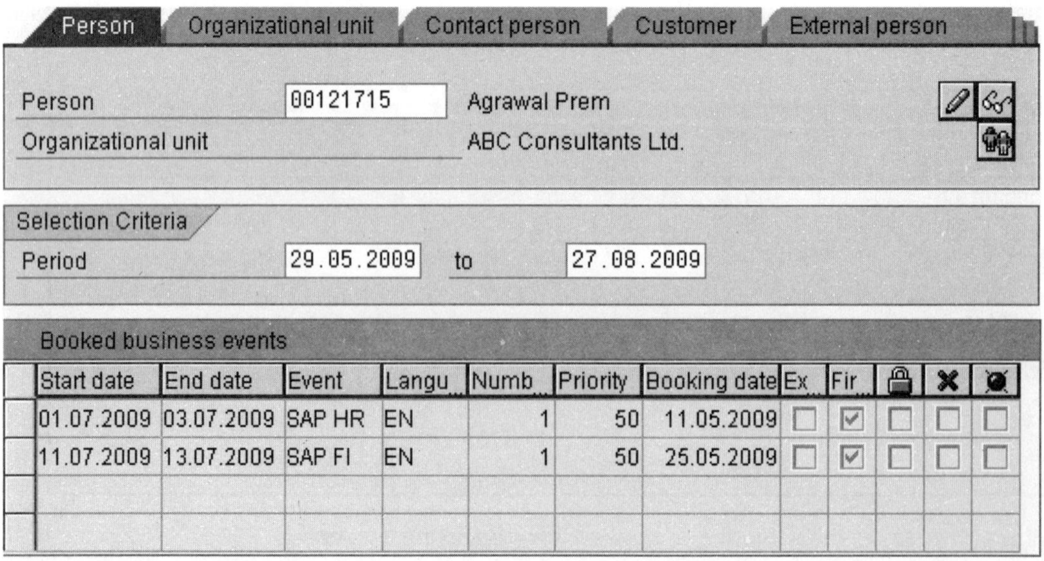

### *Replacement attendee*

You click Replacement attendee. The system gives you the screen in which you can specify the replacement attendee.

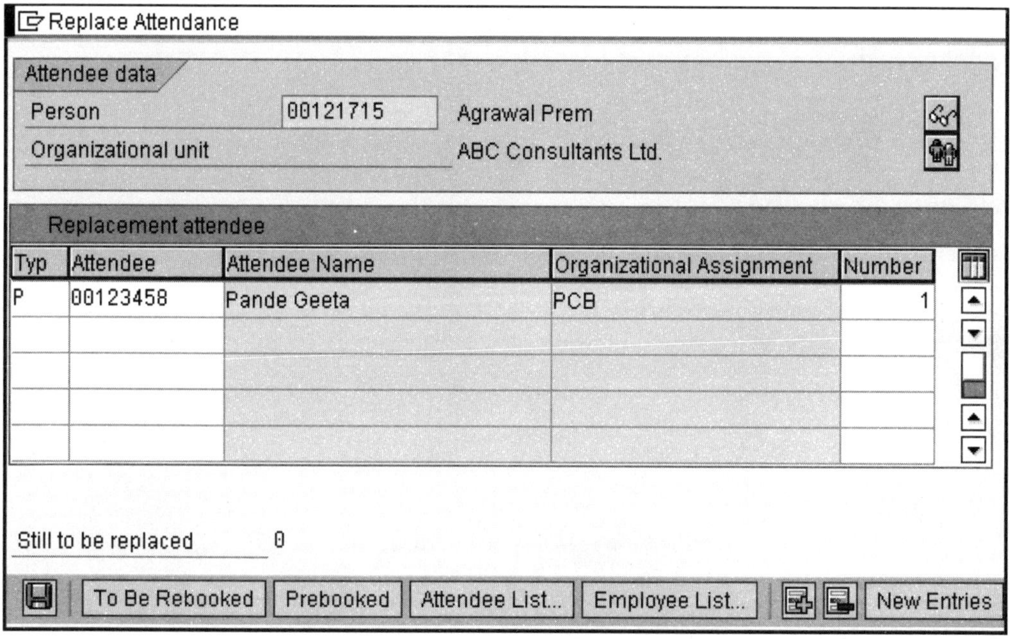


You can replace one attendee type with another attendee type. In the case of group attendees, you can specify the number. The attendee being replaced can be rebooked to another business event of the same type, or can be prebooked. You can replace group attendees completely or partially. The same checks are carried out as for booking with the exception of the capacity check. The booking priority, the price, and the fee assignment remain the same.

## 36.11 REBOOKING ATTENDANCE

| *Functional Consultant* | *User* | *Business Process Owner* | *Senior Management* | *My Rating* | *Understanding Level* |
|---|---|---|---|---|---|
| A | A | A | B | | |

### *Rebooking attendance screen*

If you have booked a business event for a certain date, but want to change to another date for the same business event type, you can rebook attendance using transaction PV01. In the initial screen you specify the personnel number. The period should cover the date of the business event you want to rebook and the period in which you want to book the attendance.

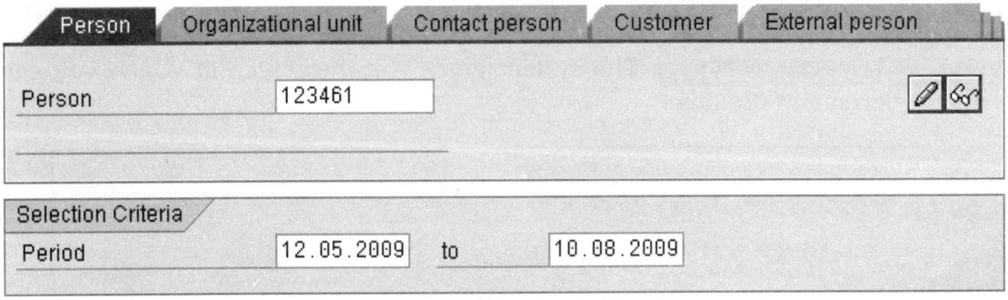


***Booked business events***

The system shows you the business events booked during the period.

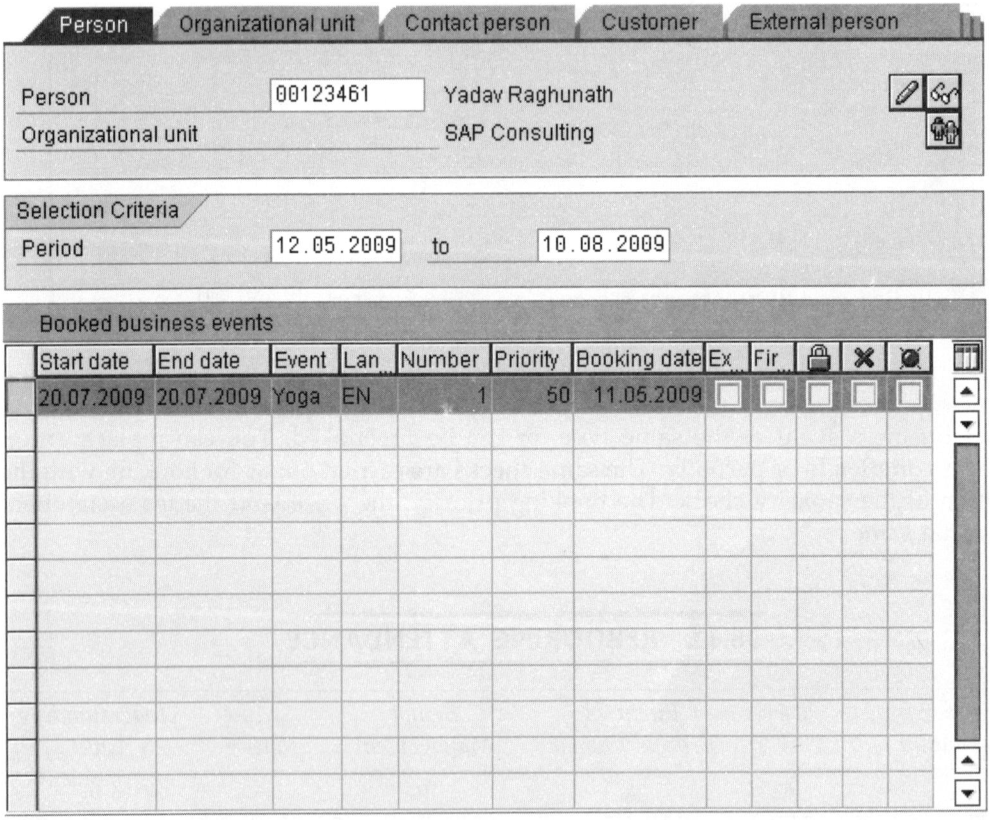

You select the business event you want to rebook and click Rebookings offered.

### *Rebooking business event*

The system shows you the business events of the same type.

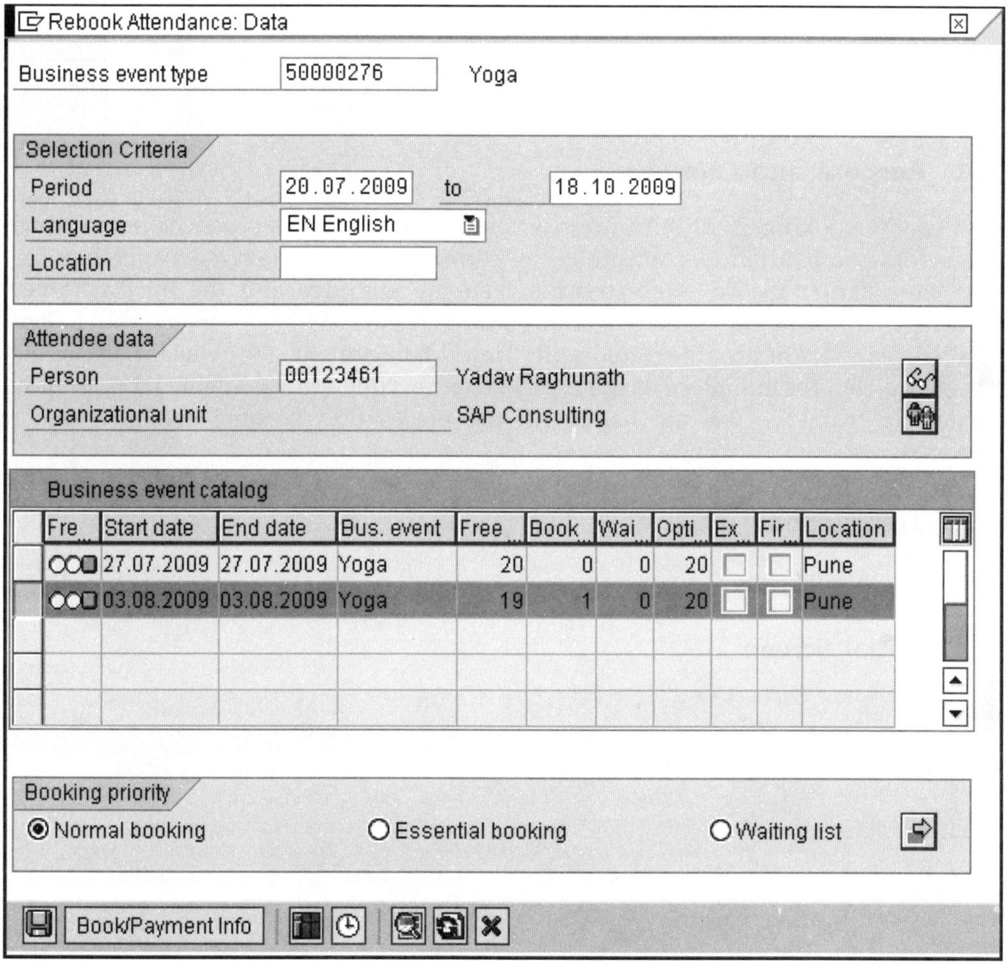


You select the business event you want to book, select the priority and save. The existing booking is cancelled and a new booking is created. The system carries out the same checks which are carried out at the time of booking. If the attendee type is person and the integration with Time Management is on, old attendance records are deleted and new attendance records are created in Time Management.

## 36.12 CANCELLING ATTENDANCE

| *Functional Consultant* | *User* | *Business Process Owner* | *Senior Management* | *My Rating* | *Understanding Level* |
|---|---|---|---|---|---|
| A | A | A | B | | |

### 36.12.1 Purpose and Overview

You can cancel bookings with any priority and for all attendee types. You can cancel bookings for group attendees partially or completely. Whenever a cancellation is made, a cancellation record is created between the attendee and the business event (relationship 040). You can specify a cancellation reason which is then used to levy cancellation fees. If you are integrated with Time Management, the relevant attendance records are deleted for attendees of the type Person in Time Management. You can move candidates up from the waiting list to fill the places that become available due to cancellations.

### 36.12.2 Transaction

PV04—Cancel Attendance

### 36.12.3 Initial Screen

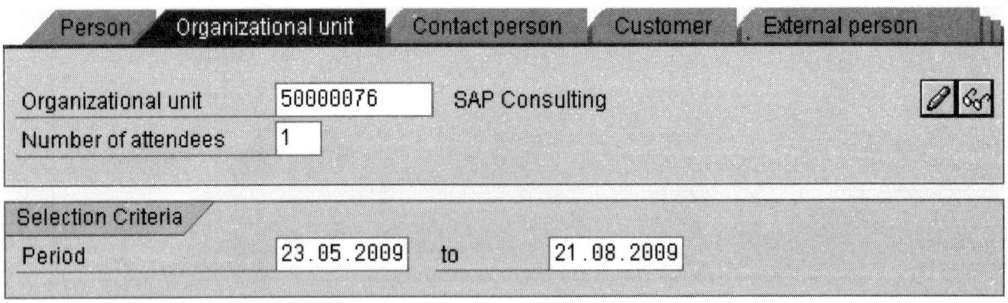

### 36.12.4 Attendance to be Cancelled

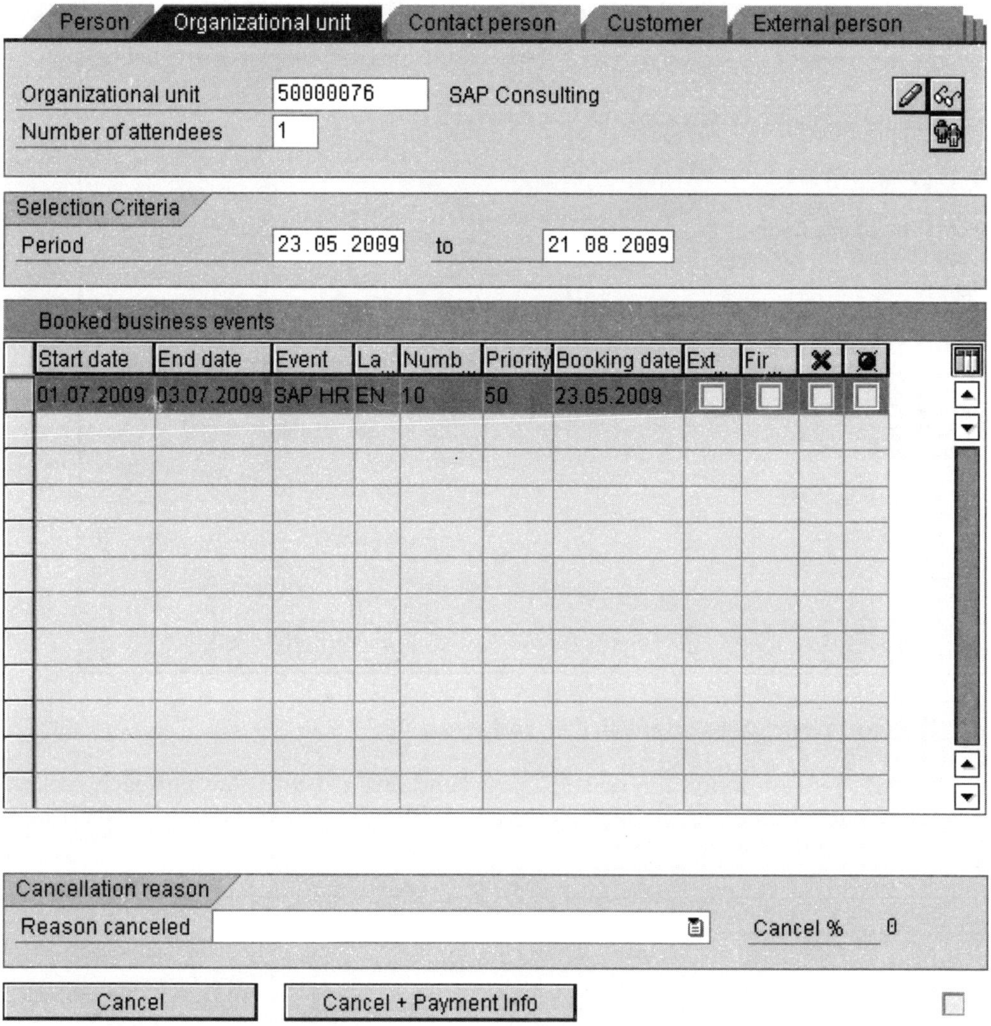

### 36.12.5 Moving-up the Waitlisted Candidates

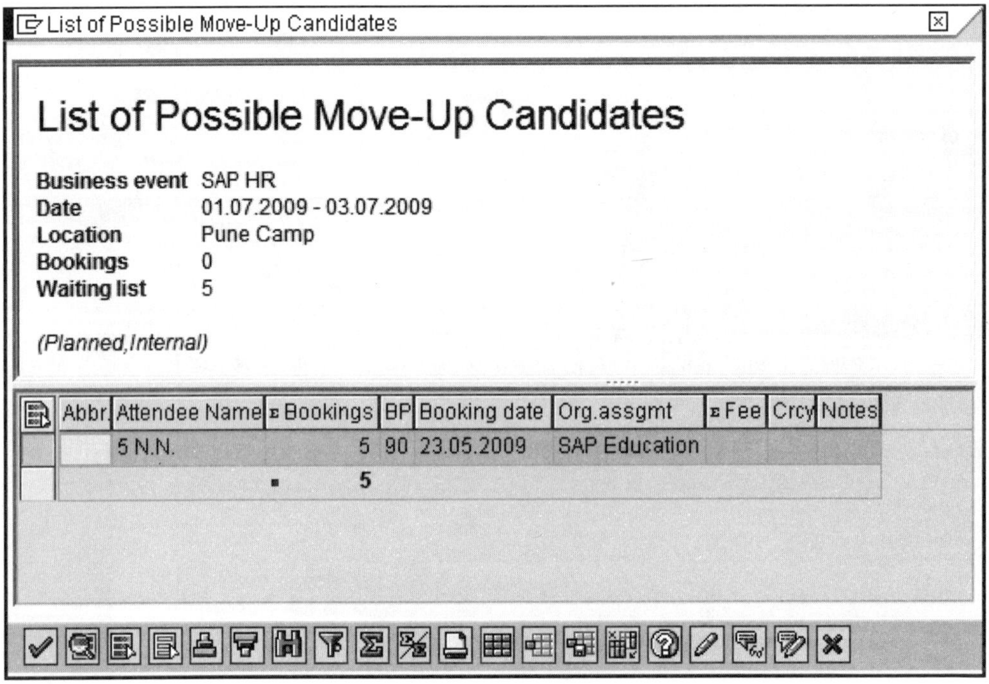

List of Possible Move-Up Candidates

**List of Possible Move-Up Candidates**

**Business event** SAP HR
**Date** 01.07.2009 - 03.07.2009
**Location** Pune Camp
**Bookings** 0
**Waiting list** 5

*(Planned,Internal)*

| Abbr. | Attendee Name | Σ Bookings | BP | Booking date | Org.assgmt | Σ Fee | Crcy | Notes |
|---|---|---|---|---|---|---|---|---|
| | 5 N.N. | 5 | 90 | 23.05.2009 | SAP Education | | | |
| | ■ | 5 | | | | | | |

### 36.12.6 Reasons for Attendance Cancellation

In view T77CAR you can define the reasons for attendance cancellation. For each reason you can specify cancellation fee as a percentage of attendance fee, or you may specify that there is no cancellation fee.

| Reas. | Reason for cancellation of attendance | Cancel % | Free of charge |
|---|---|---|---|
| | | | ☐ |
| | | | ☐ |
| | | | ☐ |
| | | | ☐ |

If no cancellation reason is specified when attendance is cancelled or if a cancellation reason has been specified for which no cancellation fee is stored in view T77CAR, default cancellation fee is charged. Default cancellation fee is stored as a percentage of attendance fees in the following parameter.

| Group | Sem. abbr. | Value abbr. | Description |
|---|---|---|---|
| SEMIN | CCDEL | 0 | Default value for cancellation fees |

### 36.12.7 Moving-up on Cancellation

| Group | Sem. abbr. | Value abbr. | Description |
|---|---|---|---|
| SEMIN | TOPMD | I | Mode for move-ups from waiting list |

Here you specify the move-up procedure for waiting list candidates to fill the places freed by cancellations. There are three options available: no move-up takes place, interactive move-up by the user, or the system automatically selects move-up candidates on the basis of booking priority and date. The move-up procedure defined here does not apply to rebookings.

## 36.13 ATTENDEE APPRAISALS

| *Functional Consultant* | *User* | *Business Process Owner* | *Senior Management* | *My Rating* | *Understanding Level* |
|---|---|---|---|---|---|
| A | A | A | B | | |

### 36.13.1 Appraising Attendees

You can run transaction PV34 to perform appraisal of attendees by a business event (instructor). The system shows you the appraisal templates available for Training and Event Management. Appraisal templates are created by consultants as per your requirements using transaction OOAM (Refer to chapter 27).

| ObjectID | Object abbr. | Object name | Start date | End Date |
|---|---|---|---|---|
| 50000443 | Business Eve | Business Event Appraisal | 01.01.1900 | 31.12.9999 |
| 50000459 | SAP HR Atten | SAP HR Attendee Appraisal | 01.01.1900 | 31.12.9999 |

You select the appropriate template. The system shows you the appraisal form. You enter the attendee, the business event, and the training period.

| | | | |
|---|---|---|---|
| Appraisal Status | In Preparation | | |
| Business Event | SAP HR | | |
| Attendee | Agrawal Prem | | |
| Training Period | 08.06.2009 | to | 10.06.2009 |

Body Data

| Nu... | Element Name | Final Appraisal | Final Appraisal (Value Text) | Fin... |
|---|---|---|---|---|
| | SAP HR Attendee Appraisal | 3.800 | | |
| 1 | Module Competencies | 3.778 | | |
| 1.1 | OM | 4 | Independent implementation ability | |
| 1.2 | Recruitment | 3 | 1 implementation or 1 year support | |
| 1.3 | PA | 5 | Mastery of the module | |
| 1.4 | Personnel Development | 4 | Independent implementation ability | |
| 1.5 | Training | 4 | Independent implementation ability | |
| 1.6 | Time Management | 4 | Independent implementation ability | |
| 1.7 | Payroll | 5 | Mastery of the module | |
| 1.8 | ESS | 3 | 1 implementation or 1 year support | |
| 1.9 | MSS | 2 | Knowledge of functionality with hands-on | |

You then Execute the appraisal, enter the appraisal data and Complete it.

### 36.13.2 Attendee Appraisals Report

You can run transaction S_PH9_46000452 to see attendee appraisals. You can filter appraisals based on appraisal template, appraisal status and period. The system shows you a list of appraisals meeting your selection criteria.

| N | App.Document Name | AppDocType | Type | Name | Type | Appraisee | App. Stat |
|---|---|---|---|---|---|---|---|
| 1 | SAP HR Attendee Appraisal | Appraisal Do | Course | SAP HR | Person | Agrawal Prem | Completed |

You can select an appraisal document and display or change it. You can even create an appraisal document from this report. You can delete an appraisal document. You can change the status of a completed document to 'In process'.

## 36.14 ATTENDANCE REPORTS

| *Functional Consultant* | *User* | *Business Process Owner* | *Senior Management* | *My Rating* | *Understanding Level* |
|---|---|---|---|---|---|
| A | A | A | B | | |

### *Attendee list*

You can run transaction S_PH9_46000434 to see the list of attendees for one or more business events. You can filter the business events selected based on period and location. You can filter the attendee list of selected business events by booking priority.

| Name ... | Start date | End date | Attendee Name | Σ Bookings | BP | Booking date | Σ Fee | Crcy | Notes |
|---|---|---|---|---|---|---|---|---|---|
| SAP HR | 08.06.2009 | 10.06.2009 | Agrawal Prem | 1 | 50 | 12.06.2009 | | | |
| SAP HR | 08.06.2009 | 10.06.2009 | Kumar Ramesh | 1 | 50 | 12.06.2009 | | | |
| SAP HR | 08.06.2009 | 10.06.2009 | Pande Geeta | 1 | 50 | 12.06.2009 | | | |
| SAP HR | 08.06.2009 | 10.06.2009 | Yadav Raghunath | 1 | 50 | 12.06.2009 | | | |
| | | | ▪ | 4 | | | | | |

### *Attendance list*

You can run transaction S_PH9_46000433 to generate attendance list of a business event. You can sort the list alphabetically, or by organizational assignment. You can take signatures of attendees on an attendance list.

Org. assignment | Alphabetically

14.06.2009 Business event attendance list 1

SAP HR from08.06.2009 - 10.06.2009

Business event language E

Please complete missing attendees' names in block letters

| Attendees | Org. assignment | Signature |
|---|---|---|
| Agrawal Prem | ABC Consultants Ltd. | ____________ |
| Kumar Ramesh | Component Factory | ____________ |
| Pande Geeta | PCB | ____________ |
| Yadav Raghunath | SAP Consulting | ____________ |

### *Employee list*

You can run transaction S_PH9_46000432 to find employees of a company, customer, interested party or organizational unit. You can also include employees of subordinate organizational units of the selected organizational unit.

| Org. assignment | EE abbr. | Employee name | Start date | End Date |
|---|---|---|---|---|
| ABC Consultants Ltd. | Agrawal | Agrawal Prem | 12.12.2008 | 31.12.9999 |
| SAP Consulting | Abhinav | Abhinav Desai | 01.01.2009 | 31.12.9999 |
| SAP Consulting | Bansal | Bansal Meenakshi | 01.01.2009 | 31.12.9999 |
| SAP Consulting | Deval | Milind Deval | 30.12.2008 | 31.12.9999 |
| SAP Consulting | Mehta | Mehta Ashish | 01.01.2009 | 31.12.9999 |
| SAP Consulting | Sharma | Sharma Vinod | 01.01.2009 | 31.12.9999 |
| SAP Consulting | Sinha | Sinha Alok | 01.01.2009 | 31.12.9999 |
| SAP Consulting | Verma | Verma Abhishek | 01.01.2009 | 31.12.9999 |
| SAP Consulting | Yadav | Yadav Raghunath | 01.01.2009 | 31.12.9999 |
| SAP Education | Gupta | Gupta Ranjana | 01.01.2009 | 31.12.9999 |

### *Bookings per attendee*

You can run transaction S_AHR_61016215 to see bookings for one or more attendees during a period. You can restrict the report to a business event type. This report does not give details of days and hours of training. If you need that information, use Attendee's training history.

| Attendee Name | Business event | Start date | End date | Σ Bookings | BP | Booking date | Σ Fee | Crcy | Notes |
|---|---|---|---|---|---|---|---|---|---|
| Agrawal Prem | SAP HR | 01.07.2009 | 03.07.2009 | 1 | 50 | 11.05.2009 | | | |
| Agrawal Prem | SAP FI | 11.07.2009 | 13.07.2009 | 1 | 50 | 25.05.2009 | | | |
| Mehta Ashish | Yoga | 06.07.2009 | 06.07.2009 | 1 | 50 | 11.05.2009 | | | |
| Abhinav Desai | Yoga | 20.07.2009 | 20.07.2009 | 1 | 50 | 11.05.2009 | | | |
| | | | | ■ 4 | | | | | |

### *Attendee's training history*

You can run transaction S_PH9_46000431 to see training history of one or more employees. A training history is a list of all training events that the attendee already has attended or is booked to attend.

| Attendee Name | Event | Event type | Bus. event | Start date | End date | Σ Days | Σ Hours | Σ Fee | Crcy | Σ B | BP |
|---|---|---|---|---|---|---|---|---|---|---|---|
| Agrawal Prem | ☑ | ☐ | SAP FI | 11.07.2009 | 13.07.2009 | 3 | 24.00 | | | 1 | 50 |
| Agrawal Prem | ☑ | ☐ | SAP HR | 01.07.2009 | 03.07.2009 | 3 | 22.00 | | | 1 | 50 |
| | | | | | | ■ 6 | ■ 46.00 | | | ■ 2 | |

### *Attendance prerequisites*

You can run transaction S_PH9_46000430 to see prerequisites for attending business events of a type. The prerequisite may be a qualification, or attending business events of a type.

| Event type | Event type | Qual. | Prerequisite | Qual.start | End date |
|---|---|---|---|---|---|
| SAP HR | ☐ | ☑ | English language | 01.01.1900 | 31.12.9999 |

If there are no prerequisites, the system gives the message 'no data found for the values entered'.

### *Attendee's qualifications*

You can run transaction S_PH9_46000429 to see an attendee's qualifications.

29.05.2009 Attendee's qualifications 1

| | |
|---|---|
| Person | Agrawal Prem |
| Selection period | 01.01.1900 - 29.05.2009 |
| Key date | 29.05.2009 |

NOTE: Expired qualifications are displayed with a dark background.

| Qualification | Validity period | Depreciation meter |
|---|---|---|
| HR | 16.02.2009 - 15.02.2019 | 10 Years |
| MM | 16.02.2009 - 31.12.9999 | |

### *Prerequisites matchup*

You can run transaction S_PH9_46000428 to check whether an attendee meets the prerequisites to attend a business event type. The result is shown in traffic lights.

| EType | Name Attendee | Prerequisite | Name Prerequisite | Analysis |
|---|---|---|---|---|
| SAP HR | Verma Abhishek | Qualification | English language | |

### *Prebookings per business event type*

You can run transaction S_PH9_46000427 to see all prebookings for one or more business event types.

| Event type | Attendee name | Start date | End date | Σ P | Pr | Prebk date | Location | Org.assgmt | Notes |
|---|---|---|---|---|---|---|---|---|---|
| SAP FI | Yadav Raghunath | 30.05.2009 | 31.12.9999 | 1 | 50 | 30.05.2009 | | SAP Consulting | |
| | | | | ■ 1 | | | | | |

### *Prebookings per attendee*

You can run transaction S_AHR_61016214 to see all prebookings for one or more attendees.

| Attendee name | Event type | Start date | End date | Σ P | Pr | Prebk date | Location | Notes | Fee | Crcy |
|---|---|---|---|---|---|---|---|---|---|---|
| Yadav Raghunath | Yoga | 24.05.2009 | 31.12.9999 | 1 | 50 | 11.05.2009 | | | | |
| Yadav Raghunath | SAP FI | 30.05.2009 | 31.12.9999 | 1 | 50 | 30.05.2009 | | | | |
| | | | | ▪ 2 | | | | | | |

### *Attendees for rebooking*

You can run transaction S_PH9_46000426 to identify attendees who need to be rebooked. Attendees who remained on waiting list of business events, or attendees of cancelled business events need to be rebooked.

| Business... | Attendee... | Org. assignment | Bus. event | Start date | End date | Σ No. | B... | L | D | Hist. |
|---|---|---|---|---|---|---|---|---|---|---|
| SAP HR | 4 N.N. | SAP Education | SAP HR | 01.07.2009 | 03.07.2009 | 4 | 90 | ☐ | ☐ | ☐ |
| | | | | | | ▪ 4 | | | | |

### *Attendance statistics*

You can run transaction S_ALR_87014085 to see the number of attendees and status of business events. You can select a business event and firmly book it, cancel it, or follow it up.

| Business event type | Business event | Start date | End date | L | Σ N... | Σ N | L | D | H | F | FB | Ext |
|---|---|---|---|---|---|---|---|---|---|---|---|---|
| SAP HR | SAP HR | 01.07.2009 | 03.07.2009 | EN | 20 | 4 | ☐ | ☐ | ☐ | ☐ | ☑ | ☐ |
| | | | | | ▪ 20 | ▪ 4 | | | | | | |

### *Attendance and sales statistics*

You can run transaction S_PH9_46000425 to see the number of bookings and total fees for each business event type which is relevant for billing, internal activity allocation and free of charge.

| Business event type | Allocation data | Σ Bookings | Σ Fee | Crcy |
|---|---|---|---|---|
| SAP HR | Relevant for billing | 0 | 0.00 | INR |
| SAP HR | Relevant for alloctn | 0 | 0.00 | INR |
| SAP HR | Free of charge | 20 | | |
| | | ▪ 20 | ▪ 0.00 | INR |

### *Cancellations per business event*

You can run transaction S_PH9_46000424 to see cancellation of attendance in business events for a period. You can also generate the list for a specific attendance cancellation reason.

| Bus. event | Start date | End date | Attendee... | Org.assgmt | Σ Canceled | Σ Fee | COCr | Reason... | Notes |
|---|---|---|---|---|---|---|---|---|---|
| SAP HR | 01.07.2009 | 03.07.2009 | 1 N.N. | SAP Consulting | 1 | | | | |
| | | | | | ■ 1 | | | | |

### *Cancellations per attendee*

You can run transaction S_AHR_61016216 to see cancellation of attendance done by an attendee. You can also generate the list for a specific attendance cancellation reason.

| Attendee Name | Business event | Start date | End date | Σ Canceled | Σ Fee | COCr | Reason... | Notes |
|---|---|---|---|---|---|---|---|---|
| Mehta Ashish | Yoga | 06.07.2009 | 06.07.2009 | 1 | | | | |
| | | | | ■ 1 | | | | |

CHAPTER 37

# Correspondence

## 37.1 AUTOMATIC CORRESPONDENCE

| *Functional Consultant* | *User* | *Business Process Owner* | *Senior Management* | *My Rating* | *Understanding Level* |
|---|---|---|---|---|---|
| A | A | A | A | | |

Training and event management can be set up for automatic correspondence with different categories of recipients, e.g. attendees, instructors, etc. The correspondence can take place in different media, e.g. e-mail, fax, postal service, etc. When a correspondence-relevant activity takes place, e.g. attendance booking or business event cancellation, appropriate correspondence automatically takes place. The content of the correspondence depends on the activity and related data. If automatic correspondence fails for any reason, administrators are informed through a workflow. They can then complete the process manually.

## 37.2 MANUAL CORRESPONDENCE

| *Functional Consultant* | *User* | *Business Process Owner* | *Senior Management* | *My Rating* | *Understanding Level* |
|---|---|---|---|---|---|
| A | A | A | B | | |

### 37.2.1 Purpose

Manual correspondence is needed if automatic correspondence fails, or if automatic correspondence is disabled by setting no output in view T77VD.

### 37.2.2 Transaction

PP40—Manual Output

### 37.2.3 Initial Screen

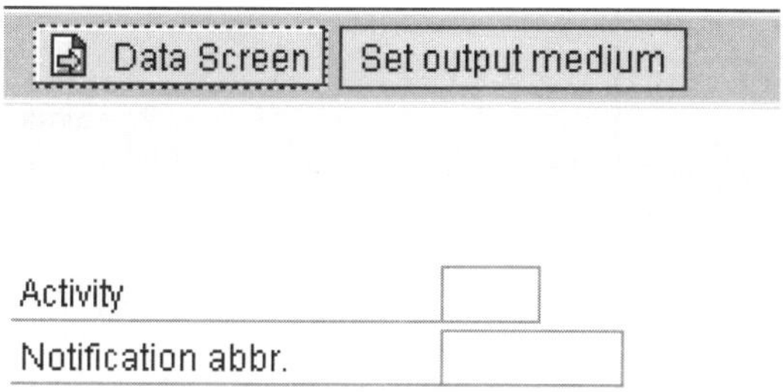


The list of activities and corresponding notification abbreviations are defined in configuration. You select from that list.

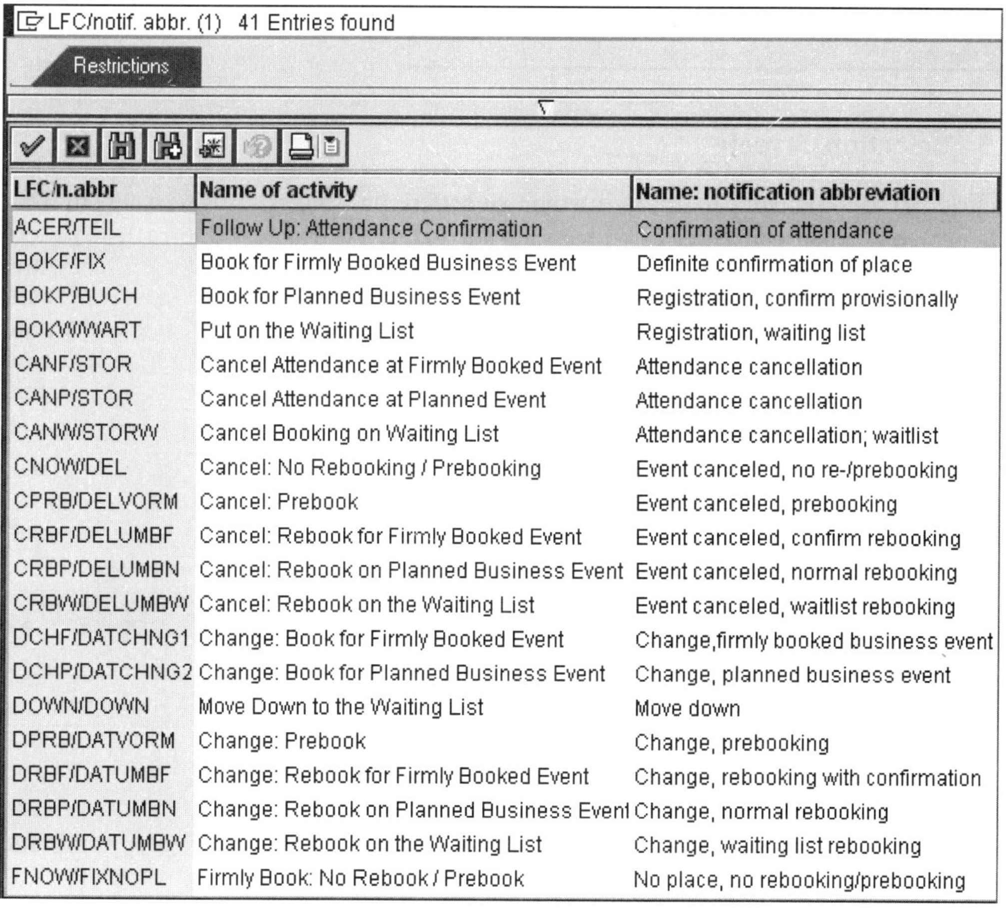


| LFC/n.abbr | Name of activity | Name: notification abbreviation |
|---|---|---|
| ACER/TEIL | Follow Up: Attendance Confirmation | Confirmation of attendance |
| BOKF/FIX | Book for Firmly Booked Business Event | Definite confirmation of place |
| BOKP/BUCH | Book for Planned Business Event | Registration, confirm provisionally |
| BOKW/WART | Put on the Waiting List | Registration, waiting list |
| CANF/STOR | Cancel Attendance at Firmly Booked Event | Attendance cancellation |
| CANP/STOR | Cancel Attendance at Planned Event | Attendance cancellation |
| CANW/STORW | Cancel Booking on Waiting List | Attendance cancellation; waitlist |
| CNOW/DEL | Cancel: No Rebooking / Prebooking | Event canceled, no re-/prebooking |
| CPRB/DELVORM | Cancel: Prebook | Event canceled, prebooking |
| CRBF/DELUMBF | Cancel: Rebook for Firmly Booked Event | Event canceled, confirm rebooking |
| CRBP/DELUMBN | Cancel: Rebook on Planned Business Event | Event canceled, normal rebooking |
| CRBW/DELUMBW | Cancel: Rebook on the Waiting List | Event canceled, waitlist rebooking |
| DCHF/DATCHNG1 | Change: Book for Firmly Booked Event | Change,firmly booked business event |
| DCHP/DATCHNG2 | Change: Book for Planned Business Event | Change, planned business event |
| DOWN/DOWN | Move Down to the Waiting List | Move down |
| DPRB/DATVORM | Change: Prebook | Change, prebooking |
| DRBF/DATUMBF | Change: Rebook for Firmly Booked Event | Change, rebooking with confirmation |
| DRBP/DATUMBN | Change: Rebook on Planned Business Event | Change, normal rebooking |
| DRBW/DATUMBW | Change: Rebook on the Waiting List | Change, waiting list rebooking |
| FNOW/FIXNOPL | Firmly Book: No Rebook / Prebook | No place, no rebooking/prebooking |

### 37.2.4 Output Medium

You can click Set output medium to set the output medium. You can further set different output media for different recipients in the output list.

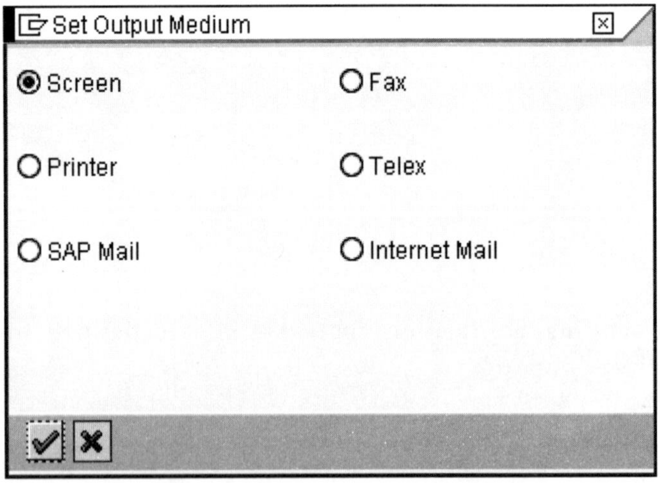


### 37.2.5 Selection Screen

You click Data Screen to input further selection parameter. Business event is a mandatory entry. You can enter attendee data to further restrict the output list.

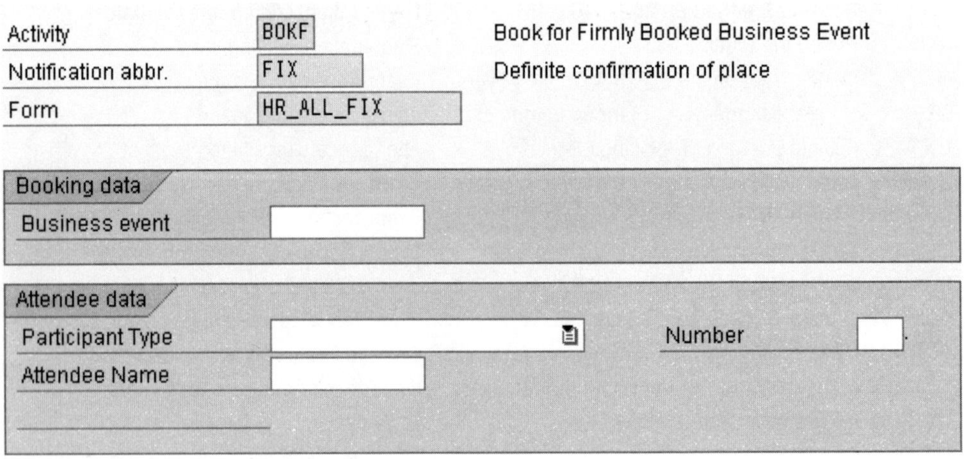

### 37.2.6 Output List

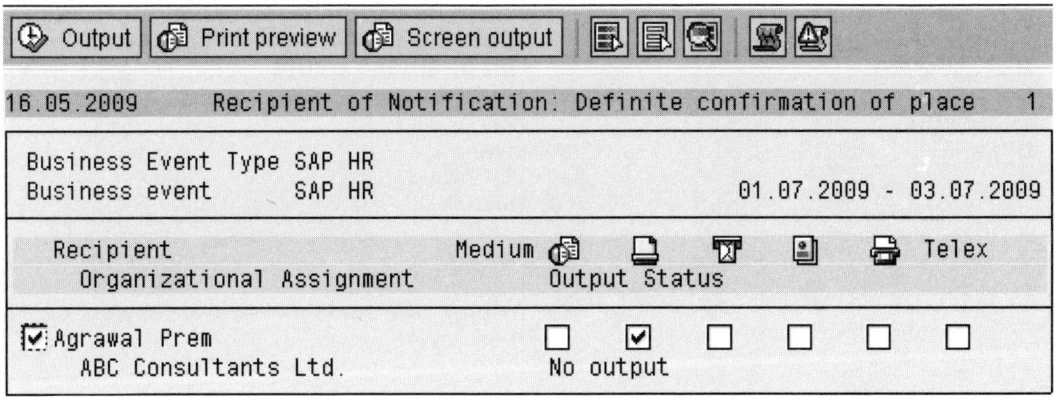


The output list shows the list of recipients and the output medium. You can select different output media for different recipients. You can see print preview, screen output, correspondence history and error log. You can output the correspondence in the specified media.

### 37.2.7 Output

ABC Consultants Ltd.
Mr Agrawal Prem
L/A-4/303,
411018 PUNE
INDIA

**Definite confirmation of place on business event**

Date
May 16, 2009
Clerk
P_PKA00137
Telephone

Fax

Reference number (Please quote in enquiries)
E 50000299

Dear Mr Agrawal,

We would like to confirm your reservation on the business event

**SAP HR (SAP HR)**

from July 01, 2009 to July 03, 2009.

The business event begins on Wednesday, July 01, 2009 at 10:00 at Pune Camp in Pune and will take place in room 101.

The attendance times are listed below.

| Date | Weekday | from | to |
|---|---|---|---|
| July 01, 2009 | Wednesday | 10:00 - | 17:00 |
| July 02, 2009 | Thursday | 09:00 - | 17:00 |
| July 03, 2009 | Friday | 09:00 - | 16:00 |

Yours faithfully,

Pioneer Education

## 37.3 CORRESPONDENCE HISTORY

| *Functional Consultant* | *User* | *Business Process Owner* | *Senior Management* | *My Rating* | *Understanding Level* |
|---|---|---|---|---|---|
| A | A | A | B | | |

### 37.3.1 Purpose

There are occasions when you want to see what correspondence has taken place with whom. This program lets you see that with a variety of search options.

### 37.3.2 Transaction

PVK0—History

### 37.3.3 Selection Screen

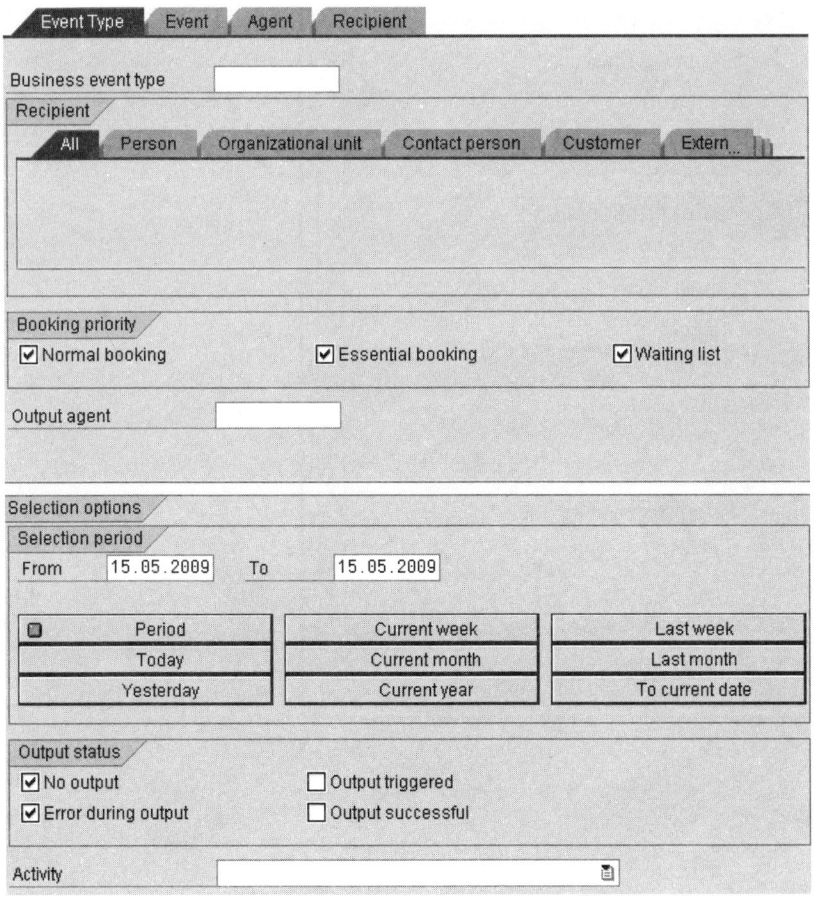

In this screen, you can specify the search criteria for a business event type, business event, agent (user) or recipient. In addition, you can specify the period, booking priority, output status and activity.

### 37.3.4 Output

| Recipient | Org. assignment | Date | Activity | Medium | Automatic |
|---|---|---|---|---|---|
| Agrawal Prem | ABC Consultants Ltd. | 16.05.2009 | Change: Book for Planned | No output | ☐ |

There are a number of fields you can add in the list by modifying the layout. Alternatively, you can see all the fields by selecting a line and clicking .

Details

| Group description | Cell Content |
|---|---|
| Recipient | Agrawal Prem |
| Organizational Assignment | ABC Consultants Ltd. |
| Plan Version | 01 |
| Plan Version Text | Current plan |
| Recipient type | Person |
| Object Type | E |
| Business event / type | Course |
| OrgAssgmtType | Organizational unit |
| Object ID | 50000299 |
| Object abbreviation | SAP HR |
| Object name | SAP HR |
| Recipient type | P |
| Recipient | 00121715 |
| Attendee Name | Agrawal |
| Org. assignment | O |
| Organizational Assignment | 50000075 |
| Org. assignment abbr | ABC Consult |
| Object Type | US |
| Object type text | User |

## 37.4 ACTIVITIES

| *Functional Consultant* | *User* | *Business Process Owner* | *Senior Management* | *My Rating* | *Understanding Level* |
|---|---|---|---|---|---|
| A | C | X | X | | |

### 37.4.1 Purpose

You need to correspond when certain activities occur, e.g. an employee books a business event. Activity definition may include more details. For example, an employee books a planned business event and an employee books a firmly booked business event may be two different activities because the correspondence would differ. SAP provides predefined activities. An activity is linked to a notification abbreviation. Notification abbreviations are linked to forms, which are correspondence templates with variable fields that get filled at runtime.

### 37.4.2 IMG Node

SM30 ➢ T77VI

### 37.4.3 Screen

| Acty | Activity | Not.abbr | Name: notification abbreviation |
|---|---|---|---|
| ACER | Follow Up: Attendance Confirmation | TEIL | Confirmation of attendance |
| BOKF | Book for Firmly Booked Business Event | FIX | Definite confirmation of place |
| BOKP | Book for Planned Business Event | BUCH | Registration, confirm provisionally |
| BOKW | Put on the Waiting List | WART | Registration, waiting list |

### 37.4.4 Primary Key

Key: Activity + Abbreviation for Notification

## 37.5 RECIPIENTS OF NOTIFICATION

| *Functional Consultant* | *User* | *Business Process Owner* | *Senior Management* | *My Rating* | *Understanding Level* |
|---|---|---|---|---|---|
| A | C | X | X | | |

### 37.5.1 Purpose

Notification abbreviations are linked to forms, which are correspondence templates with variable fields that get filled at runtime. When an event (activity) triggers a notification, it is output to a recipient group, which is specified here. Recipient group 0000, or blank, are attendees. When you do correspondence using transaction PP40, you get a selection screen which is also specified here.

### 37.5.2 IMG Node

SM30 ➢ T77VE

### 37.5.3 Screen

| Notif.abbr | Description | > | Rec | Description | Scr | Short Descript. |
|---|---|---|---|---|---|---|
| ** | Deactivate other notifications | i | | Attendances | | No data screen (lock entry) |
| BUCH | Registration, confirm provisic | i | | Attendances | 2100 | Business event with attenc |
| BUCHEX | External reg., provisional con | i | | Attendances | 2100 | Business event with attenc |
| BUCHSUP | Registration, to supervisor | i | 0006 | Supervisor (att | 2100 | Business event with attenc |

### 37.5.4 Primary Key

Abbreviation for notification

## 37.6 RECIPIENT GROUPS

| *Functional Consultant* | *User* | *Business Process Owner* | *Senior Management* | *My Rating* | *Understanding Level* |
|---|---|---|---|---|---|
| A | C | X | X | | |

### 37.6.1 Purpose

Recipient groups are the addressees of various types of correspondence generated in Training and Event Management. Recipients in a recipient group are determined by the function module specified here.

### 37.6.2 IMG Node

SM30 ➢ T77VG

### 37.6.3 Screen

| Recipient group | Description | Function module | Short text for function module |
|---|---|---|---|
| 0000 | Attendances | RH_GET_ADDR_ATTE | |
| 0001 | Cancellation | RH_GET_ADDR_CANC | |
| 0002 | Prebooking | RH_GET_ADDR_PREB | |
| 0003 | Instructor | RH_GET_ADDR_INST | |
| 0004 | Organizers | RH_GET_ADDR_ORGA | |
| 0005 | Name tags | RH_GET_ADDR_ATTE | |
| 0006 | Supervisor (atte | RH_GET_ADDR_ATTE_SUPERIOR | |
| 0007 | Supervisor (can | RH_GET_ADDR_CANC_SUPERIOR | |
| 0008 | Supervisor (pret | RH_GET_ADDR_PREB_SUPERIOR | |

### 37.6.4 Primary Key

Recipient Group

## 37.7 FORM FOR A NOTIFICATION

| *Functional Consultant* | *User* | *Business Process Owner* | *Senior Management* | *My Rating* | *Understanding Level* |
|---|---|---|---|---|---|
| A | C | X | X | | |

### 37.7.1 Purpose

Notification abbreviations are linked to forms here. Forms are correspondence templates with variable fields that get filled at runtime. You can maintain a form in multiple languages. The language of notification is determined in the following sequence: (1) Language of the attendee, (2) Language of the business event and (3) Language specified in switch SEMIN CLANG. You can also specify the default output medium. For automatic output, you must specify the output medium (such as P for printer, I for Internet Mail). For manual output, you specify 'No output'. Under Maintain global standard texts for forms, you can maintain the logo, the sender and the footer for all the forms you use. You can use the standard forms, or copy and modify them. In the latter case, you specify the modified form here.

### 37.7.2 IMG Node

SM30 ➢ T77VD

### 37.7.3 List Screen

Maintain global standard texts for forms

Change logo | Change sender | Change footer

| User grp | Not.abbr | Name: notification abbreviation | > | M | Name | Form |
|---|---|---|---|---|---|---|
| * | BUCH | Registration, confirm provisionally | | | No output | HR_ALL_BUCH |
| * | BUCHEX | External reg., provisional confirm. | | | No output | HR_ALL_BUCHEX |
| * | BUCHSUP | Registration, to supervisor | | | No output | HR_ALL_BUCHSUPER |
| * | DATCHNG1 | Change,firmly booked business event | | | No output | HR_ALL_DATCHNG1 |
| * | DATCHNG2 | Change, planned business event | | | No output | HR_ALL_DATCHNG2 |
| * | DATUMBF | Change, rebooking with confirmation | | | No output | HR_ALL_DATUMBF |
| * | DATUMBN | Change, normal rebooking | | | No output | HR_ALL_DATUMBN |
| * | DATUMBW | Change, waiting list rebooking | | | No output | HR_ALL_DATUMBW |
| * | DATVORM | Change, prebooking | | | No output | HR_ALL_DATVORM |
| * | DEL | Event canceled, no re-/prebooking | | | No output | HR_ALL_DEL |

### 37.7.4 Detail Screen

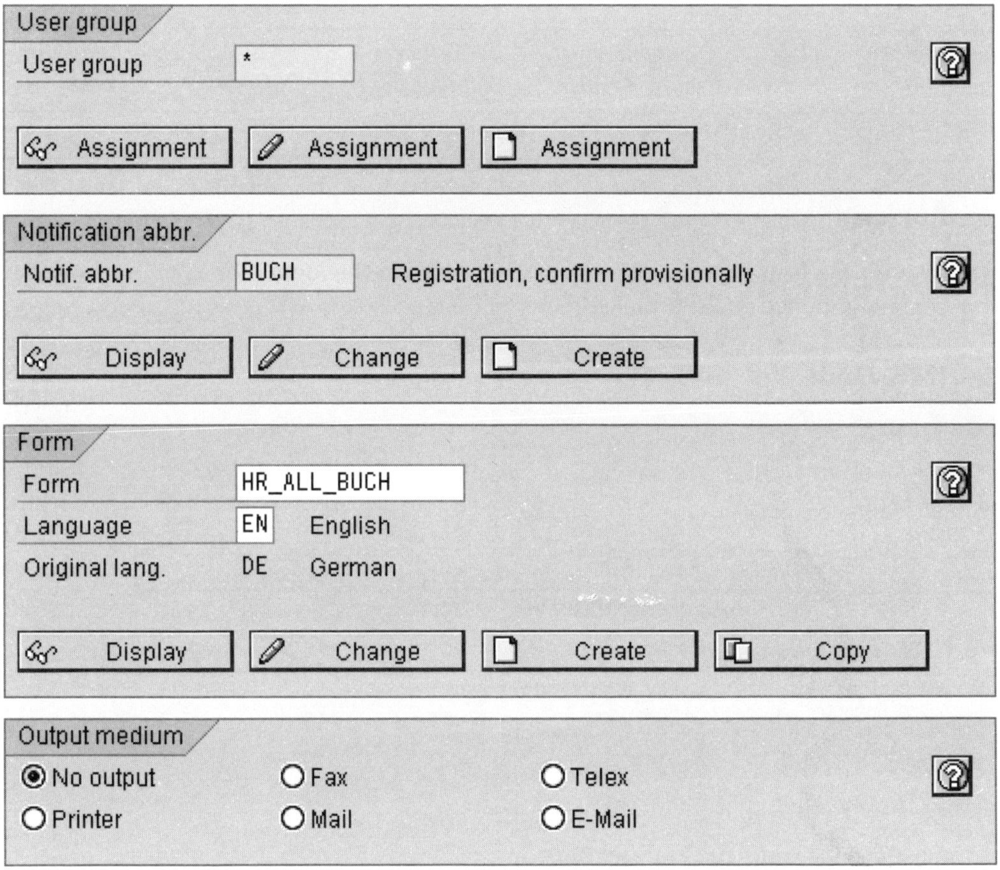


### 37.7.5 Primary Key

User group for notifications + Abbreviation for notification

## 37.8 ASSIGNMENT OF USERS TO USER GROUPS

| *Functional Consultant* | *User* | *Business Process Owner* | *Senior Management* | *My Rating* | *Understanding Level* |
|---|---|---|---|---|---|
| A | C | X | X | | |

### 37.8.1 Purpose

Here you specify the users in a user group. Depending on the logged on user, appropriate form for correspondence will be picked up.

### 37.8.2 IMG Node

SM30 ➢ T77KU

### 37.8.3 Screen

| User | User name | User group |
|---|---|---|
| | | |
| | | |
| | | |
| | | |

### 37.8.4 Primary Key

User Name + User Group for Notifications

## 37.9 DEFAULT OUTPUT MEDIUM

| *Functional Consultant* | *User* | *Business Process Owner* | *Senior Management* | *My Rating* | *Understanding Level* |
|---|---|---|---|---|---|
| A | C | X | X | | |

### 37.9.1 Purpose

Here you can specify the default output medium for each attendee type.

### 37.9.2 IMG Node

SM30 ➢ V_T77KV_3

### 37.9.3 Screen

| AT | Attendee type | M | Name |
|---|---|---|---|
| H | External person | | No output |
| P | Person | | No output |

### 37.9.4 Primary Key

Attendee Type

## 37.10 DEFAULT LANGUAGE

| *Functional Consultant* | *User* | *Business Process Owner* | *Senior Management* | *My Rating* | *Understanding Level* |
|---|---|---|---|---|---|
| A | C | X | X | | |

### 37.10.1 Purpose

The language of notification is determined in the following sequence.

1. Language of the attendee
2. Language of the business event
3. Language specified here

### 37.10.2 IMG Node

SM30 ➢ T77S0

### 37.10.3 Screen

| Group | Sem. abbr. | Value abbr. | Description |
|---|---|---|---|
| SEMIN | CLANG | EN | Default value for output language (correspondence) |

## 37.11 PRIORITY FOR WORKFLOW CORRESPONDENCE

| *Functional Consultant* | *User* | *Business Process Owner* | *Senior Management* | *My Rating* | *Understanding Level* |
|---|---|---|---|---|---|
| A | C | X | X | | |

### 37.11.1 Purpose

Here you can set priority for errors that occur in the correspondence function of Training and Event Management. The highest priority is 1 and the lowest priority is 9. If this field is blank, default priority value of 5 is used.

### 37.11.2 IMG Node

SM30 ➢ T77S0

### 37.11.3 Screen

| Group | Sem. abbr. | Value abbr. | Description |
|---|---|---|---|
| SEMIN | WFPRI | | Priority for workflow correspondence |

## 37.12 FORMS

| *Functional Consultant* | *User* | *Business Process Owner* | *Senior Management* | *My Rating* | *Understanding Level* |
|---|---|---|---|---|---|
| A | B | C | C | | |

### 37.12.1 Standard Forms

SAP provides standard forms for all notification abbreviations. If you want to have your own forms, you can copy them and modify the copied forms. You also link the copied form to the notification abbreviation in view T77VD. Alternatively, you can use the wizard at IMG node Training and Event Management ➢ Day-to-Day Activities ➢ Correspondence ➢ Wizards ➢ Correspondence Setup.

### 37.12.2 Subobjects

The forms you specify for a notification are in SAPScript which can be defined using transaction OOFO. A SAPScript form consists of subobjects shown below.

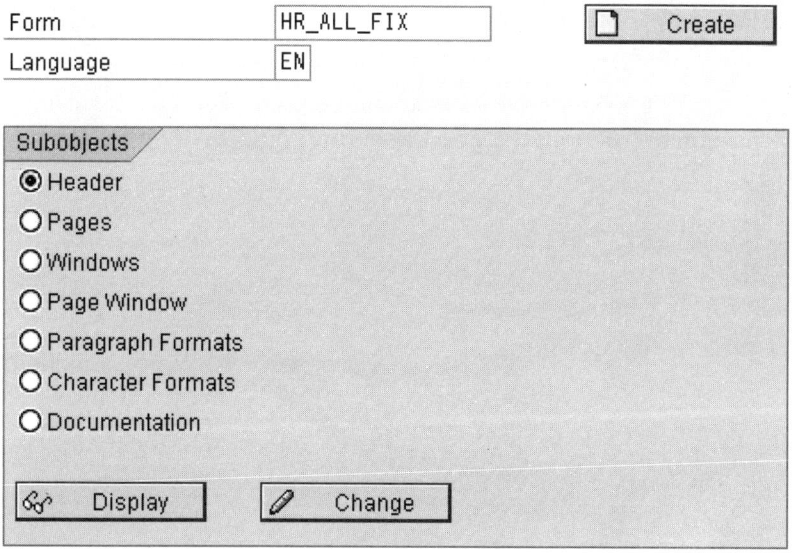


## 37.12.3 Windows

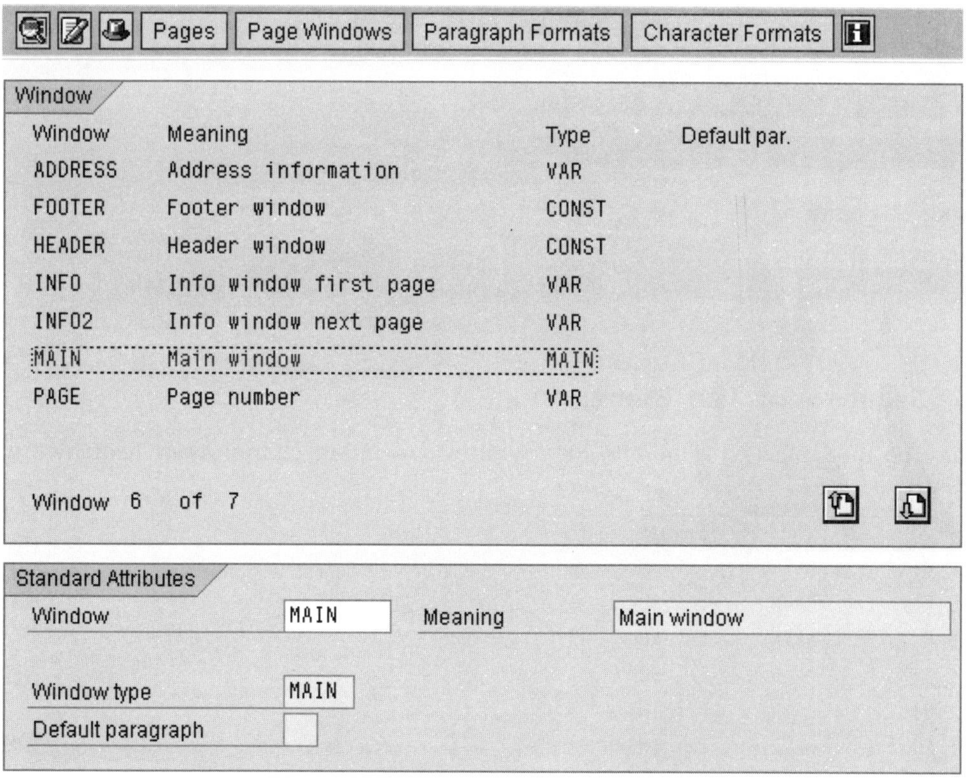


A form usually has multiple windows, each containing different types of information.

### 37.12.4 Text Elements

The real content lies in the text elements in the windows. You select a window by double-clicking it and then click . The system shows you the content. The content can be modified as per your requirements. You may need the help of an ABAP consultant.

```
TXT_BODY¶
SET·DATE·MASK·=·'MMMMM·DD,·YYYY'¶
SET·TIME·MASK·=·'HH:MM'¶
IF·&PPVAR-TANRD&·NE·&SPACE(79)&¶
Dear·&PPVAR-TANRD&·&PPVAR-TGRUS&,¶
ELSE¶
Dear·Sir·or·Madam,¶
ENDIF↵
↵
¶
IF·&PPVAR-TCANZ&·NE·'1'¶
We·would·like·to·confirm·your·reservation·of·&PPVAR-TCANZ&·places·on·the·business
event¶
ELSE¶
We·would·like·to·confirm·your·reservation·on·the·business·event¶
ENDIF¶

    &PPVAR-KSTXT&&'·('PPVAR-KSHRT')'&¶

from·&PPVAR-KBGDA&·to·&PPVAR-KNDDA&.↵
¶
IF·&PPVAR-F_ORT&·EQ·&SPACE(20)&¶
The·business·event·begins·on·&PPVAR-KBDAY&,·&PPVAR-KBGDA&&'·at·'PPVAR-
KBTIM(T)&&'·in·'PPVAR-FSTXT&&'·and·will·take·place·in·room·'PPVAR-R_NUM&.¶
ELSE¶
```

### 37.12.5 Sequence of Text Elements

There may be multiple text elements in a window. You can change their sequence in view T77VB.

| Form | Window | Element | No. |
|---|---|---|---|
| HR_ALL_FIX | MAIN | TXT_ABL | 6 |
| HR_ALL_FIX | MAIN | TXT_ABLE | 7 |
| HR_ALL_FIX | MAIN | TXT_ABLH | 5 |
| HR_ALL_FIX | MAIN | TXT_BODY | 1 |
| HR_ALL_FIX | MAIN | TXT_INS | 3 |
| HR_ALL_FIX | MAIN | TXT_INSE | 4 |
| HR_ALL_FIX | MAIN | TXT_INSH | 2 |
| HR_ALL_FIX | MAIN | TXT_MFG | 8 |

### 37.12.6 Text Variables

You can see and if necessary edit the text variables, which can be used in text elements, in view T77VC.

| Structure | Field | Short Description | > | R | Program | Subroutine | > |
|---|---|---|---|---|---|---|---|
| PPVAR | TANRD | Title: attendee | | | RHKMIT30 | GET_TANRD | |
| PPVAR | TCANZ | Number of attendees | | | RHKMIT30 | GET_TCANZ | |
| PPVAR | TCNAM | Address supplement: Attendee's address | | | RHKMIT30 | GET_TCNAM | |
| PPVAR | TGRUS | Greeting: Attendee | | | RHKMIT30 | GET_TGRUS | |
| PPVAR | TLAND | Country key: Attendee's address | | | RHKMIT30 | GET_TLAND | |

A text variable can be flagged as required for form output. If you flag a text variable as required, the form cannot be output unless the variable has been filled during the data procurement process.

### 37.12.7 Name Format for Recipients

You can define the name format for recipients in view T777N.

| Nat | N | Fmt | S | IT | Infotype Name | Field | Field | Program | Subroutine | > |
|---|---|---|---|---|---|---|---|---|---|---|
| * | All | 1 | 1 | 1034 | Name Format | ANRED | LANGU | RHNAME00 | ANREDE | |
| * | All | 2 | 1 | 1034 | Name Format | TITEL | | RHNAME00 | TITEL | |
| * | All | 2 | 2 | 1000 | Object | SHORT | STEXT | RHNAME00 | VORNAME | |
| * | All | 2 | 3 | 1034 | Name Format | VORSW | | RHNAME00 | VORSATZWORT | |
| * | All | 2 | 4 | 1000 | Object | SHORT | STEXT | RHNAME00 | NACHNAME | |
| * | All | 3 | 1 | 1034 | Name Format | TITEL | | RHNAME00 | TITEL | |
| * | All | 3 | 2 | 1034 | Name Format | VORSW | | RHNAME00 | VORSATZWORT | |
| * | All | 3 | 3 | 1000 | Object | SHORT | | RHNAME00 | NACHNAME | |

## 37.13 WIZARDS

| *Functional Consultant* | *User* | *Business Process Owner* | *Senior Management* | *My Rating* | *Understanding Level* |
|---|---|---|---|---|---|
| A | C | X | X | | |

You can also do customizing of correspondence through wizards. They also result in the same tables getting populated.

## 37.14 MAIL CONNECTION

| *Functional Consultant* | *User* | *Business Process Owner* | *Senior Management* | *My Rating* | *Understanding Level* |
|---|---|---|---|---|---|
| A | C | X | X | | |

### 37.14.1 RFC Destination

RFC destination is set by your Basis consultants using transaction SM59.

### 37.14.2 RFC Destination for Connection to Mail System

| Group | Sem. abbr. | Value abbr. | Description |
|---|---|---|---|
| MAIL | DESTN | | Specify RFC dest. for connection to mail system |

If this setting is blank, messages are sent to the current system. If you specify a RFC destination here, messages will be sent to that system. Your Basis consultant will guide you on this setting.

### 37.14.3 Subtype for Mail Connection

| Group | Sem. abbr. | Value abbr. | Description |
|---|---|---|---|
| MAIL | SAPSY | 0001 | Flagging Mail Addresses in SAP System. |

You can send mail to SAP users. If you are sending mail to an employee, his user id is determined from subtype 0001 of infotype 0105. If you are sending mail to other objects, e.g. organizational units, you take the address from infotype 1032 using subtype specified here. It is recommended that you do not change the standard setting 0001.

# CHAPTER 38 Training Integration

## 38.1 ORGANIZATIONAL MANAGEMENT

| *Functional Consultant* | *User* | *Business Process Owner* | *Senior Management* | *My Rating* | *Understanding Level* |
|---|---|---|---|---|---|
| A | A | B | B | | |

Organizational units can be booked as attendees and can organize business events.

## 38.2 PERSONNEL ADMINISTRATION

| *Functional Consultant* | *User* | *Business Process Owner* | *Senior Management* | *My Rating* | *Understanding Level* |
|---|---|---|---|---|---|
| A | A | B | B | | |

Persons from the HR master data record can be booked as attendees or reserved as instructors.

## 38.3 TIME MANAGEMENT

| *Functional Consultant* | *User* | *Business Process Owner* | *Senior Management* | *My Rating* | *Understanding Level* |
|---|---|---|---|---|---|
| A | A | B | B | | |

### 38.3.1 Integration Switch of Training with Time Management

| Group | Sem. abbr. | Value abbr. | Description |
|---|---|---|---|
| PLOGI | TIME | 1 | Integration switch: Training and Event Mgmt/ Time |

Here you can specify whether Training and Event Management is integrated with Time Management or not. If this field is blank, integration is off. If this field contains 1, integration is on. If integration is on, you can deactivate it for a business event type using the infotype 'Business Event Type Info'.

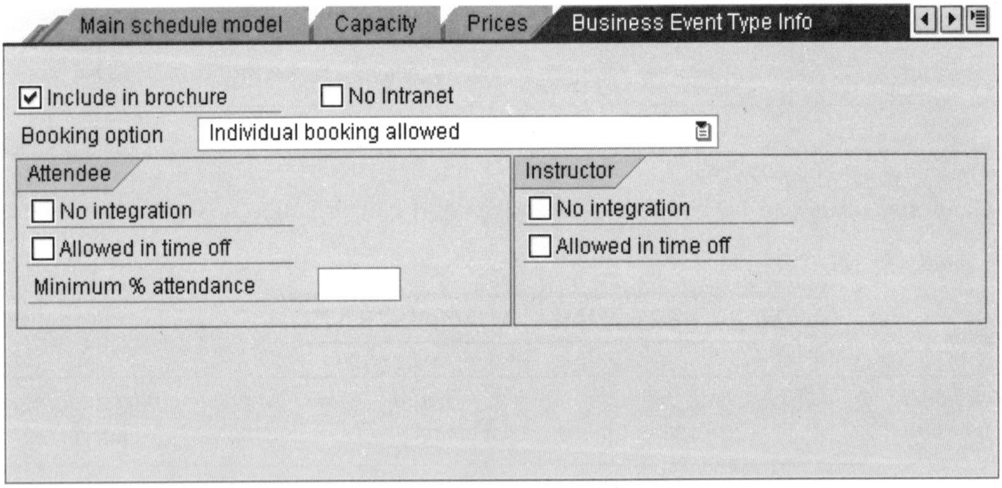


### 38.3.2 Attendance Type for Attendee

| Group | Sem. abbr. | Value abbr. | Description |
|---|---|---|---|
| SEMIN | APART | 0420 | Attendance Type for Attendance in T554S |

If integration with Time Management is active, and an employee is booked to attend a business event, his attendance record is created in Time Management. The value here is used as the attendance type of the infotype 2002 record.

### 38.3.3 Attendance Type for Instructor

| Group | Sem. abbr. | Value abbr. | Description |
|---|---|---|---|
| SEMIN | AINST | 0425 | Attendance type for instructor in T554S |

If integration with Time Management is active, and an employee is reserved to hold a business event as an instructor, his attendance record is created in Time Management. The value here is used as the attendance type of the infotype 2002 record.

### 38.3.4 Minimum Attendance Percentage

If an employee attends a business event partly, would you say that he attended the business event or would you say that he did not? Here you can specify the minimum percentage which the employee must attend to be considered present for the business event.

| Group | Sem. abbr. | Value abbr. | Description |
|---|---|---|---|
| SEMIN | TIMEP | 100 | Minimum percentage attendance |

You can also specify this value for a business event type in infotype 'Business Event Type Info'. If you do so, the value specified for the business event type is taken instead of the global value.

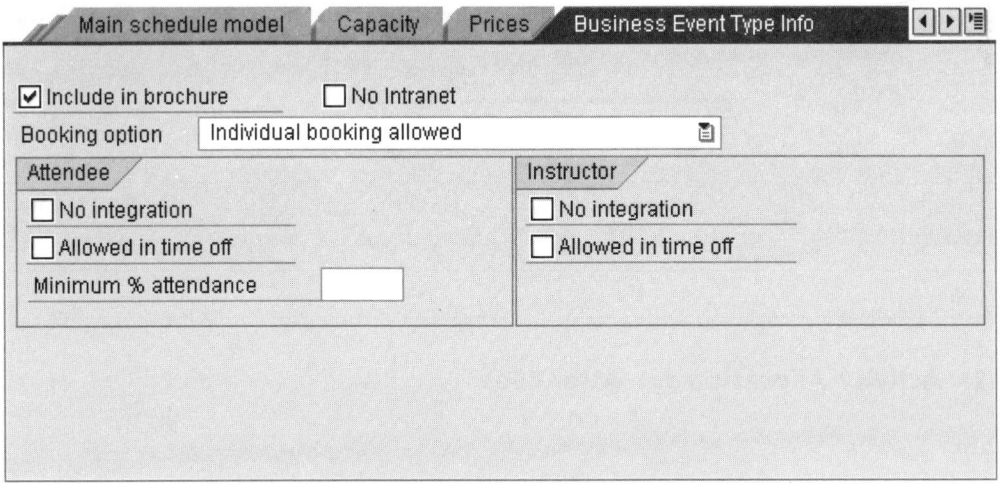


If you create absence records such that the attendance of the attendee falls below the minimum percentage, his booking for the business event is cancelled.

### 38.3.5 Incompatible Attendance and Absence Types

Refer to chapter 36.2.6.

## 38.4 PERSONNEL DEVELOPMENT

| *Functional Consultant* | *User* | *Business Process Owner* | *Senior Management* | *My Rating* | *Understanding Level* |
|---|---|---|---|---|---|
| A | A | B | B | | |

### 38.4.1 Training with Qualification

Qualifications can be prerequisites for business events. Training programs can impart qualifications. When a person completes a training program, this qualification can be added to his profile. Based on qualification deficits in profile matchup, training programs can be proposed.

### 38.4.2 Training with Development Plan Item

Change in the status of a development plan item, which is a training program, can result in the employee being booked for the training program. Conversely, booking for a training program, which is also a development plan item, can result in the change of status of the development plan item.

### 38.4.3 Training with Appraisal

You can hold business event appraisals and attendee appraisals.

## 38.5 ACTIVITY ALLOCATION

| *Functional Consultant* | *User* | *Business Process Owner* | *Senior Management* | *My Rating* | *Understanding Level* |
|---|---|---|---|---|---|
| A | A | B | B | | |

### 38.5.1 Activity Allocation for Attendees

***Purpose***

Attendance fees can be settled using internal activity allocation. The employee's cost center is debited and the organizer's cost center is credited. The amount charged is specified in the internal price field of the business event.

***Prerequisites***

- The business event should be firmly booked.
- The business event should have internal price.

- ➢ For the attendee, the business event should not be free of charge.
- ➢ The attendee should not be on the waiting list.
- ➢ The organizer must have a cost center (sender cost center).
- ➢ The employee must have a cost center (receiver cost center).
- ➢ Both cost centers must be in the same controlling area.
- ➢ Configuration given in this chapter should be maintained.

### *Activity allocation*

You run transaction PV18 to do activity allocation for attendees. You get the following screen.

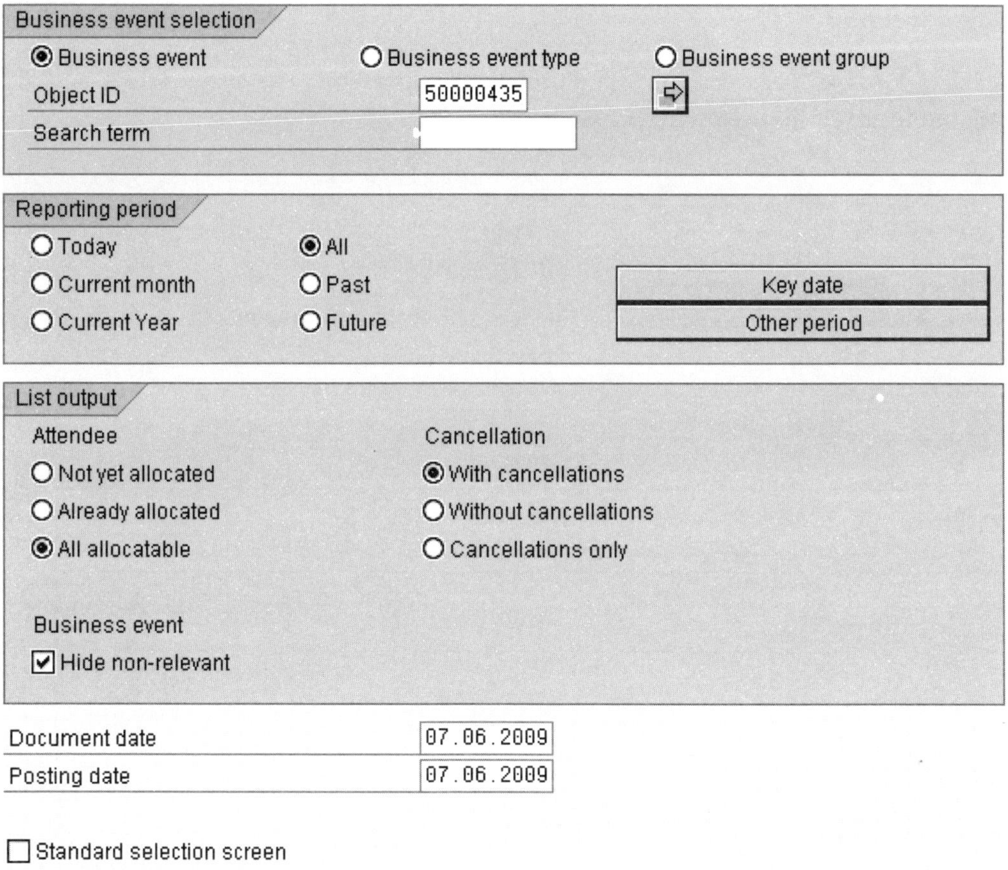


You enter the business event for which you want to do activity allocation, and other details, and Execute.

### *Activity allocation proposal*

| 07.06.2009 | Activity allocation for business events | | 1 |
|---|---|---|---|
| Business event<br>Date | Yoga<br>11.07.2009 - 11.07.2009 | | Internal<br>Firmly booked |
| **Attendees**<br>**Org. assignment** | **Sender CCtr.**<br>**Acty type** | **Internal price**<br>**Account assignment object** | **Document** |
| ☑ 1 N.N.<br>ABC Consultants Ltd. | EDUCATION<br>TRAIN1 | 2,000.00 INR<br>CTR MANAGEMENT | |

### *Activity allocation*

You click [Activity allocation] to carry out activity allocation. The system does activity allocation and gives the following message.

```
Yoga                                      ( E  50000435 11.07.2009 - 11.07.2009  )
S BK 186 Document has no errors.
S BK 003 Document is posted under number 0000000202
S PV 734 Operation stored under reference number 0000000027
```

When you click the previous screen, the system shows the reference document number.

| 07.06.2009 | Activity allocation for business events | | 1 |
|---|---|---|---|
| Business event<br>Date | Yoga<br>11.07.2009 - 11.07.2009 | | Internal<br>Firmly booked |
| **Attendees**<br>**Org. assignment** | **Sender CCtr.**<br>**Acty type** | **Internal price**<br>**Account assignment object** | **Document** |
| ✔1 N.N.<br>ABC Consultants Ltd. | EDUCATION<br>TRAIN1 | 2,000.00 INR<br>CTR MANAGEMENT | △0000000027 |

### *Reference document*

You can click [Document] to display the reference document. Note that the document number field is blank.

| | | | | |
|---|---|---|---|---|
| Ref.Doc.No. | 27 | | Document Date | 07.06.2009 |
| Document number | | | Posting Date | 07.06.2009 |
| Activity | V | Activity allocation | User Name | P_PKA00137 |
| Status | 3 | Transfer effected | | |
| Business event | 50000435 | Yoga | | |

**Document items**

| Item | O | Object ID | Amount | C... | Pe | Tot... | Activity | CO... | Sender co... | Rec. CCtr | R | W | R | R |
|---|---|---|---|---|---|---|---|---|---|---|---|---|---|---|
| 1 | 0 | 50000075 | 2,000.00 | INR | 0.00 | 0.000 | TRAIN1 | 0040 | EDUCATION | MANAGEMENT | | | | 0 |

### *Document comparison*

You place the cursor on the document number and click [Document]. The system gives the following message.

**Compare document 0000000027**

Status change from 'Transfer effected 1' to 'Transfer confirmed 2'

[Yes] [No] [Cancel]

You confirm the change of status and return to the previous page. The change in status is reflected by the icon prefixed to the document number.

07.06.2009 Activity allocation for business events 1

| | | | |
|---|---|---|---|
| Business event | Yoga | | Internal |
| Date | 11.07.2009 - 11.07.2009 | | Firmly booked |

| Attendees / Org. assignment | Sender CCtr. / Acty type | Internal price / Account assignment object | Document |
|---|---|---|---|
| ✔1 N.N. / ABC Consultants Ltd. | EDUCATION / TRAIN1 | 2,000.00 INR / CTR MANAGEMENT | 0000000027 |

If you now display the reference document, it also shows the original document number which was missing earlier.

| | | | |
|---|---|---|---|
| Ref.Doc.No. | 27 | Document Date | 07.06.2009 |
| Document number | 0000000202 | Posting Date | 07.06.2009 |

| | | | | |
|---|---|---|---|---|
| Activity | V | Activity allocation | User Name | P_PKA00137 |
| Status | 4 | Transfer confirmed | | |

Business event 50000435 Yoga

Document items

| Item | O | Object ID | Amount | C | Pe | Tot | Activity | CO | Sender co | Rec. CCtr | R | W | R | R |
|---|---|---|---|---|---|---|---|---|---|---|---|---|---|---|
| 1 | 0 | 50000075 | 2,000.00 | INR | 0.00 | 0.000 | TRAIN1 | 0040 | EDUCATION | MANAGEMENT | | | | 0 |

***Original document***

Now you can also display the original document by clicking [Original document].

Entry Data | Additional Info

| | | | |
|---|---|---|---|
| Doc. Date | 07.06.2009 | | |
| Postg Date | 07.06.2009 | Period | 6 |
| DocumentNo | 202 | Number Ranges | |
| Doc. Text | Yoga 20090711 - 20090711 | | |

Scrn var. 01SAP Cost center    Input Type L List Entry

1 Items

| ItmNo. | Send. CCtr | SAtyTyp | Rec. CCtr | Total | UM | Text | Amount | Crcy | Cost Elem. |
|---|---|---|---|---|---|---|---|---|---|
| 0001 | EDUCATION | TRAIN1 | MANAGEMENT | 1 | PC | 1 N.N. | 2,000.00 | INR | 403010 |

***Document flow***

You can see the link between the reference document and the original document by clicking [Document flow].

| | Ref. | Item | Activity | Status | Amount | Currency | Business event | Total quantity | Document |
|---|---|---|---|---|---|---|---|---|---|
| | 27 | 1 | V | 4 | 2,000.00 | INR | 50000435 | 0.000 | 0000000202 |

You can see a lot more information about the reference documents by running transaction RE_RHREFDOC0. Since these reference documents are for business events, the object type is E. For activity allocation of attendees, select V in the field 'Document Operation'.

| R | D | | Doc. Date | Postg Date | O | S | Doc. no. | PV | OT | Event | OT | ID rel.obj | Amount | Crcy |
|---|---|---|---|---|---|---|---|---|---|---|---|---|---|---|
| 27 | 1 | 1 | 07.06.2009 | 07.06.2009 | V | 4 | 0000000202 | 01 | E | 50000435 | O | 50000075 | 2,000.00 | INR |

***Log***

You can see the log by clicking [icon].

```
Yoga                                           ( E  50000435 11.07.2009 - 11.07.2009  )
S PV 000 Status change effected
```

## 38.5.2 Activity Allocation for Instructor

***Purpose***

Instructor fees can be settled using internal activity allocation. The organizer's cost center is debited and the instructor's cost center is credited. The amount charged is specified in the cost infotype of the resource type to which the instructor belongs.

***Prerequisites***

- The business event should be firmly booked.
- Instructor should have been specifically added to the business event in resource selection.
- The resource type must have a cost center (sender cost center).
- The organizer must have a cost center (receiver cost center).
- Both cost centers must be in the same controlling area.
- Cost item must be maintained for resource type for determining the amount to be transferred.
- Configuration given in this chapter should be maintained.

### Activity allocation

You run transaction PV19 to do activity allocation for instructor. You get the following screen.

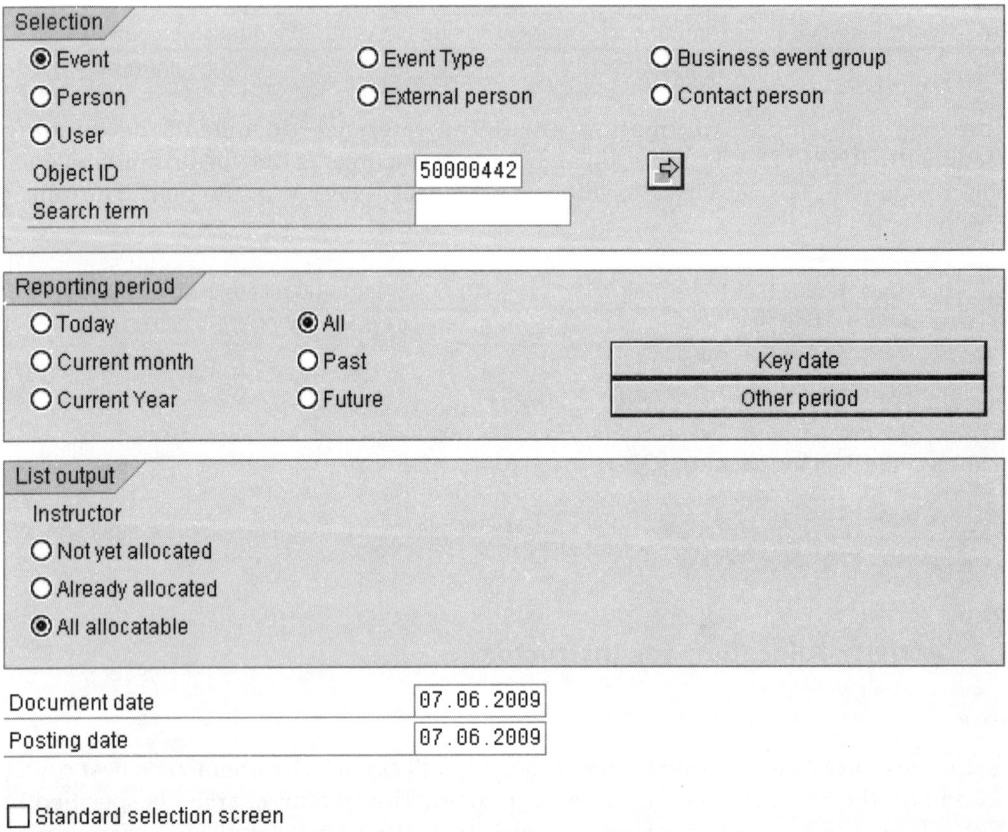


You enter the business event for which you want to do activity allocation, and other details, and Execute.

### Activity allocation proposal

07.06.2009 Activity Allocation for Instructor Function 1

| Business event | SAP HR | Internal |
|---|---|---|
| Date | 20.08.2009 - 22.08.2009 | Firmly booked |

| Instructor<br>Resource type | Sender CCtr.<br>Acty type | Internal price<br>Account assignment object | Document |
|---|---|---|---|
| ✔Naresh Kumar<br>SAP HR Instructor | MANAGEMENT<br>TEACHG | 2,400.00 INR<br>CTR EDUCATION | |

### *Activity allocation*

You click [Activity allocation] to carry out activity allocation. The system does activity allocation and gives the following message.

```
SAP HR                                          20.08.2009 - 22.08.2009
S BK 186 Document has no errors.
S BK 003 Document is posted under number 0000000204
S PV 734 Operation stored under reference number 0000000029
```

When you click the previous screen, the system shows the reference document number.

07.06.2009 Activity Allocation for Instructor Function 1

| Business event<br>Date | SAP HR<br>20.08.2009 - 22.08.2009 | | Internal<br>Firmly booked |
|---|---|---|---|
| **Instructor**<br>**Resource type** | **Sender CCtr.**<br>**Acty type** | **Internal price**<br>**Account assignment object** | **Document** |
| ✔Naresh Kumar<br>SAP HR Instructor | MANAGEMENT<br>TEACHG | 2,400.00 INR<br>CTR EDUCATION | △0000000029 |

### *Reference document*

You can click [Document] to display the reference document. Note that the document number field is blank.

| | | | |
|---|---|---|---|
| Ref.Doc.No. | 29 | Document Date | 07.06.2009 |
| Document number | | Posting Date | 07.06.2009 |
| Activity | W Instructor allocation | User Name | P_PKA00137 |
| Status | 3 Transfer effected | | |
| Business event | 50000442 SAP HR | | |

Document items

| Item | O | Object ID | Amount | Cur | Per | Total | Activity | CO | Sender cos | Rec. CCtr | R | W | R | R |
|---|---|---|---|---|---|---|---|---|---|---|---|---|---|---|
| 1 | H | 50000293 | 2,400.00 | INR | 0.00 | 0.000 | TEACHG | 0040 | MANAGEMENT | EDUCATION | | | | 0 |
| | | | | | | | | | | | | | | |

### *Document comparison*

You place the cursor on the document number and click [Document]. The system gives the following message.

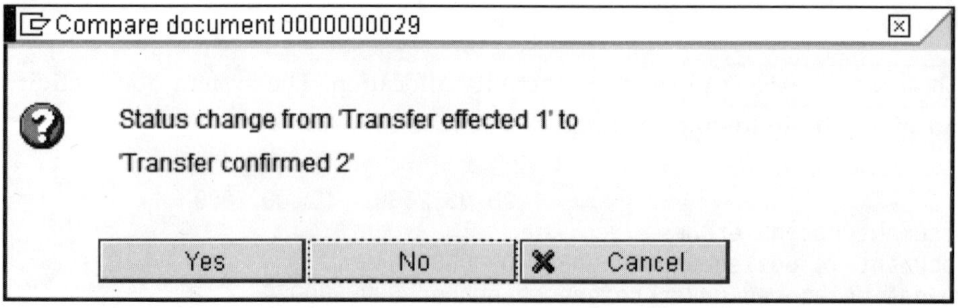


You confirm the change of status and return to the previous page. The change in status is reflected by the icon prefixed to the document number.

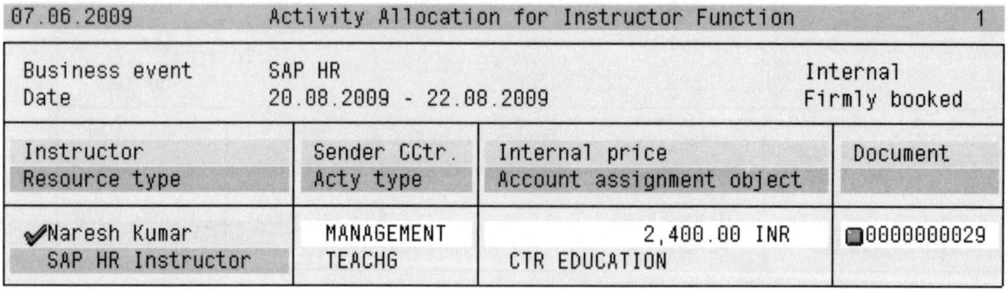


If you now display the reference document, it also shows the original document number which was missing earlier.

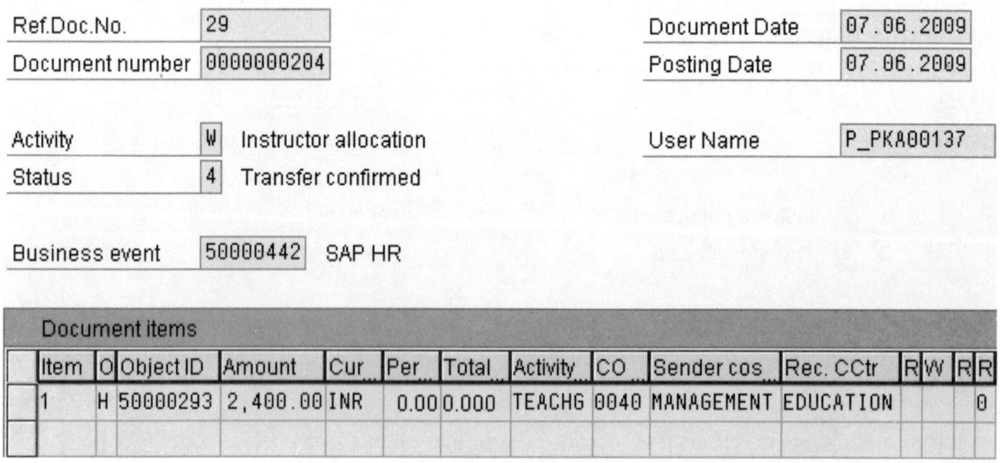

### *Original document*

Now you can also display the original document by clicking [Original document].

Entry Data | Additional Info

| | | | |
|---|---|---|---|
| Doc. Date | 07.06.2009 | | |
| Postg Date | 07.06.2009 | Period | 6 |
| DocumentNo | 204 | Number Ranges | |
| Doc. Text | SAP HR 20090820 - 20090822 | | |

Scrn var. 01SAP Cost center    Input Type L List Entry

1 Items

| Itm | Send. CCtr | SAtyTyp | Rec. CCtr | T | UM | Text | Amount | Crcy | Cost |
|---|---|---|---|---|---|---|---|---|---|
| 0001 | MANAGEMENT | TEACHG | EDUCATION | 1 | PC | H 50000293 | 2,400.00 | INR | 403010 |
| | | | | | | | | | |

### *Document flow*

You can see the link between the reference document and the original document by clicking [Document flow].

| Ref. | Item | Activity | Status | Amount | Currency | Business event | Total quantity | Document |
|---|---|---|---|---|---|---|---|---|
| 29 | 1 | W | 4 | 2,400.00 | INR | 50000442 | 0.000 | 0000000204 |

You can see a lot more information about the reference documents by running transaction RE_RHREFDOC0. Since these reference documents are for business events, the object type is E. For activity allocation of instructors, select W in the field 'Document Operation'.

| R | D | | Doc. Date | Postg Date | O | S | Doc. no. | PV | OT | Event | OT | ID rel.obj | Amount | Crcy |
|---|---|---|---|---|---|---|---|---|---|---|---|---|---|---|
| 28 | 1 | 1 | 07.06.2009 | 07.06.2009 | W | 4 | 0000000203 | 01 | E | 50000441 | H | 50000293 | | |
| 29 | 1 | 1 | 07.06.2009 | 07.06.2009 | W | 4 | 0000000204 | 01 | E | 50000442 | H | 50000293 | 2,400.00 | INR |

### *Log*

You can see the log by clicking [icon].

```
SAP HR                                     20.08.2009 - 22.08.2009
S PV 000 Status change effected
```

## 38.5.3 Activity Allocation Switch

| Group | Sem. abbr. | Value abbr. | Description |
|---|---|---|---|
| SEMIN | INLV | 1 | Integration switch: activity allocation |

If you want to use activity allocation for attendees and instructors, set this switch to 1.

### 38.5.4 Number Range

NR Object: TEM: Reference nos

Intervals

| No. | From number | To number | Current number | Ext |
|---|---|---|---|---|
| 01 | 0000000001 | 0000999999 | 0 | ☐ |

You maintain number range for reference documents using transaction OORB.

### 38.5.5 Controlling Area Selection

| Group | Sem. abbr. | Value abbr. | Description |
|---|---|---|---|
| PPINT | PPINT | 0040 | Default value for controlling area |

Here you specify the default value for controlling area in which activity allocation takes place.

### 38.5.6 Cost Center Selection

Internal activity allocation for attendance fees lets you settle costs for in-company activities between the cost object and the attendees of a business event. In this process, attendance fees are debited from the cost center of the attendee, and the cost center of the cost object is credited. In internal activity allocation for instructor, the instructor's cost center is credited and the cost center of the cost object is debited.

| Group | Sem. abbr. | Value abbr. | Description |
|---|---|---|---|
| SEMIN | COSTC | LSOCOSTC | Cost center of business event cost object |

Cost center of the cost object is found using the evaluation path specified here. Evaluation path LSOCOSTC specifies that the attendance fee be credited to, and instructor fee be debited to, the organizational units which organize the business events.

Evaluation Path: LSOCOSTC Cost object of course

| No. | Obj.Type | A/B | Relat'ship | Relationship name | Priority | Rel.obj.type | Skip |
|---|---|---|---|---|---|---|---|
| 10 | E | A | 036 | Is organized by | * | O | ☐ |
| 20 | ET | A | 036 | Is organized by | * | O | ☐ |
| 30 | O | A | 011 | Cost center assignment | * | K | ☐ |

If the system finds no cost center along the evaluation path, it takes the cost center from the following entry.

| Group | Sem. abbr. | Value abbr. | Description |
|---|---|---|---|
| SEMIN | SCOST | EDUCATION | Sender cost center for internal act. allocation |

### 38.5.7 Cost Element

| CO Area | Cost Element | Name | Long Text | C... |
|---|---|---|---|---|
| 0040 | 403010 | Training allocation | Training allocation | 43 |

Here you specify a secondary cost element for activity allocation.

### 38.5.8 Activity Type Determination

| Group | Sem. abbr. | Value abbr. | Description |
|---|---|---|---|
| SEMIN | FLWAY | LSOFLWAY | Info determination for billing and allocation |
| SEMIN | LEART | TRAIN1 | Activity type for activity allocation |
| SEMIN | RLART | TEACHG | Activity type for instructor settlement |

In order to do activity allocation for internal attendees and instructors, you determine their activity types. The activity types are determined in the following sequence.

- Activity type of the organizational unit which organizes the business event.
- Activity type of the business event type.
- Activity type for Training and Event Management.

Activity type of the organizational unit which organizes the business event and activity type of the business event type are maintained in the Billing/Allocation Info infotype. Activity type for Training and Event Management is specified in the screen above. The logic that the activity type of the organizational unit which organizes the business event should be picked up first is specified in the evaluation path LSOFLWAY.

Evaluation Path LSOFLWAY Billing/Allocation Info (infotype 1037) LSO

| No. | Obj.Type | A/B | Relat'ship | Relationship name | Priority | Rel.obj.type | Skip |
|---|---|---|---|---|---|---|---|
| 10 | E | A | 036 | Is organized by | * | O | ☐ |
| 20 | ET | A | 036 | Is organized by | * | O | ☐ |
| 30 | E | A | 020 | Is a specialization of | * | D | ☐ |
| 40 | ET | A | 020 | Is a specialization of | * | D | ☐ |

### 38.5.9 Wizard

The above settings can also be done through wizard.

### 38.5.10 Number Ranges for Controlling Documents

You need to run transaction KANK and ensure that a number range is assigned to transaction RKL in it (Controlling ➢ General Controlling ➢ Organization ➢ Maintain Number Ranges for Controlling Documents).

### 38.5.11 Activity Type

Your CO consultant will define the activity types required for the attendee and instructor functions using transaction KL01.

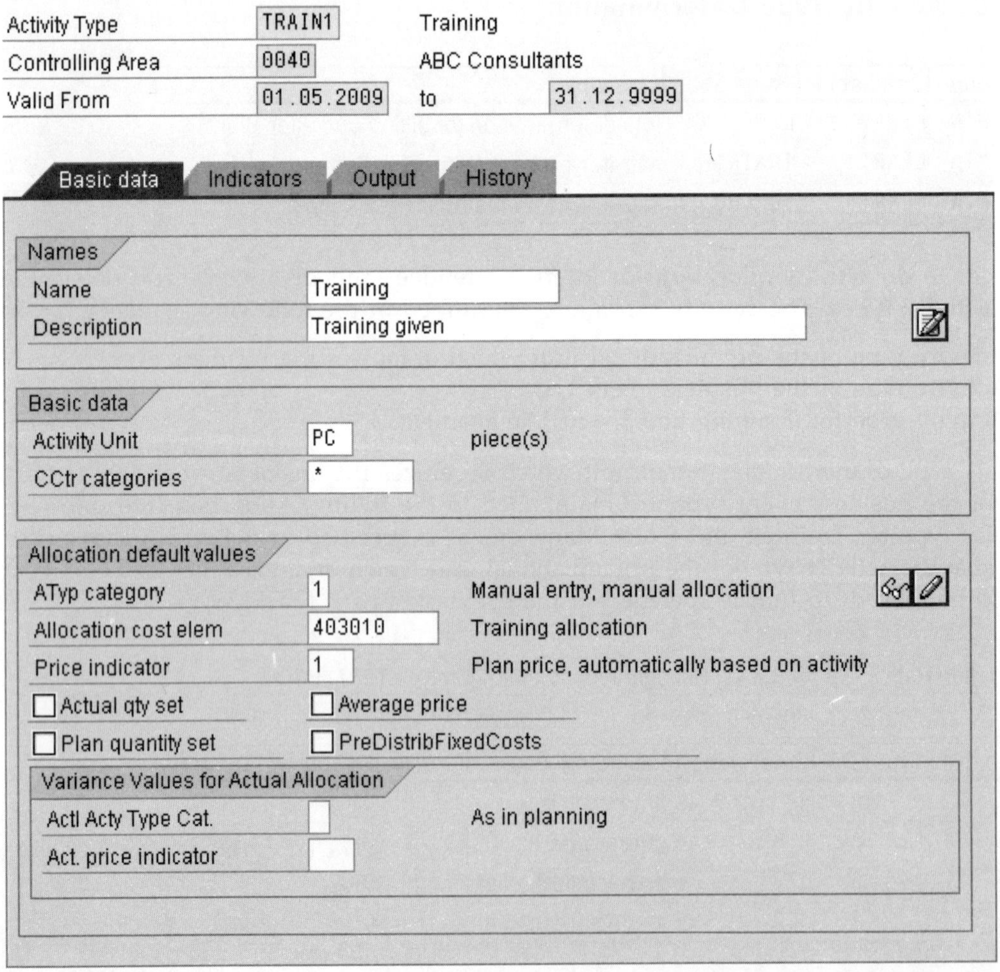

You should make the following settings.

| *Field* | *Value* |
|---|---|
| Activity unit | PC |
| Activity type category | 1 |
| Allocation cost element | Should be a secondary cost element which has cost element type 43 (internal activity allocation). Secondary cost elements are created using transaction KA06. |
| Price indicator | 1 |

### 38.5.12 Activity Price

In Controlling, you specify which cost centers produce which activities and what their prices are. In activity allocation of attendees the price comes from the internal price of the business event. Similarly, the instructor fee comes from the cost of the resource type of the instructor. Therefore, you need to define that the prices of both these activities are manual. You do so in transaction KP26 for each cost center where the activity can be produced (sender cost center). For attendees, the sender cost center is the organizer organizational unit's cost center. For instructors, the sender cost center is the cost center of the resource type of the instructor.

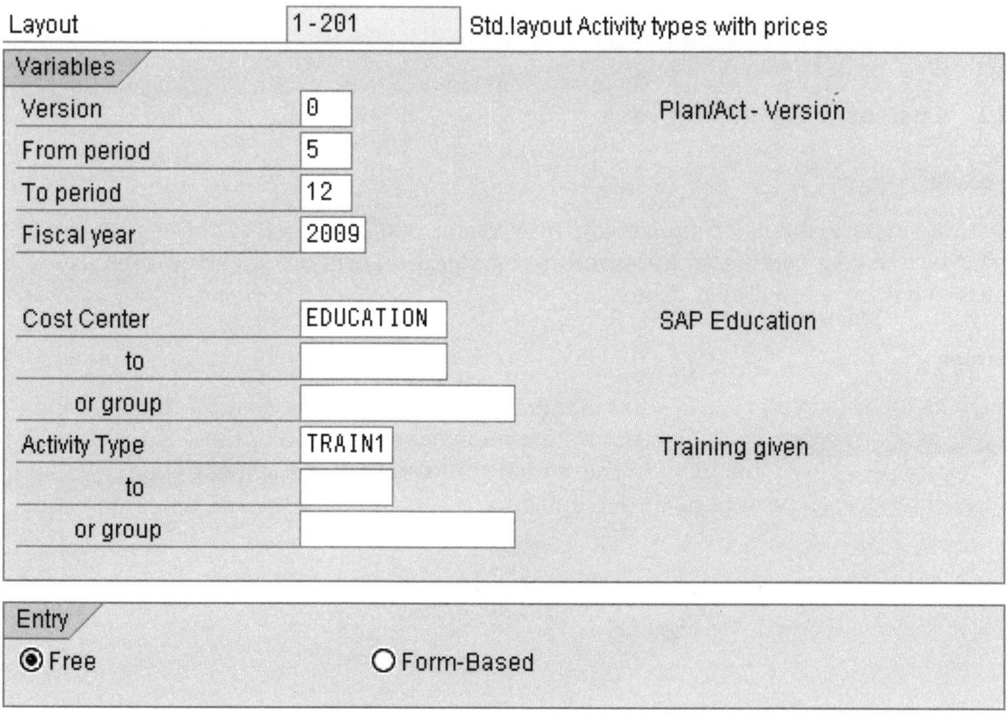

You click to specify the pricing mechanism for the activity type.

| | | | |
|---|---|---|---|
| Version | 0 | | Plan/Act - Version |
| Period | 5 | To | 12 |
| Fiscal Year | 2009 | | |
| Cost Center | EDUCATION | | SAP Education |

| ActType | Planned ... | DK | Capacity | DK | Un | Fixe ... | Vari ... | Price ... | PPI | A | Alloc. ... | C | E | A ... | T |
|---|---|---|---|---|---|---|---|---|---|---|---|---|---|---|---|
| TRAIN1 | | 2 | | 2 | PC | | | 00001 | 3 | ☐ | 403010 | 1 | | | ☐ |

Since the pricing of both attendees and instructors are defined in Training and Event Management, you do not need to specify the fixed cost, variable cost, planned activity quantity and capacity. You set the field PPI to 3, specifying that the price is determined manually.

## 38.6 COST TRANSFER POSTING

| *Functional Consultant* | *User* | *Business Process Owner* | *Senior Management* | *My Rating* | *Understanding Level* |
|---|---|---|---|---|---|
| A | A | B | B | | |

### 38.6.1 Cost of a Business Event

#### *Cost center*

When a business event is conducted, it uses resources. The cost of these resources is incurred by the cost centers of these resources. Certain costs are incurred directly by a business event in its own cost center.

#### *Cost item*

You may incur various types of costs in maintaining a resource. For example, in maintaining a PC you may incur depreciation cost and maintenance cost. Each of these is called a cost item. Details of a cost item include the amount and unit (per business event, per unit time, per attendee or per attendee per unit time).

## 38.6.2 Cost Transfer Posting

***Purpose***

The purpose of cost transfer posting is to transfer the cost of resources from the cost center of the resources to the cost center of the organizational unit organizing the business event. Costs incurred directly by a business event are also transferred from the cost center of the business event to the cost center of the organizational unit organizing the business event.

***Prerequisites***

Before you do cost transfer posting, you should ensure that

- The business event is in firmly booked status.
- The organizer of the business event is an organizational unit and it has a cost center.
- The resources used by the business event have cost centers.
- All cost centers are in the same controlling area.
- The cost data of the resources and business event is maintained.
- The customizing discussed in this chapter is done.

***Cost transfer posting***

You run transaction PV1C to do cost transfer posting. The system gives you the following selection screen.

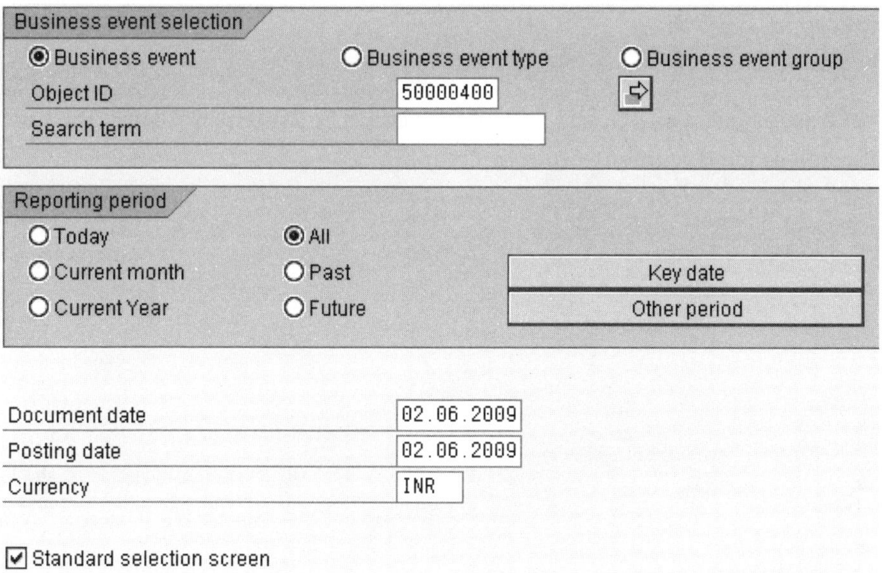


You enter the necessary details and Execute to get the cost calculation.

### *Business event cost calculation*

02.06.2009 Business event cost items 1

| Business event | SAP HR | Internal |
|---|---|---|
| Date | 25.05.2009 - 27.05.2009 | Firmly booked |

| Cost item<br>Cost origin | Sender CCtr.<br>Number | Account assignment object<br>Amount | Cost elemen<br>Ref. unit |
|---|---|---|---|
| ☑ Depreciation | MANAGEMENT | CTR EDUCATION | 403000 |
| Overhead Projector 1 | 1 | 72.00 INR | TIME |
| ☑ Depreciation | MANAGEMENT | CTR EDUCATION | 403000 |
| Personnel Computer 11 | 1 | 72.00 INR | TIME |
| ☑ Depreciation | MANAGEMENT | CTR EDUCATION | 403000 |
| Personnel Computer 12 | 1 | 72.00 INR | TIME |
| ☑ Depreciation | MANAGEMENT | CTR EDUCATION | 403000 |
| Personnel Computer 13 | 1 | 72.00 INR | TIME |
| ☑ Depreciation | MANAGEMENT | CTR EDUCATION | 403000 |
| Personnel Computer 14 | 1 | 72.00 INR | TIME |
| ☑ Depreciation | MANAGEMENT | CTR EDUCATION | 403000 |
| Personnel Computer 15 | 1 | 72.00 INR | TIME |
| ☑ Electricity | MANAGEMENT | CTR EDUCATION | 403000 |
| Overhead Projector 1 | 1 | 78.00 INR | TIME |
| ☑ Room Rent | MANAGEMENT | CTR EDUCATION | 403000 |
| Conference Room | 1 | 2,400.00 INR | TIME |
| ☑ Transfer costs | | Σ 2,910.00 INR | |

### *Cost transfer*

If the calculations are correct, you click [Cost transfer]. The system transfers the cost and gives you the reference document number created.

### *Reference document*

You can click [Document] to display the reference document. Note that the document number is blank.

| | | | |
|---|---|---|---|
| Ref.Doc.No. | 22 | Document Date | 02.06.2009 |
| Document number | | Posting Date | 02.06.2009 |
| Activity | U Cost transfer | User Name | P_PKA00137 |
| Status | 3 Transfer effected | | |
| Business event | 50000400 SAP HR | | |

Document items

| Item | Cost it | Amount | C | Qty | Unit | Cost Elem | Sender cos | Receiver c | Co | Ref | Tim |
|---|---|---|---|---|---|---|---|---|---|---|---|
| 1 | DEPREC | 72.00 | INR | 1.000 | | 403000 | MANAGEMENT | EDUCATION | 0040 | | |
| 2 | DEPREC | 72.00 | INR | 1.000 | | 403000 | MANAGEMENT | EDUCATION | 0040 | | |
| 3 | DEPREC | 72.00 | INR | 1.000 | | 403000 | MANAGEMENT | EDUCATION | 0040 | | |
| 4 | DEPREC | 72.00 | INR | 1.000 | | 403000 | MANAGEMENT | EDUCATION | 0040 | | |
| 5 | DEPREC | 72.00 | INR | 1.000 | | 403000 | MANAGEMENT | EDUCATION | 0040 | | |
| 6 | DEPREC | 72.00 | INR | 1.000 | | 403000 | MANAGEMENT | EDUCATION | 0040 | | |
| 7 | ENERGY | 78.00 | INR | 1.000 | | 403000 | MANAGEMENT | EDUCATION | 0040 | | |
| 8 | RENT | 2,400.00 | INR | 1.000 | | 403000 | MANAGEMENT | EDUCATION | 0040 | | |

Total amount 2,910.00 INR

### *Document comparison*

You place the cursor on the document number and click [Document]. The system gives the following message.

Compare document 0000000022

Status change from 'Transfer effected 1' to 'Transfer confirmed 2'

[Yes] [No] [Cancel]

You confirm the change of status and return to the previous page. The change in status is reflected by the icon prefixed to the document number. It changes from 0000000022 to 0000000022. If you now display the reference document, it also shows the original document number which was missing earlier.

Ref.Doc.No. 22 Document Date 02.06.2009

Document number 0000000101 Posting Date 02.06.2009

Activity U Cost transfer User Name P_PKA00137

Status 4 Transfer confirmed

Business event 50000400 SAP HR

Document items

| Item | Cost item | Amount | C... | Qty | Unit | Cost Elem... | Sender cos... | Receiver c... | Co... | R | T |
|---|---|---|---|---|---|---|---|---|---|---|---|
| 1 | DEPREC | 72.00 | INR | 1.000 | | 403000 | MANAGEMENT | EDUCATION | 0040 | | |
| 2 | DEPREC | 72.00 | INR | 1.000 | | 403000 | MANAGEMENT | EDUCATION | 0040 | | |
| 3 | DEPREC | 72.00 | INR | 1.000 | | 403000 | MANAGEMENT | EDUCATION | 0040 | | |
| 4 | DEPREC | 72.00 | INR | 1.000 | | 403000 | MANAGEMENT | EDUCATION | 0040 | | |
| 5 | DEPREC | 72.00 | INR | 1.000 | | 403000 | MANAGEMENT | EDUCATION | 0040 | | |
| 6 | DEPREC | 72.00 | INR | 1.000 | | 403000 | MANAGEMENT | EDUCATION | 0040 | | |
| 7 | ENERGY | 78.00 | INR | 1.000 | | 403000 | MANAGEMENT | EDUCATION | 0040 | | |
| 8 | RENT | 2,400.00 | INR | 1.000 | | 403000 | MANAGEMENT | EDUCATION | 0040 | | |

Total amount 2,910.00 INR

### *Original document*

Now you can also display the original document by clicking [Original document].

Entry Data | Additional Info

| | | | |
|---|---|---|---|
| Doc. Date | 02.06.2009 | | |
| Postg Date | 02.06.2009 | Period | 6 |
| DocumentNo | 101 | Number Ranges | |
| Doc. Text | SAP HR 20090525 - 20090527 | | |

Scrn var. 01SAP Cost center     Input Type L List Entry

8 Items

| ItmNo. | CCtr (old) | Cost ... | Amount | Crcy | CCtr (new) | To ... | UM | Text |
|---|---|---|---|---|---|---|---|---|
| 0001 | MANAGEMENT | 403000 | 72.00 | INR | EDUCATION | 1 | PC | G 50000005 OHP 1 |
| 0002 | MANAGEMENT | 403000 | 72.00 | INR | EDUCATION | 1 | PC | G 50000050 PC 11 |
| 0003 | MANAGEMENT | 403000 | 72.00 | INR | EDUCATION | 1 | PC | G 50000051 PC 12 |
| 0004 | MANAGEMENT | 403000 | 72.00 | INR | EDUCATION | 1 | PC | G 50000052 PC 13 |
| 0005 | MANAGEMENT | 403000 | 72.00 | INR | EDUCATION | 1 | PC | G 50000053 PC 14 |
| 0006 | MANAGEMENT | 403000 | 72.00 | INR | EDUCATION | 1 | PC | G 50000054 PC 15 |
| 0007 | MANAGEMENT | 403000 | 78.00 | INR | EDUCATION | 1 | PC | G 50000005 OHP 1 |
| 0008 | MANAGEMENT | 403000 | 2,400.00 | INR | EDUCATION | 1 | PC | G 50000003 Conf. Room |

### *Document flow*

You can see the link between the reference document and the original document by clicking [Document flow].

E 50000400 SAP HR

| Ref.Doc.No. | Item | Activity | Status | Amount | Cur ... | Cost item | Total quantity | Document ... |
|---|---|---|---|---|---|---|---|---|
| 22 | 1 | U | 4 | 72.00 | INR | DEPREC | 1.000 | 0000000101 |
| 22 | 2 | U | 4 | 72.00 | INR | DEPREC | 1.000 | 0000000101 |
| 22 | 3 | U | 4 | 72.00 | INR | DEPREC | 1.000 | 0000000101 |
| 22 | 4 | U | 4 | 72.00 | INR | DEPREC | 1.000 | 0000000101 |
| 22 | 5 | U | 4 | 72.00 | INR | DEPREC | 1.000 | 0000000101 |
| 22 | 6 | U | 4 | 72.00 | INR | DEPREC | 1.000 | 0000000101 |
| 22 | 7 | U | 4 | 78.00 | INR | ENERGY | 1.000 | 0000000101 |
| 22 | 8 | U | 4 | 2,400.00 | INR | RENT | 1.000 | 0000000101 |

You can see a lot more information about the reference documents by running transaction RE_RHREFDOC0. Since these reference documents are for business events, the object type is E. For cost transfer posting, select U in the field 'Document Operation'.

| R... | ▲ | | Doc. Date | Postg Date | O | S | Doc. no. | PV | O | Event | Cost item | Amount | Crcy | Qua... |
|---|---|---|---|---|---|---|---|---|---|---|---|---|---|---|
| 22 | 1 | 1 | 02.06.2009 | 02.06.2009 | U | 4 | 0000000101 | 01 | E | 50000400 | DEPREC | 72.00 | INR | 1.000 |
| 22 | 2 | 1 | 02.06.2009 | 02.06.2009 | U | 4 | 0000000101 | 01 | E | 50000400 | DEPREC | 72.00 | INR | 1.000 |
| 22 | 3 | 1 | 02.06.2009 | 02.06.2009 | U | 4 | 0000000101 | 01 | E | 50000400 | DEPREC | 72.00 | INR | 1.000 |
| 22 | 4 | 1 | 02.06.2009 | 02.06.2009 | U | 4 | 0000000101 | 01 | E | 50000400 | DEPREC | 72.00 | INR | 1.000 |
| 22 | 5 | 1 | 02.06.2009 | 02.06.2009 | U | 4 | 0000000101 | 01 | E | 50000400 | DEPREC | 72.00 | INR | 1.000 |
| 22 | 6 | 1 | 02.06.2009 | 02.06.2009 | U | 4 | 0000000101 | 01 | E | 50000400 | DEPREC | 72.00 | INR | 1.000 |
| 22 | 7 | 1 | 02.06.2009 | 02.06.2009 | U | 4 | 0000000101 | 01 | E | 50000400 | ENERGY | 78.00 | INR | 1.000 |
| 22 | 8 | 1 | 02.06.2009 | 02.06.2009 | U | 4 | 0000000101 | 01 | E | 50000400 | RENT | 2,400.00 | INR | 1.000 |

***Log***

You can see the log by clicking .

```
SAP HR                                      ( E  50000400  ) 25.05.2009 - 27.05.2009
S PV 000 Status change effected
```

### 38.6.3 Cost Transfer Switch

| Group | Sem. abbr. | Value abbr. | Description |
|---|---|---|---|
| SEMIN | UMKO | 0 | Integration switch: cost transfer posting |

If you want to use cost transfer, set this switch to 1.

### 38.6.4 Number Range

NR Object: TEM: Reference nos

Intervals

| No. | From number | To number | Current number | Ext |
|---|---|---|---|---|
| 01 | 0000000001 | 0000999999 | 0 | ☐ |

You maintain number range for reference documents using IMG node Training and Event Management ➢ Basic Settings ➢ Number Range Maintenance ➢ Define Number Ranges for External Operations.

### 38.6.5 Controlling Area Selection

| Group | Sem. abbr. | Value abbr. | Description |
|---|---|---|---|
| PPINT | PPINT | 0040 | Default value for controlling area |

Here you specify the default value for controlling area in which cost transfer takes place.

### 38.6.6 Cost Center Selection

| Group | Sem. abbr. | Value abbr. | Description |
|---|---|---|---|
| SEMIN | COSTC | LSOCOSTC | Cost center of business event cost object |

Costs are debited to the cost center of the cost object of a business event, which is found using the evaluation path specified here. Evaluation path LSOCOSTC specifies that the cost be debited to the organizational units which organize the business event.

Evaluation Path LSOCOSTC Cost object of course

| No. | Obj.Type | A/B | Relat'ship | Relationship name | Priority | Rel.obj.type | Skip |
|---|---|---|---|---|---|---|---|
| 10 | E | A | 036 | Is organized by | * | O | ☐ |
| 20 | ET | A | 036 | Is organized by | * | O | ☐ |
| 30 | O | A | 011 | Cost center assignment | * | K | ☐ |

If the system finds no cost center along the evaluation path, it takes the cost center from the following entry.

| Group | Sem. abbr. | Value abbr. | Description |
|---|---|---|---|
| SEMIN | SCOST | MANAGEMENT | Sender cost center for internal act. allocation |

### 38.6.7 Cost Items

| | | |
|---|---|---|
| Cost item | ENERGY | |
| Cost item text | Electricity | |
| Proposed amount | 3.25 | INR |

Periods

| Start | End |
|---|---|
| 01.01.1900 | 31.12.9999 |

Cost assignment per

Attendees ■ Time unit Business event

☑ Per time unit HR Hours

Cost item is

■ Relevant for transfer Not relevant for transfer

Controlling Area 0040 ABC Consultants

Cost Element 403000

Cost items are assigned to resource types, resources, business event types, and business events. Here you specify the amount which is used for cost transfer. The amount may be per attendee, per attendee per time unit, per business event or per time unit. You also specify whether the cost item is relevant for transfer and if so, what is the controlling area and cost element.

### 38.6.8 Wizard

The above settings can also be done through wizard.

### 38.6.9 Number Ranges for Controlling Documents

You need to run transaction KANK and ensure that a number range is assigned to transaction RKU1 in it (Controlling ➢ General Controlling ➢ Organization ➢ Maintain Number Ranges for Controlling Documents).

## 38.7 BILLING

| *Functional Consultant* | *User* | *Business Process Owner* | *Senior Management* | *My Rating* | *Understanding Level* |
|---|---|---|---|---|---|
| A | B | C | C | | |

### 38.7.1 Billing

Integration with Billing lets users of Training and Event Management create invoices for attendance fees for attendees of business events via the Sales and Distribution Billing interface. A billing document is generated in Sales and Distribution per customer and business event, and a billing form is output. You can run transaction PV17 to bill your customers and contact persons who attend your business events.

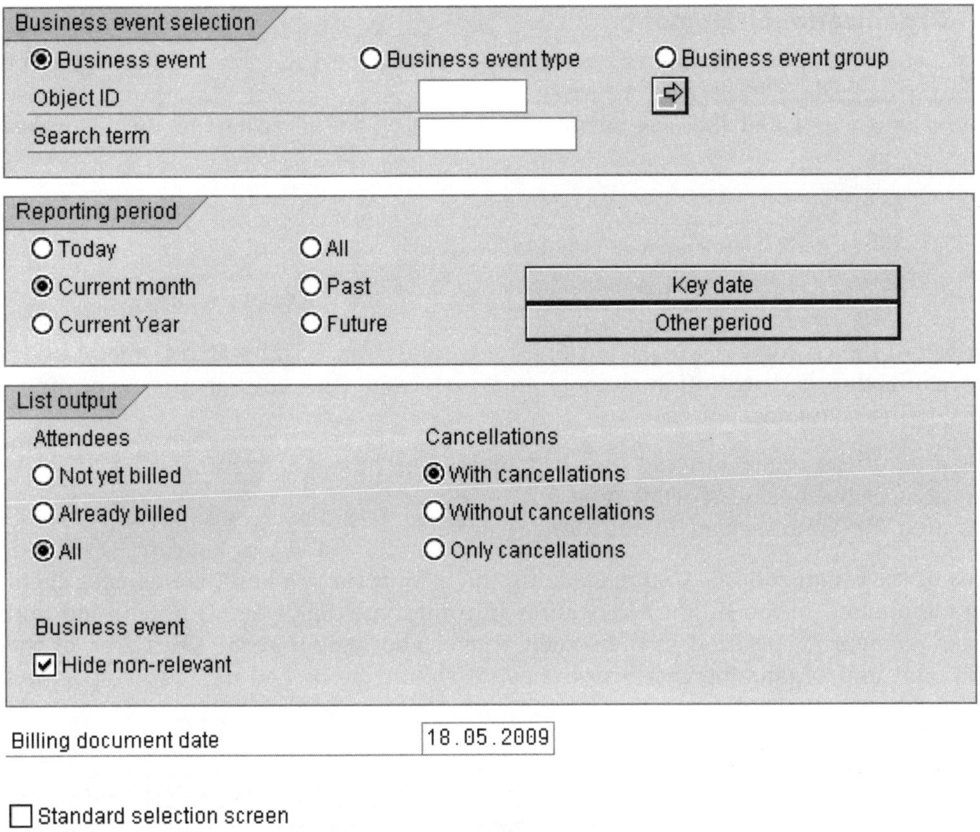


Billing document creation takes place in the same way as activity allocation or cost transfer.

***Check and repair wrong billing documents***

Report RHBELNRFIX checks for wrong billing documents and repairs them. You can do the following checks.

## 38.7.2 Integration Switch of Training with Billing

| Group | Sem. abbr. | Value abbr. | Description |
|---|---|---|---|
| SEMIN | FAKT | 1 | Integration switch: billing |

If customers and contact persons attend your business events and you would like to bill them using Sales and Distribution, you set this switch to 1.

### 38.7.3 Organizational Elements

| Group | Sem. abbr. | Value abbr. | Description |
|---|---|---|---|
| SEMIN | FLWAY | LSOFLWAY | Info determination for billing and allocation |
| SEMIN | KUCPD | | One-time customer for billing |
| SEMIN | SPART | | Division for billing |
| SEMIN | VKORG | | Sales organization for billing |
| SEMIN | VTWEG | | Distribution channel for billing |

In order to bill the customers, you determine their sales area. A sales area is made up of a sales organization, a distribution channel and a division. The sales area is determined in the following sequence.

- Sales area of the organizational unit organizing the business event.
- Sales area of the business event type.
- Sales area for Training and Event Management.

Sales area of the organizational unit organizing the business event and the business event type are maintained in the Billing/Allocation Info infotype. Sales area for Training and Event Management is specified in the screen above. The logic that the sales area of the organizational unit organizing the business event should be picked up first is specified in the evaluation path LSOFLWAY.

Evaluation Path LSOFLWAY Billing/Allocation Info (infotype 1037) LSO

| No. | Obj.Type | A/B | Relat'ship | Relationship name | Priority | Rel.obj.type | Skip |
|---|---|---|---|---|---|---|---|
| 10 | E | A | 036 | Is organized by | * | O | ☐ |
| 20 | ET | A | 036 | Is organized by | * | O | ☐ |
| 30 | E | A | 020 | Is a specialization of | * | D | ☐ |
| 40 | ET | A | 020 | Is a specialization of | * | D | ☐ |

You can also specify a one-time customer in switch KUCPD for attendees that are not assigned to any customer. One-time customers in the SAP System are customers with whom you only do business one time or not on a regular basis. It is not necessary to create a customer master record for such customers.

### 38.7.4 Invoice Creation Settings

| Group | Sem. abbr. | Value abbr. | Description |
|---|---|---|---|
| SEMIN | AUART | TA | Sales document type for billing interface |
| SEMIN | FKARA | FX | Billing type for billing interface |
| SEMIN | PSTYV | DLN | Item category for billing interface |

These settings are done on the advice of Sales and Distribution consultant. Usually the default settings are good enough.

### 38.7.5 Credit Memo Creation Settings

| Group | Sem. abbr. | Value abbr. | Description |
|---|---|---|---|
| SEMIN | GKARA | G2 | Credit memo: billing type |
| SEMIN | GPSTY | G2N | Credit memo: item category |
| SEMIN | GUART | G2 | Credit memo: sales document type |

These settings are done on the advice of the Sales and Distribution consultant. Usually the default settings are good enough.

### 38.7.6 Prices, Taxes and Account Assignment

| Group | Sem. abbr. | Value abbr. | Description |
|---|---|---|---|
| SEMIN | FLWAY | LSOFLWAY | Info determination for billing and allocation |
| SEMIN | KSCHL | PR00 | Condition type for billing |
| SEMIN | KTGRM | | Account assignment group for this material |
| SEMIN | LAND1 | | Country for tax determination in billing |
| SEMIN | PRCTR | 0 | Use of profit centers in billing |

These settings are done on the advice of the Sales and Distribution consultant. Account assignment group for this material is determined in the following sequence.

- Account assignment group for this material of the organizational unit organizing the business event.
- Account assignment group for this material of the business event type.
- Account assignment group for this material for Training and Event Management.

Account assignment group for this material of the organizational unit organizing the business event and the business event type are maintained in the Billing/Allocation Info infotype. Account assignment group for this material for Training and Event Management is specified in the screen above. The logic that the account assignment group for this material of the organizational unit organizing the business event should be picked up first is specified in the evaluation path LSOFLWAY.

Evaluation Path LSOFLWAY Billing/Allocation Info (infotype 1037) LSO

| No. | Obj.Type | A/B | Relat'ship | Relationship name | Priority | Rel.obj.type | Skip |
|---|---|---|---|---|---|---|---|
| 10 | E | A | 036 | Is organized by | * | O | ☐ |
| 20 | ET | A | 036 | Is organized by | * | O | ☐ |
| 30 | E | A | 020 | Is a specialization of | * | D | ☐ |
| 40 | ET | A | 020 | Is a specialization of | * | D | ☐ |

Condition type for billing is specified on the advice of the Sales and Distribution consultant. Attendance fees for business events are transferred to this condition type. For the purpose of tax determination, you specify a country. You also specify whether you want to use profit centers for invoice creation.

### 38.7.7 Wizard

You can also do the above settings using the wizard. Even if you do the customizing without wizard, it is helpful to run the wizard to ensure completeness. The wizard for Billing contains a lot of pointers for configuration in Sales and Distribution.

### 38.7.8 Settings for Payment Cards

If you use payment cards in Sales and Distribution, you do the necessary settings there. In that case, you can also use payment cards for payment of attendance and cancellation fees in Training and Event Management.

## 38.8 MATERIALS MANAGEMENT

| *Functional Consultant* | *User* | *Business Process Owner* | *Senior Management* | *My Rating* | *Understanding Level* |
|---|---|---|---|---|---|
| A | B | C | C | | |

### 38.8.1 Materials Procurement

You may need material to conduct business events. SAP lets you order material for a business event. You first create resource types which are material and specify that a business event type requires those resource types. You also link materials to business event types. When you create a business event with resources, you also specify that you need material resources. Material can be procured only for firmly booked business events. Once you have assigned the firmly booked status to a business event, you can order materials for it. When doing so, you can decide whether material requirements are based on the optimum or the actual number of attendees of the business event. The system automatically creates a material reservation or purchase requisition depending on the availability of material. You can use transaction PV1M to display materials from the material master (resources of the type Material) required by business events.

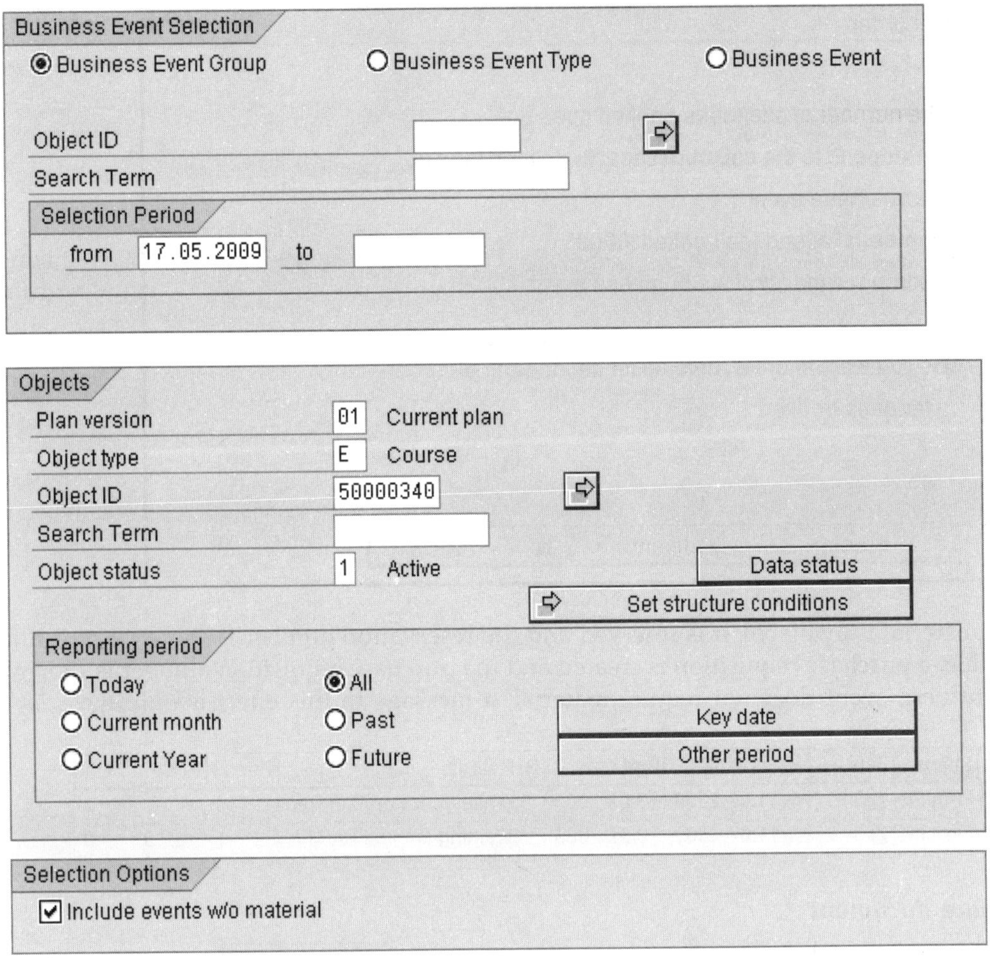


If you enter one or more business event groups, the system determines all business events belonging to the specified groups and displays their material requirements. If you enter one or more business event types, the system determines all business events belonging to the specified types and displays their material requirements. If you enter one or more business events, the system displays their material requirements.

| Busi... | Status | R | R | B | P | Start date | End date | B | Material | Per a... | Per b... | Total |
|---|---|---|---|---|---|---|---|---|---|---|---|---|
| SAP FI | Firm bk | | | | | 11.07.2009 | 13.07.2009 | | White board marker -red | 0 | 1 | 1 |
| SAP FI | Firm bk | | | | | 11.07.2009 | 13.07.2009 | | Training Manual SAP FI | 1 | 0 | 0 |

To order the above material, click Reserve material. If the number of attendees are less than the optimum capacity of the business event, the system asks you whether you will like to order material for the actual number of attendees, or for the optimum capacity.

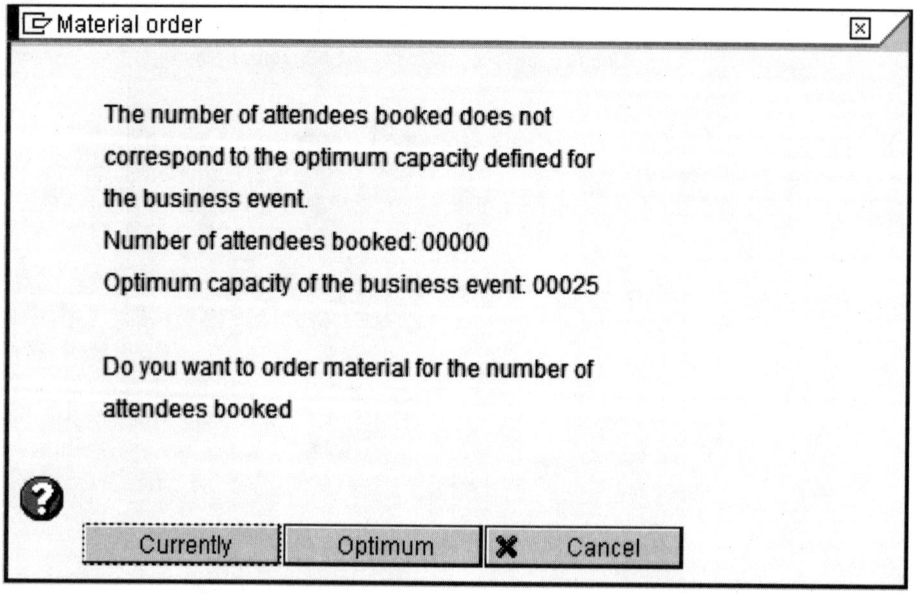


If the material is available, it is reserved and the reservation number is shown. If it is not available, a purchase requisition is created and the purchase requisition number is shown. If a business event does not require material, a message to this effect is output.

| Busi... | Status | R | R... | B | P | Start date | End date | B | Material | Per a... | Per b... | Total |
|---|---|---|---|---|---|---|---|---|---|---|---|---|
| SAP FI | Firm bk | △ | 3 | | | 11.07.2009 | 13.07.2009 | | White board marker -red | 0 | 1 | 1 |
| SAP FI | Firm bk | △ | 3 | | | 11.07.2009 | 13.07.2009 | | Training Manual SAP FI | 1 | 0 | 0 |

***Compare document***

You place the cursor on the document number and click Document. The system gives the following message.

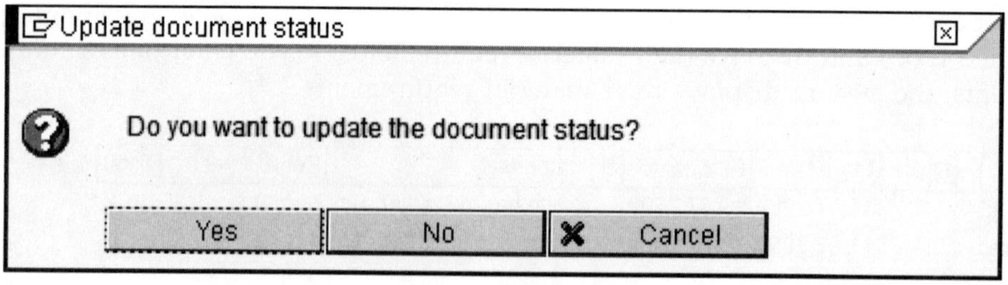


You confirm the change of status and return to the previous page. The change in status is reflected by the change of icon.

### 38.8.2 Integration Switch of Training with Materials Management

| Group | Sem. abbr. | Value abbr. | Description |
|---|---|---|---|
| SEMIN | MAT | 0 | Integration switch: materials management |

In order to reserve material or to raise purchase requisition you need to set this switch to 1.

### 38.8.3 Number Ranges

NR Object TEM: Reference nos

Intervals

| No. | From number | To number | Current number | Ext |
|---|---|---|---|---|
| 01 | 0000000001 | 0000999999 | 0 | ☐ |

You maintain number range for reference documents using IMG node Training and Event Management ➢ Basic Settings ➢ Number Range Maintenance ➢ Define Number Ranges for External Operations.

### 38.8.4 Plant and Storage Location

| Group | Sem. abbr. | Value abbr. | Description |
|---|---|---|---|
| SEMIN | PLANT | 9999 | Plant for material administration |
| SEMIN | STORE | ZCON | Storage location for material administration |

Here you specify a plant and a storage location where reservations and purchase requisitions for Training and Event Management are processed. When you specify the materials that are required for a business event type, materials in this plant and storage location are only available for selection.

### 38.8.5 Default Value for Controlling Area

| Group | Sem. abbr. | Value abbr. | Description |
|---|---|---|---|
| PPINT | PPINT | 0040 | Default value for controlling area |

Here you specify the default value for controlling area in which material costs are posted.

### 38.8.6 Cost Center of Business Event Costs

| Group | Sem. abbr. | Value abbr. | Description |
|---|---|---|---|
| SEMIN | COSTC | LSOCOSTC | Cost center of business event cost object |

Here you specify the evaluation path used to find the cost center of the cost object of a business event. Evaluation path LSOCOSTC specifies that business event costs be charged to the organizational units which organize them.

Evaluation Path LSOCOSTC Cost object of course

| No. | Obj.Type | A/B | Relat'ship | Relationship name | Priority | Rel.obj.type | Skip |
|---|---|---|---|---|---|---|---|
| 10 | E | A | 036 | Is organized by | * | O | ☐ |
| 20 | ET | A | 036 | Is organized by | * | O | ☐ |
| 30 | O | A | 011 | Cost center assignment | * | K | ☐ |

If the system finds no cost center along the evaluation path, it takes the cost center from the following entry.

| Group | Sem. abbr. | Value abbr. | Description |
|---|---|---|---|
| SEMIN | SCOST | EDUCATION | Sender cost center for internal act. allocation |

### 38.8.7 Document Type and Movement Type

| Group | Sem. abbr. | Value abbr. | Description |
|---|---|---|---|
| SEMIN | DOCTY | NB | Purchase requisition (document type) |
| SEMIN | MOVTY | 201 | Reservation: movement type |

While creating a purchase requisition, you need to specify a document type. Here you specify the document type which is used for purchase requisitions created from Training and Event Management. Similarly, while creating material reservation, you need to specify a movement type. Here you specify the movement type which is used for material reservations created from Training and Event Management. Both these are standard settings and should be changed only if recommended by the materials management consultant.

### 38.8.8 Wizard

You can also do the above configuration using wizard.

## 38.9 SAP KNOWLEDGE WAREHOUSE

| *Functional Consultant* | *User* | *Business Process Owner* | *Senior Management* | *My Rating* | *Understanding Level* |
|---|---|---|---|---|---|
| A | B | C | C | | |

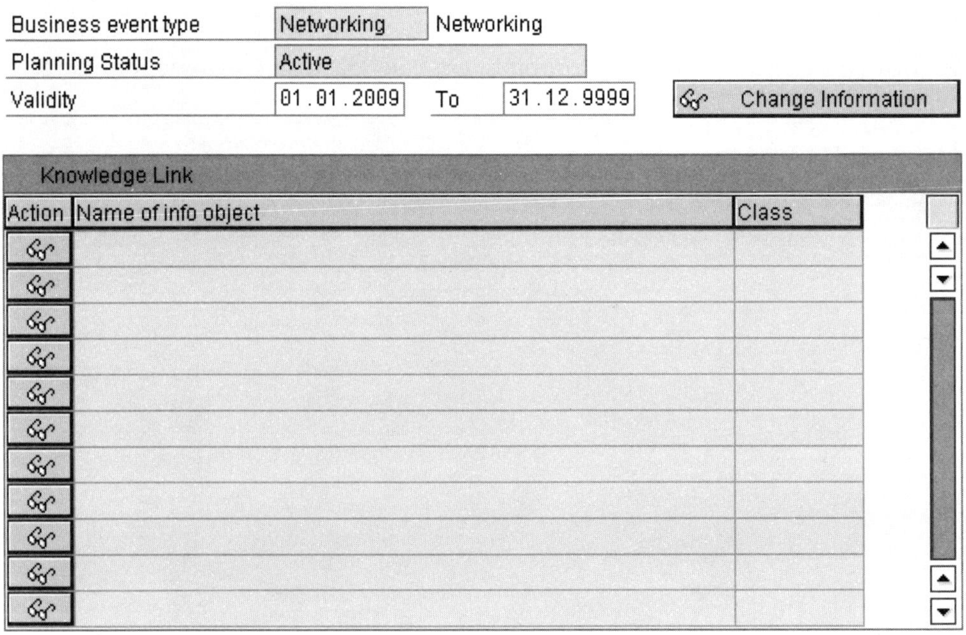


If you have installed SAP Knowledge Warehouse, you can link it with Training and Event Management by means of the Knowledge Link. You can maintain this infotype for business event types and business events.

The Knowledge Link lets you create links from business events to the information material (InfoObjects) stored in SAP Knowledge Warehouse, such as training materials or the complete online documentation in the SAP Library. You can thus access additional relevant information from business events and business event types without creating or copying it. You can display this information from Training and Event Management as well as from Employee Self-Service. When you implement SAP Knowledge Warehouse, you do the configuration given under 'SAP Knowledge Provider'. These are not specific settings required for Training and Event Management.

## 38.10 SAP APPOINTMENT CALENDAR

| *Functional Consultant* | *User* | *Business Process Owner* | *Senior Management* | *My Rating* | *Understanding Level* |
|---|---|---|---|---|---|
| A | B | C | C | | |

### 38.10.1 Appointment Calendar

In SAP Office you can maintain your appointment calendar using transaction SSC1.

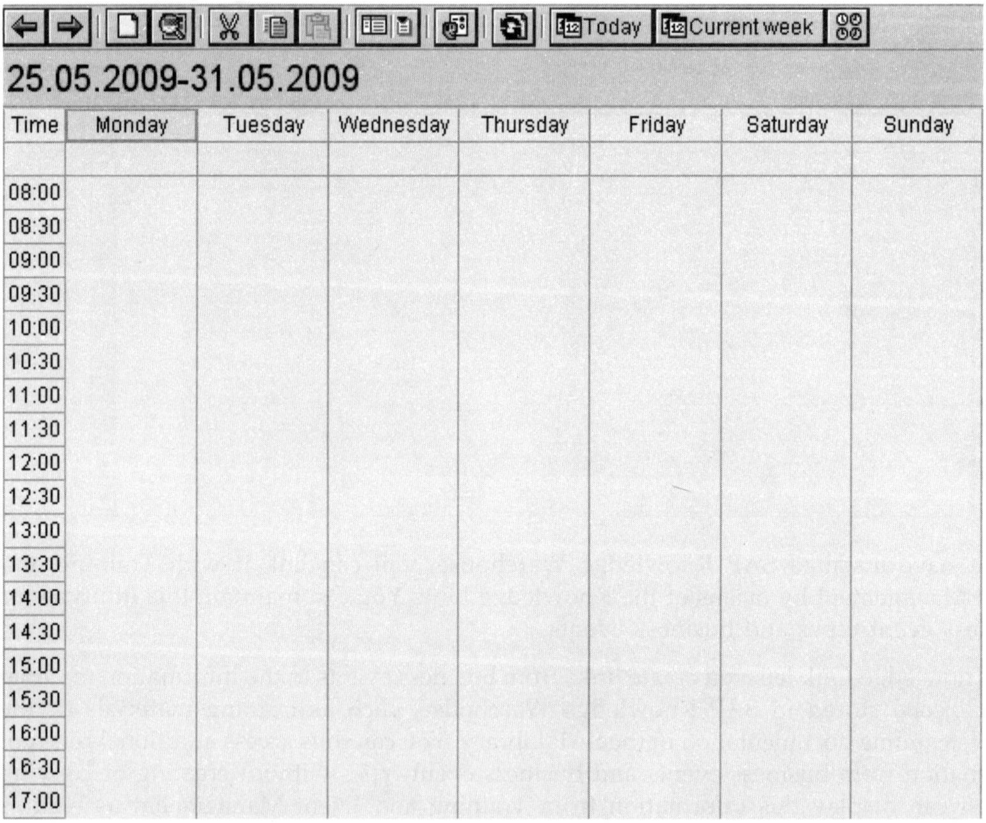


Whenever you are booked as an attendee or an instructor for a business event, the system can automatically create an entry in your appointment calendar.

### 38.10.2 Appointment Types

Appointments are categorized into appointment types. You create appointment types for attending business events and teaching at business events in view SCAPPTTYPE.

| Date Type | ATTENDEE |
|---|---|

**Appointment Type**

| Description | Attending a Business Event |
|---|---|
| Function module | |
| Color of appointments | |
| Icon for appt.types | |

☐ Title is required

| Not allowed in R/3 calendar | Not allowed outside R/3 |
|---|---|
| ☐ Create | ☐ Create |
| ☐ Change | ☐ Change |
| ☐ Delete | ☐ Delete |

### 38.10.3 Specifying Appointment Types

In view T77S0, you specify appointment types for attendees and instructors. When a person is booked to attend a business event, or to teach at one, these appointment types are used to create an entry in the appointment calendar by the system automatically.

| Group | Sem. abbr. | Value abbr. | Description |
|---|---|---|---|
| SEMIN | TINST | INSTRUCTOR | Date type for instructor function |
| SEMIN | TPART | ATTENDEE | Date type for business event attendance |

### 38.10.4 Activating Integration

You activate integration of appointment calendar with Training and Event Management by setting 1 in the following entry in table T77S0.

| Group | Sem. abbr. | Value abbr. | Description |
|---|---|---|---|
| PLOGI | APPNT | 1 | Appointment calendar integration switch |

### 38.10.5 Automatic Entry in Appointment Calendar

When an employee is booked as an attendee for a business event, or reserved as an instructor, the system automatically generates a calendar entry. The appointment calendar is for a user. When a personnel number is booked as an attendee, the system needs to determine his user id. It does so by referring to infotype 0105 subtype 0001 where the relationship between personnel number and user id is maintained.

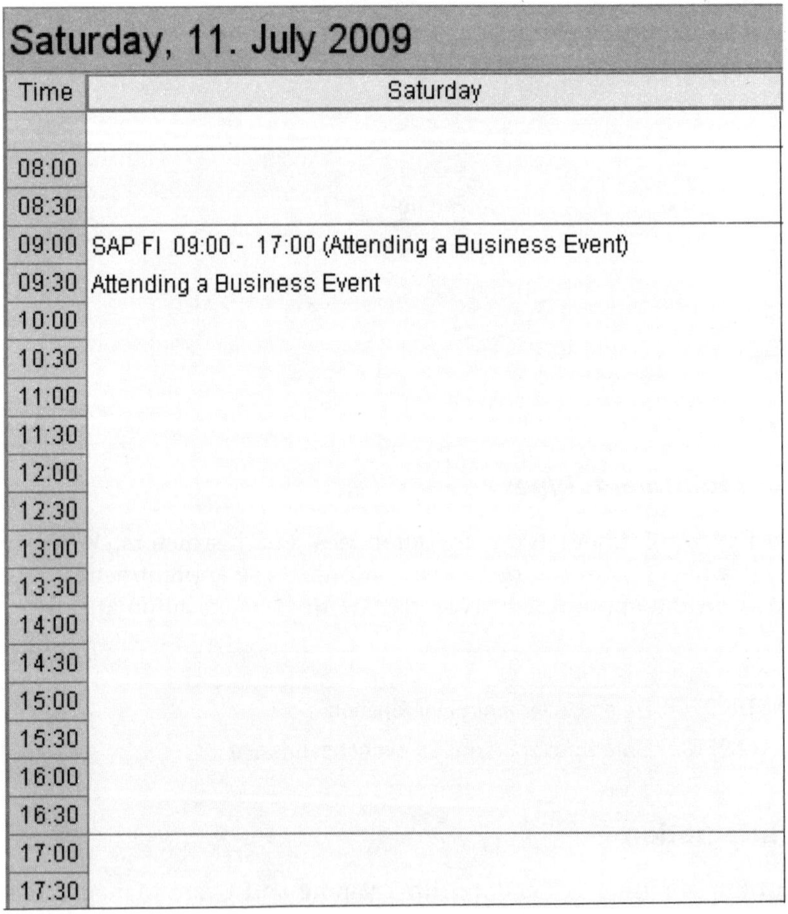

## 38.11 BUDGET MANAGEMENT

| *Functional Consultant* | *User* | *Business Process Owner* | *Senior Management* | *My Rating* | *Understanding Level* |
|---|---|---|---|---|---|
| A | A | B | B | | |

### 38.11.1 Budgeting

***Purpose***

In Training and Event Management you can create budgets for organizational units and compare the budgets with the actual costs incurred.

***Budget structure***

Usually you create budget for the entire organizational structure. The budget of a superior organizational unit includes the budgets of its subordinate organizational units. In this way managers can control budgets of higher level organizational units even when some subordinate organizational unit overspends.

While budgeting, SAP provides some flexibility. You can have, for example, a combined budget for two organizational units. SAP creates a budget structure which is usually a replica of the organizational structure. Budget units in this case have one-to-one correspondence with organizational units. However, your budget structure can differ from your organizational structure and there may be budget units which finance more than one organizational unit. However, unless you have reason to do so, it is a good practice that your budget structure mimics your organizational structure.

***Generating budget structure from organizational structure***

You run transaction PVB0 to generate the budget structure and click to create your budget structure from the organizational structure. The system gives you the following screen.

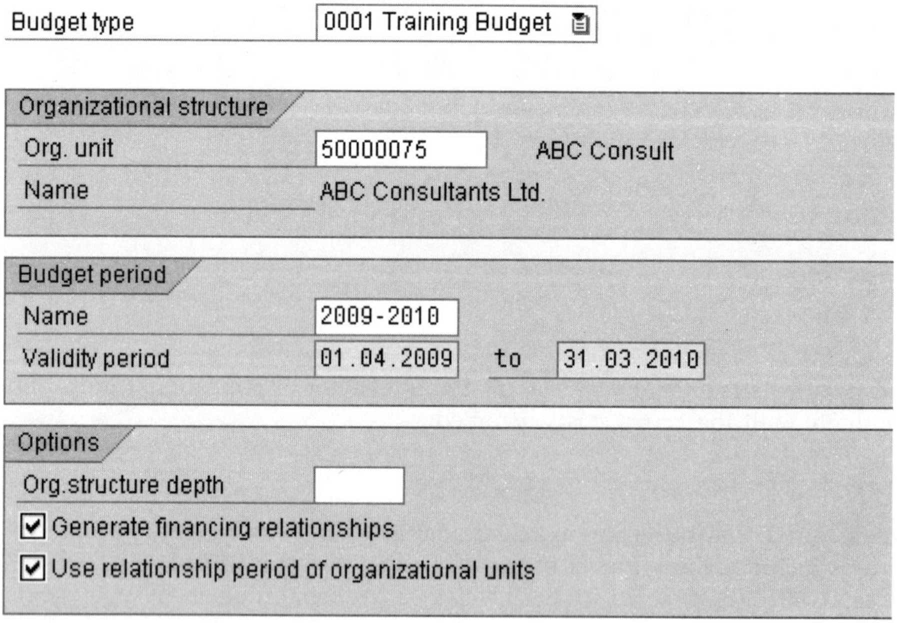


### *Budget type, organizational unit and budget period*

You specify the budget type, the organizational unit and the budget period for which you want to generate the budget structure. Note that the budget structure can be different for different budget types and periods.

### *Organizational structure depth*

If you want to generate budget structure only for certain number of levels in your organizational structure, you specify the organizational structure depth. If you leave this field blank, budget structure is generated for all the levels of the organizational structure.

### *Generate financing relationship*

A budget unit finances an organizational unit. This is specified by creating a financing relationship (314) between the two. If you tick this checkbox, the system automatically generates this relationship.

### *Use relationship period of organizational units*

What happens if your organizational structure is going to change during the budget period? If you tick this checkbox, the budget structure will also reflect that change.

### *Generate budget structure*

Click to generate the budget structure. The system shows the budget structure generated.

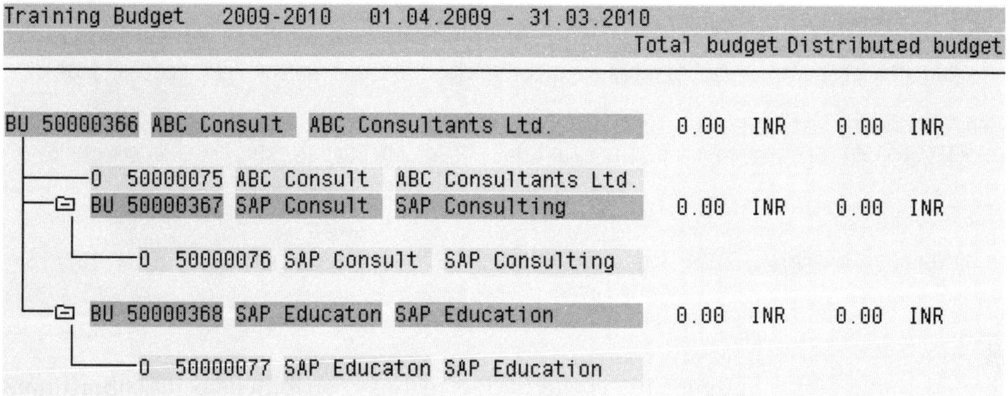


### *Specify budget amount*

You can select a budget unit and click to specify the budget amount and save.

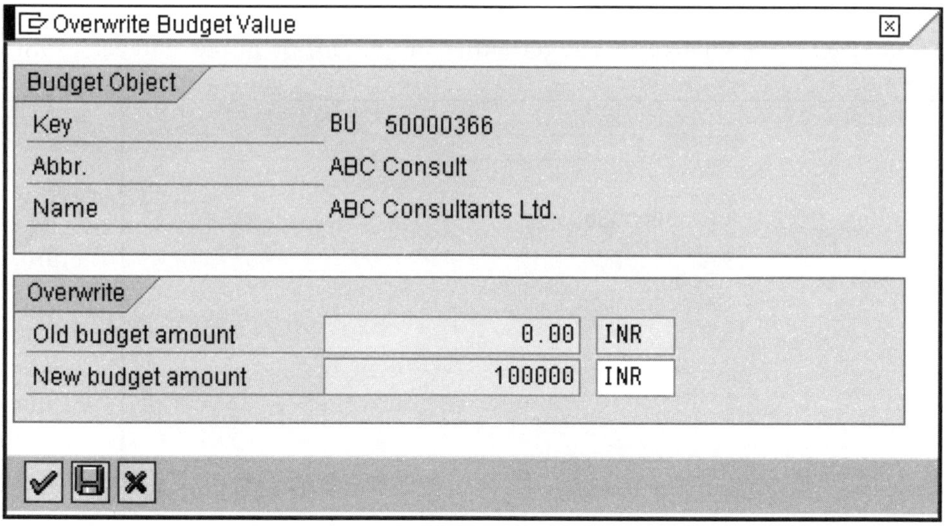

### *Distributed budget*

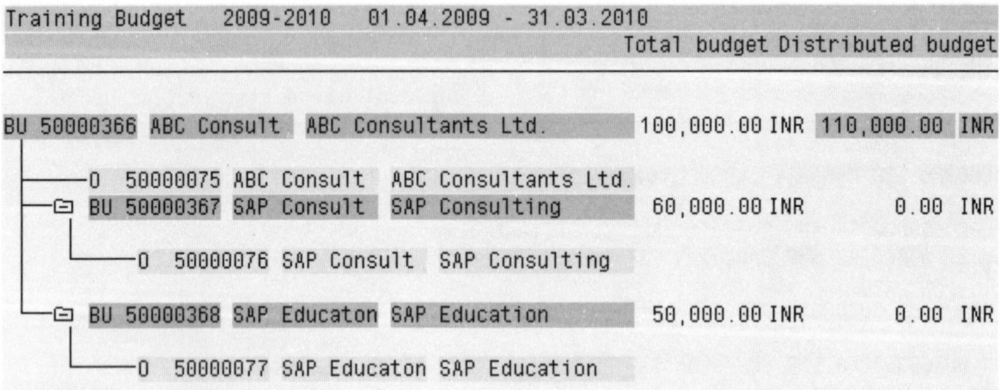


Distributed budget of a budget unit is the budget it has distributed to its subordinate budget units. If distributed budget exceeds the total budget, the system highlights it in red color. You can then change the budgets of the budget units suitably, or you may use the Revalue budget function.

### *Revalue budget*

If you select a budget unit and click [icon], the system shows the following window in which you can specify the change in budget either in amount or in percentage.

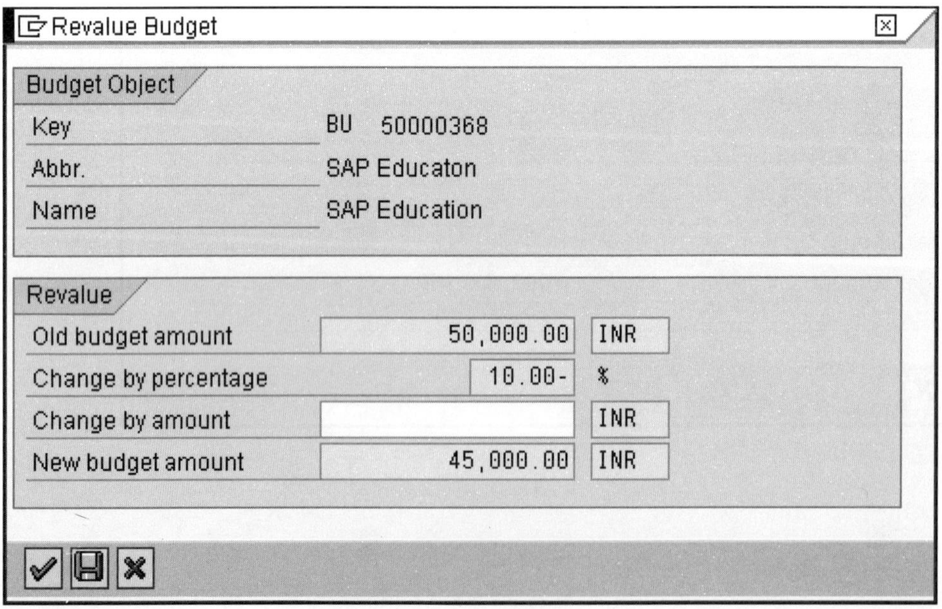

### *Releasing budget*

The budget structure is created in planned status. You release the budget structure by choosing Budget structure ➢ Set status ➢ Release. Once the budget structure is released, you can no longer edit it. Only released budgets are used for monitoring and control.

### *Maintaining budget structure*

You can change the budget structure if you want. You can also change the organizational units they finance.

### *Carrying forward budgets*

You can carry forward the unspent budget amounts. Click [Carry forward] and enter the details in the following screen.

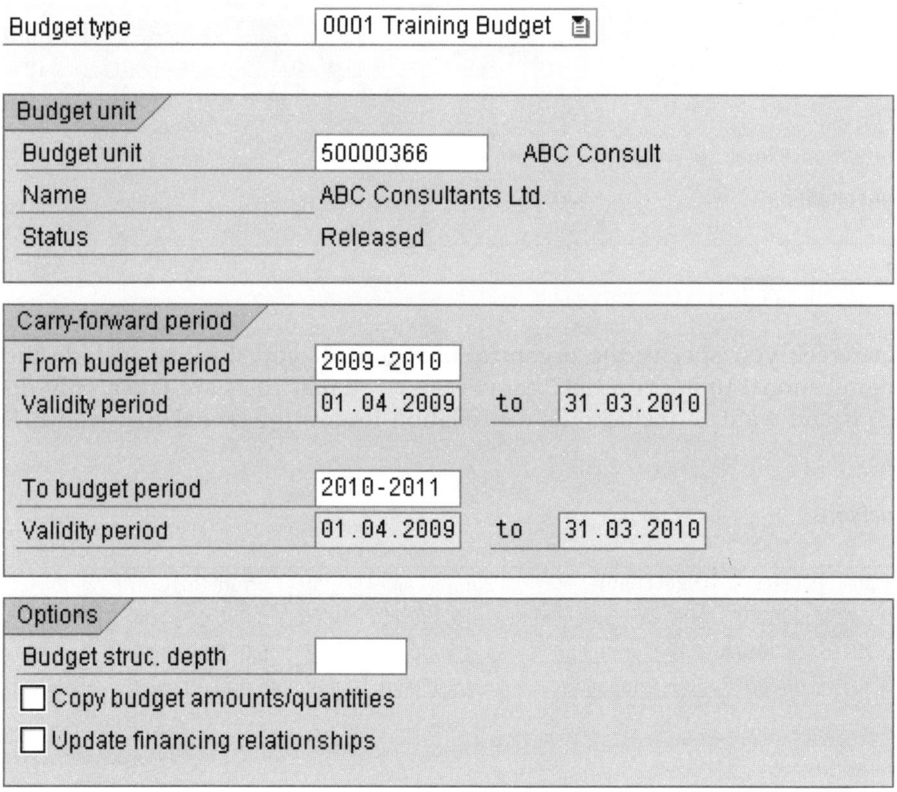


After entering the data, click [Carry forward] to carry forward the budget.

### 38.11.2 Budget Comparison

#### *Purpose*

You can run transaction PVBA or S_PH9_46000423 to compare Training and Event Management budget with the actual cost.

#### *Selection screen*

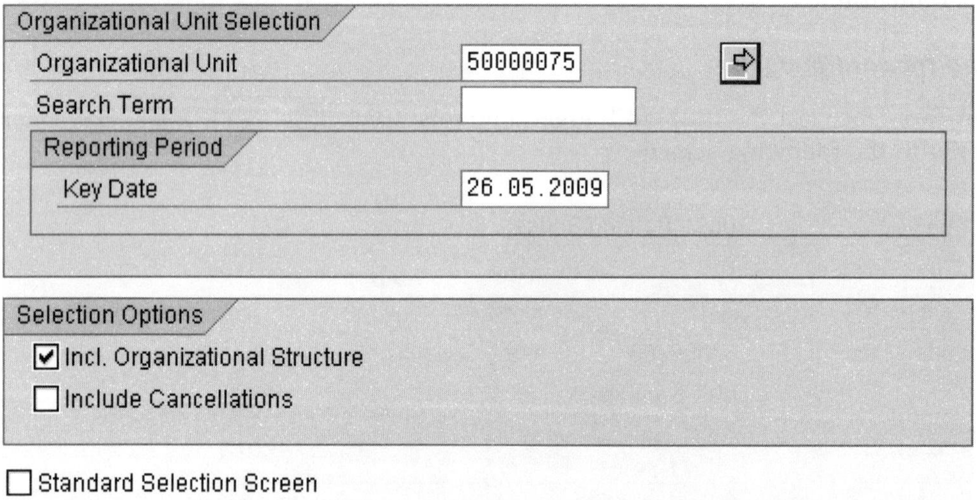


In the selection screen you specify the organizational unit. If you want to include the subordinate organizational units, you tick that checkbox. Actual costs are taken only up to the key date. If you want to include the cancellation fees in the actual cost, you tick that checkbox.

#### *Budget comparison*

| Start Date | End Date | Object ID | Object name | Budget value | Actual... | Current Bu | Currency |
|---|---|---|---|---|---|---|---|
| 01.04.2009 | 31.03.2010 | 50000075 | ABC Consultants Ltd. | 10,000.00 | 0.00 | 10,000.00 | INR |
| 01.04.2009 | 31.03.2010 | 50000076 | .SAP Consulting | 45,000.00 | 0.00 | 45,000.00 | INR |
| 01.04.2009 | 31.03.2010 | 50000077 | .SAP Education | 45,000.00 | 0.00 | 45,000.00 | INR |

### 38.11.3 Budget Currency

***Purpose***

Here you specify the currency you wish to use in budget management.

***IMG node***

SM30 ➢ V_T7PM2

***Screen***

| Budget section | 03 |
|---|---|
| Name | Training and Event Management |

| Start Date | End Date | Crcy |
|---|---|---|
| 01.01.2000 | 31.12.9999 | INR |

***Primary key***

Section of Overall Budget + End Date

### 38.11.4 Budget Types

***Purpose***

For Training and Event Management you should use the budget type 0001 in budget group 03. You should specify that it is a monetary budget, i.e. the budget type unit assigned to the budget is a currency. You should also specify that the budget is allocatable, meaning that it is allowed for budgeting.

***IMG node***

SM30 ➢ V_T7PM3_B

***Screen***

Budget type group 03 Training and Event Management

| Budg.type | Budget type name | Mon.budget | Unit | Unit name | Allocat. |
|---|---|---|---|---|---|
| 0001 | Training Budget | ☑ | | | ☑ |

***Primary key***

Budget Type Group + Budget Type

### 38.11.5 Budget Period

***Purpose***

Here you specify the period over which you want to exercise budgetary control. For example, you may create quarterly budgets and ask your organization to control their expenditure accordingly. Or, it may be okay to control the Training and Event Management budget for the financial year. The key date is the date on which the currency conversion takes place.

***IMG node***

SM30 ➢ V_T7PM9_B

***Screen***

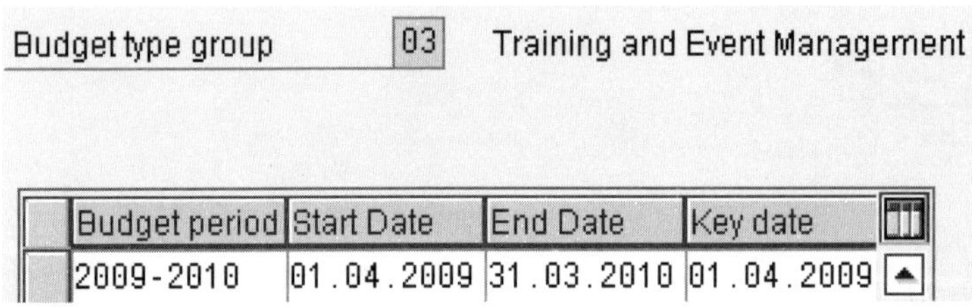


***Primary key***

Budget Type Group + Budget Period

## 38.12 INTEGRATION WITH WORKFLOW

| *Functional Consultant* | *User* | *Business Process Owner* | *Senior Management* | *My Rating* | *Understanding Level* |
|---|---|---|---|---|---|
| A | C | X | X | | |

### 38.12.1 Activating Event Linkage

| Group | Sem. abbr. | Value abbr. | Description |
|---|---|---|---|
| WORKF | ACTIV | X | Switch: Workflow Active in Update Task (X' = on) |

Set this switch to 'X' to activate automatic event linkage for Personnel Planning.

### 38.12.2 Allowed Business Object Types for HR Objects, Infotypes and Subtypes

***Purpose***

You need to maintain this table only if you have defined business objects for customer-specific infotypes, and the operations of a customer-specific infotype are used to trigger events.

***IMG node***

SM30 ➢ T777IBO

***Screen***

| OT | Object type text | IT | Infotype Name | STy. | Subtype text | Obj.type | Name |
|---|---|---|---|---|---|---|---|
| A | Work Center | 1000 | Object | | | PDOTYPE_ | Work Center |
| A | Work Center | 1001 | Relationships | B032 | Is fulfilled by | BUS7030 | Dev. Subprofile |
| A | Work Center | 1001 | Relationships | B038 | Is a potential of | BUS7030 | Dev. Subprofile |
| A | Work Center | 1001 | Relationships | B042 | Interests and pr | BUS7030 | Dev. Subprofile |

***Primary key***

Object Type + Infotype + Subtype + Object Type

### 38.12.3 Event Linkage

***Purpose***

The events that deviate from SAP standard events must be defined for the business objects concerned. The rules for event creation that deviate from the standard must be defined in a customer-specific function module.

### *IMG node*

SM30 ➢ T779X

### *Screen*

| OT | Object | IT | Infoty | STy. | Subt | U | Acty | S | Obj. type | Event | Function Module |
|---|---|---|---|---|---|---|---|---|---|---|---|
| D | Busines | 1000 | Object | | | | | 0 | PDOTYPE_D | CREATED | |
| E | Course | 1000 | Object | | | | | 0 | PDOTYPE_E | | ZUS_EVENT |
| E | Course | 1000 | Object | | | INS | | 0 | PDOTYPE_E | CREATED | |
| E | Course | 1000 | Object | | | UPD | | 0 | PDOTYPE_E | CREATED | |
| E | Course | 1001 | Relatio | A025 | Is parti | INS | BOKP | 0 | PDRELA_025 | | ZHR_EVENT_TRAINING1 |
| F | Location | 1000 | Object | | | | | 0 | PDOTYPE_F | CREATED | |
| NE | Candida | 5139 | Status | | | INS | | 0 | ERC_CDCY | | ZHR_EVENT_ERECR_SUCC |
| P | Person | 0008 | | | | INS | | 0 | BASICPAY | | ZHR_EVENT_RULES_PA0008 |
| P | Person | 0036 | | | | INS | | 0 | SOCINSCH | | HR_EVENT_RULES_PA0036 |
| P | Person | 0036 | | | | UPD | | 0 | SOCINSCH | | HR_EVENT_RULES_PA0036 |
| S | Position | 1000 | Object | | | * | CUT | 0 | PDOTYPE_SH | | HRPM_EVENT_S_1000_CUT |
| S | Position | 1000 | Object | | | * | DELO | 0 | PDOTYPE_SH | | HRPM_EVENT_S_1000_DELET |
| S | Position | 1001 | Relatio | A008 | Holder | DEL | | 0 | PDOTYPE_SH | | HRPM_EVENT_S_1001_A008 |
| S | Position | 1001 | Relatio | A008 | Holder | INS | | 0 | PDOTYPE_SH | | HRPM_EVENT_S_1001_A008 |

### *Primary key*

Object Type + Infotype + Subtype + Update Operation + Key: Activity + Sequence Number for Workflow Events

## 38.13 EMPLOYEE SELF-SERVICE

| *Functional Consultant* | *User* | *Business Process Owner* | *Senior Management* | *My Rating* | *Understanding Level* |
|---|---|---|---|---|---|
| A | C | X | X | | |

### 38.13.1 Set Up External Search Engine

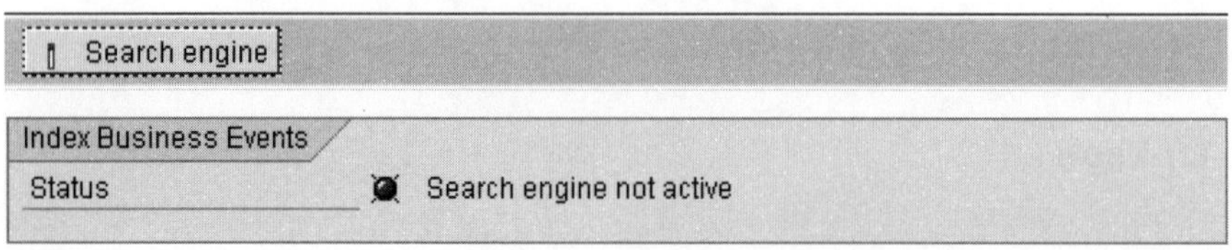


You can set up the connection to an external search engine to be used to facilitate the search for business events in the Employee Self-Service Training Center using transaction PVSEARCH_ADM.

### 38.13.2 Booking Priority for Internet

| Group | Sem. abbr. | Value abbr. | Description |
|---|---|---|---|
| SEMIN | INPRI | 51 | Booking priority for Internet |

Here you can set a booking priority for bookings made in the Employee Self-Service Training Center. If you make no entries, internet bookings are created with the same priorities as assigned by the system automatically. The priority assigned by the system depends on the number of bookings received at the time of booking.

### 38.13.3 Event Generation in Web Transactions

| Group | Sem. abbr. | Value abbr. | Description |
|---|---|---|---|
| SEMIN | REQUE | 0 | Event Generation in Web Transactions |

If you set the switch to 0, the user can book, prebook, and cancel directly on the web as long as he has the appropriate authorization. If you set this switch to 1, general event creation is activated and all these activities trigger appropriate workflows.

### 38.13.4 Cancellation Reason for Employee

| Group | Sem. abbr. | Value abbr. | Description |
|---|---|---|---|
| SEMIN | WEBST | 0005 | Cancelation reason for employee in ESS (PV8I) |

If you want to use a specific cancellation reason for ESS applications, you specify the ID of the reason here. The cancellation reason will determine the cancellation fee. If you do not make an entry, the value stored in the customizing switch SEMIN CCDEL is taken as the basis for calculating cancellation fees.

### 38.13.5 Customer-Specific Attendance Cancellation Reason

You can determine a suitable cancellation reason dynamically using the Business Add-In HRTEM00NET_WEBST, which you then transfer to the ESS application. This BAdI can be found at Training and Event Management ➢ Employee Self-Service (ESS) ➢ Business Add-Ins (BADIs) for ESS ➢ BAdI: Set Up Customer-Specific Attendance Cancellation Reason.

### 38.13.6 Customer-Specific Setup of 'My Bookings'

You can use the Business Add-In HRTEM00NET_ACTIVITY to modify the hit list of event attendance bookings that appears in the Employee Self-Service PV8I My Bookings. This BAdI can be found at Training and Event Management ➢ Employee Self-Service (ESS) ➢ Business Add-Ins (BADIs) for ESS ➢ BAdI: Customer-Specific Setup of 'My Bookings'.

## 38.14 TRAINING GENERAL SETTINGS

| *Functional Consultant* | *User* | *Business Process Owner* | *Senior Management* | *My Rating* | *Understanding Level* |
|---|---|---|---|---|---|
| A | C | X | X | | |

### 38.14.1 Changes to Historical Attendances

| Group | Sem. abbr. | Value abbr. | Description |
|---|---|---|---|
| SEMIN | HISTO | | Message type for changes to historical attendances |

This entry lets you specify the system reaction if a user tries to change (cancel, rebook, replace) an attendance booking that has a historical record flag. You can give an error, a warning, information, or no message. It is recommended that you give an error to prevent a historical record from being modified.

### 38.14.2 Specifying Data Screen Display

| Group | Sem. abbr. | Value abbr. | Description |
|---|---|---|---|
| SEMIN | DISPX | 1 | Master data: display data screen with infotypes |

When you display the master data of an object in Training and Event Management, the system can display all infotypes (value 1 here), or only those infotypes for which data has been stored (value 0 here).

### 38.14.3 Customer Enhancement for Master Data

| Group | Sem. abbr. | Value abbr. | Description |
|---|---|---|---|
| SEMIN | CALLB | | Customer Enhancement for Master Data |

Here you can specify a program that reads customer-specific object types and infotypes (such as in industry solutions) for master data of Training and Event Management.

### 38.14.4 Notes for Infotypes

In view T77NT you can make settings for formatting of notes in the editor and in print. For each combination of object type, infotype, and subtype, you specify one form and one style for the screen display and one form and one style for the printout.

**Key**

| | | |
|---|---|---|
| Object Type | * | All |
| Infotype | 1001 | Relationships |
| Subtype | A025 | Is participated in by |

**SAPscript Text Object**

| | | |
|---|---|---|
| Text Object | HR_TEMNOTE | HR: Notes in Event Management |
| Text ID | TEM1 | Remarks for processes in TEM |

**Form for Displaying Note**

| | |
|---|---|
| Style (display) | HR_TEM1 |
| Form (display) | HR_TEM_NOTE_DISP |

**Form for Printing Note**

| | |
|---|---|
| Style(printout) | HR_TEM1 |
| Form (printout) | HR_TEM_NOTE_PRN |

**Technical Settings**

| | |
|---|---|
| Note Key | HRVTXTKEY1 |
| | HRMS-TEM: Key for Note on Booking/Cancellation/Prebooking |
| Function module | RHNT_NOTE_HEADER_BOOK |
| | INTERNAL: Header for Booking Notes |

### 38.14.5 Procedure for Entering Notes

| Group | Sem. abbr. | Value abbr. | Description |
|---|---|---|---|
| SEMIN | EVATX | 1 | Protect existing comments |

Notes consist of one or more single entries. When you create a note, you create the first single entry, and each time you modify a note, you add a new single entry to the existing ones. When you modify a note, the system displays all previously created single entries and a new line editor. If this switch is on (value 1), all previously created single entries are protected. If this switch is off (value 0), previously created single entries are modifiable. If this switch is changed from 1 to 0, previously created protected entries are still not modifiable. You can run program RHNOTE00 with transaction SA38 to see and edit all existing notes.

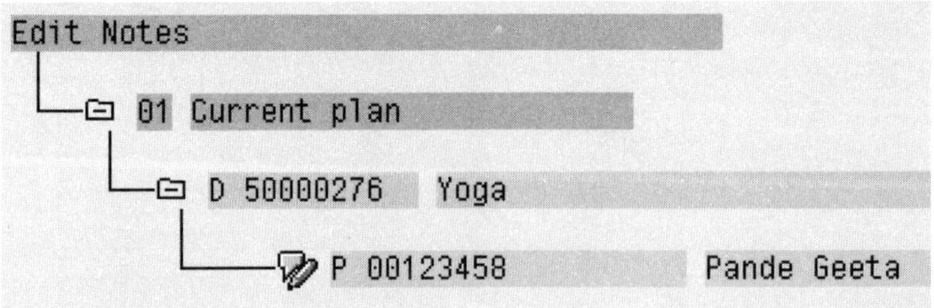


### 38.14.6 List Entry for Attendee Activities

| Group | Sem. abbr. | Value abbr. | Description |
|---|---|---|---|
| SEMIN | LIMSG | 0 | Individual messages in list entry transactions |

In list entry transactions you update several entries at once. If you want a message to be output for each entry, you set this value to 1. If you set it to 0, no message is output for each entry. A message is output on completion of the processing loop.

### 38.14.7 Pushbutton Settings for Batch Input

| Group | Sem. abbr. | Value abbr. | Description |
|---|---|---|---|
| PMAIN | OBTCI | | Switch: legacy data transfer with old pushbuttons |

This switch determines the pushbuttons used for batch input in transactions PA30 and PP02. It should be 'X' if batch input takes place using pushbuttons for Release < 4.5A; otherwise it should be blank.

### 38.14.8 Default Organizer Types

| Group | Sem. abbr. | Value abbr. | Description |
|---|---|---|---|
| SEMIN | VTYP1 | U | Default organizer type |
| SEMIN | VTYP2 | O | Default organizer type |
| SEMIN | VTYP3 | KU | Default organizer type |

Here you can maintain default organizer types.

CHAPTER 39

# Utilities

## 39.1 FUNCTIONALITY

| *Functional Consultant* | *User* | *Business Process Owner* | *Senior Management* | *My Rating* | *Understanding Level* |
|---|---|---|---|---|---|
| A | A | B | B | | |

### 39.1.1 Users

#### *Logging on*

If you are going to work in SAP, your system administrator will create a SAP logon pad on your desktop/laptop. The logon pad can be accessed either through a shortcut on your desktop, or through the Windows Start icon. When you open the SAP logon pad, you will find one or more entries in it.

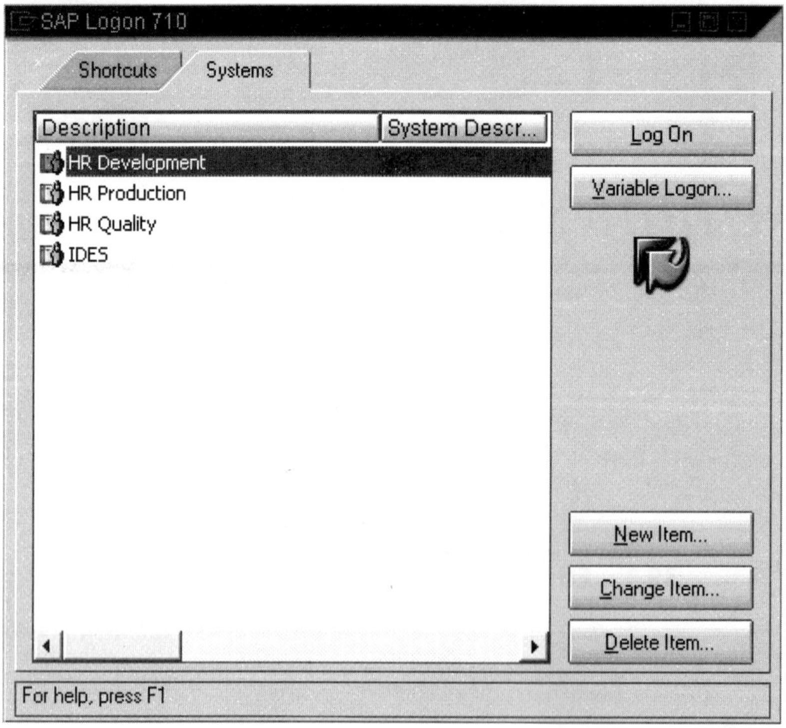


Each entry represents a server. Your system administrator will tell you the purpose for which each server is to be used. You select the server you want to work on, and click the 'Log On' icon. The system gives you the logon screen.

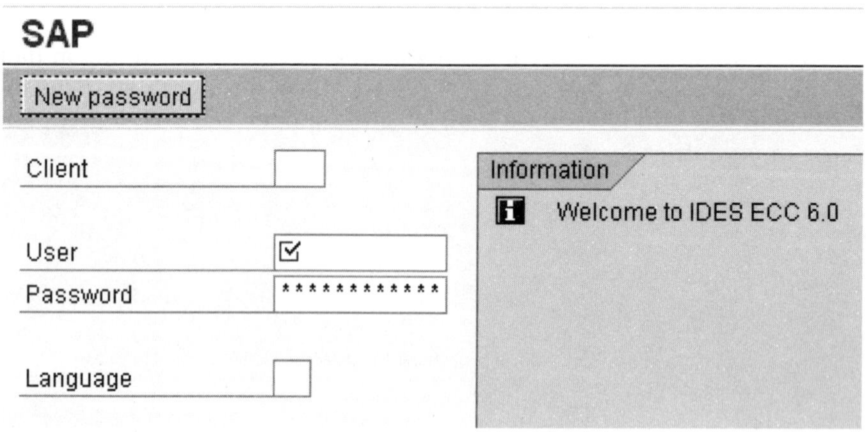


You enter the details given to you by your system administrator. You can change your password or press Enter to logon. The system gives you the SAP menu.

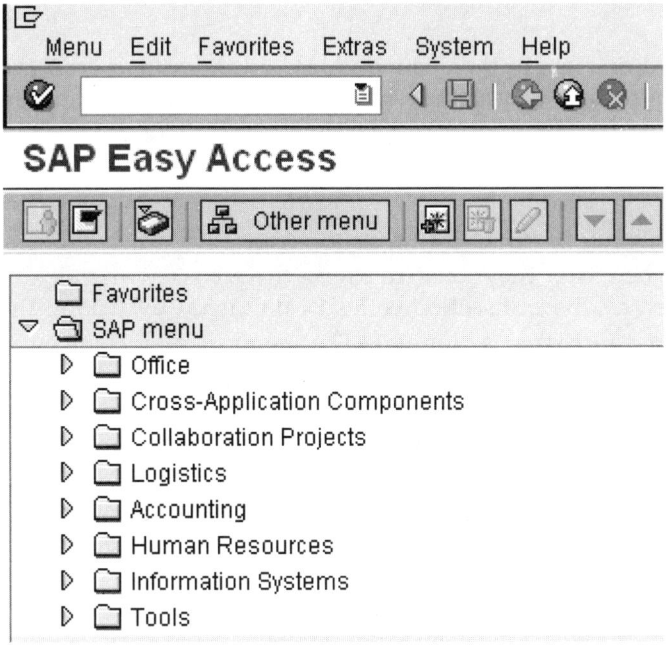


You can open the tree-like structure of the SAP menu to reach the transaction you want to carry out. You can switch to user menu, if one has been set up for you. You can add transactions to the Favorites folder, which can have sub-folders.

### *Executing a transaction in the command field*

An important part of all SAP screens is the command field, located in the top-left corner of the screen. Here, you can enter a transaction directly, instead of going through a menu. If you are already in some transaction which you want to leave, prefix the transaction with /n, e.g. /nPA30. If you want to run the new transaction in a new session, prefix the transaction with /o, e.g. /oPA30.

### *Aborting the current transaction*

You can abort the current transaction by entering /n in the command field.

### *Opening multiple sessions*

You can open another session of SAP (same server and client) by clicking icon, or by entering /o in the command field.

### *Closing a session*

You can close a session by entering /i in the command line or by closing the window. If the session you are closing is the only session on a client, you are logged off. The system asks you to confirm that you want to log off.

### Logging off

You can log off by entering /nend or /nex in the command line. In the former case, the system asks you to confirm that you want to log off. All the sessions on the client are closed.

### Displaying transaction codes

You work in SAP either through menu, or through transaction codes. Experienced users often prefer the latter method. Therefore, they need to know the transaction codes of various transactions. You can display the transaction codes in the menu by ticking the checkbox ☑ Display technical names in Extras ➢ Settings. The menu display changes as shown below.

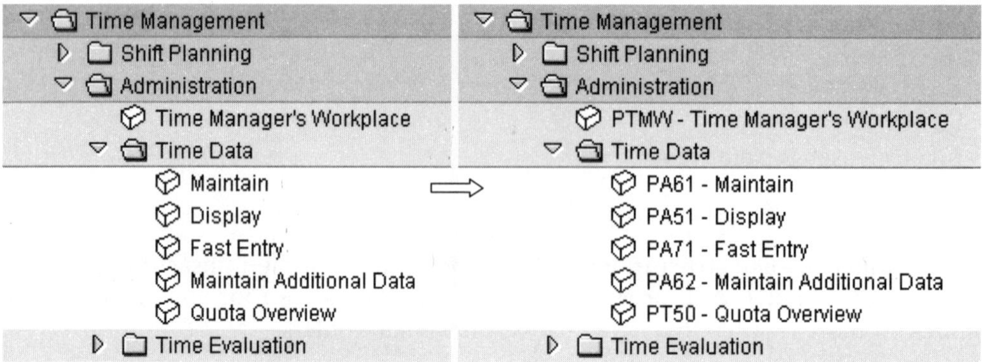


### Displaying keys in dropdown lists

In many fields, SAP provides a dropdown list from which you can choose a value. These dropdown lists usually have a key and a description. Users who like to see the key in addition to description can tick ☑ Show Keys in All Dropdown Lists . They can even sort the dropdown list by the key by ticking ☑ Sort Items by Key . You access these checkboxes by clicking ➢ Options ➢ Expert.

### Quick copy and paste

SAP provides a method of quick copy and quick paste. You enable this by ticking ✔ Quick Cut and Paste in . After that, if you press the left button of the mouse, move the mouse on some text, and leave it, the text gets copied to the clipboard. The text is not selected, as would be the case, if this feature is not enabled. Also, if you press the right button of the mouse in any field of SAP, the text is pasted from the clipboard. The text may have been copied on the clipboard from any application, e.g. Microsoft Word.

### Business workplace

SAP provides a wide range of office functionality, e.g. mail, workflow, etc. in business workplace. You can access it using transaction SBWP, or by clicking the icon as shown.

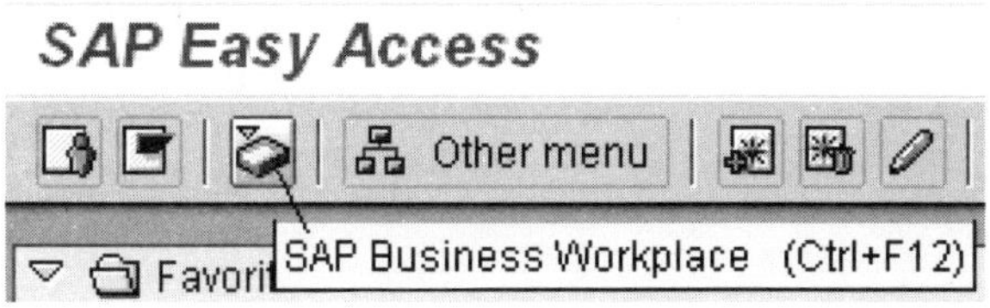


You can create document and send by selecting 'New message' from business workplace, or by running transaction SO00, or through menu (System ➢ Short Message).

### Maintain own data

You can maintain your own data using transaction SU3 (System ➢ User Profile ➢ Own Data).

### Running ABAP programs

You can run ABAP programs using transaction SA38 (System ➢ Services ➢ Reporting). It is recommended to avoid doing this by creating a transaction for every program.

### Quick viewer

You can run quick viewer using transaction SQVI (System ➢ Services ➢ QuickViewer).

### Output control

You can run transaction SP01 (System ➢ Services ➢ Output Control) to list the spool requests and output requests for a user id in a specific period. You can display their contents, print them and delete them. You can run transaction SP02 (System ➢ Own Spool Requests) to list your own spool requests.

### Batch input

You can run transaction SM35 (System ➢ Services ➢ Batch Input ➢ Sessions) to monitor, process and analyze the batch input sessions. You can see the logs using transaction SM35P (System ➢ Services ➢ Batch Input ➢ Logs). You can do recording for batch input using transaction SHDB (System ➢ Services ➢ Batch Input ➢ Recorder).

### Computer-aided test tool

You can use transaction SECATT (System ➢ Services ➢ ECATT ➢ Record) to perform computer-aided testing.

### Background jobs

You can use transaction SM36 to define and schedule a background job (System ➢ Services ➢ Jobs ➢ Define Job). You can use transaction SM37 (System ➢ Services ➢ Jobs ➢ Job Overview) to monitor and manage jobs. You can release a job, stop an active job, delete a job, display spool list, display job log and display step list. You can also check status, change status from released to scheduled, copy job, change job, repeat scheduling and move the job to a different server. You can also run transaction SMX to see your own jobs (System ➢ Own Jobs).

### *Queue*

You can use transaction SM38 (System ➢ Services ➢ Queue) to display queue.

### *Reporting authorization problems*

You can use transaction SU53 (System ➢ Utilities ➢ Display Authorization Check) to see details of authorization problems and to report to the Basis team for resolution. Immediately after you encounter the authorization problem, enter /nSU53. The system will show a comparison between authorization available and authorization required.

### *Archived documents*

You can use transaction OAAD to store and assign a new document in the content server. The transaction also provides a facility to search the archived documents.

### *Download file*

You can use transaction CG3Y to download a file from the application server to your desktop.

### *Upload file*

You can use transaction CG3Z to upload a file from your desktop to the application server.

### *SAP query*

You can start SAP queries using transaction SQ00.

## 39.1.2 Functional Consultants

### *Customizing*

Transaction SPRO is used for accessing the customizing environment. You can customize the SAP system using the SAP reference IMG (Implementation Management Guide) or you can define projects for customization, e.g. adapting the reference IMG to the needs of your company and/or subdivide the customization task into different subprojects.

### *View maintenance*

Transactions SM30 (System ➢ Services ➢ Table Maintenance ➢ Extended Table Maintenance) and SM31 are used for maintaining data in one or more tables through a maintenance view. The transaction also provides a facility to navigate to the underlying IMG node for a particular maintenance view. Transaction SM34 (System ➢ Services ➢ Table Maintenance ➢ View Cluster Maintenance) is used for maintaining view clusters.

### Customizing comparison

You can compare customizing of two systems or two clients in the same system by using transaction SCMP. You can also create comparison runs involving multiple objects using transaction SCU0 or OY19.

### Transport management

You can use transactions SE09 and SE10 for creating and releasing a customizing or workbench transport request.

### Data migration, computer-aided testing, BDC

You can use transaction LSMW to migrate legacy data to SAP. You can use transaction SCAT or SECATT for creating a test case by recording a transaction and creating and loading test data. You can record or modify a BDC and run it using transaction SHDB.

### View data in tables

You can view data in a table using transaction SE11, SE16, SE16N or SE17.

### Logon to OSS

You can use transaction OSS1 (System ➢ Services ➢ SAP Service) to logon to OSS. It is generally used to import and apply SAP notes.

### Search SAP notes

You can search SAP notes for keywords at http://service.sap.com/notes. You will need user code and password which your system administrator will provide to you.

### Search string in programs

You can use the program RPR_ABAP_SOURCE_SCAN to search strings in programs.

### Search in SAP menu

You can use transaction SEARCH_SAP_MENU to search in SAP menu.

### Search in user menu

You can use transaction SEARCH_USER_MENU to search in user menu.

### SAP query

You can use transaction SQ01 to maintain SAP queries, transaction SQ02 to maintain infoset and transaction SQ03 to maintain user groups. You can start SAP queries using transaction SQ00.

#### *Workflow builder*

You can use transaction SWDD for creating and editing workflows.

#### *System status*

You can see SAP version, operating system and database by clicking System ➢ Status. You can also see transaction, program and screen number.

#### *Translation*

You can use transaction SE63 to translate texts for various ABAP and non-ABAP objects.

### 39.1.3 ABAP

#### *ABAP programs*

You can create, modify, delete, and display source code of ABAP programs using transaction SE38. You can also execute ABAP programs using transaction SA38 or SE38. You can compare ABAP programs using transaction SE39.

#### *Function modules*

You can create, modify, delete, display and test function modules using transaction SE37. You can also maintain a function group.

#### *Dialog modules*

You can create, modify, delete, display and test dialog modules using transaction SE35. You can create menus using transaction SE41. Screens can be painted using transaction SE51 and its underlying flow logic defined.

#### *Classes*

You can create, modify, delete, display and test classes using transaction SE24.

#### *Logical databases*

You can create, modify, delete, display and test logical databases using transaction SE36. SAP provides several logical databases for HR, e.g. PAP, PCH, PNP, PNPCE.

#### *Enhancements*

You can create enhancements through transaction CMOD. Enhancements are created in projects, which are logical groups of enhancements. You can test the enhancements using transaction SMOD.

### *BAdIs*

You can use transaction SE19, to implement a Business Add-In. SAP provides predefined BAdIs for use by the customers. If you want to define your own BAdI, use transaction SE18.

### *Area menus*

You can create area menus using transaction SE43. Area menus can be used in creating role menus in transaction PFCG.

### *Tables and views*

You can create, modify, delete and display tables and table fields using transaction SE11. You can view data in a table using transaction SE11, SE16, SE16N or SE17. You can display/change technical settings of a table in transaction SE13.

### *Documentation*

You can create documentation using transaction SE61.

### *SAP scripts*

You can create SAP scripts using transaction SE71. Other transactions related to SAP script are SE72, SE73, SE74, SE75, SE75TTDTGC, SE75TTDTGD, SE76, SE77 and SO10.

### *Messages*

You can maintain messages using transaction SE91. You can then call them in your own programs. You can also use SAP-defined messages in your own programs.

### *Transactions*

You can maintain transactions using transaction SE93. It is recommended that you have a transaction for every program so that the users are not required to run programs using transaction SA38 or SE38. This provides better control on authorizations. It is also recommended that you keep the transaction code same as the program name.

### *Repository information*

SAP has created a lot of software objects. You can use transaction SE15/ SE85/ SE84 to find them.

### *BAPIs*

You can see the BAPIs provided by SAP using transaction BAPI.

#### *Object navigator*

You use transaction SE80 to organize your programming in an integrated development environment. Development objects are arranged together in object lists. Each object list contains all of the objects in a certain category, such as package, program and global class. From the object list, you can select an object by double-clicking it. When you open an object, the workbench calls up the development tool with which the object was created.

#### *ABAP dump analysis*

You can use transaction ST22 to see details of any runtime error or short dump. This will help in analyzing the root cause of the dump and finding its solution.

### 39.1.4 Basis

#### *System administration*

You can use transaction S002 to get the menu for system administration.

#### *Users*

You can maintain users using transaction SU01. You can get a variety of information about users, roles and authorizations using transaction SUIM. You can view users' logon date and password change using transaction RSUSR200. You can use transaction SM04 to check the status of the users; for example, how many users have logged on and how many sessions a user is working on.

#### *Roles*

You can maintain roles using transaction PFCG. The system automatically inserts authorization objects based on transactions selected by you (These can be maintained using transaction SU22 or SU24). You update them with appropriate values. You can see change documents for roles using transaction RSSCD100_PFCG. The same program is called by transaction RSSCD100_PFCG_USER. Transaction S_BCE_68001403 gives a list of critical authorizations.

#### *Maintain the authorization objects*

You can run transaction SU21 to maintain the authorization objects.

#### *Transport management*

You can manage transports using transactions SE01, SE03, SE09 and SE10.

#### *SAPconnect*

You can use transaction SCOT for monitoring the status of the inbound and outbound traffic through SAPconnect.

#### ALE

Customizing of ALE can be done using transaction SALE. You can monitor ALE Messages using transaction BD87.

#### Display and delete locks

Transaction SM12 is used for checking and releasing lock entries.

#### Lock/unlock transactions

You can use transaction SM01 to lock/unlock transactions.

## 39.2 TABLES AND VIEWS

| *Functional Consultant* | *User* | *Business Process Owner* | *Senior Management* | *My Rating* | *Understanding Level* |
|---|---|---|---|---|---|
| A | A | B | B | | |

### 39.2.1 Data Dictionary

#### Domains

View DD01V contains the list of domains. View DD07V contains values for domains.

#### Data elements

View DD04V contains data elements and their descriptions.

#### Tables

View DD02V contains the list of tables.

#### Table fields

Table DD03L contains table fields and DD03T their descriptions. Table DD03M contains table fields with data elements, texts, and domains. View DDVAL contains fixed values for table fields.

#### Foreign key fields

View DD08V contains foreign key relationship definitions.

#### Pool/Cluster structures

View DD06V contains pool/cluster structures.

#### *Technical settings of tables*

Table DD09L contains technical settings of tables.

#### *Matchcode objects*

View DD20V contains matchcode objects. Table DD24S contains fields of a matchcode ID.

#### *Views*

Table TVDIR contains directory of views. Table DD25T contains views, matchcode objects and lock objects. Table DD27S contains fields in a view, matchcode object or lock object.

### 39.2.2 Software Repository

#### *Packages*

All objects are developed under Packages (earlier called Development Classes), which are logical grouping of objects. Table TDEVC contains list of Packages. Packages of SAP HR can be identified by selecting entries from table TDEVC where software component is SAP_HR. Some of the important Packages are:

| | |
|---|---|
| PP00 | Organization and planning (application) |
| PP09 | Training and Event Management |
| PP0C | Organization and Planning—Customizing |
| PP2C | HR Development—Customizing |
| PP9C | Training and Event Management—Customizing |
| PPAP_HR | Appraisal Systems HR |
| PPDP | Development Plans |
| PPEM | PE Application Components |
| PPPE_HR | Personnel Development—HR |

#### *Repository objects*

Table TADIR contains the directory of repository objects, along with their development class. Tables and structures are identified by object type TABL.

#### *Objects*

Objects are stored in OBJ series of tables.

#### *ABAP programs*

Table TRDIR contains list of ABAP programs. Table D010TAB contains the tables used by ABAP programs.

#### *Transaction codes*

View TSTCV contains list of transaction codes and programs associated with them.

### 39.2.3 Users, Roles and Authorization

#### *User data*

User data is stored in USR series tables. Table USR01 stores the master list of users. Table USR04 contains the profiles attached to a user. A user's parameter IDs and their values are stored in table USR05.

#### *Role maintenance*

You can create, delete, or modify roles using transaction PFCG. Role related data is stored in tables starting with AGR.

#### *Authorization objects*

Authorization objects and their field names are in table TOBJ.

#### *Authorization objects for roles*

Table AGR_1250 contains authorization objects for a role which you see in transaction PFCG.

#### *Master list of roles*

Table AGR_DEFINE contains master list of roles.

#### *Transaction codes for a role*

Table AGR_TCODES contains transaction codes for roles.

#### *Users having a role*

Table AGR_USERS contains users for roles. Also see table AGR_USERT.

### 39.2.4 IMG Menu

Table CUS_IMGACH contains master list of IMG activities including documentation object and transaction code.

### 39.2.5 SAP Scripts

#### *SAP scripts*

SAP scripts are stored in STX series of tables.

### 39.2.6 Others

#### *Documentation*

Documentation header is stored in table DOKHL and text in table DOKTL.

#### *Reserved names*

Reserved Names for Customizing Tables/Objects are stored in table TRESC.

### 39.2.7 Delivery Class of a Table

SAP stores data in tables. Each table is assigned a delivery class which determines whether the data in the table is controlled by SAP or by the customer. Delivery class of a table can be seen in the 'Delivery and Maintenance' tab in transaction SE11.

| | | |
|---|---|---|
| A | Application table (master and transaction data) | A Support Pack of SAP is not expected to update these tables in any client. |
| L | Table for storing temporary data, delivered empty | A Support Pack of SAP is not expected to update these tables in any client. |
| G | Customizing table, protected against SAP Upd., only INS all. | A Support Pack of SAP is not expected to update these tables in any client. |
| C | Customizing table, maintenance only by cust., not SAP import | A Support Pack of SAP updates these tables in client 000 only. In other clients, these tables have to be adjusted from 000 to get these entries. |
| E | Control table, SAP and customer have separate key areas | A Support Pack of SAP updates these tables in all clients. |
| S | System table, maint. only by SAP, change = modification | A Support Pack of SAP updates these tables in all clients. |
| W | System table, contents transportable via separate TR objects | A Support Pack of SAP updates these tables in all clients. |

### 39.2.8 Search Help

When SAP designs tables, for each column it tries to provide search help. If search help is provided, you can choose a value from it. By assigning search help to table columns, the help becomes standardized. There are different types of search help. In transaction SE11, if you go to tab 'Entry help/check', you can see which columns have got entry help and of which type in the column 'Origin of the Input Help'. Different types of search help are listed below.

| | | |
|---|---|---|
| T | Input help based on data type | For example, Date (Calendar), Time. |
| D | Explicit search help attachment to data element | Attachment of a search help to the data element assigned to the field. |
| X | Explicit search help attachment to field | Data integrity is checked against search help. There is no check table. |
| P | Input help implemented with check table | Data integrity is checked using a check table. |
| F | Input help with fixed values | The field can take values only from a fixed list, which is defined in the Domain. |
| Blank | No input help | There is no input help. |

## 39.3 IMPLEMENTATION GUIDE

| *Functional Consultant* | *User* | *Business Process Owner* | *Senior Management* | *My Rating* | *Understanding Level* |
|---|---|---|---|---|---|
| A | B | B | B | | |

When a consultant implements SAP HR Organizational Management, Personnel Development or Training and Event Management for a client, how does the consultant determine the client requirement and do configuration, and how does the client know that the right configuration is done for him? The answers to these twin questions lie in the methodology you follow.

The consultant can use the structure of this book to guide the implementation. He can ask specific questions to the users, record their answers and use the answers to do the configuration. Having done the configuration, he can explain it to the users and get it approved. If the users do not have enough SAP knowledge to confirm the configuration, the consultant should record the user input and get it signed off. An auditor should then confirm that the configuration reflects the user input. The source of all configuration should be user input.

Whereas many factual inputs can come from a knowledgeable power user, policy inputs should come from senior management. In large companies, senior management is often surprised at the diversity of practices followed in different parts of the company. Implementation of SAP provides an opportunity to senior management to either commonize the practice, or approve diversity. Even when there is no diversity, decisions on policy should be approved by management.

Both user inputs and the corresponding configuration should be recorded in a configuration manual. The configuration manual should explain what has been configured and, if necessary, why. If you use the following table as the Table of Content of your configuration manual, your configuration manual will be easy to understand. Apart from what you configure, you should also indicate what is not implemented (NR) and what is SAP standard (SS). You should also add all Z developments done by you in respective chapters. Feel free to add chapters in the table of contents, but don't delete any line which has configuration in it. The support team needs to know if something is not implemented. If some configuration is not implemented, you can keep the chapter number blank, instead of creating empty chapters in the configuration manual. The Reference column contains the chapter number in the book.

In the 'Approved by' column, you should record the name of the person who has approved that particular configuration. The entries in the table below show the suggested approving level: SM – Senior Management/Steering Committee, PO – Business Process Owner, US – Power User, FC – Functional Consultant. If users are not knowledgeable enough to sign off the configuration, the users should sign off their input, and the auditor should sign off the configuration.

| *Chapter* | *Description* | *Configuration* | *NR/SS/ Done* | *Reference* | *Approved by* |
|---|---|---|---|---|---|
| **1** | **Actions** | | | | |
| 1.1 | Maintain Personnel Actions | Transaction OOMT | | 2.6.2–2.6.3 | US |
| 1.2 | Transactions for Actions | Transaction OOMT | | 2.6.4 | FC |
| **2** | **Number Ranges** | | | | |
| 2.1 | Number Ranges | Transaction OONR | | 10.2.4, 10.2.5 | US |
| 2.2 | Customer Logic for Number Assignment | Transaction CMOD | | 10.2.6 | SM |
| **3** | **Structures** | | | | |
| 3.1 | Structures Required | | | | SM |
| 3.2 | Evaluation Path | Transaction OOAW | | 12.2 | FC |
| 3.3 | Using Evaluation Paths in SAP Programs | V_T77S0AW | | 12.3 | FC |
| 3.4 | Matrix Structure Definition | T779M | | 12.6.2 | FC |
| **4** | **Infotypes** | | | **14** | |
| 4.1 | Description | | | 14.1 | US |
| 4.1.1 | Types of Description | V_778U | | 14.1.2 | US |
| 4.1.2 | Formatting of Description | T772S | | 14.1.3 | US |

| *Chapter* | *Description* | *Configuration* | *NR/SS/ Done* | *Reference* | *Approved by* |
|---|---|---|---|---|---|
| 4.2 | Department/Staff | | | 14.2 | PO |
| 4.2.1 | Department Switch | V_T77S0SC | | 14.2.2 | PO |
| 4.3 | Character | | | 14.3 | US |
| 4.4 | Planned Compensation | | | 14.4 | PO |
| 4.5 | Restrictions | | | 14.5 | PO |
| 4.5.1 | Types of Restrictions | T778C | | 14.5.3 | US |
| 4.5.2 | Reasons for Restrictions | T778X | | 14.5.4 | US |
| 4.6 | Vacancy | | | 14.6 | PO |
| 4.6.1 | Activation of Vacancy Infotype | V_T77S0SC | | 14.6.5 | PO |
| 4.7 | Account Assignment | | | 14.7 | PO |
| 4.7.1 | Enterprise Organization Activation | V_TKA06_CC | | 14.7.1 | SM |
| 4.7.2 | Enterprise Organization Creation | Transaction KEO1 | | 14.7.1 | SM |
| 4.7.3 | Inheritance of Account Assignment by Positions | V_T77S0SC | | 14.7.2 | PO |
| 4.7.4 | Default Value for Controlling Area | V_T77S0SC | | 14.7.3 | PO |
| 4.8 | Health Examinations | | | 14.8 | PO |
| 4.8.1 | Health Examinations Type | T778G | | 14.8.3 | PO |
| 4.9 | Authorities/Resources | | | 14.9 | PO |
| 4.9.1 | Authorities/Resources Type | T778W | | 14.9.3 | PO |
| 4.10 | Work Schedule | | | 14.10 | PO |
| 4.10.1 | Work Schedule Groups | T77WT | | 14.10.2 | PO |
| 4.10.2 | Work Schedule Rule Values | V_T77S0SC | | 14.10.3 | PO |
| 4.11 | Employee Group/Subgroup | | | 14.11 | PO |
| 4.12 | Obsolete | | | 14.12 | PO |
| 4.13 | Cost Distribution | | | 14.13.1 | PO |
| 4.13.1 | Cost Distribution Integration | V_T77S0SC | | 14.13.2 | PO |
| 4.14 | Quota Planning | | | 14.14 | PO |
| 4.14.1 | Quota Planning Type | V_778U | | 14.14.3 | PO |
| 4.14.2 | Planning Type and Periods | T77POSBUD | | 14.14.4 | PO |
| 4.14.3 | Calculation in Full-Time Equivalents (FTE) | V_T77S0SC | | 14.14.5 | PO |
| 4.15 | Address | | | 14.15 | PO |
| 4.15.1 | Buildings | T777A | | 14.15.2 | US |
| 4.16 | Mail Address | | | 14.16 | PO |

| *Chapter* | *Description* | *Configuration* | *NR/SS/ Done* | *Reference* | *Approved by* |
|---|---|---|---|---|---|
| **5** | **Plan Version** | | | **15** | |
| 5.1 | Maintaining Plan Version | T778P | | 15.2 | US |
| 5.2 | Active Plan Version | V_T77S0SC | | 15.4 | US |
| 5.3 | Number Assignment for All Plan Versions | V_T77S0SC | | 15.5 | PO |
| **6** | **Authorizations** | | | **17** | |
| 6.1 | Roles and Profiles | Transaction PFCG | | 17.1.4 | PO |
| 6.2 | Authorization for User | Transaction SU01 | | 17.1.5 | PO |
| 6.3 | Change Log | T77CDOC_CUST | | 17.1.7 | PO |
| 6.4 | Replace standard SAP authorization checks | BAdI HRPAD00AUTH_CHECK | | 17.1.8 | FC |
| 6.5 | Replace structural authorization checks | BAdI HRBAS00_STRUAUTH | | 17.1.8 | FC |
| 6.6 | No maintenance of structural profiles | BAdI HRBAS00_GET_PROFL | | 17.1.8 | FC |
| 6.7 | Authorization Main Switches | V_T77S0SC | | 17.2 | US |
| 6.8 | Authorization Objects for Transactions | Transaction SU24 | | 17.3 | FC |
| 6.9 | Authorization Profiles | T77PQ | | 17.4 | PO |
| 6.10 | Authorization Profile Definition | T77PR | | 17.5 | PO |
| 6.11 | Authorization Profiles to User Assignment | T77UA | | 17.6 | PO |
| 6.12 | Prefix for Batch Input Sessions | Feature BIMAP | | 17.7 | PO |
| 6.13 | User Data in SAP Memory | T77UU | | 17.8 | PO |
| **7** | **Organizational Management Integration** | | | **18** | |
| 7.1 | Integration with Personnel Administration | | | 18.1 | |
| 7.1.1 | Transfer Organizational Assignment from PA to PD (Report RHINTE00) | Transaction OOPH | | 18.1.1 | US |
| 7.1.2 | Transfer Objects from PD to PA (Report RHINTE10) | Transaction OOHP | | 18.1.1 | US |
| 7.1.3 | Create Missing Objects in OM or PA (Report RHINTE20) | Transaction OOPP | | 18.1.1 | US |

| *Chapter* | *Description* | *Configuration* | *NR/SS/ Done* | *Reference* | *Approved by* |
|---|---|---|---|---|---|
| 7.1.4 | Transfer Organizational Assignment in Batch Input Folder for Infotype 0001 (Report RHINTE30) | Transaction OOHQ | | 18.1.1 | US |
| 7.1.5 | Consistency Check | Program RHINTECHECK | | 18.1.1 | US |
| 7.1.6 | OM PA Integration Switches | V_T77S0SC | | 18.1.2 | US |
| 7.1.7 | Cost Distribution Integration Switches | V_T77S0SC | | 18.1.2 | US |
| 7.1.8 | Department Switch | V_T77S0SC | | 18.1.2 | US |
| 7.1.9 | Default Personnel Area, Subarea and Cost Center | V_T77S0SC | | 18.1.2 | US |
| 7.1.10 | Enhanced Integration | V_T77S0SC | | 18.1.2 | US |
| 7.1.11 | Extent of OM–PA Integration | Feature PLOGI | | 18.1.3 | US |
| 7.1.12 | Validity Period of Persons to Organizational Management | BAdI HREIC_RETIREES | | 18.1.5 | FC |
| 7.2 | Integration with Workflow | | | | |
| 7.2.1 | Workflow for Organizational Change | Transaction EXEORGCHEARM | | 18.3 | FC |
| 7.2.2 | Workflow Message about New Employees | Transaction WF_NEW_MAN | | 18.3 | FC |
| 7.3 | Integration with SAP Business Partners | | | 18.4 | |
| 7.3.1 | Business Partner Integration | | | | |
| 7.3.1.1 | Business Partner HR Integration | V_T77S0SC | | 18.4.2 | US |
| 7.3.2 | Business Partners in Employee Role | | | | |
| 7.3.2.1 | Creating Business Partners Automatically | V_T77S0SC | | 18.4.3 | US |
| 7.3.2.2 | Replication of Time Recording (CATS) in the Business Partner | V_T77S0SC | | 18.4.3 | US |
| 7.3.2.3 | ALE Distribution of Inactive Employees | V_T77S0SC | | 18.4.3 | US |
| 7.3.2.4 | Import Qualifications | V_T77S0SC | | 18.4.3 | US |
| 7.3.2.5 | Number Assignment of Business Partner | V_T77S0SC | | 18.4.3 | US |
| 7.3.2.6 | Subgroup of the Number Range Interval | V_T77S0SC | | 18.4.3 | US |
| 7.3.3 | Business Partners in Organizational Unit Role | | | | |

| *Chapter* | *Description* | *Configuration* | *NR/SS/ Done* | *Reference* | *Approved by* |
|---|---|---|---|---|---|
| 7.3.3.1 | Creating Business Partners Automatically | V_T77S0SC | | 18.4.4 | US |
| 7.3.3.2 | Address Necessary for Business Partner? | V_T77S0SC | | 18.4.4 | US |
| 7.3.3.3 | Standard Address of Business Partners | V_T77S0SC | | 18.4.4 | US |
| 7.3.3.4 | Business Partner Warnings | V_T77S0SC | | 18.4.4 | US |
| 7.3.3.5 | Number Assignment of Business Partner | V_T77S0SC | | 18.4.4 | US |
| 7.3.3.6 | Subgroup of the Number Range Interval | V_T77S0SC | | 18.4.4 | US |
| 7.3.4 | Data Synchronization | | | | |
| 7.3.4.1 | Synchronizing HR and Business Partners Data | Report HRALXSYNC | | 18.4.5 | US |
| 7.3.4.2 | Integration Error in IDOC | V_T77S0SC | | 18.4.5 | US |
| 7.3.4.3 | Recipient of Error Message | V_T77S0SC | | 18.4.5 | US |
| 7.3.5 | Business Partner Integration in Separate Logical Systems | | | 18.4.6 | FC |
| 7.3.6 | Mapping of Marital Status Keys | V_TB027HR_NEW | | 18.4.7 | US |
| 7.3.7 | Mapping of Form of Address Keys | V_TSAD3HR_NEW | | 18.4.8 | US |
| **8** | **Database Utilities and Dialog Control** | | | **19** | |
| 8.1 | Checking Consistency | Transaction RE_RHCHECK1 | | 19.1.6 | US |
| 8.2 | Checking Relationships | Transaction RE_RHCHECKV | | 19.1.7 | US |
| 8.3 | Installation Consistency Check | Transaction OOCH | | 19.1.11 | US |
| 8.4 | Sequence of Languages Available | T778L | | 19.2 | US |
| 8.5 | Search Function Settings | V_T77S0SC | | 19.3 | FC |
| 8.6 | Parameters for Staffing Schedule | V_T77S0SC | | 19.4 | FC |
| 8.7 | Customer Enhancements (User Exits) | Transaction CMOD | | 19.5 | FC |
| 8.7.1 | Additional Info On/Off | SAPLRHGB+CUS | | 19.5 | FC |
| 8.7.2 | Additional Info On/Off | SAPLRHGC+CUS | | 19.5 | FC |
| 8.7.3 | Further Info On/Off | EXIT_SAPLRHG B_001 | | 19.5 | FC |

| *Chapter* | *Description* | *Configuration* | *NR/SS/ Done* | *Reference* | *Approved by* |
|---|---|---|---|---|---|
| 8.7.4 | Fill Text for Customer-Specific Field | EXIT_SAPLRHG B_002 | | 19.5 | FC |
| 8.7.5 | Additional Info On/Off | SAPLRHGP+CUS | | 19.5 | FC |
| 8.7.6 | Further Info On/Off | EXIT_SAPLRHG P_001 | | 19.5 | FC |
| 8.7.7 | Fill Text for Customer-Specific Field | EXIT_SAPLRHG P_002 | | 19.5 | FC |
| 8.7.8 | Fill Header for Customer-Specific Field | EXIT_SAPLRHG P_003 | | 19.5 | FC |
| 8.7.9 | Additional Info On/Off | SAPLRHSI+CUS | | 19.5 | FC |
| 8.7.10 | Additional Info On/Off | SAPLRHSI+CUS | | 19.5 | FC |
| 8.8 | Settings for Simple Maintenance | V_T77S0SC | | 19.6 | FC |
| **9** | **Data Transfer** | | | **20** | |
| 9.1 | Transport Connection | V_T77S0SC | | 20.1 | US |
| 9.2 | Locking Infotypes for Import | T77TR | | 20.2 | US |
| 9.3 | Manual Transport | Transaction RE_RHMOVE30 | | 20.3 | US |
| 9.4 | Data Transfer through Sequential Files | Transaction SXDA | | 20.4 | US |
| 9.5 | Data Distribution using ALE | Transaction SALE | | 20.5 | FC |
| 9.6 | Data Extraction | | | | |
| 9.6.1 | Scenarios | T77SCEN_AW | | 20.6.1 | FC |
| 9.6.2 | Assignment of Queries to Scenarios | T77SCENQY | | 20.6.2 | FC |
| **10** | **Organization and Staffing Interface Customizing** | | | **21** | |
| 10.1 | Tab Pages | | | 21.1 | |
| 10.1.1 | Tab Pages (Cross-Client) | T77OMTABS | SS | 21.1.3 | FC |
| 10.1.2 | Tab Page Texts (Client-Specific) | T77OCTABST | SS | 21.1.3 | FC |
| 10.1.3 | Scenario Definition (Cross-Client) | T77OMFRAS | SS | 21.1.4 | FC |
| 10.1.4 | Scenario Attributes (Cross-Client) | T77OMFRAM | SS | 21.1.4 | FC |
| 10.1.5 | Scenario Groups (Cross-Client) | T77OMSCENF | SS | 21.1.4 | FC |
| 10.1.6 | Scenario Icons (Cross-Client) | T77OMICON | SS | 21.1.4 | FC |
| 10.1.7 | Tab Pages for Each Object Type (Cross-Client) | T77OMTABUS | SS | 21.1.5 | FC |
| 10.1.8 | Tab Pages for Each Object Type (Client-Specific) | T77OCTABUS | SS | 21.1.5 | FC |

| *Chapter* | *Description* | *Configuration* | *NR/SS/ Done* | *Reference* | *Approved by* |
|---|---|---|---|---|---|
| 10.1.9 | Services (Cross-Client) | T77OBJSER | SS | 21.1.6 | FC |
| 10.1.10 | Attributes of Services (Cross-Client) | T77OMATGT | SS | 21.1.6 | FC |
| 10.1.11 | Requests (Cross-Client) | T77OMREGIS | SS | 21.1.7 | FC |
| 10.1.12 | Requests for Object Types (Cross-Client) | T77OMIA | SS | 21.1.7 | FC |
| 10.1.13 | Requests for Object Types (Client-Specific) | T77OMIA_C | SS | 21.1.7 | FC |
| 10.2 | Columns | | | 21.2 | |
| 10.2.1 | Columns (Cross-Client) | T77COL | SS | 21.2.3 | FC |
| 10.2.2 | Column groups (Cross-Client) | T77ARRAYTP | SS | 21.2.4 | FC |
| 10.2.3 | Columns in Column Group (Cross-Client) | T77ACOL | SS | 21.2.4 | FC |
| 10.2.4 | Visibility of a Column (Cross-Client) | T77ACOLINI | SS | 21.2.4 | FC |
| 10.2.5 | Columns in Column Group and Visibility of a Column (Client-Specific) | T77ACOLC | SS | 21.2.4 | FC |
| 10.2.6 | Column/Object Type Assignment (Cross-Client) | T77COLOTYP | SS | 21.2.5 | FC |
| 10.2.7 | Hierarchical Column Groups (Cross-Client) | T77HIERATP | SS | 21.2.6 | FC |
| 10.2.8 | Hierarchical Column Groups (Client-Specific) | T77HIERATC | SS | 21.2.6 | FC |
| 10.2.9 | Column Header Types (Cross-Client) | T77COLHTYP | SS | 21.2.7 | FC |
| 10.2.10 | Column Headers (Cross-Client) | T77COLHEAD | SS | 21.2.7 | FC |
| 10.2.11 | Column Headers (Client-Specific) | T77COLH_C | SS | 21.2.7 | FC |
| 10.3 | Search Nodes | | | 21.3 | |
| 10.3.1 | Search Nodes (Cross-Client) | T77FSEAN | SS | 21.3.3 | FC |
| 10.3.2 | Search Tools (Cross-Client) | T77FSEAS | SS | 21.3.4 | FC |
| 10.3.3 | Coherence Relationships (Cross-Client) | T77FRIEND | SS | 21.3.5 | FC |
| 10.3.4 | Object Manager Scenarios (Cross-Client) | T77FOBJMAN | SS | 21.3.6 | FC |
| 10.3.5 | Search Nodes in a Scenario (Cross-Client) | T77FNODORD | SS | 21.3.6 | FC |
| 10.3.6 | Search Nodes in a Scenario (Client-Specific) | T77CNODORD | SS | 21.3.6 | FC |

| *Chapter* | *Description* | *Configuration* | *NR/SS/ Done* | *Reference* | *Approved by* |
|---|---|---|---|---|---|
| 10.3.7 | Excluding Nodes from Search Range (Client-Specific) | T77CNOD_EX | SS | 21.3.6 | FC |
| 10.3.8 | Search Tools in a Scenario (Cross-Client) | T77FSEAT | SS | 21.3.6 | FC |
| 10.3.9 | Column Group for a Search Tool (Cross-Client) | T77FSEATGB | SS | 21.3.6 | FC |
| 10.3.10 | Column Group for a Search Tool in a Scenario (Client-Specific) | V77CSEAT | SS | 21.3.6 | FC |
| 10.3.11 | Exclude Search Tools from Search Range (Client-Specific) | T77CSEAT_E | SS | 21.3.6 | FC |
| 10.4 | Excluding Infotypes when Copying Internal Objects | T77ITEX_C | | 21.4 | US |
| 10.5 | Backup Prompt | T77OMFRAMC | | 21.5 | US |
| 10.6 | Assignment of InfoSets to Object Types | T77OMAHQ_FU NCARS | SS | 21.6 | FC |
| 10.7 | Assignment of InfoSets to Object Types | T77OMAHQ_FU NCAR | | 21.6 | FC |
| **11** | **Data Model** | | | **22** | |
| 11.1 | Object Types | T778O | SS | 22.1 | FC |
| 11.2 | Essential Relationships | T77SO | SS | 22.2 | FC |
| 11.3 | External Object Types | T77EO | SS | 22.3 | FC |
| 11.4 | Structure Search | T77OS | SS | 22.4 | FC |
| 11.5 | Object Type Key | V_T77S0OT | SS | 22.5 | FC |
| 11.6 | Transactions for Maintaining Object Types | V_T77S0OT | SS | 22.6 | FC |
| 11.7 | Infotypes Master List | T778T | SS | 22.7 | FC |
| 11.8 | Infotype Time Constraints | T777Z | SS | 22.8 | FC |
| 11.9 | Object Types Allowed for an Infotype | T777I | SS | 22.9 | FC |
| 11.10 | Subtypes of an Infotype | V_778U | SS | 22.10 | FC |
| 11.11 | Customer-Specific Settings for Infotypes | T77CD | SS | 22.11 | FC |
| 11.12 | Country-Specific Infotypes | T77NI | SS | 22.12 | FC |
| 11.13 | Relationships | T778V | SS | 22.13 | FC |
| 11.14 | Relationship Characteristics | T77VA | SS | 22.14 | FC |
| 11.15 | Additional Data on Relationships | T77AR | SS | 22.15 | FC |
| 11.16 | Allowed Relationships | T777E | SS | 22.16 | FC |
| 11.17 | External Relationships | T77EV | SS | 22.17 | FC |

| *Chapter* | *Description* | *Configuration* | *NR/SS/ Done* | *Reference* | *Approved by* |
|---|---|---|---|---|---|
| 11.18 | Relationship Time Constraints | V_T777ZVK | SS | 22.18 | FC |
| 11.19 | Relationship Abbreviation | V_T77S0VK | SS | 22.19 | FC |
| 11.20 | Relationships Time Constraint Depending on Target Object Type | T77ZR | SS | 22.20 | FC |
| 11.21 | Relationships Until Birthday | T777BIRTH | SS | 22.21 | FC |
| **12** | **Qualifications Catalog** | | | **23** | |
| 12.1 | Qualifications Catalog | Transaction OOQA | | 23.2 | US |
| 12.2 | BAdI: Selection Options for "Find Objects for Qualifications" Search | BAdI HRPDV00QSEA RCH0001 | | 23.4.1 | FC |
| 12.3 | Scales | VC_T77SK | | 23.6 | US |
| 12.4 | Qualification Control Parameters | V_T77S0SC | | 23.7 | US |
| **13** | **Profiles** | | | **24** | |
| 13.1 | Creating Qualifications Sub-Profile of Several Objects | Transaction OOQM | | 24.2.1 | FC |
| 13.2 | Copying Requirements Profiles to Position Holders | Transaction OOQ5 | | 24.2.5 | PO |
| 13.3 | Subprofiles for each Object Type | | | 24.3 | SM |
| 13.4 | Personnel Development View | T77PP_VIEW | SS | 24.6 | FC |
| 13.5 | Headers | T77PP_HEAD | SS | 24.7 | FC |
| 13.6 | Headers for PD View | V_T77PR_V_H | SS | 24.8 | FC |
| 13.7 | Subprofiles Master | T77PP_PART | SS | 24.9 | FC |
| 13.8 | Subprofile for an Object Type | V_T77PR_V_H_P | SS | 24.10 | FC |
| 13.9 | Authorization Check for Accessing Subprofiles | BAdI HRPDV00 PROFILE0001 | | 24.11 | FC |
| **14** | **Career Planning** | | | | |
| 14.1 | Careers | Transaction OOQ4 | | 25.2 | PO |
| 14.2 | Suitability in Case of Over-Qualification | V_T77S0SC | | 25.3 | PO |
| 14.3 | Suitability Range | T77CS | | 25.3 | PO |
| 14.4 | Policy on User-Specific Settings | | | 25.4.5 | PO |
| **15** | **Development Plan** | | | **26** | |
| 15.1 | Development Plan Catalog | Transaction OOEC | | 26.3 | PO |
| 15.2 | Development Plan States | T77BZ | | 26.4 | PO |
| 15.3 | Permissible Further Processing | T77FUNC | | 26.5 | PO |

| *Chapter* | *Description* | *Configuration* | *NR/SS/ Done* | *Reference* | *Approved by* |
|---|---|---|---|---|---|
| 15.4 | Further Processing of Development Plan Items | T77BX | | 26.6 | PO |
| 15.5 | Confirmation of Further Processing Step | V_T77S0SC | | 26.6.5 | PO |
| 15.6 | Automatic State Management | T77BW | | 26.7 | PO |
| 15.7 | Display of Business Events in Individual Development Plans | V_T77S0SC | | 26.8 | PO |
| **16** | **Appraisals** | | | **27** | |
| 16.1 | Replace Old Appraisal System with New | V_T77S0SC | | 27.1 | FC |
| 16.2 | Appraisal Catalog | Transaction OOAM | | 27.2 | PO |
| 16.3 | Activate Extended Authorization Check | V_T77S0 | | 27.2 | PO |
| 16.4 | Appraisal Category Group | Transaction OOAM | | 27.3 | PO |
| 16.5 | Appraisal Category | Transaction OOAM | | 27.4 | PO |
| 16.6 | Appraisal Template | Transaction OOAM | | 27.5 | PO |
| 16.7 | Appraisal Criteria Group | Transaction OOAM | | 27.6 | PO |
| 16.8 | Appraisal Criteria | Transaction OOAM | | 27.7 | PO |
| **17** | **Personnel Development Integration** | | | **28** | |
| 17.1 | Integration with Personnel Administration | | | 28.2 | |
| 17.1.1 | Integration of Qualification | V_T77S0SC | | 28.2.1 | PO |
| 17.1.2 | Transfer of Qualification Data from PA to PD | Transaction OOQI | | 28.2.2 | FC |
| 17.1.3 | Integration of Appraisal | V_T77S0SC | | 28.2.3 | PO |
| 17.1.4 | Transfer of Appraisal Data from PA to PD | Transaction OOAI | | 28.2.4 | FC |
| 17.2 | Integration with Recruitment | | | 28.3 | |
| 17.2.1 | Integration of Qualification | V_T77S0SC | | 28.2.1 | PO |
| 17.2.2 | Transfer of Qualification Data from Recruitment to PD | Transaction OOQB | | 28.3.2 | FC |
| 17.3 | Integration with Strategic Enterprise Management | | | | PO |
| 17.3.1 | RFC Destination in SEM System | V_T77S0SC | | 28.6.1 | PO |

| *Chapter* | *Description* | *Configuration* | *NR/SS/ Done* | *Reference* | *Approved by* |
|---|---|---|---|---|---|
| **18** | **Business Event Catalog** | | | **29** | |
| 18.1 | Business Event Catalog | Transaction OOC3 | | 29.2 | PO |
| 18.2 | Business Event Group | Transaction OOEG | | 30 | PO |
| 18.3 | Business Event Type | Transaction OOET | | 31 | PO |
| 18.4 | Day Segment | Transaction OOTM | | 31.5.4 | PO |
| 18.5 | Time Schedule | Transaction OOTM | | 31.5.5 | PO |
| 18.6 | Standard Capacity | V_T77S0SC | | 31.6 | PO |
| 18.7 | Maximum Waiting List Capacity | V_T77S0SC | | 31.6 | PO |
| 18.8 | Message Type when Waiting List Capacity Exceeded | V_T77S0SC | | 31.6 | PO |
| 18.9 | Cost Items | Transaction OOKB | | 31.14.1 | PO |
| **19** | **Dynamic Menus** | | | **32** | |
| 19.1 | Planning Period | V_T77S0SC | | 32.1.5 | PO |
| 19.2 | Virtual Business Event Group | V_T77S0SC | | 32.1.6 | FC |
| 19.3 | Additional Line in Dynamic Menus | V_T77S0SC | | 32.1.7 | PO |
| 19.4 | Integration of Customer-Specific Reports | Transaction PVDM | | 32.2.8 | PO |
| **20** | **Resources** | | | **33** | |
| 20.1 | Resource Type | Transaction OORT | | 33.1 | PO |
| 20.2 | Room | Transaction OORA | | 33.2 | PO |
| 20.3 | Other Resource | Transaction OORE | | 33.3 | PO |
| 20.4 | Defining Service to Lock Resources | Transaction PVV0 | | 33.4.1 | FC |
| 20.5 | Assigning Service to Lock Resources | V_T77S0SC | | 33.4.2 | FC |
| 20.6 | Resource Reservation | V_T77S0SC | | 33.5 | FC |
| 20.7 | Location | Transaction OOLC | | 33.8 | PO |

| *Chapter* | *Description* | *Configuration* | *NR/SS/ Done* | *Reference* | *Approved by* |
|---|---|---|---|---|---|
| 20.8 | Switch for Business Event Locations | V_T77S0SC | | 33.8.1 | PO |
| 20.9 | Default Fa tory Calendar | V_T77S0SC | | 33.8.5 | PO |
| 20.10 | Factory Ca.endar | Transaction OY05 | | 33.8.5 | PO |
| **21** | **Business Events** | | | **34** | |
| 21.1 | Conversion of Unplaced Candidates to Prebookings | V_T77S0SC | | 34.9.6 | PO |
| 21.2 | Cancellation Reasons | T77CR | | 34.9.8 | US |
| 21.3 | Appraising Business Event | Appraisal template | | 34.12.1 | PO |
| 21.4 | Global Follow-up Actions | V_T77KV_2 | | 34.13.6 | PO |
| **22** | **Attendee** | | | **35** | |
| 22.1 | External Person/External Instructor | Transaction OOER | | 35.5 | US |
| 22.2 | Company | Transaction PVU0 | | 35.6 | US |
| 22.3 | Attendee Type Control Options | V_T77R3_1 | | 35.11 | PO |
| **23** | **Attendance** | | | **36** | |
| 23.1 | Booking Priority | V_T77S0SC | | 36.1 | PO |
| 23.2 | Attendance/Attendance Conflict | V_T77S0SC | | 36.2.3 | PO |
| 23.3 | Attendance/Instructor Conflict | V_T77S0SC | | 36.2.4 | PO |
| 23.4 | Attendee Checks | V_T77KV_1 | | 36.2.5 | PO |
| 23.5 | Incompatible Attendance and Absence Types | T77KA | | 36.2.6 | PO |
| 23.6 | Additional Checks | BAdI RHPV0001 | | 36.2.7 | PO |
| 23.7 | Checking Business Events when Prebooking | V_T77S0SC | | 36.4.2 | PO |
| 23.8 | Business Event Preview Period | V_T77S0SC | | 36.7.2 | PO |
| 23.9 | Charging Fee by Default | V_T77S0SC | | 36.7.4 | PO |
| 23.10 | Cost Maintenance | V_T77S0SC | | 36.7.4 | FC |
| 23.11 | Reasons for Attendance Cancellation | T77CAR | | 36.12.6 | US |
| 23.12 | Default Value for Cancellation Fees | V_T77S0SC | | 36.12.6 | PO |
| 23.13 | Moving-up on Cancellation | V_T77S0SC | | 36.12.7 | PO |
| 23.14 | Attendee Appraisals | Appraisal template | | 36.13.1 | PO |

| *Chapter* | *Description* | *Configuration* | *NR/SS/ Done* | *Reference* | *Approved by* |
|---|---|---|---|---|---|
| **24** | **Correspondence** | | | **37** | |
| 24.1 | Correspondence Requirements | | | | PO |
| 24.2 | Activities | T77VI | SS | 37.4 | FC |
| 24.3 | Recipients of Notification | T77VE | SS | 37.5 | FC |
| 24.4 | Recipient Groups | T77VG | SS | 37.6 | FC |
| 24.5 | Form for a Notification | T77VD | | 37.7 | FC |
| 24.6 | Assignment of Users to User Groups | T77KU | | 37.8 | PO |
| 24.7 | Default Output Medium | V_T77KV_3 | | 37.9 | PO |
| 24.8 | Default Language | V_T77S0SC | | 37.10 | PO |
| 24.9 | Priority for Workflow Correspondence | V_T77S0SC | | 37.11 | PO |
| 24.10 | Forms | | | 37.12 | |
| 24.10.1 | Forms | Transaction OOFO | | 37.12.1–37.12.4 | FC |
| 24.10.2 | Sequence of Text Elements | T77VB | | 37.12.5 | FC |
| 24.10.3 | Text Variables | T77VC | | 37.12.6 | FC |
| 24.10.4 | Name Format for Recipients | T777N | | 37.12.7 | FC |
| 24.11 | Mail Connection | | | 37.14 | |
| 24.11.1 | RFC Destination | Transaction SM59 | | 37.14.1 | FC |
| 24.11.2 | RFC Destination for Connection to Mail System | V_T77S0SC | | 37.14.2 | FC |
| 24.11.3 | Subtype for Mail Connection | V_T77S0SC | | 37.14.3 | FC |
| **25** | **Training Integration** | | | **38** | |
| 25.1 | Time Management | | | 38.3 | |
| 25.1.1 | Integration Switch of Training with Time Management | V_T77S0SC | | 38.3.1 | PO |
| 25.1.2 | Attendance Type for Attendee | V_T77S0SC | | 38.3.2 | PO |
| 25.1.3 | Attendance Type for Instructor | V_T77S0SC | | 38.3.3 | PO |
| 25.1.4 | Minimum Attendance Percentage | V_T77S0SC | | 38.3.4 | PO |
| 25.2 | Activity Allocation | | | 38.5 | |
| 25.2.1 | Activity Allocation Switch | V_T77S0SC | | 38.5.3 | PO |
| 25.2.2 | Number Range | Transaction OORB | | 38.5.4 | PO |
| 25.2.3 | Controlling Area Selection | V_T77S0SC | | 38.5.5 | PO |
| 25.2.4 | Cost Center of Business Event Cost Object | V_T77S0SC | | 38.5.6 | PO |

| *Chapter* | *Description* | *Configuration* | *NR/SS/ Done* | *Reference* | *Approved by* |
|---|---|---|---|---|---|
| 25.2.5 | Sender Cost Center for Internal Activity Allocation | V_T77S0SC | | 38.5.6 | PO |
| 25.2.6 | Cost Element | V_T77S0SC | | 38.5.7 | PO |
| 25.2.7 | Activity Type Determination | V_T77S0SC | | 38.5.8 | PO |
| 25.2.8 | Number Ranges for Controlling Documents | Transaction KANK | | 38.5.10 | PO |
| 25.2.9 | Activity Type | Transaction KL01 | | 38.5.11 | PO |
| 25.2.10 | Activity Price | Transaction KP26 | | 38.5.12 | PO |
| 25.3 | Cost Transfer Posting | | | 38.6 | |
| 25.3.1 | Cost Transfer Switch | V_T77S0SC | | 38.6.3 | PO |
| 25.3.2 | Number Range | Transaction OORB | | 38.6.4 | PO |
| 25.3.3 | Controlling Area Selection | V_T77S0SC | | 38.6.5 | PO |
| 25.3.4 | Cost Center of Business Event Cost Object | V_T77S0SC | | 38.6.6 | PO |
| 25.3.5 | Sender Cost Center for Internal Activity Allocation | V_T77S0SC | | 38.6.6 | PO |
| 25.3.6 | Cost Items | T77KB | | 38.6.7 | PO |
| 25.3.7 | Number Ranges for Controlling Documents | Transaction KANK | | 38.6.9 | PO |
| 25.4 | Billing | | | 38.7 | |
| 25.4.1 | Integration Switch of Training with Billing | V_T77S0SC | | 38.7.2 | PO |
| 25.4.2 | Organizational Elements | V_T77S0SC | | 38.7.3 | PO |
| 25.4.3 | Invoice Creation Settings | V_T77S0SC | | 38.7.4 | FC |
| 25.4.4 | Credit Memo Creation Settings | V_T77S0SC | | 38.7.5 | FC |
| 25.4.5 | Prices, Taxes and Account Assignment | V_T77S0SC | | 38.7.6 | FC |
| 25.5 | Materials Management | | | 38.8 | |
| 25.5.1 | Integration Switch of Training with Materials Management | V_T77S0SC | | 38.8.2 | PO |
| 25.5.2 | Number Ranges | Transaction OORB | | 38.8.3 | PO |
| 25.5.3 | Plant and Storage Location | V_T77S0SC | | 38.8.4 | PO |
| 25.5.4 | Default Value for Controlling Area | V_T77S0SC | | 38.8.5 | PO |
| 25.5.5 | Cost Center of Business Event Cost Object | V_T77S0SC | | 38.8.6 | PO |

| *Chapter* | *Description* | *Configuration* | *NR/SS/ Done* | *Reference* | *Approved by* |
|---|---|---|---|---|---|
| 25.5.6 | Document Type and Movement Type | V_T77S0SC | | 38.8.7 | FC |
| 25.6 | SAP Appointment Calendar | | | 38.10 | |
| 25.6.1 | Appointment Types | SCAPPTTYPE | | 38.10.2 | PO |
| 25.6.2 | Specifying Appointment Types | V_T77S0SC | | 38.10.3 | PO |
| 25.6.3 | Activating Integration | V_T77S0SC | | 38.10.4 | PO |
| 25.7 | Budget Management | | | 38.11 | |
| 25.7.1 | Generating Budget Structure from Organizational Structure | Transaction PVB0 | | 38.11.1 | PO |
| 25.7.2 | Budget Currency | V_T7PM2 | | 38.11.3 | PO |
| 25.7.3 | Budget Types | V_T7PM3_B | | 38.11.4 | PO |
| 25.7.4 | Budget Period | V_T7PM9_B | | 38.11.5 | PO |
| 25.8 | Integration with Workflow | | | 38.12 | |
| 25.8.1 | Activating Event Linkage | V_T77S0SC | | 38.12.1 | FC |
| 25.8.2 | Allowed Business Object Types for HR Objects, Infotypes and Subtypes | T777IBO | | 38.12.2 | FC |
| 25.8.3 | Event Linkage | T779X | | 38.12.3 | FC |
| 25.9 | Employee Self-Service | | | 38.13 | |
| 25.9.1 | Set up External Search Engine | Transaction PVSEARCH_ADM | | 38.13.1 | PO |
| 25.9.2 | Booking Priority for Internet | V_T77S0SC | | 38.13.2 | PO |
| 25.9.3 | Event Generation in Web Transactions | V_T77S0SC | | 38.13.3 | PO |
| 25.9.4 | Cancellation Reason for Employee | V_T77S0SC | | 38.13.4 | PO |
| 25.9.5 | Customer-Specific Attendance Cancellation Reason | BAdI HRTEM00NET_ WEBST | | 38.13.5 | FC |
| 25.9.6 | Customer-Specific Setup of 'My Bookings' | BAdI HRTEM00NET_ ACTIVITY | | 38.13.6 | FC |
| 25.10 | Training General Settings | | | 38.14 | |
| 25.10.1 | Changes to Historical Attendances | V_T77S0SC | | 38.14.1 | PO |
| 25.10.2 | Specifying Data Screen Display | V_T77S0SC | | 38.14.2 | PO |
| 25.10.3 | Customer Enhancement for Master Data | V_T77S0SC | | 38.14.3 | FC |
| 25.10.4 | Notes for Infotypes | T77NT | | 38.14.4 | FC |
| 25.10.5 | Procedure for Entering Notes | V_T77S0SC | | 38.14.5 | PO |

| *Chapter* | *Description* | *Configuration* | *NR/SS/ Done* | *Reference* | *Approved by* |
|---|---|---|---|---|---|
| 25.10.6 | List Entry for Attendee Activities | V_T77S0SC | | 38.14.6 | PO |
| 25.10.7 | Pushbutton Settings for Batch Input | V_T77S0SC | | 38.14.7 | FC |
| **26** | **Transactions** | | | | |
| 26.1 | Organizational Management | | | 39.4.1 | PO |
| 26.2 | Personnel Development | | | 39.4.2 | PO |
| 26.3 | Training and Event Management | | | 39.4.3 | PO |
| 26.4 | Utility | | | 39.4.4 | PO |

## 39.4 TRANSACTIONS

| *Functional Consultant* | *User* | *Business Process Owner* | *Senior Management* | *My Rating* | *Understanding Level* |
|---|---|---|---|---|---|
| A | X | X | X | | |

Transactions given in this chapter can be used for authorization design.

### 39.4.1 Organizational Management

| *Category* | *Transaction* | *Description* |
|---|---|---|
| User | OODT | Legacy Data Transfer |
| Customizing | OOHP | Set Up PD – PA Integration |
| Both | OOHQ | Batch Input Sessions |
| Customizing | OOMT | Actions |
| User | OOMV | Create Sequential File for PD |
| Customizing | OONR | Number Ranges |
| Customizing | OOPH | Set Up PA – PD Integration |
| Customizing | OOPP | Consistency Check for Integration |
| User | PFAL | ALE Distribution of HR Master Data |
| User | PFCT | Task Catalog |
| User | PO01 | Maintain Work Center |
| User | PO03 | Maintain Job |
| User | PO10 | Maintain Organizational Unit |
| User | PO13 | Maintain Position |

| Category | Transaction code | Description |
|---|---|---|
| User | PP01 | Maintain Plan Data |
| User | PP03 | Actions |
| User | PPME | Change Matrix Organization |
| User | PPMS | Display Matrix Organization |
| User | PPOC_OLD | Create Organizational Plan |
| User | PPOCE | Create Organization and Staffing |
| User | PPOM_MODE | Set Maintenance Interface |
| Both | PPOM_OLD, OOOE | Maintain Organizational Plan |
| User | PPOME | Change Organization and Staffing |
| User | PPOS_OLD | Display Organizational Plan |
| User | PPOSE | Display Organization and Staffing |
| User | PPSC | Create Structure |
| User | PPSM | Change Structure |
| User | PPSS | Display Structure |
| User | PSO0 | Set Plan Version |
| User | PSO3 | Object Description |
| User | PSO4 | Individual Infotype Maintenance |
| User | RE_RHAKTI00 | Change Object Status |
| User | RE_RHALECPS | Display ALE Change Pointers |
| User | RE_RHALESMD | Evaluate ALE Change Pointers |
| User | RE_RHAUTH00 | Authorized Objects |
| User | RE_RHBEGDA0 | Change Start Date |
| User | RE_RHCHECK1 | Check Database Consistency |
| User | RE_RHCHECKV | Check Relationships |
| User | RE_RHCOPL00 | Copy Plan Version w/o Comparison |
| User | RE_RHCOPLPT | Reconcile Plan Versions (Partly) |
| User | RE_RHCOPY00 | Copy Object |
| User | RE_RHCOPY10 | Copy Objects Using Selection List |
| User | RE_RHCOPYSTRUCT | Copy Structures |
| User | RE_RHDBST00 | PD Database Statistics |
| User | RE_RHDESC10 | Display Infotypes |
| User | RE_RHGRENZ4 | Set New End Date for Infotypes |
| Both | RE_RHMOVE30 | Manual Transport Link |
| User | RE_RHREPL20 | Replace User with Person |
| User | RE_RHRHAZ00 | Display PD Database Records |
| User | RE_RHRHDC00 | Delete HR Database Records via List |
| User | RE_RHRHDL00 | Delete PD Database Records |
| User | RE_RHTRANS0 | Translate Language-Dependent Records |

| *Category* | *Transaction code* | *Description* |
|---|---|---|
| User | S_AHR_61003129 | Check Integration Consistency |
| User | S_AHR_61003170 | Create Justifications |
| User | S_AHR_61003172 | Create Building Addresses |
| User | S_AHR_61003187 | Create Working Time Groups |
| User | S_AHR_61003603 | Create Health Promotion Measures |
| User | S_AHR_61007150 | Create Authorities/Resources |
| User | S_AHR_61007156 | Create Restrictions |
| User | S_AHR_61016491 | Existing Organizational Units |
| User | S_AHR_61016492 | Staff Functions for Organizational Units |
| User | S_AHR_61016493 | Organizational Structure |
| User | S_AHR_61016494 | Organizational Structure with Positions |
| User | S_AHR_61016495 | Organizational Structure with Persons |
| User | S_AHR_61016496 | Organizational Structure with Work Centers |
| User | S_AHR_61016497 | Existing Jobs |
| User | S_AHR_61016498 | Job Index |
| User | S_AHR_61016499 | Job Description |
| User | S_AHR_61016500 | Task Description for Jobs |
| User | S_AHR_61016501 | Complete Job Description |
| User | S_AHR_61016502 | Existing Positions |
| User | S_AHR_61016503 | Staff Assignments |
| User | S_AHR_61016504 | Position Description |
| User | S_AHR_61016505 | Task Description for Positions |
| User | S_AHR_61016506 | Staff Functions for Positions |
| User | S_AHR_61016507 | Authorities and Resources |
| User | S_AHR_61016508 | Planned Labor Costs |
| User | S_AHR_61016509 | Vacant Positions |
| User | S_AHR_61016510 | Correct Vacancies |
| User | S_AHR_61016511 | Complete Position Description |
| User | S_AHR_61016512 | Report Structure without Persons |
| User | S_AHR_61016513 | Report Structure with Persons |
| User | S_AHR_61016514 | Existing Work Centers |
| User | S_AHR_61016515 | Work Centers per Organizational Unit |
| User | S_AHR_61016516 | Authorities and Resources |
| User | S_AHR_61016517 | Planned Labor Costs |
| User | S_AHR_61016518 | Work Centers with Restrictions along Organizational Structure |
| User | S_AHR_61016519 | Single Work Centers with Restrictions |

| *Category* | *Transaction code* | *Description* |
|---|---|---|
| User | S_AHR_61016520 | Work Centers Requiring Health Examinations along Organizational Structure |
| User | S_AHR_61016521 | Single Work Centers Requiring Health Examinations |
| User | S_AHR_61016522 | Existing Tasks |
| User | S_AHR_61016523 | Activity Profile for Positions along Organizational Structure |
| User | S_AHR_61016524 | Activity Profile of Positions with Persons along Organizational Structure |
| User | S_AHR_61016525 | Character of Tasks in Organizational Structure |
| User | S_AHR_61016526 | Character of Individual Tasks |
| User | S_AHR_61016527 | Existing Objects |
| User | S_AHR_61016528 | Structure Display/Maintenance |
| User | S_AHR_61016529 | Structure Navigation Instrument |
| User | S_AHR_61016530 | PD Graphics Interface |
| User | S_AHR_61016531 | Display and Maintain Infotypes |
| User | S_AHR_61016532 | Infotype Reporting |
| User | S_AHR_61016533 | HR Reporting via Personnel Planning Structures |
| User | S_AHR_61018831 | Obsolete Positions |
| User | S_AHR_61018869 | Periods of Unoccupied Positions |
| User | S_PH0_48000084 | Generation of Positions for Quota Planning |
| User | S_PH0_48000085 | Freeze Planned Quota |
| User | S_PH0_48000086 | Copying the Current Required Positions into a Planning Type |
| User | S_PH0_48000087 | Copying Quota Planning into another Planning Type |
| User | S_PH0_48000088 | Delete Unoccupied Positions on Key Date |

### 39.4.2 Personnel Development

| *Category* | *Transaction code* | *Description* |
|---|---|---|
| User | APPCHANGE | Edit Appraisal |
| User | APPCREATE | Create Appraisal |
| User | APPSEARCH | Search Appraisals |
| User | HRPDV00REPORT0001 | Maintained Qualifications |
| Customizing | OOAI | Appraisal Transfer Persons |
| Customizing | OOMT | Actions |

| *Category* | *Transaction code* | *Description* |
|---|---|---|
| Customizing | OOQ5 | Copy Requirements Profile to Holder |
| Customizing | OOQB | Qualification Transfer: Applicants |
| Customizing | OOQI | Transfer Qualifications: Employee |
| User | PEPM | Profile Matchup |
| User | PEPP | Profiles |
| User | PPAD | Display Appraisals Catalog |
| User | PPCP | Career Planning |
| User | PPDPCS | Display Development Plan Catalog |
| User | PPDPIM | Change Individual Development Plan |
| User | PPDPSPFP | Find Objects which Have Completed a Plan |
| User | PPDPSPFS | Find Persons for Development Item |
| User | PPEM | Planning for Organizational Unit |
| User | PPPD | Display Profile |
| User | PPPE_SEARCH_FOR_Q | Find Objects for Qualifications |
| User | PPPM | Change Profile |
| User | PPQD | Display Qualifications Catalog |
| User | PPSP | Succession Planning |
| User | PPUP | Settings: User Parameters |
| Both | S_AHR_61003917, OOQM | Qualifications Profile: Mass Data Maintenance |
| Both | S_AHR_61003929, OOQA | Edit Qualifications Catalog |
| Both | S_AHR_61003969, PHAP_CATALOG_PA | Edit Appraisals Catalog |
| Both | S_AHR_61007168, OOEC | Edit Development Plan Catalog |
| Both | S_AHR_61007208, OOQ4 | Edit Careers |
| Both | S_AHR_61007222, OOSP | Define Authorization Profiles |
| User | S_AHR_61015524 | Evaluate Careers |
| User | S_AHR_61015532 | Profile Matchup: Positions/Holders |
| User | S_AHR_61015533 | Profiles |
| User | S_AHR_61015536 | Expired Qualifications |
| User | S_PH9_46000016 | Qualifications Overview |
| User | S_PH9_46000017 | Succession Overview |
| User | S_PH9_46000018 | Objects with Unevaluated Qualifications or Requirements |
| User | S_PH9_46000019 | Objects without Qualifications or Requirements |
| User | S_PH9_46000022 | List of Alternative Qualifications |

### 39.4.3 Training and Event Management

| *Category* | *Transaction code* | *Description* |
|---|---|---|
| Customizing | OOMT | Actions |
| User | PO07 | Maintain Other Resource |
| User | PO18 | Maintain Resource 'Room' |
| User | PO19 | Maintain External Instructor |
| User | PP40 | Manual Correspondence |
| User | PSV1 | Attendance Menu |
| User | PSV2 | Business Event Menu |
| User | PSV3 | Information Menu |
| User | PSV4 | Set Plan Version |
| User | PSV8 | Create Attendee |
| User | PSV9 | Change/Display Attendee |
| User | PSVI | User-Specific Settings |
| User | PSVO | Change/Display Organizer |
| User | PSVP | Planning Menu |
| User | PSVQ | Create Organizer |
| User | PSVR | Resource Menu |
| User | PSVT | Tool Menu |
| User | PV00 | Book: Attendee for Business Event |
| User | PV01 | Rebook Attendance |
| User | PV02 | Prebook: Attendee for Business Event Type |
| User | PV03 | Replace Attendance |
| User | PV04 | Cancel Attendance |
| User | PV06 | Prebook: Attendee List for Business Event Type |
| User | PV07 | Book: Attendee List for Business Event |
| User | PV08 | Book: Attendee for Business Event List |
| User | PV10 | Create Business Event with Resources |
| User | PV11 | Create Business Event without Resources |
| User | PV12 | Firmly Book/Cancel Business Event |
| User | PV14 | Lock/Unlock Business Event |
| User | PV15 | Follow-up Business Event |
| User | PV16 | Prebook: Attendee for Business Event Type List |
| User | PV17 | Billing |
| User | PV18 | Activity Allocation: Attendance |
| User | PV19 | Activity Allocation: Instructor Function |
| User | PV1A | Change Business Event |
| User | PV1B | Display Business Event |

| *Category* | *Transaction code* | *Description* |
|---|---|---|
| User | PV1C | Cost Transfer Posting |
| User | PV1D | Price Proposal |
| User | PV1M | Materials Procurement |
| User | PV33 | Business Event Appraisal |
| User | PV34 | Attendee Appraisal |
| User | PVB0 | Business Event Budget |
| User | PVBA | Training and Events: Budget Comparison |
| User | PVG2 | Lock/Unlock Resource |
| User | PVK0 | Correspondence History |
| Customizing | PVV0 | Create/Change Service |
| User | RE_RHAUTH00 | Authorized Objects |
| User | RE_RHCHECK1 | Check Database Consistency |
| User | RE_RHCHECKV | Check Relationships |
| User | RE_RHDBST00 | PD Database Statistics |
| Customizing | RE_RHMOVE30 | Manual Transport Link |
| User | RE_RHREFDOC0 | Reference Document Reporting |
| User | RE_RHRHAZ00 | Display PD Database Records |
| User | RE_RHRHDC00 | Delete HR Database Records via List |
| User | RE_RHRHDL00 | Delete PD Database Records |
| User | RE_RHVSTA00 | Database Statistics – Number of Objects |
| User | RE_RHVSTA10 | Database Statistics – Number of Notes |
| User | RE_RHVSTA20 | Database Statistics – Number of Object Types per Infotype |
| User | RE_RHVSTA30 | Database Statistics – Number of Infotypes per Object Type |
| User | S_AHR_61011841 | Location |
| User | S_AHR_61011843 | Building Address |
| User | S_AHR_61011844 | Time Schedule |
| User | S_AHR_61011845 | Cost Items |
| Both | S_AHR_61011885, OORA | Room |
| Both | S_AHR_61011886, OORT | Resource Type |
| Both | S_AHR_61011887, OOC3 | Master Data Catalog |
| Both | S_AHR_61011888, OOET | Business Event Type |
| Both | S_AHR_61011889, OOEG | Business Event Group |
| Both | S_AHR_61011893, OOER | External Instructor |
| Both | S_AHR_61011901, OORE | Other Resource |
| User | S_AHR_61011911 | Assign Authorization Profiles |
| User | S_AHR_61011912 | Maintain Authorization Profiles |

| Category | Transaction code | Description |
|---|---|---|
| User | S_AHR_61016214 | Prebookings per Attendee |
| User | S_AHR_61016215 | Bookings per Attendee |
| User | S_AHR_61016216 | Cancellations per Attendee |
| User | S_AHR_61016217 | Business Event Hierarchy |
| User | S_AHR_61016218 | Business Event Brochure |
| User | S_AHR_61016219 | Business Event Dates |
| User | S_AHR_61016220 | Business Event Demand |
| User | S_AHR_61016221 | Business Event Prices |
| User | S_AHR_61016224 | Resource Equipment |
| User | S_AHR_61016225 | Available/Reserved Resources |
| Both | S_ALR_87014085 | Attendance Statistics |
| User | S_ALR_87014087 | Resource Reservation |
| User | S_PH0_48000096 | Instructor Information |
| User | S_PH0_48000476 | Business Event Information |
| User | S_PH0_48000535 | Ad Hoc Query |
| User | S_PH9_46000423 | Budget Comparison |
| User | S_PH9_46000424 | Cancellations per Business Event |
| User | S_PH9_46000425 | Attendance and Sales Statistics |
| User | S_PH9_46000426 | Attendees for Rebooking |
| User | S_PH9_46000427 | Prebookings per Business Event Type |
| User | S_PH9_46000428 | Prerequisites Matchup |
| User | S_PH9_46000429 | Attendee's Qualifications |
| User | S_PH9_46000430 | Attendance Prerequisites |
| User | S_PH9_46000431 | Attendee's Training History |
| User | S_PH9_46000432 | Employee List |
| User | S_PH9_46000433 | Attendance List |
| User | S_PH9_46000434 | Attendee List |
| User | S_PH9_46000435 | Material Requirements per Business Event |
| User | S_PH9_46000436 | Resources Not Yet Assigned per Business Event |
| User | S_PH9_46000437 | Resource List per Business Event |
| User | S_PH9_46000438 | Business Event Schedule |
| User | S_PH9_46000439 | Resources Not Yet Assigned per Resource Type |
| User | S_PH9_46000440 | Resource Reservation Statistics |
| User | S_PH9_46000441 | Graphical Resource Reservation |
| User | S_PH9_46000451 | Business Event Appraisals |
| User | S_PH9_46000452 | Attendee Appraisals |

### 39.4.4 Utility

| *Category* | *Transaction code* | *Description* |
|---|---|---|
| ABAP | BAPI | Bapi explorer |
| Basis | BD87 | Status monitor for ALE messages |
| User | CG3Y | Download file |
| User | CG3Z | Upload file |
| ABAP | CMOD | Enhancements |
| ABAP | HRFORMS | HR forms workplace |
| Consultant | LSMW | Legacy system migration workbench |
| User | OAAD | Archivelink administration documents |
| Consultant | OSS1 | Logon to SAPNet |
| Consultant | OY19 | Customizing cross-system viewer |
| ABAP | PE51 | HR form editor |
| Basis | PFCG | Role maintenance |
| Basis | RSSCD100_PFCG | Change documents for role admin. |
| Basis | RSSCD100_PFCG_USER | For role assignment |
| Basis | RSUSR200 | List of users per login date |
| Basis | S_BCE_68001403 | With critical authorizations |
| Basis | S002 | Menu administration |
| User | SA38 | ABAP reporting |
| Basis | SALE | Display ALE customizing |
| User | SBWP | SAP business workplace |
| Consultant | SCAT | Computer aided test tool |
| Consultant | SCMP | View/table comparison |
| Basis | SCOT | SAPconnect – administration |
| Consultant | SCU0 | Customizing cross-system viewer |
| Basis | SE01 | Transport organizer (extended) |
| Basis | SE03 | Transport organizer tools |
| Consultant, Basis | SE09 | Transport organizer |
| Consultant, Basis | SE10 | Transport organizer |
| Consultant, ABAP | SE11 | ABAP dictionary maintenance |
| ABAP | SE13 | Maintain technical settings (tables) |
| ABAP | SE15 | ABAP/4 repository information system |
| Consultant, ABAP | SE16 | Data browser |
| Consultant, ABAP | SE16N | General table display |
| Consultant, ABAP | SE17 | General table display |
| ABAP | SE18 | Business add-ins: definitions |
| ABAP | SE19 | Business add-ins: implementations |

| *Category* | *Transaction code* | *Description* |
|---|---|---|
| ABAP | SE24 | Class builder |
| ABAP | SE35 | ABAP/4 dialog modules |
| ABAP | SE36 | Logical database builder |
| ABAP | SE37 | ABAP function modules |
| ABAP | SE38 | ABAP editor |
| ABAP | SE39 | Splitscreen editor: (new) |
| ABAP | SE41 | Menu painter |
| ABAP | SE43 | Maintain area menu |
| ABAP | SE51 | Screen painter |
| ABAP | SE61 | SAP documentation |
| Consultant | SE63 | Translation: initial screen |
| ABAP | SE71 | SAPscript form |
| ABAP | SE72 | SAPscript styles |
| ABAP | SE73 | SAPscript font maintenance |
| ABAP | SE74 | SAPscript format conversion |
| ABAP | SE75 | SAPscript settings |
| ABAP | SE75TTDTGC | SAPscript: change standard symbols |
| ABAP | SE75TTDTGD | SAPscript: display standard symbols |
| ABAP | SE76 | SAPscript: form translation |
| ABAP | SE77 | SAPscript styles translation |
| ABAP | SE80 | Object navigator |
| ABAP | SE84 | Repository information system |
| ABAP | SE85 | ABAP/4 repository information system |
| ABAP | SE91 | Message maintenance |
| ABAP | SE93 | Maintain transactions |
| Consultant | SEARCH_SAP_MENU | Find in SAP menu |
| Consultant | SEARCH_USER_MENU | Find in user menu |
| User, Consultant | SECATT | Extended computer aided test tool |
| User, Consultant | SHDB | Batch input transaction recorder |
| Consultant | SLG1 | Application log: display logs |
| Basis | SM01 | Lock transactions |
| Basis | SM04 | User list |
| Basis | SM12 | Display and delete locks |
| Consultant | SM30 | Call view maintenance |
| Consultant | SM31 | Call view maintenance like SM30 |
| Consultant | SM34 | Viewcluster maintenance call |
| User | SM35 | Batch input monitoring |
| User | SM35P | Batch input: log monitoring |

| *Category* | *Transaction code* | *Description* |
|---|---|---|
| User | SM36 | Schedule background job |
| User | SM37 | Job overview |
| User | SM38 | Queue maintenance transaction |
| ABAP | SMARTFORMS | SAP smart forms |
| ABAP | SMOD | SAP enhancement management |
| User | SMX | Display own jobs |
| User | SO00 | SAPoffice: short message |
| ABAP | SO10 | SAPscript: standard texts |
| User | SP01 | Output controller |
| User | SP02 | Display spool requests |
| Consultant | SP11 | TemSe directory |
| Consultant | SPRO | Customizing - edit project |
| User, Consultant | SQ00 | SAP query: start queries |
| Consultant | SQ01 | SAP query: maintain queries |
| Consultant | SQ02 | SAP query: maintain infoset |
| Consultant | SQ03 | SAP query: maintain user groups |
| User | SQVI | Quickviewer |
| ABAP | ST22 | ABAP dump analysis |
| Basis | SU01 | User maintenance |
| Basis | SU21 | Maintain the Authorization Objects |
| Basis | SU22 | Auth. object usage in transactions |
| Basis | SU24 | Auth. object check under transactions |
| User | SU3 | Maintain users own data |
| User | SU53 | Display authorization check |
| Basis | SUIM | User information system |
| Consultant | SWDD | Workflow builder |

# Index

# *World Government*

## *For a World Free from War, Terrorism and Poverty*

### Facts

- The world spends trillions of dollars every year on military and war equipment, while its people go hungry.
- Today the world is incapable of resolving any dispute through military actions.
- Terrorism thrives because of covert support of country governments.
- Enormous expenditure on militaries all over the world is not only a waste, but also extremely dangerous as it increases the destructive power of country governments.

### We want

- A world free from war, terrorism and poverty.

### How can it be done?

- Establish a world parliament, a world government and a world court.
- Disband militaries of all countries simultaneously.
- Use the savings to alleviate poverty.

### Will all countries agree?

- Yes! When people of the countries want it.
- We have to awaken the people of the whole world.

### How will it work?

- The world parliament will be formed through direct election of members of parliament all over the world. These members of parliament will form the world government.
- The world government will have limited but sufficient power to provide security to all countries, manage global environment and combat terrorism all over the world.
- The world government will secure the borders of all countries to ensure that there is no unauthorized entry or exit.
- The country governments will continue to manage their affairs.
- Disputes between countries will be resolved with the help of the world parliament and the world court.
- No country will disband its military first. All countries will disband their militaries simultaneously in a phased manner,

under the supervision of the world government, which will verify that the militaries are actually disbanded.

- Countries will retain their police to maintain law and order.
- Countries may have special forces to deal with terrorism and to provide relief in the event of natural disasters.

## Is it possible?

- Many people say that this is an impossible task because other people will not agree.
- This task is possible if we talk only about ourselves, and not about others. This task is big but not impossible.
- We have only one world, we can't give up on it.
- We can succeed only if we try.

## What should I do?

- Level 1: Register with WIII and become a world citizen. Even children can join.
- Level 2: Spread the message to your family, friends and neighbours. Convince five persons to join.
- Level 3: Convince five persons that each one of them would enroll five more persons.
- Level 4: Become an active volunteer.

## Act now

- Act now. Don't give up because of enormity of the task.

## You have nothing to lose

- There is no membership fee.
- You are not required to work unless you want to. But if you want, there is a lot of work to do.
- You are not required to follow any person or any belief.

## Contact

**World Integration and Improvement Initiative (WIII)**
L/A-4/303, Ajmera Housing Complex,
Pune 411018 India.
E-mail: agrawal.prem@gmail.com
Phone: 91(20)27462635

# *World Language*

## Need for a World Language

Perhaps the most important gift of nature to mankind is the ability to communicate using a language. However, this gift is not unmitigated, because we have got too much of it. We do not have a single language, but a large number of them, which sometimes is as bad as not having any language.

Lack of a common world language can greatly handicap a person, as more and more people travelling around the world discover to their dismay. With the world becoming smaller and smaller, as a result of advances in transportation and communication, the need for a common world language is felt more and more acutely. One option to overcome this hadicap is for a person to learn multiple languages, which is not only wasteful, but can be done only to a limited extent. Another way to overcome this handicap is through translation and interpretation, for which we pay a heavy price in terms of cost, time, and timeliness, and achieve at best partial communication. Scientific and technical literature available in one language cannot be used by people who do not know that language.

There is probably no one, who does not agree with the need for a world language. Only, people do not want to discuss it, fearing that accepting any language, other than their own, as world language will put them at a disadvantage. Also, people are strongly attached to their mother tongue, often considering it as revered as their mother, and feel a sense of guilt in accepting another language.

While there are some, who do not want to discuss this issue fearing that they may have to accept another language, there are others who do the same hoping that their language may become world language by default. This may well happen, but is it desirable even for them?

## Importance of a good world language

A language is a tool for communication, and we must evaluate it as we would evaluate any other tool. How effective is it in meeting its objective; and how much resources does it consume in doing so? People who hope that their language may become world language, should think again. Do we just want a common language, or do we want a really good world language—a language which provides effective, unambiguous communication with minimum effort.

This article shows that existing languages score quite badly in a rational evaluation. Let us remember that many of us use almost our entire non-sleeping time in reading, writing, and thinking—activities which depend on the efficiency of language. If we can design a language, which is more efficient than our existing language, we will gain that much extra time, which can be used for productive or recreational purposes. It has also been well accepted that languages influence our thinking, making the role of language even more important.

We must, therefore, consider ourselves lucky that we do not have a single language in the world. This gives us a choice. It is possible for us to have a well designed world language. If we had only one language, we would not have this choice, as we have no choice today in numbering system, computer keyboard, etc. We must not squander this choice away, by letting an existing language become the world language. It will be like losing a fortune, just because we refused to decide. It is also important that we decide to develop a world language as early as possible. The more time we lose, the more will be the backlog of translation, which must necessarily be done.

## Should an existing natural language be world language?

Some of the existing natural languages, particularly English, aspire to become world language. Their claim is based primarily on their widespread use in dominant segments of society all over the world, e.g. science, law, business, industry, government, etc. However, if we objectively examine their effectiveness and efficiency, they do not perform too well. Let us take a look at 'English'.

Let us start from the alphabet. English does not have a phonetic alphabet. The same letter is associated with different sounds in different words. This puts tremendous load on people learning the language. They have to learn both the pronunciation as well as the spelling. Many languages of the world have this problem, while many are free from it.

The length of the words in a language determines the effort in communication to a large extent. If the words are long, the communication time and effort is more. Natural languages being product of evolution, have not paid much attention to length of words. Consequently, the words tend to be long. The best proof of this defect in a language is the existence of short forms for long words. 'Info' for information, and 'ad' for advertisement, amply demonstrate that words can be shorter.

All languages use prefixes and suffixes to add additional meaning to the meaning of a word. By doing so, they avoid the need to define and learn a word. This practice is very good, but often there are exceptions, which are not desirable. Also, usually this concept is not utilized fully. We do not need separate words for boy and girl. We need only one word with a prefix or a suffix for gender.

The meanings of words is another area of concern. Many times the words have contextual meanings. This increases the learning effort, as all the meanings of the words have to be learnt. Also, the words often suffer from overprecision, and under-precision. There are many words which mean exactly, or nearly, the same. On the other hand there are some words, whose meaning is not precise enough.

Grammars of natural languages are usually quite complex. Agreement of number and gender between noun and verb is a case in point. Really speaking, there is no need to alter the verb for number and gender; they should be attributes of noun alone. If that was done, the language will become simpler. By unnecessarily modifying the verb for number and gender, we make the language complex, and introduce the possibility of making mistakes. Needless complexity of grammar is best understood by learners of a foreign language, who constantly compare the grammar of the new language with that of their mother tongues.

Ambiguity or lack of clarity in the meaning of a sentence also exists.

It might be argued that the defects of English may be removed to prepare it for the role of world language. However, the changes may be so many, that we may not recognise it as English at all. Also, however much we improve it, it can never be as good as a language designed from scratch. We are going to build the world language only once, and it must be the best. Evaluation of other natural languages is likely to bring us to the same conclusion.

Also, we must remember that adopting an existing language as world language will be more repugnant to the rest of the world, than adopting a newly designed language.

## Should Esperanto be world language?

If natural languages do not qualify to be the world language, what about Esperanto? After all it was created precisely for this purpose. There is no doubt that Esperanto is better suited to be the world language, than any other natural language. However, the question remains: is it possible to design a language better than Esperanto? The answer would be in affirmative, primarily because even Esperanto is based on some natural languages, and has not exercised freedom of choice in design to the fullest. However, Esperanto has definitely proved a major point—that it is possible to design a language.

## How to develop a world language?

Designing a language is not a very difficult job, but designing a good language is. Designing a language involves making a large number of decisions. How much effort is put in arriving at these decisions will determine the quality of language. Also, the process should involve wide ranging cosultations with experts in various fields. After an initial decision is made based on expert opinion, it should be widely publicized, and feedback and comments of all the people should be considered, before finalizing the decision. Even then, if there is a good reason to alter a decision previously made, it should be done. In no case should we compromise on the quality of the world language. Some ideas are discussed here to illustrate the kind of improvements possible. Obviously, they are at best the tip of the iceberg.

## Objectives of the world language

Some of the objectives of the world language would be as under. These need to be debated and enlarged. They also need to be interpreted for each sub-activity.

1. Achieve effective and unambiguous communication
   - 1.1 Between humans
   - 1.2 Between humans and machines
2. Minimize effort in communication
   - 2.1 Minimize effort in speaking and hearing
   - 2.2 Minimize effort in writing and reading
3. Minimize effort in learning the language
   - 3.1 Minimize the length and number of words
   - 3.2 Maximize the use of rules to form words and sentences. Have no exceptions.

## Designing alphabet and script

One of the most fundamental components of a language is its alphabet. The alphabet is in two forms—written and spoken. While designing the alphabet, the spoken alphabet should be designed first. The sounds produced by human beings are not discrete. From a continous spectrum, we have to select a set of sounds. If we select too few sounds, the alphabet will be small and words will be longer. On the other hand, too many sounds may cause problems in distinguishing between them. Fortunately, this science, called phonetics, is well developed, and can be used for selecting a set of sounds. The sounds should be selected in such a way that we get the maximum distinction between sounds, and the effort required in production of sound is minimum. In addition, pleasant-ness of sound in hearing may also be considered. The ability of machines to produce these sounds, and distinguish between them on hearing may also be considered.

In order to minimize learning effort, each sound should be assigned a character. Frequently occurring sound combinations may also be assigned an additional character, as in shorthand. The language should be phonetic. We already have natural languages which are phonetic, and they demonstrate the advantages offered by a phonetic language.

The script for the world language should be designed keeping in mind the ability of human hand for writing, and human eye for reading. In writing, the script should provide continuity. There should be no dotting the 'i', or cutting the 't'. This will minimize the movement of hand, and save effort. Each character should be independent, and combined sequentially. In some scripts, a part of the character is outside the main writing area, e.g. a part of 'g' is below the main line of writing. This should be avoided to conserve space. Characters should be as uniform in size as possible. Each character should be written in only one way. There should be no concept of upper and lower case, wherein the same character is written in two ways.

The effort in writing can be greatly reduced, if natural movements of body are used in the design of characters. Research should be conducted to determine which movements are easy for human hands, and which are not. For example, it is common experience that people find it easier to write 'u' than to write 'n'. So much so, that often 'n' looks like 'u'. This is not accidental, because its opposit never happens. This is an interesting example, because the two characters are mirror images of one another. It can perhaps be said that human hand can turn in quickly, but cannot turn out as quickly. Perhaps it has a natural tendency to move towards the chest as observed in case of an electric shock. Similarly, research should be conducted to determine if the human eye has any preferences in pattern recognition. We should also consider, whether the writing will be from left to right, right to left, top to bottom, or bottom to top. The suitability of the script for machine production and recognition should also be considered.

## Designing words

Words, even in natural languages, consist of parts which have independent meaning. For example, both 'un' and 'well' in unwell have independent meanings, which determine the meaning of unwell. These parts are called morphemes by linguists; we may call them roots. All languages use the concepts of roots, prefixes, suffixes, etc. But they do not use it to the fullest. For example, the word 'bad' is not needed; 'ungood' could be used in its place.

We should design word roots in such a way that their meanings are, as far as possible, independent of each other. For the same meaning there should not be more than one word root. If word roots are well defined, the learning effort will greatly reduce. Let me illustrate.

We need word roots to indicate the number and the gender. We may decide that there will be three genders—masculine, feminine, and unknown or unspecified. Similarly, we may decide that there will be three numbers—singular, plural, and unknown or unspecified. We may combine both these attributes, and assign a vowel to each of the nine combinations. We then use these vowels to suffix nouns and pronouns. Let us see the power of this simple design. We now need only one word for father, mother, and parent. Similarly, only one word will be needed for brother, sister, and sibling. Not only that the number of words will be reduced, some new words will become available, e.g. a word for either son or daughter. Speakers of Hindi, will find new words like parent and sibling, which they never had before. Also, we do not often know the sex of a bird, and use masculine, feminine, or neuter gender, depending on convention. In the new scheme, we can use the unspecified gender most of the time, and can specify it if we know the gender. Also, legal documents often use words like person(s). This is because there is no concept of unknown, or unspecified, number. We can, thus, see the power of a simple well-defined word root.

The above example is not an isolated one. By defining just three morphemes, for parent, child, and spouse, hundreds of existing and non-existing words for family relations can be eliminated. A large number of words describing young members of a species can be eliminated by using a single prefix with the word for species. Also, we can have a prefix each for first half, second half, first quarter, second quarter etc. of age, and so on. Thus, the communicator can choose the precision with which he wants to convey the age.

Word roots will be formed by assigning a sequence of characters to each concept. This should be done, using principles of classification and codification. In many branches of science, e.g. zoology and botany, such classification already exists. These should be used, so that there is no need to have a separate scientific name. Also, the frequency of their use should be considered. Highly used roots should be identified by few characters, so that the words are short.

Rules should be defined to combine roots into words. Where classification and codification gives a large word, but the frequency of use requires a small word, a synonym may be defined. Thus, synonyms will exist only for the purpose of making the language more efficient.

## Designing grammar

Grammar defines how to combine words into sentences. These rules should be as simple as possible, and there should be no exceptions. The sequence of words in a sentence should not affect its meaning. Also, preferably the sequence of words should not change, as it happens in English, where changing a sentence from affirmative to inquisitive requires a change in the sequence of words.

In many existing languages, attributes which should affect only words, are defined at the level of sentence. Number and gender are attributes of noun, and they have nothing to do with verb. Similarly, tense is an attribute of verb, and should not affect the noun. We think that a sentence is affirmative, or inquisitive (asks a question). Let us consider a simple sentence, "Are you going?". This may be interpreted as, "Are you going? (or not going)", or as "Are you? (or someone else) going". Here we can see that the question is an attribute of word, and not of sentence. Research will be needed to determine whether enquiry is always at word level, or sometimes at word level, and sometimes at sentence level.

## What do we do next?

There is no doubt that it is possible to develop a language, which is far superior to existing languages. The development of such a language will be an iterative process. It will go through several cycles of improvement, before it becomes reasonably good. If we can assign even 1% of resources being spent in linguistic research, we can easily build such a language. Then it can be improved, and compared with existing languages. Only after its superiority is clearly demonstrated, do we have to think of adopting it. This project is definitely worthy of research, and I call upon the world community to take it up.

# Good Governance

Many countries of the world face a number of problems. Are there any solutions? I believe that there are. Here are some ideas that could be helpful in solving some of our problems. There could be a structured public debate on these, and those which meet public approval could be implemented.

## Minimize government functions

- Often governments try to do too many things.
- It is not government's job to provide goods and services. It should facilitate their production and distribution and ensure competitiveness, efficiency and non-exploitation of customers.
- Government should not be looked upon to provide direct employment. It should ensure a vibrant economy in which people are gainfully engaged.

## Minimize government expenditure

- Whatever functions the government must perform, must be performed in the most efficient way, thereby reducing the cost of governance to a minimum.
- Methods of governance should be regularly reviewed, debated in public, and benchmarked with other countries and states to ensure that they are most effective and efficient.

## Taxation

- There should be a single authority in each country which can levy taxes. No one else should be allowed to collect tax from any one. However, governments should be allowed to sell specific goods and services, which the citizens should be free to buy, or not to buy.
- The taxes collected by the taxation authority should be distributed among country, state and local governments as per a pre-defined agreed formula.
- The distribution of revenue from taxes should consider both the needs of governments and their contribution to revenue.
- The needs should be determined by estimating the cost of functions the governments are expected to provide.
- It will be citizens' right to get the services for which money is provided by the tax authority.
- The tax structure should be simplified. There should be only two forms of taxes. Excise for all goods and services produced in the country, and Custom for all goods and services brought in a country from outside.
- Sales tax, octroi, income tax, etc. should be abolished.
- Collection of excise and custom should be made effective by allocating more

resources which would become available because of abolition of other taxes. In addition, the penalty for tax evasion should be very heavy, and corruption should be severely dealt with.

- It may be argued that income tax is applicable to only affluent sections of population. But, the same effect can be achieved by levying more excise on items which are consumed by these sections.

## Norm-based governance

- People have started thinking that what the government does for them is charity. As a result, while some people get too much, others don't get even the basic minimum.
- This tendency is clearly visible. Constituencies of VIPs, e.g. prime minister, railway minister, etc. get generous allocation, which suddenly dries up if the concerned minister no longer holds office.
- This tendency is often justified by saying that at least somewhere something is getting done. This argument shows how little we have come to expect from our governments.
- In order to ensure that justice is done to all, we must define the functions of government, the levels in each function, and the entitlement criteria.
- For example we may say that all villages with population between 100 and 1000 will be linked with brick road, while those with a population of more than 1000, will be linked with tar road.
- Such norms will ensure fairness to all.
- Along with norms, the mechanism to redress grievances arising from not following the norms should be specified. In case of deliberate victimization, those responsible should be punished.

## Government as service provider

- Where the government provides service, e.g. water, health care, education, roads, etc. it should be paid by the government treasury to the concerned government department for quantity and quality of service provided. This mechanism should replace the current mechanism of budgetary allocation.
- Government departments should be run as business. Their units should earn revenue, pay bills, and make profit or loss. The employees of each individual unit should be rewarded based on the financial performance of the unit.
- Citizens should be treated as customers and given bills for the service provided, showing the amount payable by them and the subsidies.
- Where possible, the quantity and quality of service should be certified by the individual customers. Where it is not possible, it should be certified by customer bodies.
- If private parties offer to provide service at a cheaper rate, the job should be given to them.

## Accountability

- Government functionaries seem to have all power but no accountability.
- For example, the encroachment department of a municipal corporation has powers to demolish an illegal building. But such powers are often exercised selectively to demolish some and leave others. The municipal corporation is not accountable to people as to why rules are being applied selectively.
- Lack of accountability breeds corruption.
- Whenever someone is given power, he should also be made accountable, preferably to the public.

- For example, if an illegal construction is found in the jurisdiction of an anti-encroachment department, its officers should be punished.

## Citizens role in governance

- Governance can be much better and easier if citizens are involved in it.
- Schemes to involve citizens in governance should clearly specify how the citizens are going to contribute.
- Citizens can contribute by providing information, monitoring situations and taking action.
- The schemes involving citizens' role should be planned keeping their convenience in mind and should utilize their contribution in a most effective way.
- For example, 'Each one teach one' is not a viable and effective method; but asking a citizen to teach for two hours in a week is both convenient to the citizen and also effective in spreading education.
- Citizens should be able to see the effect of their contribution.
- One way of involving citizens would be to have a well publicised telephone number, which citizens can use to report situations such as street lights being kept on in daytime, engine of a parked bus running, leakage in a water pipe, etc. The person manning such a telephone should contact the concerned officer, who in turn should remedy the situation. Only when citizens see their involvement resulting in action, they would participate more and more.
- Another way to involve citizens would be to assign them a small neighbourhood, which they will look after to ensure its cleanliness and orderliness. If someone digs up a road in their area, they will ensure that it is mended. They will also ensure that conservancy staff keeps their area clean. There can be many ways in which citizens can help.

## Innovation

- Innovation can greatly help in good governance. Chronic problems faced by government can be solved by innovative methods.
- For example, a municipal corporation should never award a contract merely for building roads. It should always be a contract to build and maintain roads. Then the contractor will do a good job in building the road, as he will have to spend less on its maintenance. This will benefit everyone.

## Political system

- In many countries, political system is corrupt because politics is not an economically viable profession.
- Every profession, except politics, offers a regular income.
- It is futile to argue that MLAs and MPs are paid a salary. These are the highest levels to which people reach in politics. The corruptionalisation is completed much before such levels are reached.
- We cannot expect to have politicians for free. If we do, we pay through our nose.
- Unless politics can attract young men and women and provide them a descent secure career, it is futile to expect politicians to be honest.
- Many countries have administrative or civil services. They should also create a political service in which young men and women should be recruited in an open competition. This service should conduct competitive examinations on the lines of the administrative or civil services.
- Those qualifying in the competitive examination should be trained and given

pay and perks at par with the administrative or civil services.

- Those selected for political service, should be barred from taking up any other job, or doing any business.
- They should not be given any regular work. They should do political or social work of their choice.
- Their work should be monitored by Judiciary to ensure that they do adequate amount of work. If the quantum of their work is found inadequate, they must be withdrawn from political service and assigned administrative work. If they are found to be corrupt, their services should be terminated.
- They will contest election like any other person, and if they get elected, they will be entitled to only one salary, either of the service or of the elected office.
- Only if we can attract young students, and allow them to make an honest career in politics, can we hope to end corruption some day.

## Education

- The objective of the education system is not clearly defined.
- People claim that education system has failed without even defining what education is expected to achieve.
- The objective of primary and secondary education should be to impart skills in languages and mathematics, and to create general awareness and scientific temperament.
- The objective of higher level education should be to impart skills and knowledge which a person will need in his career.
- The availability of different courses should be based on the manpower needs of a country. Consequently, in a country like India a large number of students should be educated in agriculture, horticulture, fishery, cattle rearing, etc.
- Education should not be fashionable; it should be need based and add value. It should also be easy to obtain, preferably without sacrificing the earning capacity of students.

## Judiciary

- The effectiveness of judiciary determines how civilized a society is.
- The objective of judiciary is not merely to hear cases and pronounce judgement, but also to create confidence in people that if they are wronged, judiciary will help remedy the problem. It should also create the impression that no one can do wrong and get away with it.
- From the above point of view, judiciary in many countries has failed miserably.
- Failure of judiciary is the primary reason of corruption in society.
- Judiciary must work out and implement a strategy to achieve the above objectives. Judicial management should be a part of judiciary.
- Judiciary must get its workload studied to see what part of it can be eliminated by improving the rules governing those situations. For example, Judiciary handles a large number of cases related to motor vehicle accident compensation. If rules are framed to determine this compensation based on relevant factors like age, earning capacity, number of dependants, etc. insurance companies will be able to settle most of the cases, and the number of such cases going to court will drastically reduce.
- Judiciary should work on cases in a time bound manner. It should fix time norms for different types of cases and endeavour to finish a case in the allotted time.
- Judiciary can work in a time bound manner only if it has a reasonable number of cases in hearing. Therefore, new cases should go in a queue from which they should be taken for hearing.

The cases may not be taken for hearing on a first-come first-served basis, but based on some guidelines which take into account the importance and urgency of a case.

- Judiciary must augment its capacity to meet the workload. The major resource that the judiciary requires is manpower. It is ironic that even in countries with excess manpower, this function is poorly performed due to lack of resources.
- Judiciary may take help of retired citizens to augment its capacity.
- Judiciary should review its policies to ensure that they are concomitant with speedy and effective justice.

## E-Governance

- Information Technology (IT) is having a major impact on governance. Many country and state governments are changing their business processes to take advantage of the benefits that IT offers. However, if we have to get the most efficient e-governance at minimum cost, we need to do two things: commonize business processes and develop soft IT infrastructure.

## Commonize business processes

- At present, the same business process gets computerized by different agencies in different ways. This creates islands of information which cannot talk to each other.
- A case in point is the computerization of RTO (Regional Transport Office) operations in India. Initially, different RTOs created their systems independently, and now it is proposed to scrap all those systems and replace them with a common central system. Needless to say the expenditure in independent systems could have been avoided.

## Develop soft IT infrastructure

- We are aware of the importance of IT infrastructure in the development of IT. However, we usually think only of hardware infrastructure. It is high time we start thinking of soft IT infrastructure as well, and understand its importance in the development of IT. Let me explain.
- Any computerization project requires creation of master data, e.g. citizens, business entities, real estate properties, etc. At present each system creates its own master data. In India, a citizen has one id for income tax department, another for his driving licence, and yet another for his bank. He also has an id in each of the hospitals he visits, and so on. Obviously, these systems cannot talk to each other. If each person in the world were to be given a unique person id, that id would get used by all these systems, instead of trying to create their own. This not only would save development effort but also would enable diverse systems to talk to each other.
- It is not only the persons we need to identify uniquely but also every legal entity such as businesses, each piece of land and real estate, etc. The list is endless and so are the benefits of creating such unique identities.
- Wherever possible, we should look for natural attributes in giving id to an entity. For example, we can give a number to land and real estate based on its longitude, latitude and altitude. Similarly, we can codify the primary relation between two persons as Father (F), Mother (M), Brother (B), Sister (C), Husband (H), Wife (W), Son (S) and Daughter (D). All other relations can be derived by combining these primary relations.

- It is important that standards for master data creation and codification are discussed and agreed in international bodies such as International Standards Organization. If this is not done, the world will have to incur additional cost later either in changing the systems, or in building interfaces.
- The benefits of unique identification are enormous. If each person is given a unique numeric id, we can store a telephone number and an e-mail id against him. For calling a person, you would make the call on his person id with a prefix, say 1. The prefix will indicate to the telephone system that the following number is a person id which has to be converted into telephone number. If the person's telephone number changes, only the link needs to be changed. The callers will still call the same number. Similarly, a person can be contacted on the same e-mail id, even if he changes his service provider.
- E-governance should not be creating islands of computer systems. We must have a clear vision, strategy and master plan. We must understand what to do and what not to do, if we are not to waste our precious time and resources.

## Pledge your time (samay daan)

- We citizens only criticize. We do nothing concrete.
- Things are not going to change if we expect others to change them. They will change if we act to change them.
- Those who want to change the world for better should pledge 1% of their time for society. This works out to less than 15 minutes a day and less than two hours a week.
- They can spend this time to pursue the cause of their choice. They can join an NGO, or form local groups to discuss and debate what can be done.
- Even if they just meet once a week to discuss what can be done, ideas will emerge and things will begin to happen.
- Their own efforts will shape their actions and organizations.
- The key thing is commitment and doing; not idle criticism.
- Register your time pledge (samay daan) with World Integration and Improvement Initiative (agrawal.prem@gmail.com)

# *City without Traffic Lights*

Are you fed up with traffic lights? Traffic lights at every junction. Stop, start. Stop, start. Stop, start. Do you sometimes wish that the roads of your city were like expressway. Where your car would compete with the wind and you would reach your destination in minutes.

Fortunately, this is possible. In order to use this plan, the main roads of the city need to be like a grid, as shown in Figure 1.

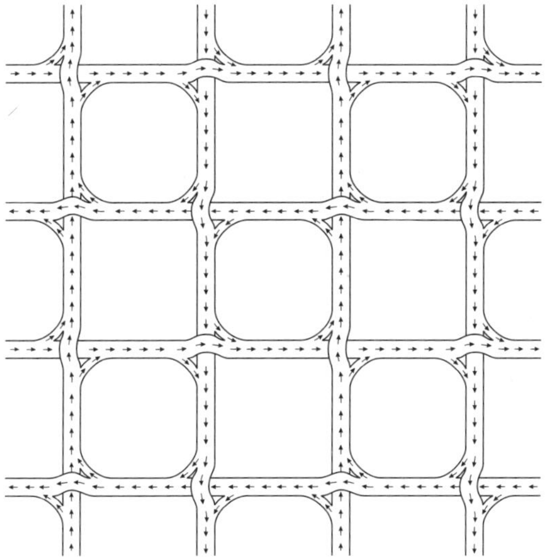

**Figure 1**

All roads will be one-way. When one road meets another at an intersection, there are two possibilities; you may either continue on your road, or you may turn on the other road in the direction of the traffic on that road. This is shown in Figure 2.

If you turn on the other road, there is no problem. But if you continue on your road, you will run into the traffic going straight on the other road. This is solved by a flyover or grade separator. Traffic on one road will go above the flyover, and the traffic on the other

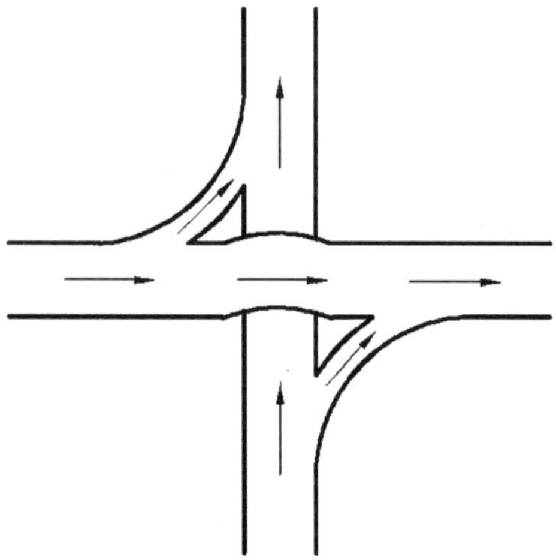

**Figure 2**

road will go under the flyover. This will ensure smooth flow of traffic without traffic light. This will be done on all intersections. Figure 1 shows this arrangement.

Sounds like a good idea. But how will the pedestrians cross the road? If the traffic moves at a fast speed, it will become impossible for the pedestrians to cross the road. The solution to this is in Figure 3.

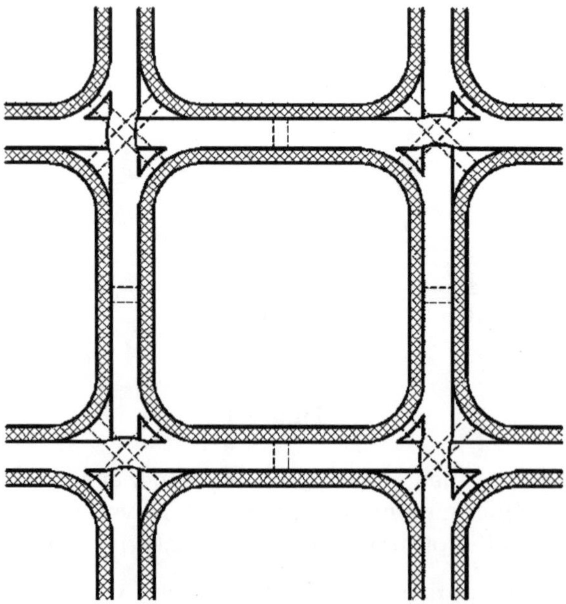

**Figure 3**

There will be a ring road for pedestrians and cyclists in each sector (the area bounded by main roads on all four sides). This pedestrian ring road will be connected to the pedestrian ring roads of adjoining sectors through subways. Thus, no pedestrian or cyclist will ever come on the main roads, allowing the vehicles to move freely on the main roads. Pedestrian roads will not be one-way. Pedestrians and cyclists will move on the pedestrian roads in both directions.

But how will a person take public transport, e.g. bus or taxi? This is explained in Figure 4.

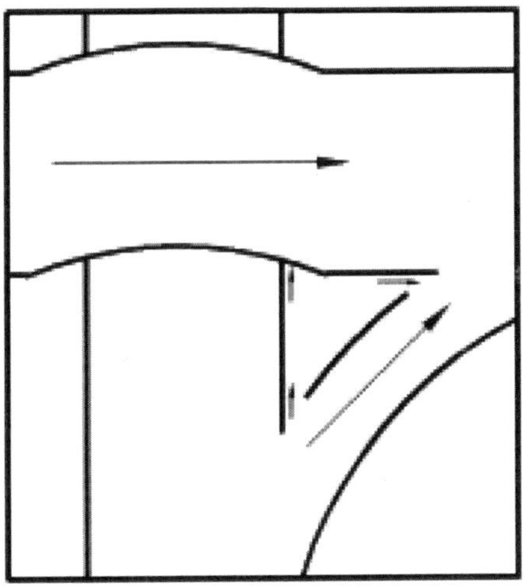

**Figure 4**

At each intersection, there are two triangular areas. Buses and taxis will go inside these triangular areas. There they will drop and pickup the passengers and come out of the triangle on the road they wish to take. These triangular areas will be connected to the pedestrian roads through subways.

Figure 5 shows the vehicle ring roads inside the sectors. This ring road will be connected to all the four main roads as well as to the internal roads of the sector. These roads will be two-way.

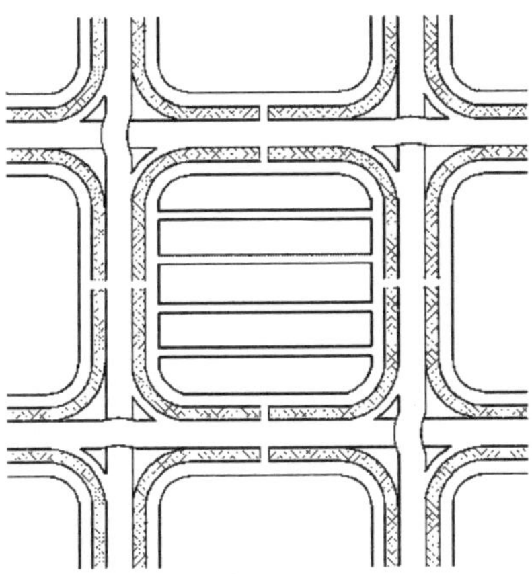

**Figure 5**

Figure 6 shows how the vehicles will move from one sector to another sector. Draw a horizontal and a vertical line from the source sector to the destination sector. You can do this in two ways. You can take either of these two ways to travel to your destination. You come out of the source sector taking the exit according to your travel path, move to the destination sector and enter it.

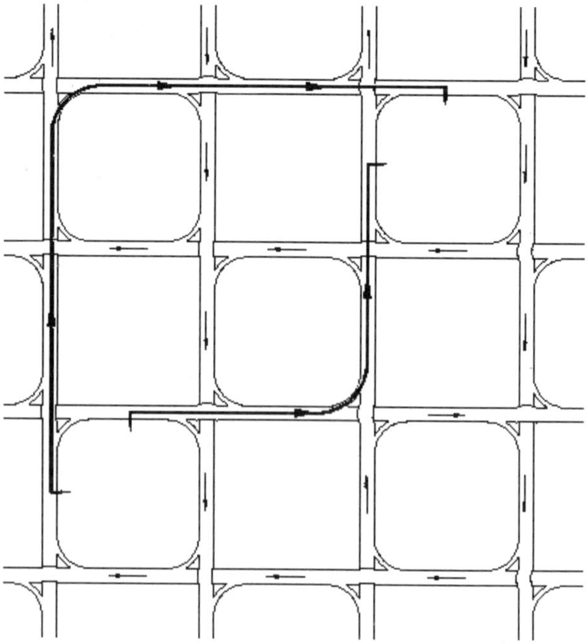

**Figure 6**

The main roads will be fenced on both sides so that no one can enter or exit them except through designated entry and exit roads. No pedestrian or cyclist will enter these roads. The vehicles will enter these roads, move to their destination and exit. Vehicles will neither stop on the main roads, nor be parked on it. Public transport will not stop on the main roads. There will be no shops or vendors on the main roads. Main roads will be like expressways. Enter, Move, Exit. No stoppage.

For further information, contact

**P K Agrawal**
L/A-4/303, Ajmera Housing Complex,
Pimpri, Pune 411018
E-mail: agrawal.prem@gmail.com
Phone: +91(20)27462635
Mobile: +919822847682

# INDEX
(709–721)